THEATRE UNDER THE NAZIS

MANCHESTER
UNIVERSITY PRESS

Theatre under the Nazis

EDITED BY JOHN LONDON

MANCHESTER UNIVERSITY PRESS
Manchester and New York

distributed exclusively in the USA by Palgrave

Published by Manchester University Press
Oxford Road, Manchester M13 9NR, UK
and Room 400, 175 Fifth Avenue, New York, NY 10010, USA
http://www.manchesteruniversitypress.co.uk

Distributed exclusively in the USA by
Palgrave, 175 Fifth Avenue, New York, NY 10010, USA

Distributed exclusively in Canada by
UBC Press, University of British Columbia, 2029 West Mall, Vancouver, BC, Canada V6T 1Z2

British Library Cataloguing-in-Publication Data
A catalogue record for this book is available from the British Library

Library of Congress Cataloging-in-Publication Data applied for

ISBN 0 7190 5912 7 *hardback*
0 7190 5991 7 *paperback*

First published 2000

07 06 05 04 03 02 01 01   10 9 8 7 6 5 4 3 2 1

Typeset by Carnegie Publishing, Lancaster
Printed in Great Britain by Bookcraft (Bath) Ltd, Midsomer Norton

Contents

Illustrations

Tables

Notes on the contributors

WILLIAM ABBEY is the Librarian at the Institute of Germanic Studies, University of London, and author of several bibliographies, including *Two into One: A Bibliography of the Wende* (1993).

GLEN GADBERRY was until recently Associate Professor in the Department of Theatre Arts and Dance at the University of Minnesota in Minneapolis. His publications are almost all centred on German theatre: the Wisconsin Kurz/Pabst Stadttheater, German/Austrian drama and theatre after 1880, and especially the theatre of Nazi Germany. He edited and contributed to the anthology *Theatre in the Third Reich, the Prewar Years* (1995) and is working on a history of German theatre *From Kaiserreich to Third Reich*, focused on the career of the actress-manager Agnes Straub.

KATHARINA HAVEKAMP has translated several plays by Franz Xaver Kroetz and published *Love Comes in Buckets* (1978), which became a bestseller in its German version, as well as numerous articles in British and German journals and anthologies. William Abbey and Katharina Havekamp have together published studies on the German PEN Group in exile (1933–45), Walter Janka and the actor Carl Balhaus.

ERIK LEVI is Senior Lecturer in the Department of Music, Royal Holloway, University of London, and a frequent contributor to *Tempo*, *Classic CD* and *BBC Music Magazine*. He has written articles for *The New Grove Dictionary of Opera* and is author of the widely acclaimed *Music in the Third Reich* (1994). As both a professional accompanist and a critic, he has made several broadcasts for the BBC.

JOHN LONDON is co-editor of *Contemporary Catalan Theatre* (1996), translator/editor of *The Unknown Federico García Lorca* (1996) and author of *Reception and Renewal in Modern Spanish Theatre* (1997). His other publications include studies of fascist sport and art, and he is on the editorial board of *Plays International*.

WILLIAM J. NIVEN is Reader in the Department of Modern Languages, Nottingham Trent University. He has published studies on the *Thingspiel*, modern German drama and the reception of *Schindler's List* in Germany. He is the author of *The Reception of Friedrich Hebbel in Germany in the Era of National Socialism* (1984) and a forthcoming book on post-1990 representations of Nazism.

REBECCA ROVIT is a theatre historian who has been Assistant Professor in the Department of Theatre, Illinois State University, among other institutions. She has published studies on contemporary German drama and performance, as well as the theatrical activities of the Jüdischer Kulturbund. She has co-edited, with Alvin Goldfarb, *Theatrical Performance During the Holocaust: Texts, Documents, Memoirs* (1999) for Johns Hopkins University Press.

Acknowledgements

My first debt of gratitude is to the other contributors to this book, for their courtesy and hard work. They have coped patiently with my requests for rewritten, restructured and augmented versions of their chapters, following my receipt of their initial drafts. Their willingness to return to their sources and their attention to the quirky details of Nazi theatre have been an inspiration in a field often characterized by oversimplification rather than accuracy. While each of us had a different emphasis within our studies, we were united by a belief that the complex variety of the people involved in the theatre industry of the Third Reich gave rise to some fascinating performances as well as several political paradoxes. At the same time, it was hard not to reach the conclusion that much of the ideological and aesthetic ugliness of the period was not unique to the Nazi regime.

The Institute of Germanic Studies, at the University of London, provided a suitable location, in December 1996, for some of the contributors to discuss their findings in the early stages of the preparation of their chapters. I am grateful to Lutz Becker for his comments during these discussions and further advice on the project. Victoria Cooper, Rosanna Eadie and Marion Kant were helpful in matters of organization and structure. Maria Delgado and Viv Gardner read earlier versions of the book and offered constructive criticism. Duncan Large and David George supplied valuable bibliographical information. Fiona Sewell's copy-editing skills were much appreciated. My editor at Manchester University Press, Matthew Frost, has been generous and considerate.

Much of my own work was carried out while I held a research fellowship from the Alexander von Humboldt Foundation at the Institut für Theaterwissenschaft within the Free University of Berlin. My thanks go to my academic sponsor during that period, Henning Rischbieter, and the attentive library staff of the Institut für Theaterwissenschaft. My subsequent study of theatre under the Nazis was financed, as part of a larger undertaking, by a special research fellowship from the Leverhulme Trust at the University of Wales, Swansea. Finally, I am grateful to the Hebrew University of Jerusalem, the institution to which I was attached during the completion of the editing process.

John London

Introduction

JOHN LONDON

Popular perceptions of theatre under the Nazis swing from one extreme to another. On the one hand, there are those who condemn everything official to do with the period. On the other, there is a general view that theatrical life under Hitler was largely untouched by the ugly violence of Nazi ideology.

Those who are keen to dismiss the theatre of the period refuse to salvage the reputation of artists from political extremism and end up claiming that hardly anything of quality was performed or written between 1933 and 1945. This leads to the kind of misconception voiced by the left-wing playwright Rolf Hochhuth, who, in 1995, associated George Bernard Shaw with drama banned under the Nazis.[1] In reality, Shaw was one of Hitler's favourite writers.

Klaus Mann took a similarly negative view in his novel *Mephisto*, whose central character, Hendrik Höfgen, was a thinly veiled portrait of the famous actor-director Gustaf Gründgens. Höfgen emerges as an arrogant, cunning liar, who is tyrannical in rehearsals and uses the new regime for his own advancement. Comforted that he is not a Jew, he none the less employs a half-Jew as a private secretary. Moreover, Mann's *roman à clef*, first published in exile in 1936, had more than one personal target: it was an aggressive caricature of many others working in the theatre under Nazi rule.[2]

And yet the German banning of Mann's novel in 1968 demonstrated that it was not easy to criticize those who had been directly involved in the theatre of the Third Reich. Indeed the prohibition (which lasted until 1980, a year before the famous film version) comforted those who believed that the theatre was somehow immune to Nazi control.[3]

Nazi state-organized racism and political persecution certainly reinforce an overwhelmingly negative aesthetic view of the period that makes Hochhuth's error and Mann's caricatures understandable. About 4000 people connected with theatre fled from the dictatorship. Jewish actors such as Fritz Kortner, Alexander Moissi and Elisabeth Bergner were forced into exile or premature retirement. Emigration was the route out for the theatre critics Alfred Kerr

I

and Alfred Polgar. Directors of the stature of Leopold Jessner and Max Reinhardt died before they could return to Germany. Estimates vary, but around 2000 writers left the country during Nazism.[4] Among the most important playwrights were Bertolt Brecht, Ernst Toller and Carl Zuckmayer. Several individuals who stayed, and were known to be ideologically opposed to the Nazis, suffered a more violent fate. Erich Mühsam, the anarchist writer and cabarettist, was put in a concentration camp and killed in 1934. From being the country with the most theatres in Europe, it looked as though Germany was destined to become an Aryan cultural desert until the end of the Second World War.

Given such a scenario, it is perhaps not surprising that the theatrical representation of the period should be dominated by the plays of exiles or those speaking on behalf of the victims of Nazism. Whereas Brecht's *Fear and Misery of the Third Reich* and *The Resistible Rise of Arturo Ui* catalogue the development of the regime, later works by Peter Weiss (*The Investigation*) and Martin Sherman (*Bent*) concentrate on the element through which the Third Reich has come to be judged for so many: the Holocaust. The underlying argument for such works, as indeed for most of the literature about fascism, is that their value derives from a position which is physically distanced from their subject and fundamentally opposed to Nazism.

However, the case of Gründgens provides a different, much less hostile approach to theatre under the Nazis. After all, Gründgens was not the only well-known personality to stay and work in Germany after the Nazi takeover. The set designer Caspar Neher and the director Erich Engel had collaborated closely with Brecht in the 1920s and went on to be active in subsidized theatres throughout Nazism. The actors Heinrich George and Bernhard Minetti played major roles after 1933, even though they had previously been involved in leftist theatre. One of the founding dramatists of German Naturalism, Gerhart Hauptmann, continued to write and have plays performed during Hitler's rule. The same goes for Richard Strauss and his music. Wilhelm Furtwängler conducted the Berlin Philharmonic. These names can hardly be construed as constituents of an artistic wasteland.

Since the early 1980s, several German studies have attempted to describe the state control of theatre and point to the continued presence of individuals and styles before and after 1933. Nevertheless, published research on Nazi theatre still has a long way to go to catch up with the amount written on art and film of the period. Some scholars, favouring a purely historical view, have ignored the artistic analysis of texts and performance altogether. Until recently, there was no collected statistical information about the quantity and nature of productions performed.[5] Only by attention to these kinds of detail is it possible to reach a more accurate picture, somewhere between the extremes of a blanket condemnation of all plays performed in the Third Reich and the simplistic assertion that the theatre remained untainted by Nazi propaganda.

Setting the scene: reactionary and Nazi theatre before 1933

Whereas it is more positive to remember the acclaimed directors and actors who stayed on in the Third Reich, the cultural doctrines dictated by the Nazis also had an established pedigree. As was the case in the political sphere, 1933 marked the triumph of Nazi groundwork and the harnessing of comparable beliefs which had been developing for decades.

One of the most prominent early representatives of extreme nationalism in the theatre was Adam Müller-Guttenbrunn, who published a scurrilous pamphlet in 1885, entitled *Vienna was a City of Theatre* (*Wien war eine Theaterstadt*). Vienna, he argued, was no longer the home to true theatre (with ethical and didactic aims), because of corrupting Jewish and foreign imports, such as French farces and operettas. Müller-Guttenbrunn also had ideas about creating a genuinely popular theatre, with cheap tickets, to reach audiences who were less well off. A chance to realize these aims came in 1898, when he was appointed director of the Kaiserjubiläums-Stadttheater, an institution established specifically to promote Christian, Aryan theatre and counteract foreign influences. He was supported by those who wanted to see a new theatre, completely free of Jews, even, if possible, among the audiences.[6]

Müller-Guttenbrunn resigned from his post in 1903, and although his successor, Rainer Simons, remained committed to an anti-semitic policy, a repertory of light opera was the only way to reverse the financial losses previously incurred. Yet even Müller-Guttenbrunn had been criticized for being insufficiently anti-semitic, and racism continued to be a potent cultural force in the Vienna with which the young Adolf Hitler would be intimately connected from 1906 to 1913. It was here that the future Führer saw the Wagner productions and the technical tricks of stagecraft which would influence his aesthetic concerns for the rest of his life. He had ambitions to write a drama and an opera, both influenced by Wagner. And it was in Vienna, as he later claimed in *Mein Kampf*, that he became an anti-semite, having observed Jewish cultural influences which he thought 'worse than the Black Death'.[7]

There was constant overlap and exchange between Austrian and German theatrical life and in Germany, similarly extremist notions also found their way into culture. When triumphant Nazi ideologues looked back on the Weimar Republic (1918–33), they were keen to adopt many reactionary projects as part of Nazi philosophy in order to prove that their ideas were not simply a 'party view'.[8] There was plenty of evidence to extend this argument for the theatre to well before the First World War. Ernst Wachler took notions of Teutonic essence once step further than Müller-Guttenbrunn. His open-air theatre in the Harz mountains was based on anti-semitic and anti-Christian beliefs. From the premiere production in 1903, Wachler presented German plays and Shakespeare at minimal admission prices, in opposition to what he viewed as the capitalist enterprises of the big cities which did not spring from German soil or represent national interests. In Wachler's productions professional actors performed alongside local residents.[9]

In 1911 Elizabeth Duncan and her husband Max Merz founded a dance school in Darmstadt on a clearly racist basis and, by 1920, the dancer and choreographer Rudolf von Laban was publishing his convictions about the inherent biological inferiority of black people. In 1914 Wilhelm Karl Gerst established the Verband zur Förderung deutscher Theaterkultur (Association for the Promotion of German Theatre Culture), set up to influence the choice of plays for theatre repertories. According to its own remit, the society intended to 'reveal once more the genuine German spirit' and thus combat 'non-culture' on German stages.[10]

The Verband diminished in importance after the creation of the Bühnen-volksbund (People's Theatre League) in 1919. Based in Frankfurt am Main, the Bühnenvolksbund was designed as a theatre-goers' organization to counter the influence of the leftist Volksbühne (People's Stage) movement and advocate the revival of a German national theatre based on Christian German values. By 1925 it had over 400,000 members, support groups in all major cities, partnerships in twelve large theatres and its own travelling theatre company. Drawing official support from the churches, right-wing parties and even President Hindenburg, the organization published a journal named after it, which stressed the need to purify German theatre from Jewish and other alien influences. Other conservative groups organized public campaigns, which, under the guise of protecting public morality against the outrages of Express-ionism or other contemporary drama, demanded the removal of 'un-German' tendencies from theatrical life.[11]

Such groups were aided by several reactionary theatre critics and literary historians. As early as 1899, a Viennese newspaper had claimed that the theatre was a victim of an international Jewish conspiracy, so there was nothing original in the reactionary reviewing of a critic like Alfred Mühr in the *Deutsche Zeitung* during the Weimar Republic. Longer, pseudo-academic analyses were available from the pro-Aryan, anti-semitic literary histories of Adolf Bartels and Josef Nadler, in which the best German literature was seen to emerge as a reaction to and in spite of pernicious foreign or Jewish influences. (Bartels had himself written some racist dramas in the 1890s.)[12]

In the musical world, more famous names became associated with radical nationalism. The composer Hans Pfitzner wrote his cantata *Of the German*

Soul (*Von deutscher Seele*) in 1921 as a meditation on German identity, following what he perceived as the national spiritual crisis caused by German defeat at the end of the First World War. At the same time, he was writing articles equating what he called the 'atonal chaos' of modern music with 'bolshevism' and declaring that German culture was under threat from internationalist Jewish influences. Likewise, the festival of Wagner's operas at Bayreuth came to represent German national defiance against the cosmopolitan decadence of the Weimar Republic. Following personal contacts between Hitler and the Wagner family, the *Bayreuther Blätter* cited Hitler and other Nazis with approval. From 1925, another periodical, the *Zeitschrift für Musik*, launched attacks on musical modernism and jazz, as well as decrying the influence of foreign and Jewish composers.[13]

After the inception of the Nazi, or National Socialist German Workers', Party in 1919, there were gestures towards promoting cultural renewal and exploiting existing tendencies seen to coincide with Nazi beliefs. The party programme of 1920 demanded the 'legal prosecution of all those tendencies in art and literature which corrupt our national life' and the 'suppression of cultural events which violate this demand'. Hitler's speeches of the early 1920s are littered with references to the harmful impact of the Jews on theatre, the need for theatre to be put at the service of the general public, and (as early as 1923) the idea of pre-performance censorship. Hitler's opinions were not isolated. In Salzburg, the attempted disruption by Catholic students of the premiere of *Everyman* (*Jedermann*), which inaugurated the Salzburg Festival in August 1920, was followed by journalistic assaults on Max Reinhardt and Hugo von Hofmannsthal, the two founders of the festival who were of Jewish origin. One critic, writing in the National Socialist *Deutscher Volksruf* in 1922, attacked Hofmannsthal's *Great Theatre of the World* (after Calderón) in the following manner: 'The content of this work falls totally within the racial context of its author, everything is dragged into the mud.'[14]

Only in the mid- to late 1920s, however, was more systematic Nazi attention paid to cultural matters. Party newspapers, such as *Der Angriff* and the *Völkischer Beobachter*, become instrumental in what was to be termed the aim of 'suppressing all detrimental influences in literature, the press, the theatre, art and cinema'. Under Josepf Goebbels's control, *Der Angriff* contained not simply the usual anti-semitic attacks, but also a token populism, in claims that the working man had neither money nor time for the products of modern culture. The *Völkischer Beobachter* was edited as the official party organ by Alfred Rosenberg, an early acquaintance of Hitler who had taken part in the failed Nazi putsch in Munich in 1923. Rosenberg later formed the Kampfbund für Deutsche Kultur (Fighting League for German Culture) in 1928 for the purpose of defending 'the value of German essence' in 'the midst of present-day cultural decadence'; for Rosenberg and his circle this meant the promotion of traditional drama and an opposition to theatrical forms such as Naturalism. The circulation of both the *Völkischer Beobachter* and *Der Angriff* had risen to over 110,000 copies each in the year before the Nazis came to power.[15]

The assaults on leftist or Jewish theatre launched from Nazi and extreme conservative quarters sometimes found expression in organized demonstrations when performances considered objectionable took place. One of the individual forerunners of such actions was the writer Artur Dinter who, in June 1914, stood up in the middle of a performance of Karl Vollmöller's spectacle *The Miracle* (*Das Mirakel*), directed by Max Reinhardt, and embarked on an anti-semitic tirade against the theatrical and cultural scene in Berlin. (Dinter would later proclaim himself a Nazi *avant la lettre*.) In 1921, during one performance of Arthur Schnitzler's *La Ronde* (*Reigen*), in Vienna, the throwing of a stink-bomb led to the theatre being stormed by demonstrators who attacked the audience and vandalized the building. When the police suspended further performances, the right-wing press declared a 'success' for 'the Christian youth of Vienna'. Gotthold Ephraim Lessing's *Nathan the Wise* (written in 1779) came under fire for its message of religious tolerance when a fascist mob heckled a film version in 1923. Jews were not the only target. In 1929 local German nationalists in Upper Silesia physically attacked and injured Polish actors.[16]

As such protests became more frequent, there were instances when the authorities were less tolerant of the plays they believed had caused the trouble. In 1924, the Viennese police had allowed a production of Toller's *Brokenbrow* (*Hinkemann*) to continue, despite the protests of swastika-bearing students. Similar attempts by rightist groups to prevent the play being performed in Berlin later that year were countered by the Prussian Ministry of the Interior. But by 1928, the Munich police were prohibiting the staging of Ernst Křenek's jazz-influenced opera *Johnny Strikes Up!* (*Jonny spielt auf!*) and a local court acquitted two Nazis who had interrupted the piece, while another two got off with light fines. In late 1932, the Berlin police banned *God, Kaiser and Peasant* (*Gott, Kaiser und Bauer*), by the Hungarian Marxist Julius Hay, following disruptions by the Kampfbund für Deutsche Kultur. And even when the law seemed to be acting correctly, it did so with a certain ambivalence: after a penalty was imposed by a Würzburg court in 1930 on Nazis who had interrupted a production by the Habimah company, the judge responsible for the verdict claimed that the performance of a foreign, Jewish theatre group was inappropriate considering the economic crisis and polarization of the German people.[17] Preventing a danger to social stability could always be an excuse for covert censorship.

Specifically Nazi ideas for theatre were not limited to criticism and the disruption of performances. Robert Rohde founded the first Nazi experimental theatre company in 1925, which underwent various transformations up until the early 1930s and performed touring shows as well as productions in Berlin. Among the plays in its later repertory were works by Dietrich Eckart and Walter Flex as well as Schiller's *The Robbers*, directed in an anti-semitic production.[18]

Of these dramatists, Eckart, who had died in 1923, was especially dear to the Nazi cause. A party member early on, he was Hitler's mentor and friend. He had little success in the theatre during his lifetime, except for his popular version of Ibsen's *Peer Gynt*. But there were also several other playwrights who subscribed to an ideology which had much in common with the Nazi creed. In *The Love of God* (*Die Liebe Gottes*) of 1919, Hermann von Boetticher used Expressionist techniques to criticize the moral and social instability caused by the war, revolution and the contamination of non-German blood. A return to Prussian values seemed to be a solution to reverse this decline. In stylistic contrast, Paul Ernst adopted more traditional forms, harking back to Greek tragedy, and wrote patriotic, historical drama during the First World War. As an example of *Blut und Boden* (blood and soil) ethics in the theatre, Hans Franck's *Klaus Michel*, of 1925, pointed out that even a successful doctor could profit from returning to the eternal merit of peasant life. Hans Kyser's virulently anti-Polish *Fire on the Border* (*Es brennt an der Grenze*, 1931) would be revived in the Third Reich.[19]

Joseph Goebbels also tried his hand at playwriting. The text of *The Traveller* (*Der Wanderer*) is now lost, but Rohde toured his own production of the play for at least two years. In a series of representative scenes phrased to convict liberal democracy, a character made his way through Germany's 'deep night', observing phenomena such as poverty, the church and the government. The play betrayed a certain Expressionism in its reduced individual psychology and fragmentary structure, but if anybody remained in doubt as to the message of the action, the Nazi anthem, the Horst Wessel Song, was played on the organ at the end of the evening.[20]

Goebbels could not compete with professional dramatists. Of those who were ready to ally themselves to the Nazis before 1933, Hanns Johst was probably the most successful. His play *The King* (*Der König*, 1920), about the need for leaders to treat their subjects with brutality rather than kindness, was seen by the young Hitler seventeen times. *Schlageter*, completed in 1932 and dedicated to Hitler, celebrated the role of the eponymous hero, who had been executed by the French for sabotage during the 1923 occupation of the Ruhr. It contains the oft-misattributed phrase: 'When I hear the word culture ... I release the safety-catch on my revolver' (Browning). The premiere of the play took place on Hitler's birthday, 20 April 1933. It was the last play

Johst wrote; from 1935 until 1945 he was president of the Reich Literature Chamber.[21]

The Nazi reorganization of the theatre profession

While certain publications and plays voiced Nazi views during the Weimar Republic, they could give only an inkling of what the Nazi control of culture would entail. A brief rehearsal for the exercise of political power came in January 1930, when the Nazi Party secured two ministries in a local coalition with other conservative groups in Thuringia. As Minister for the Interior (and culture) Wilhelm Frick appointed the leader of the local Kampfbund für Deutsche Kultur, Hans Severus Ziegler, to the post of specialist in culture, art and theatre. Frick's decree in April that year, 'Against Negro Culture – For German Tradition', meant the police could ban performances of jazz and state-subsidized concert programmes featuring modernist composers such as Stravinsky and Hindemith. Drama was also affected. In the Weimar National Theatre, which was in the region, the proportion of contemporary writers and composers performed fell from 57 per cent in 1929 to 14 per cent in 1930, with a great increase in works of a farcical nature.[22] The Nazi artistic decrees were repealed in April 1931, but they were a foretaste of the policies to be enacted once the party rose to authority at a state level.

After Hitler became Chancellor of Germany on 30 January 1933, the Nazi ascent in the cultural realm was rapidly achieved through a combination of legislature and bully tactics. An example of the latter occurred on the very day of Hitler's appointment, when ten Nazi Storm Troopers invaded the municipal theatre of Frankfurt am Main and hoisted a swastika flag on the roof of the opera house. During February a campaign of intimidation was carried out in many subsidized theatres by the more aggressive Nazis against their most easily identifiable enemies (such as Jews and Marxists). The 5 March elections gave Hitler 43.9 per cent of the vote, but he had to wait until the 'Enabling Law' of 23 March to be given the legal authority to establish a dictatorship. Meanwhile, on 13 March, Hitler had created the Ministry of Propaganda and People's Enlightenment (Reichsministerium für Propaganda und Volksaufklärung) with responsibility for culture and placed Joseph Goebbels in charge of the new organization. By April the ministry had a special theatre section (itself later divided into subsections) and the Bühnengenossen-schaft, the principal theatre employees' union, was in Nazi control. The important Civil Service Law of 7 April allowed local authorities to sack personnel regarded as politically or racially suspect.[23]

However, it was only in the autumn of 1933 that the main control mechanisms were fully in place, after the creation of the Reich Chamber of Culture (the Reichskulturkammer) on 22 September. Following a law of 1 November, professionals had to be a member of one of the seven chambers (of fine art, music, film, radio, press, literature or theatre) to work in the arts. In paragraph 10 of the November decree there was a provision explaining that individuals could be refused membership if they were shown not to possess the 'necessary reliability and suitability to exercise their activity'. This would later form the legal basis for excluding anybody who did not meet Nazi racial or political criteria, but membership was initially automatic: the Theatre Chamber was formed from two Weimar organizations, the Bühnen-Verein and the Bühngenossenschaft. With Goebbels at the hierarchical top of all the chambers, the Theatre Chamber had, by 1937, subdivisions for everything from dance to puppetry, and a membership of 41,100.[24]

Goebbels's control of cultural matters in the new Reich came as a great disappointment to his rival Alfred Rosenberg, who assumed that the activities of his Kampfbund für Deutsche Kultur would have guaranteed him exclusive authority over the arts.[25] The creation of the Chamber of Culture considerably lessened the power of the Kampfbund, although the latter was also involved in separate machinations. In 1933 it had coordinated the two largest theatre-goers' associations of the Weimar Republic, the Verband der freien Volksbühne and the Bühnenvolksbund, which were merged into the Deutsche Bühne (German Stage). The following year, the Deutsche Bühne was made a cooperative member of Robert Ley's Kraft durch Freude (Strength through Joy), a Nazi organization formed in November 1933 which arranged cultural events with discounted tickets and mass subscriptions.

The difference between the Kampfbund and Kraft durch Freude was neatly summarized by one contemporary journalist as the 'promotional and selective influence over cultural life' (of Rosenberg's movement) and 'its mediation' (through Ley's grouping). One estimate indicates that, by means of cheap tickets and compulsory outings, Kraft durch Freude brought workers to over five million theatre performances and concerts in 1935 alone.[26] But it is easy to see Kraft durch Freude and Ley's related Deutsche Arbeitsfront (German Labour Front) as threats to the Kampfbund. Together, Goebbels and Ley managed to isolate Rosenberg. In 1934 his Kampfbund became the National-sozialistische (NS) Kulturgemeinde (National Socialist Cultural Community), which organized performances for large audiences within a strictly defined Nazi ethos. By 1935 it had a membership of 1.5 million, but bureaucratic, financial and political motives meant that, two years later, the NS-Kulturgemeinde was absorbed into Kraft durch Freude under the auspices of the Deutsche Arbeitsfront. The practical demands of Ley's leisure-time organization tended to take precedence over Rosenberg's more ideological approach.

The eclipse of Rosenberg as the organizer of culture in the Third Reich did not mean that his beliefs disappeared from public view. As a kind of consolation for Goebbels's ascent, Rosenberg was granted the position of the Führer's 'Representative (*Beauftragter*) for the Supervision of the Entire Spiritual and Philosophical Training and Education of the Party' with his own little agency. Although Rosenberg was excluded from the government, his editorship of the *Völkischer Beobachter* and the publication of the theatrical periodical *Bausteine zum Deutschen Nationaltheater* (which later resurfaced as *Deutsche Dramaturgie*) provided platforms for the airing of radical opinions. Rosenberg, his colleague Walter Stang (for a long time in charge of Kampfbund theatrical policy) and their associates were vehemently anti-modernist. They were also driven by an anti-semitism and a desire to purge political undesirables from cultural life which made many government officials of the Third Reich appear benign. Indeed, whether it was condemning Expressionist styles or publicly criticizing appointments by the Theatre Chamber (on racial and ideological grounds), the Rosenberg circle kept up a constant pressure on the running of mainstream theatre. To supplement these pronouncements, the organization of mass performances by the NS-Kulturgemeinde was particularly influential in small towns, and the annual congress of the organization became Rosenberg's counterpoint to Goebbels's National Theatre Festivals.[27]

In his introductory speech about his new Propaganda Ministry, Goebbels explained that, for this 'people's government', a *Gleichschaltung* (ideological incorporation, coordination or forcing into line) between the government and 'the whole people' was one of his first tasks. And yet, besides his own sparring with Rosenberg, there were two other factors which meant that actual government policy on theatre was not 'coordinated' enough for it to be entirely coherent. As Reich Governor and Minister of the Interior in Prussia, Hermann Göring (married to the actress Emmy Sonnemann) maintained sole control over the Prussian Staatstheater (State Theatre), the Berlin Staatsoper, and each Staatstheater in Wiesbaden, Kassel and Hanover. Finally, the Führer himself could contradict official tastes by personal pronouncements. He was also responsible for guaranteeing the financial stability of Bayreuth and financing Wagner research. His own money subsidized the National Theatre in Weimar and the Berlin Volksoper.[28]

There was even a variance in policy within the Propaganda Ministry and Theatre Chamber, as different individuals gained positions of power and aesthetic directions changed. Foremost among the personalities was Rainer Schlösser, who had written a doctorate on German literature and then joined the *Völkischer Beobachter* as cultural-political editor. Schlösser was appointed National Reichsdramaturg in the Propaganda Ministry, a title which in effect meant that he was chief theatre censor for the duration of the Third Reich. The most prominent of his colleagues were the playwrights Sigmund Graff and Eberhard Wolfgang Möller. Meanwhile, the first president of the Theatre Chamber was the former actor Otto Laubinger. The Rosenberg Dienststelle (administration section) criticized the appointment because of Laubinger's Jewish name and appearance (in spite of the fact that he was the son of a Protestant minister).[29]

When Laubinger died in 1935, Goebbels used the opportunity to reorganize the chamber. He appointed Schlösser as president of the Theatre Chamber in addition to his position in the Propaganda Ministry. Schlösser worked with Albert Eduard Frauenfeld, who, as Geschäftsführer, was responsible for the daily running of the Theatre Chamber (1935–41), and Hans Hinkel, who, as Reichskulturwalter of the Chamber of Culture, had started a purge within the system. Together they arranged for the formal dissolution of the Bühnen-Verein and the Bühnengenossenschaft, the membership and assets of which became the constituents of a new organization, the Fachschaft Bühne. This new entity would be more tightly supervised by the Propaganda Ministry and the Theatre Chamber. There was also an attempt to ensure a higher degree of conformity between the theatre department of the ministry and the chamber. Schlösser remained Reichsdramaturg, but he left his post as president of the chamber in 1938 – Goebbels did not think he was good at administration – and the actors Ludwig Körner and Paul Hartmann were appointed presidents of the Theatre Chamber for 1938–42 and 1942–45 respectively. Radio drama and even an embryonic form of television were organized through similarly varying degrees of Propaganda Ministry supervision. The whole system resembled a set of Russian dolls, so that even the most subsidiary activities and organizations came under the control of larger, politically responsible entities.[30]

The two main aims behind the increased power of the Theatre Chamber were to facilitate ideological-bureaucratic control and accelerate the exclusion of undesirables. With regard to censorship, much of the task had been accomplished within the first year of the Reich. Repertory lists for individual theatres had to be submitted to Reichsdramaturg Schlösser for approval, but there were no uniform lists of forbidden dramatists, and complications were usually avoided in advance by publishers who had already cleared works with Schlösser before publication (in order to avoid banning after printing). In spite of the attempted *Gleichschaltung*, the prohibition of one play could be effective in only one region or consist in limiting the number of performances, rather than outright banning. Rebecca Rovit's study in the present volume (Chapter 4) reveals a considerable degree of improvisation by the censor's office, in relation to both the racial identity of the dramatists concerned and the texts themselves. Living playwrights proved extremely malleable when faced with proposed cuts; there is no evidence that any dramatist refused to comply with the authorities. One writer, Georg Fraser, had a reserve of potential textual changes ready should the censor object. Jewish and Marxist authors were obviously forbidden, but overt anti-semitism often came under censure: one directive from the Reichsdramaturg's office to a publisher in 1934 forbade the anti-semitism of a play, not because it was 'wrong', but because it was 'completely superfluous with regard to domestic policy' (since Jewish influences had already been eliminated) and 'harmful to foreign politics'. In any case, the overall results of the censorial spirit were immediate: German plays of the Weimar Republic, which had constituted roughly 30 per cent of the total repertory during 1929–33, dropped to 5.56 per cent in the first full season (1933–34) of the new regime and sank further in the subsequent years of the Third Reich. One of the richest periods of modern German drama had virtually disappeared.[31]

As far as the exclusion of 'undesirable' professionals from theatrical life was concerned, the fulfilment of Nazi intentions was a longer procedure. The initial campaign of terror did have its effects. By April 1933 there had been thirty-six changes of *Intendanten* (theatre managers/artistic directors) all around the country. The Communist actor Hans Otto was clubbed to death by Nazi Storm Troopers in November of the same year. But Nazi declarations were ambitious. *Der Angriff* referred to the urgency of overcoming 'fourteen years of cultural Bolshevism' during which the 'complete Judaization of the theatre' had occurred. Another commentator thought it was 'impossible' for a Jewish actor to represent a German character on stage with credibility.[32] It would therefore be necessary to eliminate Jews from any active part in German culture.

Judicial measures helped in this process. Following the important paragraph 10 of the November 1933 decree, the Unified Theatre Law of 15 May 1934 increased Propaganda Ministry control over private theatres (which constituted 20 per cent of theatre companies) and state theatres, by making them equally subject to national racial and artistic policies. It also gave Goebbels the power to appoint theatre managers and artistic directors and ban the performance of works 'if he consider[ed] it necessary for the fulfilment of the cultural task (*Kulturaufgabe*) of the theatre'. There were addenda to this decree, but the Nuremberg Laws of 1935 proved crucial for effective exclusion, since they revoked German citizenship for non-Aryans. Expulsions from the Theatre Chamber were carried out from the autumn of 1935 through most of the following year. By 1938, 535 members had been forced to leave and the racist atmosphere was so pronounced that social associations with Jews were being officially discouraged. One actress was investigated by the chamber after she had been spotted climbing into the car of a Jewish doctor. Members of the Theatre Chamber had to present proof of their Aryan descent well into 1937.[33] Given that jobs advertised in the theatrical magazine *Die Bühne* demanded this proof, together with a photograph of the applicant, it is tempting to see

Die Stelle eines

INTENDANTEN

für die Kurhessische Landesbühne in Kassel
(Wanderbühne) ist zu besetzen.

Bewerbungen m. beglaubigten Zeugnisabschrif-
ten, Lichtbild, Lebenslaufschilderung und Ariernachweis (bei Verheirateten auch für die Ehefrau)
sowie mit Angabe von Gehaltsansprüchen an den

Kurhessischen Gemeinde-Kulturverband
Kassel, Ständeplatz 8

I   An advertisement for the post of theatre manager in Kassel in the magazine *Die Bühne*
(1939). Among the material requested with the application is a photograph (*Lichtbild*) and proof
of Aryan status (*Ariernachweis*), for the candidate, and for his wife if he is married.

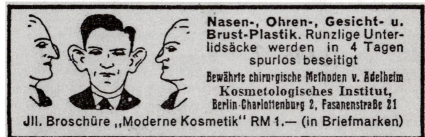

Nasen-, Ohren-, Gesicht- u.
Brust-Plastik. Runzlige Unter-
lidsäcke werden in 4 Tagen
spurlos beseitigt
Bewährte chirurgische Methoden v. Adelheim
Kosmetologisches Institut,
Berlin-Charlottenburg 2, Fasanenstraße 21

JII. Broschüre „Moderne Kosmetik" RM 1.— (in Briefmarken)

2   Changes possible through plastic surgery, as advertised in *Die Bühne* (1937).

advertisements for plastic surgery in the same publication as an opportunity
for candidates to transform their un-Aryan appearance (Figures 1 and 2).

There were laughable aspects to this extreme nationalism. Local functionaries wanted to exclude even non-Germanic words from the theatre, so that
Parkettplatz (seat in the stalls) was replaced by *Erdgeschoß*, and *Balkon* (circle)
by *Hauptrang*. More sinister were Goebbels's attempts to purify audiences by
preventing Jewish attendance at concerts, cabarets, theatres, cinemas, circuses
and lectures with an order of 1938. The measure was only enforceable in
September 1941, when German Jews were ordered to wear yellow stars.[34]

It would be wrong to think that Nazi theatrical organizations were watertight, even by 1936, and that nobody escaped the restrictions. Members of the various chambers did not have to be members of the Nazi Party. According to one estimate, less than 20 per cent of those in the Theatre Chamber joined the party. Furthermore, conflicts within and between local, regional and central departments sometimes provided the opportunity for individual exceptions. (The manager/artistic director of the local theatre was often answerable in the first instance to the mayor of the town.) Goebbels was sometimes ready to grant dispensations for membership of one of the chambers. The daughters of the Jewish composer Friedrich Korolanyi were allowed one such dispensation because of their artistic achievements and the fact that, as the official argument ran, 'externally they exhibit no Jewish characteristics'. A Jew in the Music Chamber, Manfred Kropf, used forged documents to remain a member until 1943. Richard Mohaupt was expelled from the Music Chamber in 1936, because of his political unreliability, but then gained admittance to the Theatre Chamber for his theatre work and stayed a member until 1938.[35]

Rivalry among Nazi leaders and professional ability were often reasons for blatant ideological contradictions. As Gauleiter of Vienna from 1939, Baldur von Schirach offered personal protection to Richard Strauss (against Goebbels's wishes) and promoted composers who had lost favour in Berlin. The well-known dancer Gret Palucca enjoyed the protection of the SS, even though she was a half-Jew according to the Race Laws. Göring appointed Gustaf Gründgens director of the Berlin Staatstheater, despite the actor's overt homosexuality and his left-wing antecedents in Hamburg cabaret. Gründgens remained in his post throughout the increasingly official Nazi persecution of gay men.[36]

Similar exceptions occurred for the performance of works by dead authors and composers. Having been the object of anti-semitic attacks during his lifetime, Hugo von Hofmannsthal was condemned at the start of the Third Reich. None of his plays was performed after 1934. And yet Strauss's *Arabella* (for which Hofmannsthal wrote the libretto) was continually produced and became one of the most popular operas of the period. Hofmannsthal was then excused as only quarter-Jewish in Nazi circles. Another strange anomaly was that Jewish composers stayed on record company catalogues until 1938.[37] The debate over differing musical and dramatic styles deserves separate attention. Equivalent difficulties in applying general rules meant that atonalism and theatrical Expressionism (both targets of much Nazi venom) did not disappear entirely from the Third Reich, even after 1936.

Those who managed to remain within the Theatre Chamber were treated to concerted attempts to improve standards and conditions. In 1934, a minimum wage was decreed for those working in Berlin theatres. The Goebbels Foundation for Theatre People organized a welfare fund. Although some pension schemes were very successful, the same cannot be said for the initiative to set an examination for the chamber, which was started in 1934, but then abandoned the following year. This may be one of the factors which allowed official figures to indicate that total employment in the theatre world had risen from 22,045 in 1932–33 to 36,441 in 1938–39. By the 1942–43 season, with the opening of German theatres in the assimilated and occupied territories, the total was 42,678. While these figures undoubtedly concealed the fact that jobs were sometimes temporary, they still provide a stark contrast to the high unemployment of the Weimar Republic. Moreover, for those with salaries, the rewards could reach astounding proportions. Well-known actors were especially well recompensed, earning 1000 Reichsmarks (RM) a day for film work (when the average annual salary of a skilled worker was 2500 RM). As Gustaf Gründgens was to say after the war: 'There is no doubt that, superficially and as far as money was concerned, German actors never had it so good as in the last years before the [Nazi] collapse.'[38]

The state subsidies for theatre to sustain this wage inflation were correspondingly high: they increased almost five-fold from 1934 to 1942, to reach over 22 million RM a year. Of all the activities subsidized by the Propaganda Ministry, theatre was the most privileged, even above active, direct propaganda. Ticket prices were reduced by up to half and the subscription systems of organizations like Kraft durch Freude made attendance even cheaper. The claim in 1942 that audiences had doubled from ten years earlier is not difficult to believe. By that same year in the Second World War, there were 362 German-language theatres within the expanded Third Reich from which to choose.[39]

Contradictions in dramatic theory and practice

In conjunction with the prohibitions of drama and personnel, many claims were made about the radically different repertoire offered to growing theatre audiences under the Nazis. And yet, despite an initial impression of uniformity, these claims were never totally consistent, partly because of the differing opinions held by the individuals involved and partly because the notions themselves were self-contradictory or at best unclear.

It was usually easy to condemn past styles. Naturalism was the common enemy, because of its association with Socialism and what one critic called its 'artistic inbreeding'. Another commentator added: 'Naturalism desecrated and brutalized the theatre. Its drama did not belong to ideas, but to the propaganda methods of political parties.' One of the foremost Nazi authorities on contemporary drama, Hermann Wanderscheck, voiced another important line of attack: 'In Naturalism, the I not the We [...] reigned supreme.' Wanderscheck asserted that contemporary dramatists, unlike the Naturalists, knew that theatre was not life 'as it is', but poetry/fiction (*Dichtung*), and poetry is 'superelevated life'. According to an encomium of the Nazi dramatist Eberhard Wolfgang Möller, 'real drama' did not concern itself with guilt and innocence, but took for granted 'absolute morality'.[40]

Even in these statements there were inconsistencies. Naturalism could not be art for art's sake (artistic inbreeding) and at the same time so overtly political. Leftist ideologies were ostensibly concerned with mass movements, but Wanderscheck, objecting to the omnipresent 'I' of much recent theatre, labelled it with the oxymoron 'individualist-Marxist theatre'.[41] Moreover, the concept of absolute morality was patently open to a political gloss.

The idea which served to obscure these contradictions consisted in one word, with a strong Romantic heritage: the *Volk* (nation, people). There were, however, fundamental problems with the term in a theatrical context. The Berlin Volksbühne (or People's Stage) had been set up in 1890, under the influence of emergent Socialist groups. Expressing a desire to extend audiences beyond the bourgeoisie, its main founder, Bruno Wille, declared that 'art should belong to the people (*Volk*), and not be the privilege of one section of the population or one social class'. By 1914, the movement had its own theatre in Berlin, inscribed with the motto 'Art for the people', although we have already seen how organized competition over the theatrical allegiances of the 'people' had evolved in 1919 with the creation of the right-wing Bühnenvolks-bund.[42]

It was therefore obvious that the Nazis would have to appropriate completely the terms of leftist intentions, while switching political direction, avoiding the promotion of playwrights like Gorky and Schnitzler, and giving the impression of a new aesthetic terrain. The Nazis (or National Socialists) would thus claim to be as anti-bourgeois as their left-wing predecessors, and as sympathetic to the working class. And so, to exaggerate their difference, apologists for the Nazi regime argued that previous (leftist) attempts to take theatre to the people had been singularly unsuccessful. 'Irresponsible young people like Bertolt Brecht' were wrong in thinking that contemporary drama had filled the theatre with masses of people; on the contrary, 'it had depopulated (*entvölkert*) theatres'. When the Nazis took over the Berlin Volksbühne they were not afraid to rename it the Theatre on Horst-Wessel-Platz and simultaneously exploit its previous ethos by retaining 'Art for the people' as a statement printed in the deceptive house magazine.[43]

Echoes of the original Volksbühne ideology can be found throughout the Nazi hierarchy in the first year of the regime. Before the setting up of the Chamber of Culture, Goebbels had proudly proclaimed: 'We want to take art back to the people (*Volk*), to be able to take the people back to art.' Rainer Schlösser thought that it was hardly possible to know for whom the theatre was intended in the past decade. Yet, at the same time, from the camaraderie on the front line in the First World War, an answer to the question had emerged: 'For the people!' The first president of the Theatre Chamber, Otto Laubinger, was likewise convinced that 'the theatre of the new state must be a people's theatre (*Volkstheater*, also meaning "folk theatre")'.[44]

Schlösser's mention of a German 'blood brotherhood' obviously gave this *Volk* a racial definition which was missing from leftist conceptions. Goebbels later explained that the art in which the 'deepest inner expression of a people' was mirrored could not be international. And yet the appeal to a broad audience remained. As the Dramaturg Klaus Jedzek argued, 'the theatre belongs to the people'. It is 'like a religion, a "property" of the people' and the 'people' encompassed a broad definition: 'People (*Volk*) are not a proletarian class. People are not the bourgeois upper strata of society in tails and dinner-jackets. People are the unity of feeling, of language, of piousness/ uprightness, of sadness, of humour and of happiness. *People are a unity of a feeling of being alive (Lebensgefühl).*' In his context, Expressionism was not, according to Jedzek, 'a theatre for the people'.[45]

Some affirmed that the *Volk* should not be linked indelibly with a quantity of people and that artistic levels should not be lowered to reach everybody. However, the need to attract a relatively uneducated public led to arguments in praise of the worker as well as the more practical activities of the NS-Kulturgemeinde and Kraft durch Freude. A series of rather awkward articles appeared in the theatrical press lauding the erudition, good behaviour and theatrical instinct of workers. But unity remained the priority. In the words of one enthusiast, the theatre audiences, where young and old, office workers and manual labourers, sat side by side, constituted a 'community based on [common] experience (*Erlebnisgemeinschaft*)'. Or, as Sigmund Graff put it, having declared the end of personal drama and writing from his position in the Propaganda Ministry: 'People do not need pity, they need leadership. People are not a class, but a community (*Gemeinschaft*).'[46]

Otto zur Nedden, the academic and Dramaturg in Weimar, thought that it was precisely this idea of 'community theatre' (*Gemeinschaftstheater*) which connected contemporary German theatre with the theatre of antiquity. Goebbels, insisting on the need for German writers to be political, claimed that contemporary politics was itself writing 'a people's drama (*Volksdrama*)'. And because acting had to establish an inner relationship with the *Volk*, the Rosenberg camp argued that the *individual* stars of the Weimar Republic (many of whom happened to be Jewish) were automatically excluded.[47]

Thus the *Volkstheater* of the new Germany was essentially envisaged as a national theatre, although the nature of the repertoire was never certain. During the Second World War, Ludwig Körner claimed that the amount of soldiers who visited Bayreuth proved that there was more real art in Germany for the people than in Britain. But in 1942 the theatre director Paul Rose was still discussing the exact nature of the texts to be performed: the *Volksstück*, standing as a replacement for cultic drama, was essentially a play in dialect, so, although it should concern and appeal to workers and farmers, its language inevitably limited its effective distribution. Meanwhile, the transformation of Max Reinhardt's Grosses Schauspielhaus in Berlin into the Nazi Theater des Volkes had continued Reinhardt's ambitions of creating unified, mass audiences (although the Jewish Reinhardt could not be acknowledged as part of the process). As for the incorporation of different social strata into established bourgeois theatre, recent research has shown that, apart from the special performances reserved or organized by Kraft durch Freude, the success was limited: in the case of Frankfurt municipal theatre, of the 3765 season-ticket holders in the 1936–37 season, only sixty-five could be classified as 'workers'. And as if to prove that the entire concept of a German-influenced 'theatre for the people' still had an untainted validity, an English critic called, in 1945, for the creation of 'a real *Volksbühne*' in London.[48]

Undoubtedly the most concerted effort to realize Nazi theory and establish a theatre for the people was the *Thingspiel* or *Thing* play movement, a genre acknowledged by zur Nedden as a latter-day exemplification of *Gemeinschaftstheater*: now the people were supposed to join in celebrating stories of mythic leaders who led Germany out of Weimar decadence. Open-air performances on *Thingplätze* and other venues increased the community spirit: in the summer of 1933, sixty-three open-air stages had welcomed 820,000 members of the public (an increase of 300,000 on the previous year). In one such production in 1935, of the *Thing* play by Heinrich Lersch, *Evolving People* (*Werdendes Volk*), even a collective sense of smell was involved, as stagehands fanned the audience with the scent of herbs and pine needles dropped into flaming torches.[49] But however much these experiences contributed to the feeling of a *Volksgemeinschaft* (national people's community) with audiences of 20,000 and more, the *Thing* plays were (as William Niven shows in Chapter 1 of the present study) stylistically, and sometimes even ideologically, redolent of the precedents to which so many Nazis objected: Expressionism and left-wing workers' plays (*Arbeiterdrama*). Authors central to the *Thing* play movement, such as Kurt Heynicke and Richard Euringer, had actually started out as Expressionists.

One element of the *Thing* plays which seemed ideal for the denial of the individual and the promotion of the community was the *Sprechchor* or declamatory chorus. The genre had an independent existence and was used in schools for consolidating a Nazi ethos:

> We're all related through blood and soil [*Blut und Boden*]
> on the same land we come to toil.

And another:

> Flag! We love you dear!
> Flag! We follow you near!

The Nazi writer Gerhard Schumann composed a series of slightly more sophisticated poems along the same lines, which were broadcast on radio. Again, however, the genre was not free from the contamination of a condemned epoch. Apart from the liturgical echoes of communal recitation (hardly suitable for pagan Nazism), the *Sprechchor* was essentially Marxist in origin. The fact the Nazi poems of unity could be chanted as well as declaimed brought them into a common realm and made the identity of the *Volksgemeinschaft* purely nominal rather than instrinsic to a particular form of expression. Besides the possible superficial resemblance to leftist songs of unity, there had been a remarkable attempt to develop didactic choral forms for Jewish unity in a *Lehrkantate* ('teaching cantata'), following Brecht's *Lehrstücke*, and based on the Hanukah story.[50]

Another obvious communal theatrical form was dance. The modern dance of the 1920s was felt to be relatively uncontaminated, largely because most of the greatest names in the profession were ready to agree to Nazi racial policy. A reaction against the 'individualist' aspects of *Ausdruckstanz* (dance of expression/free dance) had already begun before 1933 and mass choral forms took on a new attraction in the Third Reich. As one dancer argued: 'The history of dance shows us [...] that rising nations (*Völker*) always have a highly developed art of dance.' This dance would have to be collective and racially defined. The famous dancer and choreographer Mary Wigman talked in the Nazi period of the 'call of blood, which involves us all', a phrase whose potency is confirmed by her personal anti-semitism.[51]

Rudolf von Laban, meanwhile, ensured official support for modern dance and a correspondingly hostile view of ballet. It was a surprising triumph for an avant-garde and neo-primitivist view of the German body: here was a territory with blood ties to German identity in which the search for specifically German movements and rhythms could take place. These conceptions of unity through movement culminated in much of the choreography for the 1936 Berlin Olympic Games, above all the festival of *Olympic Youth*, staged on the opening night. Choreographed by Wigman, Palucca, Harald Kreutzberg and Dorothee Günther, the show had a cast of 10,000, divided according to sex, age and gender, but united in obedience to Hitler. It involved a spoken text, mock war and lamentations for the dead.[52]

The enthusiasm for such pioneering work could not last. Wigman never received another major commission from the government and Goebbels did all he could to sideline what he called such 'philosophical dance'. The regime moved back to more classical styles and Wigman, by reverting to numerous solo performances (in an implicit refusal to subordinate the artist to the *Volksgemeinschaft*), became the victim of criticism from the Rosenberg circle. Laban was denounced and had to leave Germany in 1937.[53]

The reversal of policy on dance typified the artistic conservatism which took hold after the first three years of the Third Reich. As well as the *Thing* play experiments in drama, the early stages of the regime had accommodated movements towards developing a Nazi strand of Expressionist art (some of which was much admired by Goebbels). But in 1935, the magazine which formed the basis for these ideas – *Kunst der Nation* – was banned. The same year saw a prohibition on the use of the terms *Thing* play and *Thingplatz* in connection with the Nazi Party and the suppression of Catholic theatre performances not directly connected to the Nazi cause. By 1936, the use of *Sprechchöre* was forbidden and two years later Hitler denounced cultic plays and cultic mysticism (while at the same time continuing to exploit cultic elements in public ceremonies and meetings).[54] Following the manipulative openness of the Olympic Games, the theatrical experiments to promote the *Volksgemeinschaft* appeared to have run their course.

The banning of theatre criticism in 1936

Goebbels's prohibition of art criticism in November 1936 reinforced the new stringency. It seemed like the hangman's rope to any meaningful debate on the nature of the *Volk* and the possible creative directions a theatre for the *Volk* could take.

An examination of the steps which preceded this radical decree reveals that it was far from inevitable. Those who welcomed the Nazi regime were predictably keen to distance themselves from the theatre criticism of the recent past. Critics like Alfred Kerr had been far too subjective, and the 'affected literary apes' or 'clowns' of the Weimar Republic had been more interested in themselves than in the productions they were supposed to be reviewing. The new era banished this decadent, negative approach. Gerhard Riesen even believed that the near future could produce a drama – he thought a *Thing* play – so brilliantly accessible that criticism would be superfluous. In the meantime, however, he took inspiration from famous names in German literature such as Herder, Kleist, the Schlegel brothers and Ludwig Tieck. Theatre criticism should teach the *Volk* about art, point out what was good and bad, explain what made a play politically valuable for the nation and, through all this work, become an essential part in the creation of a true German national theatre. Guidelines were established for the judgements theatre reviews should include, about, for example, language, performance and national-political worth.[55]

If these imperatives seem dogmatic, it is important to realize that they also contain a sense of excitement. Hans Knudsen, who was responsible for theatre criticism within the Reichsverband Deutscher Schriftsteller (Reich Association of German Writers), called critics 'comrades in arms (*Mitkämpfer*) in a new age' and appealed to their 'responsibility' in the face of the nation; they had to be capable of appreciating the culture of a new state and might well need extra qualifications to understand new genres (such as the *Thing* play). All this new criticism would not be free from argument. As another commentator put it: 'The livelier theatre criticism is in a town, the more fascinatingly it puts the concept of "theatre" up for discussion. Where there's a fight (*Kampf*) there's life as well.'[56]

At the same time, others were demanding more control. In the first year of the Third Reich a lawyer complained about negative criticism published in a Nazi Party newspaper: it was inconceivable that a play by Hans Rehberg, who had joined the party in 1930, could be treated in this fashion. In 1934 the actor Karl Vogt suggested that theatre criticism should stop, because the bourgeoisie – as opposed to the *Volk* – borrowed the 'crutches' of criticism to limp to a decision as to whether or not it liked a production. Vogt's idea was that, since no objective truth existed, the audience should rely on the unconditional validity of its own judgement and experience.[57]

By 1935 Goebbels was still condemning the 'anarchic state' of the German press before the Nazi takeover: everybody wrote what they wanted without taking into account the needs of the German people. His banning of criticism of the arts in 1936 implied that the situation had not changed sufficiently after more than three years of Nazi rule, although Goebbels's explanations in the decree are a crafty, simultaneous appeal to populism and elitism. He mentioned the 'increasing number of complaints about criticism, both from the ranks of artists themselves and from other sections of the population', but he also argued that the great critics of the past – such as Lessing, Kleist and Tieck – had completed creative work before writing reviews. Those with creative talent, Goebbels claimed, are less worried about criticizing than about creating. The great critics were not judges (unlike their Jewish colleagues), but just wanted 'to serve art'. This argument justified the abolition of criticism in favour of 'commentary/reporting on the arts (*Kunstbericht*)'. The reporters would need a licence to practise.[58]

In a mordant poem, Brecht wrote that Goebbels had banned theatre criticism 'to forbid criticism of the government by the people' – a logical move, because

Nazi achievements (in the socio-political sphere) were 'mainly in a theatrical realm'. One of Brecht's greatest suppporters, Herbert Ihering, was expelled from the Press Chamber in 1936, although the general effects of Goebbels's ban are more difficult to assess. The head of the German Press Association, Wilhelm Weiß, defended the prohibition by explaining how the 'measure of good and bad must be overcome and replaced by the understanding of the idea of a work of art'. Thus, according to another enthusiast, writing in 1942, reporters of the new breed were conscious of the harm their comments could cause and also aware of the encouragement they could give.[59]

These official assessments concealed the continued tensions within journalism. Critics such as Karl Heinz Ruppel and the music specialist Heinrich Strobel developed codes which could contain criticism within description. Wolf Braumüller, a committed Nazi in the Rosenberg camp, attacked individual directing styles and policies (for example, Saladin Schmitt's obsession with the classics in Bochum).[60] The complaints did not dry up either. During the war, the Hamburg critic Wolf Schramm was called before the Propaganda Ministry because of his reviews and, through the intervention of a sympathetic representative, subsequently spared by being transferred abroad to work on a German newspaper in Paris. It proved difficult to control journalists in the occupied and assimilated territories, even when they were ostensibly sympathetic to the Nazi cause. The cast of a German Shakespeare production in The Hague was described by a Dutch critic as having 'few high points', with one actor being especially 'silly', while the set made 'little impression'. In 1940 Goebbels was moaning in his diary about the difficulties the director Lothar Müthel was having with the critics in Vienna.[61]

Contemporary drama

As the performance of German plays written in the 1920s and early 1930s declined to less than 1.5 per cent of the repertoire in the last season under the Nazis (1943–44), they were replaced by a different kind of contemporary German drama which constituted well over half the total repertory of the Third Reich. According to Walter Stang, recent dramatists before 1933 had 'battled against the cornerstones of age-old German morality, against honour and duty, against family and marriage, against national consciousness'.[62] It would therefore be logical to suppose that the new dramas promoted or even tolerated after 1933 as smaller-scale counterparts to the *Thing* plays would support the notions which had apparently been so undermined in the Weimar Republic. As well as being removed from Expressionism and Naturalism, they would be patriotic and anti-Marxist.

There were indeed many plays with such ideological content. One of the most-cited examples of a drama of the *Blut und Boden* genre is Friedrich Griese's *Man Made out of Earth* (*Mensch aus Erde gemacht*), premiered two months before the Nazis came to power. Much of the message about German values rooted in the soil of generations came from the stubborn peasant protagonist, Hans Biermann: 'I'm a man [...] a man made out of earth, out of a clod of earth, as the Bible says. I can't make myself be anything else. I could stuff earth down my throat, I'd chew it, and it would taste good.' These words may sound ridiculous, but they were voiced by an actor of the stature of Heinrich George in a major production of the play, directed by Jürgen Fehling at the Berlin Staatstheater in 1933.[63] Richard Billinger's *The Giant* (*Der Gigant*) likewise extolled the virtues of farming life, with a stern lesson about the penalty to be paid for abandoning the ancestral home in favour of the cosmopolitan city.

Yet it would be wrong to assume that all the writers eager to replace the dramatists of Weimar followed a similar path. It is estimated that only a fifth of the films made in the Third Reich were overtly propagandistic, and the figure for drama could be much less, largely because direct allusions to the present were officially limited. Goebbels issued a decree on 8 December 1937 prohibiting positive or negative references in theatres to politics, the state, religion, the police and the army. It was difficult to enforce, but subsequent orders in May 1939 and December 1940 showed how seriously the matter was taken. The reduction of possibilities included a ban on the Nazi salute in the theatre and, as we have already seen, measures against primitive anti-semitism.[64]

In the face of these strictures, more remote history was (as Glen Gadberry explains in Chapter 2) an attractive terrain, although even here there were constraints. In 1937 a law was passed forbidding the frivolous imitation of German historical characters, such as Frederick the Great and Bismarck, in circuses and variety theatres. Apart from the obvious need to respect the past, perhaps officials had realized that the mass of inferior work in circulation was bound to provoke parody. One account tells of 500 scripts about the Germanic hero Arminius which were submitted in 1933. And yet parallels from other countries were available. Hermann Heinz Ortner's *Isabella of Spain* (*Isabella von Spanien*) included a powerful Inquisition and negative Jewish characters. It was given ninety-four productions. A year before the premiere in 1938 the author had divorced his Jewish wife.[65]

Another successful author, the committed Nazi Friedrich Bethge, praised strong political control in relation to the theatre by stating that 'liberalism and drama are opposites', because liberalism tended to side-step decisions rather than face up to them. He defined his own style as 'heroic realism'. Thus, the hero of his *Veterans' March* (*Marsch der Veteranen*) is a Prussian officer in Napoleonic Russia who incarnated the need to bring discipline to a huge country. With chanting and the stress on the 'honour of the nation', the text seemed like an ideal parallel to contemporary preoccupations, although it was not used as propaganda in the Second World War, because of the presence of the war wounded in the play (and initially because of the Molotov–Ribbentrop pact). A similar fate befell the much subtler text by Sigmund Graff and Carl Ernst Hintze, *The Endless Road* (*Die endlose Straße*), premiered in 1930. Set on the 1917 battlefront in northern France, it painted a humane portrait of soldiers and was far from a tone of bombastic heroism. Although it won the first Dietrich Eckart Prize at the end of 1933, it was, on Graff's suggestion, withdrawn two years later from the list of officially sanctioned plays after Rainer Schlösser had demanded changes in the text.[66]

Despite the allegories and serious historical dramas, about half the drama performed in the Third Reich can be classified as 'light entertainment' (which included farces and classic comedies from previous centuries). An author of comic plays, Wolfgang Müller, considered that the purpose of his craft could be called 'medical', although he might have added that a conservative morality was usually part of the treatment. Women, for example, had their fixed place in society. In Jochen Huth's *The Four Companions* (*Die vier Gesellen*), four women tried to make work their first objective in life, but by the end, three have husbands to take precedence, while the fourth gives herself over to art. (The play was so successful that a film was made of it in 1938 starring Ingrid Bergman.) One of the most famous comedies was the 1930 *Much Ado about Iolanthe* (*Krach um Iolanthe*), by August Hinrichs. Originally written in dialect, the text conveyed a kind of peasant, *Volk* justice through the return of a pig taken as a substitute for taxes. The play was enormously popular and Hitler apparently saw it three times.[67]

For the famous authors who stayed in Germany, the situation was more difficult. The playwright who had come to represent Expressionism, Georg Kaiser, was faced by Nazi protests at the premiere of *Silverlake* (*Der Silbersee*) in February 1933, after which his plays were banned. Kaiser continued to write, published secret editions of his allegorical poems about the regime, and emigrated to Switzerland in 1938.[68] The fate of the master of Naturalism, Gerhart Hauptmann, typifies the divide between those who were reluctant to dismiss entirely a great talent and those Nazis who felt confident enough to apply the conclusions of their politics with the utmost thoroughness.

Those who wanted to adopt Hauptmann for the Nazi cause had to ignore certain aspects of his character. His declared philosemitism and his mockery of Nazi speeches before 1933 could find no place in the new order. Alfred Rosenberg, in his 1930 book *The Myth of the Twentieth Century*, had dismissed Hauptmann outright, and the Nazi anti-Naturalist strain meant that the dramatist's epic picture of industrial misery, *The Weavers* (*Die Weber*, 1892), was banned. (Reichsdramaturg Schlösser was ready to allow the play, but was overridden by Goebbels.) However, Hauptmann's increasing nationalism and his literary prestige, despite his support for Weimar, indicated directions to be exploited. The peasant tragedy *Florian Geyer* (1896) was misused for Nazi propaganda (even in the Berlin Volksbühne), while there were several productions of other plays, including performances in Italy and the occupied territories. A large edition of his complete works appeared during the war, but Goebbels agreed with Rosenberg that Hauptmann was ideologically suspect and made sure that his eightieth birthday celebrations in 1942 were limited in extent and not associated with the Nazi Party. Heinz Hilpert was prevented from directing Hauptmann's realistic vision of Berlin poverty *The Rats* (*Die Ratten*), at the same time, in a proposed production in honour of the author. Hauptmann himself wrote a classical cycle during the war and, in his last interview before his death in 1946, was welcoming the new productions of his work in the Soviet-occupied zone of Germany and declaring himself ready for the reconstruction of his homeland.[69]

When a figure as important as Hauptmann proved so problematic, it is understandable that numerous officials felt unsure about the success of Nazi goals in the theatre. The Rosenberg sector was always ready to criticize much-performed dramatists such as Billinger and Curt Langenbeck. What is more remarkable is that unconcealed disapppointment about contemporary drama evolved into a public admission of inadequacy by those representing more central policies of the regime. The attraction of the Nazi martyr Horst Wessel as a subject led to a host of inferior plays within the first year of the Reich. Hanns Johst classified one of the many contributions as 'complete patriotic kitsch!' Two years later, after all the energy channelled into *Thing* plays, Goebbels confessed to the party that 'unfortunately we still don't have the playwrights who possess the visionary power to mould the mental substance of our age into dramatic form'.[70]

Such comments did not stop after the ban on criticism in 1936, above all in longer considerations of current theatre. In his book surveying drama of the twentieth century, Otto zur Nedden claimed: 'There are all too many writers who imagine they have written a political and valid drama, relevant for our age, if the words "Fatherland", "German" and the expression "blood and soil" occur at least twice on every page of their manuscript.' While still wanting to salvage a kind of political theatre, he went on to mock dramas which began with Germanic heroes and ended with prophecies of the Third Reich, or viewed every peasant war leader as a precursor of the new Germany. The comments stayed in the third edition of zur Nedden's book, published in 1944, and, despite the absence of specific authors, they seemed to defame a whole genre. To complicate matters further, a curious discussion of contemporary drama – published days before the closure of all theatres in the same year – proposed a synthesis of Naturalist and classical styles as a way of combining reality with a conflict of ideas. Naturalism did not appear to be so contemptible after all. That such comments should be printed in an official theatre magazine so late in the regime expresses, to say the least, a quirky degree of uncertainty about recent endeavours.[71]

The German classics

Given the difficulties caused by contemporary drama, the German classics seemed like safer ground. Those in the Rosenberg camp were not afraid of making comparisons on the subject: 'The dramatic work of our classic writers (among whom we also count Shakespeare) has [...] a poetic, formally fashioned character which is unfortunately all too often missing in living dramatists.' The guarantee was ideological as well. For Hitler, these artists were untouched by the cultural decay of Dadaism and Cubism and free from modernism's disdain for the past. According to one strand of anti-religious Nazi literary theory, the 'Nordic' figures of Schiller, Kleist and Hebbel signalled the end of a gap in German literature for which Christianity had been responsible. For other supporters of the regime, such authors were suitably 'anti-bourgeois' and they became relevant during the Second World War, because they spoke of 'the challenge of destiny'. More importantly, they reinforced the idea of a national German theatre, with Weimar – the home of Goethe and Schiller – at its centre (as a fortress against the ills of the Weimar Republic). Goebbels's conviction that Germany was 'the motherland of world theatre' could be proven by the performance of its greatest dramatists, who had themselves aspired to the creation of a national theatre.[72]

That, at least, was the theory. In practice, plays were not so conveniently open to exploitation. Gotthold Ephraim Lessing, for example, was an attractive focal point because of his famous plea, in 1767–69, for a national theatre. But, besides the author's friendship with Moses Mendelssohn, his *Nathan the Wise* had shown clear sympathy towards Jews. Hence the convoluted attempts by Nazi commentators to apologize for Lessing's tolerance and explain how the play was, in fact, anti-semitic. Adolf Bartels and Werner Zimmermann went as far as to argue that Lessing would have been anti-semitic in contemporary Germany.[73] Despite writing of this nature, *Nathan the Wise* was banned from Nazi stages. It was left to the Jewish cultural organization, the Berlin Jüdischer Kulturbund, to perform the play for Jewish audiences, while less contentious pieces, such as *Minna von Barnhelm*, graced mainstream theatres. Even with the prohibition of *Nathan*, the percentage of Lessing productions doubled compared with the last years of the Weimar Republic to reach 1.33 per cent of the total repertory.

Schiller, on the other hand, was the most-performed dramatist of the Third Reich, jostling with Shakespeare for first place and eventually beating him. Part of the Nazi rhetoric to manipulate Schiller was already in place before 1933. Hitler had seen *William Tell* when he was twelve years old. A year before the Nazi takeover, the party published a book by Hans Fabricius entitled *Schiller as Hitler's Comrade in Arms* (*Schiller als Kampfgenosse Hitlers*), which, as the subtitle clarified, sought to demonstrate the 'National Socialism in Schiller's plays'. Fabricius viewed the dramatist not just as a prophet but as a guide to the Nazis, and analyzed the relevant political concepts of each drama, such as 'soldiership and politics' (in *Wallenstein*). The book was republished in 1934 and, although not everybody within the regime agreed on the extent of Nazification Schiller could undergo, official promotion included lavish celebrations of the writer's 175th birthday in Bochum, Weimar and Marbach am Neckar. Thousands took part in processions and homages linked to the glorification of the Third Reich.[74]

There were also approaches to directing Schiller which gave the group, rather than the individual, the illusion of power. Hans Meissner's 1933 inaugural production of *The Robbers* in Frankfurt placed heroic emphasis on the band of outlaws. The following year, the renamed Theater des Volkes in Berlin opened with a large-scale version of the same play. Perhaps to suggest a parallel with the number of empowered actors on stage, the premiere was free for workers. During the war, the political message was blunter: both *Maria Stuart* and Schiller's Joan of Arc story, *Die Jungfrau von Orleans*, had anti-English potential.[75]

However, Schiller was not so easily moulded to the Nazi cause. In the third act of *Don Carlos*, the Marquis de Posa's plea to King Philip – 'Give us freedom of thought' – was greeted with applause in Hamburg, Dresden, Munich, Bremen and, most notably, the Deutsches Theater in Berlin (for Heinz Hilpert's production). *William Tell* was initially very popular. It was broadcast on radio on 5 March 1933. In the 1933–34, 1934–35 and 1938–39 seasons it was Schiller's most-performed play. It was also the first (or often only) play studied by fourteen- and fifteen-year-old children. Then, in June 1941, Hitler personally banned it, probably fearing the notion of the legitimate murder of a tyrant which the text contained. The ban covered the use of *William Tell* in schools, and measures were taken to limit the reprinting even of extracts from the play. By the end of the regime it was the far less political *Intrigue and Love* (*Kabale und Liebe*) which had received the most (a total of 213) productions in the Third Reich.[76]

Hesitations over Schiller were as nothing compared to the challenge at first

3 Schiller's *William Tell*, at the Staatstheater, Dresden, premiered 11 June 1933. Director: Rudolf Schröder. Set designer: Adolf Mahnke.

provided by Goethe, whose plays were slow in recovering their former popularity. Rosenberg relegated Goethe to the sidelines for the coming decades, because the poet had hated 'the violence or force of a character-forming idea' and had refused to accept 'any dictatorship of thought'. (Without such a dictatorship, Rosenberg affirmed, a *Volk* cannot remain a *Volk* or ever create a real state.) It was left to Hans Severus Ziegler, director of the National Theatre in Weimar, to head the construction of a Nazi Goethe, by basing the writer's aesthetics on the *Volk* and labelling him an anti-semite. Faust became a leader figure for the regime, with special emphasis placed on Mephistopheles's statement when the pact between the two is made: 'Blood is a juice of exceptional quality.' By wartime, there were over 300 performances each year of the first part of Goethe's tragedy (among them Gründgens's portrayal of Mephistopheles). Mathias Wieman, who played Faust in a production of both parts of the play in Hamburg, claimed that the peformances had taken on a great new relevance on two occasions: when German troops had landed in Norway and when they had marched into Holland and Belgium. *Faust* was then the 'daring and faithful picture of our character', a character other nations could never possess. It now seems ironic that Faust's final invocation of a 'free people' on 'free soil' was used in Nazi rituals and reprinted in anthologies.[77]

Hebbel was considered easier to accept, but likewise suffered enormous distortions. His anti-Communism and his belief in the need for German unification could be welcomed wholeheartedly, although he had to be divorced from liberalism and praised for conquering individualism. There were Hebbel weeks in Bochum (1939) and Vienna (1942), yet even the plays most lauded underwent a form of censorship. *Die Nibelungen* found favour as a Nordic drama, but also contained many Christian elements. Thus, references were often cut and the 1938 production at the Munich Prinzregententheater disposed of the Christian characters altogether. In 1940, Bernd Rehse's version of *Der Diamant* was premiered in Chemnitz. It incorporated textual changes which exposed the Jewish character Benjamin to ridicule and, in a spurious addition, had him led off at the end to be tried. These transformations are even more repellent, given the fate of Hebbel's play about a famous Jewish character, *Judith*: having been performed 850 times in the Weimar Republic, it received not one production in the theatres of the Third Reich and, like *Nathan the Wise*, was consigned to the Jüdischer Kulturbund.[78]

During the Bochum Kleist week in 1936, one talk described Kleist's biography as a 'path to *Volk*, state and fatherland', and it was this kind of interpretation which encouraged the renewed popularity of the dramatist under Nazism. The protagonist of *The Battle of Arminius* (*Die Hermannsschlacht*) was identified with Hitler. The play justified the concept of the chosen leader, upheld the idea of total war and propagated the *Volksgemeinschaft*. School essay topics reinforced these angles: students were asked to prove the accuracy of Hitler's statement 'It is not the quantity that tips the scales, but the will' with reference to the play. *Prinz Friedrich von Homburg* was also submitted to the demands of Nazi propaganda, by inspiring unquestioning obedience and devotion in young men prepared for combat. Jürgen Fehling's 1938 production had the actors proclaim the final patriotic lines directly to the audience from the front of the stage. There was entertainment to be had from Kleist as well. Emil Jannings gained such a reputation as the judge in *The Broken Jug* (*Der zerbrochene Krug*) that Gustav Ucicky recorded Jannings's performance in a film version of the comedy.[79]

Grabbe's status was considerably improved by Reichsdramaturg Rainer Schlösser's presidency of the Grabbe Society. Hailed by Schlösser as 'the single *Volk* visionary of his time', Grabbe's plays were welcome portrayals of German heroism. Detmold, the town of his birth, initiated a Grabbe week in 1936. The incorporation of Georg Büchner into Nazi theatres is much more difficult to explain. Büchner may have been a nineteenth-century forerunner of Expressionism, but some defended his plays. '*Woyzeck* is not a socialist work', ran one argument, 'but rather a metaphysical work of confession.' Among the noteworthy Büchner productions were those of *Danton's Death* (*Dantons Tod*) in Munich (1937, directed by Otto Falckenberg) and Berlin (1939, under Gründgens's direction).[80]

The recommended styles for the great dramatists of the past were predictably traditional in appearance. A note published in 1936 mocked an experimental Aeschylus production in London in which the Chorus was to appear wearing a dinner jacket. Yet the German heroic approach was not always so apparent. Ernst Legal was taken to task for underplaying the political aspect of *Maria Stuart* (in Berlin's Schiller-Theater) and turning the text into a drama of intrigue. In the penultimate season of the Reich, complaints came from the Rosenberg camp that productions were not sufficiently *völkisch* (national, of the people) and that directors were still following the 'alien' directing style of Max Reinhardt. Yet national respect had to be adapted for the present. It was suggested that long plays by Schiller and Hebbel should be cut, because the current generation no longer had the time to sit through four- or five-hour performances.[81] Once again, it seemed that not everybody had been satisfied by concerted attempts to honour Germany's literary legacy.

Theatre during the Second World War

Part of the challenge faced by those attracted to National Socialism was that the reality of larger spectacles outside normal auditoria appeared infinitely more theatrical than the bourgeois theatre the Nazis claimed to despise (and yet ended up embracing). At the root of much of the dissatisfaction already mentioned with regard to contemporary writing and performance was the conviction that drama could hardly rival the excitement of political developments. From the first year of Nazi rule, it was obvious to non-German observers that charismatic ceremonies were just as important to the new regime as the radical changes enforced on the theatre industry. A new calendar of Nazi ritual allowed school children to recite the creed of the Third Reich and commemorate anniversaries of Nazi successes. Hitler's own speeches, witnessed by thousands, were small dramas following ritualistic, triumphant narratives. Despite the *Thing* play experiment, it was difficult for theatre to compete with events like the Nuremberg Rallies and the Olympic Games, both ideal for Leni Riefenstahl's sophisticated cinematic treatment glorifying the Führer. Such shows continued in 1937 with *Berlin in Seven Centuries of German History*, a massive, choreographed extravaganza performed in the Olympic Stadium, involving over 12,000 participants, whose bodies formed symbols such as the swastika. In the same year, the overlap between theatre and political life became most apparent when the Reich Stage Designer, Benno von Arent, decorated Unter den Linden in Berlin for the state visit of Mussolini.[82]

There had been attempts to incorporate the energy of activities such as sport into traditional dramatic performances, but the new boost to the immediate, communal aspect of Nazi theatre was conveniently provided by the Second World War. Since, according to one Nazi argument, political drama had grown from the experience of battle, the current conflict inspired Germans to create what one critic called their 'national drama'. A representative of the Propaganda Ministry in occupied Holland set the scene more globally: 'The time is ripe: is not the whole of world history a simultaneously comic and tragic drama, worthy of an Aristophanes and an Aeschylus?' Ludwig Körner, then president of the Theatre Chamber, placed dramatic artists on a level with warriors and sailors, as 'one of the examples of people who fight directly for their lives on a daily basis with all their body and soul'.[83]

Of course, aggressive nationalist plays with war (or the threat of it) at their centre had been prominent before 1939. Friedrich Bethge's *Reims*, of 1934, had heroicized self-sacrifice in battle above family ties. Hans Christoph Kaergel's anti-Czech drama and Bethge's anti-Polish work were given a new relevance once hostilities began. Authors such as Rudolf Stache provided anti-English drama for the radio. As unpalatable as these plays seem today, one should remember that such theatrical nationalism was not exclusive to Germany during the war. Glinka's 1836 opera *A Life for the Tsar* – full of Russian heroes and Polish villains – was given a lavish, retitled production in Moscow in 1939 and then revived in Berlin the following year. When Hitler turned against the Soviet Union in the summer of 1941, the recent patriotic drama of Vladimir Solovyev, set during Napoleon's invasion of Russia, took on more significance. In the USA, the Soviets' status as new allies meant that Robert Sherwood had to withdraw his play *There Shall be No Night*, about a Finnish scientist who had joined his country's war against Russia.[84]

Speaking in November 1939 in the Berlin Theater des Volkes, Goebbels announced that Germans were defending not just their '*Lebensraum*, daily bread and machines against plutocratic enemy powers', but also 'German culture'. He concluded: 'We are a *Volk*; we want to become a *Weltvolk* (world people).' A logical step towards fulfilling this ambition in the realm of culture was the German theatrical activity at the front and in the occupied territories. A Viennese sympathizer gave Goebbels's words a less conflictual gloss: the German drama performed all over Europe in the early 1940s was a continuation of the fruitful exchanges and collaborations which had characterized the history of German theatre. This 'European mission of German theatre' did not pursue 'egocentric goals', but rather represented 'an important connecting link in the new evolving Europe'. Such statements justified the setting up of theatres in occupied and assimilated territories (analyzed by William Abbey and Katharina Havekamp in Chapter 6), although policies differed from country to country. While Polish theatre was crushed into the function of frivolous escapism, German plays rose from 15 per cent to 45 per cent of the repertoire of Belgian theatres within one year of the occupation. Meanwhile, entertainment for soldiers was magnified into a part of the front-line action. From 1942, any member of the Theatre, Film or Music Chambers could be summoned for up to six weeks each year for *Truppenbetreuung* (Troops' Welfare entertainment). There was even a primitive form of television drama broadcast to military hospitals.[85]

Kraft durch Freude continued to transport wounded soldiers and armament workers to the Bayreuth Festival until 1944. (In 1943, 30,000 guests were accommodated.) Yet a less serious form of entertainment came to be accepted officially. At the start of the war, Schlösser issued a circular urging against the performance of depressing and pessimistic plays. By 1943 Goebbels was boasting that the government was doing everything possible to support 'opportunities for relaxation' (theatres, concert halls and cinemas) needed by 'the working *Volk* in this difficult time'. The shows on offer included diversions which proved problematic for the authorities and contradicted previous dismissals of decadence in the Weimar Republic. Female high-kicking legs were a great attraction of the *Truppenbetreuung*. The Führer himself was a fan of the American Tiller Girls, so a bowdlerized German substitute evolved, called the Hiller Girls. There was a ban on military choreographies, but nearly naked 'beauty dances' continued in the war, despite the complaints from the Berlin police about bare breasts and buttocks. It was all a far cry from Nazi claims for high culture.[86]

Whether it consisted of light pornography or more serious fare, theatrical activity showed no sign of slowing down. Cutbacks did occur, but in 1942 Hitler was reportedly affirming that there were not enough theatres in Germany and that Berlin, for example, should have four or five opera houses (instead of the three it already had). A year later, a foreign visitor to the capital explained that the theatre was so popular that the only way of seeing a production was to book at least a week in advance. As the bombs dropped, the Theatre Chamber was still expelling members in 1944: one for fleeing Berlin after an air raid, another for fraternizing with a French prisoner of war. Then, in August of the same year, as part of the 'total war' effort, Goebbels ordered that all the theatres of the Reich should be shut down. The decree took effect on 1 September.[87]

Isolated performances of one sort or another nevertheless continued. The theatre, music and art sections of the Propaganda Ministry were merged into one cultural department under Schlösser's leadership. At the same time, the Theatre Chamber continued to function, ordering expulsions, even in 1945. Although many actors were sent to factories, a few opportunities for artistic work remained. In November there were still two Berlin cabarets (open from midnight to 5 a.m.) offering entertainment to soldiers in transit. Actors such as Bernhard Minetti gave recitals of drama and poetry in front of members of the army and navy. As late as April 1945, Will Quadflieg gave recitals of Hölderlin's writing in the Olympic village as part of a mass event with the Berlin Philharmonic to see off soldiers to the Western Front. He then went to the north coast to read scenes from Goethe's *Faust* to submarine sailors. Even theatre buildings were granted small-scale performances. The Viennese Josefstadt Theatre held evenings of recitals until 2 April 1945. Despite serious bomb damage the Berlin Staatsoper hosted extracts from operas by Smetana and Puccini, while the State Schauspielhaus kept the literary drama going with scenes from *Faust*, *The Robbers* and *Hamlet*, as well as concerts which lasted well into April. The last operatic concert (extracts from *Tosca* and *The Barber of Seville*) took place on 22 April, ten days before Berlin's unconditional surrender.[88]

The theatre of the repressed

Accounts of theatrical opposition to the Nazis tend to describe the nuances in mainstream productions of well-known plays, by directors such as Jürgen Fehling and Erich Engel. Gestures, costumes and – as we have seen in the case of Schiller – original lines could convey antagonism to the regime. Stories about political power by Shakespeare and Shaw had contemporary ramifications. As Erik Levi explains (in Chapter 3), even musical forms had the potential to criticize and parody. But although textual references were sometimes cut and productions were sometimes banned, the danger involved was rarely as great as the risks run by those designated from the start as enemies of the Nazis.

Groups who were so obviously victims had their culture eliminated or reduced to ghetto status. The Jüdischer Kulturbund (analyzed in Chapter 4) became the only legal outlet for Jews working in the theatre and was limited to exclusively Jewish audiences. By 1938 the seventy-six branches had 50,000 members and had presented 1638 play performances. Some Communist theatre companies split up after Hitler's takeover and their members tried to exert their influence over amateur dramatic societies. Others on the left, like the dancer and sculptress Oda Schottmüller, combined public work with clandestine opposition. There is also anecdotal evidence about the diffusion of forbidden leftist texts in theatrical circles of the Third Reich. During the shooting of a film in 1942, actors sat behind the scenes between takes, singing songs from *The Threepenny Opera* (*Die Dreigroschenoper*). They were soon told to omit Brecht's words and therefore just hummed Weill's tunes.[89]

The most fascinating example of open opposition is the work of the cabaret performer Werner Finck. Finck was master of ceremonies at the Berlin Kata-kombe and his sketches danced on the delicate tightrope of political satire. In one scene, a patient refusing to open his mouth had connotations about the fear of expressing one's opinion. His tailor sketch, acted with Ivo Veit in March 1935, mocked the contemporary horror within a matter of minutes:

> TAILOR [...]   What would you like then? Sportswear? Something for camping?
> CUSTOMER   Everyone's winding up in camps these days.
> TAILOR   Would you like it all one colour or with stripes?
> CUSTOMER   We've had enough of all one colour. But no stripes by any means!

Amazingly, Finck received positive reviews in the *Völkischer Beobachter*, but there were Nazi protests. Despite Finck's self-defence – he claimed the tailor skit ridiculed draft evaders – he was imprisoned in a concentration camp, along with several members of another cabaret club, the Tingel-Tangel. (Later released, he was expelled from the Theatre Chamber, but survived the war.)[90]

This level of audacity was exceptional. Most of the overt criticism emerged from a much more comfortable position: exile. The Zurich Schauspielhaus became the principal centre for the drama forbidden in the Third Reich. The story of anti-Nazi aesthetics is not, however, simple. About 500 German plays were written in exile, but many of the best-known examples, such as Ferdinand Bruckner's *The Races* (*Die Rassen*) and Brecht's *Fear and Misery of the Third Reich*, concentrate on small-scale human conflicts and the Nazi influence on everyday situations. There was a need for grand statements about loyalties, leadership, sacrifices and belief – precisely the elements prominent in National Socialist drama. Yet apart from fearing the Nazi connotations of these notions, several writers seem to have been worried by the irrationalist and Expressionist origins of their own drama. As one recent critic puts it: 'The articulation or dissemination of a conviction itself became a suspect literary project in these years.'[91]

In between Nazi rule in Germany and freedom in exile lies a forgotten episode in cultural history: the theatre of occupied and assimilated countries. Sometimes the venues themselves provided a site for protest. On Monday nights at the Comédie Française in Paris, students fired paper darts down into the area where German officers were sitting. The relatively restrained censor-ship in the French capital allowed Sartre's first plays to be performed, although few understood their intended message. Elsewhere, criticism had to be much more covert. In the Netherlands, audiences were left to pick up nuances in legal productions or attend one of the illegal private performances called 'black evenings'. In Poland, Tadeusz Kantor carried out his extraordinary theatrical experiments entitled *Balladyna* (1942) and *The Return of Odysseus* (1944), the latter staged in a destroyed room to which actors brought objects from the debris, such as a soldier's uniform and a cartwheel smeared with mud.[92]

At the same time, German soldiers were enjoying a different sort of peformance. Inside Auschwitz, German theatre companies acted before SS guards. One group of actors was surprised to see that the prisoners waiting on them were wearing only their usual overalls in the depths of winter. Those who were destined to stay in captivity had to survive daily within that kind of reality. Concentration camp internees had organized performances before the war began. There was a permitted cabaret in Buchenwald for the 1938 New Year. Vaudeville entertainment took place as well as underground political cabaret with satirical dialogue (imitating a drunken leader of the camp and an equally drunk Robert Ley). In Dachau, Jura Soyfer composed a song which parodied the motto 'Work makes you free' ('Arbeit macht frei').[93]

After 1939, many prisoners of war formed another category to be detained in different locations. The late French president François Mitterrand remembered with fondness the poetry and music performed in the German prisoner-of-war camp where he was interned. Most imprisoned Jews did not live to enjoy that privilege. Initially, the areas of confinement prior to the Final Solution provided the most organized entertainment. In the Warsaw ghetto (from 1940 to 1942) six small theatres offered Polish and Jewish plays. In the Dutch transit camp Westerbork, revues (supported by SS Commandant Konrad Gemmeker) made fun of the conditions prisoners had to suffer. (Many boycotted the shows because they found them tasteless and sacrilegious.) In Theresienstadt, Jews played music by Schubert and Brahms. There was a production of the children's opera *Brundibár* by Hans Krása and Adolf Hoffmeister. It was the first of over twenty shows with which František Zelenka, the innovative Czech set designer, was involved in Theresienstadt. Reduced activities went on in the camps. In one of the labour detachments of Auschwitz, actors recited extracts from Yiddish plays. Small-scale sketches took place. One of the lesser-known activities was the work of female puppeteers in Ravensbrück and an internment centre near Riga.[94]

Post-1945: the end or the continuation of an era?

After the war, when the Soviets used some of the camps to imprison Germans, limited performances continued to take place in such restricted circumstances. The head of Berlin's Schiller-Theater, Heinrich George, helped entertain fellow prisoners after his transfer to Sachsenhausen. George never had the chance to act in normal theatres again: he died on 25 September 1946.[95]

Assessing the acting styles of the final seasons of the Third Reich in 1948, the critic Herbert Ihering thought that the most common trap into which practitioners had fallen was that of a 'heroic manner'. Those who had been character actors converted even dramatic antagonists into heroes. The pressure for such an approach did not come merely from the theatre: according to Ihering, the 'illusion of the period' was that of an 'unproblematic heroism'. While not suffering Heinrich George's fate, other actors paid a considerable price for working within this illusion. Gustaf Gründgens was imprisoned by the Soviets for nine months. Werner Krauss, having played Jewish caricatures in the anti-semitic film *Jew Süß* (*Jud Süß*), was at first forbidden to work and heavily fined. Support from Carl Zuckmayer and George Bernard Shaw helped in his rehabilitation.[96]

A few playwrights received similar punishments. Probably the most severe was the decision of a denazification court concerning Hanns Johst in 1949: he was sentenced to three years in a labour camp, the confiscation of half his property and a ten-year publication ban. However, anomalies remained. Friedrich Bethge was let off, despite the nature of his drama and his political activities. (As evidence of his commitment to the Nazi cause he used to wear his SS uniform to work when he was Dramaturg in Frankfurt.)[97]

Other transitions seem equally incongruous. By 1958, the former Nazi critic Hermann Wanderscheck ended up praising Expressionist writers he had previously insulted as spiritually 'degenerate'. Commentators like Otto zur Nedden and Joseph Gregor, once eager to develop Nazi aesthetics, took refuge in academic appointments and freelance work. For many theatre professionals, there was even less of a sense that they had been in any way compromised. After a period in Munich, the director Erich Engel settled in Communist East Germany and renewed his contacts with Brecht. The set designer Caspar Neher was also welcomed back by Brecht in spite of the choice he had made to stay in Nazi Germany.[98]

One of the prime concerns of the present study is the extent to which those involved in theatre during the Third Reich can be called 'willing executioners' of Nazi policy (to quote the title of Daniel Goldhagen's polemical book about the Holocaust). Distinctions obviously need to be made. Neher's work as a librettist with Rudolf Wagner-Régeny can, for example, be viewed as a form of anti-totalitarian opposition (as is suggested in Chapter 3). Heinz Hilpert, the director who was head of the Deutsches Theater, showed genuine courage in saving work companions from Nazi persecution and publicly mourning the death of his former colleague, Max Reinhardt, in 1943.[99]

Most individual cases lack such clarity and are further complicated by the obfuscation of those concerned. After *Thing* play author Richard Euringer was allowed to write again, in 1948, he underlined his Catholic faith (which had conveniently been apparent even during his adherence to Nazism). One of the most prominent of Third Reich authors, Eberhard Wolfgang Möller, wrote fiction and poetry condemning the modernism of post-war culture and always portraying others (not himself) as the 'barbarians'. Despite his close involvement in Nazi bureaucracy, he claimed he was 'just a writer' at the time of Hitler's regime. Möller's political commentaries continued none the less, now criticizing the behaviour of Russians on the Eastern Front (from 1941 to 1943). During the Cold War, it was a more acceptable stance than Möller's previous anti-semitism. Möller still found supporters, especially when his obituary had to be written in 1972.[100]

The sophistry of writers like Euringer and Möller reveals its obscenity by explicit self-exculpation. Actors who had worked during Nazism adopted a less direct approach. There were instances of self-justification by the strong denial of Nazi ideology and anti-semitism, but an analysis of fifty-nine actors' autobiographies shows that, even when these assertions occur, the pervasive implication is that actors were just doing their job, almost oblivious to contemporary politics. It is hard not to conclude that this wilful ignorance goes on, for not one of the memoirs surveyed makes any mention of the documentary evidence about Nazi theatre which has been widely available since the 1960s (above all in Joseph Wulf's compilation). This omission is not just academic. Some actors do seek to provide general introductions to Nazi influence on theatre and even quote specific episodes, without giving an impression of the full extent of Nazi control.[101]

Perhaps actors have no other choice. You cannot consign a whole profession to the moral scrapheap. To do so would be to tarnish the public who appreciated their performances. When Gustaf Gründgens stepped onto the Berlin stage in 1946 after months of a prolonged denazification procedure, he could not start acting for several minutes. The audience, fully aware of what he had been through, broke into spontaneous applause. They may well have been cheering for a great artistic Germany which had survived the Nazis. The clapping also articulated a collective relief that other cultural bystanders would be proclaimed innocent. Over forty years later, Heinz Rühmann, a member of the Berlin Staatstheater from 1938 to 1944 and one of the best-paid actors of the Third Reich, was asked on television if, granted the opportunity to live another life, he would do anything differently. When he replied that he would do exactly what he had done, the eighty-six-year-old was greeted with applause.[102]

This was not the only way of dealing with the past. Those eager to define themselves as victims of the Nazis had a correspondingly radical definition of collaboration. The underground press in occupied Holland issued appeals to its readers not to attend concerts and plays approved by the German forces. Those who did not follow the boycott received severe criticism years after the war. In 1985 a veteran Dutch actor accused audiences who had enjoyed a few hours' entertainment in the legalized theatres of the period: even if they had been using theatre as a drug to escape from the harshness of daily existence, they were still, he claimed, guilty of collaboration.[103]

If debates about the guilt of individuals continue, the nature of theatre repertoires in post-war Germany would seem to indicate a clear break with National Socialism. Indicative of this change was the production of Lessing's *Nathan the Wise*, a play banned by the Nazis, which reopened the Berlin Deutsches Theater in September 1945. A similar gesture came from the Vienna Burgtheater, which presented Hofmannsthal's *Everyman* as its first new production in June of the same year. Contemporary mainstream European plays, as well as previously neglected North American dramas, were soon being performed all over West Germany, without the limits of Nazi censorship.

Yet these salient differences conceal the common features which link the post-war period with Nazi rule. It may have been left for Erica Jong to rediscover the Heidelberg *Thingplatz* (in her 1973 novel *Fear of Flying*), but many of the dramatists active in 1933–44 were in no need of resuscitation. Of the 1269 authors of German drama from the 1930s and 1940s whose works were performed in the Third Reich, 232 had plays produced from 1945 to 1956. Hans Rehberg, Richard Billinger and Curt Langenbeck premiered new works. As far as great drama from the more distant past was concerned, there were also similarities with the Nazi period. In West Germany from 1955 to 1975, Shakespeare and Schiller were still the two most performed playwrights, although, in a reversal of the situation in the Third Reich, Shakespeare occupied first place.[104]

While Nazi propaganda is obviously not the reason for the make-up of the post-war repertoire, the overlap between the pre- and post-war periods has been accompanied by a surprising degree of forgetfulness about Nazi ideology and aesthetics. Actual allegiances during the 1930s could appear unimportant. By the 1960s, the British theatre critic Harold Hobson was perversely arguing that Brecht had written work 'calculated to assist Hitler' between 1938 and 1942. By praising cowardice in *Mother Courage*, Hobson thought that Brecht wrote 'what was in effect Nazi propaganda'. On the other hand, styles hijacked by the Nazis now seem free from any malign potential. A lengthy journalistic consideration of choral theatre was recently published in German, including several German examples. It mentioned how large groups moving and speaking in unison formed an anti-realistic, anti-naturalist, anti-psychological theatre; how choral theatre was like a drug; how it promoted a mythic, utopian vision.

Although these were precisely the features which attracted the Nazis, their ambitious contributions to the genre were apparently neglected in favour of an Ancient Greek background and modern international models.[105]

Against such a background of distorted historical awareness, recent revivals of genuine Nazi drama have granted the theatre of the Hitler regime a curious afterlife. There were, for instance, productions of Hanns Johst's *Schlageter* in the 1970s and 1990s. However well intentioned – as polemical reconstructions or didactic exercises – these productions could be said to legitimize a play whose extreme nationalism formed an integral part of the ethos of the Third Reich. Many of the theatres built specifically for *Thing* plays are now used for operas and concerts, just as large choreographed spectacles continue to be important for sporting events around the world. Nor are the parallels in the field of drama exclusive to Germany. In 1999 a show about Charles de Gaulle called *The One Who Said No* (*Celui qui a dit non*), with a cast of 100, was put on in the 3700-seat Palais des Congrès in Paris. De Gaulle said 'no' to the Nazi occupation, the NATO alliance and British membership of the Common Market, so a definite nationalism was being celebrated on a large scale. Apart from implications about the need for a similar stance in current politics, there was a direct connection with the present: at the end of the premiere performance, the ruling Gaullist President Jacques Chirac publicly thanked the producer and director of the production from his seat in the audience.[106]

Of course, current theatrical examples of nationalism in European theatre are not created within systems of rigid censorship, racial persecution and totalitarian control. Nevertheless, the studies which follow reveal elements one might not expect to find in a declaredly repressive regime. By explaining contradictions in theory and practice and describing a certain variety of repertoire and theatrical debate, the contributors are not writing a revisionist apology for their subject. On the contrary: they are suggesting that many of the characteristics of theatre under the Nazis were not limited to the twelve years of Nazi rule. The resulting confusion about the role of individuals within the Nazi system and the nature of the drama performed is therefore not entirely unwarranted. Only the details can provide the answers.[107]

Notes

1 Rolf Hochhuth, 'Der Stellvertreter', *Der Tagesspiegel*, 29 April 1995.

2 Klaus Mann, *Mephisto: Roman einer Karriere*, rororo, 1490 (Reinbek bei Hamburg: Rowohlt, 1981), pp. 243 (comforted at not being Jewish), 340 (employment of half-Jew).

3 On the banning, see Eberhard Spangenberg, *Karriere eines Romans: Mephisto, Klaus Mann und Gustaf Gründgens: ein dokumentarischer Bericht aus Deutschland und dem Exil 1925–1981* (Munich: Ellermann, 1982).

4 Bogusław Drewniak, *Das Theater im NS-Staat: Szenarium deutscher Zeit-geschichte 1933–1945* (Düsseldorf: Droste, 1983), p. 145 (4000 theatre people); Ronald Taylor, *Literature and Society in Germany: 1918–1945*, Harvester Studies in Contemporary Literature and Culture, 3 (Brighton: Harvester Press; Totowa, NJ: Barnes & Noble, 1980), p. 214 (2000 writers).

5 Drewniak (*Das Theater*, p. 9), for example, admits that he is not concerned with theatrical or literary analysis, although he has also been criticized for placing too much emphasis on the totalitarian nature of the regime. See the useful review of Drewniak's book by another expert in the field, Uwe-Karsten Ketelsen, *Forum Modernes Theater*, 1 (1986), 103–8. The statistical information referred to is found in a database of traceable productions (40,267 in all), set up in the Institut für Theaterwissenschaft, Free University of Berlin, dating from the 1929–30 season (in the Weimar Republic) until the last season in the war, 1943–44. The database is a valuable source for German-language performances, but needs to be used with caution: it does not include operas or revues and is far from being complete with regard to the recording of open-air premieres, unauthorized performances and productions in the occupied territories during the war. The generic classification of plays is also, on occasion, problematic. My statistical information is based on this database and my own additional research, unless another source is cited. Despite the deficencies of the database, a study using it has conclusively contra-dicted many of Drewniak's statements. See Thomas Eicher, 'Theater im "Dritten Reich": eine Spielplananalyse der deutschen Schauspieltheater 1929–1944' (unpub-lished doctoral thesis, Free University of Berlin, 1992), pp. 23, 175, 262, 328. By stressing how rapidly the Nazi takeover had an effect on theatre repertories, Eicher explains (pp. 399–404) how the statistics also contradict some arguments of another important study, Konrad Dussel, *Ein neues, ein heroisches Theater?: Nationalsozialistische Theaterpolitik und ihre Auswirkungen in der Provinz*, Literatur und Wirklichkeit, 26 (Bonn: Bouvier, 1988).

6 Adam Müller-Guttenbrunn, *Wien war eine Theaterstadt*, Gegen den Strom, 2 (Vienna: Graeser, 1885). For Müller-Gruttenbrunn's beliefs and theatre in context, see Richard S. Geehr, *Adam Müller-Guttenbrunn and the Aryan Theater of Vienna: 1898–1903: The Approach of Cultural Fascism*, Göppinger Arbeiten zur Germanistik, 114 (Göppingen: Kümmerle, 1973); W. E. Yates, *Theatre in Vienna: A Critical History, 1776–1995* (Cambridge: Cambridge University Press, 1996), pp. 168–9, 173–7. For a general outline of anti-semitic tendencies in Austrian theatre until 1938, see Hilde Haider-Pregler, 'Ausgrenzungen: Auswirkungen anti-semitischer Tendenzen in der Kulturpolitik auf das österreichische Theater von der Jahrhundertwende bis 1938', in *Theatralia Judaica: Emanzipation und Anti-semitismus als Momente der Theatergeschichte: von der Lessing-Zeit bis zur Shoa*, ed. by Hans-Peter Bayerdörfer, Theatron, 7 (Tübingen: Niemeyer, 1992), pp. 184–204.

7 Yates, pp. 176–7 (Simons), 175 (insufficiently anti-semitic); Brigitte Hamann, *Hitlers Wien: Lehrjahre eines Diktators*, Serie Piper, 2653 (Munich: Piper, 1998), pp. 87–98, 117–18 (Hitler and theatre in Vienna); Ian Kershaw, *Hitler*, 2 vols (London: Penguin, 1998–), I: *1889–1936: Hubris*, pp. 39–40 (Hitler's dramatic and operatic ambitions); Adolf Hitler, *Mein Kampf*, trans. by Ralph Manheim (London: Pimlico, 1992), pp. 59 (anti-semite), 54 ('Black Death'). Hamann argues (pp. 496–503), somewhat controversially, that, despite the general cultural

tendencies of the time, Hitler did not show strong anti-semitic sentiments in Vienna and that they were a retrospective construction in *Mein Kampf*.

8   Paul Meier-Benneckenstein, untitled preface, in *Das Schrifttum des National-sozialismus von 1919 bis zum 1. Januar 1934*, ed. by Erich Unger (Berlin: Junker und Dünnhaupt, 1934), p. vi. See also Walter Sagitz, *Bibliographie des National-sozialismus* (Cottbus: Albert Heine, 1933).

9   Bruce Zortman, *Hitler's Theater: Ideological Drama in Nazi Germany* (El Paso, TX: Firestein Books, 1984), pp. 21–5 (Wachler).

10 Lilian Karina and Marion Kant, *Tanz unterm Hakenkreuz: eine Dokumentation* (Berlin: Henschel, 1996), pp. 49–51 (Duncan and Laban); Dussel, p. 28 ('reveal once more').

11 On the Bühnenvolksbund and reactionary tendencies in the theatrical life of the Weimar Republic, see Jens Malte Fischer, ' "Die jüdisch-negroide Epoche": Anti-semitismus im Musik- und Theaterleben der Weimarer Republik', in *Theatralia Judaica*, ed. by Bayerdörfer, pp. 228–43; Klaus Petersen, 'Censorship and the Campaign against Foreign Influences in Film and Theater during the Weimar Republic', in *Zensur und Kultur/Censorship and Culture: Zwischen Weimarer Klassik und Weimarer Republik mit einem Ausblick bis heute/From Weimar Classicism to Weimar Republic and Beyond*, ed. by John A. McCarthy and Werner von der Ohe, Studien und Texte zur Sozialgeschichte der Literatur, 51 (Tübingen: Niemeyer, 1995), pp. 149–58.

12 Yates, p. 187 (Jewish conspiracy); Steven N. Fuller, *The Nazis' Literary Grand-father: Adolf Bartels and Cultural Extremism, 1871–1945*, Studies in Modern German Literature, 62 (New York: Lang, 1996), pp. 65–81, 84–94, 154–6.

13 Erik Levi, *Music in the Third Reich* (Basingstoke: Macmillan, 1994), pp. 3–4 (Pfitzner), 7–8 (*Zeitschrift*); Annette Hein, *'Es ist viel "Hitler" in Wagner'*: *Rassismus und antisemitische Deutschtumsideologie in den 'Bayreuther Blätter' (1878 bis 1938)*, Conditio Judaica, 13 (Tübingen: Niemeyer, 1996), pp. 175–84, 397–8 (Bayreuth, racism and Hitler).

14 *Nazism, 1919–1945: A Documentary Reader*, ed. by Jeremy Noakes and Geoffrey Pridham, 4 vols (Exeter: University of Exeter Press, 1983–98), I: *The Rise to Power 1919–1934* (1983), p. 16 (1920 programme); Adolf Hitler, *Sämtliche Aufzeich-nungen: 1905–1924*, ed. by Eberhard Jäckel and Axel Kuhn, Quellen und Darstellungen zur Zeitgeschichte, 21 (Stuttgart: Deutsche Verlags-Anstalt, 1980), pp. 719 (decline of theatre), 965 (service of general public), 863 (censorship); *Deutscher Volksruf*, 26 August 1922 (quoted in Michael P. Steinberg, *The Meaning of the Salzburg Festival: Austria as Theater and Ideology, 1890–1938* (Ithaca, NY: Cornell University Press, 1990), p. 167).

15 Gottfried Feder, *Was will Adolf Hitler?: das Programm der N.S.D.A.P,* 5th edn (Munich: Franz Eher, 1932), p. 11 ('suppressing'); Russel Lemmons, *Goebbels and 'Der Angriff'* (Lexington: University Press of Kentucky, 1994), pp. 33 (token popu-lism), 41–2 (circulation); 'Die Geisteswende', *Mitteilungen des Kampfbundes*, January 1929 (quoted in Alan E. Steinweis, *Art, Ideology, & Economics in Nazi Germany: The Reich Chambers of Music, Theater, and the Visual Arts* (Chapel Hill: University of North Carolina Press, 1993), p. 23: 'German essence'); Dussel, pp. 109–20 (theatrical views of the Rosenberg circle); Oron J. Hale, *The Captive Press in the Third Reich* (Princeton, NJ: Princeton University Press, 1964), p. 31 (circulation of *Völkischer Beobachter*).

16 Günter Hartung, 'Artur Dinter: A Successful Fascist Author in Pre-Fascist Germany', in *The Attractions of Fascism: Social Psychology and the Aesthetics of the 'Triumph of the Right'*, ed. by John Milfull (New York: Berg, 1990), pp. 103–23 (pp. 108–9); Yates, pp. 202–3 (*La Ronde*); Jo-Jacqueline Eckardt, *Lessing's 'Nathan the Wise' and the Critics: 1779–1991* (Columbia, SC: Camden House, 1993), p. 59; Drewniak, *Das Theater*, p. 98 (Upper Silesia).

17 Ernst Toller, *Hinkemann*, ed. by Wolfgang Frühwald, Universal-Bibliothek, 7950 (Stuttgart: Reclam, 1971; repr. 1985), p. 92; Petersen, 'Censorship', pp. 157–8 (Krenek, Habimah); Wayne Kvam, 'The Nazification of Max Reinhardt's Deutsches Theater Berlin', *Theatre Journal*, 40 (1988), 357–74 (pp. 358–9: Hay); Mendel Kohansky, *The Hebrew Theatre: Its First Fifty Years* (Jerusalem: Israel Universities Press, 1969), p. 121 (Habimah).

18 Bruno Fischli, *Die Deutschen-Dämmerung: zur Genealogie des völkisch-faschisti-schen Dramas und Theaters (1897–1933)*, Literatur und Wirklichkeit, 16 (Bonn: Bouvier, 1976), p. 352, n. 189 (1930–31 repertory); Ruth Freydank, *Theater in Berlin: von den Anfängen bis 1945* (Berlin: Argon, 1988), pp. 426–7 (Nazi theatre in Berlin, *The Robbers*). For more on Nazi theatre productions before 1933, including those of the *Gaubühnen* (regional theatres), see George Mosse, 'Die NS-Kampfbühne', trans. by Reinhold Grimm, in *Geschichte im Gegenwartsdrama*, ed. by Reinhold Grimm and Jost Hermand, Sprache und Literatur, 99 (Stuttgart: Kohlhammer, 1976), pp. 24–38.

19 For an introduction to such extreme nationalist plays before the Third Reich, see Fischli, and, in English, H. F. Garten, *Modern German Drama* (London: Methuen, 1959), pp. 219–29. For the increase in performances of Kyser's play, see Drewniak, *Das Theater*, p. 236; Eicher, p. 405; Fischli, p. 120.

20 Fischli, pp. 231–6. For Horst Wessel, see n. 47 in Chapter 1 of the present study (p. 93).

21 *Zeit und Theater*, ed. by Günther Rühle, 6 vols (Frankfurt am Main: Ullstein/ Propyläen, 1980), V: *Diktatur und Exil*, pp. 19 (17 times), 87 ('When I ...'). Johst's *Thomas Paine* (1927) would later be exploited by the Nazis. See Chapter 2 of the present volume (pp. 96, 101–3).

22 Dussel, pp. 30–1 (decree); Levi, p. 11 (percentages). For more on the Nazi cultural experiment in Thuringia, see Hildegard Brenner, *Die Kunstpolitik des National-sozialismus* (Reinbek bei Hamburg: Rowohlt Taschenbuch, 1963), pp. 31–5, 169–70.

23 Bettina Schültke, 'The Municipal Theatre in Frankfurt-on-the-Main: A Provincial Theatre under National Socialism', trans. by Laura Tate and Günter Berghaus, in *Fascism and Theatre: Comparative Studies on the Aesthetics and Politics of Performance in Europe, 1925–1945*, ed. by Günter Berghaus (Providence, RI: Berghahn Books, 1996), pp. 157–71 (p. 161: swastika); Bogusław Drewniak, 'The Foundations of Theater Policy in Nazi Germany', trans. by Glenn R. Cuomo, in *National Socialist Cultural Policy*, ed. by Glenn R. Cuomo (New York: St. Martin's Press, 1995), pp. 67–94 (pp. 75–6: subsections of Theatre Department); Steinweis, p. 38 (Bühnengenossenschaft).

24 David Welch, *The Third Reich: Politics and Propaganda* (London: Routledge, 1995), pp. 155–6 (English translation of 22 September law); Albert E. Frauenfeld, *Der Weg zur Bühne*, 2nd edn (Berlin: Wilhelm Limpert, 1941), p. 46 (paragraph 10); Gerhard Menz, *Der Aufbau des Kulturstandes* (Munich, 1938), pp. 35–6 (repr.

in Joseph Wulf, *Theater und Film im Dritten Reich: eine Dokumentation*, Ullstein Buch, 33031 (Frankfurt am Main: Ullstein, 1983), p. 39: subdivisions of Theatre Chamber); Levi, p. 25 (diagram of hierarchy of Culture Chamber); Steinweis, p. 6 (41,100). Steinweis (pp. 32–49) is an excellent guide to the setting up of the various chambers, particularly on how they were based on professional associations of the Weimar era and how advocates of neo-corporatism were exploited.

25 On the clash between Goebbels and Rosenberg, see Reinhard Bollmus, *Das Amt Rosenberg und seine Gegner: Studien zum Machtkampf im nationalsozialistischen Herrschaftssystem* (Stuttgart: Deutsche Verlags-Anstalt, 1970), pp. 39–103.

26 *Frankfurter Zeitung*, 31 December 1937 (quoted in Dussel, p. 105: 'promotional and selective'); Dussel, p. 132 (5 million). For subsequent figures, which, although large, contradict Dussel's official amounts, see Ronald Smelser, *Robert Ley: Hitler's Labor Front Leader* (New York: Berg, 1988), pp. 216–17.

27 On a context (with regard to a precise choice of repertory) for the different views of Rosenberg and Goebbels, see Glen W. Gadberry, 'The First National Socialist Theatre Festival – Dresden 1934', in *Theatre in the Third Reich, the Prewar Years: Essays on Theatre in Nazi Germany*, ed. by Glen W. Gadberry, Contributions to the Study of World History, 49 (Westport, CT: Greenwood Press, 1995), pp. 121–39 (especially pp. 131–4).

28 Welch, *The Third Reich*, p. 137 (Goebbels's speech); Hein, pp. 177–8 (Hitler's subsidy of Bayreuth); Levi, p. 35 (Hitler's subsidies).

29 Dussel, pp. 93–4 (biographical summaries for Schlösser, Graff and Möller); Drewniak, *Das Theater*, p. 26 (Rosenberg criticism); *Die Bühne*, 1 November 1935, pp. 1–6 (florid assessments of Laubinger).

30 Steinweis, p. 55 (reorganization of the Theatre Chamber); Drewniak, *Das Theater*, p. 59 (TV); Wolfram Wessels, *Hörspiele im Dritten Reich: zur Institutionen-, Theorie- und Literaturgeschichte*, Abhandlungen zur Kunst-, Musik- und Literaturwissenschaft, 366 (Bonn: Bouvier, 1985), pp. 78–108 (radio). A list of all the personnel in the Theatre Chamber was included every year in the *Deutsches Bühnen-Jahrbuch*. It is worth mentioning that Hinkel, Hanns Johst (president of the Reich Literature Chamber) and even Laubinger (!) were veterans of the Kampfbund für Deutsche Kultur, although they now came under Goebbels's control. In the occupied Soviet Union, Rosenberg, who had been made Minister for the East, developed his own propaganda organization (Drewniak, pp. 32–3).

31 Steinweis, p. 136 (publishers); Barbara Panse, 'Censorship in Nazi Germany: The Influence of the Reich's Ministry of Propaganda on German Theatre and Drama, 1933–1945', trans. by Meg Mumford, in *Fascism and Theatre*, ed. by Berghaus, pp. 140–56 (pp. 143–4: no evidence, analysis of percentages 1929–34); Eicher, pp. 17–19 (Fraser, anti-semitism). The study of Lille in the present volume (Chapter 6) also reveals how plays were rejected for a specific repertoire (pp. 270–2).

32 'Das deutsche Volk – die deutsche Kunst – der deutsche Aufbauwille überwinden 14 Jahre Kulturbolschewismus', *Der Angriff*, 1 March 1933; Kurt Engelbrecht, *Deutsche Kunst im totalen Staat* (Lahr in Baden: publisher unknown, 1933), p. 20 (repr. in Wulf, *Theater*, p. 255: Jewish actor).

33 Frauenfeld, pp. 52–60 (May 1934 law, subsequent theatre laws in 1934–35); Levi, p. 48 (expulsions); Steinweis, p. 114 (actress); *Die Bühne*, 1937, p. 575 (repr. in Wulf, *Theater*, p. 262: proof of Aryan descent).

34 Bettina Schültke, *Theater oder Propaganda?: die städtischen Bühnen Frankfurt am*

Main 1933–1945, Studien zur Frankfurter Geschichte, 40 (Frankfurt am Main: Waldemar Kramer, 1997), pp. 161–2 (Germanic lexical replacements); Steinweis, p. 115 (preventing Jewish attendance).

35 Steinweis, pp. 29 (less than 20 per cent, calculated on Steinweis's survey of 1419 Theatre Chamber files), 117 (Korolanyi), 110 (Kropf); Levi, p. 33 (Mohaupt).

36 Levi, p. 37 (Schirach); Karina and Kant, p. 202 (Palucca). On the persecution of homosexuals see, for example, *Hidden Holocaust?: Gay and Lesbian Persecution in Germany 1933–45*, ed. by Günter Grau, trans. by Patrick Camiller (London: Cassell, 1995).

37 Levi, pp. 176 (*Arabella*), 139–46 (record companies); Drewniak, *Das Theater*, p. 188 (quarter-Jew).

38 Steinweis, pp. 80 (1934 decree), 100 (welfare fund), 86–9 (examinations), 95, 150 (employment figures); Drewniak, *Das Theater*, pp. 149–55 (earnings); Gustaf Gründgens, *Briefe, Aufsätze, Reden*, ed. by Rolf Badenhausen and Peter Gründgens-Gorski, dtv, 694 (Munich: Deutscher Taschenbuch Verlag, 1970), p. 56. Dussel (pp. 80–7), on the other hand, argues against exaggerated views of the prosperity of those who worked in the theatre.

39 Drewniak, *Das Theater*, pp. 38–9 (subsidy); Richard Grunberger, *A Social History of the Third Reich* (Harmondsworth: Penguin, 1991), p. 458 (doubling of audiences). Other figures claim a tripling of audiences within the first five years of the regime. According to one estimate, 30 million theatre tickets were sold in 1936 (Dussel, p. 132, n. 3).

40 Dr Richard Elsner, *Die deutsche Nationalbühne*, Deutsche Zukunft, 1 (Berlin: Wolf Heyer, 1934), p. 22 (Socialism, 'inbreeding'); Herbert A. Frenzel, *Eberhard Wolfgang Möller* (Munich: Deutscher Volksverlag, 1938), pp. 21 ('desecrated'), 22 ('real drama'); Hermann Wanderscheck, *Dramaturgische Appassionata* (Leipzig: Max Beck, [1943]), p. 39 ('I', theatre is not life). For the Nazi criticism of Naturalism, see also Chapter 1 of the present study (p. 59).

41 Wanderscheck, p. 64. By lamenting the absence of the 'we' in Naturalism, Wanderscheck was therefore not promoting a Socialist collective entity, but rather the 'we' of the *Volksgemeinschaft* (national people's community), as explained below.

42 Julius Bab, *Wesen und Weg der Berliner Volksbühnenbewegung* (Berlin: Ernst Wasmuth, 1919), p. 6 (quotation from Bruno Wille's speech of 29 July 1890); John Willett, *The Theatre of the Weimar Republic* (New York: Holmes & Meier, 1988), pp. 19–24 (setting up of the Volksbühne). In 1905, the anti-semitic critic Adolf Bartels had invoked the concept of *Volk* to promote a national theatre in Weimar (free from foreign and Jewish influences) and help create a festival which targeted German school children. However, the conservative *Festspiele*, which enjoyed the Kaiser's sporadic financial support and took place while Bartels exercised an influence (1909–15), consisted mainly in the performance of German classics and Shakespeare (Fuller, pp. 88–94).

43 Elsner, *Die deutsche Nationalbühne*, p. 52 (against Brecht); Drewniak, *Das Theater*, pp. 54–5 (Nazi takeover); *Blätter der Volksbühne* [sic] Berlin, November–December 1937, p. 1 (motto retained).

44 'Rede des Propagandaministers Dr. Joseph Goebbels vor den Theaterleitern am 8. Mai 1933', *Das Deutsche Drama in Geschichte und Gegenwart*, 5 (1933), 28–40 (p. 37); Rainer Schlösser, 'Der alte und der neue Weg!', *Der neue Weg*, 62, no. 6 (20 April 1933), 122–3 (p. 122); Otto Laubinger, 'Aufgaben des Theaters im Dritten

Reich', *Die Deutsche Bühne*, 25, no. 13 (16 October 1933), 214–25 (p. 214). For examples of how the concept of *Volk* was exploited with regard to foreign drama, see Chapter 5 of the present study.

45 Schlösser, p. 122; 'Stellenvermittlung und Bühnennachwuchs', *Frankfurter Zeitung*, 16 June 1937 (repr. in Wulf, *Theater*, pp. 49–50: 'inner expression'); Klaus Jedzek, *Theater als politische Kraft* (Eisenach: Erich Röth, 1935), pp. 10–11 ('theatre belongs to the people' etc.), 19 (Expressionism). The appearance of Jedzek's booklet is a fascinating confusion of artistic eras: the cover has inventive sans-serif lettering which could be from the 1920s, while the typeface inside is wholly in the pseudo-Gothic cultivated by the Nazis.

46 Dr Richard Elsner, 'Der Weg zum deutschen National-Theater', *Das Deutsche Drama in Geschichte und Gegenwart*, 5 (1933), 40–5 (pp. 52–3: quantity, artistic levels); Elsner, 'Haben wir eine Nationalbühne?', *Das Deutsche Drama in Geschichte und Gegenwart*, 6 (1934), 9–25 (p. 21: quantity); Kurt Fischer, 'Besucherorganisation – Erlebnisgemeinschaft?', *Blätter der Volksbühne Berlin*, September–October 1935, pp. 10–11 (p. 11: 'common experience'); Sigmund Graff, 'Wohin geht der Weg?', *Die Deutsche Bühne*, 25, no. 9 (13 July 1933), 152–3 (p. 152). For examples of articles in praise of the worker, see Karl Broeger, 'Der Arbeiter und sein Buch', *Blätter der Volksbühne Berlin*, March–April 1935, pp. 11–12; Ludwig Körner, 'Von der Kultur des Theaterbesuches', *Die Bühne*, 5 December 1938, pp. 447–8; Dr [!] Werner Kurz, 'Der deutsche Arbeiter und das Theater', *Bausteine zum Deutschen Nationaltheater*, 2 (1934), 357–62.

47 Dr Otto C. A. zur Nedden, *Drama und Dramaturgie im 20. Jahrhundert: Abhandlungen zum Theater und zur Theaterwissenschaft der Gegenwart*, 'Das Nationaltheater': Schriftenreihe des Theaterwissenschaftlichen Instituts der Friedrich-Schiller-Universität Jena, 4 (Würzburg: Konrad Triltsch, 1940), p. 18; Goebbels, 'Rede', p. 31; Dr Ferdinand Junghans, 'Schauspielkunst und Volk', *Bausteine zum Deutschen Nationaltheater*, 2 (1934), 105–10 (on acting).

48 Ludwig Körner, '"Sprich eine Lüge und bleib dabei!": die *Times* wird interviewt', *Die Bühne*, 25 July 1940, pp. 194–202 (p. 202); Paul Rose, 'Gedanken über das Volksstück, seine Elemente, sein Publikum und sein Theater', *Deutsche Dramaturgie*, 1, no. 12 (December 1942), 275–81; Yvonne Shafer, 'Nazi Berlin and the *Grosses Schauspielhaus*', *Theatre Survey*, no. 34 (May 1993), 71–90 (on the Theater des Volkes); Schültke, *Theater*, p. 442 (65 workers); Edward J. Dent, *A Theatre for Everybody: The Story of the Old Vic and Sadler's Wells* (London: T. V. Boardman, 1945), p. 134 ('real *Volksbühne*'). For a discussion with regard to the exploitation of the genre of *Volksoper*, see Chapter 3 of the present volume (pp. 145–6, 153–4).

49 Nedden, p. 18; Jutta Wardetzky, *Theaterpolitik im faschistischen Deutschland: Studien und Dokumente* ([East] Berlin: Henschel, 1983), p. 88 (figures on open-air theatres); Zortman, p. 75 (*Werdendes Volk*).

50 *Sprechchöre für die nationalsozialistische Deutsche Schule*, ed. by Franz Türk (Frankfurt am Main: Moritz Diesterweg, 1935), pp. 7, 29 (cited for schools); Klaus Vondung, 'Das Bild der "faschistischen Persönlichkeit" in der nationalsozialistischen Literatur nach 1933: am Beispiel chorischer Dichtungen Gerhard Schumanns', in *Fascism and European Literature: Faschismus und europäische Literatur*, ed. by Stein Ugelvik Larsen and Beatrice Sandberg, with Ronald Speirs (Berne: Lang, 1991), pp. 58–64 (on Schumann); Dr M. Grünewald, *Licht und Volk:*

eine Lehrkantate (Mannheim: H. Adler, 1930) (Hanukah story). The Nazi author Eberhard Wolfgang Möller, in a remarkable echo of Brecht's term, saw his 1936 play *The Frankenburg Dice-Game* (*Das Frankenburger Würfelspiel*) as 'the first German *Lehrspiel* (didactic play)'. See Jörg Bochow, 'Berliner Theater im Dritten Reich: repräsentative Ästhetik oder/und "Bewahrer kultureller Werte"?: Linien und Brüche der Moderne im Berliner Theater der dreißiger Jahre', in *Berliner Theater im 20. Jahrhundert*, ed. by Erika Fischer-Lichte, Doris Kolesch and Christel Weiler (Berlin: Fannei & Walz, 1998), pp. 147–69 (p. 154); Chapter 1 of the present volume (p. 91, n. 11).

51 Hedwig Müller, 'Tanz ins Dritte Reich', in Hedwig Müller and Patricia Stöckemann, '... *jeder Mensch ist ein Tänzer': Ausdruckstanz in Deutschland zwischen 1900 und 1945*, exhibition catalogue (Gießen: Anabas, 1993), pp. 108–17 (p. 116: against individualism); Gustav Fischer-Klamt, 'Weltanschaulicher Appell an das deutsche Tänzertum' (1936), repr. in Müller and Stöckemann, pp. 121–2 (p. 121: 'rising nations'); Karina and Kant, pp. 75 (Wigman's anti-semitism), 136 ('blood', quoted from Mary Wigman, *Deutsche Tanzkunst* (Dresden: Carl Reissner, 1935), p. 12).

52 Karina and Kant, pp. 142–4 (Laban and anti-ballet); Inge Baxmann, 'Tanz als Kulturkritik und Projekt der Gemeinschaftsbildung', in *Entre Locarno et Vichy: les relations culturelles franco-allemandes dans les années 1930*, ed. by Hans Manfred Bock, Reinhart Meyer-Kalkus and Michel Trebitsch, 2 vols (Paris: CNRS, 1993), I, 527–48 (specifically German movements); Susan A. Manning, *Ecstasy and the Demon: Feminism and Nationalism in the Dances of Mary Wigman* (Berkeley: University of California Press, 1993), pp. 194–202 (*Olympic Youth*, with photographs). Manning interestingly describes the vagaries and constants in Wigman's career, from Weimar to post-war Germany.

53 Manning, pp. 201–2 (Wigman); Joseph Goebbels, *Die Tagebücher von Joseph Goebbels: sämtliche Fragmente*, Teil I: *Aufzeichnungen 1924–1941*, 4 vols, ed. by Elke Fröhlich (Munich: K. G. Saur, 1987), III, 187; Hedwig Müller, 'Heimat-Front', in Müller and Stöckemann, pp. 186–200 (p. 197: Rosenberg circle); Karina and Kant, pp. 93, 182 (Laban's departure).

54 Stefan Germer, '*Kunst der Nation*: zu einem Versuch, die Avantgarde zu nationalisieren', in *Kunst auf Befehl?: Dreiunddreißig bis Fünfundvierzig*, ed. by Bazon Brock and Achim Preiß (Munich: Klinkhardt & Biermann, 1990), pp. 21–40; Steinweis, pp. 137–8 (suppression of Catholic theatre); Glen W. Gadberry, '*The Stedingers*: Nazi Festival Drama of the Destruction of a People', *Theatre History Studies*, 10 (1990), 105–26 (pp. 120–2: context of Hitler's denunciation).

55 Dr Gerhard Riesen, *Die Erziehungsfunktion der Theaterkritik*, Neue Deutsche Forschungen: Abteilung Neuere Deutsche Literaturgeschichte, 5 (Berlin: Junker und Dünnhaupt, 1935), pp. 34–5 (on Kerr), 49 (on *Thing* play), 48 (good), 58 (politically valuable), 77 (national theatre), 65–6 (Wilhelm von Schramm's guidelines quoted); C. M. Köhn, 'Kritik und Theater', *Die Deutsche Bühne*, 27, no. 9 (9 July 1935), 151–5 (p. 153: 'literary apes').

56 Hans Knudsen, *Wesen und Grundlagen der Theaterkritik* (Berlin: Langen/Müller, 1935), pp. 9 ('responsibility'), 10 ('comrades'), 15 (genres); Köhn, p. 154 ('The livelier').

57 Wulf, *Theater*, pp. 25–6 (lawyer's complaint in letter); Karl Vogt, 'Volkskunst', *Der neue Weg*, 63, no. 12 (15 August 1934), 261.

58 Joseph Goebbels, 'Kunst und Volk', *Der neue Weg*, 64, no. 10 (15 June 1935), 286–7 (p. 286: 'anarchic state'); Joseph Wulf, *Die bildenden Künste im Dritten Reich: eine Dokumentation*, Ullstein Buch, 33030 (Frankfurt am Main: Ullstein, 1983), pp. 127–9 (Goebbels's prohibition; English translation in Welch, *The Third Reich*, pp. 168–9).

59 Bertolt Brecht, *Werke*, ed. by Werner Hecht and others, 30 vols (Berlin: Aufbau-Verlag; Frankfurt am Main: Suhrkamp, 1988–98), XII: *Gedichte 2: Sammlungen 1938–1956* (1988), p. 79; Schültke, *Theater*, p. 206 (Weiß); Dietmar Schmidt, 'Wege der Kunstbetrachtung', in *Berliner Theater-Almanach: 1942*, ed. by Axel Kaun (Berlin: Paul Neff, [1942]), pp. 13–21 (p. 20: conscious). Ihering ended up with a lucrative job in the Vienna Burgtheater (Drewniak, *Das Theater*, p. 155).

60 M. Kirsch, 'Die Bochumer Festwoche', in *Deutsche Klassiker im Nationalsozialismus: Schiller: Kleist: Hölderlin*, ed. by Claudia Albert (Stuttgart: Metzler, 1994), pp. 86–99 (p. 87: Braumüller). On the jargon and reading between the lines in theatre criticism of the Nazi period, see, for example, Hans Daiber, *Schaufenster der Diktatur: Theater im Machtbereich Hitlers* (Stuttgart: Günther Neske, 1995), pp. 158–73; Bergita Gradl, 'Rudolf Geck: Theaterkritiker der *FZ* 1898–1935' (unpublished doctoral thesis, Free University of Berlin, 1968), pp. 161–76; Schültke, *Theater*, pp. 208–9.

61 Erich Lüth, *Hamburger Theater 1933–1945: ein theatergeschichtlicher Versuch* (Hamburg: Verlag der Werkberichte Justus Buekschmitt, 1962), p. 32 (Schramm); B. V. Eysselsteijn, Review of *Twelfth Night* at the Deutsches Theater in The Hague, *Haagsche Courant*, 27 April 1943; Joseph Goebbels, *Die Tagebücher*, IV, 423. Further examples of the overt and covert criticism of plays after 1936 are to be found in the present volume in the assessments of history plays (Chapter 2) and of much foreign drama (Chapter 5).

62 Eicher, pp. 391–2 (percentages); Walter Stang, *Grundlagen nationalsozialistischer Kulturpflege* (Berlin: Junker und Dünnhaupt, 1935), p. 11.

63 Friedrich Griese, *Mensch aus Erde gemacht* (Berlin: Langen/Müller, 1933), p. 35. See also the analysis with the extracts quoted in Uwe-Karsten Ketelsen, *Von heroischem Sein und völkischem Tod: zur Dramatik des Dritten Reiches*, Abhandlungen zur Kunst-, Musik- und Literaturwissenschaft, 96 (Bonn: Bouvier, 1970), pp. 127–36, 263–5.

64 David Welch, 'Nazi Film Policy: Control, Ideology, and Propaganda', in *National Socialist Cultural Policy*, ed. by Cuomo, pp. 95–120 (p. 107: one fifth); Peter Jelavich, *Berlin Cabaret* (Cambridge, MA: Harvard University Press, 1993), pp. 245–6 (decrees of 1937, 1939, 1940); Schültke, *Theater*, p. 267 (Nazi salute); Barbara Panse, 'Antisemitismus und Judenfiguren in der Dramatik des Dritten Reiches', in *Theatralia Judaica*, ed. by Bayerdörfer, pp. 299–311 (on anti-semitism in Nazi drama).

65 Wulf, *Theater*, p. 45 (1937 law); Eckart von Naso, *Ich liebe das Leben: Erinnerungen aus fünf Jahrzehnten* (Hamburg: Wolfgang Krüger, 1953) (quoted in George L. Mosse, *Nazi Culture: Intellectual, Cultural and Social Life in the Third Reich*, trans. by Salvator Attanasio and others (New York: Grosset & Dunlap, 1968), pp. 185–8 (p. 186: Arminius)); Drewniak, *Das Theater*, p. 224 (Ortner's wife).

66 *Zeit und Theater*, ed. by Rühle, VI, 760 ('opposites'), V, 229 ('honour'); Wulf, *Theater*, p. 222 ('heroic realism'); Panse, 'Censorship', p. 150 (banning of *The*

Veterans' March, although Panse curiously does not mention the Nazi–Soviet alliance). For Nazi criticism of *The Veterans' March* in 1935, see Bochow, p. 148. The exception to the ban on plays about Russian themes (declared in 1943) was Herbert Reinecker's *The Village by Odessa* (*Das Dorf bei Odessa*). For an analysis of *The Endless Road*, see William Sonnega, 'Theatre of the Front: Sigmund Graff and *Die endlose Straße*', in *Theatre in the Third Reich*, ed. by Gadberry, pp. 47–64.

67 Wolfgang Müller, 'Das Lustspiel und die Gegenwart', in *Berliner Theater-Almanach*, ed. by Kaun, pp. 345–54 (p. 353); Drewniak, *Das Theater*, p. 221 (Hitler). On the morality of comedies, see Regina Wallner, 'Erfolgreiche Komödien im Nationalsozialismus' (unpublished Magisterarbeit, Free University of Berlin, 1991).

68 Audrone B. Willeke, *Georg Kaiser and the Critics: A Profile of Expressionism's Leading Playwright* (Columbia, SC: Camden House, 1995), pp. 29–31, 69–70 (protests, banning); Ralf Schnell, *Dichtung in finsteren Zeiten: deutsche Literatur und Faschismus*, Rowohlts Enzyklopädie, 55597 (Reinbek bei Hamburg: Rowohlt Taschenbuch, 1998), pp. 149–60 (Kaiser's poetry).

69 *Gespräche und Interviews mit Gerhart Hauptmann (1894–1946)*, ed. by H. D. Tschörtner and Sigfrid Hoefert, Veröffentlichungen der Gerhart-Hauptmann-Gesellschaft, 6 (Berlin: Erich Schmidt, 1994), pp. 109–11 (philosemitism), 176 (last interview); Karl S. Guthke, 'Der "König der Weimarer Republik": Gerhart Hauptmanns Rolle in der Öffentlichkeit zwischen Kaiserreich und Nazi-Regime', *Schweizer Monatshefte*, 61 (1981), 787–806 (p. 803: mockery of speeches); Alfred Rosenberg, *Der Mythus des 20. Jahrhunderts: eine Wertung der seelisch-geistigen Gestaltenkämpfe unserer Zeit*, 147–8th edn (Munich: Hoheneichen, 1939), pp. 439, 444. For Hauptmann and the Third Reich, see also Drewniak, *Das Theater*, pp. 190–210; Eberhard Hilscher, *Gerhart Hauptmann: Leben und Werk: mit bisher unpublizierten Materialien aus dem Manuskriptnachlaß des Dichters* (Frankfurt am Main: Athenäum, 1988), pp. 403–30; Walter Requardt, 'Gerhart Hauptmann und der Nationalsozialismus – die Nationalsozialisten und Gerhart Hauptmann', in *Nationalsozialismus und Widerstand in Schlesien*, ed. by Lothar Bossle and others, Schlesische Forschungen, 3 (Sigmaringen: J. Thorbecke, 1989), pp. 41–71.

70 Drewniak, *Das Theater*, pp. 220 (Langenbeck), 223 (Billinger); Wulf, *Theater*, p. 100 ('kitsch'); Goebbels, 'Kunst und Volk', p. 286.

71 Nedden, p. 81 (3rd edn, 1944, p. 74); Gert von Klaß, 'Das Gegenwartsdrama und der Geist unserer Zeit', *Die Bühne*, 20 August 1944, pp. 113–14 (Naturalism and classical drama).

72 Wolf Braumüller, 'Die Spielzeit der Klassiker: Überblick über die ersten drei Monate der Theaterspielzeit 1935/36', *Bausteine zum Deutschen Nationaltheater*, 4 (1936), 5–10 (p. 5: 'The dramatic work'); Hitler, *Mein Kampf*, pp. 235–6; William J. Niven, *The Reception of Friedrich Hebbel in Germany in the Era of National Socialism*, Stuttgarter Arbeiten zur Germanistik, 142 (Stuttgart: Hans-Dieter Heinz, 1984), pp. 83–4 (anti-religious theory); Max Geisenheyner, 'Antibürgerliche Klassik', in *Berliner Theater-Almanach*, ed. by Kaun, pp. 196–209 (p. 198: anti-bourgeois, relevant in war); Günther Rühle, 'Einleitung', in *Zeit und Theater*, ed. by Rühle, V, 7–75 (pp. 48–9: on Weimar); *Rhein-Ruhr-Zeitung*, 14 June 1938 (repr. in Wulf, *Theater*, p. 51: 'motherland'). Proposals for a new national theatre under the Nazis, such as Richard Elsner's *Die deutsche Nationalbühne*, were full of references to previous German writers' aspirations to the supposedly identical notion (of a national theatre).

73 Eckardt, pp. 41, 45, 56–60 (Nazi critics on Lessing).

74 Hitler, *Mein Kampf*, p. 15 (*William Tell*); Hans Fabricius, *Schiller als Kampfgenosse Hitlers: Nationalsozialismus in Schillers Dramen* (Bayreuth: N. S. Kultur-Verlag, 1932; 2nd edn, Berlin: Deutsche Kultur-Wacht, 1934); Georg Ruppelt, *Schiller im nationalsozialistischen Deutschland: der Versuch einer Gleichschaltung* (Stuttgart: Metzler, 1979), pp. 33–8 (1934 celebrations).

75 Schültke, *Theater*, pp. 282–3 (*The Robbers* in Frankfurt, showing photograph with what looks like the Nazi salute); Shafer, pp. 78–9 (production at Theater des Volkes).

76 Friedrich Schiller, *Sämtliche Werke*, ed. by Gerhard Fricke and others, 5th edn, 5 vols (Munich: Carl Hanser, 1973–6), II (1974), 126 ('freedom of thought'); Ruppelt, pp. 113–14 (applause), 40–5 (on *William Tell*).

77 Rosenberg, p. 515; Karl Robert Mandelkow, *Goethe in Deutschland: Rezeptionsgeschichte eines Klassikers*, 2 vols (Munich: Beck, 1980–89), II: *1919–1982* (1989), pp. 80–101 (Nazi views of Goethe); Johann Wolfgang Goethe, *Sämtliche Werke*, ed. by Karl Richter and others, 21 vols (Munich: Carl Hanser, 1985–98), VI. 1: *Weimarer Klassik: 1798–1806*, ed. by Victor Lange (1986), p. 582 ('blood'), XVIII. 1: *Letzte Jahre: 1827–1832*, ed. by Gisela Henckmann and Dorothea Hölscher-Lohmeyer (1997), p. 335 ('free people'); Drewniak, *Das Theater*, p. 171 (performance figures of Goethe's plays in the war); Mathias [*sic*] Wieman, 'Faust in Kriege', in *Berliner Theater-Almanach*, ed. by Kaun, pp. 253–6; Gerhard F. Probst, 'Zur Klassik-Rezeption im Dritten Reich: prinzipielle Überlegungen und Analyse eines "Hausbuches"', *Jahrbuch für Internationale Germanistik*, Reihe A5 (1979), 148–57 (p. 155: Faust's speech in Nazi ritual).

78 Niven, *The Reception*, pp. 18–19, 31 (liberalism, individualism), 85 (*Die Nibelungen*), 118–21 (*Der Diamant*), 106–7 (*Judith*).

79 Kirsch, p. 95 ('path'); William C. Reeve, *Kleist on Stage, 1804–1987* (Montreal: McGill-Queen's University Press, 1993), pp. 146–8 (*Hermannsschlacht*), 166–7 (*Prinz*), 29 (Jannings).

80 Drewniak, *Das Theater*, p. 175 ('visionary'); R. Lindemann, in *Der 30. Januar: Braune Blätter der Städtischen Bühnen* (1936–37) (quoted in Schültke, *Theater*, p. 211: *Woyzeck*). For more on Grabbe see *Grabbe im Dritten Reich: zum nationalsozialistischen Grabbe-Kult*, ed. by Werner Broer and Detlev Kopp (Bielefeld: Aisthesis, 1986).

81 'Immer wieder einmal ...', *Die Bühne*, 15 November 1936, p. 674 (Aeschylus); Karl H. Ruppel, 'Eine Berliner Spielzeit', in *Berliner Theater-Almanach*, ed. by Kaun, pp. 22–104 (pp. 89–90: *Maria Stuart*); Bruno Koch, 'Inszenierungsfragen bei klassischen Werken', *Deutsche Dramaturgie*, 2, no. 1 (January 1943), 8–10 (complaints).

82 Calvin B. Hoover, *Germany Enters the Third Reich* (London: Macmillan, 1933), pp. 115–16 (ceremonies), 149, 171 (changes in theatre); Gerhard Hellwig, *Nationalsozialistische Feiern im Rahmen eines Hitlerjahres für Schule und Gemeinde des 3. Reiches* (Berlin: N. B. Buchvertrieb, 1934) (new calendar); Peter J. Mellen, 'The Third Reich Examined as the Dramatic Illusion of Ritual Performance' (unpublished doctoral thesis, Bowling Green State University, 1988), pp. 231–7 (Hitler's speeches); Patricia Stöckemann, 'Die neue Gemeinschaft', in Müller and Stöckemann, pp. 140–9 (pp. 146–8: *Berlin in Seven Centuries*; 113, 140–2: photographs); *Art and Power: Europe under the Dictators 1930–45*, ed. by David Britt, exhibition

catalogue (London: Hayward Gallery, South Bank Centre, 1995), pp. 280–1 (Arent's decoration and Albert Speer's architecture of light the previous year in the Olympic Stadium). For an approach to fascist theatre as ritual, see Günter Berghaus, 'The Ritual Core of Fascist Theatre: An Anthropological Perspective', in *Fascism and Theatre*, ed. by Berghaus, pp. 39–71.

83 Dr Hans Zigelski, 'Sport und Bühnenspiel', *Bausteine zum Deutschen National-theater*, 4 (1936), 193–9 (sport in theatre); Wanderscheck, pp. 56 (experience of battle), 23 ('national drama'); Prof. Dr T. Goedewaagen, one of several articles with the collective title 'Zur Eröffnung des Deutschen Theaters in den Nieder-landen', *Maandblad der Nederlandsch-Duitsche Kultuurgemeenschap/Monats-schrift der Niederländisch-Deutschen Kulturgemeinschaft*, November 1942, pp. 1–2 (p. 2: 'time is ripe'); Ludwig Körner, '1. Teil: von des deutschen Shauspielers theatralischer Sendung', in Frauenfeld, pp. 5–12 (p. 11).

84 Drewniak, *Das Theater*, pp. 233–6 (Kaergel, Bethge); Schültke, 'The Municipal Theatre', pp. 166–7 (Bethge); Wessels, pp. 496–503 (anti-English drama); Norman Davies, *Europe: A History* (Oxford: Oxford University Press, 1996), pp. 994–5 (Glinka); Harold B. Segel, 'Drama of Struggle: The Wartime Stage Repertoire', in *Culture and Entertainment in Wartime Russia*, ed. by Richard Stites (Bloomington: Indiana University Press, 1995), pp. 108–25 (Solovyev and other examples of Rus-sian dramatic nationalism); C. W. E. Bigsby, *A Critical Introduction to Twentieth-Century American Drama*, 3 vols (Cambridge: Cambridge University Press, 1982–85), III: *Beyond Broadway* (1985), pp. 1–2 (Sherwood).

85 'Rede zur Jahrestagung der Reichskulturkammer und NS-Gemeinschaft "Kraft durch Freude"', *Die Bühne*, 5 December 1939, pp. 460–2 (Goebbels); Heinz Kin-dermann, *Die europäische Sendung des deutschen Theaters*, Wiener Wissenschaftliche Vorträge und Reden, 10 (Vienna: Verlag der Ringbuchhandlung, 1944), p. 55 ('European mission'); Etienne Verhoeyen, *Belgie bezet: 1940–1944: een synthese* (Brussels: BRTN-Instructieve Omroep, 1993), p. 228 (Belgian theatres); Drewniak, *Das Theater*, p. 59 (TV).

86 Drewniak, 'The Foundations', p. 73 (Bayreuth); Dussel, pp. 326–7 (Schlösser circular); Joseph Goebbels, *Goebbels Reden: 1932–1945*, ed. by Helmut Heiber, 2 vols (Düsseldorf: Droste, 1971–72), II, 194; Müller and Stöckemann, pp. 191 (photographs of legs), 137–8 (Hiller Girls); Jelavich, pp. 252–6 (Tiller Girls, beauty dances); Steinweis, pp. 164–6 (police complaints, measures against nudity).

87 Steinweis, p. 148 (cutbacks), 155, 172 (expulsions); *Hitler's Table Talk: 1941–44: His Private Conversations*, trans. by Norman Cameron and R. H. Stevens, 2nd edn (London: Weidenfeld and Nicolson, 1973), pp. 320–1; F. De Crucciati, 'Itinerario teatrale attraverso l'Europa in guerra', *Scenario*, 12 (1943), 114–16 (foreign visitor).

88 Jelavich, p. 257 (cabarets); Bernhard Minetti, *Erinnerungen eines Schauspielers*, ed. by Günther Rühle (Stuttgart: Deutsche Verlags-Anstalt, 1985), p. 146; Will Quadflieg, *Wir spielen immer: Erinnerungen* (Frankfurt am Main: Fischer, 1976), pp. 134–7; Drewniak, *Das Theater*, p. 76 (Josefstadt); Freydank, pp. 462 (Staats-oper), 470–1 (Schauspielhaus); Günther Bellmann, *Schauspielhausgeschichten: 250 Jahre Theater und Musik auf dem Berliner Gendarmenmarkt* (Berlin: Christoph Links, 1993), p. 226 (Schauspielhaus). The unconditional surrender of *all* German territory took place on 7 May 1945.

89 Herbert Freeden, 'A Jewish Theatre under the Swastika', *Leo Baeck Institute Yearbook*, 1 (1956), 142–62 (pp. 158–9: figures of members and performances);

Len Crome, *Unbroken: Resistance and Survival in the Concentration Camps* (London: Lawrence & Wishart, 1988), p. 36 (Communists); Hedwig Müller, 'Die andere Seite', in Müller and Stöckemann, pp. 202–16 (pp. 202–4: Schottmüller); Heinrich Goertz, *Lachen und Heulen: Roman* (Munich: Paul List, 1982), p. 302 (*Threepenny Opera*). The Rote Kapelle and Weiße Rose are two of the better-known leftist opposition groups (Daiber, pp. 251–3).

90 Jelavich, pp. 236–41 (on Finck, Tingel-Tangel); Werner Finck, *Alter Narr, was nun?: die Geschichte meiner Zeit* (Munich: Herbig, 1972), pp. 66–7 (tailor sketch); trans. in *Cabaret Performance*, 2 vols, ed. and trans. by Laurence Senelick (New York: PAJ; Baltimore, MD: Johns Hopkins University Press, 1989–93), II: *Europe 1920–1940: Sketches, Songs, Monologues, Memoirs* (1993), pp. 278–9.

91 Rühle, 'Einleitung', p. 68 (numbers of plays written and performed in exile); Tom Kuhn, 'Forms of Conviction: The Problem of Belief in Anti-Fascist Plays by Bruckner, Toller and Wolf', in *German Writers and Politics 1918–39*, ed. by Richard Dove and Stephen Lamb (Basingstoke: Macmillan, 1992), pp. 163–77 (on the uncertainty experienced by dramatists in exile; quotation, p. 174).

92 Marie-Agnès Joubert, *La Comédie-Française sous l'occupation* (Paris: Tallandier, 1998), p. 342 (paper darts); Drewniak, *Das Theater*, p. 117 (on violent demonstrations against German music tours in France); Ingrid Galster, *Le Théâtre de Jean-Paul Sartre devant ses premiers critiques: les pièces créées sous l'occupation allemande: 'Les Mouches' et 'Huis clos'* (Tübingen: Gunter Narr; Paris: Jean-Michel Place, 1986) (Sartre's plays); Hans Mulder, *Kunst in crisis en bezetting: een onderzoek naar de houding van Nederlandse kunstenaars in de periode 1930–1945* (Utrecht: Het Spectrum, 1978), pp. 221–2, 225 (nuances), 220, 284–7 (black evenings); Tadeusz Kantor, *A Journey Through Other Spaces: Essays and Manifestos, 1944–1990*, ed. and trans. by Michal Kobialka (Berkeley: University of California Press, 1993), pp. 36, 72–4, 118, 120–1, 147–8, 259, 271–8.

93 Wulf, *Theater*, pp. 212–13 (theatre for SS guards, recounted personally by the actor Dieter Borsche to Wulf); Alvin Goldfarb, 'Theatrical Activities in Nazi Concentration Camps', *Performing Arts Journal*, 1, no. 2 (Fall 1976), 3–11 (p. 6: Buchenwald); *Gehn ma halt a bisserl unter: Kabarett in Wien von den Anfängen bis heute*, ed. by Walter Rösler, 2nd edn (Berlin: Henschel, 1993), pp. 286–7 (Dachau song).

94 François Mitterrand, *Mémoires interrompus: entretiens avec Georges-Marc Benamou* (Paris: Odile Jacob, 1996), p. 17; *Lachen in het donker: Amusement in Kamp Westerbork*, ed. by Dirk Mulder and Ben Prinsen, Westerbork Cahiers, 4 (Hooghalen: Herinneringscentrum Kamp Westerbork; Assen: Van Gorcum, 1996), pp. 13, 87, 109 (programme, photographs of revues); Jelavich, pp. 263–8 (Westerbork revues); Joža Karas, *Music in Terezín 1941–1945* (New York: Beaufort Books, 1985), pp. 41 (Schubert, Brahms), 93 (*Brundibár*); *František Zelenka: Scenographer: 1904–1944*, exhibition catalogue (London: London Institute, 1994), p. 15 (list of Zelenka's productions); Goldfarb, pp. 4 (Auschwitz), 8 (near Riga); Jan Malík, *Puppetry in Czechoslovakia*, trans. by B. Goldreich (Prague: Orbis, 1948), pp. 32–6, 52–3 (puppetry in occupied Prague, Theresienstadt, concentration camps). For an introduction to theatre in Nazi concentration camps, see *Theatrical Performance During the Holocaust: Texts, Documents, Memoirs*, ed. by Rebecca Rovit and Alvin Goldfarb (Baltimore, MD: Johns Hopkins University Press, 1999). I am grateful to Zdenka Ehrlich for talking to me about her acting in Theresien-

stadt (Terezín in Czech) in a personal interview (London, 29 November 1996) and
to the Canadian puppeteer Ronnie Burkett for information on puppetry during
the war.

95   Berta Drews, *Wohin des Wegs: Erinnerungen*, 4th edn (Munich: Langen Müller,
1987), pp. 240–56 (sympathetic account of George's imprisonment by his widow,
who considers him an innocent victim); Christoph Funke, 'Heinrich George – ein
Komödiant im Dritten Reich: Versuch einer Deutung', in *Sachsenhausen bei Berlin:
Speziallager Nr. 7 1945–1950*, ed. by Günter Adge (Berlin: Aufbau Verlag, 1994),
pp. 216–28 (documented account).

96   Herbert Ihering, *Junge Schauspieler*, 2nd edn (Berlin: Henschel, 1948), pp. 57–9;
William R. Elwood, 'Werner Krauß and the Third Reich', in *Theatre in the Third
Reich*, ed. by Gadberry, pp. 91–101 (recent assessment of Krauss). Gründgens ran
a theatre group during his imprisonment. See Andreas Weigelt, 'Jamlitz – Spezial-
lager Nr. 6 (September 1945–April 1947)', in *Speziallager des NKWD: Sowjetische
Internierungslager in Brandenburg 1945–1950*, ed. by Jörg Morré (Potsdam:
Brandenburgische Landeszentrale für Politische Bildung, 1997), pp. 33–42 (p. 40).

97   Taylor, p. 248 (Johst); Schültke, *Theater*, pp. 131–2 (Bethge).

98   Willeke, p. 30 (Wanderscheck); Willett, pp. 201–4 (Brecht and Neher after the
war).

99   Daniel J. Goldhagen, *Hitler's Willing Executioners: Ordinary Germans and the
Holocaust* (New York: Alfred A. Knopf, 1996); Alfred Dreifuss, *Deutsches Theater
Berlin: Schumannstraße 13a: Fünf Kapitel aus der Geschichte einer Schauspiel-
bühne* ([East] Berlin: Henschel, 1987), p. 217 (Hilpert). There is evidence for
Hilpert saving the life of a homosexual actor. See Pierre Seel, *Liberation was for
Others: Memoirs of a Gay Survivor of the Nazi Holocaust*, trans. by Joachim
Neugroschel (New York: Da Capo Press, 1997), p. 167. Sympathetic accounts of
the lives of actors such as Gründgens and George assert that they protected Jewish
colleagues.

100 Jürgen Hillesheim, 'Heil Dir Führer! Führ uns an! ...': der Augsburger Dichter
Richard Euringer* (Würzburg: Königshausen & Neumann, 1995), pp. 98–9, 153
(Euringer's Catholicism); Stefan Busch, *'Und gestern, da hörte uns Deutschland':
NS-Autoren in der Bundesrepublik: Kontinuität und Diskontinuität bei Friedrich
Griese, Werner Beumelburg, Eberhard Wolfgang Möller und Kurt Ziesel*, Studien
zur Literatur- und Kulturgeschichte, 13 (Würzburg: Königshausen & Neumann,
1998), pp. 169–208 (Möller's post-war career).

101 Helmar Harald Fischer, 'Was gestrichen ist, kann nicht durchfallen', *Theater
Heute*, 30, no. 9 (September 1989), 1–3, 6–19 (analysis of autobiographies). Will
Quadflieg is one of the few exceptions in the acting world. He admitted to Fischer
personally (p. 17) what he had not written in his memoirs: that he had not wanted
to know certain things during the Nazi period and that this was inexcusable.

102 Friedrich Luft, *Stimme der Kritik*, 2 vols (Frankfurt am Main: Ullstein, 1982), I,
66 (applause for Gründgens); Drewniak, *Das Theater*, pp. 151, 162–3 (Rühmann's
pay), 164 (Rühmann divorced his 'non-Aryan' wife during the Third Reich);
Fischer, 'Was gestrichen ist', p. 18 (interview quoted).

103 'Kultuurkamer als splijtzwam', *Het Parool*, 4 May 1985 (quoted in Hans van den
Heuvel and Gerard Mulder, *De illegale pers in Nederland 1940–1945: het vrije
woord* (The Hague: SDU, 1990), p. 125: Dutch actor, F. Sterneberg). On the boycott urged by clandestine journals, see also *'De Vrije Kunstenaar' 1941–1945:*

facsimilé herdruk van alle tijdens de bezetting verschenen afleveringen (Amsterdam: B. R. Grüner & John Benjamins, 1970), pp. 9, 29.

104 Erica Jong, *Fear of Flying: A Novel* (London: Minerva, 1994), pp. 70–2; Eicher, pp. 405–6 (1930s and 1940s drama); Simon Williams and Wilhelm Hortmann, *Shakespeare on the German Stage*, 2 vols (Cambridge: Cambridge University Press, 1990–98), [II]: *The Twentieth Century* (by Hortmann, 1998), p. 181 (Shakespeare, Schiller).

105 Harold Hobson, 'Brecht the Misunderstood', *Sunday Times*, 16 May 1965; Hajo Kurzenberger, 'Sprachkörper im Bühnenraum: chorisches Theater der neunziger Jahre', *Neue Zürcher Zeitung*, 26–27 June 1999.

106 Florian Radvan, 'Überlegungen zur Wiederaufführung nationalsozialistischer Dramatik auf deutschen Bühnen: Hanns Johsts Schauspiel *Schlageter* (UA 1933) als Beispiel', *Forum Modernes Theater*, 13 (1998), 165–83 (on revivals of *Schlageter*); William Niven, Chapter 1 of the present volume, pp. 88–90 (recent uses for *Thingplätze*); Charles Bremner, 'France Examines its Conscience as de Gaulle Says "No" Again', *The Times*, 28 September 1999 (on *The One Who Said No*); Clarisse Fabre, 'Soirée gaulliste pour l'homme qui a dit "oui" à Jacques Chirac', *Le Monde*, 2 October 1999 (Chirac's thanks).

107 I am grateful to Lutz Becker, Glen Gadberry and William Niven for their comments on an earlier version of this introduction.

The birth of Nazi drama?
Thing *plays*

WILLIAM NIVEN

Between 1933 and 1936, literally hundreds of new German plays celebrated the advent of the Third Reich. Many of these plays were written spontaneously in response to a sense of national renewal; others were written at the instigation of the Nazi authorities. Selected plays of both origins were labelled *Thingspiele*, or *Thing* plays, and hailed as the supreme dramatic expression of National Socialism. Commonly regarded as the National Socialists' only original contribution to the development of German drama, the *Thing* plays were an essential component of Nazi theatre in the early years of the regime. By tracing important administrative measures, it is possible to see exactly how this new dramatic genre was promoted. A considerable body of theory was combined with official support. Yet, although the resulting plays had a certain coherence, they were rarely successful. Moreover, they relied heavily on styles which were in ostensible political opposition to the new regime.

Prime reasons for the collapse of the *Thing* movement in 1936 may have been technical and financial in nature. However, it had also become clear that the *Thing* plays were rooted in the culture of the Weimar Republic and therefore ultimately more of a hindrance to the inculcation of National Socialism than a help. While apparently epitomizing the essence of Nazi ideology, the *Thing* plays in fact had much in common with Expressionist and workers' drama (*Theater der Arbeiterbewegung/Arbeiterdrama*). An initially lauded element of Nazi aesthetics became a threat to the political system it was supposed to be celebrating.

Measures taken to promote a new form of drama

One area which interested the Nazis from the outset was outdoor theatre, which they brought under their control by a number of measures. On 7 July 1933, the Reichsbund der Freilicht- und Volksschauspiele (Reich League of

Outdoor and People's Theatre) was set up, with Otto Laubinger as president and Joseph Goebbels as patron. On 8 August, all outdoor theatre groups were forced to join the Reichsbund, and in October 1933 such groups had to acquire explicit permission to perform plays. In March 1935, the Reichsbund was divided up into three areas of responsibility, including one for *Thing* plays.

One of the Reichsbund's functions was purely economic. The aim was to curb the unemployment of professional actors – which had reached 48 per cent in 1932 – by forcing amateur outdoor theatre groups to employ professional actors, at least for lead roles. Other functions of the Reichsbund were to transform the performance of existing plays into more cultic events and to create new plays which would celebrate national values. This celebration was to be enhanced by outdoor performance on sites of significance in German history, thereby stressing the organic links between contemporary culture, Nordic nature and the glorious German past. These new plays, by using mass choruses and marching groups, would also help to foster a sense of national community among participants and encourage the audience to identify with the events on stage.

The term *Thing* play (*Thingspiel*), which quickly became accepted as the name for this new drama, was introduced by the Germanist Professor Carl Niessen on 29 July 1933.[1] A number of measures were taken to foster the development of a *Thing* play movement. To write the new kind of drama, a circle of authors was set up, including nationalist writers such as Hans Friedrich Blunck, Eberhard Wolfgang Möller and Heinz Steguweit.[2] Model performances of plays were organized to give writers a feeling for the general dramaturgical direction. It was with this in mind that Kurt Eggers's *The Play about Job, the German* (*Das Spiel von Job dem Deutschen*) was premiered in Cologne on 16 November 1933, with 500 actors in front of an audience of 4200 people. Drama competitions took place, such as the one organized by the Deutsche Arbeitsfront (German Labour Front) late in 1933, to which 489 entries for mass-cast plays and 694 works for choruses were submitted.

Steps were taken to create a context for the large-scale production of the new dramas. In September 1933, the first Spielgemeinschaft für nationale Festgestaltung (Play Community for the Organization of National Festivities) was set up in the Rhineland. Others followed. The aim of these organizations was to plan at least two large-scale national festivals a year which would serve as vehicles for the *Thing* plays. By March 1934, eleven Play Communities had been set up; by the end of June the number had risen to sixteen.[3] One of the first, and probably most successful, of the planned festivals was the Reichsfestspiele (Reich Festival of Plays) in Heidelberg in 1934. Within the context of this Festival of Plays, Richard Euringer's *German Passion 1933* (*Deutsche Passion 1933*) was performed.[4] The original intention had been to perform the play on a specially built *Thingplatz*, but the huge outdoor theatre on the Heiligenberg near Heidelberg was not built in time for the production, so it had to be staged instead in the courtyard of Heidelberg Castle.[5]

The Nazis started a massive building programme to construct outdoor stages (*Thingplätze* or *Thingstätten*) for the *Thing* plays all over Germany. Initially, the Propaganda Ministry and the Freiwilliger Arbeitsdienst (League of Voluntary Workers) agreed on the building of twenty such stages, but soon 400 were envisaged. Regional offices of the Propaganda Ministry were responsible for finding locations. The building of the *Thingplätze*, initially at least, was a project on as grand a scale as the building of motorways. By the end of 1934, five stages were finished: in Halle, Holzminden, Jülich, Schmiedeberg and Stolzenau. By the end of 1935, sixteen stages were playable. These stages were usually the focal point of vast outdoor theatres built to accommodate thousands of people. The *Thingplatz* auditorium in Braunschweig could hold 15,000, the one at Annaberg up to 50,000 people (including standing room). Arguably, the architecture was more important than the plays. At the opening of the Heidelberg *Thingplatz* in 1935, Goebbels talked of 'National Socialism in stone' and of the Heidelberg *Thingplatz* giving 'a living, tangible and monumental expression' to 'our concept of life'. Goebbels claimed that the *Thingplätze* would testify to the creative energy of National Socialism for centuries to come, and compared the new theatres to the Autobahns. Only then did he stress that cultural life would emanate from these stages.[6] The hope was that the building of impressive stages would stimulate a correspondingly impressive form of drama.

Theoretical principles of the new drama

In addition to the administrative steps, there were a number of important theoretical proposals setting out what the new drama should be like. These proposals stressed the need for several essential elements.

Community

The new form of drama was to be *völkisch* (national, of the people). All theoretical pronouncements stress this. Hence Reichsdramaturg Rainer Schlösser underlined concepts such as 'the *völkisch* blood-brotherhood' and 'communal experience' in connection with the new drama.[7] Wilhelm von Schramm put the same idea in slightly different terms: 'The German should no longer experience himself as private person and isolated individual, but as part of the public and of the people's community (*Volksgemeinschaft*)'.[8] In contrast to traditional theatre, the Nazis strove to create a form of theatre in which the German people itself constituted the focus of the drama, not an individual or a collection of individuals, or a class, or even a society. German theatre was no longer to be 'bourgeois', a shallow form of entertainment for the moneyed classes, but a serious cultural experience for the people as a whole. Consequently, the new drama would have to demonstrate the relevance of the dramatic action to *all* citizens, if not directly, then at least indirectly. Schlösser maintained that what was required was a drama which raised historical events to a mythical level *above* reality: the fate and character of the German people had to be visible in any dramatic representation.[9] The actors on stage were thus not individuals, but exemplary figures. Von Schramm stated that, in contrast to what he termed 'individualistic' theatre, the actor would no longer play an 'individual', but a 'type'; he would represent not an 'individual soul', but a 'common soul'. The new drama would also to a large extent be choric in character. Von Schramm even defined it as 'choric-*völkisch*' (Figure 4).[10] Obviously, a collective dramatic persona could suggest representativeness and *völkisch* qualities far better than a single character.

A cultic experience

The audience was therefore invited to identify with the stage action. Indeed, actors and audience were as one, participants in a dramatic acting out of the

4 An example of choric-*völkisch* drama: Kurt Heynicke's *Road to the Reich* on the **Heidelberg** *Thingplatz* in 1935.

German soul. The *Thing* plays were designed to rekindle or strengthen those ethnic spiritual and moral values which had been smothered or at least weakened by the alienation of the Weimar Republic. If defamiliarization, to use Shklovsky's term, was the function of Brechtian drama, the *Thing* play aimed at refamiliarization.[11] It was hoped that the plays would help to cement a sense of belonging to the *Volksgemeinschaft* and thus become an almost cultic ceremony in which the people celebrated their own racial identity. *Thing* play author Euringer produced a series of thirteen *Thing* play theses, of which the tenth reads: 'Cult, not "art" is the purpose of the *Thingplatz*.'[12] And von Schramm talks of the 'political and cultic' character of *Thing* plays.[13]

The passing of judgement

In theory, *Thing* meant 'place of judgement'. When he conceived the term *Thing*, Carl Niessen was thinking of Tacitus's *Germania*, in which the Latin author mentioned gatherings of Germanic clansmen during which political decisions regarding peace and war-making were made, leaders elected, various contracts discussed and issues of law decided upon. Tacitus even wrote of masculinity rites, which seemed to come closer to capturing the spirit of the *Thing* plays than anything else.[14] The term *thing* has survived in the words for European parliaments such as those in Norway (Storting), Iceland (Folketing) and even the Isle of Man (Tynwald). The common Indo-Germanic root is probably *teng*, *thing*, *Ding*. Niessen gave his reasons for coining the term *Thing*:

> The new Germany is again striving to leave the stone deserts of the towns. Parliamentary meetings in stuffy rooms served the interests of a period of subversion and incitement. The real community of the people, who have been liberated from the politics of self-interest, finds its wonderful symbolic expression in the wide realm (*Lebensraum*) of nature.[15]

The literary critic and Nazi ideologue Wolf Braumüller took up Niessen's idea, arguing though that the new form of *Thing* should not be a working group deciding on political issues, but rather a celebration designed to unite the people and the nation.[16] And Euringer writes in his third *Thing* play thesis of the 'site, where the court will meet'.[17] Thus the *Thing* plays were supposed to imitate a process of collective decision-making and give the audience the feeling they were participating in ancient Germanic rites, sharing power and responsibility as their ancestors did in the distant past.

Heroism

The emphasis on choric drama and collectivity did not mean, however, that individual characters were to be mere mouthpieces of the group. It was

Schlösser who talked of National Socialism's 'affirmation of the right to personality' and of the need for 'personalities' who would stand at the centre of the dramatic action. At the same time, Schlösser stressed that cultic theatre must develop a 'more profound concept of the tragic'.[18] National Socialism tended to reject Naturalism, dismissing Naturalist plays as 'milieu pieces' and Naturalism, to quote von Schramm, as 'nihilistic'.[19] While Naturalism suggested that man was the passive plaything of his genetic inheritance and social environment, Nazi drama aimed to show man as a heroic struggler who rises above his environment and who, while often 'tragically' losing his struggle, points the way forward in an act of creative martyrdom. This was the essence of Goebbels's 'steely Romanticism'.[20]

There is a contradiction between the notion of heroic personality and the idea that even heroes were 'bound to their community', as Schlösser expressed it.[21] One's behaviour cannot be at once shaped by ties of blood and race (biological determinism) and free to transcend these. But in the *Thing* plays there were indeed lead characters who were quintessentially *völkisch* and yet more dynamic and individual than the people they represented.

A total art form

Schlösser, talking of traditional popular plays, identified five essential elements: oratorio (a programme alternating between choruses and the pronouncements of individual speakers); mime/symbolism (such as allegory or the consecration of the flags); processions (parades, festive processions and mass meetings); dance (ballet, expressive dance or gymnastics); and music. While music was traditionally the binding element, Schlösser emphasized that what was now required as a means of fusion was 'the dramatic law' – a conclusion he had come to in conversation with the dramatist Möller.[22] From this it was clear that the *Thing* play was to offer a kind of total artistic and aesthetic spectacle, both visual and aural, within an overarching dramatic framework. It was to be a popular *Gesamtkunstwerk* (total work of art) with a mass appeal, in which all the elements of drama, sport, music, dance, and political parade would be merged. This conceptual totality corresponded to the monumentality of the *Thingplätze*. Just as the *Thingplatz* was the ultimate stage, so the new drama was to be the ultimate in art, a syncretic experience of inimitable immensity.

Problems of definition

If this was the theory, what of the plays themselves? In a sense, there are problems in defining exactly which plays can be designated *Thing* plays. It would be possible to examine all Nazi drama performed outdoors and select those whose content accords with the above principles, but this would be an ultimately subjective process. In any case, the theory does not necessarily precede the practice. In fact, only some of the plays performed as *Thing* plays were written in response to the call for a new form of drama: Kurt Heynicke's *Road to the Reich* (*Der Weg ins Reich*, 1935) and Euringer's *Dance of Death* (*Totentanz*, 1934) are two better-known examples.[23] Others, however, were written before the term '*Thing* play' had been coined by Niessen, and both Heynicke's *Neurode*[24] and Eggers's *The Play about Job, the German* were completed in 1932, before the Nazis had come to power. Even Euringer's *German Passion 1933*, one of the best known of all Nazi plays, was conceived, if not completed, in December 1932.

Another criterion might be to define as *Thing* plays everything performed on *Thingplätze* (Figure 5). However, this is not a reliable measure, given that *Thingplätze* were also the site of summer solstice plays and semi-sacral acts of inauguration, and that some plays performed there were actually designed for performance on other sites, such as Gustav Goes's *Germany Rises!* (*Aufbricht Deutschland!*) of 1933, which was in fact a stadium play or *Stadionspiel*.[25] Conversely, plays intimately associated with *Thingplätze*, such as Heynicke's *Neurode*, were not always performed there: *Neurode* was performed by the Lower Saxon Outdoor Drama Community in the sports stadium at Hanover-Linden in 1934, while Eggers's *The Play about Job, the German* was first performed in a trades-fair hall in Cologne in 1934.

Another problem is that some of the plays performed on *Thingplätze* were

5 The *Thingplatz* in Heidelberg, completed in 1935.

not originally intended for outdoor performance. Euringer's *German Passion 1933*, for instance, was written as a radio play and first broadcast on all German radio channels on Maundy Thursday (13 April) 1933. Similarly, Hans Jürgen Nierentz's *Work Symphony (Symphonie der Arbeit)*[26] was written for radio and was first broadcast on 1 May 1933 as an accompanying programme to the Nazi celebration of this traditionally left-wing occasion on the Tempel-hofer Field in Berlin. While Euringer's *German Passion 1933* was broadcast as a Germanic alternative to the Christian Easter Passion Play, Nierentz's *Work Symphony* was used as part of the attempt to propagate a non-Socialist, Nazi view of the function of 1 May. In other words, these plays were embedded within an act of political propaganda and thus robbed of their purely theatrical or aesthetic function.

The Nazis produced two official lists of *Thing* plays, one in 1934 and the other in 1935.[27] It might seem reasonable to take these lists as a starting point for critical analysis, since they represent what the Nazis themselves saw as the archetypal *Thing* plays. However, some of the plays included in the 1934 list did not feature in the 1935 list. The authorities clearly vacillated on what they considered appropriate.[28] Quite why they changed their minds is hard to establish, though in the case of Nierentz's *Farmers' Blessing* it may have been because this work is more of a paean of praise to the Almighty than a celebration of National Socialist chthonian values. It is interesting none the less that most of the plays in one or both of the lists – especially those by Eggers, Heynicke, Euringer and Erich Müller-Schnick – were among the frequently performed works on the *Thingplätze* and featured regularly in public discussions of the *Thing* play movement. The lists are therefore a valid criterion for definition, despite reservations. In addition, the examination of other plays performed on *Thingplätze* can be illuminating when they share certain features with the plays on the lists.

Plots

The plots of the *Thing* plays are very similar in terms of their essential structure and direction. Two typical examples can serve as illustrations. In Euringer's *German Passion 1933*, a dead soldier emerges from the grave and is shocked that he cannot find the great Germany he used to know. Characters such as the War Cripple, the Unemployed Man, a number of children and a girl complain bitterly at the treatment meted out to Germany by the Allies, who are accused of having blamed the war on Germany, stripped it bare of weapons and then imposed savage reparations, thus inflicting poverty on innocent little children who move from scene to scene lamenting their fate: 'Need – need – need – / Hunger. And no bread' (p. 19).

The play vigorously condemns Communism and internationalism, which are interpreted respectively as self-emasculation and orgiastic racial intermingling of the most distasteful kind. The Evil Spirit, who symbolizes moral decline, welcomes 'Sodom and Gomorrah in Berlin' (p. 27) and the fact that 'Europe is getting to be one big brothel.' 'Hold your nose – it stinks here – / mass orgies they call revues' (p. 27), he expostulates sarcastically. The returning soldier, triggered by such dilapidation into a state of agonized enlightenment, cries for a strong leader and calls the people to order, demanding of them a moral self-purification by commitment to work. His message comes across powerfully, the people turn to the future with renewed zest and the play ends with the Evil Spirit himself now stunned into enlightenment: 'So it really does exist, this Third Reich!' (p. 47).

In Heynicke's *Neurode*, Wilhelm Radke returns home to his native village and takes the place of his brother, who has been killed in a mining accident. A little later, a second mining accident claims the lives of 152 miners, and the syndicate of owners takes the opportunity to call for the closure of the mine, ostensibly because of safety reasons, but in reality for economic motives. Villagers arrive from a neighbouring town. They have been entrusted with the job of demolishing the mine. Radke and other miners try to stop them. The remainder of the play is taken up with speech-making scenes, the fate of the mine hanging in the balance until the Stranger arrives to offer the support of the Reich for the ailing mine:

> THE STRANGER   Everyone in Germany for all of Germany, all Germany for every German! The Reich puts in an offer too and saves the mine – because you – have been loyal! Loyal – to Germany – Germany – and to yourselves!! (p. 60)

In typical fashion, the play ends with a rousing final chorus involving all the actors and clearly stating the symbolic nature of the action. As in all *Thing* plays, National Socialism redeems the people, but their determination and hard work are a prerequisite for revival. State and citizens are united in a single-minded effort of national will.

The indictment of the Weimar Republic

What is the essential character of the *Thing* plays? It might be most profitable to begin by considering them as acts of judgement – a quintessential component of the original theoretical conception – because such a consideration enables us to gain a better impression of what the plays are about. With the exception of Möller's *The Frankenburg Dice-Game* (*Das Frankenburger Würfelspiel*, 1936), *Thing* plays do not depict the passing of judgement in a literal manner.

This is not large-scale court-room drama with judge and jury. But the element of judgement is nevertheless strongly present at an implicit level, and that this judgement is passed in the name of a reawakened national and moral consciousness is also made clear. For the most part, it is the Weimar Republic which is put on trial and condemned. Behind such biblical titles as Euringer's *German Passion 1933* or Eggers's *The Play about Job, the German* is an allegorical intention, Christ's Passion or Job's sufferings being equated with those of the German people at the hands of the Weimar Republic. Heynicke's *Neurode* is not explicitly set in the Republic, but it clearly reflects its social and economic problems.

Most of the plays portray Weimar as corrupt from inception to end. It started off on a note of duplicitous pacifism and stab-in-the-back betrayal, was pusillanimously parliamentarian, passively accepting of the Versailles Treaty, internationalist, yet at the same time rampantly capitalistic, contemptuous of nationalism, and a den of iniquity, excessive artistic licence and racial chaos. Politically, economically and morally, in other words, it lacked any sort of fibre. It is this Weimar world and/or its associated problems of inflation, industrial strife, unemployment and poverty which are most frequently evoked.

It is a characteristic of some of the *Thing* plays that they interpret all those aspects of Weimar which they despise as conspiratorially interlinked. This is the implication behind syncretic images such as the Golden Doll in Euringer's *Dance of Death*, which embodies the lure of gold, champagne, Socialism and sexual abandon: 'Naked and made of purest gold / I am the lust of this world!' (p. 16). In Goes's play *The Sacrificial Flame of Work* (*Opferflamme der Arbeit*, 1933) it is Ahasuerus[29] who personifies Jewry, pacifism, Marxism, class conflict, inflation and parliamentarianism, while the Evil Spirit is at the root of all problems in Euringer's *German Passion 1933*, and the Antichrist plays a similar role in Becker's *The End of German Hardship*. Other *Thing* plays, while avoiding total personifications, nevertheless posit suggestive links. In Eggers's *The Long March*, the group responsible for incitement to revolution in 1918 is termed the 'Chorus of Degenerates', thus connecting Socialist revolution with immorality. And in Müller-Schnick's *Soldiers of the Soil*, which charts the suffering of German farmers from the Thirty Years War through to the Weimar Republic, the First Speaker for Internationalism proclaims: 'We don't need meadows, nor lakes, nor woods. / What we need is asphalt, asphalt, asphalt' (p. 29). He is therefore as committed to destructive industrialization and urbanization as the Speaker for Capital.

That Socialism means internationalism and therefore outside interference in Germany's affairs is a point often made in *Thing* plays. Internationalism, moreover, is perceived as signifying an 'open-doors' policy inviting racial intermingling and orgiastic abandon – the death-knell to German racial purity.

The Evil Spirit in Euringer's *German Passion 1933* compares Europe to a brothel, continuing: 'Export to all countries. What's wanted is racial contamination!' (p. 28). Another idea is that Socialism is divisive because it leads to class conflict and even to unmitigated self-interest. In all cases there is a strong suggestion of an intimate connection between Socialism and degeneracy, which leads to the perception of Socialist ideas as comparable to a bacillus. In Euringer's *German Passion 1933*, the War Cripple talks of democrats, Jews, pacifists and Marxists 'getting into milk and flour' (p. 22), while the Speaker in Müller-Schnick's *Soldiers of the Soil*, in reference to the victory of internationalism, speaks of 'poisonous odours drifting through the country' and of 'evil thoughts eating into our brains' (p. 27).

Women are placed in the same degenerate category as Socialists. The embodiment of vice in Eggers's *The Play about Job, the German* is a woman, and the representative of the Versailles Treaty in Goes's *Germany Rises!* is a white-tunicked female who soon reveals a close-fitting, snake-like costume befitting her seductive treachery. Sexually self-confident women seem to have been a hallmark of Weimar's urban culture, and conservative males clearly felt threatened by them. Authors of *Thing* plays stigmatize such sexual overtness by associating it with a wide range of perceived forms of political and moral corruption. Alternatively, one could argue that they construe a link between such overtness and moral degeneracy to undermine the moral authority of Socialism and internationalism in particular.

Thing dramatists identified unemployment as a central cause of the problems in the Weimar Republic. Euringer's *German Passion 1933* features a grumpy, disillusioned Unemployed Man, and the central theme of Heynicke's *Neurode* is the prospect of mass unemployment hanging over the mining community. However, even unemployment is linked to Socialism. In Becker's *The End of German Hardship*, the sounds of Socialist rebellion are immediately followed by the Epic Speaker's claim – 'The factories close their massive doors. [...] The grey army of the unemployed swells like an ocean' (p. 14) – as if this were the direct result of Socialist industrial protest. In *German Passion 1933*, the Mother attributes Germany's industrial inactivity to the Communists, while a Proletarian maintains that he deserted his wife and workplace in the name of (the presumably Socialist prospect of) 'paradise' (p. 20), thereby implying that Communist-influenced workers resign voluntarily and thus increase unemployment.

The national revolution

Unemployment in *Thing* play historiography is a political consequence of Socialist class warfare rather than of rationalization and economic crisis.

Logically, then, an end to this warfare will create employment. The *Thing* plays portray a coming together of all classes, whose differences are forgotten as they recognize what they have in common, namely their Germanness. This renewed awareness of ethnic identity generates a sense of national responsibility, which finds expression in a sudden zest for hard work. At the end of *German Passion 1933*, citizens from all walks of life and classes assert in rapid succession the need to work in order to save Germany. In Heynicke's *Neurode*, workers and management combine to save the mine (representative of Germany) and march united into the future, the chorus declaiming 'Work is the people's blessing!' (p. 62). A medley of German workers marches on stage from the auditorium at the conclusion of Müller-Schnick's *Soldiers of the Soil*, singing:

> Our German land needs deeds,
> Enough words have been spoken.
> Germany, you most beautiful of lands,
> It is to you we dedicate the work of our hands!
> We serve you with the spade,
> Because we are soldiers, work soldiers. (p. 36)

The association of work with militarism is strengthened by the application of the term 'work soldiers' to these marching groups, and by the fact that, like real soldiers, the work soldiers also have weapons slung over their shoulders – spades instead of guns.

The military image of marching people is inherently nationalistic and implies an end to internationalism within Germany's borders: the Weimar Republic is sentenced to extinction as the Germans reoccupy their own country, overcoming the enemy within. In some *Thing* plays, such as Eggers's *The Long March*, the marching is also associated with the need to find new land, implying the necessity of a revanchist foreign policy. Marching conveys a disciplined, determined harmony of purpose, total integration and vigour. It also suggests a moral regeneration. While men are not the only ones to march, they dominate the groupings, and the implication is that the women among the marchers must adopt masculine customs. The militarization of women meant an end to their emancipation, which had threatened moral health. Militarization generally suggests a revitalization of interest in honour, disciplined codes of conduct and rigour. It is therefore this display of marching which represents the national revolution in all areas of life. The central contradiction here, of course, is that marching groups are a strangely inappropriate image for an act of self-liberation. Military marching rather conveys a loss of self-determination.

Indeed, the return to hard work celebrated by the marching groups clearly involves a return to traditional labour values. Müller-Schnick's *Soldiers of the*

Soil denigrates urbanization and industrialization in favour of a return to agriculture. Such a return would bind the industrial worker to the soil and thus rob him of what few union rights and social privileges he had acquired in the city. But clearly not all workers can return to the countryside. The Nameless Soldier in Euringer's *German Passion 1933* describes a process whereby the proletarian should return to the people, while the Boy in Eggers's *The Long March* talks of giving the worker back to the nation and the nation back to the worker. What this means is that those workers who remain in the cities should abandon their ostensibly uncooperative attitude and laziness – the supposed result of Socialism – and return their loyalty to the principle of labour, which is identified as the national interest. 'Discipline, poverty and humility liberate the people' (p. 34), declares the Nameless Soldier in Euringer's *German Passion 1933*. The Young Worker in Eggers's *The Long March* asserts that the bright light of the future will be reached when all Germans have accepted voluntary poverty and the sense of sacrifice.

This sense of sacrifice knew no bounds in the *Thing* plays. In Heynicke's *Neurode* the bankrupt mine is initially saved only when the workers agree to go on working there without wages, the character Radke coining the term 'spiritual wages' in defence of this policy (p. 49). The renewal of industrial and agrarian life evoked in the *Thing* plays is thus dependent on a submissive attitude, harking back to the days before trade unions, when the worker's function was to work, suffer and not complain. *Thing* dramatists present this submissiveness as an enriching spiritual experience, almost as the route to illumination, obscuring the fact that it leads to self-denial and the loss of hard-earned industrial rights and forms the basis of exploitation, even slavery. So while it is true to say that the *Thing* plays (like many of the workers' dramas of the Weimar Republic) end with a revolution, it is a conservative revolution. And it is a revolution which has already happened. While Social Democratic dramas impugn the status quo in calling for a revolution, the *Thing* plays impugn the status quo ante and celebrate the transition to the status quo. *Thing* plays thus take over the revolutionary thrust of workers' drama only to redirect it, in a thinly concealed form, and turn it, in fact, against itself. Revolutionary became anti-revolutionary.

The spirit of humble self-denial brings us back to the issue of Weimar immorality. Self-denial means doing without, the exact opposite of the sensual and sexual overfeed perceived by conservative writers to be the moral cancer of the Republic's urban culture. Collective hard work is *per se* a form of self-denial, since it relegates the interest of the self to second place in the name of economic growth. Hard work means little free time and little free will. Moreover, the unity of all classes asserted at the end of the *Thing* plays is also a form of self-denial, not just because the self is subordinated to the whole, but also because group interests are subordinated to whatever is considered to be the national interest. The Communist and Socialist insistence on defending the interests of the worker becomes unimportant; indeed, it is stigmatized as destructive and divisive in the context of the message that national unity is a prerequisite for recovery.

Identification with audiences

The marching groups in the *Thing* plays represent the German people synecdochically, while the national revival they bring about symbolizes the 1933 seizure of power. The plays thus construct a mythology of popular revolution. The audience is invited to participate in the 're-enactment' of this act of national self-determination. The invitation is facilitated by the unspecific characterization of the *Thing* plays. The 'characters' are not so much individuals as representative types with whom different sectors of the audience can identify. In Eggers's *The Long March* we encounter figures such as the Girl, the Young Worker, the Boy and the Woman. There are also many choruses, often culminating, as with Müller-Schnick's *Soldiers of the Soil*, in a rousing conclusion involving all choruses, in imitation of an opera or oratorio. The choruses are collective entities with which the audience can easily associate itself once more. Müller-Schnick's *Soldiers of the Soil* features a Farmers' Chorus and a Workers' Chorus. Nierentz's *Work Symphony* also has a Workers' Chorus. The audience was encouraged to see *itself* on stage, and this identification with the action was supported by a number of other factors.

First, there was no clear physical separation between actors and audience. The stages of the *Thingplätze* often merged with the first row of the audience, as in Heidelberg. Second, productions of plays, and indeed the plays themselves, were often designed so that groups of marching people would descend through the audience towards the stage or walk from the stage through the auditorium. Müller-Schnick, in his stage directions for *Soldiers of the Soil*, requires four choruses to be positioned in the audience, as well as two speakers who express the views of the farmers and the workers. These speakers and choruses intercede towards the end of the play, voicing their views and then marching onto the stage. The audience is supposed to believe *it* has interceded in the action. A third integrative factor is the language used by the choruses. They often speak in the first person plural. This is logical given their collective identity, but the form is unspecific enough to imply the inclusion of the audience in the making of the utterance. Second person singular forms also abound, sometimes in the imperative, or in reference to nouns such as 'people' or 'nation': the audience feels directly addressed.

It is also important to note the breaking down of barriers between amateur and professional actors. The Arbeitsdienst was responsible for building many of the *Thingplätze*, and they provided men for the choruses and marching groups in the *Thing* plays themselves. Newspaper reports also refer to the participation of the Bund deutscher Mädel (League of German Girls), Sturmabteilung/SA (Storm Troopers), Jungvolk (Young People/*Volk*), and Hitler Youth in the productions. Hundreds, sometimes even thousands, of walk-on parts were written into the *Thing* plays, giving young people especially the chance to take part in the action. One can well imagine that parents came to the *Thing* plays in the hope of catching a glimpse of their son Hans or daughter Helga as he or she marched across the stage, creating a sense of family unity across boundaries of stage and audience.

While the *Thing* plays claimed to have brought an end to the theatre of illusion, the myth of collective enterprise imposed on historical events became the grandest illusion of all. It was an illusion with an important mass-psychological effect. Audiences could share in a retrospective act of self-celebration for a role as historical agent which they never had. Moreover, because the *Thing* plays end with marching groups asserting in the indicative or imperative mood a vigorous sense of purpose, they suggest that the action continues beyond the temporal and physical bounds of the play. This is the conclusion to Heynicke's *Neurode*:

ONE MAN	Get into line!
ALL	Get into line!
ONE MAN	Step up!
ALL	Step up, you working man!
ONE MAN	Close up the ranks!
ALL	Close up the ranks!
	It must be all of Germany! [...]
	We are eternally united.
	All Germany marches with us! (pp. 63–4)

The audience is meant to leave with the feeling that it can, as it were, pick up where the play leaves off and shape present and future by popular will and dynamism. This feeling of influence was important. After all, Hitler had presented his movement as both nationalist and Socialist: there were genuine hopes of broad-based participation. But after 1933, as Hitler consolidated his personal hold on Germany, there was little room for the realization of these hopes in the political arena. It became the job of the theatre to fulfil them by ersatz means, by illusion and myth. One could argue, then, that the *Thing* plays blinded the population to its actual powerlessness. On the other hand, they may have had a quite different effect, keeping alive the wish for real power-sharing and engendering a feeling of frustration, perhaps even helping to foment disruptive wishes for a second revolution.

Individual and collective

Despite this dramatic manifestation of the power of the people, individuals nevertheless play a significant role. Indeed, the prominence given to choruses and groups often seems like an attempt to disguise the fact that they are activated by individuals. These individuals tend to be heroic, even superhuman. Just as the *Thing* plays have their absolute personifications of evil, so they have, as a necessary contrast, their absolute personifications of good. These clean-minded, big-hearted, nationally minded Germans can be dead soldiers emerging from the grave, such as the Nameless Soldier in Euringer's *German Passion 1933* (Figure 6), or returning soldiers, as in Becker's *The End of German Hardship*. They are also represented in the homecomers who have been abroad for a while, like Radke in Heynicke's *Neurode* and the Home-comer in Heynicke's *Road to the Reich*. Other strong individuals are impassioned youngsters like Hans and the Young Worker in Eggers's *The Long March*. These individuals embody the spirit of true Germanness, from which many Germans have been alienated. They sense the discrepancy between Germany as it is and Germany as it should be, suffer because of this

6 The Nameless Soldier prior to his awakening in Euringer's *German Passion 1933* (courtyard of Heidelberg castle, 1934).

discrepancy, but are unshakeably convinced that it can be overcome and that a national sense of responsibility will triumph. At the beginning of the plays these heroes are outsiders, and they are often exposed to ridicule, discrimination and marginalization. (The Evil Spirit mocks the Nameless Soldier in *German Passion 1933*.) Yet, like the outsiders whose arrival shatters the social order in the plays of German Naturalism (which the National Socialists claimed to despise), the heroic individuals in the *Thing* plays have a radical impact on their environment.

These heroes are, as dramatic characters, infinitely dull. They are perfect in almost every respect: determined, robust, patient, visionary, dynamic, selfless repositories of absolute virtue. Their moral sheen singles them out from their corrupt or dilatory environment, and their sense of wonder at the disarray of the world around them is matched only by their proselytizing vigour. *Thing* plays frequently include political speech-making scenes in which the heroes gather the other characters around them and try to win them over, always successfully. At such points the plays become political broadcasts on behalf of National Socialism (Figure 7). A case in point is the Nameless Soldier, who gives a decisive turning-point speech in Scene IV of Euringer's *German Passion 1933*, as does the Stranger in Heynicke's *Neurode*. The heroic individuals are similar to Christ in that their capacity for suffering is limitless to the point of martyrdom – an example for the people to follow. The Nameless Soldier in *German Passion 1933* suffers a two-fold passion, during the First World War and then subsequently in the Weimar Republic. The Boy in Eggers's *The Long March* is shot when he tries to mediate between conflicting groups, and the German Job in Eggers's *The Play about Job, the German* is an archetypal martyr figure. His sons are killed in the war, he loses house and land, is afflicted by poverty, stricken by plague and tempted by vice. His spiritual strength does not waver, and it is his unrelenting faith which prompts the Holy of Holies to celebrate the Germans:

HOLY OF HOLIES   German!
                 I bless you and your faith.
                 German, I celebrate you
                 For your strength [...]
                 German!
                 Your country
                 Is the fount of the world,
                 Enlivening and sustaining
                 All peoples. (p. 61)

The final moments often feature the glorification of the good German and the destruction or banishment of the personification of evil. The Evil Enemy

7 Hans Niedecken-Gebhard (left) vigorously directing one of the many speech-making scenes in Euringer's *German Passion 1933* (courtyard of Heidelberg castle, 1934).

is sent down to perdition by the Holy of Holies in Eggers's *The Play about Job, the German*; by contrast, God makes Job world regent. The Evil Spirit descends into the abyss in *German Passion 1933*, whereas the Nameless Soldier ascends to Heaven as the Good Spirit. The removal of evil and elevation of good constitute the final act of judgement, but it is a process of judgement often influenced more by individuals than by the people. True, these individuals are often given generic names, such as the Homecomer, and in the case of *The Long March* there are three leader-figures; but the principle of leadership is nevertheless triumphant. While the choruses usually do provide the final determined flourish, thereby ultimately supplying the transformational energy, they often seem to be following the lead they have been given. The heroic Germans show the way, answer the questions, and this is reflected in the tendency of the choruses to repeat the words of these individuals rather than formulate their own ideas. The *Thing* plays thus certainly did as much to encourage the Führer cult as they did to support the notion of the people as political power.

The cult of the dead

The dead of the First World War also help to bring about the national revolution in the *Thing* plays. In many ways, the plays were cults of the war dead and thus a continuation of a tradition which had begun in the Weimar Republic. From 1926, the second Sunday in March was the official Day of Mourning for the dead of the Great War, the *Volkstrauertag*.[30] Radio programmes and theatres, as well as religious services, encouraged nationwide remembrance. In 1927, some critics were already lamenting the increasingly revanchist and nationalistic tone of many of the commemorations,[31] and this tone became the hallmark of the *Thing* plays. As Euringer puts it in his ninth *Thing* play thesis: 'The *Thingplatz* is the place for a cult of the dead. The dead rise up and the spirit cries out from the stones.'[32] In *German Passion 1933*, Euringer has a dead soldier emerge Christ-like from the grave and transform the Weimar Republic. In *Dance of Death* he goes even further by having the dead soldiers emerge from their graves and literally strangle the representatives of Weimar. This direct intervention is justified by the oft-stated thesis that the dead are more alive than the living, who have been zombified by ingesting too much Weimar corruption.

Elsewhere, the role of the dead is more subtle. In Goes's *Germany Rises!*, as a vestal virgin lights a fire on stage and torches are passed round, a chorus of war dead can be heard reminding the living that they died for them:

> We demand loyalty in return for our loyalty
> No more, and yet it's a great deal,
> A very great deal! It's our reward
> And it's your task!
> We will demand honour, loyalty, duty
> Back from you. (p. 25)

In Becker's *The End of German Hardship*, the Homecomer sees in his dreams fields of crosses, on one of which he reads: 'I fell for you on the fifth of May in Flanders, only for you!' (p. 18). The Homecomer sees himself as a 'vassal' in relation to the war dead. There is the suggestion here that the 1914–18 losses have created a moral debt which must be repaid by the living in the form of a reawakening of national consciousness and a rebuilding of Germany's greatness. Another notion is that the sacrifices of the war dead are in some more mystical sense the fount from which the future must spring, an idea which can take organic form in the notion of blood fertilizing the soil. The images and structure of Eggers's *The Long March* are informed by a teleological view of history, whereby the sacrifices of 1914–18 were an important and even indispensable part of a process which resulted in the triumph of National Socialism. The soldiers died to make Hitler possible; conversely, Hitler's accession to power fulfilled their destiny (Figures 8 and 9).

The plays thus seem set on giving retrospective meaning to the war deaths. At the same time, the Third Reich is legitimized by being presented as the result of a mechanism of loss and compensation, debt and payment, an idea that is inherently capitalistic for all its metaphysical appearance. By interpreting history as something governed by rigorous moral laws, the playwrights introduced a concept of fate in the light of which the German people and the individual heroes were the instruments of a higher purpose. It is therefore legitimate to call these authors dramatic mythmakers. Euringer, in his fifth *Thing* thesis, in fact talks metaphorically of the *Thingplatz* as the 'day of myth'. In the context of this mythologizing historiography, the Weimar Republic comes across as an historical anomaly, a piece of interference, and the origins of the Third Reich are glorified, thus discouraging too close an analysis of the real causes of its emergence, namely violence, hoodwinking, and exploitation of the economic crisis.

The end of the *Thing* play movement

If the *Thingplätze* were, as Goebbels put it, 'National Socialism in stone', then the *Thing* plays themselves were National Socialism in word, movement and general ethos. The condemnation of the Weimar Republic, the celebration of the war dead, of national and heroic virtue, of morality and purity, of the people and the strong visionary leader, the cult of participation: all of this certainly reflected the political and cultural ideology of Hitler's movement. It may come as a surprise, then, that official support for the *Thing* plays should have been replaced, in 1935 and especially 1936, by a policy of repression. Indeed, the *Thing* play movement was stifled and ultimately snuffed out. The first step towards this was the order to liquidate the Play Communities responsible for organizing the *Thing* plays, an order issued by the Propaganda Ministry on 7 September 1935.[33] Following that, on 23 October 1935, the Propaganda Ministry issued an edict forbidding the use of the term *Thing* play or *Thing* in connection with the Nazi Party. The edict also stipulated that the term 'cult' should no longer be associated with National Socialism.[34] Finally, in May 1936, Goebbels went so far as to ban the use of declamatory choruses (*Sprechchöre*), which he found banal and bombastic.[35]

8 Dead soldiers emerge from their graves in Euringer's *German Passion 1933* (courtyard of Heidelberg castle, 1934).

9 The War Cripple gives his speech in Euringer's *German Passion 1933* (courtyard of Heidelberg castle, 1934).

Given that such choruses were a fundamental constitutive element of the *Thing* plays, this more or less brought an end to the genre. 'Immediately all the singing, marching, banner waving and torch-bearing ceased, and all the people's choruses were silenced', writes one post-war commentator.[36] This is perhaps an exaggeration, but not a misdirected hyperbole.

Financial and technical difficulties

One of the reasons given by Reichsbund President Franz Moraller for the dissolution of the Play Communities – the initial nail in the coffin of the *Thing* plays – was the fact that they had made huge losses.[37] Were the *Thing* plays therefore unsuccessful with audiences? This is difficult to answer. Newspaper reports from the period tend to focus on first performances only, but if these are anything to go by, the *Thing* plays attracted large numbers of people. More than 12,000 people watched Heynicke's *Road to the Reich* on the Heidelberg *Thingplatz* in July 1935.[38] On the *Thingplatz* in Halle in 1934, Euringer's *German Passion 1933* was able to attract 4000 people, while the actors and walk-on parts in the production themselves numbered an incredible 2000. These vast numbers, however, did not necessarily convert into huge sums of money. When *German Passion 1933* was first performed in the courtyard of Heidelberg castle in 1934, prices ranged from one to three Reichsmarks. No fortune was to be made on that basis. Productions of this enormous size undoubtedly cost a great deal and, given that they were often staged for only a few nights in the summer, one can well imagine that box-office receipts did not cover expenses.

The plays also posed a number of acoustic problems which were never adequately solved. Individual speakers had difficulties projecting their voices over such huge auditoria. Choruses could be enormous, so that the words were indistinct and, because these choruses were often amateur, they did not always manage to speak with the precise coordination and clarity required. Microphones were used to increase the volume, but they also distorted the sound. When employed for the premiere of Heynicke's *Road to the Reich* in Heidelberg in 1935, they carried the noise of the Torchbearer's flaming torch blowing in the wind more clearly than his voice.[39]

Summer rainstorms also created audibility problems, quite apart from soaking the audience. If newspaper critics are to be believed, however, audiences were particularly resilient. When Euringer was asked what becomes of a *Thing* play if it rains, he answered: 'Just as the masses stood [...] through storms and showers waiting for Hitler to descend from the clouds in his aeroplane when he was fighting for the hearts of his people, so the people will not give in now when it comes to strengthening the blood-bonds of the community.' Euringer went on to stress that the *Thingplatz* was no place for tender plants and complaining women, and advised them to stay away from the holy place if they could not face the 'severity of the demands'.[40]

Poor quality and questionable taste

Surely a more important reason for displeasure with the *Thing* plays was their poor quality. The Nazis had proclaimed the dawning of a new era of drama and built special theatres as a vehicle for this drama. Inevitably, official expectations were high, so that the meagre results were both a disappointment and an embarrassment. That quality was felt to be lacking is evident from newspaper reviews of productions of *Thing* plays, all of which were written before Goebbels banned the criticism of art and theatre in 1936. While the general tone of the theatre critics is positive, they often seem more satisfied with the scale of the productions and with the spectacle (marching, singing and torch-waving) than with the plays themselves. The composers of the accompanying music – such as Werner Egk in the case of Eggers's *The Play about Job, the German* and Herbert Windt in that of Euringer's *German Passion 1933* – often received more praise than the dramatists. Again and again the observation was made that the *Thing* plays written thus far were important steps in the right direction, but no more than that. Herbert Ihering, a critic who established his reputation in the Weimar Republic and whose opinion can be considered reliable, described Heynicke's *Road to the Reich* as an 'interesting attempt which future *Thing* drama will soon leave behind'. Another critic described Eggers's *The Long March* as 'little more than an admittedly noteworthy attempt'.[41]

Critics rarely outlined precisely what it was about these 'attempts' that fell short of the mark, but two principal objections can be read between the lines. First, the *Thing* plays lack dramatic action, focusing more on the static and declamatory; groups and individuals jostle uneasily on stage rather than truly interacting. Second, the plays follow the same basic plot, namely the transformation from the evils of Weimar Republicanism to the infinite light of National Socialism. The problem with this revolutionary pathos was that, while it may have been interesting in 1933, by 1934 and especially 1935, it would have become very familiar.

Those few *Thing* plays which abandoned the 1918–33 pattern in favour of a focus on the post-1933 period were even more static. They shied away from the presentation of even the most rudimentary plot, as a plot presupposes the existence of tensions and problems, phenomena which Hitler's accession had consigned to the past. Thus, instead of portraying issues, Nierentz's *Thing* plays *Work Symphony* and *Farmers' Blessing* have recourse to ecstatic celebrations of the regeneration of industrial and agricultural life in the Third Reich. Both these works are inherently undramatic and read stiffly like oratorios. What Nierentz's *Thing* plays also do is mirror in their language, syntax and sparse content the processes of the life they evoke (the functionality of industry, the working of the soil) and stress the integration of man into these processes. They thereby help to reflect and underpin aesthetically the dynamic mechanization of society which typified the Third Reich. But this did not make them any more interesting to watch.

The focus on the Weimar Republic in many of the *Thing* plays was, however, itself problematic. Writers went to great lengths to portray all the aspects of its corruption and sinfulness. Only at the end did National Socialism win out over its adversary, often in a manner that is tacked on and arbitrary. The negative appeared, therefore, to outweigh the positive. The negative, moreover, was not all that negative to start with. Nationalistic writers vented their spleen on the corruption of the Weimar Republic, yet described this corruption with an eye for detail and in images of indignation which resonate with admiration and even fetishistic fascination. 'The towns of the Reich are in the grip of a dastardly frenzy' (p. 7), proclaims the Epic Speaker in Becker's *The End of German Hardship*, while the Homecomer in the same play speaks with unconvincing distaste of the emergence of 'a generation of the night' and 'women without a hint of honour' (p. 6). This inherent ambivalence is evident above all in Euringer's *Dance of Death*, where dead soldiers dance intimately with Weimar's representatives, killing them by something akin to a necromantic sexual union, and becoming part of the general dissolution they despise. Without going so far as to claim that *Thing* plays were more of a swansong for Weimar than its judge, jury and executioner, there were elements of nostalgia in its portrayal. The Sodom and Gomorrah portrayed in the *Thing* plays are more interesting than the groups of boringly good Germans who come to demolish evil. Negative characters such as the Evil Spirit in Euringer's *German Passion 1933* or the Evil Enemy in Eggers's *The Play about Job, the German* are more impressive than their positive counterparts. The Weimar Republic did not end in 1933: it lived on in the *Thing* plays through the jazz, the dancing, the eroticism, the internationalism and the sense of 'living for today'. This was quite possibly one of the reasons why the Nazis ultimately banned the new genre from the stage.

Suspect ideological connotations: Christianity

The *Thing* plays were thus steeped in the atmosphere of the Weimar Republic, an atmosphere which was in many ways also one of doom and gloom. Parts of the plays are weighed down by the oppressiveness of poverty, unemployment and a sense of directionlessness. In the Weimar Republic there were many radio plays which dealt with the theme of unemployment and the effect of spiritual desolation which it generated. The most famous of these is possibly Hermann Kasack's *The Call* (*Der Ruf*, 1932), in which the suicidal Martin is rescued at the last moment by a communal will to work. Euringer himself also wrote a radio play with the title *The Unemployed* (*Die Arbeitslosen*, 1933).[42]

The tenor of these unemployment dramas was often pessimistic, occasionally with an unconvincingly optimistic conclusion. While *Thing* plays are not as asymmetrical, some, especially Heynicke's *Neurode*, inherited a certain bleakness from these radio plays. The implication that the Germans are the helpless playthings of a hostile fate sits uneasily with the notion of heroic assertiveness which ends the texts. It also runs contrary to the National Socialist image of the German as robust and self-confident. In a newspaper review of a production of Euringer's *German Passion 1933* in Halle, one critic wrote: 'Passion – road of suffering; that is a passive, submissive endurance. The road taken by the German people was, however, quite different. [...] Struggle was the German road, dramatic struggle, not a road of Passion.'[43]

Euringer's play admittedly heroizes helplessness by reinterpreting it as a tenacious and productive ability to withstand adversity: the Germans' infinite capacity for enduring negative influences, so Euringer implies, makes a better future possible. The same message emerges from Eggers's *The Play about Job, the German* and from Müller-Schnick's *Soldiers of the Soil*. But this praise of patient suffering and unshakeable faith represents an adoption of Christian notions of Passion and submissiveness. This is perhaps not surprising given that one of the inspirational forces behind the *Thing* movement was Wilhelm Karl Gerst, who had been active in the Catholic Bühnenvolksbund (People's Theatre League) since 1919 and took over the position of secretary under Laubinger in the Reichsbund. Gerst undoubtedly hoped to use the *Thing* movement as a vehicle for the inculcation of a Christian-Germanic nationalism. Many writers obliged by producing *Thing* plays which presented the route to the national revolution in a heady mixture of Christian symbolism and Germanic patriotism. The idea that the German people had suffered a passion between 1914 and 1933 was expressed again and again in the plays, especially in Euringer's *German Passion 1933* and Beyer's *Düsseldorf Passion* (*Düsseldorfer Passion*, 1933). Just as Christ arose from the dead, so Germany had its resurrection in 1933. The biblical Passion is the supreme example of death and rebirth, an example of unquestionable status which could be used to lend authority and validity to the tendentious interpretation of recent historical events in the plays. The Germanic people became the supreme martyr, their suffering elevated and glorified. At the same time, however, if Germany's fate was a re-enactment of the Passion, then the national revolution remained but an imitation of its biblical predecessor, a copy, not an original. This was what may have upset officialdom. Rather than being its own justification, the Nazi cause was being legitimized by following an existing pattern hallowed by Christianity.

The *Thing* plays also made frequent use of apocalyptic motifs, symbols and structures. In passages in the Old Testament Book of Daniel, and particularly throughout the New Testament Book of Revelation, the eschatological future of the world is envisaged in the following terms: an accelerating decline in the moral and spiritual condition of mankind; an intense conflict between good and evil, personified in the divine struggle with Satan in his various manifestations; the direct intervention of God in the world's affairs, bringing universal judgement and the punishment of wayward mankind; and the dawning of an age of salvation, heralded in the Book of Revelation by the second coming of Christ, in which the cosmos will be radically transformed.

This pattern of synchronic and diachronic moral dualism is also present in the *Thing* plays. There is an implicit and occasionally explicit identification of Weimar with Babylon and of the Third Reich with the Thousand-Year post-apocalyptic empire – an identification of which Nazi propaganda was itself immensely fond. Satanic figures are confronted and overcome by Christ-like figures in the *Thing* plays. It is the figure of the German in Goes's *Sacrificial Flame of Work* who triggers the protest which topples the evil Ahasuerus and sends him scuttling off to Paris. At the end of Becker's *The End of German Hardship*, the ultimate victory over Satan is anticipated, the audience being invited to imagine that the advent of Hitler is the fulfilment of a holy prophecy:

THE WOMAN   The Antichrist's head awaits the One
      Who will come on sturdy legs,
      Empowered as a servant of God [...]
      Who will dig out and extinguish the seed
      Of the devil in the name of
      The Almighty.
      And will take the skull in his hands
      And carry its face to the end of the universe. (p. 27)

The *Thing* plays also celebrate the dead in the way in which Christ's martyrs are celebrated in the Book of Revelation, where those who have died for Christ protest at the condition of the world and plead with God to take vengeance (Revelation 6.10). Later, they rise from the dead and rule together with Christ over the thousand-year empire. This sharing of power is presented in the Bible very much as a reward for and vindication of all the sufferings they have undergone. In the *Thing* plays, dead war soldiers also rise from the dead and help to shape the new order as a reward for their sufferings.

The appropriation of apocalyptic thinking lent credence to the conservative view of recent German history, while at the same time suggesting that Hitler's revolution was prefigured by – and thus secondary to – the Second Coming. The banning of the term *Thing* on 23 October 1935 and the explicit wish of the Party to dissociate its organizations from the use of the word 'cult' or 'cultic' was in part, according to the edict, a response to complaints from the Church.[44] One can well imagine that the Church would have viewed the appropriation of Christian symbolism and allegory in the *Thing* plays with suspicion.[45] It certainly seems as if a Christian form is being filled with new content and thus estranged from the message it was designed to transport. Christian symbols, moreover, alternate quite freely with elements of nature worship. The lighting of fires to help stimulate renewal at the end of Eggers's *The Long March* and Goes's *Sacrificial Flame of Work* is a practice which derives from pagan nature mysticism:

THE YOUNG WORKER Pile up wood,
So that there's a fire all over Germany,
A fire of awakening.
THE OLDER MAN   A fire of confession!
A WOMAN   A fire of community!
THE PEOPLE   A fire of freedom!

(Eggers, *The Long March*, p. 68)

The associated notions of awakening in *Thing* plays also evoke Germanic myths such as that of the sleeping Barbarossa, a former German emperor who, according to legend, will wake up in Germany's hour of need to lead the country to glory.

On the other hand, it is doubtful that the edict was really issued in deference to the clergy's objections to this sort of profane combination of superstition and Christian ideas. Hitler had signed a concordat with the Vatican on 20 July 1933 which guaranteed Catholics certain rights, and the Third Reich supported the 'German Christians' within the Protestant Church. But this did not stop discrimination against Christians, and it certainly did not provide a basis for allowing the Church to determine Nazi cultural policy. A likelier explanation is that the Nazi Propaganda Ministry objected to the imposition of Christian mythological patterns and motifs upon recent events. Whether intended or not, there is the implication in the plays that these patterns are historical determinants shaping secular history, a view which makes of the Nazi movement an instrument rather than showing it to be *sui generis*, the product of its own inherent dynamism. Moreover, the obsession with the apocalyptic past and the process of martyrdom implies that the Nazi movement was the means to an end (liberation and compensation) rather than the end itself, an idea which cannot have been welcome in the Propaganda Ministry.

Suspect aesthetic associations: workers' drama and Expressionism

While the *Thing* plays owed much to the dramatic traditions of Catholic theatre, such as the Oberammergau Passion plays, their apocalyptic elements were also a feature of workers' theatre, which had been a strong theatrical presence in the Weimar Republic. Against the background of the dashed hopes of revolution in the immediate post-war years, inflation, rationalization and unemployment led to a desperate longing for another, successful revolution in Socialist and even Social Democratic circles.

A comparison of some twenty of these workers' plays with the official *Thing* plays reveals close thematic, conceptual, structural and linguistic similarities.[46] Both sets of plays are filled with a sense of despair at economic hardship, and both agree that materialism, capitalism, selfishness and moral decay are among Weimar's problems. Both forms of drama lament the broken relationship with nature as a result of industrialization. Both call for unity in the face of these problems, for self-determination and brotherhood. Both portray a dualistic struggle and the gradual transition from slavery to liberation, from darkness to light. In both sets of plays doubters and the indifferent are won over. In both, the revolutionary group dynamic is frequently a response to an individual spirit of enterprise. In both, the dead of various wars or revolutions give their blood so that others can live, and there is a cult of these dead martyrs. Both sets of plays end with the dream of change either being fulfilled, ecstatically anticipated or indignantly called for; choruses march across the stage and there is much singing and flag-waving.

Of course there are differences. In the *Thing* plays, the emphasis is on the Germans, the German workers or all the Germans, whereas the left-wing workers' theatre focuses on the proletariat. There is a different historiography and teleology at work in the two types of drama. The left-wing plays look back to the tradition of the French, Russian and sporadic post-First World War German revolutions. These are interpreted as milestones on the road to a world-wide emancipation of the proletariat. Obstacles along this road are nationalism, war and militarism, which are interpreted as the extreme expression of unfettered capitalism. The *Thing* plays look back to the tradition of the Thirty Years War, Prussian greatness, Bismarck and the Kaiser. These are viewed as stages in the progression towards Germany's national emancipation. Obstacles to this progression are defeat in the First World War and subsequent oppression by the Allies in the form of the Versailles Treaty, Ruhr

occupation and war reparations. While the workers' plays naturally see
National Socialists as the principal enemy, the *Thing* plays see the Socialists
as the main threat. At the end of the workers' plays, choruses sing the
Communist Internationale, or the Ode to Joy from Beethoven's Ninth Symphony, and wave red flags; in the *Thing* plays, the German national anthem
and Horst Wessel Song are sung, and swastikas are unfurled.[47]

Despite these differences of internationalism and nationalism, it is the
impression of similarity which predominates.[48] Both the *Thing* plays and the
workers' drama express the same longing for transcendence, for a people's (or
peoples') revolution and a new empire as the means of redemption. The shift
in favour of nationalism which constitutes the main distinguishing feature of
the *Thing* plays was a step which Max Barthel, one of the leading writers
of workers' drama in the Weimar Republic, clearly did not find too hard to
take. After 1933 he wrote Nazi drama and one of his plays was on the 1934
official list of *Thing* plays: *A Play about the German Working Man*. In the
Thing play *The Long March* by Eggers, moreover, the Young Worker who
leads the combined might of workers, farmers and soldiers into the future is
a former Communist turned nationalist. The play has a didactic aspect, but
the implication is that such a conversion is possible because the worlds of
Socialism and nationalism are not far apart.

It has already been pointed out that several of the *Thing* plays were written
before 1933. This serves to confirm that the origins of the *Thing* plays are
not in post-1933 Nazi cultural policy, but part of the very longing for
transcendence that was a hallmark of Weimar culture. They are also rooted
in the ideological landscape of Weimar, where Nazism (National Socialism)
evolved as an alternative to Socialism, as a combination of ethnicity with
collectivity. This original brand of National Socialism left its stamp on all the
Thing plays. Even those which were written after Hitler's accession reiterate
the idea. Thus while the *Thing* plays are undoubtedly nationalistic and
conservative in their orientation, there is nevertheless a certain Socialist
resonance in their ecstatic flexing of mass muscle. This may have been
acceptable in 1933, but it was not acceptable in 1935, by which time the
Socialist element in National Socialism was unwelcome: Hitler was in control,
not the people. There was a danger that the glorification of the national
revolution in the *Thing* plays might have had a different effect in 1935 or 1934
to the effect it had in 1933.

As the date of Hitler's accession receded in time, portrayals of revolution
would have taken on a prospective and prescriptive dimension, for all their
retrospective pathos. It might have seemed as if they were calling for a second
revolution in which the people played more of a role than Hitler was willing
to assign to them – a call also associated with Ernst Röhm, who, along with

many of his supporters, was liquidated by Hitler in the summer of 1934 in the Night of the Long Knives. The *Thing* plays thus came to acquire a certain subversiveness for all their national tub-thumping, and this is probably one of the unstated reasons why they were banned. That the Propaganda Ministry objected to the choruses is a clear indication that it was aware of Socialist elements in the plays. In a 1936 article, the second Reichsbund president Franz Moraller explicitly criticized the fact that the origins of the *Sprechchor* were Marxist, not National Socialist.[49]

Besides the visionary zeal of the biblical apocalypse, the conflation of Catholicism, transcendentalism and revolutionary bravura, there was another element which united the new Nazi dramatic genre with Weimar workers' theatre: the spirit of Expressionism. The poet Gottfried Benn, who later threw in his lot with the Nazis, summed up the essence of Expressionism as 'vision–protest–transformation',[50] a characterization which also fits the *Thing* plays. Expressionism is thought of as a cry of the spirit (*Geist*) against the dehumanizing influence of bourgeois materialism, industrialization and technology. The language of Expressionism is ecstatic, but vague, and the abstract character of the poetry and prose is matched by ambiguity in matters political. Some scions of Expressionism welcomed the First World War as a chance for renewal, but others condemned its violence. In the course of 1918 and subsequently, Expressionism became increasingly pragmatic and political in orientation, and its representatives tended to drift either to the right or to the left.

Several of the most significant writers of *Thing* plays, such as Euringer, Heynicke and Becker, were former Expressionists. Heynicke, for instance, had contributed to Herwarth Walden's quintessentially Expressionist magazine *Der Sturm* ('The Storm'). The case of Heynicke is particularly illuminating because his 1935 *Road to the Reich* was preceded in 1922 by a volume of ecstatic essays entitled *Road to the Self* (*Der Weg zum Ich*). The latter stresses self-realization, but also the values of love and brotherhood: 'Love is the law of all laws', Heynicke writes. By 1933, Heynicke had clearly rejected inwardness, love, and what he called in *Road to the Self* the 'higher cosmic vision' in favour of outwardness, aggression and nationalism. Nevertheless, the seeds of this development are visible already in *Road to the Self*, which is not free of Nietzschean elitism or contempt for contemporary culture.[51]

The fact that many Expressionists with left-wing sympathies, such as Heynicke and Hanns Johst, drifted to the right does make one wonder to what extent Expressionist revolutionary pathos was from the beginning shot through with elements which made such a drift possible. To talk of a 'split' in the Expressionist ethos is to deny its inherent predisposition for proto-fascist thinking: the anti-bourgeois feeling, the often destructive-sounding zest for renewal and artistic elitism, were there in Expressionism from the very beginning. In the case of some writers, these elements never triumphed over an essentially humanist message, over the vision of an ultimately liberated and united humankind. But in the case of others, the chauvinistic elements won the day. Even those left-wing writers whose political credentials are not in doubt, such as Ernst Toller and Bruno Schönlank, never quite freed themselves from the tainted origins of Expressionism. Indeed, blood-and-soil mysticism – usually thought of as typically Nazi – is evident in Toller and Schönlank, as is an aggressive distaste for the moral depravity of the Weimar Republic.[52]

Nevertheless, Expressionism was regarded with suspicion by the National Socialists because of its links with the political left. The element of visionary protest in, as well as the anti-materialist thrust of, Expressionism were unwelcome once the Nazis had succeeded in establishing themselves: a drama of consolidation and confirmation was required instead. Elements of such anti-materialism survived in Euringer's *German Passion 1933* and Heynicke's *Neurode*, where the spirit triumphs over money, the hero Radke professing the hope that 'the common purpose will conquer the rigidity of figures' (p. 52). In the Expressionist tradition, the *Thing* plays by Euringer, Eggers's *The Long March* and Heynicke's *Road to the Reich* feature types rather than individuals. While this was quite consistent with the Nazi idea of *völkisch* representativeness, the typology sometimes degenerated into caricatured depiction, reminiscent of the worst Expressionist social criticism, or resulted in what were felt to be abstractions rather than real flesh-and-blood figures. Critics also objected to a certain 'theatricality' in the *Thing* plays which was seen as inappropriate to their cultic purpose.[53] The *Thing* plays are characterized by much of the ecstatic assertiveness of Expressionist language, and by many acoustic and visual effects. These were complemented by Expressionist styles of production, as in the case of Euringer's *German Passion 1933* in Heidelberg (1934), where extreme gestures were used, as well as symbolic colours: green for the barbed wire, red for the diabolic Evil Spirit, grey for the dead soldiers and gold for the Regiments of Young Germany.[54] There was a danger this symbolic style would create distance, encouraging critical reflection in the audience rather than emotional identification. The Nazi clamp-down on Expressionism in 1935 and 1936 may therefore also have been aimed at the *Thing* plays.

Thing plays and *Thing* theatres after the ban: The Frankenburg Dice-Game

On 2 August 1936, Eberhard Wolfgang Möller's play *The Frankenburg Dice-Game* was premiered on the newly built Dietrich-Eckart-Bühne in Berlin as part of the accompanying programme to the Olympic Games (Figures 10 and 11).[55] Plans for building this stage had existed as early as 1933, in response to Hitler's personal request for a big open-air theatre.[56] But the Dietrich-Eckart-Bühne was never referred to in official documentation as a *Thingplatz*, presumably because Laubinger did not want to irritate the Olympic Committee

10   Scene from Möller's *The Frankenburg Dice-Game* (Dietrich-Eckart-Bühne, Berlin, 1936).

11   Dietrich-Eckart-Bühne in Berlin, completed in 1936.

(who were also involved in the organization of the Games) by using nationalistic terminology. The Dietrich-Eckart-Bühne had 20,450 seats. It therefore had more seating space than any other open-air theatre constructed by the Nazis. Moreover, the first performance of Möller's play in front of 20,000 people, many of whom were foreigners, was quite possibly the most spectacular theatrical event involving Nazi drama in the history of the Third Reich.[57] It was designed as a piece of propaganda. According to Stommer, Goebbels intended, as early as 1933, to make the Olympic Games not just a sporting but also a cultural competition.[58] The stage and the play were designed to demonstrate Germany's cultural superiority.

Möller was one of the founding fathers of the *Thing* play idea, and *The Frankenburg Dice-Game* is in many ways an archetypical *Thing* play. The audience witnesses a recreation of an historical incident from 1625, when Protestant farmers were persecuted and killed during the Counter-Reformation. They were made to play dice against one another to decide who would survive and who would be executed. This recreation is embedded by Möller within the framework of a trial: von Herbersdorf, the Emperor Ferdinand, Maximilian of Bavaria, Lamormaini and Caraffa are charged with acts of inhumanity, and as no one seems prepared to accept responsibility, history is repeated so that a clearer picture can be gained. But history is repeated with a twist at the end. When von Herbersdorf calls for the executioner to dispose of the farmers who threw the lowest numbers, a figure in black armour appears and makes von Herbersdorf, Ferdinand, Maximilian, Lamormaini and Caraffa throw dice against him. He throws infinity, and the five are condemned and cursed.

On one level the play is about a retroactive application of justice exercised by a later era, of which the seven judges who appear at the beginning to open the trial are the representatives.[59] The play is preceded by a foreword in which the fact is stressed that the judges are but representatives of the audience, 'Your will is here the judge' (p. 339), suggesting in true *Thing* play fashion that the judgement dispensed here is a collective enterprise. On another level, however, the play is like a Day of Judgement, as it is ultimately the god-like Figure in Black, a veritable *deus ex machina*, who dispenses justice.

The play represents a radicalization of the *Thing* play, because it is an explicit trial of history rather than an implicit one. It is also a radicalization of another kind. In the *Thing* plays of Euringer and Eggers the injustices of history are compensated for by the act of national regeneration in 1933. In Möller's play, history is rewritten by the intervention of the Figure in Black. The course of history is reversed in the name of a higher justice. Thus Möller's play might be seen as the apogee of the *Thing* play movement, even though it was performed after the banning of the term *Thing* and rarely referred to as a *Thing* play by the Nazis themselves, any more than the Dietrich-Eckart-

Bühne was referred to as a *Thingplatz*.[60] This seems an appropriate irony. The very first *Thing* plays, such as Euringer's *German Passion 1933*, were written before the term existed; and the last was written after its banning (Möller did not write his play until January 1936). In the case of the early plays to which the label *Thing* play was later affixed, the terminological designation serves as a linguistic marker of appropriation. Euringer's *German Passion 1933* is passionate, and passionately nationalist. But only the tag 'Thing Play' *explicitly* identifies it as Nazi property. Conversely, if Möller wrote what is in essence a *Thing* play after the term and the whole notion had fallen out of official favour, this is also an act of appropriation, a defiant attempt to retain a spurned invention. There may even be critical elements in Möller's drama. While the Figure in Black may be Hitler, he might equally well be interpreted, in the words of one recent critic, as a 'reminder that we will all some day be judged for our actions' and therefore as a warning against overstepping limits.[61] The intervention of the Figure in Black in the name of the right of the farmers to practise their religion might be seen as Möller's breaking a lance for tolerance of difference: certainly a critical message in the Third Reich.

In certain ways, however, Möller's play is different from the *Thing* plays. There is no revolutionary dynamic in *The Frankenburg Dice-Game*. On the contrary, the idea seems to be that the Figure in Black, as well as the secular judges, represent a higher established order which must be protected against transgression. This has a conservative political impetus. While the recognized *Thing* plays did stress the importance of a strong leader-figure, Möller attributes *total* powers to the strong individual, who is not so much a guide to better times as a god-like redeemer and executor of divine judgement. The people are not inspired by the Figure in Black; they are utterly dependent upon him for their salvation. There are choruses, but by and large, perhaps as a result of the forbidding of the *Sprechchor*, they tend to comment on the action rather than participate in it and are more like choruses in classical Greek drama. Möller's play could be read as a plea for absolutism. The *Thing* plays, on the other hand, celebrated collective control under strong guidance, not the dictatorial principle. Moreover, *The Frankenburg Dice-Game* is written largely in the style of a nineteenth-century historical drama, has a reasonably detailed plot, and turns back to the Germanic past for its inspiration rather than to the turmoils of the Weimar Republic. It therefore follows the line prescribed by Nazi ideologue Alfred Rosenberg.

In contradistinction to the *Thing* play, which was supported by Goebbels, Rosenberg had called for a return in drama to central and symbolic episodes in national history, to a portrayal of the struggle between Germanic and Catholic, for instance, as in Möller's play. Rosenberg, as the head of the

Nationalsozialistische Kulturgemeinde (National Socialist Cultural Community), had encouraged the building of the Stedingsehre stage, which was conceived as an alternative to the Heidelberg *Thingplatz*.[62] By 1937, the site accommodated audiences of up to 15,000 for the performance of August Hinrichs's play *The Stedingers* (*Die Stedinger*), about the slaughter of Stedinger peasants by an army of crusaders.[63] Möller's drama has as much in common with this style of drama as it does with the *Thing* plays.

Thing play authors and *Thingplätze* after 1936

In a sense, Möller's play represents the victory of the historical drama or historical *Volksstück* (people's play) over the more allegorical *Thing* play, and in fact other authors of *Thing* plays started to turn their hand to historical drama. A case in point is Eggers. In 1941 his play *The Just One* (*Der Gerechte*) was premiered in Magdeburg. It depicts the period after the battle of Fehrbellin. Here, Corporal Görg Binder, unhappy with life in Germany after the battle, forms his own little mercenary army. His spirit is pure, but he takes too much authority into his own hands, and at the end of the play is executed. The Elector treats him nobly by having him shot rather than hanged, but ultimately Eggers comes down in favour of established authority, in contrast to the revolutionary elements of his *Thing* plays.[64] Euringer turned his hand to writing novels after 1936, Heynicke to writing comedies such as *Woman in the House* (*Frau im Haus*), which was first performed in Berlin in 1936 with Gustaf Gründgens in the cast, under the direction of Wolfgang Liebeneiner.

Euringer's career after 1945 was chequered. He was interned at the end of the war and was forbidden from writing in 1946. But this ban was lifted in 1948, by which time Euringer was considered adequately denazified. Euringer spent the last years of his life producing reworkings (of, for example, Calderón's dramas), but in 1952 he also published diary entries in which he tried to present himself as a victim of maltreatment in Allied internment camps. This was a characteristic reaction of many former Nazis, who were only too keen to deflect attention by pointing the finger at others.[65]

Heynicke's career continued successfully after 1945. His seventieth birthday was celebrated in West German newspapers, which in their laudations conveniently excised the part of his biography which had to do with *Neurode* and *Road to the Reich*. (Not a single copy of the latter play seems to have survived in German libraries.) Hanns Elster, in a 1957 article on Heynicke, even goes so far as to claim that the Nazis neglected Heynicke's plays – an extraordinary assertion. The same critic also talks of Heynicke's deep religiosity and warm humanity, a somewhat one-sided image to say the least.[66]

The *Thingplätze* did not lie empty after the banning of the *Thing* plays.

They were used instead for operas, oratorios, Nazi celebrations and plays considered more suitable for public consumption than the *Thing* plays. Schiller's *Bride of Messina* (*Die Braut von Messina*) was performed on the *Thingplatz* in Heidelberg in 1939. Between 1937 and 1939, the Braunschweig *Thingplatz* was used for performances of *Alceste* by Gluck, Hebbel's *Die Nibelungen* and Beethoven's Ninth Symphony.

There was continued use of several *Thingplätze* even after 1945, and some are still active today. The Bad Segeberg *Thingplatz*, opened in October 1937, is the home of the now famous Karl May Festival Plays.[67] (Karl May was a German writer of Westerns and one of Hitler's favourite authors.) The Loreley *Thingplatz* (near St Goarhausen) is known for its rock concerts. Most interesting is the case of the Heidelberg *Thingplatz*. In 1945 the American occupying forces used it for basketball matches (the Harlem Globe Trotters played there), the performance of musicals and exercising of troops. After some years of subsequent neglect it was, as of the early 1970s, used for everything from pop festivals and a hunting-horn concert to religious services. In May and June 1977, the stage having become damaged, forty English pioneers of the 73rd Independent Field Squadron set about repairing it. However, the damage continued (due not just to wind, weather and age, but also to vandalism, camp-fires and wild parties) and the auditorium and stage had to be extensively repaired. The local authorities spent 150,000 marks in 1985 on the *Thingplatz*, and another 433,000 marks in 1987. The refurbished *Thingplatz* subsequently took on a new lease of life. Beethoven's Ninth Symphony was performed there on 13 June 1987, and in the same year Plácido Domingo and Josefina Arregui sang there to an audience of 8000 people. Park-and-ride systems, roofing and 90,000-watt loudspeakers made these concerts more amenable than *Thing* play performances could ever have been. On 5 July 1991, Konstantin Wecker and Wolfgang Dauner sang to an audience of 3000, and two days later 8000 visitors attended a monumental performance of Carl Orff's *Carmina Burana*, which was sung by nine choirs (400–500 singers) and played by seventy musicians, not to mention the nine dancers. In the summer of 1996, Montserrat Caballé sang on the *Thingplatz*.

The Mannheim concert organizer Matthias Hoffmann once called the Heidelberg *Thingplatz* 'the finest concert venue in West Germany'.[68] Although the local authorities in Heidelberg did have long discussions in the 1980s as to whether the *Thingplatz* should be used, given its 'brown' Nazi past, it was simply too good a venue not to be exploited. As with the German motorways and the House of Art in Munich, the *Thingplätze*, whatever the stigma of their origins, have proven to be of practical value for later generations. Performances on *Thingplätze* could be seen as a retroactive legitimation of the cultural activities of the Third Reich, or as somehow compromised by the tainted history of these stages. A contrasting point of view is that concerts by such celebrated stars as Plácido Domingo and Konstantin Wecker on the Heidelberg *Thingplatz* can only serve to liberate the venue from its original associations. The performance of Carl Orff's *Carmina Burana*, however, given that it was premiered in the Third Reich and is arguably coloured by elements of National Socialist ideology, seems unlikely to create fresher, more democratic associations.

Conclusion

Not much by way of even acceptable drama resulted from the amount of time and organizational zest invested in the creation of *Thing* drama. The failure to produce successful plays must largely be put down to the fact that the works seen as a suitable starting point, such as Euringer's *German Passion 1933* or Eggers's *The Play about Job, the German*, were products of the Weimar Republic and the desire for renewal. They were spontaneous utterances which could not be channelled without incurring the danger of banal, even insincere, and ultimately subversive repetition.

In a sense, the plays also became superfluous, since many of their constituent elements were also elements of Nazi propaganda exercises such as the Nuremberg Rallies. Here too there was marching, torch-bearing and flag-waving, here too ecstatic self-celebration. The celebration of the dead in the *Thing* plays was mirrored by the Heldengedenktag (Heroes' Commemoration Day) – the Nazi version of the Day of Mourning – on 16 March. And the celebration of the return to the soil was catered for by the Summer and Winter Solstice and Harvest Festivals regularly staged by the Nazis. 'Staged' is the right word. These ritualistic days of celebration were a piece of theatre, aesthetically draped propaganda, designed to produce a comprehensive inculcation of Nazi values. Given such a state-driven programme, there was ultimately little need for the *Thing* plays. They had outstayed their welcome.

Notes

1   Wolfgang Kloss, 'Die nationalsozialistischen Thingspiele: die Massenbasis des Faschismus 1933–1935 in seinem trivialen Theater: eine parataktische Darstellung' (unpublished doctoral thesis, University of Vienna, 1981), p. 90.
2   Rainer Stommer, *Die inszenierte Volksgemeinschaft: die 'Thingbewegung' im Dritten Reich* (Marburg: Jonas, 1985), p. 34.
3   Stommer, p. 83.
4   Richard Euringer, *Deutsche Passion 1933: Hörwerk in sechs Sätzen* (Oldenburg/ Berlin: Gerhard Stalling, 1933).
5   A detailed account of the building of the Heidelberg *Thingplatz* and the accompanying problems is provided by Meinhold Lurz, *Die Heidelberger Thingstätte:*

die Thingbewegung im Dritten Reich: Kunst als Mittel politischer Propaganda (Heidelberg: Schutzgemeinschaft Heiligenberg, 1975).

6 The source for this inaugural speech by Goebbels is 'Weihe der Heidelberger Thingstätte', *Heidelberger Neueste Nachrichten*, 24 June 1935 (quoted in Stommer, p. 111).

7 Rainer Schlösser, *Das Volk und seine Bühne: Bemerkungen zum Aufbau des deutschen Theaters* (Berlin: Albert Langen, 1935), pp. 42, 57.

8 Wilhelm von Schramm, *Neubau des deutschen Theaters: Ergebnisse und Forderungen* (Berlin: Schlieffen, 1934), p. 39.

9 Schlösser, p. 55.

10 Schramm, p. 42.

11 However, according to one commentator, Johannes Reichl, Brecht was not just a proponent of the alienation effect. Reichl argues that Brecht's *Lehrstücktheorie* (theory of didactic drama) advocates the emotional engagement of the audience in the action, and that the Nazi dramatist Eberhard Wolfgang Möller's dramatic concept represents a 'modified fascist reception' of this Brechtian theory. (Möller had discussed ideas of didactic drama with Brecht.) See Johannes Reichl, *Das Thingspiel: über den Versuch eines nationalsozialistischen Lehrstück-Theaters* (Frankfurt am Main: Mißlbeck, 1988), p. 110; also, the introduction to the present volume, pp. 45–6, n. 50.

12 Richard Euringer, 'Thingspiel-Thesen I', *Der Führer*, no. 182 (5 July 1934).

13 Schramm, p. 48.

14 See Kloss, p. 90; *Germania*, especially Chapters/Sections 11–12, 24, 31, 39. For further details on the distorted reception of *Germania* in the Third Reich, see Allan A. Lund, *Germanenideologie im Nationalsozialismus: zur Rezeption der 'Germania' des Tacitus im 'Dritten Reich'* (Heidelberg: Universitätsverlag C. Winter, 1995).

15 Carl Niessen, 'Thingplätze und ihre Aufgaben', radio manuscript of a lecture broadcast on 18 October 1934, Theaterinstitut, University of Cologne, 7c/500 (quoted in Kloss, p. 91).

16 Wolf Braumüller, 'Die Landschaftsbühne: Wesen und Wege einer neuen Theaterreform', *Bausteine zum deutschen Nationaltheater*, 2 (1934), 205–13.

17 Euringer, 'Thingspiel-Thesen'.

18 Schlösser, pp. 59, 58.

19 Schramm, p. 25.

20 'Rede des Reichspropagandaministers Dr Goebbels vor den deutschen Theaterleitern im Hotel "Kaiserhof" zu Berlin über "Die Aufgaben des deutschen Theaters" vom 8. Mai 1933', in *Die Nationalsozialistische Revolution 1933*, ed. by Axel Friedrichs, Dokumente der deutschen Politik, 1, 3rd edn (Berlin: Junker und Dünnhaupt, 1938), pp. 286–300 (p. 296).

21 Schlösser, p. 59.

22 Schlösser, pp. 53–4.

23 Kurt Heynicke, *Neurode* and *Der Weg ins Reich* (Berlin: Volkschaft-Verlag, 1935); Richard Euringer, *Totentanz: ein Tanz der lebendig Toten und der erweckten Muskoten* (Hamburg: Hanseatische Verlagsanstalt, 1935).

24 Kurt Heynicke, *Neurode: ein Spiel von deutscher Arbeit* (Berlin: Volkschaft-Verlag, 1934).

25 Gustav Goes, *Aufbricht Deutschland: ein Stadionspiel der nationalen Revolution* (Berlin: Traditions-Verlag Kolk, 1933).

26 Hans Jürgen Nierentz, *Symphonie der Arbeit: ein chorisches Erntespiel* (Berlin: Langen/Müller, 1933).

27 According to Kloss (p. 196, n. 7), the original 1934 list consisted of the following plays: Barthel's *A Play about the German Working Man* (*Spiel vom deutschen Arbeitsmann*) (Berlin: Volkschaft-Verlag, 1934), Julius Maria Becker's *The End of German Hardship* (*Deutsche Notwende*) (Munich: Val. Höfling-Verlag, 1933), Eggers's *The Long March* (*Das Große Wandern*) (Berlin: Volkschaft-Verlag, 1934), Euringer's *German Passion 1933*, Heynicke's *Neurode*, Nierentz's *Farmers' Blessing* (*Segen der Bauernschaft*) (Berlin: Langen/Müller, 1933) and *Work Symphony*, and Roßkopf's *The Festival by the Sea* (*Das Fest am Meer*, 1934). In 1935 the following were added: Richard Euringer's *Dance of Death*, Kurt Heynicke's *Road to the Reich*, and Heinrich Zerkaulen's *In Honour of Work* (*Der Arbeit die Ehr'*) (Berlin: Volkschaft-Verlag, 1935). According to Stommer (p. 286, n. 127), Müller-Schnick's *Soldiers of the Soil* (*Soldaten der Scholle*) (Berlin: Langen/ Müller, 1935) as well as Johannes G. Schlosser's *Call to the People* (*Ich rief das Volk*) (Berlin: Langen/Müller, 1934/35 [*sic*]) and *German Celebration* (*Deutsche Feier*) (Berlin: Langen/Müller, 1935) were also added, but this is not confirmed by Kloss. I should like to thank Hans Koch for providing me with many of the above plays. I have included a list of all the traceable published *Thing* plays, together with selected theory on the genre, in the bibliography of the present volume (pp. 296–7).

28 Stommer's presentation of the two lists implies that the 1935 version contained additions, but no deletions; Kloss, however, who quotes his source, makes it clear that there were four deletions: Roßkopf's *The Festival by the Sea*, Nierentz's *Farmers' Blessing* and *Work Symphony*, and Barthel's *A Play about the German Working Man*.

29 Gustav Goes, *Opferflamme der Arbeit: ein Freilichtspiel* (Berlin: Traditions-Verlag Kolk, 1934). According to legend, a Jew named Ahasuerus insulted Jesus on his way to the cross by refusing to let him rest a while by his house; for this he was condemned to wander forever without rest or death. The name is probably more reminiscent of this legend than of the Ahasuerus of the Book of Esther.

30 For more on the *Volkstrauertag* and other days of national celebration cultivated by the Nazis, see Klaus Vondung, *Magie und Manipulation: ideologischer Kult und politische Religion des Nationalsozialismus* (Göttingen: Vandenhoeck & Ruprecht, 1971), pp. 74–87.

31 See for instance M. F. M., 'Volkstrauertag im Rundfunk', *Der Neue Rundfunk*, 12 (20 March 1927), 313–14.

32 Euringer, 'Thingspiel-Thesen'.

33 Stommer, p. 121.

34 This edict is contained in the Bundesarchiv, Koblenz, ZSg 101/6 (quoted in Kloss, p. 75).

35 Dr Goebbels, 'Bekanntmachung der Reichspropagandaleitung', printed under the heading 'Stimmen zum Sprechchorverbot', *Das Deutsche Volksspiel*, no. 3 (1935–36), 220–1.

36 Bruce Harold Zortman, 'The Theater of Ideology in Nazi Germany' (unpublished doctoral thesis, University of California, Los Angeles, 1969; Uni. Microfilms, Ann Arbor, MI), p. 206.

37 Stommer, p. 121.

38 Erik Krünes, 'Thingspiel auf dem Heiligen Berg', *Der Montag*, 22 July 1935.

39 Herbert Ihering, '*Der Weg ins Reich*: Kurt Heynicke's Aufbau-Spiel vor Zehntausend', *Berliner Tageblatt*, 22 July 1935.

40 Richard Euringer, 'Zur heutigen Uraufführung der *Deutschen Passion 1933*', *Volksgemeinschaft*, 28 July 1934.

41 Ihering, '*Der Weg ins Reich*'; G. He., 'Zwei Thingspiele uraufgeführt', *FAZ (R)*, 21 September 1934.

42 For these two plays, see Hans-Jürgen Krug, *Arbeitslosenhörspiele 1930–1933* (Frankfurt am Main: Lang, 1992), pp. 26, 396–417.

43 Dr Ramlow, 'Passion im Thing', *Der Deutsche*, no. 185 (11 August 1934).

44 See Kloss, p. 75.

45 The *Thing* plays never caught on in Catholic southern Germany, the *Thingplatz* in Heidelberg being the only site of significance. For more on Catholic objections, see Zortman, pp. 213–14.

46 The workers' dramas used as a basis for comparison are: Max Barthel, *Parade* (*Aufmarsch*) (Berlin: Deutscher Arbeiter-Sängerbund, 1930); Hendrik de Man, *Us!* (*Wir!*) (Berlin: Arbeiterjugend-Verlag, 1932); Hermann Dombrowski, *Ours is the Deed* (*Unser die Tat*) (Leipzig: Arbeiter-Theaterverlag Alfred Jahn, 1929); Erich Grisar, *The Gate* (*Das Tor*) (Waldenburg-Altwasser in Schlesien: Altenberger, 1929); Berta Lask, *Consecration of Youth* (*Weihe der Jugend*) (Berlin: Kommune Ernst Friedrich, 1927); Felix Renker, *On the Spinning-Wheel of Time* (*Am Webstuhl der Zeit*) (Leipzig: Arbeiter-Theaterverlag Alfred Jahn, 1931); Martin Roolf, *The Nameless Proletarian* (*Der namenlose Proletarier*) (Leipzig: Arbeiter-Theaterverlag Alfred Jahn, 1929); Fritz Rosenfeld, *The Dead Accuse!* (*Die Toten klagen an!*) (Leipzig: Arbeiter-Theaterverlag Alfred Jahn, 1931); Hans aus Sachsen, *Man and Machine* (*Mensch und Maschine*) (Leipzig: Arbeiter-Theaterverlag Alfred Jahn, 1927); Hans aus Sachsen, *The Liberated Heart* (*Das befreite Herz*) (Leipzig: Arbeiter-Theaterverlag Alfred Jahn, 1927); Bruno Schönlank, *Redemption* (*Erlösung*) (Berlin: A. Seehof, 1924); Bruno Schönlank, *Day of Youth!* (*Jugendtag!*) (Berlin: Arbeiterjugend-Verlag, 1925); Walter Troppenz, *The Revolution* (*Die Revolution*) (Leipzig: Arbeiter-Theaterverlag Alfred Jahn, 1925); Walter Troppenz, *The Rough Road to the Stars* (*Über rauhen Weg zu den Sternen*) (Leipzig: Arbeiter- Theaterverlag Alfred Jahn, 1925); Friedrich Wendel, *The March of the Red Flags* (*Der Marsch der roten Fahnen*) (Berlin: Reichsausschuß für sozialistische Bildungsarbeit, 1927); Paul Wille, *The Victor* (*Der Sieger*) (Leipzig: Arbeiter-Theaterverlag Alfred Jahn, 1925); Karl Ziak, *A Poem of Youth* (*Ein Gedicht der Jugend*) (Berlin: Arbeiterjugend-Verlag, 1927).

47 Horst Wessel (1907–30) was a young Berlin SA leader who became a venerated martyr of the National Socialist movement. He composed the simple marching song known as the Horst Wessel Song, which was elevated to the level of a national anthem by the Nazis.

48 For more information on links with left-wing drama, see Henning Eichberg, 'Das nationalsozialistische Thingspiel: Massentheater im Faschismus und Arbeiterkultur', *Ästhetik und Kommunikation*, no. 26 (July 1976), 60–9.

49 Franz Moraller, 'Der Sprechchor in der nationalsozialistischen Feiergestaltung', *Unser Wille und Weg*, 6 (1936), 118–21 (p. 119). Stommer also believes the Socialist elements to have been the reason for the ban: 'The ban of the *Sprechchor* must be seen within the context of the removal of all traces of Socialist thought, which

had long survived – and continued to do so – particularly [...] within the Hitler Youth and SA' (Stommer, p. 133).

50 Quoted in Otto F. Best, 'Einleitung', in *Expressionismus und Dadaismus*, ed. by Otto Best (Stuttgart: Reclam, 1974), pp. 11–21 (p. 18).

51 For the quoted extracts see Kurt Heynicke, *Der Weg zum Ich: die Eroberung der inneren Welt* (Prien [Upper Bavaria]: Anthropos, 1922), pp. 10, 106.

52 For more information on the questionable elements in Toller and Schönlank, see my article, 'Apocalyptic Elements in National Socialist *Thingspiele* and in Drama of the Weimar Republic', *German Life and Letters*, 48 (1995), 170–83.

53 One critic wrote of the Heidelberg 1935 production of Heynicke's *Road to the Reich*: 'Heynicke's play is afflicted by the problem that it is too much of a play and not enough of a cultic act' (Heinrich Koch, *Berliner Börsenzeitung*, 22 July 1935).

54 For a description of the use of light in the production, see '*Die Deutsche Passion 1933*', *Frankfurter Zeitung*, 31 July 1934.

55 Henning Eichberg points out that there are striking similarities between the Olympic tradition – with its flag and fire-lighting ceremonies, hymns and oaths – and many aspects of the *Thing* plays. The 1936 Olympics thus represent a coming together of related cultural and sporting phenomena. See Eichberg, 'Das nationalsozialistische Thingspiel', p. 68. Page references to Möller's play are to the edition in *Zeit und Theater*, ed. by Günther Rühle, 6 vols (Frankfurt am Main: Ullstein/Propyläen, 1980), V: *Diktatur und Exil*, pp. 335–78.

56 Stommer, p. 134.

57 See Bruno E. Werner, 'Gegenwart sitzt zu Gericht', *Deutsche Allgemeine Zeitung*, 3 August 1936.

58 Stommer, p. 138.

59 Reichl argues that Möller's interest in court scenes owes much to the influence of Brecht, who used such scenes frequently in didactic plays such as *The Measure* (*Die Maßnahme*). See Reichl, p. 115.

60 An exception is the *Völkischer Beobachter* of 4 August 1936, which did use the word *Thing*, maintaining that Möller's play is 'the first successful attempt to master the laws of form which lead to the *Thing* play' (quoted in Rühle, VI, 790).

61 Glen Gadberry, 'Eberhard Wolfgang Möller's *Thingspiel Das Frankenburger Würfelspiel*', in Henning Eichberg and others, *Massenspiele: NS-Thingspiele, Arbeiterweihespiel und olympisches Zeremoniell* (Stuttgart: Frommann-Holzboog, 1977), pp. 235–51 (p. 248).

62 Stommer, p. 89. For a detailed discussion of the differing cultural policies of Goebbels and Rosenberg with regard to the *Thing* play, see Konrad Dussel, *Ein neues, ein heroisches Theater?: Nationalsozialistische Theaterpolitik und ihre Auswirkungen in der Provinz*, Literatur und Wirklichkeit, 26 (Bonn: Bouvier, 1988), pp. 121–31.

63 Stommer, p. 115. For a discussion of *The Stedingers*, see Glen Gadberry, '*The Stedingers*: Nazi Festival Drama of the Destruction of a People', *Theatre History Studies*, 10 (1990), 105–26.

64 See Wilhelm Westecker, 'Soldat des Rechts', *Berliner Börsen-Zeitung*, 12 May 1941.

65 The work in question bears the strange title *Life, as Wide as a Coffin: We are Internees* (*Die Sargbreite Leben: wir sind Gefangene*) (Hamm: Grote, 1952). For

an analysis of Euringer's life after 1945, see Jürgen Hillesheim, *'Heil Dir Führer! Führ uns an! ...': der Augsburger Dichter Richard Euringer* (Würzburg: Königshausen & Neumann, 1995).

66 Hanns Martin Elster, 'Von der "Sturm-Lyrik" zum Unterhaltungsroman', *Tagesspiegel*, 20 September 1957.

67 See Katrin Sieg, 'Wigwams on the Rhine: Race and Nationality on the German Stage', *Theatre Forum*, no. 6 (Winter–Spring 1995), 12–19.

68 Quoted in 'Probeweise zwei Konzerte in der Thingstätte', *Rhein-Neckar-Zeitung*, 17 July 1986. I am indebted to the staff at Heidelberg Town Hall Archive for helping me retrieve information on the post-war history of the local *Thingplatz*.

2

The history plays of the Third Reich

GLEN GADBERRY

It is 'a peculiar characteristic of our time to see the majority of its events through the lens of history'.

(Bochum Theatre Notes, Premiere of Jelusich's *Cromwell*, 5 May 1934.) [1]

On 30 March 1927, Hanns Johst's proto-Nazi history play *Thomas Paine* opened in Baden-Baden, Bremen, Cologne, Danzig (Gdansk), Düsseldorf, Hanover, Karlsruhe and Lübeck. The simultaneous premiere occurs somewhat frequently in German theatre history; less common is that such a nationalist work was produced at all during the early or middle years of the liberal Weimar Republic.[2] And perhaps as a sign of shifting sentiments, *Thomas Paine* was singularly popular, with forty-eight performances in the original productions and over 200 in the remainder of 1927. After 1933, it became one of the most-performed new serious dramas and was accordingly called 'the first political drama of the new Germany'.[3] As such, *Paine* would set impossible expectations for other German history plays.

This genre has been a major dramatic form since the Egyptians and Greeks, if one accepts that many spectators in Behdet (Edfu) or Athens viewed *The Triumph of Horus* or *Oedipos Tyrannos* as an account of national or local history, rather than what we sometimes dismiss as dramatic ritual or myth. With this view of ancient drama and its reception, Aristotle's distinction in the *Poetics* between poetry (i.e. tragedy) and history gains new vitality. As a poetic expression, drama or tragedy is more philosophical and speculative than prosaic and 'factual' history. Serious historic dramas like *The Trojan Women* or *Thomas Paine* interpret and reconfigure events and actions from the past, influencing the intellectual and cultural life of the present.

The concern with motivation – why people acted as they did – is particularly appealing to the practices of traditional, Aristotelian theatre, where role definition, probability and necessity are central to composition and performance. And when a traditional stage is dominated by star-quality actors, as in Nazi Germany, it is not surprising that history plays would be written and produced in great numbers. The genre also seems to be prevalent during periods of revolution, and the Third Reich did present itself as a major ideological and political upheaval, with Hitler's legal appointment as Chancellor hailed as a 'seizure of power' (*Machtergreifung*) on 30 January 1933.[4] Revolutions necessarily make a new assessment of the past: the heroes of previous regimes may be exposed as oppressors, while one-time criminals or traitors emerge as helpless victims or martyrs. Everywhere are found the harbingers of the new state, which honours these visionaries for authenticating the inevitability of the revolution. The theatre is a viable and memorable means to reassess the past.

Historical subjects, viewed through the mediating lens of National Socialism, would be invaluable for serious German playwriting. This was the view of the Reichsdramaturg, the literary advisor and censor for all German theatre, at the beginning of 1934. In a speech that was reprinted in the press and subsequently published in a volume that became a major source of national theatre theory and practice, Dr Rainer Schlösser asked:

> Is there *any* historic material which would not be given a totally new face when advanced into the light of our natural and legitimate myth of blood and honour? Is there any group of [historical] questions which does not change completely as soon as it is put in relation to Nordic conceptions? We thought we had come to the end of the world and had exhausted all subjects, but now through the national revolution, the entire world, for a second time, is given to us once again.[5]

Schlösser's charge to 'realize the cultural principles of National Socialism in the world of German theatre' gave his endorsement of historical drama an official status denied other traditional genres.[6] German playwrights redoubled their efforts to produce history plays of all types and styles, but with varying degrees of artistry.

Theorists sometimes categorize history plays according to factual accuracy, from implausible invention to referenced documentary. While factual fidelity has been a recurring concern, the advice of the venerable Abbé d'Aubignac seems preferred: 'One should never insist on the details of history when they do not suit the beauty of the theatre.'[7] At the end of 1940, a critic argued that play-wrights should take Schiller's *Don Carlos* and Goethe's *Egmont* as models of inventive historical drama, letting 'history fall by the wayside. Only in this way can [your] work grow away from realistic text-book descriptions of history and fulfil its true structuring function.'[8] The artist is allowed, or expected, to bring invention and supposition to the account; in Nazi Germany, as in any politicized age, embellishment could be for ideological as well as aesthetic reasons.

Some interpretative categories are suggested in *German Drama of the Present* (*Deutsche Dramatik der Gegenwart*, 1938), one of the most valuable sources on Nazi drama, by Berlin critic and author Hermann Anders, who, adding letters to his name, published under the pseudonym Hermann Wanderscheck. Somewhat equivalent categories are provided in 'German Literature and the World of History', an address by the novelist Heinrich Zillich to the First Greater-German Writers' Congress in Weimar, on 28 October 1938.[9] Wanderscheck separated the 'Costume Play' (*Historienstück*), which merely exploits historic milieu for background colour, from the more serious categories of 'History Play' (*historisches Schauspiel*) and 'Historical Drama' (*geschichtliches Drama*). The History Play is essentially focused on the past, for its own sake, presented to the audience as if contemporary; application to other events or periods is left to the spectator's imagination. Historical Drama is more difficult and valuable; it may use the same events or personalities, but its focus is not Romantic milieu, or the past, *per se*, but the political present and future. Historical Dramas often develop new forms and use 'an ideological and politically militant style' to 'elevate historical material into the super-real' realm of National Socialist understanding. 'Historical Drama without contemporary content is meaningless for a living theatre' (p. 205).

Zillich spoke in a complementary way, rejecting, for example, those popular authors who merely exploit an historical moment or character in 'a shallow, fragmentary manner', without giving an accurate or effective voice to the past (p. 1187). Like Wanderscheck, he privileged ideological treatments of history, but only those done in a conscientious manner. He summarily rejected those political 'opportunists (*Nutznießer der Stunde*) who forcefully bring the ideas of the present into their representations of the past' (p. 1187). He thus suggests that the specific programmes and ideas of the Third Reich are temporally determined, and cannot simply be applied to the deeds and words of people in the past; authors who do so produce the worst kind of historical distortion, seeking their own political advantage. Such works (he provided no examples) pervert not only history, but also a clear understanding of the emergence of the Third Reich. The truly political author will be drawn exclusively to German history, and will focus on German destiny; he will 'not fall into the error of misapplying the spirit of his time to the past, but should instead seek out the historic diversity of the German peoples and represent its fate' (p. 1189). The true historical author will focus on the ebb and flow of German identity as *Volk* (nation, people) and will redeem the past for the present and future of the Third Reich.

While one could continue anatomizing history plays, generating specialized terms to differentiate multiple forms, including all the permutations offered by genre, these few will suffice. They should be taken as open categories, to allow for the considerable variety found in the period. The output of new historical drama will be described and then selected plays, beginning with *Thomas Paine*, can be considered.[10] To highlight stage vitality, reviews of premieres or signficant productions will be cited. This has been a satisfactory approach, because many German critics, before and after 1933, were particularly insightful about stage performance (some, like Herbert Ihering and Bernhard Diebold, reviewed both Weimar and Third Reich productions). Newspaper critics also typically assess the contributions of the full variety of theatre artists to stage success.[11] Whenever possible, criticism in the Nazi Party newspaper, the *Völkischer Beobachter*, will be included; while not government-sanctioned, and subject to censorship as well, these reviews frequently suggest the radical Third Reich context of interpretation.

Some statistics

Hundreds of plays were written and produced in the period. Wilhelm Frels tabulated German-language premieres and unproduced but published dramas in the journal *Die neue Literatur*. For the sake of comparison and to avoid complications offered by the occupied territories and the Second World War, the figures are for 1927–32 and 1933–38.[12] Premieres of domestic and newly translated plays in Germany increased after 1933 (from 1201 to 1297), while unproduced plays (frequently 'dramatic poems' and other closet works) declined, from 396 to 239. Premieres of foreign plays in all German-language European theatres declined by more than half (444 to 208), largely due to Nazi cultural planning. Because premieres in Vienna, Innsbruck, Zurich, Prague and Strasbourg, and at other German-language theatres outside Germany, remained the same (240), the overall increase of German plays (from 1393 to 1568) is largely due to playwriting in the Third Reich. Although the increase (12.6 per cent) did not meet Nazi expectations, it is impressive, especially considering the number of playwrights in exile or those who adopted that strategy of separation from the regime which has been called 'inner emigration'.[13]

Frels apportioned plays by genre (tragedy, comedy, farce and so on) and by source material (Table 2.1). History plays accounted for 42 per cent of

Table 2.1 *Plays by genre and source material, 1927–32 and 1933–38*

| | 1927–32 | | 1933–38 | |
	Total	Yearly Average[a]	Total	Yearly Average
Histories	483	80	627	104
Biblical/Christian legend	50	8	25	4
Saga/fairy tale/fantasy	241	40	188	31
Contemporary	808	135	663	110
'Unknown'	255	42	273	45
Total number of plays in all categories	1837	306	1776	296

Note: [a] Averages are rounded to whole numbers.

premieres, published dramas and foreign premieres in translation, a 30 per cent increase over the last years of Weimar. The most favoured periods continued to be 1550–1788 and 1789–1914; medieval subjects were also popular (Table 2.2):

Table 2.2 *History plays, 1927–32 and 1933–38*

| | 1927–32 | | 1933–38 | |
	Total	Yearly Average	Total	Yearly Average
Ancient	35	6	40	7
Medieval	66	11	95	16
Renaissance	59	10	61	10
1550–1788	88	15	143	24
1789–1914	118	20	167	28
Great War	55	9	51	8
Post-war	61	10	68	11
Multi-era	1	0	2	0
Total	483	80	627	104

Hostile critics assumed this preference for historical subjects represented 'flight behaviour': rather than risk censure (or worse) from an unpredictable government, playwrights simply fled into the safety of the past. Yet Wanderscheck, Zillich and others argued that dramatists had actively embraced history to address the truly 'important problems of life, of the *Volk*, and its very history. [...] *The highest dramaturgic law*' was not to confront the 'mundane shape of changing political events', but to write *'from the "Volk" for the "Volk"*.'[14] In this emphasis upon the past, Wanderscheck acquiesced to the Propaganda Minister, Joseph Goebbels, who told the theatre community in 1936 that artists should not deal with contemporary events and issues, because they were typically in flux; only when they had been resolved and relegated to history could current events be refashioned into dramatic form.[15]

Wanderscheck duly cited the prominent playwright and Dramaturg Eberhard Wolfgang Möller on how the Nazi *Weltanschauung* had created a new opportunity, much as Rainer Schlösser had expressed it three years earlier:

> Everything that had seemed to be long researched, registered and labelled, has once again become problematic. From the vantage of our racial perceptions, the whole area of history itself has become once again a new, unresearched area. All human situations and conflicts appear fresh to us, in any case, *ripe for assessment*.[16]

Möller's charge was expanded by Zillich, when he encouraged German novelists (and by implication, all writers) to deal with historic events and figures

> whose totality encorporates the *Volk* as the essential hero of the tale. [You are to create] an epic, which as each memorable work does, seizes important material – the destiny of states, the community of suffering, and the quests of humankind, the wars, the hopes, the spiritual and religious developments, the enduring values of soil, blood, culture. Like the epics, such a work [...] would unite the solitary human being with common destiny. (p. 1192)

Not to treat these larger issues of *Volk* destiny was an irresponsible flight from the world and from history.

Thomas Paine as prototype

It is not surprising that what Wanderscheck called the 'first political drama of the New Germany' (p. 93), should deal with a foreign revolutionary, and that it should premiere outside Berlin. Johst had to fly into foreign history because most producers in 1927 would never have selected a play about a German nationalist. And because Berlin theatre was dominated by commercialism and Jews – according to Nazi historiography – *Paine* would necessarily premiere in the provinces.[17] As a reborn Expressionist, Johst (1890–1978) believed the writer could spark rebellion; Paine was particularly appealing as a gifted wordsmith who actually created a revolution.

In Johst's inventive biography, Paine's writings, rhetoric and national hymn inspire and shape the American revolution, but fail to humanize the post-Revolutionary French Republic fifteen years later. Paine is imprisoned for opposing the execution of 'Louis Capet' (the name for Louis XVI after the revolution), and after seventeen years in prison (historically nine months), he returns to an America which has forgotten him. Paine commits suicide. Yet, standing over Paine's body, an old comrade remembers, and speaks the words of Paine's hymn as others join in:

GRIGNAN   How old would the world be,
               Without the forests, the mountains,
               The youth of America …!
VOICES (*from everywhere, even offstage*)
               The youth of America …!! […]
GRIGNAN (*possessed by his memories, he seems younger, a spiritual
           image of Paine as he saw him singing at the camp fire*)
               America would be nothing,
               If we weren't Americans,
               We comrades, we!!
ALL (*with spirit and power*)
               We comrades, we …!!

The lights go out. From the darkness, like a hymn:

               We comrades, we …!! [18]

The curtain falls on this life transfigured into myth and patriotic 'melody'.[19] *Paine* is unashamedly rhetorical and theatrical, full of pathos and sentiment, and to use two specially favoured terms of the time, it is 'militant' and 'manly'. It is in that style Propaganda Minister Joseph Goebbels called 'steely Romanticism', and playwright Thilo von Trotha, from the rival Rosenberg camp, called 'heroic objectivity'.[20]

Johst gives new motivations to some facts and his inventions are given the façade of documentary by the immanence of performance and by a chronology accompanying the text.[21] Although its politicized themes may be found in most patriotic drama, *Paine* relates closely to the emerging prejudices of National Socialism, as a parable of an individual achieving immortality in the life of the *Volk*. The play is anti-capitalist and anti-French, pro-community and pro-expansionist for 'living space' (*Lebensraum* – an idea found in Paine's *Public Good* of 1780): in the second scene, Paine and General George Washington study a map spread across a campaign drum. The western lands of the continent are unknown territory where civilization stops and armies fear to go. Paine says it is all America, it is what this war is about: 'Land! … Land!! Washington! Earth … space, that's what we're fighting for … Fatherland!' (p. 46). It was a message understood by most Germans, particularly those on the political right, and those who had read Hans Grimm's novel of racial and national manifest destiny, *People Without Space* (*Volk ohne Raum*, 1926).

Paine finally came to Berlin on 16 November 1935, achieving its most accomplished production at the Staatstheater, the independent flagship stage of Prussian Governor Hermann Göring. In part to celebrate Johst as new President of the Writers' Union, it was produced for the 1935 Congress of the Chambers of Culture. Directed by Jürgen Fehling, designed by Traugott Müller, and featuring Lothar Müthel as Paine, along with Eugen Klöpfer, Gustaf Gründgens and Bernhard Minetti, the production earned critical acclaim. Respected critic Herbert Ihering called it the best Berlin production he had seen in twenty-five years. Considering the host of famous performances he had reviewed – including major productions by Reinhardt, Piscator and Jessner, now discredited by the Nazis – it was high praise indeed.[22] Writing in the *Völkischer Beobachter*, Wolf Braumüller compared 'our comrade' Paine to stage biographies of Nazi martyrs *Schlageter* (by Johst) and *Horst Wessel* (by Kurt Sommerer), both from 1933, 'for their avowal of our *Volk* and our era'. But only when Paine convinced Washington to take the revolution across the continent did the play become a *'manifestation of heroic theatre*, binding the stage to the cultural will of our new state'.[23]

Fehling's production was subsequently revived for the Third National Theatre Festival in Munich (May 1936) and for the two-week Olympic season in August, to demonstrate German cultural pre-eminence. *Thomas Paine* was the only contemporary German play produced in the two sanctioned traditional theatres in Berlin during the Eleventh Olympics, which was so important for Nazi self-promotion; it shared the stage with *The Oresteia*, *King Lear*, *Hamlet* and *Faust*. No other new serious work fared so well in Hitler's Germany, and it helped establish the history play as a major Third Reich genre.

English rebels and costume plays

Nearly half of Nazi history plays focus on a dominating personality, like *Thomas Paine*, while most feature a broad event, with a number of central characters. Personality histories probably dominated production because they offered greater unity (a recurring concern of 1930s dramatic theory) and the opportunity to feature an actor or actress, often as a militant Führer figure. Some of the most desirable subjects were revolutionaries, from any world culture. The 1602 'Essex Rebellion' became *Rebell in England* by Hans Schwarz (1890–1967).[24] Written in 1926, *Rebell* was not produced until 1934, when the political and artistic climate had shifted to the political right.[25] In effect 'correcting' Ferdinand Bruckner's 'decadent Jewish' psychoanalytic portrait (*Elisabeth von England*, 1930), Schwarz focused on an Elizabethan rebel who lacked the essential 'blood bond' to the *Volk*.

A more successful revolutionary was refigured by Austrian Mirko Jelusich (1886–1969), who used material from his doctoral course (philosophy, Slavonic and Sanskrit studies) to authenticate a series of historical works. In 1934 he converted his novel *Oliver Cromwell* (1933) into a play with the same title. Audiences saw clear parallels with Hitler, although Jelusich denied that had been his intent.[26] The monumental play glorifies Cromwell for dissolving an extravagant monarchy and corrupt parliament to forge his new state. 'From his lonely heights', Cromwell 'gives everything for his idea. The vision of the dying Cromwell – a unified, creative *Volk* – is the vision of our era and our Führer.'[27] He expresses those dreams and his accomplishments in a deathbed speech to his family and friends:

> Since God has given me his grace, I have had only one goal: the Nation. I have seen it in my dreams, I have created it, I have served it, I have sacrificed everything for it. The idea is so simple – every great idea is simple: the many, united to each other, can do more than the individual – and someone must be the first to make this idea a reality. (*He becomes visionary.*) The proudest courts of Europe now bow down to us! [...] Scholars and artists create eternal works which will proclaim the glory of our land through all time! And in the country-side the plough slices sacred wounds in the earth: tens of thousands turn their own land into bread for hundreds of thousands! That is what shapes my nation! (*Powerfully.*) Yes, that's what I have created! Me – one among millions, – me – through the grace of God! They might bless or curse me – but my deed cannot be taken from me; it lives and endures and will outlive them all: this united, one great nation – the nation! (*He sinks back and dies; people cover their faces and break into tears.*)
>
> LADY CROMWELL (*with deep fervour*) No! Don't cry! He has achieved grace![28]

Jelusich's portrayal conveniently overlooked the Restoration of the Stuart monarchy and the ultimate triumph of Parliament, thereby maintaining his heroic image of Cromwell. He also did not mention that the Lord Protector allowed the Jews to return to England (an historical act which led Hitler's anti-semitic mentor Dietrich Eckart to dismiss Cromwell's Protectorate as a precursor to the Führer state).[29]

Cromwell premiered in Bochum in May 1934 and came to Berlin in December, for the Youth Division of Rosenberg's NS-Kulturgemeinde (National Socialist Cultural Community). Jelusich enthusiasts and Rosenberg radicals responded with stormy applause, but the critics were less kind. They wrote that Jelusich should have remained satisfied with his novel, and that he tended to put Cromwell into grand tableaux without dramatic opponents – a recurring criticism of the personality history play. Some critics could not get beyond their favourable memories of *Oliver Cromwell's Mission* (*Oliver*

Cromwells Sendung, 1932), Walter Gilbricht's theatrical vehicle for Eugen Klöpfer. And so Jelusich's *Cromwell* had 'no storm, not even a murmur; no steel, only lead'. It was 'boring, undramatic, a poor copy' and, most damning of all, 'dilettante kitsch', a phrase echoing the harsh assessment of Nazi playwriting in 1934 by Goebbels.[30] Braumüller praised the proto-Nazi rhetoric and the parallels with Hitler; at Rosenberg's *Völkischer Beobachter*, ideology superseded artistic excellence.[31]

Gerhard Aichinger (the pseudonym of Gerhard Aick, 1900–78) was a journalist who worked for the Nazis in Austria. He had great success with the sentimental costume play *Jewel Fetched from the Silver Sea* (*Kleinod in die Silbersee gefaßt*).[32] Alternately known as *Caroline von England*, the play deals with the Braunschweig princess who married the Prince of Wales in 1796. It was a political union, and Caroline soon deserted England for Italy. She returned for the coronation of her husband as George IV (1820), but when Parliament tried to dissolve the union, Caroline successfully fought for her marriage and title. She died in 1821, under mysterious circumstances. In Aichinger's retelling, the beautiful Caroline charms Parliament and wins popular support for her cause (a specious addition in Braumüller's estimation).[33] Deeply troubled that she won this fight because she was a woman, not because she was right, Caroline takes poison. She accepts she acted out of pride and recognizes the 'higher truth' consistent with Nazi family values: 'Power is man's disposition, but love is the existence of woman.' Although the Berlin edition of the *Völkischer Beobachter* did not initially review the play and Wanderscheck slighted it as a mere criminal story (p. 229), it was popular, as thin and well written as Scribe's *Glass of Water*, with solid roles and theatrical moments. It premiered in Munich in 1936 and, as a sign of its success with Goebbels, it was mounted in Bochum in 1937 for his six-city Fourth National Theatre Festival. It was the first Austrian play to be featured at these annual celebrations, one year before the *Anschluß*.

Another successful example of the costume history play – these ideologically indifferent (or carefully obscured) entertainment pieces, usually on themes of romance and identity – is Liliane Wied's *Roving Queen* (*Die Wanderkönigin*, 1936). Famed actress/producer Agnes Straub discovered Wied (1913–?) and created the title role of Queen Christine of Sweden. The title refers both to Christine's wanderings in Europe and to her indecisiveness, yet one critic thought: 'whoever seeks insight into the puzzle of Christine from the woman's perspective of Liliane Wied must be disappointed', for instead of a revealing psychological approach, Wied settled for 'heroic pathos'.[34] As with Caroline, Christine simply 'being a woman destroys her mission' – a perspective which the *Völkischer Beobachter* found flat and simplistic; it was clearly the work of a beginner, produced 'not for literary value', but as a star vehicle.[35] As was so often the case with successful personality histories, it was the actor or actress who animated the title role, and with it the play, beyond what seemed possible.

Forgotten Germans and the revaluation of history

Nazi playwrights were enormously adept at reviving 'forgotten Germans', wherever they had settled. Like Jelusich, Hans Friedrich Blunck (1888–1961) was principally a novelist. In 1934, this first president of the Nazi Writers' Union (1933–35) turned to 'history' substantiated by 'common knowledge' for his tragedy *Land in the Twilight* (*Land in der Dämmerung*): Diderik Pining, German-born, Danish-empowered governor of Iceland, supposedly 'discovered' the New World twenty years before Columbus, an achievement then accepted by Scandinavian historians and populist reference works like *Knaurs Lexikon*.[36] Blunck's Pining wants to bring his Icelandic *Volk* to that more fertile land to the west. He dreams of a new state, governed by compassionate laws rather than the whims of kings and priests, or the blood codes of clan warfare. But he is opposed by his own family and the farm leader Grettir, who thinks it ludicrous to 'desert our ancient homeland for the dream of a better world'.[37] Grettir finally assassinates Diderik.

Walter Stang, director of Rosenberg's NS-Kulturgemeinde, saw two aspects of the eternal German in the play: the Faustian searcher for a better world, 'to whom cultures from Iceland to India owe their origin' (Pining), and Nordic man, with 'hard, unwavering fidelity to his native land, bound by the laws of God and nature' (Grettir). Their opposition constituted a uniquely German tragedy. *Twilight* had a major Berlin premiere in 1934, with Fehling as director, Caspar Neher as designer, Friedrich Kayßler as Pining and Walter Franck as Grettir. Yet it did poorly, in part because Blunck had written it in stiff 'book German', a serious fault emphasized in production by slow pace and lengthy pauses.[38] Stang blamed Fehling for suspiciously abstract overstylization and for cutting the last line, an imperative to Pining's son, and the audience: 'Not God, YOU must decide your future, you German.' The line focused the essential opposition of Germanic-Nordic self-sufficiency and Judaeo-Mediterranean 'slave' Christianity, repeatedly defined by Rosenberg in his speeches, articles and especially his ponderous 1930 'masterpiece': *The Myth of the Twentieth Century*.[39] Fehling, responsible for some of the most intriguing productions in Nazi Germany, dropped the line and continued to irritate Nazi radicals.[40]

After transforming *Twilight* to better advantage in the novel *The Great Journey* (*Die große Fahrt*, 1934), Blunck returned to playwriting in 1938 with *Jakob Leisler* (*Fight for New York*) (*Kampf um New York*). Although it made a respectable showing at the Berlin Volksbühne Theatre on Horst-Wessel-Platz in 1939, it had no abiding success. Another tragedy about Leisler, better written, performed and received, had preceded it – Curt Langenbeck's *The Traitor* (*Der Hochverräter*, 1938). Unlike Blunck, Langenbeck (1906–53) was primarily a dramatist, Dramaturg and visionary for a new political drama; he best knew how to dramatize the fate of Leisler, a German emigré, who, with populist approval, seized the colonial government of New York during the Glorious Revolution. Although he ceded power to the new English Governor, Leisler and his aide John Stoll were executed for treason in 1691.

Blunck focused on the last year of Leisler's rule and his realistic account turned melodramatic when the governor has a heart attack as Leisler dies. As one character underlined the message: 'If a German falls, an Englishman will follow him into the grave.' Blunck called *Leisler* 'a parable, a reminder' that 'destiny punishes any conflict between Germans and the English', at a time when those relations were strained.[41] Langenbeck's verse tragedy portrays Leisler's last twenty-four hours; the work observes the unities of time, place and action, has a chorus of four elders of New York, and was to be performed without intermission 'in 2¼ hours'. Langenbeck wrote that 'historic accuracy' in setting or costumes was 'not desired', presumably to universalize the action and suggest a contemporary context.[42] Here was that formalist, but essentially classical, experiment which would typify Wanderscheck's category of 'Historical Drama'.

The play dramatizes the 'tragic conflict of two principles of world order' (Wanderscheck, p. 151): elitist moneyed aristocracy and *Volk*-sanctioned Führer state. Leisler finally admits his arrogance and, facing a firing squad, he accepts his execution:

> I have paraded around with my beliefs and have
> Not known God. And so I did everything selfishly
> And yes, made God a witness to my fine title.
> Pride grew in me. [...]
> At the end I accomplished much, sacrificed nothing. [...]
> Now I will pay the bitter price – and will be free. (p. 432)

Although Leisler failed to establish an enduring, independent *Volk* state, his martyrdom pointed to final victory:

LEISLER   I proclaim there are still miracles, you children of man!
         And nothing has been lost or stolen from you, as long as
         My fate burns like a sacrificial flame and rallies
         Hearts, who will tend it for their *Volk*!
         Now then, sergeant, in the name of our king: Hail!
         We trumpet it with the fanfares of victory:

(*Together with* STOLL)   Hail New York!

SLOUGHTER   Lieutenant?

NICOLLS   Governor! They must live!

LIEUTENANT (*softly*)   Fire.

NICOLLS *turns away and falls to his knees; salvo;* LEISLER *and* STOLL
collapse. (p. 437)

The New York Elders, witnesses to the execution, conclude that it is hard to
die, but that God shall receive Leisler and Stoll as his heroes.

Eberhard Wolfgang Möller (1906–72) also examined significant lives in the
New World, such as Johann Suter in *Californian Tragedy* (*Kalifornische
Tragödie*) and Ferdinand de Lesseps in *Panama Scandal* (*Panamaskandal*, both
premiered in 1930). However, more typically, like Heinrich Zillich, he found
inspiration in German history. *Martin Luther, or The Hellish Journey* (*Martin
Luther, oder Die höllische Reise*) was staged in 1933, during celebrations of
the 450th anniversary of Luther's birth. It premiered in Königsberg, where
Möller served as Dramaturg. He intended to present the complex of persons
around Luther 'as living beings: not out of reverence to history but *as
contemporary people*', in other words, as a legitimate 'History Play'. But he
also wanted to provide 'a mirror of the religious controversy of today [1933],
which has once again become a German controversy'.[43] Accordingly, *Luther*
rests somewhere between History Play and Historical Drama, or as one critic
tried to express it, it was a 'play of the contemporary German past'.[44]

A factual outer frame carries us from Luther's appearance at Worms in
1521 through his forced flight to the Wartburg, at the start of the Peasant
Wars; it encloses private scenes of Luther torn by doubt and regret for the
rebellion he encouraged, but betrayed. According to the *Völkischer Beobachter*,
the play's parallels with 'today's struggle for a belief system' were Möller's
greatest gift to the nation and *Luther* should be performed on all German
stages beyond the Vistula (in other words, in the cities of East Prussia, some
like Königsberg still German Lutheran, but others, thanks to Versailles, Polish
Catholic).[45] But this endorsement did not guarantee a prolonged stage life: like
Twilight and many of the plays of this period, *Luther* was only available as
an unpublished theatre script. Luther remained a problematic figure in the
Third Reich, as a reform Christian with anti-peasant and the more acceptable
anti-semitic tendencies. Many Third Reich playwrights sought to resolve
Luther's ideological inconsistencies, and claim him for National Socialism.[46]

Möller achieved greater notoriety in 1934 with *Rothschild is the Victor at
Waterloo* (*Rothschild siegt bei Waterloo*), a 'satirical' portrait of the London
banker. It is 'history' based upon an untrue but 'known anecdote' popularly
accepted as accurate. As a witness to Napoleon's defeat, Nathan Rothschild

races to London. At the English Stock Exchange, he cleverly drops the false news that Wellington has been defeated. His report causes economic panic, financial collapse, at least one suicide and fears of national bankruptcy. He uses this disorder to become enormously wealthy when his agents buy up huge amounts of momentarily worthless stock.[47] Möller wrote that this fraud was evidence of that sinister force which makes 'numbers out of people, market objects out of men, profit from life, capital from blood. [...] [*Rothschild*] is the anecdote of capitalism.' In 1970, Möller said it was 'incidental' that Rothschild was Jewish and that his play therefore 'was not anti-semitic'.[48]

Reinforcing the economic interpretation, Möller uses Rothschild's name infrequently in the play, preferring the official title of 'Banker'. And there is only one other direct Jewish reference in the text: amid a string of insults Rothschild hurls at O'Pinnel, his head clerk, who has quit to protest against the market fraud, he uses the word '*Meschugge*' (Yiddish for 'crazy', p. 125). German spectators were thus reminded of Rothschild's Jewish heritage, in case they had forgotten his well-known family history. The Third Reich audience probably found Rothschild's attempt to invent a different biography 'typically' deceptive:

ROTHSCHILD   I'm a simple person, I come from a humble background like you, from a military background, I should say. My father was a patriot and military man in Frankfurt. He gave his life for the Fatherland. [...]

O'PINNEL   Your father, I think, was a banker in Frankfurt.

ROTHSCHILD   Quite right, as I said, a banker, a devout banker and a very active churchgoer for business reasons. (pp. 47–8)

Möller's intention, however, was that Rothschild, like the other, non-Jewish brokers and bankers in the play, celebrated crass capitalism: 'The London Stock Market is our Fatherland. We fall and rise with the rate of exchange' (p. 93).

Finally giving in to his moral core, O'Pinnel will expose 'The truth. Someone must tell it':

ROTHSCHILD   Why?

O'PINNEL   (*beside himself*)   Because I'm a good person. [...] People didn't die so you could make money off them. And in such a shabby manner.

ROTHSCHILD   You liar.

O'PINNEL   Thieves always defend themselves with insults. You've robbed the dead.

ROTHSCHILD   Of what?

O'PINNEL   Of their honourable graves. (pp. 127–9)

The other brokers are outraged by Rothschild's fraud – and perhaps a little jealous – but they apparently have no recourse to regain their lost money. Rothschild will be shunned, a fabulously wealthy outcast from the human community.

The play's most prominent production was at the Third National Theatre Festival in Munich in 1936, sponsored by the Propaganda Ministry. The director, Otto Falckenberg, stressed the racial issue by staging it as 'a satire against *Jewish* capitalism' (emphasis added).[49] He also reinforced conspiracy theories about the First World War, how capitalists (Jewish and otherwise) had profited from the blood of 'real Germans', much as Rothschild, the 'monstrous money-maker', cheats what one critic called the 'soldiers and fisherfolk – honourable, straightforward, modest humanity' in the play.[50] The *Völkischer Beobachter* revelled in this portrayal of the 'old, fixed mask of the Eternal Jew', as played by Friedrich Domin, and praised the settings of Eduard Sturm, especially his English Stock Exchange: 'this round temple of money, its walls stock listings and its dome the globe; the oriental [i.e. Jewish] faces and gestures were remarkably effective in this corrupt money-space'.[51] Citing the Goebbels-inspired opinion of the Reichsdramaturg ('Möller wrote it with the means of steely Romanticism') and Greek theatre history, a major Munich critic called *Rothschild* a sardonic 'satyr play' in contrast to the serious works in the Festival, *Thomas Paine* and Friedrich Bethge's *Veterans' March* (*Marsch der Veteranen*, 1934), both of which portrayed true 'national virtue'.[52]

The medieval era generated scores of histories demonstrating the varieties of national virtue, such as *The Last Prussian* (*Der letzte Preuße*, 1938). This 'Tragedy of the Destruction of a People' was by Rolf Lauckner (1887–1954), who, like Blunck, trained as a lawyer. Herkus Monte is chief of the pagan East Prussian Natangers, who were massacred by the Teutonic Order in 1273. We see Herkus in his relationship with the Christian knight Hirzhals. Friends since childhood, but political and religious opponents, the two are given ample opportunity for noble action. Hirzhals is captured and is to be sacrificed; to spare his friend having to deny his own people by trying to save him, Hirzhals leaps onto the sacrificial pyre. Subsequently betrayed by 'a treacherous bastard, a mongrel' (the kind of mixed-race 'subhuman' haunting Nazi ideology), the Natangers are slaughtered. Herkus's body is cremated on stage, a distasteful, overblown ending which the *Völkischer Beobachter* recommended cutting.[53] The Stuttgart premiere came on the fifth anniversary of the *Machtergreifung* (30 January 1938), ample opportunity for a relevant ideological context, but *The Last Prussian* had more resonance for Lauckner's other career as opera librettist than for the 'steely Romanticism' of Goebbels and Schlösser.

The Stedingers (*Die Stedinger*) by August Hinrichs (1879–1956) is another work subtitled 'Play of the Destruction of a People'. It is a festival 'event history' mourning the 1234 massacre of the northwest coastal German people known as the Stedingers. Anxious to seize the fertile Stedinger lands, the Archbishop of Bremen declares the territory interdict, the people heretics, and sends crusader armies to destroy them. Heiko, a young monk, deserts the church and its crusade after he sees his village and the land which fostered his Stedinger values:

HEIKO   I have beaten my back bloody and prayed and prayed, trying
to forget the green meadows – it wasn't easy to do. I learned to bow
down and to do everything my order demanded – twenty years – my
entire youth – twenty years! [...] And then, when I saw that Stedinger
land again – the dikes, the red roofs and meadows – and saw you
standing there in need – my own countrymen and brothers – I
couldn't any more! And my blood screamed: stand by them! And then
– it came to me – may God forgive me – if you're heretics, then I am
too! [54]

Except for a few youths who ensure the continuing life of these people, the Stedingers, including Heiko, are slaughtered.

The play premiered at the historic site, on the 700th anniversary of the massacre, 27 May 1934. Dedicated by Rosenberg – whose radical ideology matched the play's anti-Christian and pro-*Volk* agenda – the outdoor festival theatre ultimately included a dozen medieval buildings in Thilo von Trotha's 'heroically objective' style, 650 professional and amateur actors and seating for 15,000. Annual performances recreated, personalized and reassessed this dark episode from German history. Once reviled as shameless heretics, the Stedingers, like the Natangers, became martyrs, whose blood hallowed German soil, encouraging the emergence of the heroic Third Reich.[55] In its final vision of Stedinger heroism and survival, it became an Historical Drama, looking forward to 1933.

Reassessment of the historical record is also central to Erwin Guido Kolbenheyer's *Gregor und Heinrich*, Edmund Kiß's *Wittekind* and Ernst Bacmeister's *Emperor Constantine's Baptism* (*Kaiser Konstantins Taufe*). Each gives the lie to 'accepted facts' for a new, Nazi reading of the past, fully supporting Möller's later views of playwriting opportunity. *Gregor und Heinrich* had a simultaneous premiere in six cities on 18 October 1934; a meaningful context was immediately provided by that date – the anniversary of the 1813 battle of Leipzig, when 'the concept of the united Greater Germany (*Großdeutschland*) began to appear in the hearts of fiery patriots for the first time' (Wanderscheck, p. 213). Dedicated 'to the rising German spirit', the play was produced by most major German theatres, finally coming to Berlin in 1940 and Nazi Vienna in 1942.

The massive work – with over seventy characters and taking up to five hours to perform – revisits the familiar conflict of the Mediterranean papacy (Gregory VII) and the German empire (Heinrich IV), which culminated in Heinrich's humiliation before Gregory at Canossa in 1077. That interpretation of the past was challenged in the 1930s; as Kolbenheyer (1878–1962) demonstrated, Heinrich was the real victor by feigning the penitent to secure independence for his German Reich. Responding to the Dresden premiere (the one Kolbenheyer attended) Franz Köppen complained that the play 'trivialized' a complex 'intellectual and ideological problem', whereas the *Völkischer Beobachter* praised the timely symbolism: 'through heroic self-restraint, Germanic will freed itself from a Roman, from a foreign yoke. The great connection to the present is open ended, but the national stage has once again been justified as a "moral institution".'[56]

Herbert Ihering commended Kolbenheyer's layers of dialectics, but thought the play merely a double monologue, with each title character wrestling with his unseen enemy over the Alps.[57] Pope and emperor share only one short scene (the last) and, rather than engaging in full conflict or action, each resorts to ritual prayers and pronouncements. Heinrich directly assails Gregory with his exit line: 'Christ's empire has a soul and body; you, Bishop of Rome, be lord and refuge of the soul, and leave to the king what belongs to the king.'[58] Kolbenheyer, who had studied psychology along with zoology on his way to a doctorate in philosophy, was urged to drop narrow historical accuracy altogether, rewrite the play, and bring the central characters on stage as true dramatic opponents, as Schiller had done in the third act of *Maria Stuart*.[59] In this way, Historical Drama would be truer and more philosophical than the mere facts of history. But Kolbenheyer did not follow this critical advice, because he had moved on to other literary projects.

Wittekind (or Widukind) was a Saxon farmer and chieftan who fought Charlemagne and Christianity for twenty years, until 785, when he sued for peace, submitted to baptism and surrendered Saxony to Charlemagne's Christian league. One of Charlemagne's chroniclers, Alcuin of York, recorded a miracle, but Kiß (1886–?) challenged that pious 'history' in his tragedy, written in 1928. Unable to bring a military solution to the Saxon problem, Kiß has Church Legate Isidorus persuade Charlemagne to capture the women of Saxony and give Wittekind an ultimatum: he must submit to the church and Charlemagne, or 60,000 Saxon wives and daughters will be interned with rank criminals, traitors and the 'human scum' from the Mediterranean basin, from 'the Nile delta, from Arabia's plague-infected harbour cities, Jews, Greeks, Italians and Moors'.[60] To save his race, Wittekind submits and is sworn to secrecy about this pact, to allow Alcuin to invent his account 'as so much smoke' (p. 61).

To avoid insulting Mussolini, 'Italians' may have been changed to 'Asiatics' (in other words, 'Jews' in Rosenberg jargon) for the premiere in Hagen in 1935.[61] Yet *Wittekind* continued to offend the church, and priests denounced the play and tried to stop the production. At the second performance, Catholic students began to hoot and whistle, shouting 'History shall not be falsified' – suggesting their inflexible view of the past – until they were cleared from the gallery by local police. There was an unprecedented storm of commentary in the press, in Germany and abroad, and subsequent performances (fifteen of twenty-five) were restricted to the state teachers' union or to members of Rosenberg's ideological NS-Kulturgemeinde.[62]

In 1936, Kiß converted his play into the novel *Wittekind der Große*, wherein Isidorus is revealed as a Jew, who works with the church to destroy the independent German *Volk*.[63] Although he was not played as a Jewish stereotype in Hagen, Isidorus held the kind of hatreds Nazi prejudices ascribed to Jews. When Charlemagne returns the Saxon women unpolluted, for example, he rages: 'As long as German blood remains unmixed, the church will lose, even in a thousand years' (p. 66). Isidorus's Judaeo-Christianity demands the genetic disintegration of the German *Volk*. Seen in the light of his later novelistic identity, Isidorus, like Rothschild, becomes one of those rare examples of the Nazi stage Jew as a major character. Both plays demonstrate how Jews work to shape events and history, to their own advantage. In this his only play, Kiß, novelist and chief of the Prussian Construction Office in Kassel, embraced and exceeded the programmatic demands of Möller and Zillich. He created one of the darkest Third Reich histories, which also demonstrates how power shapes history – in the account by Kiß *and*, more than a thousand years earlier, by Alcuin.

Ernst Bacmeister (1874–1971) subtitled *Emperor Constantine's Baptism* (1937) a 'Tragedy of Religion', but it is no pious *in hoc signo vinces*. The emperor will dedicate his magnificent new capital to the 'true God' and calls upon the fifty-three faiths, sects and cults of Byzantium to invoke their divinities. To claim the city, a divinity must appear within twenty-four hours, 'Be it a daemon or demiurge, / A hero, angel, devil or god; / The many in one or the one only.'[64] Constantine will prostrate himself to this being and dedicate his capital, empire and rule to a Christian, Olympian, Germanic, Mid-Eastern, Egyptian or even Jewish faith.[65] Yet Constantine is assured no god will appear; he has erected a colossal statue of himself holding the all-powerful goddess Fate, atop a black porphyry column (his statue remains out of sight of the audience). The monument bears the words *Soli victrici comiti* (To the Sun, the Victorious Guide), and the citizens variously assume the city will be dedicated to Apollo, Fate, Jesus Christ or even Constantine himself. As a reviewer wrote, 'in drunken Imperial-Popery, Constantine declares himself God of Byzantium', but Constantine is not another self-deified Roman emperor.[66] He proclaims himself a model and champion of militant human will, independent of any 'imagined divinity'. As he has conceived and built this glorious city and reshaped the empire, so too each person must act according to individual will:

> Why grasp emptiness?
> Why grasp after a god? Since all of this is through us!
> You are not proud enough, you sons of men.
> You don't take risks with all that you could
> And with what you are, or could be, if you wanted.
> So then take me as the measure, Byzantines,
> For I created the empire anew out of ruins,
> More secure and greater than the world
> Has ever seen. I as my own god. (p. 56)

At the height of Constantine's self-confidence, the news arrives that his competent nephew and heir has been killed by his incompetent son, out of jealousy. The Christians see this murder as a laudable retribution for Constantine's blasphemy and are urged on to rebellion by the radical Athanasius, bishop of Alexandria. Even the emperor's own elite guard of Goths has become infiltrated by Christianity and cannot be trusted. A bloody civil and religious war seems immanent.

Constantine now seeks guidance from his old teacher. Although he advocates religious freedom and the ultimately unknowable mystery of the divine, Sopater argues that Christianity is an unfortunate historic inevitability. Lest the dogmatic bigotry of Athanasius envelop the empire and erase the emperor's vision of free human will and action, Constantine must submit to baptism:

> You must lead, Emperor, and not wait
> Until you are led by the stupid world.
> It is outgrowing you. And so become Christian
> And make it develop, AS YOU WILL:
> At the head of God's service.
> And so solve the riddle of who He is,
> For then you are He. Who cares about the name? (p. 81)

Because he cannot live in such a Christian empire, even under the stewardship of Constantine, Sopater takes poison.

Constantine asks Athanasius to perform the rite of baptism, but the bishop insists Constantine make full confession first. Recognizing how such knowledge would empower the bishop and the church, Constantine appeals to Athanasius's practicality and pride: certainly a willing bishop could be found to perform the rite, but it is only the zealous and strict Athanasius, who successfully fought the Arian Heresy, who is truly worthy of performing this historic and serviceable ritual (p. 97). Thus flattered and assuaged, Athanasius agrees and Constantine undergoes baptism, without confession. He now commissions a magnificent church, 'its great space a poem in stone'. This church – rebuilt by the Emperor Justinian as the massive Hagia Sophia, or Church of Sacred Wisdom – will be consecrated to Sopater's 'Divine Mystery. But to no God!' (pp. 98–9). Constantine will continue to rule, as Sopater counselled, with his 'pagan heart, yet a Christian skin' (p. 81).

Wanderscheck thought this political drama belonged 'on every stage of the Reich, in [our] time of conflict between the church's will to rule and the self-assured state, faithful to the *Volk*' (p. 58). After its successful premiere in Stuttgart, this work was selected as the first of a 'community' of ideological plays to be published in a new series, the 'Library of Dramatic Literature'. Two brief essays, by Curt Langenbeck and Wolf Braumüller, append Bacmeister's text. As introduced by this 'Tragedy of Religion', the series would be, in Braumüller's estimation, a 'phalanx to overcome the traditional realistic forms on the German stage', as well as a guide for the new Nazi drama. 'And before this phalanx stands the flag of victory as a rising battalion.'[67] Braumüller certainly saw that flag emblazoned with a swastika.

The spectre of France

Few plays were located in antiquity – whether 'historical' (*Constantine*) or 'mythical' (Hermann Burte's *Prometheus*, 1933). The most popular period was post-Renaissance, and France, chronic enemy and Nazi paradigm of modernist decadence, was a recurring subject. Paul Joseph Cremers (1874–1941), born in Aachen and raised in Cologne (cities with histories of French occupation), dramatized France's most successful politician in *Richelieu, Kardinalherzog von Frankreich* (1934). By any means, and unhindered by his priestly vows, Richelieu forges a centralized monarchy, against the rebels of the Fronde and even against the weakling Louis XIII. Most serious history plays reinforced or instructed Nazi ideology as they attempted true Historical Drama, but a selfless, powerful servant (Richelieu) empowering an incompetent ruler (Louis) provided a mixed political message for Hitler's Germany. Wanderscheck tried, unsuccessfully, to give the play a Nazi context by arguing that Louis was, like Hitler, a 'God-sent Führer, whose highest ethic is the well-being of the *Volk*' (p. 129). Structurally, Cremers's Richelieu had no opponents in what a critic dismissed as a 'cleverly stitched Gobelin tapestry, with strong colours and typical figures in lively scenes, but none the less lifeless, static and woven in low relief'.[68] In a Munich production in 1938, it was Louis – a flawed, contradictory and hence more complex character – who overshadowed the less interesting Richelieu; casting, direction and music made that production a success, despite the inherent weaknesses of Cremers's text.[69]

Even more politically problematic is Walter Gilbricht's *Marie Charlotte Corday* (1936), a drama focused on political assassination. Corday, who came from Caen, killed the bloody Jean Marat out of patriotism and admiration for the noble Brutus. We first see her in the second act, combing through accounts of the assassination of Julius Caesar, by Plutarch, Corneille and Shakespeare, while her lamp casts her 'grotesquely enlarged shadow across the wall' – a design that recalls German Expressionism.[70] Corday's life story, from assassination to execution, was thought undramatic, 'an episode, and a silent one at that', in the annals of history; when asked if she had anything to say to the charges, Corday merely said: 'Nothing, except that I have succeeded.' A dramatist must expand upon her brevity, 'and so Gilbricht lets her voice her views from the start'; she is made to fulfil a 'clearly thought out, self-chosen martyr's fate', without wavering or doubt.[71]

While rhetoric replaces character development and dramatic conflict, some moments are replete with irony. At Corday's trial the prosecutor Tinville charges that Marat 'gave himself helplessly into your hands':

CORDAY   God did that. Marat took every care. He thought me a mere woman, *that* was his mistake.
TINVILLE   You stabbed a sick man.
CORDAY   He wasn't picked for his virtue. (*Uproar from the judges.*) [...]
MONTANÉ   Marat's last words?
CORDAY   You'll have to invent them yourselves. What he said isn't worth the marble to carve them in: 'You've earned a good spot at the Place de la Révolution' [her reward for betraying the Girondists]. That was the last I heard him say. When the state places his bust across from St Lepelletier, these words can be set in gold lettering.
(*Uproar from the Judges*) You're mocking the dead friend of the people!
CORDAY   You're mistaken, I only wanted him to have more memorable last words. (pp. 59–60)

This unrepentant, outspoken Corday is condemned to death by guillotine, at an even better 'spot at the Place de la Révolution'. In the last scene, the path of her tumbril is blocked by Marat's large funeral cortège – his famed bath closed over as his coffin. Attracted to the greater spectacle of this beautiful, proud woman facing death, Danton and Desmoulins desert the mourners – including Robespierre and Saint-Just, who begin to suspect

Danton's political reliability. Gilbricht (1891–1974) thus sets the scene for the events in Georg Büchner's *Danton's Death* (*Dantons Tod*, 1835), a documentary history play to which *Corday* was often unfavourably compared.

In 1936, at the Berlin Deutsches Theater, the flagship theatre of the Propaganda Ministry, Angela Salloker played Corday as a second Joan of Arc, a 'passionately inflamed idealist who sacrifices herself for France'.[72] This simple maid from Nordic Normandy (an ethno-geographic heritage favoured in the Third Reich) is the only noble character in the play, yet she delivers up the Girondists and her lover to gain access to Marat; her murder of Marat merely ushers in greater bloodshed under Robespierre. Did the play imply Germany was experiencing its own Reign of Terror, built on a series of political murders? Was it advocating assassination? Perhaps sensing these awkward questions, Berlin critic Wilhelm Westecker argued the essential contemporary context was not Nazi Germany, but civil-war-torn Spain, and the *Völkischer Beobachter* dismissed *Corday* as mere 'historical reportage [...] of the French Revolution, its filth and heroism, its murders, vulgar misdirection and soaring enthusiasm – an impossible task, even for Büchner'.[73] It is likely *Corday* was taken as further evidence of French barbarism, without acceptable parallels with Germany in 1936.

Two years later, Gilbricht had a less controversial success with his entertaining stage biography of Napoleon's mother, *Letizia* (1938). In this family portrait, which one critic thought 'Shavian', Letizia cannot accept her child as the emperor, but merely someone she can still 'take by the hand or by his imperial ear'.[74] The French emperor was the most popular historical figure in German playwriting from 1933 to 1938, with at least a dozen plays focused on various periods of his life; Fritz Helke's *The Duke of Enghein* (*Der Herzog von Enghien*, 1938) is unusual in this regard, because Napoleon does not appear as a character, although he controls the action of the play. An official in the Hitler Youth, Helke (1905–67) adapted his 1937 novel *Der Prinz von Frankreich* to focus on the 1804 kidnapping, trial and execution of Louis de Bourbon-Enghien. According to historical accounts, this heir to the French throne was a passive figure, but Helke made him a patriot who rejects his royal heritage to serve the new France. However, he is betrayed by *Realpolitiker* Talleyrand, under orders from Napoleon. The innocent Enghien will be shot, but the firing squad baulks, fearing for its honour; Napoleon forces the execution, 'thereby betraying the ideals of the Revolution, the Republic and even more those of morality'.[75] Kleist's *Prinz Friedrich von Homburg* (1821) was supposedly a major influence upon Helke's purpose to demonstrate that 'power and glory are mutable, while the fatherland is eternal and immutable, as long as there are people who are ready to lay down their lives for its sake'.[76] Helke's Enghien becomes an unfortunate martyr to his French fatherland.

'Der alte Fritz' and metatheatrical plays

While Napoleon was the most popular dramatic character, the complicated and bloody saga of German history – or more accurately, the histories of hundreds of separate German states before the formation of the German empire – attracted the most literary attention, as Zillich had advised. Frederick the Great (*Friedrich der Große* or, affectionately, *Der alte Fritz*) was the second most frequently dramatized historical personality, and Hans Rehberg (1901–63) made the most stock out the Hohenzollern family. He was one of the most lauded of the younger generation, 'who have pledged themselves to the [Nazi] movement with body and soul, and who have been moved exclusively by its militant spirit to be writers'.[77] Rehberg's five 'Prussian dramas' (1934–37) culminate in *The Seven Years War* (*Der Siebenjährige Krieg*), which had a gala premiere at the Berlin Staatstheater on 7 April 1938, with Gründgens directing and playing Frederick. Rehberg focused on the difficult period from 1759 to 1762, from a Prussian military defeat to final victory over the Austrians, securing Frederick's claim to Silesia. The *Völkischer Beobachter* put this work ahead of the 'hurrah patriotism' and 'bloodless vacuity' of other Frederick plays by 'largely mediocre authors' before and after 1933.[78] Rehberg provided an assessment of Frederick that authenticated the history of Prussia and the Third Reich.

We first see the Prussian king sitting at a table covered with campaign maps, asking about the mythological Phaethon, who died driving the chariot of the sun to determine whether he was truly the son of Helios. Major Kleist provides the pertinent comparison for the audience:

> His destiny, your majesty, none the less changed the world. Peoples were destroyed, peoples were turned to ash, mountains burned. But the bold sceptic of his time must be acknowledged: he was the son of the god Helios! Certainly misfortunate, but he proved his divine ancestry to the whole world – Phaethon was a god. And if the words 'Not entirely successful, defeated by striving too high', appear on a tombstone, your majesty, then those who follow will know that one of Phaethon's race lies there, and that he changed his world.[79]

The play baldly suggests Frederick was another Phaethon, but one who learned to show moderation in his demands, to the greater glory of his country, and without self-destruction.

In the brief but telling scene that follows, Frederick meets with Ephraim, Moses Isaac and Daniel Itzig, members of the Jewish community, who are helping to fund his war. Frederick is surprised at their rich attire, especially when compared to his own dishevelled appearance ('I can't believe it. – War has turned my Jews into princes'). Rehberg presents these historic characters as clever usurers and war profiteers, who, with 'fast talk and the cunning of David', have collected Jewish gold in Eastern Europe. But their investors in Warsaw and Prague have demanded the equivalent of a ten per cent return, while Frederick urges six. Necessity forces the higher, exorbitant figure upon the king and if victory comes, it will be particularly costly (pp. 453–4). While this scene is a minor moment in the totality of the play, it reinforces the official anti-semitism of the Third Reich, which the real humanist Frederick would have found offensive.[80]

Wanderscheck would have preferred a more forceful Frederick to dominate the entire play. He decried Rehberg's artistic 'falsification' of history by presenting Frederick 'more as a passive hero than as an active dramatic figure'. The play was a series of mixed scenes, functioning as separate dramas reflecting the 'struggling and striving' king, who at the end is 'alone and facing the peace which finally comes; he is exhausted and larger than life at the same time' (Wanderscheck, pp. 154–5). The benign conqueror makes plans for the rebuilding of Silesia and, mindful of Phaethon, does not pursue other territorial aims against Austria. He tells the defeated General Laudon: 'Fate's sharp shears have clipped the wings, the wings. [...] (*Pointing to his heart.*) It's exhausted General, – it's exhausted. Seven years have exhausted me. [...] How old we have become, General' (pp. 499–500). The play, and Rehberg's series of Prussian dramas, end with this grandfatherly image of *Der alte Fritz* having brought glory to his country and peace to the land, at great personal cost.

With Göring and his wife (the former Staatstheater actress Emmy Sonnemann) in the royal box, the premiere earned that special response granted to the best productions – a moment of awed silence before stormy applause for the production as a whole and especially for Gründgens as director and star. An ironic context was added by the *Anschluß* – Hitler had moved into Austria less than a month before (12 March 1938), and a plebiscite followed on 10 April (the play was performed that evening as well). The audience knew only too well that the Austrian Hitler had realized the dream of *Großdeutschland* which Frederick had not attempted, even in his defeat of Austria.

The Witch of Passau (*Die Hexe von Passau*), by Richard Billinger (1893–1965), is set in and around the Austrian border town of Schärding – the district of Billinger's (and Hitler's) birth. It is a 'non-historical history', inventing a doomed peasant revolt against the prince–archbishop of Passau, and the burning of an actress, Valentine Ingold, charged with witchcraft. Both plots are more or less plausible within the demonstrably historic milieu, but as several critics observed, they are poorly related, and motivation is thin; while Herbert Ihering agreed with this common assessment, he had special praise for Billinger's ability to feature the regional dialect: 'Without this language, it would be only one of many peasant plays, and not the best. With this authentic, sensuous language, it is art.'[81]

The two plots are brought closer together when masses of peasants arrive to witness the hanging of the rebel leaders and the burning of the actress. Suggesting the inherent power of the *Volk*, Count von Klingenberg, the bishop's commandant, observes: '9000 people have travelled to Passau – there's never been so many peasants together! [...] If they ever gather under *one* flag – then there will be a thunderous storm! It'll be heard in Munich, in Vienna, everywhere.'[82] Because he now believes that the German *Volk*, united under one flag and one Führer, can reshape society according to its own preferences, Klingenberg abandons the cruel bishop. The play closes on the count bellowing out the peasant song of rebellion and taking command of a renewed revolt. Spectators might well imagine a subsequent *Volk* victory in this German/Austrian land, or, knowing the recurring outcome of such rebellions in the past, they must mourn another *Volk* defeat.

Beyond its reinforcement of *Volk*/peasant superiority, *The Witch of Passau* also features a religious Passion play within the play, in rustic rehearsal in a tavern (pp. 156–63) and impromptu performance on a platform stage in the town square (as ordered by Klingenberg, so that the churchmen may experience what they have condemned unseen (pp. 177–81)). Although the churchmen remain adamant, Klingenberg and the peasants are deeply moved by the message of forgiveness and by the naive sincerity of Valentine's portrayal of reformed sinner Mary Magdalene. Billinger assumed the real audience beyond the proscenium would share in the emotional response; this was certainly true of the 1935 Berlin premiere, which featured Käthe Dorsch as Valentine, playing the role of Magdalene. Complex layers of performance have traditionally contributed to the success of metatheatrical plays, whether they are based on fictional or real characters.

As in the case of conventional histories, metatheatrical histories have the full range of approach and style, from shallow Costume Play to ideological Historical Drama. They also allow or encourage reflective commentary about playwriting, production or the health of the arts in general. Dramas about theatre artists abounded in the Third Reich: the 1942 edition of the *Dramen-Lexikon* notes nine plays on Heinrich von Kleist and five on Shakespeare (including Karl Faehler's *Tragödie Kleist* (1933) and Ernst Geyer's Elizabethan comedy *At the Mermaid* (*Zur Meermaid*, 1937)). There are also plays about actors (Deburau and Talma, in Walther Marschall's *Shadows of the Emperor* (*Kaisers Schatten*, 1936)), actor-playwrights (Hans Kyser's *Molière will Perform* (*Molière spielt*, 1937)) and actress-managers (*Caroline Neuber*, alternatively *Die Neuberin*, 1934).[83]

Die Neuberin is one of the more intriguing works of the type. It was commissioned by the well-known actress Agnes Straub, whose career had been compared to that of Neuber (1697–1760), the first luminary of the German theatre.[84] Published and produced as the work of 'Christian Förster-Munk', the play was actually written by Eberhard Keindorff (1902–75) and Günther Weisenborn (1902–69), the latter marginalized by the Third Reich.[85] Because Straub had also earned the suspicion of Goebbels and Rosenberg, we might expect that this play about eighteenth-century stage reform, produced while the Nazis were reforming the German stage, might challenge the artistic policies of the Third Reich. That is, it might be a true 'Historical Drama', which looked to the aesthetic and political present and future, but which subverted Wanderscheck's National Socialist understanding of the term.

The play seems an innocuous costume drama, except for the alterations in theatre history and the powerful ending. After his sexual advances are spurned, this historically inaccurate Johann Christoph Gottsched seeks to destroy Neuber's integrity (and German theatre) by funnelling lewd farces and the weak plays of favourites onto the stage. As Neuber complains, 'You call them artists? They're miserable, tedious feather-scratchers! Don't compare dilet-tantes to real writers!' (p. 58). Gottsched finally uses the state to shut down Neuber's company. Soldiers strip costumes, props and furniture from her once vital theatre, and push back the supposed 'front' curtain to reveal the 'dark and empty, gaping auditorium' beyond (p. 102). The conception is brilliant and baroque: across a stripped (back)stage, the 1935 audience could contem-plate the void the German theatre had become under new dilettantes and arts dictators. Neuber stands in a naked space before an empty house and talks to an absent – and present – public, as a woman, as Neuber, as Straub, as a performer denied her stage, and as all actors, all theatre in an age of enforced decline. Defiance yields to anguish and, as she speaks, she puts out the stage lamps, one by one. She is in darkness as she bids farewell to the German stage (p. 106).[86] Die Neuberin seems a powerful protest against the loss of a rich theatre that met and challenged German intellectual and emotional needs. It was not too difficult to transfer the action to the 1930s, especially since changes in theatre history called attention to the Keindorff–Weisenborn–Straub collaboration.

The premiere produced ovations which brought Straub and the company repeatedly before the house. That response might be expected, for first nights are traditionally dominated by theatre people, who could best appreciate the metatheatrical format. Subsequent audiences and critics were less impressed: one reviewer thought the play should not have been written, since it departed from history in ways he could not understand.[87] Writing in the Völkischer Beobachter, Wolf Braumüller tried to put this play into a Nazi perspective: while the German theatre did rebound after this momentary 'defeat of Neuber', he complained her spirit was missing in '*the theatre of today*', which depended too much on 'foreign comedies'.[88] Like many history plays of the Third Reich, *Die Neuberin* altered truth for greater contemporary significance, but in this case, it was to challenge the prevailing (aesthetic) ideology. It was the only one to do so, in this sample. Doubtless there are others to be found in this expanding field of study.

Conclusion

If one can generalize about hundreds of plays by scores of dramatists, Nazi history plays taught and pleased, sometimes celebrated or mourned two thousand years of German history, or the lives of peoples related by blood, ideology or analogy. They often recorded some more or less well-known, remarkable life which had personal appeal to the playwright. In 1925, one year after joining the Italian Fascist Party, Luigi Pirandello called these kinds of author 'historical writers', who 'narrate a particular affair, lively or sad, simply for the pleasure of narrating it'.[89] Plays of this type probably comprise the majority of Third Reich historical drama, and include costume plays, non-historical history plays and Wanderscheck's simple 'History Plays'.

More significant to Pirandello are the products of a 'philosophical writer', someone comparable to Shaw's 'artist-philosopher' or Wanderscheck's 'Historical Dramatist'. These authors write for pleasure as well, but they also 'feel a more profound spiritual need on whose account they admit only figures, affairs, landscapes which have been soaked, so to speak, in a particular sense of life and acquire from it a universal value' (p. 244). Most of the plays in this sample – and those intended to appear in the Langenbeck–Braumüller vision of the 'Library of Dramatic Literature' – are of this sort. They form an ideological community reflecting the variety of National Socialist beliefs contained under the umbrella of Hitler's prejudices.

While these works cover a wide range of human history, there is a predictable ideological correctness which permeates the playwriting. Some of the more interesting plays radically realign 'the historical record', but most simply honour *Vaterland*, the *Volk* and the would-be Führer, with recurring sameness. There is pride in all things German, with repetitive rhetorical images and themes, but little art. When he was not dismissing new German drama as 'kitsch', Goebbels was promising the immanence and future glory of authentic Third Reich theatrical art, but his promises remained empty propaganda.

Style and content were similar in these histories, not only because the state tried to maintain a level of aesthetic and ideological purity through its trade unions and webs of control (albeit sporadically enforced), but also because the Third Reich had such a distinct and absolute view of the past and human progress, informed by the core principle of Nazi ideology: racial hierarchy – which may be expressed outright, or in such loaded terms as 'Volk' and 'blood'. At the apex of this theorized pyramid are those heroic Aryan/Nordic/Germanic peoples, as Walter Stang expressed it, 'to whom cultures from Iceland to India owe their origin'.[90] At its base are the 'culturally destructive' peoples from Africa or 'oriental' Jews, who seek, according to Nazi doxology, to reduce everyone to their own lowest common denominator through miscegenation, through Bolshevist art, and more broadly, through the anti-völkisch, grand phrases and intersecting ideologies of liberté, égalité, fraternité, of Christianity, capitalism, Communism and democracy.[91] Nazi ideologues felt history recorded or obscured the ongoing and shifting struggles between creative peoples seeking to ensure their continuation, and those who would demean and destroy superior races and their achievements.

While this world view suggests a dramatic, universal struggle of peoples, the ironic and recurring complaint about the history plays of Nazi Germany, even from their most sympathetic critics, is that they were constructed without essential conflict. And without conflict, there was no drama, according to the prevailing dramaturgic wisdom of the time; only rhetoric, bathos, zealotry or petulance. With rare exceptions, Nazi playwrights gave us flat historic tableaux or 'Gobelin tapestries'; we witness ancient massacres and humiliations, stabs in the back, fraud and other criminal acts against the Volk, without complexity or mediating considerations, or we see how some völkisch hero easily triumphs over adversity and shadow enemies.

If true drama requires real antagonists and motivated actions, Nazi historiography and most Third Reich historical playwrights were loath to create a balanced or complex struggle. Well-rounded or believable antagonists were incompatible with an absolute historical view based upon race, and so playwrights were satisfied with caricatures, cartoon figures or poster drama; audiences and critics were less impressed. Only a few of these new histories attained anything close to a prolonged stage life or popularity, and there were ongoing complaints that Nazi dramatists were mere 'dilettantes or profiteers' (Wilhelm von Schramm), producing 'routine scribblings' (Braumüller) or 'the most tedious kitsch' (Goebbels).[92] It was high praise when a critic wrote that Aichinger's Caroline von England avoided 'black and white treatment, pathos and words of thunder. The sublime is seldom loud, and a great thought is best served without noise; that is something the younger representatives of our writers' generation need to take note of.'[93] Unfortunately, Aichinger's 'great thought' – power is the realm of men and love that of women – was hardly great or sublime.

Perhaps Nazism was too assured of its prejudices, and too intrusive in the process of artistic production, to yield great drama, historical or otherwise. The noblest output of the period may be those rare and carefully veiled works, like *Caroline Neuber*, which found a way to question Nazi ideology without raising suspicions of subversion. One hopes more will be discovered. That truly memorable plays had not emerged was a grievous fault understood and mourned by many Nazi critics, but widely celebrated by exile and post-war historians, because it reinforced their assumptions that great art was impossible under such a regime.

Although significant new plays had not appeared, German audiences continued to experience remarkable performances. In Berlin and other German cities, old and new texts were animated by accomplished directors, actors, designers and musicians, many of whom, ironically, had trained or been featured in the 'decadent' or Jewish theatres of the 1920s. Hilpert, Krauss, Dorsch and Klöpfer staged and performed the new German plays, as best they could – they were professionals, after all, most of them committed more to their art than to shifting national politics. The drama of the Third Reich mixed into the standard, albeit reconfigured, repertoire. *Wittekind* and *Land in the Twilight*, with their radical views of the past and of the inevitability of national and racial rebirth, remained a minority drama in annual schedules of sophisticated or shallow comedies, together with the likes of Goethe's *Faust*, Shaw's *Saint Joan* and Shakespeare's *Hamlet*. All were performed with commitment, style and substance, fully in line with the traditions of twentieth-century German stage art.

Appendix:
Performance data of major Third Reich history plays

Premiere and significant production(s). The number of performances, during the first season, is indicated in parentheses.

Aichinger, Gerhard, *Jewel Fetched from the Silver Sea (Kleinod in die Silbersee gefaßt)*, Munich Residenztheater, 26 September 1936 (14). Directed by Hans Schweikart, designed by Otto Reigbert, music by Robert Tants; Anne Kersten as Caroline.

Bochum 16 June 1937, as part of Fourth National Theatre Festival (4). Directed by Saladin Schmitt, designed by Harry Mänz; Heidi Kuhlmann as Caroline.

Bacmeister, Ernst, *Emperor Constantine's Baptism (Kaiser Konstantins Taufe)*, Stuttgart Kleines Haus, 28 May 1937 (7). Directed by Heinz Haufe, designed by Felix Cziossek; Walter Richter as Constantine and Rudolf Fernau as Sopater.

Billinger, Richard, *The Witch of Passau* (*Die Hexe von Passau*), Augsburg (2) and Regensburg (4), 12 November 1935.
    Berlin Deutsches Theater, 13 November 1935 (25). Directed by Heinz Hilpert, designed by Ernst Schütte, music by Hans Steinkopf; Käthe Dorsch as Valentine, Siegfried Breuer as Klingenberg.

Blunck, Hans Friedrich, *Jakob Leisler (Fight for New York)* (*Jakob Leisler* [*Kampf um New York*]), Saarbrücken, 3 April 1938 (6).
    Berlin Volksbühne Theatre on Horst-Wessel-Platz, 27 January 1939 (34). Directed by Heinz Kenter, designed by Cesar Klein, music by Kurt Heuser; Carl Kuhlmann as Leisler.
    Land in the Twilight (*Land in der Dämmerung*), Berlin Staatliches Schauspielhaus, 13 April 1934 (6). Directed by Jürgen Fehling, designed by Caspar Neher; Friedrich Kayßler as Pining, Walter Franck as Grettir.

Cremers, Paul Joseph, *Richelieu, Cardinal-Prince of France* (*Richelieu, Kardinalherzog von Frankreich*), Bochum, 23 November 1934 (4). Directed by Saladin Schmitt.
    Munich Residenztheater, 26 August 1938 (24). Directed by Arnulf Schröder, designed by Kurt Gutzeit, music by Robert Tants; Hellmuth Renar as Richelieu.

Förster-Munk, Eberhard (Eberhard Keindorff and Günther Weisenborn) *Caroline Neuber/Die Neuberin*, Berlin Deutsches Künstlertheater, 22 May 1935 (31). Directed by Wolfgang Liebeneiner, designed by Hellmuth Käutner; Agnes Straub as Caroline.

Gilbricht, Walter, *Letizia*, Berlin Deutsches Theater, 29 April 1938 (14). Directed by Heinz Hilpert, designed by Ernst Schütte; Hedwig Bleibtreu as Letizia.
    Marie Charlotte Corday, Wuppertal, 12 November 1936 (5). Directed by Günther Stark, designed by Cajo Kühnly; Dorothea Constanz as Corday, Arthur Mentz as Marat.
    Berlin Deutsches Theater, 13 November 1936 (19). Directed by Ernst Karchow, designed by Willi Schmidt; Angela Salloker as Corday, Herbert Prigann as Marat.

Helke, Fritz, *The Duke of Enghien* (*Der Herzog von Enghien*), Dresden, 12 March 1938 (11). Directed by Karl Hans Böhm, designed by Adolf Mahnke; Werner Hessenland as Enghien, Paul Hoffmann as Talleyrand.

Hinrichs, August, *The Stedingers* (*Die Stedinger*), Altenesch, 27 May 1934 (10). Directed by Gustav Rudolf Sellner; Iwo Braak as Heiko.

Jelusich, Mirko, *Cromwell*, Bochum, 5 May 1934 (8). Directed by Saladin Schmitt, designed by Johannes Schröder; Willy Busch as Cromwell.
  Berlin, Youth Association of the NS-Kulturgemeinde in the Deutsches Künstlertheater, 7 December 1934 (7). Directed by Jürgen von Alten, designed by Stefan Welke; Herbert Dirmoser as Cromwell.

Johst, Hanns, *Thomas Paine*, 30 March 1927:
  Baden-Baden Städtisches Theater (5)
  Bremen Stadttheater (4)
  Cologne Schauspielhaus (10)
  Danzig Stadttheater (5)
  Düsseldorf Kleines Haus (12)
  Hanover Schauspielhaus (6)
  Karlsruhe Landestheater (5)
  Lübeck Stadttheater (1).
  Berlin Staatliches Schauspielhaus, 16 November 1935 (25). Directed by Jürgen Fehling, designed by Traugott Müller; Lothar Müthel as Paine.

Kiß, Edmund, *Wittekind*, Hagen, 24 January 1935 (25). Directed by Horst Hoffmann, designed by Hans Gaßner; Walter Segler as Wittekind and Kurt Wilcke as Isidorus.

Kolbenheyer, Erwin Guido, *Gregor und Heinrich*, 18 October 1934:
  Dresden Schauspielhaus (16)
  Erfurt Deutsches Volkstheater (4)
  Hanover Schauspielhaus (25)
  Karlsruhe Staatstheater (6)
  Königsberg Neues Schauspielhaus (12)
  Mannheim Nationaltheater (11).
  Frankfurt am Main Schauspielhaus, 11 December 1937 (15). Directed by Herbert Wahlen, designed by Caspar Neher, music by Bruno Hartl; Max Noack as Gregor and Hermann Schomberg as Heinrich.
  Munich Prinzregententheater, 15 September 1940 (19). Directed by Arnulf Schröder, designed by Otto Reigbert, music by Robert Tants; Alexander Golling as Gregor and Paul Wagner as Heinrich.
  Berlin Schiller-Theater, 20 November 1940 (40). Directed by Ernst Legal, designed by Paul Haferung, music by Leo Spies; Paul Wegener as Gregor and Horst Caspar as Heinrich.
  Vienna Burgtheater, 19 September 1942 (27). Directed by Adolf Rott,

designed by Fritz Judtmann, music by Franz Salmhofer; Ewald Balser as Gregor and Siegmar Schneider as Heinrich.

Langenbeck, Curt, *The Traitor* (*Der Hochverräter*), Erfurt Städtische Bühne (10) and Düsseldorf Stadtbühne (16), 15 March 1938.
    Berlin Staatliches Schauspielhaus, 28 October 1939 (26). Directed by Karlheinz Stroux, designed by Traugott Müller; Friedrich Kayßler as Leisler.

Lauckner, Rolf, *The Last Prussian* (*Der letzte Preuße*), Stuttgart Staatstheater, 30 January 1938 (6). Directed by Richard Dornseyff, designed by Felix Cziossek; Walter Richter as Herkus.

Möller, Eberhard Wolfgang, *Martin Luther, or The Hellish Journey* (*Martin Luther, oder Die höllische Reise*), Königsberg Neues Schauspielhaus, 19 November 1933 (12). Directed by Kurt Hoffmann, designed by Karl Wilhelm Vogel; Carlheinz Emmerich as Luther.
    Rothschild is the Victor at Waterloo (*Rothschild siegt bei Waterloo*), Aachen Stadttheater (5) and Weimar Deutsches Nationaltheater (4, directed by Hans Severus Ziegler), 5 October 1934.
    Munich Kammerspiele im Schauspielhaus, for Third National Theatre Festival, 13 May 1936 (5). Directed by Otto Falckenberg, designed by Eduard Sturm; Friedrich Domin as Rothschild.
    Berlin Rose-Theater, 25 November 1936 (32, performed with Möller's *Die graue Eminenz*). Directed by Paul Rose, designed by Harry Breuer; Georg August Koch as Rothschild.

Rehberg, Hans, *The Seven Years War* (*Der Siebenjährige Krieg*), Berlin Staatliches Schauspielhaus, 7 April 1938 (22). Directed by Gustaf Gründgens, designed by Traugott Müller, music by Mark Lothar; Gründgens as Friedrich.

Schwarz, Hans, *Rebell in England*, Berlin Staatliches Schauspielhaus, 30 May 1934 (10). Directed by Gustaf Gründgens, designed by Rochus Gliese; Paul Hartmann as Essex.

Wied, Liliane, *The Roving Queen* (*Die Wanderkönigin*), Berlin Agnes-Straub-Theater (Theater am Kurfürstendamm), 11 March 1936 (22). Directed by Ernst Stahl-Nachbaur, designed by Caspar Neher; Agnes Straub as Christine.

Notes

1 In Wegra, 'Uraufführung in Bochum: *Cromwell*, ein Schauspiel in 5 Aufzügen von Mirko Jelusich', *General-Anzeiger Krefeld*, clipping file, Schloß Wahn, Theaterwissenschaftliche Sammlung, University of Cologne (hereafter Wahn). The people who collected these reviews seldom provided the full bibliographical material, and in some cases, the newspaper issues no longer exist. These references are to materials in the Sammlung's author/play files. I wish to thank the librarians and staff of the Sammlung for their kind and professional assistance with this project.

2 While some playwrights who had major careers after 1933 were produced prior to 1927, most of these early plays are inappropriate or peripheral to rising German nationalism or to later Nazi aesthetic demands. For example, Eberhard Wolfgang Möller's debut came in 1923, at the Realgymnasium Mariendorff – a school production. His true professional career only began in 1928. For extreme nationalist playwrights of the Weimar Republic, see the introduction to the present volume (pp. 7–8). *Thomas Paine* is privileged in discussions of Third Reich theatre history, not only because of its content, but also by its early and multiple stage production.

3 Hermann Wanderscheck, *Deutsche Dramatik der Gegenwart* (Berlin: Bong, 1938), p. 93. Wilhelm Westecker had come to the same conclusion in his newspaper review of the 1935 Berlin production; 'Geschichtliches Gleichnis: Hanns Johst: *Thomas Paine* im Staatlichen Schauspielhaus', Wahn.

4 As Robert Pois has suggested, the Nazi 'revolution' was in favour of belief systems already held by large portions of the middle class, allowing popular revolutionary fervour without the need to change essential opinions and prejudices. See his article 'The National Socialist *Volksgemeinschaft* Fantasy and the Drama of National Rebirth', in *Theatre in the Third Reich, the Prewar Years: Essays on Theatre in Nazi Germany*, ed. by Glen W. Gadberry, Contributions to the Study of World History, 49 (Westport, CT: Greenwood Press, 1995), pp. 17–31 (p. 18). As the third chapter in his assessment of Hitler scholarship, John Lukacs takes up this issue anew, arguing for an overwhelmingly modern and revolutionary component in Hitler's ideology, and subsequently in Nazi Germany; Lukacs, 'Reactionary and/or Revolutionary?', *The Hitler of History* (New York: Alfred A. Knopf, 1997), pp. 76–112.

5 Rainer Schlösser, 'Vom kommenden Volksschauspiel: der Reichsdramaturg über Grundlagen und Umrisse des Dramas im neuen Staat', *Völkischer Beobachter*, 26 January 1934 (subsequent references to this important newspaper are from the Berlin edition). The speech was published as the '*Thingspiel*' chapter of Schlösser's *Das Volk und seine Bühne: Bemerkungen zum Aufbau des deutschen Theaters* (Berlin: Langen/Müller, 1935), pp. 40–64.

6 'Entschließung vom 21.8.1933', in Joseph Wulf, *Theater und Film im Dritten Reich: eine Dokumentation* (Gütersloh: Sigbert Mohn, 1964), p. 39. See also Otto Laubinger, 'Die Aufgaben der Reichsdramaturgen', in Wulf, *Theater* p. 40.

7 *Remarques sur Sophonisbe* (1633), quoted in Marvin Carlson, *Theories of the Theatre: A Historical and Critical Survey, from the Greeks to the Present* (Ithaca, NY: Cornell University Press, 1984), p. 104.

8 L. Schlotermann, 'Das Wagnis der "Dritten Bühne": zur Aufführung von Kolben-

heyers Schauspiel *Gregor und Heinrich*', *Berliner Börsen-Zeitung*, 21 December 1940. The play is discussed below (pp. 111–12).

9 Zillich's 'Die deutsche Dichtung und die Welt der Geschichte' was subsequently published in *Das Innere Reich*, 5, no. 10 (January 1939), 1179–96. Subsequent references to Wanderscheck and Zillich will appear in the text.

10 Production figures for all history plays, from Shakespeare to Johst, would be another way to gauge the importance of such works in this period. A full production database would be invaluable for this line of inquiry; a first attempt at such a database is found at the Institut für Theaterwissenschaft, Free University of Berlin.

11 Reviews became more supportive after Joseph Goebbels decreed stage criticism become positive reviewing (27 November 1936). Reviews remain important, however, sometimes to suggest alterations of text: while it frustrates historians, German theatre has the healthy tradition of revising texts for performance. In this period, directors and Dramaturgs typically cut plays to focus the dramatic action; they seldom shuffled scenes or added new material, in the manner of Piscator, Meyerhold or postmodern *auteur* directors (i.e. theatre artists who rewrite existing playtexts – typically those in the public domain – to give expression to their own creative visions).

12 Data are compiled from the monthly *Die neue Literatur*; Frels's appraisals typically appear in the June issue. His categories are not entirely clear: works which he could not identify by title or other information are lumped into an 'Unknown' category. We cannot know which plays were counted this way, and in many cases, specific information about the plays no longer exists. His categories are also idiosyncratic: he will count a Prometheus play among 'Histories', but would put a play about Herod into 'biblical'. Whenever possible, his figures have been adjusted; for example, he will count an unperformed play when it is published, but then count it a second time when it is performed. Such plays are counted only once in these figures. Uwe-Karsten Ketelsen uses the statistics of Frels, but without making these adjustments; Ketelsen, *Heroisches Theater: Untersuchungen zur Dramentheorie des Dritten Reichs*, Literatur und Wirklichkeit, 2 (Bonn: Bouvier, 1968), pp. 66–7.

13 See, for example, *Exil und innere Emigration*, ed. by Reinhold Grimm and Jost Hermand (Frankfurt am Main: Athenäum, 1972).

14 Wanderscheck, p. 15. He also cites the critic Hans Knudsen on the same issue (p. 206).

15 'Reichsminister Dr Goebbels auf der Jahreskundgebung der Reichstheaterkammer: Rechenschaft über das deutsche Theaterwesen', *Völkischer Beobachter*, 13 May 1936.

16 Wanderscheck, p. 15. He emphasized the last three words, to stress the importance of re-evaluating standard historical sources. The published version of Möller's speech did not treat those words differently; Möller, *Rede in Lauchstädt* (Merseburg: Landeshauptmann der Provinz Sachsen, 1938), p. 30. The speech was delivered on the occasion of the Theatre Chamber meeting during the first 'Regional Cultural Week' of the Halle-Merseburg district, 2 March 1938. Möller was credited by Schlösser for contributing to the ideas found in his 1934 address: 'In many conversations I had with individual writers, and particularly often with Eberhard Wolfgang Möller, probably the most talented among younger

dramatists, we came again and again to the founding perception [for the *Thing-spiel*]'; 'Vom kommenden Volksschauspiel', pp. 53–4.

17 For example, see Hans Knudsen, 'Der Jude auf dem deutschen Theater', *Völki-scher Beobachter*, 21 August 1940, in Wulf, *Theater* p. 235; '"Deutsches Theater" – von ehedem: das Theater der Piscator, Jessner, Reinhardt und Barnay', *Deutsche Allgemeine Zeitung* (Reichsausgabe), 28 August 1936.

18 Johst, *Thomas Paine* (Munich: Albert Langen, 1927), pp. 119–20.

19 'Zu Thomas Paine', preface to *Thomas Paine*, p. 5. In part, it reads 'Thomas Paine – leader and danger [...] passion, yearning, humility and courage, disappears as individual fate, to become melody'. Most plays at this time were performed with music, often specially composed for the premiere. Since many scores have not survived, a significant indicator of the stage experience has been lost. The 1936 Berlin production featured music by Mark Lothar, Staatstheater composer and conductor.

20 'Rede des Reichspropagandaministers Dr Goebbels vor den deutschen Theater-leitern im Hotel "Kaiserhof" zu Berlin über "Die Aufgaben des deutschen Theaters" vom 8. Mai 1933', in *Die Nationalsozialistische Revolution 1933*, ed. by Axel Friedrichs, Dokuments der deutschen Politik, 1, 3rd edn (Berlin: Junker und Dünnhaupt, 1938), pp. 286–300 (p. 296); Trotha, 'Heroische Sachlichkeit: Ge-danken über einen neuen Stil', *Völkischer Beobachter*, 14 March 1934.

21 'Historische Daten zu Thomas Paine', in *Paine*, p. 121. The chronology is mislead-ing and contradicts the play; the action has Paine in prison for seventeen years, while the chronology has ten. Similarly, Johst has Paine commit suicide, while the chronology suggests 'Paine's end is unknown' (in fact, he succumbed to illness and alcohol in 1809).

22 'Zum Jahrestag der Reichskulturkammer: Hanns Johsts *Thomas Paine*: Festvor-stellung im Staatlichen Schauspielhaus', 18 November 1935; Wahn.

23 'Hanns Johst: *Thomas Paine*: Festvorstellung anläßlich der Jahrestagung der Reichskulturkammer', *Völkischer Beobachter*, 18 November 1935.

24 Although Schwarz's date of death has come to light, attempts to discover the dates of death of several other playwrights in this chapter have been unsuccessful. Some certainly died in the Second World War, either on the front or in the bombing of cities.

25 See the accompanying appendix of production information (pp. 124–7), which suggests the initial popular response to these plays. Data derive from the monthly *Deutscher Spielplan* – a valuable listing of production schedules, dependent upon reports from the theatres themselves. Unfortunately, it is not without error.

26 Wegra, 'Uraufführung in Bochum', quoting Jelusich's essay on his own work which was printed in the programme notes.

27 G. M. Vonau, 'Im Kasseler Staatstheater: Mirko Jelusich: *Cromwell*', *Kasseler Neueste Nachrichten*, Wahn.

28 Mirko Jelusich, *Cromwell* (Vienna: F. G. Speidel, 1934), p. 176.

29 Dietrich Eckart, *Der Bolshewismus von Moses bis Lenin: Zwiegespräch zwischen Adolf Hitler und mir* (Munich: Hoheneichen, 1924), p. 14.

30 '*Cromwell*: Jugendgruppe der NS-Kulturgemeinde im Deutschen Künstlertheater', Wahn. In a speech to leading playwrights and theatre people at his national theatre festival, Goebbels called the new plays the 'most tedious kitsch' (*ödester Kitsch*). The speech, in its entirety, was published twice in the *Völkischer Beobachter*: 'Das

deutsche Theater im neuen Reich', 1 June 1934; 2 June 1934. For a more complete account of Goebbels's remarks in context, see Glen Gadberry, 'The First National Socialist Theatre Festival – Dresden 1934', in *Theatre in the Third Reich*, ed. by Gadberry, pp. 121–39.

31 Braumüller, '*Cromwell*: Erstaufführung der Jugendgruppe der NS-Kulturgemeinde im deutschen Künstlertheater', *Völkischer Beobachter*, 9–10 December 1934.

32 The title is from Shakespeare's *Richard II*, 'This precious stone set in the silver sea' (II. 1.46), in the August von Schlegel translation.

33 'Gerhard Aichingers *Kleinod in die Silbersee gefaßt* in Bochum', Wahn. Braumüller's review did not appear in the *Völkischer Beobachter*, as did others cited in this chapter. The review which did appear there is uncommonly brief: Friedrich W. Herzog, 'Reichstheaterfestwoche 1937: Glanzvolle Festvorstellung in Bochum: *Kleinod in die Silbersee gefaßt* von Gerhard Aichinger', *Völkischer Beobachter*, 18 June 1937.

34 W. K., 'Agnes Straub als Christine: Uraufführung des Iambenstücks *Die Wanderkönigin* von Liliane Wied', *12 Uhr Blatt* (Berlin); Agnes Straub Archive, Gries, Austria.

35 Erwin H. Rainalter, '*Die Wanderkönigin: Christine von Schweden*: Uraufführung im Agnes-Straub-Theater', *Völkischer Beobachter*, 14 March 1936.

36 *Knaurs Lexikon, A–Z* (Berlin: Knaur, 1939), p. 1194.

37 Walter Stang, 'Hans Friedrich Blunck als Dramatiker: *Land in der Dämmerung*: Berliner Erstaufführung im Staatlichen Schauspielhaus', *Völkischer Beobachter*, 17 April 1934. The play was not published separately, and the stage text appears not to have survived.

38 Bernhard Diebold, '*Land in der Dämmerung*: Uraufführung von Hans Friedrich Bluncks dreiaktigem Schauspiel im Staatlichen Schauspielhaus am Gendarmenmarkt', Wahn; see also Hans Flemming, 'Blunck: *Land in der Dämmerung*/Staatstheater', Wahn.

39 For example, see Rosenberg, *Der Mythus des 20. Jahrhunderts: eine Wertung der seelisch-geistigen Gestaltenkämpfe unserer Zeit*, 87–90th edn (Munich: Hoheneichen, 1935), pp. 155–68, which details the coming of 'the idea of Christian love into the Germanic world', with 'nine million dead heretics on this road of love'.

40 Fehling's *Richard III*, for example (Staatstheater, 2 March 1937), with its overt comparisons to the Third Reich, by some accounts, nearly cost Fehling his life. See William Grange, 'Ordained Hands on the Altar of Art: Gründgens, Hilpert, and Fehling in Berlin', in *Theatre in the Third Reich*, ed. by Gadberry, pp. 75–89 (pp. 85–7). For a different reading, see Chapter 5 of the present volume (pp. 247–9).

41 Blunck, quoted in Fritz Johannes, 'London oder Neuyork: *Jakob Leisler* – Blunck-Uraufführung im Stadttheater Saarbrücken', *Völkischer Beobachter*, 7 April 1938. This was the conclusion Christian Jenssen also came to in his comparative review in *Die neue Literatur*, 39, no. 5 (May 1938), 260. See also Blunck, 'Kampf um Neuyork: die Geschichte von Jakob Leislers Aufruhr', *Völkischer Beobachter*, 24 January 1939. Blunck subsequently reworked the material into a novel, *Kampf um New York, die Geschichte des Pfälzers Jakob Leisler* (Flensburg: Wolff, 1951).

42 Curt Langenbeck, *Der Hochverräter*, in *Zeit und Theater*, ed. by Günther Rühle, 6 vols (Frankfurt am Main: Ullstein/Propyläen, 1980), V: *Diktatur und Exil*, pp. 379–438 (p. 381).

43 Möller, quoted in F. G. Hermann, 'Möllers Lutherspiel wird geprobt: zur heutigen Uraufführung des Werkes im Neuen Schauspielhaus', *Ostpreußische Zeitung* (Königsberg); H. G., 'Aus dem Königsberger Theaterleben: Uraufführung eines Luther-Dramas'; both undated cuttings, Wahn.

44 epb [*sic*], 'Eberhard Wolfang Möller: *Martin Luther oder die höllische Reise*: Uraufführung im Königsberger Schauspielhaus', *Königsberger Hartungsche Zeitung*, Wahn.

45 l. [*sic*], 'Königsberger Neues Schauspielhaus: *Martin Luther* oder *Die höllische Reise*: erfolgreiche Uraufführung des Schauspiels von Eberhard Wolfgang Möller', *Völkischer Beobachter*, 24 November 1933.

46 See, for example, Karl Irmler's festival play *Luther's Fight and Victory* (*Luthers Kampf und Sieg*), premiered in Zwickau, 10 November 1933 and also published (Dortmund: H. Selzer, 1933); Josef Buchhorn's *The Changeover in Worms* (*Wende in Worms*) (Cottbus: Albert Heine, 1937); or Arthur M. Miller's *Knight, Death and Devil* (*Ritter, Tod und Teufel*, 1937), a 'musical tragedy' only partially focused on Luther; the stage manuscript was apparently available through Heinrich Buchner in Munich.

47 Möller writes in his 'Forward' that the story is 'very famous and very disputed', but whether true or not, it 'belongs to the undying anecdotes of world history', to be treated by 'writers and not historians'; *Rothschild siegt bei Waterloo* (Berlin: Langen/Müller, 1934), p. 5. One critic demonstrated the anecdote was false, from a number of different sources. For example, there was no sharp fluctuation in the English stock market after Waterloo; O. G., 'Nathan Rothschilds "Sieg" bei Waterloo', hand-dated 17 January 1937, Wahn.

48 Forward, p. 6; personal interview with Möller in Bietigheim, Germany, 13–14 June 1970.

49 Quoted in A. W., 'Falckenberg inszeniert *Rothschild siegt bei Waterloo*: die Kammerspiele in der Reichstheaterfestwoche', Wahn.

50 J. M. Wehner, '*Rothschild siegt bei Waterloo*: auf der Kammerspiele in der Reichstheaterfestwoche', *Münchner Neueste Nachrichten*, Wahn.

51 Hans Gstettner, 'Reichstheaterfestwoche in München: *Rothschild siegt bei Waterloo*: erfolgreiche Aufführung des Schauspiels von Wolfgang Eberhard Möller [*sic*]', *Völkischer Beobachter*, 15 May 1936.

52 Wehner, '*Rothschild*'.

53 K. Buchmann, 'Rolf Lauckners *Der letzte Preuße*: erfolgreiche Uraufführung am Württembergischen Staatstheater', *Völkischer Beobachter*, 2 February 1938. Buchmann, and other 'reviewers', were beginning to criticize the premieres they witnessed, despite the November 1936 directives of Goebbels against art and theatre criticism.

54 August Hinrichs, *Die Stedinger: Spiel vom Untergang eines Volkes* (Oldenburg: Rudolf Schwartz, 1935), p. 27.

55 See Glen Gadberry, '*The Stedingers*: Nazi Festival Drama of the Destruction of a People', *Theatre History Studies*, 10 (1990), 105–26. The play is a fine example of the popular literature of 'blood and soil' (*Blut und Boden*, or *Blubo*), and of Rosenberg's open-air theatre competitor to the *Thing* plays of Goebbels; see William Niven's assessment of the *Thing* play genre in Chapter 1 of the present book.

56 Köppen, 'Kolbenheyer: *Gregor und Heinrich*: Eindrücke von der Uraufführung in Dresden', Wahn; Kurt Arnold Findeisen, 'Kolbenheyers *Gregor und Heinrich*:

Uraufführung im Staatlichen Schauspielhaus Dresden', *Völkischer Beobachter*, 21–22 October 1934.

57 '*Gregor und Heinrich*/Kolbenheyer-Uraufführung in Hannover', *Berliner Tageblatt*, Wahn.

58 Kolbenheyer, *Gregor und Heinrich*, in *Zeit und Theater*, ed. by Rühle, V, pp. 259–334 (p. 334).

59 L. Schlotermann, 'Das Wagnis der "Dritten Bühne"'.

60 Kiß, *Wittekind* (Leipzig: Koehler & Amelang, 1935), pp. 58–9. This was one of four Wittekind plays which premiered that 1934–35 season; the others were by Friedrich Forster, Berthold von Biedermann and Heinrich Rogge.

61 Only one reviewer noted this substitution, v. Bo. [von Bories], 'Eine seltsame Ehrenrettung Wittekinds: zur Uraufführung des Schauspiels *Wittekind* von Edmund Kiß in Hagen', *National-Zeitung* (Essen), 26 January 1935. He may have done so for several other reasons, of course, including mishearing the line in the first place, or applying his own sense of decorum.

62 See 'Erneuter Protest gegen das Wittekind-Drama', *Germania* (Berlin), 1 February 1935; and Wulf, *Theater*, pp. 176–7.

63 Kiß, *Wittekind der Große* (Landsberg/Warthe: Max Bölkow, 1935).

64 Ernst Bacmeister, *Kaiser Konstantins Taufe: Religionstragödie* (Berlin: Langen/Müller, 1937), p. 15. Uwe-Karsten Ketelsen describes the play, with a lengthy section of dialogue, in *Von heroischem Sein und völkischem Tod: zur Dramatik des Dritten Reiches*, Abhandlungen zur Kunst-, Musik- und Literaturwissenschaft, 96 (Bonn: Bouvier, 1970), pp. 67–70. He follows the same format for several of the plays already treated in this chapter: *Rothschild* (pp. 104–9), *Thomas Paine* (pp. 136–8), *Der letzte Preuße* (pp. 255–7), *Jakob Leisler* (pp. 282–5), *Gregor und Heinrich* (pp. 285–8) and *Der Hochverräter* (pp. 311–13). His other examples include other historical works and *Thing* plays.

65 Conversion to Judaism is specifically mentioned (p. 14) and represents an ideological error on Bacmeister's part. The Nazis typically categorized Jews as a separate race, not as diverse believers in a single faith. The objectionable line might well have been cut from the premiere and subsequent productions.

66 Wilmont Haake, 'Bacmeisters *Kaiser Konstantin*: Uraufführung in Stuttgart', Wahn.

67 Braumüller, 'Das Drama im Buch: Aufruf zu einer neuen Phalanx der Lesenden', in Bacmeister, pp. viii–xiv (p. xiii). See also Curt Langenbeck, 'Sein und Pflicht einer neuen Bibliothek zeitgenössischer Dramen', pp. ii–vii. (Although the Roman numerals suggest otherwise, the essays appear at the end of the volume.)

68 Bk., 'Bochum: *Richelieu* von Paul Joseph Cremers', Wahn.

69 Peter Trumm, '*Richelieu, Kardinalherzog von Frankreich*, erstaufgeführt im Residenztheater', *Münchner Neueste Nachrichten*, Wahn.

70 Walter Gilbricht, *Marie Charlotte Corday* (Berlin: Arcadia, 1935), p. 19.

71 H. G., '*Marie Charlotte Corday*: Erstaufführung im Deutschen Theater', Wahn.

72 Wilhelm Westecker, 'Eine Frau tritt der französischen Revolution entgegen: *Marie Charlotte Corday* im Deutschen Theater', Wahn. For the ambiguous character of Joan of Arc in the Third Reich, see Chapter 5 of the present volume (pp. 237–9).

73 Westecker, 'Eine Frau'; Job Zimmermann, 'Gilbrichts *Corday* – Drama bei Hilpert', *Völkischer Beobachter*, 15 November 1936.

74 Respectively, B. E. Werner, 'Familie Bonaparte: *Letizia* – Deutsches Theater'; Hubert Maushagen, 'Deutsches Theater: *Letizia*'; both Wahn.

75 W. Grohmann, 'Uraufführung im Reich: Fritz Holke [*sic*]: *Der Herzog von Enghien*', Wahn.

76 Helke, quoted in Döring-Manteuffel, 'Der Dichter Fritz Helke', Wahn.

77 'Beobachtet-Festgehalten', *Die Bühne*, 1 March 1936, p. 129, cited in Wulf, *Theater*, p. 179.

78 Günther Stöve, 'Hans-Rehberg-Uraufführung: preußisches Menschentum: *Der Siebenjährige Krieg* im Staatlichen Schauspielhaus Berlin', *Völkischer Beobachter*, 9 April 1938.

79 Hans Rehberg, *Der Siebenjährige Krieg*, in *Zeit und Theater*, ed. by Rühle, VI: *Diktatur und Exil*, pp. 439–500 (p. 452).

80 The Jews' names appear in the text, but not in the cast of characters; the general category 'Jews' comes after 'officers, soldiers, actors, musicians, masqueraders'. Dietrich Eckart used those historical figures to demonstrate how even 'the most just Friedrich' and his new coinage were compromised by Jewish influence: 'Frederick on the outside, Ephraim on the inside' (Eckart, *Der Boshewismus von Moses bis Lenin*, pp. 21–2).

81 Respectively, Erwin H. Rainalter, 'Billingers *Hexe von Passau*: Erstaufführung im Deutschen Theater', *Völkischer Beobachter*, 15 November 1935; Ihering, '*Die Hexe von Passau*/Uraufführung im Deutschen Theater', Wahn. The Berlin critic Otto Ernst Hesse complained that Billinger set his unhistorical play ten years after the last documented witch-burning in Germany (1775) and objected to the incongruous medieval costumes and props; '*Die Hexe von Passau*: der neue Billinger im Deutschen Theater', Wahn. For the opera based on Billinger's text see Chapter 3 of the present volume (pp. 153–4).

82 Richard Billinger, *Die Hexe von Passau*, in *Gesammelte Werke*, 12 vols (Graz: Stiasny, 1956–60), IX (1960), pp. 129–214 (p. 202).

83 See the entries in Friedrich Ernst Schulz, *Dramen-Lexikon* (Berlin: Drei Masken, 1942).

84 See, for example, Herbert Mylo's 'Agnes Straub, die *Neuberin* unserer Zeit erzählt', *Koralle*, 43 (27 October 1935), 1362–3. For the text of the play, see Christian Förster-Munk, *Caroline Neuber* (Berlin: Fischer, 1934).

85 Most of Weisenborn's plays, like *U-Boot S4* (1928), and novels (*Barbaren*, 1931) were banned, and he suffered a writing prohibition. Subsequently active in the resistance, he was arrested and sentenced to death in 1942, but was freed by the Allies. Neither Weisenborn nor Keindorff appear in Wanderscheck's listing of German playwrights, or in Franz Lennartz's *Die Dichter unserer Zeit*, 3rd edn (Stuttgart: Alfred Kröner, 1940), a sure sign of their marginal status. Straub had also run into difficulties with the Nazis, for her 'decadent' Weimar productions (such as Hans Henny Jahnn's *Schwarze Medea* in 1926) and for her relationship with Jewish actor/director Leo Reuß; see Bogusław Drewniak, *Das Theater im NS-Staat: Szenarium deutscher Zeitgeschichte, 1933–1945* (Düsseldorf: Droste, 1983), p. 148.

86 The play closes on rumours that Gottsched's Harlequin has been cast out of Hamburg and Königsberg, that Neuber's lead actor, Johann Schönemann, is trying to re-establish a legitimate stage, and that everywhere there are signs that 'the theatres awake' (p. 106). Straub, the playwrights and the privileged audience

certainly had the same hopes for German theatre under the Nazi art dictatorship with its 'miserable, tedious feather-scratchers'.

87 M., 'Agnes Straub als *Neuberin* im Deutschen Künstlertheater', *Kreuz-Zeitung* (Berlin), 28 May 1935.

88 'Uraufführung in den Deutschen Künstlertheater: Eberhard Förster-Munk: *Die Neuberin*', *Völkischer Beobachter*, 28 May 1935.

89 Luigi Pirandello, preface to *Six Characters in Search of an Author*, trans. by Eric Bentley, in *Drama in the Modern World: Plays and Essays*, ed. by Samuel A. Weiss (Lexington, MA: Heath, 1964), pp. 243–50 (p. 243).

90 Stang, 'Hans Friedrich Blunck als Dramatiker'. This theory of pervasive Aryan culture is addressed in Léon Poliakov, *The Aryan Myth: A History of Racist and Nationalist Ideas in Europe*, trans. by Edmund Howard (New York: Meridian, 1977).

91 In *Mein Kampf*, Hitler describes graphically how Aryan womanhood is under perpetual threat from 'the black-haired Jewish youth', with 'satanic joy in his face', or from African troops during the Rhine/Ruhr occupation after the First World War, brought there by their French-Jewish overlords; *Mein Kampf*, trans. by Ralph Manheim (London: Pimlico, 1992), p. 295. See also Rosenberg, *Mythus* (p. 252) on the binaries of Judaeo-Catholic stasis versus Nordic-western dynamism, and (p. 321) on the unholy partnerships of Judaeo-Christian internationalism, Marxist 'Internationale' and democratic 'humanity'. His work is also replete with references to miscegenation.

92 Schramm, 'Praktische Dramaturgie: Erfahrungen im Bühnenvertrieb', *Deutsche Allgemeine Zeitung* (Berlin, Reichsausgabe), 27 January 1935; Braumüller 'Weltanschauung und Theater: Rückschau auf das deutsche Theater 1934/35', *Völkischer Beobachter*, 18 June 1935; Goebbels, 'Das deutsche Theater im neuen Reich'.

93 Werner Fiedler, 'Reichs-Theater-Festwoche: in der "Goldgräberstadt": Aichinger: *Kleinod in die Silbersee gefaßt*', *Wahn*.

3

Opera in the Nazi period

ERIK LEVI

The Third Reich's omnipresent system of artistic censorship has remained strangely elusive to the historian. Far from the stereotype of the coldly efficient, centralized, totalitarian model of control, it was a fluid and amorphous agglomeration of official proscriptions, unofficial pressures, and self-imposed constraints. Improvised amid the early power struggles of the Nazi era rather than erected from a master plan, its structures were asymmetrical, ambiguous, and often contradictory.[1]

Few areas of artistic activity better illustrate the assertion that cultural policy in the Third Reich was beset with ambiguities and contradictions than the development of opera between 1933 and 1945. Of particular concern to cultural ideologues, musicologists and critics was the establishment of an operatic repertoire that fully mirrored the political characteristics of the Nazi era. Although this issue occasioned much debate in various music journals, it was never fully resolved and the notion of a so-called 'opera crisis' persisted throughout the period.[2] In many respects, musicologists of the time had little idea as to what constituted the ideal Nazi opera, and much of their writing on this subject clutches at vague definitions. All too often, one senses that critics were somewhat helpless, placing their trust upon the rather unpredictable reception of audiences in determining whether an opera was, or was not, ideologically acceptable. In many cases, attempts to boost the claims of a composer with supposedly impeccable Nazi political credentials misfired, while arguments that justified the success of a particular opera on purely ideological grounds appeared contrived and unconvincing.

Such evidence would surely lend credibility to the contention that not one palpably Nazi opera was written during the Third Reich.[3] At the same time, an analysis of the contemporary repertoire performed at this time evinces certain features which fully accord with the ideological climate of the period: for example, a resurgent nationalism, a conservative/traditional choice of subject matter and a preoccupation with *völkisch* (national, of the people) themes. It is more questionable, however, as to whether these ingredients *per se* counteract the claim stated above. The problem lies not so much in the relevance or otherwise of certain chosen subject matters as in their musical treatment. In this respect, composers presented a much greater variety of stylistic approaches than one might have expected. While a few effected a retrogressive imitation of nineteenth-century musical styles, many others embraced aspects of modernism. Indeed, contrary to some of the propaganda of the period, the distinctions between the musical styles of opera composers during the Weimar Republic and those of the Nazi era were often blurred, many composers rejecting the structures of through-composed post-Wagnerian music-drama and preferring to retain the neo-classical number opera or neo-baroque oratorio conceptions that had been fashionable at the height of 1920s *Neue Sachlichkeit* (New Objectivity).

Although it is important to emphasize elements of continuity within twentieth-century German opera, certain aspects of Nazi operatic policy still remain unique. In attempting to stamp their own identity on the cultural environment, the Nazis found it necessary to pursue a programme of censorship on an unprecedented scale. Hand in hand with this process, the regime also encouraged a reappraisal and revival of repertoire of the past, frequently promoting composers of an unequivocal Aryan background, or libretti that could be interpreted in an anti-semitic light.

Censorship and control of operatic repertoire

To achieve their desired goal, Nazi censorship of operatic repertoire took place in two phases. Broadly speaking, these moved from organized public demonstrations to the enactment of legal measures. During the early months of 1933 the Nazis relied on the support of the Storm Troopers (SA/Sturmabteilung) and party agitators to disrupt performances of works considered to be tarnished by association with the Weimar Republic. Probably the most public demonstration of this process was manifested at performances of *Silverlake* (*Der Silbersee*), a play by the Expressionist writer Georg Kaiser with music by Kurt Weill, whose first performance took place simultaneously in three theatres at Leipzig, Erfurt and Magdeburg on 18 February, nearly three weeks after Hitler seized power. Although the premiere appears to have been an emphatic success, an ever-increasing crescendo of threats in the Nazi press, together with barracking from audiences who were sympathetic to the new regime, generated a campaign to withdraw the work. A community declaration from the local Nazi Party in Magdeburg, issued three days after the premiere, effectively sealed its demise:

With indignation and the sharpest of protests, the German public in Magdeburg objects to the degradation of art to the one-sided, un-German propaganda of Bolshevist theories that has taken hold in the Magdeburg Stadttheater. The performance of the play by Georg Kaiser and Kurt Weill is a slap in the face of the national population. [...] The public [...] therefore demands in the name of countless citizens [...] the immediate withdrawal of the play.[4]

While *Silverlake* managed to survive at least in Leipzig until 4 March, other theatres throughout Germany were soon capitulating to this sort of pressure and suppressed any potentially controversial repertoire planned for the latter part of the 1932–33 season. Amongst the most significant works sacrificed in this manner were Berthold Goldschmidt's *The Magnificent Cuckold* (*Der gewaltige Hahnrei*) (Berlin Städtische Oper), Franz Schreker's *Christophorous* (Freiburg), Manfred Gurlitt's *Nana* (Mannheim), Alexander von Zemlinsky's *The Chalk Circle* (*Der Kreidekreis*) (Berlin Staatsoper, Cologne and Frankfurt), Stravinsky's *Soldier's Tale* (*L'Histoire du Soldat*) (Bremerhaven), Milhaud's *The Abandonment of Ariadne* (*L'Abandon d'Ariane*) (Chemnitz) and Alban Berg's *Wozzeck* (Stettin and Mannheim).

Although this list appears to be quite substantial, containing music by some of the principal composers of the period, it needs to be placed in a wider context. One should remember that by the time the Nazis came to power, German opera houses had experienced several seasons of severe financial austerity. After the Wall Street Crash of 1929, local authorities could no longer afford to subsidize theatres to the levels experienced in the late 1920s. Opera personnel were reduced and, in an attempt to secure stable box-office returns, theatres offered a far more cautious diet of repertoire than before.

As an illustration of this development, it is worth examining the repertoire policy pursued by a medium-sized company, such as the Essen Opera House, from the 1920s to the 1930s. Between 1922 and 1928 Essen had developed a reputation for promoting adventurous twentieth-century repertoire, but in the wake of the financial crisis, their policy showed a marked change of outlook, as Table 3.1 demonstrates.

Table 3.1 *Operas performed at the Essen Opera House, 1928–33*

Season	Total number of operas performed	Total number of twentieth-century operas performed
1928–29	26	11
1931–32	26	6
1932–33	16	3

A more detailed analysis of these statistics reveals that in the 1928–29 season, nine of the eleven twentieth-century operas were works by modernist composers, as opposed to two out of six in 1931–32. Yet in the following year the Essen opera management were no longer prepared to countenance promoting adventurous works, the three twentieth-century operas featured that season having been composed by late Romantic composers in the period before the 1920s.[5]

From such evidence, it seems that a conservative artistic policy was already in place in some provincial theatres well before Hitler's rise to power. While the suppression of controversial repertoire became a major propaganda issue for the regime, its effects were limited to only a few theatres. A more significant change was brought about by the removal of all theatre administrators, conductors and directors who were deemed unacceptable to the regime – a process which had already begun in February 1933, but continued until the beginning of the 1933–34 season. By installing politically compliant substitutes into many of these posts, the Nazis hoped to avoid future controversies and smooth the path towards their ultimate goal of a centrally co-ordinated plan for all German theatres under the direction of Reichsdramaturg Rainer Schlösser.

As well as censoring plays, Schlösser ensured that a watchful eye would be kept over any proposed operatic repertoire. But Schlösser's ability to influence artistic policy appears to have been limited by his subordination to Goebbels and to Hans Hinkel, the assistant president of the Reich Chamber of Culture. In addition, he had no jurisdiction over the policy of the Berlin Staatsoper, which remained under the control of Göring.[6]

Because of these divided responsibilities and the impression that politicians were sometimes working at cross-purposes, performances of works by composers nominally outlawed by the Nazis managed to slip through the net. For instance, in 1934 Hinkel apparently sanctioned performances of three operettas by the Jewish composer Offenbach in Koblenz, an action which had earlier been rejected by Schlösser.[7] The Berlin Staatsoper mounted a performance of *Der Kreidekreis* by the half-Jewish Zemlinsky in 1934, although one year earlier the opera had been removed from production in Stettin after protests from local Nazi Party activists. Controversy also raged over the work of Aryan opera composers. The world premiere in Dresden in 1935 of Richard Strauss's *The Silent Woman (Die schweigsame Frau)* was marked by a boycott by the Nazi leadership and open hostility in the pages of *Die Musik* – a journal under the control of Alfred Rosenberg and the NS-Kulturgemeinde (National Socialist Cultural Community). Further divisions affected other new works, for example Höffer's *The Mistaken Waldemar (Der falsche Waldemar)* and Reutter's *Dr Johannes Faust* (both misleadingly branded as atonal in some quarters), Mohaupt's *The Widow of Pinsk (Die Wirtin von Pinsk)*, Egk's *Peer Gynt* and Orff's *The Clever Young Woman (Die Kluge)*.

Although these works aroused much heated debate at the time of their first performance, it should be emphasized that the majority of opera houses managed to avoid conflict and controversy simply by pursuing a policy of self-censorship. The inevitable consequence of such action, however, was to produce a repertoire that lacked enterprise and studiously avoided the unfamiliar. Surveying the 1934–35 season, one commentator remarked upon the fact that only eighteen out of forty-six theatres had managed to perform repertoire by a living German composer, and that in seven of these theatres the composers represented were established old masters such as Richard Strauss and Hans Pfitzner. To alleviate this situation, he proposed that each theatre should devote at least 10 per cent of its attention to premiering German operas, and that in an annual season of twenty operas, at least two should have been composed by living Germans.[8]

Appraising the repertoire presented in individual opera houses, as documented in the 1937 edition of the *Deutsches Bühnen-Jahrbuch*, it appears that many theatres heeded such advice. In Essen, for example, four out of the nineteen operas featured in their 1935–36 season were composed by living Germans (Egk, Graener, Sehlbach, Strauss), while in Hamburg the number stood at three (Graener, Strauss, Egk) out of twenty. Similar statistics apply to the 1937–38 season in each opera house, although in the following year both companies reverted to less adventurous material – a factor which no doubt prompted Schlösser to issue a directive in 1939 compelling German opera companies to devote more attention to contemporary German music, and insisting that every opera company stage at least one new production of a German opera composed after 1900.[9]

Redrawing and expanding repertoire from the past

Mozart and Wagner

Although trying to create the necessary conditions for the promotion and performance of contemporary operas, the Nazis were equally concerned with imposing their influence on the established classics of the repertoire. Wolfgang Amadeus Mozart and Richard Wagner, two of the greatest German-speaking opera composers, were specifically appropriated for this purpose, though with rather different consequences. In the case of Mozart, the central preoccupation seems to have been the desire to 'Aryanize' the libretti of the three operas (*Don Giovanni, Le nozze di Figaro, Così fan tutte*) the composer wrote in collaboration with the baptized Jew Lorenzo da Ponte. Although no official directive was issued to this effect, the climate of anti-semitism that percolated through all aspects of cultural life during this period encouraged numerous opportunists to present their 'purified' arrangements of these texts before the public. As a further incentive and justification for their actions, many noted the need to ensure that opera houses throughout Germany no longer persisted in rehearsing these operas in published editions made by the German-Jewish conductor Hermann Levi.[10]

While Mozart remained a fringe concern in the question of Nazi cultural politics, Wagner was elevated to the very centre, as the spiritual godfather to the party. The association was sealed during the 1920s when Hitler became a frequent visitor to Bayreuth and received strong political support from members of the Wagner family, most notably the racial historian Houston Stewart Chamberlain. A defining moment in this process was the reopening of the Bayreuth Festival ten years after the outbreak of the First World War, and during the following years Bayreuth became one of the major rallying points for organized conservative and nationalist opposition to the Weimar Republic. The degree to which Bayreuth had become appropriated by such forces can be exemplified by the increasingly xenophobic material which was published in conjunction with the Festival. Two issues were predominant: the need to emphasize an irresistible link between Wagner and Hitler as joint redeemers of German society, and the attempt to interpret Wagner's operas in the light of the current political climate. Commenting on the 1930 *Ring* cycle at Bayreuth, the critic of the *Völkischer Beobachter*, for example, suggested the work to be a parable of the age, with the giant Fafner as a symbol of the indolent upper classes at the time of Wilhelm II that had failed to foresee the coming revolution, and Hagen as representative of the politicians that had stabbed the German army in the back in 1918. Inevitably, Siegfried was depicted as the 'symbol of young Germany which is now preparing to replace the remnants of a collapsing bourgeois-Marxist state and to erect a new Germany, the Third Reich'.[11]

Apart from the growing Nazification of Wagner, Bayreuth also came to be regarded as one of the last bastions of Germanic values standing in opposition to such artistic preoccupations as modernism and Expressionism. It is not surprising, therefore, that Nazi sensibilities were especially riled when modernists dared to subject their beloved composer to such reinterpretation during the Weimar Republic. One Wagner production of the 1920s that particularly incensed the Nazis was that of *The Flying Dutchman* (*Der fliegende Holländer*) mounted at the Kroll Opera in Berlin in 1929 with Otto Klemperer as conductor, Jürgen Fehling as director and Ewald Dülberg as designer. The production caused offence on a number of counts: the severe rectilinear sets, the Expressionist acting of the singers, the proletarian-style costumes of the major protagonists and the hard-driven musical interpretation of the score. But it was the Kroll's attempt to demythologize Wagner, stripping away many of the composer's most overt manifestations of national romanticism, that aroused the greatest fury and hastened the demise of the Kroll Opera in 1930.[12]

Although by the early 1930s few opera houses dared to follow the Kroll's example by staging anti-traditional productions of Wagner, two further controversies surrounding the composer confronted the Nazis in the early months of the Third Reich. The fiftieth anniversary of Wagner's death happened to take place on 13 February 1933, and the regime lost no time in exploiting the event for its own purposes. But while Hitler, Göring, Frick and the Wagner family attended a much-publicized commemorative celebration at the Gewandhaus in Leipzig, a new and innovative production of the composer's *Tannhäuser* opened at the Berlin Staatsoper under Otto Klemperer, with Fehling as director and sets by Oskar Strnad. Once again, the provocative nature of the production, which challenged traditional conceptions of the work in both staging and musical interpretation, aroused a chorus of indignation in the right-wing press, playing admirably into the hands of the Nazis, who now demanded that the new regime exert an even tighter control of cultural policy. Not surprisingly, one of the earliest victims of this charge was Otto Klemperer, who left Germany in April 1933.[13]

Another artist forced into exile partly as a result of his anti-traditional interpretation of Wagner's outlook was the novelist Thomas Mann. Mann's lecture entitled 'The Suffering and Greatness of Richard Wagner', delivered at the University of Munich on 10 February (and subsequently published in *Die Neue Rundschau* in April 1933), warned of the inherent dangers of adopting a totally uncritical attitude towards Wagnerian ideology. Inevitably, by expressing such opinions at the very moment when the Nazis were attempting to silence opposition to their policies, Mann entered on a collision course with the new regime. The campaign of denunciation against Mann gathered pace, particularly after a group of Munich intellectuals, including the composers Richard Strauss and Hans Pfitzner, put their names to a published letter of protest against the lecture.[14]

Once the Nazis had managed to silence any independent notions of Wagner's place in cultural history, they set about consolidating and perpetuating the traditional conception of Wagner as epitomized by Bayreuth in the 1920s. Moderately adventurous stagings of his operas were discarded in favour of a homogenized style that favoured realism and promoted official ideology. Wagner propaganda was further supported by the publication of innumerable books and articles on the composer. For example, the July 1933 issue of the *NS-Monatshefte* was devoted exclusively to Wagner. Entitled 'Richard Wagner and the New Germany', the articles concentrated on subjects such as 'Wagner and Hitler', 'Richard Wagner as the leader of the future', '*Parsifal* and National Socialism' and 'Wagner and Nordic Philosophy'.[15]

In a more overtly public arena, Wagner's work became unmistakably associated with the regime's most significant cultural celebrations. With its rousing final chorale 'Germans awake! Soon will dawn the day', the opera *Die Meistersinger* was shamelessly exploited by Goebbels as an anthem to the Nazi Party. Thus on 13 March 1933, the day which formally inaugurated the Third Reich, festivities began with the convening of the new Reichstag and culminated in a gala performance of the work at the Berlin Staatsoper. From then on, the opera was performed at many important party and state occasions. In particular, the transmogrification of *Die Meistersinger* into a quintessentially Nazi opera was realized at the annual Nuremberg Party Rallies, where Benno von Arent's monumental staging of the final act, with its massed crowds and celebratory flags and banners, consciously mirrored the events taking place outside the opera house.

A further opportunity to exploit the link between Wagner and the Third Reich came with the 1933 Bayreuth Festival. Hitler and other party officials attended the opening performances, and local crowds celebrated their appearance with frenzied enthusiasm. Almost every subsequent year Hitler made the annual pilgrimage to Bayreuth, and after 1939 he reconstituted the event as a *Kriegsfestspiel* (war festival) so as to enable regular attendance by German war veterans. The festival managed to retain a modicum of artistic independence by avoiding subjugation to officials controlling the Chamber of Culture. Thus, although traditional stagings remained the order of the day at Bayreuth, the combined efforts of conductor Heinz Tietjen and director Emil Preetorius steadfastly avoided the blatant pandering to Nazi ideology as manifested by Benno von Arent in Berlin and Nuremberg.

Other composers

Setting aside specific attempts to Nazify Mozart and Wagner, a broader appraisal of traditional opera repertoire suggests less apparent divergence in taste between the Weimar Republic and the Third Reich than one might have expected. According to the critic Wilhelm Altmann, the fifteen most popular operas during the 1930–31 season were Bizet's *Carmen*, Wagner's *Tannhäuser*, Weber's *The Freeshooter* (*Der Freischütz*), Wagner's *Lohengrin*, Mozart's *Magic Flute* (*Die Zauberflöte*), Mascagni's *Cavalleria rusticana*, Leoncavallo's *I pagliacci*, Verdi's *Il trovatore*, Puccini's *Madame Butterfly*, Offenbach's *Tales of Hoffmann*, Wagner's *Flying Dutchman*, d'Albert's *The Lowlands* (*Tiefland*), Puccini's *La Bohème*, Verdi's *La traviata* and Beethoven's *Fidelio*.[16] The same operas by Bizet, Leoncavallo, Puccini and Weber remained as popular eight years later, together with others by Wagner and Verdi. Of course, the Jewish composer Offenbach could no longer be performed, so the only other striking difference between the two sets of statistics rests in the considerable rise in popularity of the operas by the nineteenth-century composer Lortzing.[17]

Although the Nazis imposed a total ban on the performance of Jewish nineteenth-century opera composers such as Offenbach, Jacques François Halévy and Meyerbeer, policy decisions regarding operas with libretti by those who were either Jewish or half-Jewish seem to have been far more capricious.[18] The continued popularity of Bizet's *Carmen* should be noted, despite the composer's partly Jewish origins and a collaborative libretto in which one of the partners, Ludovic Halévy, was wholly Jewish. Yet there was no active campaign to damage the work's reputation, and it was notably excluded from the wholesale ban on compositions from enemy countries issued during the Second World War. While Strauss's *The Silent Woman* was removed after only a few performances because of Stefan Zweig's libretto, no objections were raised with regard to performances of *Der Rosenkavalier*, *Elektra* and *Arabella*, despite the fact that Hugo von Hofmannsthal was half-Jewish. Even Nazi Party loyalists such as Paul Graener and Georg Vollerthun were excused for having composed operas with the Jewish playwright Rudolf Lothar, who was in exile during the Third Reich.

All these exceptions to the Nuremberg Laws of 1935, which effectively forbade any artistic partnership between Aryan and Jew, illustrate the contradictory and ambiguous nature of Nazi censorship. At the same time, there are other examples where the campaign to expunge Jewish influence from German cultural life produced notable changes. The three operas Mozart composed in collaboration with the baptized Jew Lorenzo da Ponte, for example, have already been cited as a high-profile *cause célèbre*. Likewise, Nazi propaganda forced opera companies to abandon Franz Werfel's highly successful German translations of some of Verdi's operas, such as *La forza del destino* (1925), *Simon Boccanegra* (1929) and *Don Carlos* (1932), and encourage the creation of alternative adaptations of these works.[19]

Despite the much-publicized proscription of Werfel because of his Jewish origins, the so-called Verdi renaissance, which had been largely initiated by the Austrian novelist's efforts, continued apace throughout the Nazi era. Another area of continuity with the Weimar Republic was the Handel revival, which had begun in the small town of Göttingen in 1920. Although initially confined to small theatres whose modest orchestral pits were more suitable for the performance of baroque music, Handel's operas soon began to attract the attention of much larger companies. Thus during the Second World War one finds surprisingly frequent performances of his work; for example, *Giulio Cesare* at the Berlin Staatsoper (1939), *Rodelinde* in both Berlin and Vienna (1940), *Xerxes* in Hamburg, Danzig (Gdansk) and Schwerin (1943) and *Radomisto* at Hagen and Wuppertal (1943).[20]

The revival of early music which was initiated in the 1920s, in particular with Handel, extended to other areas of the baroque and classical repertoire. Two composers featured prominently: Monteverdi, whose *Orfeo* in the arrangement by Carl Orff featured at the Dresden Staatsoper in 1940, and Gluck, whose work was particularly celebrated during the 150th anniversary of his death; during the 1937–38 season there were revivals of the two Iphigénie operas in Dresden and Regensburg and of *Paride e Elena* in Weimar, and a Gluck Festspiel at the Dietrich-Eckart-Bühne in Berlin.

Attempts to revive long-forgotten operas from the nineteenth century met with rather less success. Despite positive criticism in Nazi music journals, such works as Conradin Kreutzer's *A Night's Shelter in Granada* (*Die Nachtlager in Granada*), E. T. A. Hoffmann's *Aurora* and Schumann's *Genoveva* sunk without trace after only a few performances. Hermann Goetz's *The Taming of the Shrew* (after Shakespeare) enjoyed greater exposure, achieving performances in several theatres, but the major beneficiary of this nineteenth-century revival was Lortzing, the archetypal composer of German popular opera.

Of Lortzing's twenty operas only *Tsar and Carpenter* (*Zar und Zimmermann*, 1837), *The Poacher* (*Der Wildschütz*, 1842), *Undine* (1845) and *The Armourer* (*Der Waffenschmied*, 1846) were regularly featured in German opera houses before 1933. But this changed in the wake of widespread demands for the revival of the German *Volksoper* which followed the Nazi takeover. In the 1933–34 season, for example, performances of the long-forgotten *Casanova in Murano* (Braunschweig), *Hans Sachs* (Stuttgart) and *Scenes from Mozart's Life* (*Szenen aus Mozarts Leben*) (Danzig/Gdansk) set a trend for further intensive activity on Lortzing's behalf which resulted in more stagings of these works, and revivals of the equally neglected *The Two Shooters* (*Die beiden Schützen*) (Magdeburg, 1935) and *Prinz Caramo* (Mannheim, 1937, and Berlin, 1938).

There are a number of reasons why the Nazis were favourably disposed towards Lortzing. The composer's frequently proclaimed desire to produce quintessentially German music-theatre works provided much of the justification. But equally significant was Lortzing's penchant for writing simple melodious music and uncomplicated comic libretti, neither of which made great intellectual demands on an audience. It is also worth noting that, whereas a number of his most notable contemporaries managed to achieve success elsewhere in Europe, Lortzing's work failed to gain any foothold outside German-speaking countries. Thus the Nazis could also argue that Lortzing was unique in being a German composer writing exclusively for German audiences.

Although the fashion for revisiting long-forgotten *Volksopern* extended to the later nineteenth century (for example, Alexander Ritter's *Lazy Hans* (*Der faule Hans*) (Munich, Augsburg) or August Bungert's *Student from Love*

(*Student aus Liebe*, or *Die Studenten von Salamanka*) (Krefeld)), the whole process remained a somewhat piecemeal affair, largely dependent upon the particular enthusiasms of a local theatre administrator. The Propaganda Ministry began to take a more concerted interest in such matters only after the outbreak of war. On 1 May 1940, the Reichsstelle für Musikbearbeitungen (Government Panel for the Arrangement of Music) was unveiled as a new organization within the Music Section of the Ministry. Although the director was Dr Heinz Drewes, who was also responsible for overseeing all other musical affairs in the ministry, the real driving force behind the Reichsstelle was Drewes's deputy, the musicologist Hans-Joachim Moser. In an article published in the *Jahrbuch der deutschen Musik 1943*, Moser outlined some of the major objectives of the Reichsstelle:

> Decisive for its foundation is the desire to see the repertory of German theatres of serious as well as light entertainment extended and enriched in that particular direction so that material important to the Reich is faithfully promoted, while works of a purely commercial and objectionable nature are avoided. At the same time, no restrictions are to be placed upon healthy and responsible publishing. In any case, this task is carried out in an amicable agreement with the Reichsdramaturg, the main activities being divided into two areas: older works are to be revised, and suitable contemporary works should also be commissioned.[21]

As a distinguished musicologist, Moser's principal concern had been to rescue neglected operas, operettas and *Singspiele* (song-plays) from the eighteenth and nineteenth centuries, and make them more palatable to contemporary audiences by effecting the necessary literary and musical alterations. The initial list of projects, summarized in the January 1941 issue of *Zeitschrift für Musik*, looked impressive and included the late operas of Gluck, as well as Spohr's *Jessonda* and Weber's *Euryanthe*. The latter two works constituted two of the most historically significant early Romantic German operas, though this reputation rested almost entirely upon their music, rather than their libretti. In the event, however, Moser's ambitions of resuscitating Weber and Spohr never materialized, and of Gluck's late operas, only *Iphigénie en Tauride* was unveiled before the German public with a new German text by Joseph Maria Müller-Blattau.

It is entirely possible that the failure to initiate Moser's original ambitions with regard to serious operas was symptomatic of wider concerns, in particular Goebbels's demands that entertainment had to take precedence over erudition and enlightenment during the war. This would explain why greater energy was channelled into supporting the *Volksoper* revival. Once again, Lortzing appears to have been a major preoccupation, with two neglected operas, *The*

Two Shooters and *Casanova in Murano*, subjected to adaptation by the contemporary German composer Mark Lothar.[22]

Although I have placed considerable emphasis on the Reichsstelle's seemingly commendable policy of resuscitation, extra-musical concerns inevitably overshadowed such work. In particular the organization was deputed to oversee the texts of popular operettas and revise them in the light of the current political situation. Thus, the setting for Millöcker's *The Beggar Student* (*Der Bettelstudent*) was changed from the Cracow of Augustus the Strong to the Breslau of Prince Eugen, while Oskar Nedbal's *Polish Blood* (*Polenblut*) was renamed *Harvest Bride* (*Erntebraut*) and the geographical background was altered from Russian-occupied Poland to that of the Sudetenland. With Suppé's *Fatinitza*, originally cast at the Battle of Sebastopol in 1854, the Reichsstelle proposed updating the historical background to the 1940s and the so-called Bulgarian war of liberation. Countless other works were subjected to this kind of treatment, most notably the 'Aryanized' textual adaptations of Handel's biblical oratorios. Yet it remains unclear whether all German theatres followed the instructions of the Reichsstelle to the letter. In matters of artistic censorship, the situation remained ambiguous and confusing, even during the war.

Characteristics and reception of new German operas, 1933–45

The older generation of composers: Schillings, Graener, Vollerthun and Siegfried Wagner

Having effectively outlawed most of the contemporary operatic repertoire that had enjoyed such prominence during the later years of the Weimar Republic, the Nazis were faced with the obvious problem of finding suitable alternatives. While an easy option would have been to allow opera houses simply to stick to tried and tested classics, such a move could easily have backfired during the early months of the regime by suggesting that, instead of the much-trumpeted notion of national regeneration, the Nazis had in reality instigated a period of cultural stagnation. To counteract such a possibility, the regime rewarded the most prominent of its musical supporters with stagings of their operas.

Amongst the leading beneficiaries of this policy were the composers Max von Schillings, Paul Graener, Georg Vollerthun, Siegfried Wagner (the son of the Bayreuth master, who died in 1930) and, to a lesser extent, Hans Pfitzner. Broadly speaking, all these musical figures subscribed to a similar, conservative, post-Wagnerian conception of opera, and had largely rejected the modernism and experimentalism that had prevailed during the 1920s. While

Pfitzner always enjoyed a certain degree of eminence prior to the Third Reich, largely as a result of his conservative music-drama *Palestrina* (1917), the other composers were ignored by the major opera houses, and became increasingly embittered by their failure to achieve lasting success during the Weimar Republic. With the changing political and cultural climate of the early 1930s, they hoped for better prospects.

In the short term, they were not disappointed. Taking overall control of Berlin's Städtische Oper midway through the 1932–33 season, Max von Schillings replaced proposed performances of Goldschmidt's *The Magnificent Cuckold* with stagings of Vollerthun's *The Volunteer Corporal* (*Der Freikorporal*, 1931) and Graener's *Assumption of Hannele* (*Hanneles Himmelfahrt*, 1930). Similar gestures were made at other metropolitan opera houses, as newly installed theatre managers responded to a campaign orchestrated, particularly in conservative music journals, to revive contemporary operas that were deemed unfashionable during the Weimar Republic.[23] Although one can argue that the process of replacing modernist opera with more traditional late Romantic material had begun some years before the Nazis came to power, there was a notable upsurge in this activity during the latter part of the 1932–33 season, when, for instance, such operas as *Mona Lisa* and *Der Moloch* by Max von Schillings enjoyed swiftly mounted revivals, and Pfitzner's most recent opera *The Heart* (*Das Herz*, 1931) was featured in opera houses that had previously refused to stage the work.[24]

The trend for promoting these and other conservative Romantic composers continued through the 1933–34 and 1934–35 seasons. Statistics released in connection with the latter season suggest that, among living composers, the operas of Richard Strauss and Pfitzner ranked first and second in popularity, with Graener, the Italian Wolf-Ferrari, and Vollerthun occupying third, fourth and fifth places respectively. But while Strauss and Pfitzner maintained this pre-eminence to the very end of the Third Reich, Graener and Vollerthun suffered a considerable reversal of fortunes in the following years. To a certain extent, this reversal was not unexpected, for although Graener and Vollerthun may have curried greater favour in Nazi Party circles than either Strauss or Pfitzner, as composers they ranked at a much lower level. Personal difficulties may also have played a part, as in 1936 Vollerthun's career was almost curtailed by a homosexual scandal.[25] Likewise, Graener's prestige was damaged by financial improprieties and his mismanagement of the budget allotted to the Composers' Section of the Reich Music Chamber.[26]

Given the unanimous chorus of approval that greeted Nazi cultural policy decisions in loyal music journals such as *Zeitschrift für Musik* and *Die Musik*, it is interesting to note that as early as October 1933, critical opinion appears to have turned against composers like Graener and Vollerthun, regarding their work as outdated and ideologically suspect. Referring in particular to Graener's *Friedemann Bach* and Vollerthun's *The Volunteer Corporal*, the writer and opera director Hans Költzsch condemned these works for their 'cold ideology and snobbery', and for their reliance on a 'hypocritical, artificial and unhealthy tyranny of style':

> These works are still more or less descended from an almost *Biedermeier* (i.e. petit-bourgeois) way of life, or at least from a pre-war middle-class spirit. Their characters, tales and subject matter are petty and narrow-minded, their interpretation of German history is debased, and never suggests the symbolism of national greatness, and the German Middle Ages are inevitably seen through the sentimental and trivialized eyes of the nineteenth century. Judged purely by artistic merit and quality, German national traditions, such as they exist, are simply added on – they are an artifice, or a cheap varnish, bereft of artistic principle or real creativity.[27]

This perception of artifice and a lack of real creativity was reinforced by the relative failure of the operas written by both composers after 1933. Despite the fact that Graener's much-trumpeted opera *Der Prinz von Homburg* enjoyed a prestigious first staging at Germany's largest opera house, critical reaction was cool, suggesting in particular that the composer had failed to sustain effectively the dramatic tension of Kleist's play (*Prinz Friedrich von Homburg*). Although *Der Prinz von Homburg* was taken up by a few provincial theatres during the following season, it was never revived, and the composer's last effort in the genre, *Schwanhild* (1942), aroused little more than polite approval. While Graener continued to enjoy a powerful position within German music, having replaced Richard Strauss as head of the Composers' Section of the Music Chamber in 1935, his reputation had diminished. This impression is further confirmed by the obsequious and somewhat desperate tone of a letter sent directly to Hitler in 1936, begging the Führer to attend a performance of 'his national opera' *Der Prinz von Homburg*.[28]

A similar fate befell Georg Vollerthun. After a few seasons, *The Volunteer Corporal*, granted official approval by Hitler for the conspicuous use of popular military marches in its final act, disappeared from the repertoire. In 1942 Vollerthun tried to rescue his flagging reputation with *The Royal Sacrifice* (*Das königliche Opfer*). Set during the Napoleonic wars, the libretto deals with the conflict between love and patriotism – a familiar topic of the Nazi era. But once again, Vollerthun's music failed to match the serious nature of the subject matter, and the opera disappeared after only one season.

Of the late Romantic figures who had died before the Third Reich, special attention was devoted to Siegfried Wagner, a prolific composer with eighteen operas to his credit. During the Weimar Republic, performances of these

12 Paul Graener, *Der Prinz von Homburg* (Berlin Staatsoper, 1934–35). Director: Rudolf Hart-mann. Stage designer: Benno von Arent. Note the festive banners and raised arms, which are analagous to von Arent's famous sets for the Third Act of Wagner's *Die Meistersinger*, performed annually at the Nuremberg Party Rallies.

works, which drew their inspiration from fairy tale or supernatural events often set within an historical context, were infrequent, and confined to provincial theatres such as Rostock and Karlsruhe. But after 1933, there was a concerted effort, orchestrated to a certain extent by the composer's widow Winifred, to secure a wider dissemination of his output. How far this promo-tion rested on historical sentiment, given the prominence accorded to Bayreuth and its Wagnerian legacy in official Nazi propaganda, is unclear. Neither is there any evidence to suggest that the justification for such a reappraisal of his work rested with a perceived ideological relevance of his chosen subject matter.[29] None the less, the policy seems to have paid off in that some leading German opera houses not only mounted new productions of long-forgotten works, but in Cologne in December 1933 presented the world-premiere of *The Heathen-King (Der Heidenkönig)*, an opera which had actually been composed in 1913. Yet, as in the cases of Graener and Vollerthun, no amount of effort on the part of theatre managers and music critics could bring about a widespread acceptance of a composer of relatively minor stature.

Richard Strauss

Of all the composers of the older generation, it was Richard Strauss who maintained a dominating presence throughout both the Weimar Republic and the Third Reich. Doubtless, Nazi propagandists, especially on the Rosenberg wing of the party, would have preferred Hans Pfitzner to occupy this pre-eminent position. But the rivalry between the two, fuelled by arguments from the Pfitzner supporters that their composer manifested a purer assimilation of the Wagnerian tradition, had little impact; there was little tangible increase in the number of performances of Pfitzner's operas between the 1920s and the 1930s, and their frequency lagged far behind those of Strauss. It should also be noted that while Strauss continued to pour his creative energies into writing operas during the period, Pfitzner effectively bade farewell to the genre with *The Heart*, two years before the Nazis came to power.

In many other respects, Strauss gained the upper hand on his contemporary. While both composers experienced difficulties with the Nazi regime, it was Strauss rather than Pfitzner who was elevated to the post of president of the Music Chamber in 1933. In contrast, Pfitzner was rewarded with a less high-profile position in the Cultural Senate of the Reich. Although Strauss suffered the humiliation of enforced dismissal from the presidency of the Music Chamber in 1935, the composer continued to accept and fulfil prestigious commissions up to the end of the regime. Pfitzner was also honoured with many commissions, though his new works never attracted the same degree of publicity as those of Strauss. Ironically, Pfitzner's conservative and nationalist cultural pronouncements, which were already aired in the early 1920s, more obviously accorded with the Nazis. Yet the composer remained essentially an outsider whose intellectualism and asceticism aroused deep suspicion in some sectors of the Nazi hierarchy.

While Pfitzner actively engaged in polemics, Strauss remained far more aloof from public pronouncements.[30] This equivocal position has inevitably aroused greater debate as to the extent to which Strauss was, or was not, a willing accomplice to Nazi cultural policies. More relevant to the present argument is the question of whether the operas he composed during the 1930s and 1940s either reflect or negate the prevailing ideological climate. According to one view, Strauss's aesthetic position and his inability to distinguish between art and kitsch made him a passive accomplice to the culture of fascism:

> Strauss, as the modern he had been and remained in part, was affected by a discourse of nihilism, which meant that there could be no principle which would allow him to distinguish between art and kitsch. [...] Such differing forms of incomplete nihilism were all taken up by the culture of Nazism, which may be defined, almost, as an artificial attempt to preserve values manipulatively, while knowing the lack of grounds for them, knowing their readiness to succumb to the charge of relativism.[31]

An opposing argument rejects the notion that Strauss ever composed in a style 'congenial to fascism, or composed fascist music, as some critics, including Thomas Mann, insinuated', and that 'so long as the parameters of fascist aesthetics are undefined, such remains merely subjective conjecture'.[32]

In defence of the latter view, it would be difficult to suggest that the comic farce of The Silent Woman (Die schweigsame Frau, 1935), or the debate between words and music in opera portrayed in Capriccio (1942), are the most obvious subjects to lend themselves to a purely fascist interpretation. Likewise, although the exploration of ideas drawn from classical mythology, manifested in Daphne (1938) and The Love of Danae (Die Liebe der Danae, 1944), is common to other contemporary German operas of the period, Strauss's approach differs little from that of his earlier works such as Ariadne on Naxos (Ariadne auf Naxos, 1916) and The Egyptian Helen (Die Aegyptische Helena, 1927).

Arguably the most controversial opera Strauss composed during the Third Reich is Day of Freedom (Friedenstag, 1938). Written in the wake of Strauss's removal from the presidency of the Music Chamber and his enforced severing of ties with the Jewish writer Stefan Zweig, the opera remains the least well-known and least characteristic of his entire output.[33] Not only does the subject matter, which concerns the defence of a garrison during the Thirty Years War, mark a departure from the composer's usual preoccupations, but the opera's major protagonists, including the commandant and his wife, seem archetypal embodiments of the Nazi ideal of the heroic man and the submissive woman. Further central themes of the opera – self-sacrifice, loyalty and redemption from evil forces – can also be linked to the prevailing ideological climate and to other contemporary operas of the period. The following description of the opera's plot, published after its first performance in Vienna in 1939, admirably summarizes these aspects:

> The terrors of war and the cries for peace of a battle-scarred rural community drive the fortress almost to surrender. But this is resisted to the end by the iron will and soldierly courage of the commandant. Embedded delicately in this brutal outer tale is the moving struggle of a loving woman, the wife of the commandant, who at last wants to win for herself her husband's heart which has been given over entirely to soldierly honour.[34]

Although this particular aspect of the opera, manifested in an extended duet between the commandant and the wife, inspires Strauss to compose some of his most intense neo-Wagnerian music, interpretation of the work's final section, depicting a sudden and unexpected cessation of hostilities and a jubilant choral celebration of peace, is far more ambiguous. In some respects, the clamour for peace could be regarded as an act of subterfuge designed to counter the authoritarian policies of the Nazis.[35] But the musical style at this juncture, couched in Strauss's most monumental E flat major, suggests empty triumphalism and veers dangerously close to kitsch. Interestingly, this inability to compose an entirely convincing musical apotheosis to the opera was noted by critics at the time, though the work initially enjoyed strong approval and was performed in the presence of Hitler.

The younger generation

After Strauss, the most successful opera composers in the Third Reich came from a much younger generation. Many of these figures had received their musical education during the 1920s and were keen to capitalize on opportunities which followed the mass exodus of major creative talent in 1933. Inevitably, opportunism resulted in some interesting stylistic and political compromises. One should note, for example, that Ottmar Gerster, composer of three highly successful operas during the Third Reich, had previously written workers' choruses for the Social Democratic Party; that Hermann Reutter, whose *Dr Johannes Faust* (1936) constituted one of the most frequently performed contemporary operas in Nazi Germany, had in 1930 composed the *Lehrstück* (didactic piece) *Job* (*Hiob*), inspired by Brecht; that Carl Orff, whose stage works *Carmina Burana* (1937) and *The Moon* (*Der Mond*) (1939) attracted considerable enthusiasm, had set texts by Brecht and Werfel for unaccompanied chorus in 1931; and that the equally favoured Rudolf Wagner-Régeny had earlier been an active participant at the annual avant-garde music festivals of the 1920s held in Baden-Baden.

By and large, all these composers managed to shake off their past associations without encountering the sort of high-profile controversy experienced by a figure such as Hindemith. At the same time, question marks hang over the degree to which their operas are genuine products of National Socialist culture. On the one hand, these composers heartily embraced the prescribed attempt to revive the *Volksoper* tradition, contributing popular representations of escapist fairy tales (Egk, *The Magic Violin* (*Die Zaubergeige*); Orff, *The Moon*) or idealized depictions of peasant life (Gerster, *The Witch of Passau* (*Die Hexe von Passau*)). Yet it is equally interesting to note that many of these works survived in the post-war repertoire of opera houses in both West and Communist East Germany, suggesting that there were sufficient ambiguities in their scenarios and musical styles to withstand the charge of complete political collusion.

A good test-case for such an argument is Gerster's opera *The Witch of Passau*, first performed in Düsseldorf in 1941, and frequently revived after the Second World War in East German opera houses. The libretto, by the well-known playwright Richard Billinger, contains some ideologically apposite ingredients – implied anti-semitism in the third scene, anti-clericalism, and a peasants' revolt that culminates in self-sacrifice for the sake of the people. Yet despite these elements, the political dimension remains curiously enigmatic. On the one hand, the opera's sequence of picturesque episodes and its undemanding musical score could have met Goebbels's demands for escapist entertainment in support of the war effort. But the work failed on two counts: the lack of ideological clarity and the absence of the kind of humour that might have enhanced national morale.[36]

Similar ambiguities of interpretation can be found in Werner Egk's *Peer Gynt*, first performed in Berlin in 1938. The reception history of this opera is particularly interesting, since it initially received a controversial press, but then experienced a dramatic reappraisal after Hitler had signalled his strong approval of the work. One explanation for this apparent volte-face was that Hitler was simply indulging in mischief-making and enjoyed the prospect of stirring up bitter rivalries between Goebbels and Göring, who were both present at the performance.[37] In his autobiography, the composer further suggested that Hitler had somehow managed to ignore some of the more overtly satirical aspects of the score.[38] Particularly controversial in this respect was the Troll scene, which, according to Egk, represented a lampooning of Nazi rituals and the activities of the Storm Troopers.[39] In addition, the score contained many unequivocal references to the music of the 1920s (jazz idioms, harsh dissonances, coarse instrumentation and imitations of the idiom of Kurt Weill).

It is possible that Hitler's response to the opera was simply capricious, and that he had misunderstood the subversive elements in the work. Yet Egk's argument is not entirely convincing, particularly since, after securing Hitler's approval, the opera was awarded a national prize at the 1939 Reich Music Days in Düsseldorf, and continued to be performed, not only in Germany, but also in Prague in 1941 and at the Paris Opéra in 1943. To provide a plausible explanation for Hitler's approval and for the continuing success of the opera, one needs to understand that the work's modernist elements appear exclusively in the sections which deal with negative aspects of the plot. Furthermore, it should be noted that Egk's approach in these sections was illustrative and journalistic rather than interpretative. Far from representing a negative allegory of the National Socialist State, the hideous world of the Trolls appeared to Hitler to be a reflection of the 1920s and the degenerate elements of the Weimar Republic.[40] One aspect of the music which supports this contention is the grotesque musical quotation, at the end of the Troll scene, of the cancan from Offenbach's *Orpheus in the Underworld* – an unmistakable reference to a famous work by a composer outlawed by the Nazis on account of his Jewish origins.

Although arousing a good deal of controversy for grafting modernist elements into an opera, Werner Egk not only escaped censure, but secured active

13, 14   Gustav Vargo's set designs for Ottmar Gerster's *The Witch of Passau* (*Die Hexe von Passau*) (Städtische Bühnen, Düsseldorf, 1941–42). Using a libretto by the well-known dramatist Richard Billinger, Gerster attempted to emulate the *Volksoper* tradition of the nineteenth century, though with only moderate success.

approval from the highest authorities. His colleague Rudolf Wagner-Régeny, on the other hand, achieved a more problematic relationship with the Nazis. The composer wrote three operas during the 1930s in collaboration with the stage designer and librettist Caspar Neher, who had been closely associated with Brecht and Weill, for example producing the libretto for Weill's opera *The Pledge* (*Die Bürgschaft*) in 1932. In view of this, one might have expected a cautious critical response to their first work, *The Favourite* (*Der Günstling*), performed in Dresden in 1935. Yet the work scored an instant success with the public and sustained frequent performances in several German opera houses.

Once again, post-war critics have tended to stress the anti-totalitarian features of Neher's text, with its allusions to the executioner's axe, a land laid waste and the overthrow of a tyrant. Yet such issues appear to have escaped the notice of contemporary reviewers, who made no mention whatsoever of Neher's Brechtian connections. Without exception, critical reception appears to have been favourable to both Neher's text and the freshness and neo-Handelian simplicity of Wagner-Régeny's music. In examining the musical structure, the use of separate numbers, as encountered in baroque or classical opera, is clearly indebted to 1920s 'New Objectivity' as formulated by composers such as Hindemith. The effect is not dissimilar to that of the epic music-theatre of Brecht. That such an idiom appeared palatable to the Nazis in this context is not surprising, since Wagner-Régeny had gone out of his way to strip his musical language of direct association with the immediate past. Thus his score, though austere and monumental in sound, contains precious little harsh dissonance, and the instrumentation avoids the kinds of texture that were redolent of the 1920s.

While *The Favourite* was quickly recognized as one of the most significant operas to have been composed during the Third Reich, its successor, *The Burghers of Calais* (*Die Bürger von Calais*) (Berlin, 1939), fared less well. In drawing their inspiration for this work from the anti-war drama that the Expressionist playwright Georg Kaiser had written in 1914, Neher and Wagner-Régeny were certainly taking a calculated risk. Yet Neher's adaptation of the story, which concerned the English siege of the French port and the townsfolk's heroic resistance to such oppression, was sufficiently ambiguous not to offend Nazi sensibilities. By placing the emphasis upon the willingness of individuals to sacrifice their lives for the sake of the community, Neher was certainly exploiting a theme frequently encountered in Nazi literature. A more uncomfortable aspect of the opera, however, was the appearance on stage of a beleaguered and downtrodden group of people desperately brokering for peace, especially at the very moment that Germany was preparing for war.

The opera, conducted by Herbert von Karajan, ran for only six performances before it was suddenly removed. The Rosenberg wing of the Nazi Party had raised particular objections to Neher's libretto, which it was claimed hardly accorded with 'the world view of the new Germany'.[41] Further suspicions were targeted on Wagner-Régeny's score, which, with its austere orchestration featuring a pair of alto saxophones, provided unequivocal reminiscences of Stravinsky, Hindemith and Kurt Weill.

Wagner-Régeny's reputation reached its lowest ebb in the Third Reich with his third opera, *Johanna Balk* (Vienna, 1941), commissioned by the former Hitler Youth leader and Gauleiter of Vienna Baldur von Schirach. With this work, both the libretto and the music proved controversial. Neher's original scenario had concerned the actions of a seventeenth-century Hungarian prince who raped and overpowered German Saxons in Wagner-Régeny's birthplace in Siebenbürgen. But on the orders of the Propaganda Ministry, Neher changed the Hungarian names to German ones, out of consideration for Germany's current alliance with the Hungarian regime. Ironically, this enforced change put a somewhat different gloss on the drama, for the German prince now was perceived as a villain and a tyrant with an obvious likeness to Hitler. The satirical attack on dictatorship reached its climax in a final scene whose dramatic structure was unmistakably reminiscent of the Brecht/Weill *Threepenny Opera*. Wagner-Régeny's music similarly recalled Weill, not so much in melodic and harmonic terms as in both its saxophone-oriented texture and its driving percussive rhythms.

In a gesture of defiance and in an attempt to assert his cultural autonomy, Baldur von Schirach steadfastly resisted attempts from Berlin and the Propaganda Ministry to have the work removed, and it was revived in Vienna during the following season. But elsewhere in the German Reich, *Johanna Balk* was officially proscribed. Wagner-Régeny's composing career during the early 1940s was soon terminated; he was drafted into the army in 1942.

The archetypal Nazi opera?

In assessing the operatic achievements of German composers during the Nazi era, there is an obvious tendency on the part of scholars to concentrate the greatest attention upon those works which aroused the greatest degree of controversy, either by appearing to contradict the prevailing ideological climate, or by offering the potential after 1945 for a subversive or anti-totalitarian interpretation. But this approach creates a somewhat misleading picture, for the overwhelming majority of new operas were conformist and largely conservative in outlook.

More significant, perhaps, is the evidence that in a highly politicized period such as the Third Reich, the most successful and frequently performed contemporary operas, such as Norbert Schultze's *Black Peter* (*Schwarzer Peter*) (1936), Mark Lothar's *Tailor Wibbel* (*Schneider Wibbel*) (1938), or even Werner Egk's *The Magic Violin* (1935), fail to deal with obvious ideological issues, preferring instead to provide audiences with uncomplicated, comic, escapist and entertaining material that in effect provide a twentieth-century equivalent to the *Volksopern* of the much-admired Lortzing. Furthermore, the few opera composers who attempted to write works which were more overtly political in content were unable to secure unequivocal approval either from critics or from audiences. One notable example of such a failure was *The Homecoming of Jörg Tilman* (*Die Heimfahrt des Jörg Tilman*) by Ludwig Maurick. Commissioned by Alfred Rosenberg's NS-Kulturgemeinde for its 1935 festival in Düsseldorf, the opera was published by the NS-Musikverlag, but was mounted in only two other theatres.[42] The scenario concerns the experiences of a wounded German soldier, imprisoned by the Russians during the First World War, who loses his memory, but manages to return to his homeland after a series of improbable escapades. Constructed almost like an oratorio, with the chorus apparently symbolizing the soul and destiny of the German people, this so-called *Gemeinschaftsoper* (community opera) fell well short of its declared intentions. As an experimental music-theatre piece, the opera aroused somewhat contrasting reactions from the two principal music journals of the period. While the reviewer in Rosenberg's journal *Die Musik* expressed misgivings about some aspects of the score, he praised the composer's 'astonishing musical intensity', and hoped that other opera houses would be prepared to 'open the door' to this new *Gemeinschaftsoper*.[43] On the other hand, a much less favourable response to Maurick's work emanated from the pages of the *Zeitschrift für Musik*:

> Maurick's *Gemeinschaftsoper* is the only work amongst present-day music-theatre pieces which deals with contemporary material – a task which demands the highest creative power. Unfortunately, Maurick's strengths do not belong to a creatively expressive, pulsating, robust and strong present, but to a weak, soft, effeminate, hedonistic and outmoded past. This overflowing unrestrained music which is utterly without self-discipline manages to create exactly the opposite of the intended binding of a community.[44]

There are numerous other examples from the 150 new German operas performed between 1933 and 1945 where critical reaction was similarly dismissive, pointing either to a composer's inability to bring convincing dramatic intensity to an ideological message, or to an over-reliance upon a derivative musical language that in many instances veered dangerously close to kitsch. Yet although it is difficult to cite a wholly successful example of an archetypal Nazi opera, there are still certain common preoccupations of subject matter which connect much contemporary operatic work during this period. To a certain extent, one could argue that opera in the 1930s reverted to specific trends that had been identified by German music historians before the Weimar

15, 16   Ludwig Maurick, *The Homecoming of Jörg Tilman* (*Die Heimfahrt des Jörg Tilman*) (Württembergische Staatstheater, Stuttgart, 15 October 1936). Director: Otto Kraus. Stage designer: Gustav Vargo. Commissioned by the NS-Kulturgemeinde, this rare excursion into the genre of *Gemeinschaftsoper*, exploring themes of self-discipline and heroism in the context of the First World War, failed to achieve wide currency.

Republic. In his book *Die Musik seit Richard Wagner*, published in 1913, Walter Niemann appraises various alternative contemporary approaches to operatic writing, including popular comic opera, fairy tale opera, and historical and redemption dramas.[45] With few exceptions, most operas of the 1930s easily fall into similar categories. Since music historians of the period, such as Ludwig Schiedermair, drew attention to these unifying factors, it may be useful to summarize them below with specific examples:[46]

1 Traditional settings of classic German literature: Henrich, *Melusine* (Goethe); Henrich, *Beatrice* (Schiller); Klenau, *Michael Kohlhaas* (Kleist); Graener, *Der Prinz von Homburg* (Kleist).

2 Settings of 'classic' world literature: Egk, *Peer Gynt* (Ibsen); Kusterer, *The Servant of Two Masters* (*Der Diener zweier Herren*) (Goldoni); Hess, *Twelfth Night* (*Was ihr wollt*) (Shakespeare); Wödl, *The Comedy of Errors (Die Komödie der Irrungen)* (Shakespeare); Gerster, *Enoch Arden* (Tennyson).

3 Historical and patriotic drama: Schliepe, *Marienburg*; Von Borck, *Napoleon*.

4 Destiny of creative and inventive genius: Klenau, *Rembrandt van Rijn*; Sehlbach, *Galilei*; Egk, *Columbus*.

5 Heroism and self-sacrifice: Zillig, *The Sacrifice (Das Opfer)*; Wagner-Régeny, *The Burghers of Calais*.

6 Parables of homecoming: Egk, *Peer Gynt*; Maurick, *The Homecoming of Jörg Tilman*.

7 Settings of classic mythological episodes: Reutter, *Odysseus*; Trantow, *Odysseus near Circe* (*Odysseus bei Circe*); Souchay, *Alexander in Olympia*; Strauss, *The Love of Danae*.

8 Fairy tales: Orff, *The Moon*; Egk, *The Magic Violin*.

Performance and reception of non-German operatic repertoire

In his scurrilous pamphlet *Degenerate Music: A Reckoning (Entartete Musik: eine Abrechnung)*, Hans Severus Ziegler cited 1930 as the year in which he believed German musical life had reached its lowest point of existence. Ziegler's hostility was particularly targeted at the directors of German opera houses for staging first performances of operas by Jews and foreigners, instead of providing a platform for purely German composers to have their works presented.[47] In this respect, Ziegler was simply reiterating an argument frequently adopted by the Nazis that the cultural environment of the Weimar Republic had been polluted by an internationalist conspiracy which had sought to undermine and denigrate national traditions.

Given the atmosphere of intense xenophobia that erupted during the first months of Nazi rule, one might have expected newly installed theatre managers in Germany's opera houses to have upheld a policy of cultural isolationism, making a conscious decision to ban the performance of all contemporary non-German operatic repertoire. Yet no such action was forthcoming. While administrators were sufficiently zealous to effect an almost comprehensive purge of repertoire by Jewish composers, their attitude towards new works from other countries was less predictable. In this respect, decisions on whether to perform a contemporary non-German opera were normally determined by such factors as a perception of commonly held racial and cultural ties, a desire to maintain long-standing special relationships between a particular composer and a specific theatre, or a necessity to promote a specific work for political expediency.

Arguably the major benefactors of the racial/cultural argument should have been the Scandinavians, with whom the Nazis believed Aryan Germans shared identical aspirations. As in the case of drama, propaganda to promote Nordic art surfaced from the outset of the Nazi era, frequently orchestrated by influential critics such as Fritz Stege, himself the librettist of a Nordic *Volksoper*. Commenting on the proposed purification of the German opera repertoire that would follow from the Nazi takeover of German opera houses, Stege suggested in May 1933 that although 'foreign art could not be completely eliminated in favour of German music, it would be preferable to give precedence to Nordic opera over racially alien productions by Slavs, Magyars, and others'.[48]

Despite the fact that contemporary operatic activity in Scandinavia hardly matched the scale achieved in Germany, Italy or France, such demands were soon realized at the beginning of the 1933–34 season. As early as December 1933, Braunschweig mounted the German premiere of *Engelbrekt*, an opera written in 1929 by the Swedish composer and veterinary surgeon Natanael Berg. Prior to this performance, Berg's music was hardly known in Germany, but this did not deter Ernst Stier, in the *Zeitschrift für Musik*, from going out of his way to praise the composer's musical credentials and the topical relevance of his new work, which was described as the 'first Hitler opera':

Early in the opera, there is a desire for a saviour who will lead the people from bondage and servitude. With ardent fervour, the hero Engelbrekt risks his life in heavy battle, loses through lack of real support, and only after his death are his true values and intentions recognized. In effect, Engelbrekt becomes a national hero and is sincerely mourned by the whole nation.[49]

Two months later, the same theatre followed up Berg's work with the German premiere of *Fanal* (*Flammendes Land*) by another, much better-known Swedish composer, Kurt Atterberg.[50] This opera could have proved more controversial with the authorities, since Atterberg's chosen subject derived from the Jewish poet Heine's *The Knave of Bergen* (*Der Schelm von Bergen*). None the less, reviews published in *Zeitschrift für Musik* and *Die Musik* seem to have overlooked this issue, preferring instead to argue that the opera's setting of the 1525 Peasants' War was propitious. As in his review of Berg's *Engelbrekt*, Ernst Stier interpreted Atterberg's opera as a parable of the contemporary situation, which in political, social, economic and religious terms paralleled the years 1929–32, 'when the desire for freedom, peace and unity was fulfilled against all expectations by the Führer'.[51]

Contemporary reviews suggest that both Swedish operas were received enthusiastically by the Braunschweig audience. Yet no other German theatre chose to stage *Engelbrekt*, and further productions of *Fanal* were confined to only three theatres (Lübeck in 1936, and Chemnitz and Dortmund in 1937). Although one might argue that the literary connection with Heine hindered the possibility of *Fanal* being given more extensive exposure, Atterberg's next opera, *Härvard the Harpist* (*Härvard harpolekare*), a work originally composed in 1919 but revised for a production in Chemnitz in March 1936, attracted relatively little interest elsewhere. Five years later, Atterberg tried once again to establish himself in Germany with his recently composed opera *Alladin*, premiered in Chemnitz. But this work fared no better than his previous attempt, and was not performed elsewhere.

Further endeavours to advance the cause of new Scandinavian opera by other composers suffered in a similar manner. By and large, the bigger metropolitan opera houses simply ignored such repertoire, leaving provincial companies to make the occasional fitful gesture.[52] Despite propaganda to the contrary, the Germans showed little appetite for promoting unknown Scandinavian composers, preferring instead to enhance the reputation of established figures such as Sibelius.[53] Although neither an opera composer *per se* nor a supporter of the Nazis, Sibelius had forged strong links with Germany from the turn of the century, and the relationship flourished through various changes of political system.

While few non-German composers attained the same level of prestige in the Third Reich as Sibelius, there were a number of other figures whose relationship with the German musical scene remained largely secure, despite the different cultural circumstances of the Third Reich. Amongst the most notable was the Italian Gian Francesco Malipiero. A prolific composer of operas, Malipiero enjoyed extensive patronage in German theatres during the Weimar Republic.[54] Yet despite Malipiero's iconoclastic style of the 1920s, which often juxtaposed musical archaisms with sudden eruptions of violent dissonance, and the sometimes irrational nature of his chosen subject matter (for instance, the enigmatic symbolism in *Night Tournament* (*Torneo notturno*)), the composer continued to profit from his ties with Germany. In January 1934, Braunschweig mounted the first performance of the composer's most recent opera *The Changeling* (*La favola del figlio cambiato*), and used the occasion to cement cultural and political ties with the Italian Fascist regime. According to the report in the *Zeitschrift für Musik,* the Italian ambassador attended the performance, arriving from the station under protection from local Storm Troopers.[55] Although Alfred Schlee, writing in the American periodical *Modern Music*, suggested that Malipiero's opera scored a 'tremendous success' at its first performance, neither Malipiero's music nor Luigi Pirandello's libretto found much favour with the anonymous critic in Rosenberg's *Die Musik*, who lambasted the work as 'pale, intellectual and overburdened'.[56]

Whether in fact the performance of Malipiero's opera helped to promote cultural understanding between the two countries is unclear. Certainly, the work failed to be taken up by other German theatres, and the libretto by Pirandello proved sufficiently controversial for the opera to have been banned in Italy some months later on the orders of Mussolini.[57] Yet in spite of this setback, Malipiero's subsequent operas, couched, it must be emphasized, in a simpler musical style and utilizing more conventional dramatic scenarios, were all staged in Germany.[58] Critical reception of these works was positive rather than effusive. Malipiero's musical asceticism and his rejection of the traditional division of operatic structure into sequences of arias, choruses and ensembles would have challenged traditionalists, inspiring respect rather than wholehearted enthusiasm.[59]

Another figure who maintained strong ties with Germany throughout the Nazi era, while enjoying more prestigious support, was the Swiss late Romantic composer Othmar Schoeck. Like Richard Strauss, Schoeck established a special relationship with the Dresden Staatsoper, which premiered the majority of the stage works he composed during the 1920s. During the Third Reich, Dresden remained loyal to Schoeck, giving the first performance in 1937 of his new opera *Massimilla Doni* (after Balzac's story of the same name), under the conductor Karl Böhm, in front of a distinguished audience that included Goebbels. Schoeck's subtle score, contrasting aesthetic debate about the respective roles of words and music in opera (an interesting forerunner of Strauss's *Capriccio*) with amorous intrigue, was not geared to populist sensibilities, and the work failed to make headway elsewhere in Germany. None the less, the modest success which *Massimilla Doni* enjoyed hardly damaged Schoeck's reputation, for his next and final opera *Dürande's Castle* (*Das Schloß Dürande*), with a text by the Nazi writer Hermann Burte (after Eichendorff) and set during the French revolution, was commissioned and premiered by the Berlin Staatsoper in 1943.[60]

17 Emil Preetorius's design for Othmar Schoeck's *Dürande's Castle* (*Das Schloß Dürande*) (Berlin Staatsoper, 1942–43). Director: Wolf Völker. As during the Weimar Republic, the Swiss late Romantic composer Schoeck was accorded prestigious first performances of his operas in major German theatres. Yet, despite boasting a text by the Nazi poet Hermann Burte, the apocalyptic nature of the opera, culminating in the destruction of the castle, offended official Nazi sensibilities.

Ideologically, certain aspects of Schoeck's opera would have appealed to the Nazis; in particular, the central character of Gabriella seems to have represented the ideal of Nazi womanhood. But the work was given its first performance at an inappropriate time. Not only did Schoeck's sometimes dissonant score (occasionally reminiscent of the composer's earlier quasi-Expressionist opera *Penthisilea*) arouse consternation, but the violent nature of the scenario, which culminated in several murders, a suicide and a blowing up of the castle, disturbed audiences who were experiencing increasing Allied bombings of the German capital. Yet although Göring sent a furious telegram of protest to the Staatsoper about the libretto, performances of the opera continued.[61]

While Schoeck experienced somewhat mixed fortunes during the Third Reich, his younger compatriot Heinrich Sutermeister achieved considerable acclaim. The world premiere of his opera *Romeo und Julia* in Dresden in 1940 was a glittering affair attended by theatre managers, conductors and singers from every corner of the Reich. Critical response was almost unanimously favourable and the opera was soon championed in numerous theatres throughout Germany. Writing about the Dresden premiere in the *Zeitschrift für Musik*, the critic Ernst Krause praised Sutermeister for composing 'genuinely operatic music', and described his talent as a 'great promise for the future'.[62] The composer had certainly exploited a vein of escapist late Romanticism which provided necessary emotional relief from the harsh realities of war. But one commentator went even further in claiming that Sutermeister had succeeded in overcoming inherent problems that had beset contemporary opera for many years, by re-establishing the future 'viability' of lyrical bel canto opera.[63]

After the success of *Romeo und Julia*, Sutermeister was commissioned to write a further Shakespeare opera *Die Zauberinsel* (based on *The Tempest*) for Dresden. The premiere of the new work took place in 1942, and once again featured a prestigious cast under the musical direction of Karl Böhm. Although the opera appears to have received a warm reception, it failed to register the same degree of interest as *Romeo und Julia*. Whether its reduced impact was simply a result of increased difficulties which Germany faced three years into the war, or that Sutermeister's musical inspiration operated at a lower ebb, remains unclear.[64]

Setting aside specific cases of operas by Malipiero, Schoeck and Sutermeister, decisions regarding the performance of non-German operatic repertoire during the Third Reich were shaped not so much by questions of artistic merit as by matters of political expediency. This certainly appears to be the case when examining the cultural interaction which flourished between the Nazis and the Italian Fascist regime. Naturally, opera played a significant role in this process. Examining the repertoire of various German opera houses, one can find a reasonable representation of contemporary Italian operas, and the Italians appear to have reciprocated, particularly after 1938, by staging works by Wilhelm Kempff, Ottmar Gerster, Werner Egk and Carl Orff at La Scala, Milan.[65]

From reading contemporary reports, it appears difficult to glean a wholly accurate estimate of the impact of new Italian opera on German audiences. In some cases, critics may well have been inhibited by Goebbels's dictum of 1936 that they should simply report cultural activities, rather than impart aesthetic judgements on specific works. Thus a better litmus test of critical reception may rest with other factors, in particular the number of times an opera was staged, and whether it was revived or performed again at another theatre. The evidence here suggests that the German public were more inclined towards works by the conservative *verismo* composers or successors to Puccini (such as Riccardo Zandonai and Franco Alfano) than those of the 'generation of the 1880s' (such as Alfredo Casella and Ildebrando Pizzetti). In the latter case, Casella's *La donna serpente* (after Gozzi) was staged in 1934 at Mannheim without a revival, while Pizzetti's *Orsèolo*, performed in Cologne in 1941, received a somewhat muted response, partly one suspects on account of the opera's conclusion, in which the protagonist renounces all notions of revenge on his enemies – a position that would have been regarded as incompatible within the context of war.

Although one can find a smattering of performances of new operas by less well-established figures in provincial theatres, the major focus for the Italians remained Berlin. The first German performance of Ottorino Respighi's opera *The Flame* (*La Fiamma*) at the Berlin Staatsoper in 1936, for example, attracted widespread interest, and the work was revived successfully in 1939 in Danzig (Gdansk). In Germany, Respighi was regarded as the most significant twentieth-century Italian composer after Puccini, and the reception of his new work was normally warm. None the less, in appraising new works by conservatives such as Respighi, Zandonai and Alfano, German critics enthused mainly about the composers' perceived stylistic links with native musicians such as Strauss, and tended to look down somewhat at any intrinsically Italianate features such as a tendency towards melodrama.[66]

While it is possible to justify the continued performance of contemporary Italian opera in Germany on the grounds of the strong political ties that existed between National Socialism and Fascism, the sporadic promotion of operas by composers from Eastern Europe and Russia appears to have been a more cynical exercise in cultural diplomacy. What, for example, should one make of the much-heralded German premiere in Hamburg in 1935 of *Halka* by the nineteenth-century Polish composer, Stanislaw Moniuszko? Performed, somewhat incongruously, within the context of an International Festival of Contemporary Music, one might have expected this strongly patriotic work, which proclaimed Slavic nationalism in every bar, much in the manner of Smetana's *Bartered Bride* or Glinka's *A Life for the Tsar*, to have been regarded with disdain by the authorities. Yet the opera was highly successful, enjoying not only a revival in 1939 in Hamburg, but also stagings in Berlin (1936) and Chemnitz (1938).

To explain the opera's success in Germany, one might point to certain obvious features such as the anti-Russian aspects of the scenario, or the tuneful accessibility of Moniuszko's musical idiom. But a more plausible explanation for its acceptance can be gleaned from a contemporary review by H. W. Kulenkampff, published in the *Blätter für Kunst und Kultur*, the official magazine of the Hamburg branch of Rosenberg's NS-Kulturgemeinde. In summarizing the dramatic narrative in *Halka*, Kulenkampff attempts to draw parallels between the oppression experienced by Poles in the late eighteenth century, and the humiliation suffered by the German people in the aftermath of the First World War.[67] Emphasizing the *völkisch* elements in Moniuszko's opera, Kulenkampff seems to have deliberately overlooked the indisputably

Polish elements in the work, and once again drawn specific attention to the composer's apparent indebtedness to Germanic models. This kind of argument would be rehearsed several times in positive reviews of the other 'nationalist' operas by Eastern Europeans that were performed in Nazi Germany. Significantly, few such works enjoyed the sustained exposure of *Halka*, a notable exception being the comedy *Ero the Joker* (*Ero s onoga svijeta*), by the Croatian composer Jakov Gotovac, which enjoyed consistent popularity throughout Germany after its premiere in Karlsruhe in 1938. One can argue, of course, that this success was determined to a certain extent by Germany's political alliance with Croatia. But Gotovac's portrayal of Croatian peasant life through the eyes of a Till Eulenspiegel-like protagonist was also deemed palatable to German audiences, since the music and dramatic action clearly attained a simplicity and directness of expression that was analogous to the nineteenth-century German *Volksoper*.

The musical ramifications of the brief German–Soviet pact between 1939 and 1941 have yet to be investigated in full. However, the sudden and short-lived preoccupation with performing Russian opera during this period, particularly at such major venues as the Berlin Staatsoper and the Vienna Opera, can almost certainly be accredited to the political situation, as can the staging of operas based upon Russian subject matter but composed by non-Russians (for example, the premiere of Boris Blacher's *Empress Tarakanova* (*Fürstin Tarakanowa*) at Wuppertal-Barmen and Amilcare Zanella's *The Government Inspector* (*Il revisore*, after Gogol) at Dessau in 1941.[68] Perhaps the most salient observation to make about Nazi Germany's brief flirtation with Russian opera was its consistent avoidance of performing anything composed after the Russian Revolution. One might argue that in any case, precious little of this repertoire was directly accessible to the Germans, and it would be difficult to imagine that works by Prokofiev or Shostakovich could have been deemed palatable on either musical or dramatic grounds.

Significantly, the only contemporary Russian opera to have been staged in Germany during this period was composed by the staunchly anti-Bolshevik Stravinsky. In 1938, the composer's recently completed stage work *Perséphone* featured in a double bill with Kodály's *The Spinning Room* (*Székely fonó*) at a Festival of Contemporary Opera in Braunschweig and was also performed at Baden-Baden. The acceptance of the modernist Stravinsky may seem curious, particularly since the performances took place five years after the Nazis came to power. Yet one should also take into account the composer's political stance, which at this stage was still resolutely supportive of Mussolini.

Apart from the isolated example of Stravinsky's *Perséphone*, no opera by a widely recognized modernist composer was performed in Nazi Germany.[69] None the less, a general survey of non-German repertoire performed throughout this period reveals a few surprises. The revival in 1939 of Busoni's *Doktor Faust* seems unexpected, given that the Italian-German composer played such a significant role in shaping musical styles during the Weimar Republic. Even more extraordinary is the sustained popularity of Janáček's *Jenufa*, which maintained a place in the repertoire of several opera houses in the 1930s and throughout the Second World War. It is difficult to offer a satisfactory explanation for the opera's continued success, given that Janáček was an ardent Moravian nationalist, and, more particularly, that the recognized German translation of his most famous work had been undertaken by the Jewish writer Max Brod. Whether or not such issues were simply overlooked by officials is unclear, but there seems to be no evidence to suggest that Brod's translation was ever suppressed.[70] Perhaps this was one of those cases where officialdom was insufficiently vigilant to have noticed an anomaly.

If composers from Scandinavia, Italy, Eastern Europe and Russia managed to gain a nominal foothold in German opera houses, the same was certainly not the case with those from France. As far as nineteenth-century repertoire is concerned, only Bizet's *Carmen* remained an almost permanent fixture with theatre managers, while the once-popular operas of Ambroise Thomas and Charles Gounod were subjected to an official ban at the outbreak of the Second World War. Even before 1939, German opera houses had contrived to neglect twentieth-century French opera almost entirely. Neither Debussy's *Pelléas et Mélisande* nor Ravel's *The Child and the Spells* (*L'Enfant et les Sortilèges*) was revived, and the only recent opera to have received a German premiere at this time was Jacques Ibert's *The King of Yvetot* (*Le roi d'Yvetot*), which was staged in Düsseldorf in 1936. Originally scheduled for the 1932–33 season, the belated performance of this knockabout comedy of village life presumably came about as a result of Ibert's appointment to the post of vice-president of the Nazi- organized International Society for Co-operation amongst Composers. Ibert's musical style, an ingenious mixture of Gallic frothiness and Stravinskian modernisms, could hardly have caused major offence, but the opera evidently failed to excite sufficient interest to enjoy either a revival or a staging elsewhere in Germany.

Historical context: the decline of modernism in opera

Because of the idiosyncratic nature of opera policy, not to mention the capricious reception of non-German repertoire during the Nazi regime, scholars have tended to isolate operas composed in Germany between 1933 and 1945 from the European mainstream. However, a broader appraisal of operatic developments during this period suggests that musico-dramatic accessibility and the rejection of modernism, forcefully superimposed by totalitarian states such as Nazi Germany and Stalinist Russia, also characterizes the majority of new operatic works premiered in countries which preserved democratic forms of government. Surveying some of the operas first performed during the 1930s in such countries as France, Switzerland and the United States, it is noticeable that, with only one or two exceptions, very few works adhere to the modernist styles embraced during the 1920s. Moreover, those operas that attained some degree of public approval seem to revert to a much more traditional language than earlier in the century, placing greater emphasis on utilizing folk idioms, or making a conscious effort to effect a directness of expression.[71] The uncomfortable conclusion to be drawn from this evidence is that opera in Nazi Germany actually retains much closer links to its non-German counterparts than one might like to think.

Appendix:
List of opera first performances and significant revivals of earlier repertory in Germany, Austria and the Protectorate of Bohemia and Moravia, 1933–44

The list below encompasses first performances in Germany of all contemporary operas, by both Germans and non-Germans, and, from 1938, works premiered in Austria and the Protectorate of Bohemia and Moravia. Also included in the list (represented in **bold**) are selected examples of rearrangements/revivals of some earlier repertory which have usually been adapted, on either political-ideological or racial grounds. The titles of operas by non-German composers are normally presented both in their original language and in German translations.

Bold	= revival or arrangement of earlier material
Italic	= *non-German opera premiere*
arr.	= arranged by

Non-German composers from:

A = Austria	N = Norway
B = Belgium	P = Poland
C = Croatia	R = Russia
Cz = Czechoslovakia	Ro = Romania
F = France	S = Switzerland
G = Greece	Sp = Spain
H = Hungary	Sw = Sweden
I = Italy	USA = United States

* = planned performance, but aborted after Allied bombing raids
[ ] = rehearsal performance – staging prohibited owing to Goebbels's declaration of 'total war' in August 1944

Date	Title	Composer	Librettist	Place
1933				
11 February	Der Roßknecht	Winfried Zillig	Richard Billinger	Düsseldorf
8 March	Kaukasische Komödie	Otto Wartisch	Otto Wartisch	Nuremberg
29 April	Die Schmiede	Kurt Striegler	Waldemar Staegemann	Hanover
1 July	Arabella	Richard Strauss	Hugo von Hofmannsthal	Dresden
17 August	Godiva	Ludwig Roselius	Ludwig Roselius	Nuremberg

Date	Title	Composer	Librettist	Place
1933–34				
1933				
13 October	Szenen aus Mozarts Leben	Albert Lortzing	Albert Lortzing	Danzig (Gdansk)
14 October	Undine	E. T. A. Hoffmann	E. T. A. Hoffmann (arr. H. von Wolzogen)	Leipzig
15 October	Sein Schatten	Friedrich Flotow	Richard Genée (arr. H. and S. Scheffler)	Hamburg
21 October	Madame Liselotte	Ottmar Gerster	Franz Clemens/Paul Ginthum	Essen
25 October	Soleidas bunter Vogel	Max Donisch	Curt Böhmer	Krefeld
4 November	Michael Kohlhaas	Paul von Klenau	Paul von Klenau (after Kleist)	Stuttgart
5 November	Aurora	E. T. A. Hoffmann (arr. Lukas Böttcher)	Franz von Holbein	Bamberg
25 November	Franzosenzeit	Hermann Wunsch	Hermann Wunsch (after Fritz Reuter)	Schwerin
26 November	Das Herzwunder	Friedrich Hölzel	Wilhelm von Scholz	Altenburg
6 December	Münchhausen	Mark Lothar	Wilhelm Treichlinger	Dresden
8 December	*Engelbrekt*	*Natanael Berg [Sw]*	*Natanael Berg*	*Braunschweig*
16 December	Der Heidenkönig	Siegfried Wagner	Siegfried Wagner	Cologne
1934				
11 January	*Die Legende vom vertauschten Sohn (La favola del figlio cambiato)*	*Gian Francesco Malipiero [I]*	*Luigi Pirandello*	*Braunschweig*
16 January	Der Kreidekreis	Alexander von Zemlinsky	Alexander von Zemlinsky (after Klabund)	Stettin (Szczecin)
21 January	Die Verdammten	Adolf Vogl	Hans von Gumppenberg	Leipzig
26 January	Das Lambertusspiel	Franz Ludwig	Prosper Heil	Bremerhaven
17 February	*Flammendes Land (Fanal)*	*Kurt Atterberg [Sw]*	*O. Ritter/J. Wellem-insky (after Heine, 'Der Schelm von Bergen')*	*Braunschweig*
23 February	Der Herr von Gegenüber	Ernst Schliepe	Ernst Schliepe	Danzig (Gdansk)
4 March	*Frau Schlange (La donna serpente)*	*Alfredo Casella [I]*	*C. Lodovici (after Gozzi)*	*Mannheim*

Date	Title	Composer	Librettist	Place
10 March	Rübezahl	Friedrich Flotow	Gustav Putlitz (arr. Rudolf Senger)	Braunschweig
3 April	Wilhelm Tell	Gioacchino Rossini	Jouy etc. after Schiller (arr. Julius Kapp)	Berlin
28 April	Casanova in Murano	Albert Lortzing	Albert Lortzing (arr. Fritz Tutenberg)	Braunschweig
28 April	Familie Gozzi	Wilhelm Kempff	Erich Noether	Stettin (Szczecin)
5 May	Hans Sachs	Albert Lortzing (arr. H. Rücklos)	Philip Reger (arr. O. Kühn)	Stuttgart
18 May	Münchhausens letzte Lüge	Hans-Heinrich Dransmann	Theo Halton	Frankfurt/Kassel/ Darmstadt
20 June	Das Wahrzeichen	Bodo Wolf	Eugen Rittelbusch	Darmstadt

1934–35

1934

Date	Title	Composer	Librettist	Place
6 October	Blondin im Glück	Hans Grimm	Hans Grimm	Hanover
18 October	Liebesnächte (Stjernenaetter)	Gerhard Schjelderup [N]	Gerhard Schjelderup	Lübeck
20 October	Lucedia	Vittorio Giannini [USA/I]	Karl Flaster/G. Sala	Munich
23 October	Die kleine Stadt (adaptation of Hans Sachs)	Albert Lortzing	Paul Haensel-Haedrich (after A. von Kotzebue)	Rostock
7 November	Der Moloch	Max von Schillings	E. Gerhäuser	Berlin
18 November	Der Meister von Palmyra	Hans-Ludwig Kormann	Carl Willnau (after Wilbrandt)	Altenburg
12 December	Der falsche Waldemar	Paul Höffer	Paul Höffer (after Willibald Alexis)	Stuttgart

1935

Date	Title	Composer	Librettist	Place
16 January	Annelise	Carl Ehrenberg	Carl Ehrenberg (after H. C. Andersen)	Lübeck
26 January	Taras Bulba	Ernst Richter	Johann Kempfe (after Gogol)	Stettin (Szczecin)
26 January	Der Tod des Johannes A Pro	Wolfgang Riedel	Wolfgang Riedel (after Ernst Zahn)	Darmstadt
1 February	Die Stadt	Erich Sehlbach	Erich Sehlbach	Krefeld
20 February	Der Günstling	Rudolf Wagner-Régeny	Caspar Neher (after Hugo)	Dresden
23 February	Arminio	Georg Frideric Handel	A. Salvi (arr. H. J. Moser and M. Seiffert)	Leipzig
10 March	Die heilige Not	Carl Grovermann	Walter Förster	Kassel
14 March	Der Prinz von Homburg	Paul Graener	Paul Graener (after Kleist)	Berlin
24 March	Melusine	Hermann Henrich	Hermann Henrich (after Grillparzer)	Karlsruhe
30 March	Die betrogene Betrügerin	Karlheinz Appel	Karl Best	Ratibor (Racibórz)

Date	Title	Composer	Librettist	Place
31 March	Der abtrünnige Zar	Eugen Bodart	Carl Hauptmann	Cologne
7 April	Heirat wider Willen	Engelbert Humperdinck (arr. Adolf Vogl)	H. Humperdinck (arr. W. Humperdinck)	Leipzig
9 April	Ulenspiegel der Geuse	Karl August Fischer	J. A. Wilutzky (after de Coster)	Munich
17 April	Der vertauschte Sohn (Die beiden Schützen)	Albert Lortzing	Albert Lortzing (arr. Arthur Treumann-Mette)	Magdeburg
14 May	Halka	Stanisław Moniuzsko [P]	W. Wolski	Hamburg
14 May	Legende von Kitezh und Fevronia (Skazaniye o nevidimom Kitezhe i deve Fevronii)	Nikolai Rimsky-Korsakov [R]	V. Belsky	Duisburg
22 May	Die Zaubergeige	Werner Egk	Ludwig Andersen (after Pocci)	Frankfurt
9 June	Die Heimfahrt des Jörg Tilman	Ludwig Maurick	Ludwig Maurick	Düsseldorf
11 June	Die Studenten von Salamanka	August Bungert	August Bungert and Hermann Gräff (arr. Günther Bungert)	Krefeld
13 June	Der Fremde	Hugo Kaun	F. Rauch (after Brothers Grimm)	Weimar
24 June	Die schweigsame Frau	Richard Strauss	Stefan Zweig	Dresden

1935–36

1935

28 September	Der Student von Prag	Erich Mirsch-Riccius	Heinrich Noehren (after Heinz Ewers)	Wiesbaden
25 October	Don Juans letztes Abenteuer	Paul Graener	Otto Anthes	Hamburg
14 November	Viola	Hanns Holenia [A]	Oskar Widowitz (after Shakespeare)	Munich
1 December	Das Stuttgarter Hutzelmännchen	Marc-André Souchay	Marc-André Souchay (after Mörike)	Stuttgart

1936

5 January	Leon und Edrita	Charles Flick-Steger	Aline Sanden (after Grillparzer)	Krefeld
12 January	Der Eulenspiegel	Hans Stieber	Hans Stieber	Leipzig
1 February	Beatrice	Hermann Henrich	Hermann Henrich (after Schiller)	Karlsruhe
18 February	Der Dreispitz	Hans-Ludwig Kormann	Carl Willnau (after Alarcón)	Altenburg
20 February	Der König von Yvetot (Le roi d'Yvetot)	Jacques Ibert [F]	J. Limozin/A. de la Tourasse	Düsseldorf
23 February	Rembrandt in Uselfingen	Hans-Albert Mattausch	Ernst H. Bethge	Liegnitz (Legnica)

Date	Title	Composer	Librettist	Place
21 March	Der Diener zweier Herren	Arthur Kusterer	Arthur Kusterer (after Goldoni)	Freiburg
30 March	Der Sohn der Sonne	Max Peters	Max Peters (after Ingo Krauss)	Hanover
31 March	**Lottchen am Hofe**	**J. A. Hiller**	**C. F. Weisse (after Goldoni)**	**Darmstadt**
31 March	Der verlorene Sohn	Robert Heger	Robert Heger	Dresden
7 April	Skandal um Grabbe	Paul Strüver	Caroline Creutzer (after Grabbe)	Duisburg
12 April	Ilona, oder Das Fest in Budapest	Bodo Wolf	Eugen Rittelbusch	Meiningen
26 April	**Zum Grossadmiral**	**Albert Lortzing**	**Albert Lortzing arr. Treumann-Mette**	**Schwerin**
26 May	Dr Johannes Faust	Hermann Reutter	Ludwig Andersen	Frankfurt
7 June	*Die Flamme (La fiamma)*	*Ottorino Respighi [I]*	*Claudio Guastalla (trans. by J. Kapp)*	*Berlin*
13 June	Die Brücke	Max-Richard Albrecht	Rudolf Gahlbeck	Chemnitz
13 June	Gänsegret, die Fürstin aus dem Volke	Paul Roeder	Ernst H. Bethge	Saarbrücken

1936–37

1936

Date	Title	Composer	Librettist	Place
13 October	**Montezuma**	**Karl Heinrich Graun**	**Frederick the Great (arr. F. Neumeyer)**	**Saarbrücken**
14 November	Das Wunder / Hyazinth Bißwurm	Hugo Herrmann / Hugo Herrmann	Georg Schmückle / Georg Schmückle	Stuttgart / Stuttgart
15 November	Enoch Arden	Ottmar Gerster	K. M. von Levetzow (after Tennyson)	Düsseldorf
26 November	Hirtenlegende	Eugen Bodart	Friedrich Walther (after Lope de Vega)	Weimar
6 December	Schwarzer Peter	Norbert Schultze	Walter Lieck (after H. Traulsen)	Hamburg
6 December	Puszta	Hans-Albert Mattausch	Ernst H. Bethge	Görlitz (Gierloz)
27 December	*Il campiello*	*Ermanno Wolf-Ferrari [I]*	*Mario Ghisalberti (after Goldoni)*	*Munich*

1937

Date	Title	Composer	Librettist	Place
13 January	De Uglei	Paul Wittmack	Otto Hallig	Kiel
23 January	Rembrandt van Rijn	Paul von Klenau	Paul von Klenau	Berlin
31 January	Schlaraffenhochzeit	Siegfried Walther Müller	Karl Hellwig (after A. Kopisch)	Leipzig
10 February	Galilei	Erich Sehlbach	Erich Sehlbach	Essen
27 February	**Prinz Caramo**	**Albert Lortzing**	**Albert Lortzing (arr. Georg Richard Kruse)**	**Mannheim**
2 March	*Massimilla Doni*	*Othmar Schoeck [S]*	*Armin Rueger (after Balzac)*	*Dresden*
5 March	Das heilige Feuer (La battaglia di Legnano)	Giuseppe Verdi	S. Cammarano (arr. J. Kapp)	Bremen

Date	Title	Composer	Librettist	Place
7 April	Das verbotene Lied	Franz Werther	Gustav Quedenfeldt (after Paul Hubl)	Ratibor (Racibórz)
10 April	Die Prinzessin und der Schweinhirt	Casimir von Paszthory	Casimir von Paszthory (after H. C. Andersen)	Weimar
14 April	Inka	Albert Henneberg [Sw]	Fritz Tutenberg	Chemnitz
14 April	Dibux (Il dibuk)	Ludovico Rocca [I]	R. Simoni (after S. Anski)	Breslau (Wrocław)
15 April	Baronin Vansdensland	Hans Schilling	Hans Schilling (after de Coster)	Oldenburg
21 April	Tranion oder Das Hausgespenst	Ludwig Hess	Eberhard König	Bonn
22 April	Genoveva	Alexander Ecklebe	Alexander Ecklebe	Hagen
30 April	Kalif Storch	Walter Girnatis	Rüdiger Wintzen (after Hauff)	Hamburg Radio
14 May	Radamisto	Georg Frideric Handel	N. Haym (arr. H. Buths)	Düsseldorf
5 June	Perséphone	Igor Stravinsky (R)	André Gide	Braunschweig
8 June	Carmina Burana	Carl Orff	Carl Orff	Frankfurt
17 June	Till Eulenspiegel	Emil Nikolaus von Reznicek	Reznicek	Cologne
20 June	Scipione	Georg Frideric Handel	N. Haym (trans. by E. Dahnke-Baroffio)	Göttingen

1937–38

1937

Date	Title	Composer	Librettist	Place
2 October	Magnus Fahlander	Fritz von Borries	Fritz von Borries	Düsseldorf
8 October	Der Holzdieb	Heinrich Marschner	F. Kind	Berlin
16 October	Spanische Nacht	Eugen Bodart	Eugen Bodart (after Heinrich Laube)	Mannheim
17 October	Ein Fest auf Haderslevhus	Kurt Gerdes	Kurt Gerdes (after Theodor Storm)	Krefeld
21 October	Die Erzgräber	Karl Ueter	Walther Reymer	Freiburg
26 October	Die Glucksnarren (Rolands Knappen)	Albert Lortzing	Albert Lortzing (arr. Paul Haensel-Haedrich)	Kassel/Rostock
7 November	Volpino il calderaio	Renzo Bossi [I]	L. Orsini (after Shakespeare, 'The Taming of the Shrew')	Lübeck
12 November	Das Opfer	Winfried Zillig	Reinhard Goering	Hamburg
14 November	Die Heirat (The Marriage)	Modest Mussorgsky (completed Alexander Tcherepnin)[R]	Gogol	Essen
24 November	Tobias Wunderlich	Joseph Haas	H. H. Ortner and Ludwig Andersen	Kassel
27 November	Die Fastnacht von Rottweil	Wilhelm Kempff	Wilhelm Kempff	Hanover

1938

Date	Title	Composer	Librettist	Place
9 February	Spinnstube (Székely fonó)	Zoltán Kodály [H]	B. Sczabolcsi	Braunschweig

Date	Title	Composer	Librettist	Place
10 February	Die Wirtin von Pinsk	Richard Mohaupt	Kurt Nanne (after Goldoni)	Dresden
12 March	Der Hammer (La grançeola)	Adriano Lualdi (I)	Adriano Lualdi (after A. Bacchelli)	Leipzig
19 March	Signor Caraffa	Erich Sehlbach	Erich Sehlbach	Duisburg
31 March	Livia	Toni Thoms	Toni Thoms	Lübeck
3 April	Ero der Schelm (Ero s onoga svijeta)	Jakov Gotovac [C]	Milan Begović	Karlsruhe
3 May	**Ingwelde**	**Max von Schillings**	**F. von Sporck**	**Berlin**
11 May	Orpheus (La favola d'Orfeo)	Alfredo Casella[I]	C. Pavolini (after A. Poliziano)	Stuttgart
11 May	Der Teufel im Kirchtum (Il diavolo nel campanile)	Adriano Lualdi [I]	Adriano Lualdi (after Poe)	Stuttgart
12 May	Schneider Wibbel	Mark Lothar	Hans Müller-Schlösser	Berlin
23 May	Simplicius Simplicissimus	Ludwig Maurick	Ludwig Maurick (after Grimmelshausen)	Düsseldorf
24 May	Der Sohn	Joseph Lichius	Werner Jäckel	Königsberg (Kaliningrad)
30 May	Odysseus bei Circe	Herbert Trantow	Herbert Trantow	Braunschweig
2 June	Das Brandmal (The Scarlet Letter)	Vittorio Giannini[USA/I]	Karl Flaster (after N. Hawthorne)	Hamburg
17 June	Irrwisch	Ernst Meyer-Olbersleben	Olga Brugger	Wiesbaden
19 June	**Tolomeo**	**Georg Frideric Handel**	**N. Haym (trans. by E. Dahnke Baroffio)**	**Göttingen**
24 July	Friedenstag	Richard Strauss	Joseph Gregor	Munich

1938–39

1938

Date	Title	Composer	Librettist	Place
2 October	Die Gänsemagd	Lill Erik Hafgren [Sw]	Lill Erik Hafgren (after Brothers Grimm)	Mannheim
15 October	Daphne	Richard Strauss	Joseph Gregor	Dresden
24 October	Der Gnom	Richard Lerch	Richard Lerch	Breslau (Wrocław)
1 November	Die Lügnerin	Carl Seidemann	Carl Seidemann	Hagen
6 November	Rosalind	Florence Wickham [USA]	Florence Wickham (after Shakespeare, 'As You Like It')	Dresden
11 November	Carina Corvi	Fritz Neupert	Alois Hofmann	Dessau
24 November	Peer Gynt	Werner Egk	Werner Egk (after Ibsen)	Berlin
27 November	Der Bär	Kuno Stierlin	Hans Brenner (after L. Uland and J. Kerner)	Osnabrück
6 December	Julius Cäsar (Giulio Cesare)	Gian Francesco Malipiero (I)	Malipiero (after Shakespeare) (arr. G. Winkler)	Gera

Date	Title	Composer	Librettist	Place
1939				
7 January	Die pfiffige Magd	Julius Weismann	Julius Weismann (after L. Holberg)	Leipzig
14 January	Dafnis und Eglé (Dafni)	Giuseppe Mulé[I]	E. Romagnoli	Düsseldorf
27 January	L'amante in Trappola	Arrigo Pedrollo [I]	Giovanni Franceschini	Dortmund
27 January	Scampolo	Ezio Camussi [I]	Dario Niccodemi	Dortmund
28 January	Die Bürger von Calais	Rudolf Wagner-Régeny	Caspar Neher (after Georg Kaiser)	Berlin
2 February	Königsballade (Harald Haarfanger)	Rudolf Wille	Otto Emmerich Groh	Vienna
5 February	Der Mond	Carl Orff	Carl Orff (after Brothers Grimm)	Munich
5 February	Das böse Weib	Arno Hufeld	Arno Hufeld (after Hans Sachs)	Tilsit (Sovetsk)
21 February	Die Schweinewette	Jaap Kool	Jaap Kool	Weimar
25 February	Antonius und Cleopatra (Antonio e Cleopatra)	Gian Francesco Malipiero [I]	Malipiero (after Shakespeare)	Bremen
25 February	Nabucco	Giuseppe Verdi	T. Solera (Aryanized version arr. Julius Kapp)	Kassel
4 March	Es gärt in Småland (Det jäser i Småland)	Albert Henneberg [Sw]	Fritz Tutenberg	Chemnitz
21 March	Die kleine Sängerin (La canterina)	Joseph Haydn	A. Zeno etc. (arr. Max See)	Bielefeld
24 March	Dorian	Hans Leger	Caroline Creutzer (after Wilde)	Karlsruhe
25 March	Elisabeth von England	Paul von Klenau	Paul von Klenau	Kassel
29 April	Gudrun	Ludwig Roselius	Ludwig Roselius	Graz
14 May	Katarina	Arthur Kusterer	Arthur Kusterer	Berlin
17 May	Die Nachtigall	Alfred Irmler	Rudolf Gahlbeck (after H. C. Andersen)	Düsseldorf
6 June	Der Kobold	Siegfried Wagner	Siegfried Wagner	Berlin
7 June	Wera	Ernst Schiffmann	Ernst Schiffmann	Dortmund
10 June	Artz wider Willen (Il medico suo malgrado)	Salvatore Allegra [I]	Alberto Domini (after Molière, 'Le médecin malgré lui')	Kassel
10 June	Rast vor dem Jenseits (I viandanti)	Salvatore Allegra [I]	Vittorio Andreaus	Kassel
18 June	La Dama Boba	Ermanno Wolf-Ferrari [I]	Mario Ghisalberti (after Lope de Vega)	Mainz

Date	Title	Composer	Librettist	Place
1939–40				
1939				
24 October	Der goldene Becher	Hans Grimm	Hans Grimm	Nuremberg
1940				
23 January	Dolores	Wolfgang Deinert	Wolfgang Deinert	Kaiserslautern

Date	Title	Composer	Librettist	Place
2 February	Ring der Mutter (The Mother's Ring)	Manolis Kalomiris [G]	Agnis Orfikos	Berlin Volksoper
4 February	Dalibor	Bedřich Smetana	J. Wenzig (arr. Julius Kapp) (suppression of Czech nationalist elements in libretto)	Coburg
7 February	Der eingebildete Kranke (Il malato immaginario)	Jacopo Napoli [I]	Mario Ghisalberti (after Molière)	Mannheim
7 February	Das Leben für den Zaren (A Life for the Tsar)	Mikhail Glinka	Baron G. F. Rozen	Berlin
28 February	Brautfahrt	Hans Maria Dombrowski	Werner Oehlmann and Joachim Poley	Oberhausen
5 March	Die verkaufte Braut (The Bartered Bride)	Bedřich Smetana	K. Sabina (arr. P. Ludikar and Ilse Hellmich)	Munich
14 March	Dame Kobold	Kurt von Wolfurt	E. Kurt Fischer (after Calderón)	Kassel
16 March	Königin Elisabeth	Fried Walter	Christoph Schulz-Gellen	Hamburg
12 April	Palla de' Mozzi	Gino Marinuzzi [I]	Giovacchino Forzano	Berlin
13 April	Romeo und Julia	Heinrich Sutermeister [S]	Heinrich Sutermeister (after Shakespeare)	Dresden
20 April	Alexander in Olympia	Marc-André Souchay	Marc-André Souchay	Cologne
27 April	Die Liebe der Donna Ines	Walter Jentsch	Walter Jentsch (after Stendhal)	Wilhelmshaven
4 May	Lukrezia	Ottorino Respighi [I]	Claudio Guastalla (after Shakespeare, 'The Rape of Lucrece', and Livy, 'Ab urbe condita libra')	Gera
4 May	Amelia geht zum Ball (Amelia Goes to the Ball)	Gian-Carlo Menotti [I/USA]	Gian-Carlo Menotti	Gera
5 May	Kampfwerk 39	Marc-André Souchay	Marc-André Souchay	Stuttgart
14 June	Dorothea	Friedrich Bayer	Max Morold	Vienna

1940–41

1940

4 October	Orpheus	Claudio Monteverdi (arr. Carl Orff)	Alessandro Striggio	Dresden
20 October	Guntram	Richard Strauss (revised version)	Richard Strauss	Weimar
23 October	Kniesenack oder Der Soldatenglück	Carl Friedrich Pistor	Benno Rinow/Peter Andreas (after John Brinckmann)	Schwerin
29 October	Die 7 Schwaben	Richard Rossmayer	Maria Kastl	Vienna

Date	Title	Composer	Librettist	Place
5 November	Faust und Helena	Marc-André Souchay	Marc-André Souchay (after Goethe)	Halle
17 November	Hille Bobbe	Hans Ebert	Hans Ebert	Nuremberg/Darmstadt
19 November	Das Herrenrecht	Wilhelm Stärk	Eva Hermecke-Engelhardt	Weimar
19 December	Andreas Wolfius	Fried Walter	Christoph Schulz-Gellen	Berlin
1941				
2 February	*Der Revisor (Il revisore)*	*Amilcare Zanella [I]*	*Antonilo Lega (after Gogol)*	*Dessau*
5 February	Fürstin Tarakanowa	Boris Blacher	Karl O. Koch	Wuppertal-Barmen
16 February	*Julius Cäsar (Giulio Cesare)*	*Gian Francesco Malipiero [I] (revised version)*	*Malipiero (after Shakespeare)*	*Hamburg*
25 February	Der Uhrmacher von Straßburg	Hans Brehme	Paul Ginthum	Kassel
8 March	Bretonische Hochzeit	Gustav Kneip	Willi Schäferdiek	Karlsruhe
21 March	Komödie der Irrungen	Franz Wödl	Roland Gugg (after Shakespeare)	Beuthen (Bytom)
29 March	Der goldene Topf	Wilhelm Petersen	Wilhelm Petersen (after E. T. A. Hoffmann)	Darmstadt
30 March	Was ihr wollt	Ludwig Hess	Ludwig Hess (after Shakespeare)	Stettin (Szczecin)
30 March	*Orsèolo*	*Ildebrando Pizzetti [I]*	*Ildebrando Pizzetti*	*Cologne*
4 April	Johanna Balk	Rudolf Wagner-Régeny	Caspar Neher	Vienna
4 May	*Donata*	*Gaspare Scuderi [I]*	*Gaspare Scuderi*	*Karlsruhe*
11 May	Die Frauen des Aretino	Kurt Gillmann	Franz bei der Wieden	Mannheim
12 May	Die Windsbraut	Winfried Zillig	Richard Billinger	Leipzig
18 May	Ein Tag im Licht	Hans Grimm	Hans Grimm	Erfurt
28 June	*Winternachtstraum (Winternachtsdroom)*	*August de Boeck [B]*	*Leonce du Castillon*	*Cologne*
28 June	*Seevolk (Gens de Mer/Zeevolk)*	*Paul Gilson [B]*	*George Garnir (after Hugo)*	*Cologne*

1941–42

1941

11 October	Die Hexe von Passau	Ottmar Gerster	Richard Billinger	Düsseldorf
11 October	*Der Jakobiner (Jakobin)*	*Antonín Dvořák [Cz]*	*M. Czervinkova-Riegrová*	*Mannheim*
25 October	Die Abenteuer des Don Quichotte	Robert-Alfred Kirchner	Robert-Alfred Kirchner	Schwerin
18 November	*Alladin*	*Kurt Atterberg [Sw]*	*B. Hardt-Werden and J. Welleminsky*	*Chemnitz*
22 November	Das Dreinarrenspiel	Hans Uldall	Walter Gättke	Braunschweig

Date	Title	Composer	Librettist	Place
1942				
4 January	Schwanhild	Paul Graener	Otto Anthes	Cologne
13 January	Columbus	Werner Egk	Werner Egk	Frankfurt
24 January	Marienburg	Ernst Schliepe	Ernst Schliepe	Danzig (Gdansk)
7 February	Der Dombaumeister	Hans Stieber	Hans Stieber	Breslau (Wrocław)
25 February	Die Spielereien einer Kaiserin	Franz Bernhardt	Max Dauthendey	Bielefeld
7 March	Die schönen Mädchen von Haindelbrück	Hans Joseph Vieth	Fritz Clodwig Lange	Troppau (Opava)
28 March	Der leichtsinnige Herr Bandolin	Eugen Bodart	Eugen Bodart	Mannheim
15 April	Die Hochzeitsfackel	Clemens Schmalstich	Max Dreyer	Königsberg (Kaliningrad)
15 April	Dornröschen	Cesar Bresgen	Otto Reuther	Strasbourg
19 April	Antje	Herbert Trantow	Herbert Trantow	Chemnitz
25 April	Claudine von Villa Bella	Alfred Irmler	Alfred Irmler	Weimar
3 May	Die Musici	Hermann Henrich	Hermann Henrich	Schwerin
16 May	Sarabande	Eugen Bodart	Eugen Bodart	Altenburg
16 May	Das königliche Opfer	Georg Vollerthun	Oswald Schrenk	Hanover
20 June	Die Geschichte vom schönen Annerl	Leo Justinus Kauffmann	E. Reinacher/ E. Bormann	Strasbourg

1942–43

Date	Title	Composer	Librettist	Place
1942				
19 September	Napoleon	Edmund von Borck	Edmund von Borck (after Grabbe)	Gera
26 September	Überliestete Eifersucht oder Maestro Bernardo	Kurt Gillmann	Franz bei der Wieden	Schwetzingen
7 October	Odysseus	Hermann Reutter	Rudolf Bach	Frankfurt
28 October	Capriccio	Richard Strauss	Clemens Krauss	Munich
30 October	*Die Zauberinsel*	*Heinrich Sutermeister [S]*	*Sutermeister (after Shakespeare, 'The Tempest')*	*Dresden*
1 November	Das Buch der Liebe	Alexander Ecklebe	Otto Rombach	Beuthen (Bytom)
1 November	Der Garten des Paradieses	Felix Petyrek	Hans Reinhart (after H. C. Andersen)	Leipzig
14 November	Der Roßdieb	Richard Müller-Lampertz	Müller-Lampertz (after Hans Sachs)	Bremen
14 November	*Don Juan de Manara*	*Franco Alfano [I]*	*Ettore Moschino*	*Berlin*
20 December	*Morana*	*Jakov Gotovac [C]*	*A. Muradbegović*	*Hanover*
1943				
7 February	Das Urteil des Paris	Cesar Bresgen	Otto Reuther	Göttingen
13 February	Die schlaue Müllerin	Cesar Bresgen	Cesar Bresgen	Essen

Date	Title	Composer	Librettist	Place
20 February	Die Kluge	Carl Orff	Carl Orff (after Brothers Grimm)	Frankfurt
6 March	Die Fackel	Hans-Hendrik Wehding	Curt Böhmer	Karlsbad (Karlovy Vary)
12 March	I capricci di Callot	Gian Francesco Malipiero [I]	Malipiero (after E. T. A. Hoffmann, 'Prinzessin Brambilla')	Dortmund*
24 March	Rafaela	Hans-Hendrik Wehding	Karl Schueler	Görlitz (Gierloz)
1 April	Das Schloß Dürande	Othmar Schoeck [S]	Hermann Burte (after Eichendorff)	Berlin
22 April	Adelina	Nino Neidhardt	Herbert Kuchenbuch	Dresden
8 May	Schinderhannes	Gustav Kneip	Willi Schäferdiek	Karlsruhe
13 May	Der Zaubertrank (Le vin herbé)	Frank Martin [S]	Martin (after Joseph Bédier's 'Roman de Tristan et Iseult')	Braunschweig
27 May	Die kluge Wirtin	Hajo Hinrichs	Friedrich Lindemann	Oldenburg
27 May	Paracelsus	Hugo Herrmann	Marta Sills-Fuchs	Bremen
4 June	Der Kuckuck von Theben (Gli dei a Tebe)	Ermanno Wolf-Ferrari [I]	Mario Ghisalberti and Ludwig Andersen	Hanover
20 June	Signor Formica	Hans Grimm	Hans Grimm	Nuremberg
20 June	Das Leben ein Traum (La vita è sogno)	Gian Francesco Malipiero [I]	Malipiero (after Calderón)	Breslau (Wrocław)

1943–44

1943

6 November	Catulli Carmina	Carl Orff	Carl Orff	Leipzig
7 November	Das kalte Herz	Norbert Schultze	Kurt E. Walter	Leipzig
10 November	Mariora	C. G. Cosmovici [Ro]	Carmen Sylva	Heilbronn
13 November	Dorfmusik	Fried Walter	P. Beyer/E. Tramm	Wiesbaden
4 December	Las Golondrinas	José María Usandizaga [Sp]	G. Martínez Sierra	Frankfurt
5 December	Das Werbekleid	Franz Salmhofer	Franz Salmhofer	Salzburg

1944

7 January	Der Wunderschrank (A bűvös szekrény)	Ferenc Farkas (H)	G. Kiszély	Erfurt
12 March	**Casanova in Murano**	**Albert Lortzing (arr. Mark Lothar)**	**Albert Lortzing**	**Berlin**
17 June	Die Trug einer Nacht	Viktor Junk	Viktor Junk (after Calderón)	Thorn (Toruń)
2 July	Die Hochzeit des Jobs	Joseph Haas	Ludwig Andersen	Dresden
22 July	Das Perlenhemd	Leo Justinus Kauffmann	Erich Bormann	Strasbourg
[16 August	Die Liebe der Danae	Richard Strauss	Joseph Gregor	Salzburg]

Notes

1 Alan Steinweis, *Art, Ideology, & Economics in Nazi Germany: The Reich Chambers of Music, Theater, and the Visual Arts* (Chapel Hill: University of North Carolina Press, 1993), p. 132.

2 Although this perceived 'opera crisis' in Germany was much discussed in the musical press before 1933, it is particularly interesting to note that the issue was still debated as late as 1942. See Otto Eckstein-Ehrenegg, 'Die tieferen Ursachen der Opernkrise und der Weg zu ihrer Überwindung', *Zeitschrift für Musik*, 109 (1942), 62–4.

3 Michael Meyer, *The Politics of Music in the Third Reich*, American University Studies: Series 09, 49 (New York: Lang, 1991), p. 309.

4 Quoted in Jürgen Schebara, *Kurt Weill: An Illustrated Life* (New Haven, CT: Yale University Press, 1995), p. 203.

5 Fritz Feldens, *75 Jahre Städtische Bühnen Essen: Geschichte des Essener Theaters 1892–1967* (Essen: Rheinisch-Westfälische Verlagsgesellschaft, 1967), pp. 252, 287, 297.

6 For more on these methods of control, see the introduction to the present volume (pp. 8–14).

7 Steinweis, p. 134.

8 Fritz Stege, 'Zum deutschen Opernspielplan', *Zeitschrift für Musik*, 101 (1934), 1267–9.

9 Steinweis, p. 137.

10 Erik Levi, *Music in the Third Reich* (Basingstoke: Macmillan, 1994), pp. 75–7.

11 The review of the 1930 *Ring* Cycle at Bayreuth by Josef Stolzing-Czerny was published in the *Völkischer Beobachter*, 2 August 1930, and is quoted in Frederic Spotts, *Bayreuth: A History of the Wagner Festival* (New Haven, CT: Yale University Press, 1994), p. 157.

12 Peter Heyworth, *Otto Klemperer: His Life and Times*, 2 vols (Cambridge: Cambridge University Press, 1983–96), I: *1885–1933*, pp. 275–80.

13 Heyworth, pp. 402–4.

14 English translations of Mann's essay and the 'Letter of Protest from the City of Munich' can be found in Allan Blunden, *Thomas Mann: Pro and Contra Wagner* (Chicago: University of Chicago Press, 1985), pp. 91–152.

15 A photocopy of the frontispiece of the *NS-Monatshefte* Wagner number (July 1933) is reproduced in Hartmut Zelinsky, *Richard Wagner – ein deutsches Thema: eine Dokumentation zur Wirkungsgeschichte Richard Wagners 1876–1976* (Frankfurt am Main: Zweitausendeins, 1976), p. 219.

16 Wilhelm Altmann, 'Opernstatistik August 1930 bis Juli 1931', *Zeitschrift für Musik*, 99 (1931), 948–68.

17 Levi, pp. 192–3.

18 For a more detailed examination of Meyerbeer's reception during this period see Michael Walter, *Hitler in der Oper: deutsches Musikleben 1919–1945* (Stuttgart: Metzler, 1995), pp. 131–74

19 See, for example, Alfred Heuss, 'Weg mit der Werfelschen Bearbeitung von Verdis *Die Macht des Schicksals*', *Zeitschrift für Musik*, 100 (1933), 1123–6. This article reviews a new vocal score by Georg Göhler and Kurt Soldan of Verdi's opera *La*

forza del destino, published by C. F. Peters in Leipzig. During the following years, Peters would bring out further newly arranged adaptations of Verdi's operas.

20 It should be noted that the overwhelming majority of Handel's Italian operas were performed in German translation during this period, thus affording the opportunity to impose some kind of ideological adaptation of the text. A frequently performed example was Hans-Joachim Moser's arrangement of *Arminio*, first performed in the Handel anniversary year of 1935, which concluded with an arrangement of a chorale to a patriotic text.

21 Hans-Joachim Moser, 'Von der Tätigkeit der Reichsstelle für Musikbearbeitungen', *Jahrbuch der deutschen Musik* (Leipzig: Breitkopf und Härtel, 1943), p. 78.

22 A further revival, sponsored by the Reichsstelle, was of a little-known early Romantic opera, *The Homecoming of the Proscribed* (*Die Heimkehr des Verbannten*), by Lortzing's contemporary Otto Nicolai, which took place at the Berlin Staatsoper in February 1943, almost 100 years after its first performance. Originally composed in Italian, the opera served a useful dual purpose of emphasizing further cultural links between Germany and Italy, and placing before the public a melodious and patriotic work by a composer whose chief claim to fame remains the Shakespearian comic opera *The Merry Wives of Windsor* (*Die lustigen Weiber von Windsor*).

23 Werner Ladwig, 'Oper im neuen Zeichen', *Die Musik*, 25 (1933), 643–9; Wilhelm Altmann, 'Für einen deutschen Opernspielplan', *Die Musik*, 25 (1933), 901–4; Fritz Stege, 'Die Reinigung des deutschen Opernspielplans', *Zeitschrift für Musik*, 100 (1933), 487–8; Georg Vollerthun, 'Meine Absichten in der Oper und für ihre Erneuerung', *Zeitschrift für Musik*, 100 (1933), 844–5; Hans Költzsch, 'Der neue deutsche Opernspielplan', *Zeitschrift für Musik*, 100 (1933), 996–1000.

24 In the case of Schillings, the promotion of his best-known opera, *Mona Lisa* (1916), during the Third Reich posed a dilemma for some critics of a more puritan disposition. At issue was the deliberately sensationalist nature of the plot, which concerns the gruesome deaths by suffocation of Mona Lisa's husband and lover in fifteenth-century Florence. See Alfred Heuss, 'Wie steht es mit der *Mona Lisa* von Max von Schillings im neuen Deutschland?', *Zeitschrift für Musik*, 100 (1933), 624–5. Although Schillings's other operas had fallen out of the repertoire during the Weimar Republic, the revival of *Der Moloch* (1908) on 7 November 1934 in Berlin was deemed especially propitious given that the scenario could be interpreted as a symbol of legalized anti-semitism. The opera, inspired by an incomplete fragment by the Romantic dramatist Friedrich Hebbel, concerns the action of the high priest Hiram, who forces his way into a foreign land and attempts to make the natives of Thule believe in his religion, and to subjugate their culture for his own purposes. Anti-semitic elements are also implicit in Pfitzner's *The Heart*, particularly its central character, the restless Jewish doctor Daniel Athanasius, who attains supernatural powers that are capable of raising the dead.

25 Michael H. Kater, *The Twisted Muse: Musicians and their Music in the Third Reich* (Oxford: Oxford University Press, 1997), p. 29.

26 Kater, p. 26.

27 Hans Költzsch, 'Der neue deutsche Opernspielplan', *Zeitschrift für Musik*, 100 (1933), 997.

28 The letter is reproduced in Joseph Wulf, *Musik im Dritten Reich: eine Dokumentation* (Gütersloh: Sigbert Mohn, 1963), under the heading 'Mein Führer!' (pp. 95–6).

29 It is interesting to note that at least two of Siegfried Wagner's operas could have offended official sensibilities. In *The Smith of Marienburg (Der Schmied von Marienburg)* (1920; revived at the Berlin Staatsoper in the 1935–36 season), the pompous pledge of the thirteenth-century German knights to accept the status quo and reject all notions of personal freedom and dogmatism is ridiculed by the composer. More subversively, Siegfried's final opera, *The Little Curse that Everyone Experiences (Das Flüchlein, das Jeder mitbekam,* 1929–30), is set during the 1920s, tackling controversial issues such as unemployment and the rise of fascism, and in the case of the latter, not necessarily in a flattering light. Not surprisingly, the Wagner family made strenuous efforts to suppress the work, and it was performed for the first time in 1984.

30 The joint signatures of both composers on a manifesto condemning Thomas Mann's 1933 Wagner lecture (above, p. 142) proved to be one rare instance when Pfitzner and Strauss publicly supported the same argument.

31 Jeremy Tambling, *Opera and the Culture of Fascism* (Oxford: Clarendon Press, 1996), p. 202.

32 Kater, pp. 208–9.

33 It should be noted that although the opera's text was written by Joseph Gregor, much of the idea for the opera and even portions of its text emanated from Strauss's previous literary collaborator, Stefan Zweig.

34 Viktor Junk, 'Wiener Musik', *Zeitschrift für Musik*, 106 (1939), 860.

35 See Pamela Potter, 'Richard Strauss's *Friedenstag*: A Pacifistic Attempt at Political Resistance', *Musical Quarterly*, 69 (1983), 408–20.

36 For a more detailed discussion of Gerster's opera see Walter, p. 274.

37 Fred K. Prieberg, *Musik im NS-Staat* (Frankfurt am Main: Fischer, 1982), pp. 319–20.

38 Werner Egk, *Die Zeit wartet nicht*, 2nd edn (Mainz: Wilhelm Goldmann, 1981), pp. 311–13.

39 In his review of a performance of *Peer Gynt* in Dresden in March 1940, the critic Ernst Krause noted that Egk had revised the score, removing the Troll hymn – a decision which supports Egk's post-war contention that this particular section was critical of Nazi rituals. See Ernst Krause, 'Konzert und Oper: Dresden', *Zeitschrift für Musik*, 107 (1940), 170.

40 Walter, p. 118.

41 Herbert Gerigk, 'Neue Oper', *NS-Monatshefte*, March 1939, p. 278.

42 It is interesting to note that Caspar Neher designed the sets for the Düsseldorf performance. In view of Neher's associations with Brecht and Weill, one might speculate as to his reasons for associating himself with such an overtly Nazi political project. Unfortunately, the published literature on Neher remains silent about this episode.

43 Alfred Burgartz, 'Düsseldorfer Musiktagebuch: junge Komponisten in Front auf der Reichstagung der NS-Kulturgemeinde', *Die Musik*, 27 (1935), 736–41.

44 Hans Költzsch, 'Neues deutsches Opern-Schaffen', *Zeitschrift für Musik*, 102 (1935), 1100–5 (pp. 1103–4).

45 Walter Niemann, *Die Musik seit Richard Wagner* (Leipzig: Schuster und Loeffler, 1913), pp. 20–68.

46 Ludwig Schiedermair, *Die deutsche Oper: Grundzüge ihres Werdens und Wesens*, 2nd edn (Bonn: Dümmler, 1940), pp. 311–16.

47 Hans Severus Ziegler, *Entartete Musik: eine Abrechnung* (Düsseldorf: [Völkischer Verlag], 1938), p. 20 (quoted in *Entartete Musik: eine kommentierte Rekonstruktion*, ed. by Albrecht Dümling and Peter Girth (Düsseldorf: Kleinherne, 1988), p. 137). The Jewish works specifically cited by Ziegler were Schoenberg's *From Today till Tomorrow* (*Von heute auf morgen*), Weill's *Rise and Fall of the City of Mahagonny* (*Aufstieg und Fall der Stadt Mahagonny*), Grosz's *Attention! Performance!* (*Achtung! Aufnahme!*) and Toch's *The Fan* (*Der Fächer*). Amongst the foreign works mentioned by Ziegler were the 'Czech' Krenek's *Life of Orestes* (*Leben des Orest*), the Pole Rathaus's *Strange Earth* (*Fremde Erde*), the Frenchman Milhaud's *Christophe Colomb* and the American Antheil's *Transatlantic*.

48 Fritz Stege, 'Die Reinigung des deutschen Opernspielplans', *Zeitschrift für Musik*, 100 (1933), 488. See also Stege's articles 'Musiker im Gespräch: Gerhard Schjelderup', *Zeitschrift für Musik,* 100 (1933), 840–1; 'Deutsch und nordische Musik', *Zeitschrift für Musik*, 101 (1934), 1269–70. Stege's opera text *Northerners in Distress* (*Norden in Not*), designated a '*Nordische Volksoper*', with music by the Austrian composer Roderich von Mojsisovics, was broadcast on Leipzig Radio in 1936.

49 Ernst Stier, 'Konzert und Oper: Braunschweig', *Zeitschrift für Musik*, 101 (1934), 90.

50 A highly respected figure whose music already enjoyed considerable exposure in Germany, Atterberg became a staunch proponent of the Third Reich, lending active support to the International Society for Cooperation amongst Composers – an organization established by the Nazis in 1934 in opposition to the 'avant-garde' International Society for Contemporary Music.

51 Ernst Stier, 'Konzert und Oper: Braunschweig', *Zeitschrift für Musik*, 101 (1934), 330.

52 Excluding the three works by the Swede Atterberg, between 1934 and 1944 only four Scandinavian operas were performed in provincial German theatres: *Nights of Love* (*Liebesnächte*), a neo-Wagnerian confection by the Norwegian Gerhard Schjelderup (Lübeck, 1934); *The Goose-Maiden* (*Die Gänsemagd*), by Swedish-German Lill Erik Hafgren (Mannheim, 1938); and *Inka* and *Es gärt in Småland* by the Swede Albert Henneberg (Chemnitz, 1937 and 1939 respectively). Despite the signal failure of any Swedish opera to make any impact at a major German theatre, Stockholm's Royal Opera House seems to have accepted Nazi propaganda about the irrefutable racial and cultural ties between Scandinavia and Germany, and reciprocated by giving a platform to new German operas, for example Fried Walter's *Queen Elizabeth* (*Königin Elisabeth*, 1939).

53 During the Third Reich, Sibelius was the only non-German composer to have been awarded the Goethe Prize (in 1936). In 1943, Heinz Drewes, director of musical affairs in the Propaganda Ministry, established the German Sibelius Gesellschaft.

54 It is worth noting that eight of the eleven operas Malipiero composed between 1920 and 1931 were given their first performances in German opera houses: *Orfeo* and *The Death of the Masks* (*La morte delle maschere*) (Düsseldorf, 1925); the *Three Plays by Goldoni* (*Tre commedie goldoniane*) (Darmstadt, 1926); *The Pretend Harlequin* (*Il finto Arlecchino*) (Mainz, 1928); *Night Tournament* (*Torneo notturno*) (Munich, 1931); and *The Eagles of Aquileia* (*Le aquile di Aquileia*) (Coburg, 1932).

55 Ernst Stier, 'Konzert und Oper: Braunschweig', *Zeitschrift für Musik*, 101 (1934), 215.

56 Alfred Schlee, 'German Opera in Transition', *Modern Music*, 11, no. 2 (1934), 149. Significantly, the anonymous reviewer in Rosenberg's journal confines comment on Malipiero's opera within a report largely devoted to Braunschweig's other non-German operatic premiere, Atterberg's *Fanal*. See 'Eine Schwedische Oper vom Rhein', *Die Musik*, 26 (1934), 441. For a summary of the plot of Pirandello's libretto for the opera and the subsequent banning, see Chapter 5 of the present volume (pp. 225–6).

57 John C. G. Waterhouse, 'La favola del figlio cambiato', *The New Grove Dictionary of Opera*, ed. by Stanley Sadie, 4 vols (London: Macmillan 1992), II, 140.

58 The Shakespeare opera *Antonio e Cleopatra* was given in Bremen in 1939, *Life is a Dream* (*La vita è sogno*, after Calderón) in Breslau in 1943 and *Giulio Cesare* (after Shakespeare) in Gera in 1938 and at the Deutsch-Italienische Kunstwoche (German-Italian Arts Week) in Hamburg in 1941, while the planned performance of *I capricci di Callot* (after E. T. A. Hoffmann) in Dortmund in 1943 was aborted after Allied bombing raids.

59 See, for example, the review of *Antonio e Cleopatra* by Professor Dr Kratzi in *Zeitschrift für Musik*, 106 (1939), 418.

60 The piano reduction of the opera, published by Universal Edition in Vienna, was made by Anton Webern in 1942.

61 Ronald Crichton, 'Othmar Schoeck', *The New Grove Dictionary of Opera*, ed. by Sadie, IV, 236; Derrick Puffett, *The Song-Cycles of Othmar Schoeck* (Berne: Paul Haupt, 1982), p. 56; Peter Andraschke, 'Das Schloß Dürande', in *Pipers Enzyklopädie des Musiktheaters*, 7 vols (Munich: Piper, 1986–97), V (1994), 602..

62 Ernst Krause, 'Heinrich Sutermeister *Romeo und Julia*: Uraufführung in Dresden', *Zeitschrift für Musik*, 107 (1940), 293–4.

63 Otto Eckstein-Ehrenegg, 'Die tieferen Ursachen der Opernkrise.

64 In his admittedly selective autobiography, the conductor Karl Böhm attributes the relative failure of the score to Sutermeister's contrived attempt to appeal to the public, and to an unconvincing concluding scene in C major which fails to aspire to the heroic apotheosis embodied in a work like Beethoven's *Fidelio*. See Karl Böhm, *Ich erinnere mich ganz genau* (Frankfurt am Main: Gutenberg, 1968), pp. 74–5.

65 A useful summary of some of the principal musical activities that resulted from the Berlin–Rome axis is contained in Harvey Sachs, *Music in Fascist Italy* (London: Weidenfeld and Nicolson, 1987), pp. 189–90. In the context of the performance of contemporary German opera in Italy, it should be noted that the published score of Kempff's *Familie Gozzi* bore a personal dedication to Mussolini.

66 See, for example, Fritz Stege's review of *The Flame* in 'Berliner Musik', *Zeitschrift für Musik*, 103 (1936), 831–2. After 1939, however, the same critic followed official cultural policy in emphasizing mutual stylistic links between German and Italian operas.

67 Dr H. W. Kulenkampff, 'Polens Nationaloper *Halka*: deutsche Uraufführung in der Hamburgischen Staatsoper', *Blätter für Kunst und Kultur – Hamburger Theater-Woche*, 3, no. 21 (1935), 8.

68 At the same time, it should be noted that a number of nineteenth-century Russian operas were performed before 1939, for example: Tchaikovsky, *Eugene Onegin* (Berlin Staatsoper, 1934); Tchaikovsky, *Queen of Spades* (*Pique Dame*) (Essen, 1935); Glinka, *A Life for the Tsar* (Stuttgart, 1936); Mussorgsky, *Sorochintsy*

Fair (*Der Jahrmarkt von Sorotschinsk*) (Koblenz, 1936; Essen, 1937); Mussorgsky, *Boris Godunov* (also Berlin, 1934). Hamburg staged the original version of *Boris Godunov* in 1935 and Borodin's *Prince Igor* in 1938. Operas by Rimsky-Korsakov also featured in the repertory, for example *The Legend of the Invisible City of Kitezh* at the Berlin Staatsoper in 1937 and the *Tale of Tsar Saltan* in Darmstadt in 1938. As far as the two contemporary works are concerned, Blacher's work soon fell out of favour when the Rosenberg wing of the party discovered evidence to the effect that the composer was quarter-Jewish. Zanella's opera, however, enjoyed greater favour, particularly since Gogol's play had earlier been praised by the Nazis (see Chapter 5 of the present volume (p. 233)).

69 When Erich Kleiber conducted fragments from Berg's opera *Lulu* at a concert in Berlin in November 1934, critical response, particularly from the reactionary journals such as *Zeitschrift für Musik* and *Die Musik*, was so hostile that the conductor soon realized that he could no longer work in Germany. In any case, although no question marks hung over Berg's racial origins, the composer's strong association with Schoenberg, not to mention the 'decadent' nature of the libretto, almost certainly ruled out any prospect of a performance of the opera in Germany. For a useful resumé of the critical reception of Berg's work see Alfred Burgartz, 'Alban Bergs Lulu Musik: Uraufführung im Berliner Staatsopernkonzert', *Die Musik*, 27 (1935), 262–3. See also the editorial: 'Unsere Meinung: Alban Berg und die Berliner Musikkritik', *Die Musik*, 27 (1935), 263–4.

70 A recent communication from Universal Edition in Vienna to the author (13 September 1999) has revealed that, when the vocal score was reprinted in 1939 and 1941, Brod's name was discreetly removed from the title page of the publication.

71 Works which follow such musical principles include Howard Hanson, *Merry Mount* (New York, 1934), Vaughan Williams, *Riders to the Sea* (London, 1937), and Holst, *The Wandering Scholar* (Liverpool, 1934). One could even argue that Gershwin's *Porgy and Bess* (New York, 1935) is, in essence, an opera about ordinary folk using putative folk music materials.

4

Jewish theatre: repertory and censorship in the Jüdischer Kulturbund, Berlin

REBECCA ROVIT

In September 1933, a group of Jewish artists in Berlin submitted a play manuscript for examination to SS Kommandant Hans Hinkel, state commissar for Jewish cultural affairs. The play, entitled *God's Hunt* (*Die Jagd Gottes*), was written by the German Jewish rabbi Emil Bernhard (Cohn). Seeking permission for performance, the theatre directors scheduled this as the first Jewish play for their first winter season in 1933. The predominantly German-born Jewish artists belonged to the newly sanctioned Kulturbund Deutscher Juden (Cultural League of German Jews) – known after 1935 as the Jüdischer Kulturbund in Germany. This organization, based exclusively on member subscriptions, became the only long-term, legitimate cultural outlet for Jewish musicians and theatre practitioners in Germany after the Nazis had the capacity to bar Jews from their professions on 7 April 1933 with the Civil Service Law.

On 22 September 1933, the Reich Chamber of Culture Law initiated the process, implemented strictly in 1935, whereby Jewish artists were denied membership in the theatre, film, radio, music, literature, visual arts and press chambers.[1] Some Jewish artists in large cities like Berlin maintained part-time employment in German theatres and film studios, despite the official bans. Yet they eventually lost their membership in the chambers of culture and joined the Kulturbund if they had not already emigrated.[2] Those Jewish artists who stayed in Germany suddenly found themselves separated from their former non-Jewish colleagues and forced to create specifically termed 'Jewish' art in the Kulturbund, exclusively among Jews.

Jewish theatre- and opera-goers in Berlin were not immediately barred from German theatres and concert halls in April 1933, however. Many Jews continued to attend performances at German theatres until at least 1935, and in fact, even as late as 1938.[3] They could more easily remain anonymous and integrate themselves into all-German audiences in large cities than they could in provincial towns. But as a result of increasing social and cultural isolation, many Jews had preferred to join the Jewish Kulturbund, where they were welcomed and could belong to some kind of community.

A crucial cultural and national struggle for identity lies at the heart of this German Jewish cultural organization, whose network spread from Berlin's centre to theatre branches across the new Reich. The struggle reveals itself not only in the identity with which the organization's directors wished to imbue their undertaking, but also in their choices for a viable and authorized dramatic repertory for their theatre. In a cultural domain characterized by epistolary sparring, Kulturbund managing director, musicologist and medical doctor Kurt Singer forged, together with Hinkel, a careful, necessary collaboration to procure permissions and to secure both administrative protection and parameters within which to develop a theatrical and orchestral repertory. Their collaboration also enabled other cities, like Hamburg in 1934 and, over the next years, groups of neighbouring towns in the Ruhr valley and former Silesia, for example, to establish their own Jewish cultural leagues or Kulturbünde. From his Berlin-Charlottenburg office and, after autumn 1935, from the theatre on Kommandantenstraße in Berlin's centre, Singer served as middle-man between Jewish artists in other urban centres and Hinkel's office. He orchestrated the flow of manuscripts and permissions, directed warnings to Jewish centres, and arranged touring concerts from Berlin to Jewish communities in Germany's provinces. By mid-1935, these local Jewish cultural agencies had become centralized in Berlin under the umbrella organization the Reichsverband der jüdischen Kulturbünde (the Reich Association of Jewish Cultural Leagues).

After Singer left Berlin for Holland in November 1938, Hinkel and his staff continued to oversee the Jewish theatre enterprise and to cooperate with Singer's successors, Werner Levie until 1939, and the actor Fritz Wisten until the organization's dissolution by the Nazis on 11 September 1941. A similar Jewish theatre had formed in Amsterdam, Holland, earlier that same summer of 1941, under the leadership of former Berlin Kulturbund personnel Werner Levie and cabaret artist Max Ehrlich.[4] The Dutch version of a Jewish theatre ensemble in Nazi-occupied Holland represents the more macabre aspects of a Jewish theatre struggling to survive against the odds in the wake of the Nazi plan to eliminate Jews; less than a year later, on 12 July 1942, the Nazis converted the Joodsche Schouwburg theatre into a deportation depot for Holland's Jews, who were sent to the Westerbork transit camp and subsequently transported eastward to Auschwitz.[5]

This study on Jewish theatre during the Third Reich focuses on the Kulturbund in Germany, specifically Berlin. In examining the Kulturbund it

is necessary to examine first the man at the theatre's helm: *Intendant* Kurt
Singer. How did the director obtain authorization for performances? And how
did the mercurial system of Nazi censorship work in regard to the Kulturbund's
choice of programming? Using correspondence from Hinkel's office to theatre
directors and original playscripts from the main theatre in Berlin, a concentration on the Kulturbund's dramatic repertory will highlight examples of
censorship to which playtexts and programmes were exposed. Berlin's Jewish
theatre represents the Kulturbund phenomenon as the primary pulse of a
network of cultural organizations across Germany. It was the Kulturbund
centre with the largest audience membership and most extensive personnel; in
fact, some of its performers often travelled across Germany to perform with
troupes at other Jewish cultural centres.[6] The main organization's headquarters
in the capital of the Reich gave Berlin's theatre extra legitimacy. First, Singer
had a special alliance with Hinkel's office at the Propaganda Ministry. He
also kept close ties with the administrative organization in Berlin for Jews in
Germany, the Reichsvertretung der deutschen Juden (by 1939, incorporated
into the centralized Jewish organization, the Reichsvereinigung der Juden in
Deutschland).

My focus on Berlin exemplifies the dilemmas faced by the Kulturbünde in
general. Such dilemmas included providing unemployed artists with work,
shaping cultural programmes whose content would appeal to members, and
cooperating with the authorities and their censorship rules. My concern with
Singer, his allegiance to the Kulturbund and its theatrical repertory will shed
light on the operations within branch organizations of the original Berlin
Kulturbund. An examination of official censorship and the Jewish theatre
repertory may also raise new questions regarding the Dutch 'experiment', for
the actors and managers of the Jewish theatre in Amsterdam were mainly
German refugee artists.

Problems of interpreting the Kulturbund

There has already been a good deal of work on Nazi-occupied Holland in
English and German. Yet current research on the Kulturbund in Germany is
limited to but a few studies. In English, more frequent are references to the
Kulturbund within broader studies on German Jews in Nazi Germany. Many
often dismiss the Kulturbund as a Nazi ploy to subordinate Jews and their
culture to Nazi plans and to 'foreshadow the Nazi ghetto' by creating a
'pretence of internal autonomy' on the part of the Jews, more or less, until
their eventual deportation.[7]

English-language essays on the Kulturbund have focused mainly on an
historical recapitulation, based on the account of former Dramaturg Herbert

Freeden.[8] In fact, until the efforts made by Berlin's Akademie der Künste to mount an exhibition in 1992, Freeden had remained the authority on the subject. But then other eye-witnesses, former Kulturbund artists who were interviewed, started to contradict the historical accounts. Their personal recollections provoke questions about how one may understand the Kulturbund in hindsight, given the atrocities committed by the Nazis during the 1930s and 1940s. The debate on the Kulturbund could move beyond moral judgements of whether the Kulturbund was right or wrong, a 'failed institution that was forced to exist', or a prelude to the ghettoization of Europe's Jews.[9] But researchers must present balanced studies of Kulturbund activities in all their complexity. Such studies could benefit as much from discussions of theatrical representation and collaboration, for example, as from pronouncements that Jews misunderstood the Kulturbund's significance and stayed in Germany until their inevitable deportation.

Even the most recent analyses of the Kulturbund reveal the limited scope of present conceptions. Many questions regarding the Kulturbund still remain – questions of representation and identity, collaboration and censorship, for example.[10] No one to date has ventured a close examination of the actual playscripts performed by the Kulturbund in connection with censorship and performance issues, beyond a mere cataloguing of play titles and performance dates. The most recent study of the second-largest Kulturbund theatre, in Hamburg, echoes familiar themes regarding the theatre's function: spiritual resistance through theatre. A primary focus on Hamburg's theatre centre reinforces already-published observations on Kulturbund centres, specifically the one in Rhenish-Westfalen (Frankfurt). Finally, the Kulturbund Jews' link to their German and Jewish identity has already been established.[11]

It is time to integrate disparate interpretations in order to examine an area still under-researched: Nazi censorship and how it affected the Kulturbund repertory. The examination of playscripts proposed for performance and evaluated by the Nazis reveals that the Nazis' demands for the Jewish theatre were contradictory to the spirit of those Kulturbund Jews and to the Nazis' aims to promote a separate Jewish culture. Nazi supervisors interpreted repertory choices with too Jewish an emphasis (such as themes of Messianism) as subversive and potentially dangerous to the new German Reich. Such plays, however, might have helped to promote a sense of Jewish identity for the Jews, many of whom viewed themselves as German citizens. Attempts by the Nazis to censor plays which they deemed part of German culture undermined the Jews' cultural programmes. In conclusion, this analysis will suggest that the Kulturbund challenged both Jews and Nazis throughout its existence.

Berlin Jews, Jewish theatre and the Kulturbund in Berlin

Throughout the nineteenth century, Jews in Germany had assimilated German customs in their quest for equality as citizens of the early empire. Their formal emancipation finally came in 1871. But even then, German Jews were still denied high posts in state-dependent institutions like the military and the universities. By the time of the Weimar Republic (1918) large percentages of Jews had gravitated to such independent occupations as trade, commerce, law, medical practice and the arts. Jews in Germany had long regarded themselves as German citizens of the 'Israelite' or 'Mosaic' faith. Many well-known Jews had undergone baptism or converted to Christianity in order to gain full acceptance in German society.[12] Generally speaking, the artists of the Berlin Kulturbund were brought up according to the liberal traditions of the Weimar period; politically, they were for the most part, liberals or Social Democrats. They had been exposed in German schools to the humanist concepts of *Bildung* and *Sittlichkeit*, morals and manners.[13]

The number of Jews in Germany by January 1933 was 525,000, over two-thirds of whom lived in cities. Berlin alone was home to one-third of Germany's Jews.[14] Urban centres like Berlin had also been the destination for the influx of East European Jewish immigrants, the *Ostjuden*, during the last decades of the nineteenth century. These Jews did not assimilate the dress, language or cultural attitudes of their German hosts. They populated Berlin's central eastern district, the Scheunenviertel, maintained their Yiddish language, preserved their Orthodox religious rituals, and even nurtured Yiddish theatre traditions in the first two decades of the twentieth century.[15] This was also the neighbourhood where, in the 1920s, touring Jewish troupes from Eastern Europe (the Habimah and Jewish Academy Theatres) staged foreign tales of Hebrew and Yiddish lore using a non-realistic presentational style.

Martin Buber and Leo Baeck, who both served on the Kulturbund's advisory council, had instigated a Jewish revival in their search to define a religious community and to transmit knowledge about Judaism throughout the 1920s.[16] The Kulturbund directors knew the work of Buber and Baeck and were aware of the Jewish theatre troupe visits to Berlin. The first set designer for the Kulturbund, Heinz Condell, remembered those stylized modes of theatre as being 'original, expressive and un-European', in forms which 'greatly excited' him and his colleagues. Many people identified such forms with 'a "Jewish" theatrical style'. Because Jewish theatres after 1933 had to work 'more economically and more intellectually' than subsidized state theatres, Condell claimed that a more spartan design should emanate from each play's style and spirit.[17]

The majority of the Kulturbund founding and ensemble members, like

Condell, were typical acculturated German Jews – 'barely practising Jews', as one former musician later acknowledged about his family life. These artists considered themselves German by birth, culture and language. But some of them believed that while feeling German was 'in all of us, having lived as Germans for many generations, [...] we always felt like Jews'.[18] The German-born Kulturbund artists appear to have been strongly conscious of their dual roots of German and Jew, of being both part of a society and apart from it, particularly after 1933. Singer and his literary advisor, Julius Bab, sought to reflect this duality in their programmes. By acknowledging the Jewish heritage of the theatre's members, they proposed lectures on Bialik and theatrical adaptations of Sholom Aleichem's stories, for example. Buber's early enthusiasm for Chassidism had allowed writers to establish the image of the *Ostjude* as the genuine Jew. This only further distinguished East European Jews from their German counterparts.[19] Moreover, Kulturbund directors promoted a repertory rooted primarily in the West European cultural tradition, which members knew better than 'authentic' Hebrew and Yiddish models from the East.

There was a small contingent of Orthodox and Zionist Jews in Berlin's theatre-going community. Some of the Kulturbund artists were born outside Germany, like the actor Kurt Katsch from Poland and the singer Mascha Benyakonski (Benya-Matz) from Lithuania. They had developed a strong sense of Judaism and they were familiar with Yiddish folk art. Before his emigration to the United States in 1935, however, Katsch's onstage roles were limited to such classics as Lessing's Nathan and Shakespeare's Othello in 1933 and 1934. The Kulturbund directors also discouraged Benya-Matz's desire to promote Yiddish and Hebrew folklore on their stage. In spite of her training in an area which might have been termed 'Jewish culture', she sang an aria in French for her 1937 audition to the ensemble. She subsequently sang such operatic roles as Verdi's Gilda in the Kulturbund's *Rigoletto* (in German).

None the less, from the Kulturbund's beginning, pressures from the Zionist minority within Berlin's Jewish community, as well as from the Nazis, urged Singer and his colleagues to produce plays which would reflect 'Jewish' concerns.[20] These pressures mounted after autumn 1936. That is when the theatre hired a Dramaturg, Herbert Friedenthal, alias Freeden, to steer the repertory in a more Jewish direction. Benya-Matz finally had a chance to sing in Hebrew on occasion; prior to her emigration, she enhanced the 'Oriental' atmosphere with Hebrew and Yemenite folksongs at an introductory matinee for a play by a Jewish writer from Palestine, Shulamit Batdori, entitled *The Trial* in May 1938.[21] Several months later, she sang in the world premiere of Chelmo Vinaver's opera, *The Pioneers* (*Ha'Chalutzim*), which took place in a synagogue. While the actors performed plays by Osip Dimov, H. Leivick and Jacob Gordin in German translation, Nazi censors oversaw the theatrical enterprise with particular attention to the goal of 'Jewish' theatre. This meant that censors had to decide whether the 'Jewish' plays would be contrary to the rules of the new Germany, especially when presented by Jewish performers.

Nazi censors and Jewish directors: a tenuous coalition

The process by which the Nazis evaluated the Kulturbund's first proposed Jewish playtext, *God's Hunt*, offers an insight into the difficulties faced by the Jewish theatre in shaping a repertory, particularly in the early years of the Third Reich. The play 'takes place in a Jewish village high in the Carpathian mountains, of a forgotten name and forgotten time',[22] and opens inside an ancient synagogue. Amid a 'deathly silence', the entire community waits behind locked doors:

THE VOICE OF THE COSSACK-GENERAL   You Jew sows! You god-
damned swine! Stinking pack of crooked noses! Pickled garlic bellies! Shall we smoke you out like a load of lice? Shall we bait your women? Shall we slaughter your babies? We're going away, today, you pigs! But don't celebrate yet; we'll be back!
Outside, shouts, then the sound of horses' hooves receding. Silence.
A CHILD *begins to cry softly.*
MOTHER   Shh – shh —
WOMAN'S VOICE   Rabbi!
GABBE (PINCHAS)   Shhhhh!
   Silence.
VOICE   Rabbi!
GABBE   Pssst!
Silence.
VOICE   We've been sitting in here for three days while the Cossacks shout in our alleys. And we've got no more to eat.
MAN'S VOICE   For three years, they've been living in our mountains. They reap our earth; they steal our livestock. The woods are burning around us. And we can't get over the mountains.
WOMAN'S VOICE   The Cossacks keep coming back, and our blood keeps flowing.
MAN'S VOICE   The Cossacks are gone now, but we still can't get over the mountains; the forests are burning!
RABBI   Chonenu, adonoi, chonenu, ki umlolim anochnu (Have mercy on us, Lord, have mercy on us, for we are in misery).

Thus begins the playscript that Hans Hinkel forwarded to Reichsdramaturg

Dr Rainer Schlösser. Hinkel's secretary enclosed an accompanying note that succinctly sums up the Kulturbund's situation and, in a way, eerily replicates the dramatic opening of Bernhard's play: 'The events of the "KDJ" [Kultur-bund] take place exclusively with Jewish actors and lecturers in closed performances for exclusively Jewish audiences.'[23]

God's Hunt incorporates such themes as Jewish community cohesion and a renewed spirit of Judaism, the notion of a Messiah, or a political deliverer, and the sacrifice of a martyr, Naftali, to the Cossacks. These themes stress love over hate; for, in the end, the Jews' community prevails over the threat by the Cossacks, whose actual stage presence never materializes, except in sound (voices, shouts, destruction and horses' hooves). But the Reichs-dramaturg banned the Kulturbund's performance of the play, which had already been cast and set for a December premiere by the time Dr Singer heard of the rejection. A glance at Schlösser's report to Hinkel on the Jewish drama that never reached the Kulturbund stage suggests the potential dangers of a public performance of Bernhard's play:

Dear Herr Staatskommissar,

Having examined the drama *God's Hunt* by Emil Bernhard, I hasten to inform you that the performance by the Kulturbund of German Jews does not appear to me as very opportune. The whole thing is a kind of 'solace of Judaism', a kind of 'restorative' for Jews. In itself, the play is not tendentious and would be harmless if one had performed it during the last Reich. The Third Reich, however, had recognized Judaism in its imminent danger, thus making the matter appear quite objectionable, especially since the play's background is a Russian rabble of soldiers which mistreats Jewry. One can imagine with whom the suggested Cossacks will be identified.

Heil Hitler!

A note in the bottom left-hand corner reads, '1 manuscript back to Jews on 31 October'.[24] This is when Hinkel finally responded to Singer, who had already waited a month before asking whether they could proceed with rehearsals for the play. Hinkel warned Singer, however: 'Your proposal for a performance of *God's Hunt* by Emil Bernhard was examined with the result that permission for a performance of the play may not be granted. You should take notice of this.' With scarcely more than a month until the play's putative premiere (the play was already announced as a coming attraction in galley-proofs sent to Singer), Singer submitted a request to perform Hebbel's biblical (apocryphal) *Judith* instead, suggesting that he from then on submit three to four scripts at a time for examination.[25] Hebbel's play centres on the title character in his version of Judith's murder of the enemy military captain,

Holofernes. Hebbel reveals conflict in his Judith, a woman who had seemingly murdered for love of her country, yet is plagued by her hurt pride and her misdeed. In late October, Singer received word that he could proceed with Hebbel's *Judith*; but by this time, he had postponed that production 'for technical reasons', and asked to produce Shakespeare's *Othello*. Thus began a new phase of negotiation, resulting in a December production of *Othello*.

This is but an example of the volley of written permission requests, formal approvals, civil warnings and deferential pleas between Singer and Hinkel to establish a theatre repertory for Jewish artists and theatre-goers within a framework of censorship. A fortnight of correspondence between the two men might typically yield as many as ten letters related to requests and authoriz-ations. Singer would trigger the process by submitting a script to the Propaganda Ministry for examination. While Dr Schlösser personally examined some of the submissions, other Nazi functionaries, who were more loyal to the principles of the new Reich's 'national revolution' than to cultural matters, also decided what might be performed.

Exceptions for German stages

It should be noted that this process was not reserved for Jewish theatres; indeed, all German (or Aryanized) theatres were subject to similar, restrictive procedures in selecting their repertory seasons. The Reichsdramaturg required all prospective repertory lists for the Reich to be submitted for approval before the season in question began.[26] Evidently, however, top propaganda officials made specific exceptions for German theatres. Especially in the early years, before almost all Jewish artists were successfully 'purged' from the Reich Chamber of Culture, Schlösser (and Hinkel) appeared to make up the rules for theatres as they went along. In the correspondence between Schlösser and Hinkel, one notices the almost haphazard way in which these men discussed whether the work of some Jewish artists was acceptable for German theatres in specific situations. Although the men's letters focus on the work of Jews in German theatres, some of the issues raised by the Reichsdramaturg in his letters suggest that exceptions may have been made by these same officials for the Kulturbund.

It is useful to consider some examples from Schlösser's correspondence regarding German theatre in order better to understand the censorship of the Jewish theatre repertory and the seeming fluidity of the Nazis' guiding principles. In March 1934, for instance, Schlösser responded to a request from Hinkel's office about composers whose work was considered objectionable. The censor had asked specifically about Meyerbeer, Bizet and Offenbach, while adding that his office did not expect any objections. Schlösser's letter indicates that Hinkel made decisions in the realm of music without necessarily checking with Schlösser. Apparently, Hinkel had permitted a German theatre in Koblenz to stage three Offenbach operettas, although Offenbach's work was supposedly banned from Aryanized stages. Schlösser's letter makes clear that he understands from a musically critical standpoint Hinkel's 'generosity' (*Freizügigkeit*) vis-à-vis these productions. This is provocative because it suggests that Hinkel may have also decided on specific repertory choices for the Jewish theatre after negotiating only with Singer.[27] Schlösser ends his letter by disagreeing with Hinkel's decision, 'given the unmistakable sensitivity of the masses regarding the Jewish Question'.[28]

But exceptions were made for some artists, in spite of their belonging to the wrong 'race'. In a letter to Hinkel, Schlösser noted that 'for reasons of international relations', he had allowed some of Ralph Benatzky's work to be performed. This did not mean, however, that undesired 'non-Aryan' composers like 'Kálmán, Leo Fall, Jarno, Offenbach, Meyerbeer, etc.' were permissible.[29] Evidence suggests that allowances for work by supposedly 'undesirable' composers very much depended on where the performance was to take place. Ironically enough, the Kulturbund theatre had become a haven for the work of 'undesirables'; Jews could and did produce the work of these banned composers. But repertory offerings at German state-subsidized theatres, especially in Berlin, had to reflect the racial purity espoused by Nazi cultural politics. This is clear in Schlösser's answer to a censor regarding Herybert Menzel's opera, *Annerl and Kasperl*, with music written by Ernst Viebig, who was half-Jewish. Schlösser expressed heavy objections to a performance of the opera, at least at a 'state-subsidized theatre'. For one would have to imagine many performances of the work; and this at a time when 'the pure Aryan artists on our stages have not yet received justice'. Nor would this set the right example for other half-Jewish composers, who would expect similar treatment. Therefore, 'in the interest of a consolidation of the *Kulturpolitik* (cultural politics) of the national revolution, a world premiere of the opera in question would be premature', Schlösser concluded.[30]

Schlösser appeared to have been more likely to make exceptions for productions either in private theatres or theatres outside Berlin than in state-sponsored national theatres. Even after the Nuremberg Racial Laws had been passed in 1935, discussion continued regarding exceptions for plays on which Jews, or half-Jews, had collaborated. Schlösser wrote to Hinkel in April 1937 about a widow's request for a performance of her late husband's play, *The Happy Excellency* (*Die selige Exzellenz*), which had been written together with a Jew:

I certainly do not want to close my eyes to Frau Presber's difficult social situation, but if I as Reichsdramaturg even allow but one Berlin private theatre a play by a Jewish author, then immediately all hell will certainly break loose at all the others [theatres]. I have remained quite stubborn on this point since 1933 and would prefer to remain so in the future with full agreement from you. In the provinces, of course, which would not bring in much in the way of royalties, I would let myself be talked to. Please respond.[31]

If Schlösser and Hinkel discussed various scenarios for allowing the work of Jewish authors in German theatres under a variety of circumstances, then they probably also made exceptions for the Jewish Kulturbund theatre. Indeed, obvious exceptions were made in the interest of international relations during the 1936 Olympics – and prior to the Second World War – when foreign journalists gained permission to attend and review Kulturbund productions.[32] All of the above examples suggest some inconsistency on the part of official censors in deciding which composers, writers and works were taboo. The Nazi officials who censored Aryanized theatres were the same ones who decided about the Jewish Kulturbund repertory. They appear to have made decisions under rules which often changed, depending on the situation or particular work in question.

The Kulturbund repertory and censorship

In the case of the Kulturbund theatre, the Reichsdramaturg or a clerk would eventually report to Hinkel, who, in turn, reported back to the Jews. On occasion, as was the case with German theatres, Hinkel himself made decisions on the playscripts and musical programmes submitted by the Jews. The next steps were internal ones in the theatre with the *Indendant* relaying all necessary revisions to the play's director, and ultimately to the cast. The Nazis' guidelines for Jewish theatre rejected plays and musical works by all non-Jewish Germans by 1936 and non-Jewish Austrians (after the *Anschluß* in 1938) and barred many topics which were either misunderstood or might be subject to misinterpretation. In addition, the Kulturbund was forbidden to transfer royalties out of the country to living playwrights. Foreign playwrights who had been dead for over fifty years, however, could be performed, as royalty payments were no longer necessary. Some dramatists, such as Ferenc Molnár and J. B. Priestley, gave up their right to royalties to allow for performances of their plays.

Over 80 per cent of the plays performed by the Kulturbund were plays not originally in German. Texts by such German-speaking Jews as Richard Beer-Hofmann, Arthur Schnitzler and Stefan Zweig were the exception. Among the Shakespeare scripts used were the well-known translations by Dorothea Tieck and A. W. von Schlegel. Among the classics were *Reclam* editions of German translations like Sophocles' *Antigone* (by Georg Thudicum) or the plays of Ibsen (by Wilhelm Lange), already part of theatre repertories prior to 1933. The Kulturbund Dramaturgs, Herbert Freeden and Leo Hirsch, translated modern scripts from abroad, like Shulamit Batdori's *The Trial*, Leivick's *The Golem* or Priestley's *People at Sea*, from Hebrew, Yiddish and English. While examining the extant original performance scripts, it is vital to remember that revisions and deletions in the scripts must be viewed in context. Some revisions and deletions in translations by Kulturbund Dramaturgs may have been simply due to directorial problems with phrasing, word flow, rhythm and script length. At the same time, it is possible to discover in these original scripts clear examples of official Nazi censorship.

'We put on Shakespeare, Ibsen, modern plays. It was not a Jewish theatre', a former actress of the Kulturbund told me.[33] She played Shakespeare's Viola, Ibsen's Hedvig in *The Wild Duck*, and, among Pirandello's *Six Characters in Search of an Author*, the Daughter, during two seasons in 1934 and 1935. She recalled nothing of censorship, nor was she ever aware of the 'big Nazis' in the audience. But censorship occurred. Two of the plays she performed in, Zweig's biblical *Jeremiah* (*Jeremias*) and a modern Jewish fairy tale by Osip Dimov, *Bronx Express*, were censored. The Gestapo actually banned *Bronx Express* after only ten performances.[34] Apparently, another of Dimov's plays was abruptly taken out of the repertory, because the author had said an 'unkind word' about Hitler somewhere in America.[35] In *Bronx Express*, Dimov captures one Chassid's conflict between the temptations of the New World and the love for the old world (and wife) he left behind. The play, performed in 1935 by Berlin's Kulturbund, portrays a protagonist who falls asleep in a New York subway and dreams of such consumerist commodities as chewing gum and cigarette girls. However, another play by Dimov set in the shtetl with a fairy tale motif, *Jusik*, played in the autumn of 1940 without apparent mishap or censorship.

But by 1940, some principles had been established to which the censors could adhere. As officially stated in January 1940, long after the Nuremberg Laws were passed, the guiding principles (or *Richtlinien*) for the Jewish theatre were fairly straightforward: 'on principle, theatre is allowed. There are no reservations about Shakespeare. All authors of German descent or those who belong to the Reich Theatre Chamber are excluded from consideration.'[36] 'German descent' for the Nazis did not include those Jews who were born in Germany. Beyond these basic parameters, there still appears to have been room for negotiation. Nevertheless, as has already been intimated, reservations remained about the thematic and semantic make-up of the texts themselves.

Establishing categories for authorized performances

Some play censors clearly enjoyed an opportunity to show off their knowledge and ability to criticize drama. Singer submitted a copy of Arthur Schnitzler's one-act *Paracelsus* as a substitute for a proposed work by Yitskhok Leyb Peretz in 1933, for example. Hinkel received a report which stated: 'No objections to a performance of this "intellectual albeit a bit too artistically" constructed one-act by the Viennese Jew, Schnitzler. Much ado about nothing – an absolutely great opportunity to "milk the brain" and give our "Jewish friends" some fun. – I know better things by Schnitzler.' The same censor embellished his report on Wolf-Ferrari's opera *The Curious Ladies* (*Die neugierigen Frauen*) with: 'Just a side note: content-wise, extraordinarily thin and boring; the librettist plays with words which may lead to ambiguity and then the most ridiculous jokes. No objections to a performance.'[37] Yet most Nazi censors from the Reich Chamber of Culture seemed to care little about a dull plot-line or whether the Jews enjoyed an intellectual evening out. Rather, they believed that the play's content had to be not distinguishable as part of Germanic culture and had to be distinctly Jewish – without being too Jewish.

What may we assume from Dr Schlösser's report on *God's Hunt*? A play's acceptance was best secured if no parallels might be drawn between the Jews' present situation and one of mistreatment in the past. This may be clearly seen in *God's Hunt*. Nor was it wise to choose a play in which the Jewish community (or a protagonist) might show themselves capable of rising up against a perceived enemy; this included the Messianic protagonist, Naftali, in *God's Hunt*, a prophet of God in Zweig's biblical *Jeremiah* (performed in 1934, but substantially censored), and the general theme of Messianism in *The Golden Chain*, by the East European Jew Peretz. Hinkel himself had objected to this work in November 1933, approving the Schnitzler one-act in its place.

After Hinkel informed Singer that *The Golden Chain* was forbidden, Singer tried to convince Hinkel that the 'drama of a Chassidic family' was not harmful; in fact, he said that they had never 'wished to perform all three acts, rather only the first act by itself as a complete, balladic poem'. 'For in this act', Singer continued, 'the relationship of Jews to the non-Jewish world is not touched on. Instead, a pure inner-Jewish tragedy is present.' In conclusion, Singer asked that Hinkel reconsider permission for the play's first act only. Hinkel tersely responded: 'Please take note that I CANNOT agree even to a performance of only the first act of *The Golden Chain*.'[38] The play's chain refers to the unbreakable chain of religious faith begun by the Baal Shem Tov and maintained by successive generations of miracle rabbis (the play features three generations). The expressionistic playscript used for a Kulturbund performance of seven episodes in September 1936, is much rewritten. But the first act (which was originally banned) remains virtually intact in its portrayal of Shlomo, the charismatic rabbi and great-grandfather, who wishes for an 'eternal Sabbath' that will bring about redemption. His words incite among the Chassids an ecstatic dance in a circle: 'The world should go to ruin! But we, the joyous Sabbath-celebrating Jews, free of rejoicing for absolution, stride over the rubble.'[39] Such undaunted proclamations of religious zeal by Jews may account for a marginal note Hinkel wrote to himself on Singer's letter as a reason for the ban: 'precisely the first act' ('grade der 1. Akt').[40]

According to Arthur Eloesser, who knew the play and reviewed its 1936 production, the first act made a powerful impression in 'lyrical outbursts of single voices and choral echoes', which swelled into 'an ecstatic state'. He commented that this act, in fact, could have been the final act or catastrophe.[41] In another review for a north German newspaper, an Aryan critic warned that the 'strange' play embodied the 'Jewish nationalist dream for dominance'; his review ends with his suggestion that the realization of that dream – 'Judaeo-bolshevism' in contemporary Spain – could endanger Germany.[42]

Such Nazi fears of Jewish dominance ostensibly caused censors to require extensive cuts in the Kulturbund script of Zweig's *Jeremiah*. The modern verse story of the biblical leader and prophet Jeremiah, leading the Jews beyond the destruction of the Temple in ancient Israel, shares themes with *The Golden Chain*. The deleted passages include over three-quarters of the ninth, and final, scene of the play, entitled 'The Eternal Path' ('*Der ewige Weg*'). One may infer from such deleted references to determined Jews the volatility of the idea that Jews together could overcome adversity and proclaim themselves a proud people. In addition to deleted references to Jeremiah's cry to arms, where he tells his people not to cower, but rather to be strong, proud Israelites, the last lines from the play are also completely deleted; the Chaldean watches the Jews depart and invokes their invincible spirit:

> CHALDEAN   See, see, how they stride in the sun! There is a glow about this people, an aura of dawn upon their heads! Their God must be powerful.
>
> THE CHALDEAN GENERAL   Their God? Have we not ruined His altars? Have we not conquered Him?
>
> CHALDEAN   One cannot conquer the Unseen! One can kill men, but not the God who lives within them. One can vanquish a people, but never its spirit.[43]

This exchange, and much of Zweig's play, represent the ongoing historical Jewish quest for emancipation. The Nazis took all measures to censor literature which espoused the desire for political and spiritual deliverance. Messianism

18   Stefan Zweig's *Jeremiah* (Jüdischer Kulturbund, Berlin, 7 October 1934). Director: Fritz Jessner. Set and costume designer: Heinz Condell.

may have been exploited initially in the Aryan *Thing* plays, but it was unthinkable in Jewish theatre. Censors followed the central Nazi ideology and sought to eliminate Jewish influences from penetrating and contaminating German 'pure culture'.

Assimilation as anathema

Any mention of both German and Jewish culture in one breath was termed 'assimilation', and was therefore suspect. Take, for example, an essay on art and Judaism in Germany which Hinkel banned for a Kulturbund publication because, as the censor suggested, the author defied Hinkel's aims. Instead of sharply separating Jewish and German cultures, 'the essay seeks with all means to mix these cultures', the censor wrote to Hinkel; and he demanded 'final assurance from Herr Dr Singer that all such efforts will cease for good'. Hinkel indicated the problem to Singer, citing the author in question. The author had written: 'In the writings and music of Germany, the share of Jewish forces is known to everyone and generally recognized.' This was Hinkel's warning to Singer: 'The government wishes to reject all assimilation. [...] Today the expression must be seen as sabotage.'[44]

If such a statement of Jewish influence in the arts may be called 'sabotage' and was therefore forbidden, it is not surprising that in February 1935, Richard Beer-Hofmann's drama *Jacob's Dream* (*Jaákobs Traum*) would be subject to the same reprisals. In the Old Testament, Jacob, the father of the Israelites, tricked his brother out of his birthright. Beer-Hofmann's modern verse drama of the biblical brothers, Jacob and Esau, required substantial cuts, specifically in its second part where the two estranged brothers confront one another at a cliff precipice. Jacob cuts his finger, draws blood, and wants to mix it with his brother's fresh blood; through this symbolic act, they will overcome their dividedness and become one again. The parallels with German rituals of fraternal bonding implicit in this tale of blood-brothers may have been potentially too volatile to be permitted on the Jewish stage, for this particular scene appears to have been struck from the script before production.[45] Based on the Nazi aversion to assimilation, it appears that artists were denied subsequent requests for public recitation of this particular scene.

The following year, however, Georg Hermann's popular novel from 1906, *Jettchen Gebert*, was adapted for the Kulturbund stage (July 1935), in spite of the play's depiction of an assimilated German Jewish family in 1840s Berlin. The play's heroine, Jettchen, engages in a love affair with the non-Jewish doctor, Kösling, to the dismay of her great uncles. Despite the family's assimilated status, they force Jettchen to marry a distant cousin, Julius Jacoby. Jettchen and Kösling, however, profess their love for one another and Jettchen does not appear on her wedding day. The audience last sees her as she plaintively throws from a window violet petals from flowers given to her by Dr Kösling. Then she exits. The play remained virtually uncensored, barring such line changes as 'pastor' to 'rabbi' or cut references to 'the Protestant Church newspaper'.[46] Given the subject matter, might there have been some inconsistency in censorship? Or could this have been due to a premiere which occurred before the passage of the Nuremberg Laws in September 1935? Perhaps the overt suggestion in the final act that Jettchen will commit suicide because of her love (which was out-of-faith) was indication enough for the play to be permitted. A similar theme appears in Peretz's *The Golden Chain* with the ostracism of Lea, Shlomo's granddaughter, after her marriage to the outsider, Dr Bergmann. In the play's final *coup de théâtre* (which was performed) Lea returns to her father's house with her blind baby, begging for help.

There is little question that the censors tightened their control after the Nuremberg Laws in 1935 and the Kristallnacht pogroms in November 1938. For example, Shakespeare's *The Winter's Tale*, eventually performed in February 1939, suffered major cuts, whereby almost an entire scene was scratched from the director's script; the censors apparently found passages objectionable which suggested cross-breeding – albeit among plant life. In Act IV, scene 4, much of the discussion between Perdita, as shepherdess, and Polixenes was deleted. Gone from the script are Polixenes's words extolling the art of marrying 'a gentler scion to the wildest stock, / And make conceive a bark of baser kind / By bud of nobler race. This is an art / Which does mend Nature – change it, rather – but / The art itself, is Nature' (ll. 93–7).

Without a doubt, Shakespeare's play reverberates with murky suspicions of adultery and illegitimate children, as well as references to the cross-breeding of social classes. But on a more overt level, Perdita would certainly have been lost for good had she been allowed to speak of 'nature's bastards' (l. 83) on any stage in the German Reich – let alone at the Jewish Kulturbund. By 1939, intermarriage with Aryans or any practice involving *Mischlingen* (people of mixed race) was not only unlawful, but severely punished. 'Hitler made clear what we were', a one-time Kulturbund musician told me when he referred to himself as a 'Jewish artist', not a 'German' one.[47]

By December 1939, the National Socialist state and its censors had clearly announced their official rejection of 'assimilatory' aims in drama. Singer's second successor, Fritz Wisten, reported in a protocol note from a meeting with Nazi authorities that his request to perform Ferenc Molnár's comedy *The Pastry Baker's Wife* (*Die Zuckerbäckerin*) had been rejected because of its 'assimilatory character'. Confused by this verdict, Wisten wrote: 'I cannot see any assimilatory aims in *The Pastry Baker's Wife*; however, I will [...] check against such tendencies. My will is strong; my spirit is weak.'[48] The play, set in a Budapest pastry shop, and written by a Hungarian Jew, may have been indicted as 'assimilatory' because it authentically portrays a pastry baker and his wife who might very well have been Viennese. (The comedy actually was premiered in Vienna in 1935.) The plot turns on a misunderstanding that the baker's wife is romantically involved with a customer who helps with the taxes. The Kulturbund director's script of *The Pastry Baker's Wife* is unmarked. However, Wisten had cast the play and also determined the royalty fees, actors' weekly wages and production costs.[49] Molnár's references in the play to 'our Fatherland' and to bourgeois values, along with the characters' command of German, specifically Viennese expressions like 'Küß die Hand' (good day) and the names for sweets and pastries of the Reich (*Rosenzucker* and *Linzentorte*, for example), may have been considered too fluent for Jews to pronounce with the blessing of the Propaganda Ministry.

But Molnár was 'not fundamentally forbidden as a submission' for future seasons, according to Wisten's minutes from a later meeting at the Propaganda Ministry on 31 July 1940.[50] As was the case in Aryanized theatres, the censors for the Jewish stage appear to have been improvising the conditions for play approval as they went along. This underlines the tendency towards inconsistency on their part. It also suggests that, by 1940, each play submission, regardless of author, would be considered individually, based on content.

Other texts by Molnár were granted performances on the Kulturbund stage, *Delilah* (1936) and a play within a play, *The Play's the Thing* (premiered in 1935 and revived in 1941). The original acting scripts have been lost. Based on the plot-lines of these two romantic comedies, however, evidently the contents could hardly have been construed as assimilatory drama. In the modern version of the well-known biblical story, for example, the modern Delilah recognizes her husband's strength not in his hair but in his bank savings book.

Censors may not have objected to a modern parody based on the Bible, but they did cut all references in song, poetry, drama and prose – written, recited or uttered by Jews – to mixed ancestry, baptism and other Christian rites, and indigenous dialects from Berlin and Vienna. Finally, references to revered Germanic writers or thinkers, including the Scandinavian playwrights Strindberg and Ibsen, and even to soccer players were subject to revision. An example of this kind of censorship is in the libretto to Emmerich Kálmán's operetta *Countess Mariza* (*Gräfin Mariza*), performed by the Kulturbund to great acclaim in July and August 1939.[51] Deletions and changes made to the script by the director, Fritz Wisten, support my explanation for the ban of *The Pastry Baker's Wife*, making clear what kinds of reference were off-limits to the Jews. Offending lines referred specifically to Goethe, Schiller and a popular Viennese sports star, Uridil.

The operetta centres on the romance between the Countess and Count Tassilo Endrody-Wittemburg. In the fourth scene of the first act in the script, Prince Populescu (Moritz Dragomin), the gypsy prince, and Count Tassilo are on a castle terrace awaiting Countess Mariza. Pointing to a statue in its niche, Populescu asks: 'Who is that? Schiller or Goethe?' Tassilo rejoins, 'That is Uridil'; the stage directions state, '*famous soccer player in Vienna*'. Populescu then responds: 'I think it's Navratil.' This witty, topical exchange reveals Populescu's ignorance about artistic matters; the exchange is crossed out in the text. It is clear from the red-pencilled revisions directly across the page and from the deleted sections that the director, Wisten, reworded these lines. His revisions reword Populescu's question to 'Napoleon or Dante?' Tassilo says: 'That is Apollo of Belvedere.' And Populescu shows his ignorance once more by answering, 'Ah, the world weightlifting champion.' This revised dialogue is also crossed out in pencil.[52]

Exceptions to the rule?

While the Nazis rejected plays, or parts of them, which too closely reflected familiar German culture, they also evidently regarded plays which emphasized Judaism too strongly as harmful to the Reich. Dramas for the Kulturbund

19 Shulamit Batdori's *The Trial* (Jüdischer Kulturbund, Berlin, May 1938). Director: Fritz Wisten.

were deemed unacceptable if the plays' themes stressed Jewish political or religious power. I have already noted this in *God's Hunt*, as well as in *The Golden Chain*, *Jeremiah* and *Jacob's Dream*. And yet, for some reason – in spite of one play's provocative subject matter – exceptions may have been made for the Kulturbund's world premiere of *The Trial* in May 1938, a play written by the Jewish playwright living in Palestine, Shulamit Batdori.

Batdori focused on Zionism in her portrayal of the three warring factions within Palestine: the British, the Arabs and the Jews. The play, originally written in Hebrew in 1936, captures the tensions of the times when Jews were fighting for the independent state of Israel. Radio broadcasts and a night raid on a kibbutz open the play.[53] A 'Speaker' narrates the six episodes. He interacts with the other characters and remains outside the action as commentator. In the closing moments, a young British soldier, an Arab youth and a Jewish settler question how they might coexist peacefully. The play ends with the Speaker's pronouncement that the young people must find a solution, for they are 'our future'.

The censors overlooked the contemporary socio-political relevance of the drama. The theatre produced the play without incident, regardless of the parallels to the plight of Jews in Germany. Perhaps such an oversight occurred, in part, because of the play's didacticism, whose focus on the Middle East was clearly beyond German borders. The Zionist Organization hosted a matinee introduction to Palestine for guests prior to the first performance. The play was also premiered at a time when the Nazis still actively encouraged emigration to Palestine.

Such facts become more interesting in light of the Kulturbund German-language premiere of J. B. Priestley's *People at Sea*.[54] The play was premiered in April 1939, at a time when life for Jews in Germany had become increasingly intolerable. Many anxiously awaited quota numbers to emigrate, and emigration dreams were realized only via ship passage to foreign ports. These were the concerns of some of Berlin's Jewish artists and audience members. Priestley's play takes place on board a ship, the *Zillah*, somewhere on 'Middle American seas'. The mood and tone of the play are bleak; the characters are a motley collection of British and American passengers in limbo on a 'wrecked ship' which might not stay afloat. The drama begins on the morning after an explosion. The captain and several crew members have been lost overboard.

Priestley heightens the sense of physical isolation by portraying people who are also socially isolated from one another and from reality. The 'washed up' actress, Diana Lismore, is a self-centred pill freak who has lost touch with reality, according to Professor Pawlett, whose own philosophy is that reality is an illusion. Karl Velburg has no home and no identification papers; he says: 'I am nothing [...] have no papers', in spite of the fact that on three occasions, he had stolen passports and landed up in jail.[55] Lismore's maid plays on Velburg's weakness and convinces him to commit suicide with her. The play ends on a taut note: one passenger realizes that he is financially ruined; the professor has committed a murder on board; and even while the actress stamps on her sleeping pills, as if to shatter an addiction, the last image is one of the professor tearing up his philosophy manuscript.

It is unclear what is more illusory, the reality of the characters' predicament before their rescue or that of the future they face when they get off the boat. An exchange between Lismore and her ex-lover, Valentine Avon, a drunkard and has-been writer, is especially telling, particularly in the lines deleted in the Kulturbund script which suggest official censorship: Lismore tells Val, 'The World War has been long over', which he counters with 'Are you certain?'[56] Priestley's message in his original English-language script is even more direct: Val responds to Diana that the 'Great War' has not been over long. He says: 'It's never stopped. And for all we know, the Still Greater War might have started now.'[57] In light of Germany's intent to invade Poland and the onset of the Second World War, such dialogue, even if tempered by Hirsch in adaptation, is ominous. Whatever the cuts, one can only speculate on the analogies which theatre-goers might have drawn from the fate of the characters while watching this play in performance.[58]

Priestley's play was premiered only months before Great Britain became Germany's active military enemy. After the outbreak of the war, Aryan theatres blacklisted most plays by British authors (although exceptions were made for Shaw and Shakespeare). On their stages, Priestley's play would have represented political betrayal. On the Jewish stage, as we have seen, many works were performed which had often been banned from German theatres. One could argue, as has Freeden, that in an ironic twist of logic, the Jews' performance agenda was like 'a breath of freedom', since it included plays deemed unacceptable in Nazi theatres: plays by Jews for example, even biblical problem plays by Zweig and Beer-Hofmann, or plays by foreigners whose countries opposed Germany in war.[59] At the same time, Jewish artists played such classics as *Antigone*, *Pillars of Society* and *A Midsummer Night's Dream*. This may seem surprising, given that these particular plays had been staples of pre-Hitlerian German repertories, besides being performed on Aryanized stages in Nazi Germany. And yet, while the Jewish theatre had the freedom to perform such plays as well as texts banned elsewhere during the Third Reich, censorship could considerably alter the production scripts used for performance.

Pillars of a repertory: political censorship

An examination of the extant Kulturbund scripts, especially those by well-known European playwrights, suggests that censors did not risk references to political philosophies such as Darwinism or Socialism. Passages which touted democratic ideas, even ideas concerning the emancipation of women, were also subject to revision. This is evident in the Kulturbund's production script of George Bernard Shaw's *You Never Can Tell* (translated by Siegfried Trebitsch). Wisten directed Shaw's comedy in December 1935, without references to Charles Darwin, John Stuart Mill and Herbert Spencer. The names of writers critical of society like Aldous Huxley and John Tyndall were also removed. These references in the second act stem from the conversation between Mrs Clandon and the lawyer, M'Comas. M'Comas's lines have even been rendered free of his apparent dislike for Socialism.[60] It appears that any kind of 'radical' philosophy of freedom for the individual, or equality for the masses, was not to be uttered on stage by or for Jews.

The Nazis had already exploited Darwin's notion of the survival of the fittest for their own Aryan uses. A character on stage, labelled a proponent of 'Darwinism' and played by a Jew, could seem to promote a brand of Messianism. Looking at Shaw's play from this vantage point reveals how other progressive ideas espoused in the play could have appeared objectionable in performance: in Act III, for example, Valentine likens the battle of the sexes to the proliferation of the defence system in war. The Kulturbund audience never heard the witty discussion surrounding this analogy, because it too was completely struck from the script.[61]

The Kulturbund auditorium may have been reserved for Jews only, but that made it a most suitable meeting place for the onstage exchange of ideas among Jews, and thus a potential centre for public discussion and dispute. With this in mind, we may consider substantial cuts made to the actors' rolebooks for Creon in *Antigone* and community leader Bernick in Ibsen's *Pillars of Society*. Sophocles' play was performed in the spring of 1936 (including on Hitler's birthday) and Ibsen's play premiered in autumn 1937.

Especially interesting in *Antigone* are the many lines cut within the Haemon–Creon dialogue. Cut from Creon's speeches are references to fathers' siring sons to side with them against their foes (ll. 641–7) and the relationship between one's worthiness at home and within the governing state (ll. 661–71), as well as Haemon's metaphor of the too-tight steering of a ship resulting in its ruin (ll. 715–17).[62] Also cut from the script are lines where Haemon chides his father for sinning against right and desecrating Heaven's honour (ll. 742–7). Finally, script changes which resemble double cuts appear to have been made to the lines where Haemon insists, to his father's wrath, that one man does not make a state and suggests that Creon is sole ruler of a deserted city (ll. 736–9). In the Kulturbund script, the lines are both reworded to keep the original meaning and crossed out. There is no way to know whether the brief exchange was first cut and then reworded or vice versa; however, a look at the cuts made to Ibsen's text suggests that this particular example of cutting has nothing to do with the style of the translation and everything to do with content. It would appear that lines unfavourable to the king in *Antigone* were cut altogether before performance.

20   Sophocles' *Antigone* (Jüdischer Kulturbund, Berlin, March 1936). Director: Fritz Jessner.

According to reviews of the play, these cuts appear not to have affected the onstage performance potential. From the liberal Jewish newspaper to the Zionist one, Wisten's performance as Creon was commended for showing a tyrant's 'unbending will'; his use of playing the 'psychologizing defensive' made him all the more sympathetic at the end. Only one critic saw the portrayal of Haemon as 'unconvincing'. Youthful energy was attributed to the actor playing Haemon; his performance was deemed 'adequate', and 'sympathetic', although he lacked direction in 'mastering' Sophocles' speech.[63] The reviewers were probably familiar with the play and may have been aware of changed lines or omitted passages. Meanwhile, actors may have used intonation and gesture to convey their characters on a subliminal level.

We cannot know for certain how Ibsen's *Pillars of Society* was performed. Reviewers do not refer to any line changes or omissions (reviews themselves, of course, were also subject to censorship). But, in the Kulturbund script of Ibsen's drama, there is a most remarkable cut in Act III: the entire scene between Bernick and Rörlund where Bernick seeks consolation for his bad conscience.[64] In the play, Bernick – for selfish, cowardly and ostensibly communal reasons – uses his breakthrough railway investment venture as a pretext for his discussion with Rörlund. We know, however, that the consul has more at stake than business deals for the communal good, including new coastal access by train to his community. He has knowingly commanded an unseaworthy foreign ship to sail; he does so more for personal reasons than for the communal good. By Act III, tweaks of remorse cause Bernick to voice the idea of sacrificing one for the good of many. This entire discussion is struck from the Kulturbund script, as is Bernick's justification to the ship worker, Aune, in Act II for commanding the American ship to sail, seaworthy or not; I refer specifically to Bernick's cut line: 'The particular must [...] be sacrificed to the general good.'[65]

The many cuts made to Bernick's discussion of the railway scheme clearly deprived a Kulturbund audience from knowing the full lie upon which the consul had built his reputation. And why was Act III's pivotal scene in the development of Bernick's character eliminated? Surely, no director would delete this scene purely for artistic reasons. We can speculate that a discussion suggesting martyrdom, on a Jewish stage in 1937 Germany, may have been perceived as potentially inflammatory. Thus there appear to be two phases of censorship regarding the cuts in Sophocles' and Ibsen's texts: what was permissible for a German audience, and what could be permitted for an exclusively Jewish one.

A Nazi censor would initially seek to rid a text of any material critical of the regime. In both examples, the actions of leaders (Bernick and Creon) are questioned, making the men appear weak. On an Aryan stage, a strong leader remains strong; there can be no pangs of conscience. The censorship for plays in German theatres may be summed up fairly easily: no Jews or Communists (seen in a positive light); no traitors (unpunished); no democratic ideals. The idea of an individual sacrifice for the communal good, and for the Führer, was welcomed. In fact, *Pillars of Society* was one of Ibsen's plays whose stagings were used in German theatres precisely for propaganda purposes.[66] But for these same censors examining texts for a Jewish theatre, a second phase of censorship had to be considered: Jews were viewed as a separate race and group within the Reich. Even a separatist inner Jewish tragedy attempted on stage might have been too threatening. Obviously, references which appeared critical of a government would be banned before such passages might provoke recognition – or unrest – within theatre-goers.

The missing reference to a sacrifice 'to the general good' in the Ibsen text is, in effect, what Naftali the Jew – and martyr – represents in the Kulturbund's banned play *God's Hunt*. Naftali's self-sacrifice results in strengthening the persecuted Jewish community. Allied to this was Dr Schlösser's reason for banning that play: to hinder the wrong sort of identification among Jews. First, it is clear that any themes of Messianism would have encountered the censors' hostility. And allied to the notion of a charismatic leader or liberator like Zweig's Jeremiah, for example, is the potential problem for censors that Jews could have regarded themselves as persecuted victims who sacrificed a great deal to the Nazis, even as early as 1933. By removing the whole moral dilemma of Act III from the Ibsen script, a censor could prevent any embarrassing misinterpretations on the part of his superiors and maintain the status quo vis-à-vis the Jewish question.

It is not surprising, then, to see further cuts in the fourth act of the Kulturbund's *Pillars of Society* which tone down the effect that Consul Bernick has on his fellow townspeople. All references to the gifts and to the laudatory applause which Bernick receives are cut in the scene where he is honoured as a model citizen. Cut too are Rörlund's lines about the railway, which resound today with a most ominous ring:

> It is true that the railway may expose us to the risk of admitting elements of corruption from without; yet it could equally be a quick way of getting rid of them. Even as it is now, we cannot always stop undesirable elements coming in from outside.[67]

Such deletions suggest that Nazi censorship incorporated not only Nazi suspicions about Jews, but also what Jews represented to them. None the less, even if they believed Jews to be 'elements of corruption', the Nazis chose to censor lines which could be misconstrued if declaimed on a Jewish stage. One can imagine with whom the Jews might have identified those easily transportable 'elements of corruption' – particularly by 1937, when they knew that their hosts saw them as unwelcome parasites. Compare this to Rörlund's deleted line in Act I: 'Not but [...] there aren't some tares among the wheat here too, I'm sorry to say; but these we honestly try to weed out as best we can.'[68] Jews in Germany were at the mercy of German society. A former actress admitted that the theatre was a 'big showcase for the Nazis' to show the world how well the Jews were treated in Germany. She claimed that the artists all knew it, but wondered 'what were the Jews to do?'[69]

Besides permits and passage: the Kulturbund final seasons

Prior to war, in August 1939, many of the Jewish artists and audience members persevered in their attempts to emigrate, but they had to wait months for permits, affidavits from abroad and quota numbers. In the meantime, they lived their lives as best they could, in the worsening conditions for Jews. By 1939, only one communal Jewish newspaper was permitted to exist, the *Jüdisches Nachrichtenblatt*, which the Nazis censored. In a special issue on 11 August, Dramaturg Leo Hirsch spelled out the need to nurture one's inner life with cultural events as one dealt with the reality of leaving Germany. His article, 'What one Needs besides Permits and Passage', was a plea to readers to join the Kulturbund, and thereby support the organization.[70] The theatre was for many their only means of economic gain. Others apparently found refuge in the theatre when they were not working in enforced labour for the Germans (begun after September 1939).

After the invasion of Poland the Nazis closed the Kulturbund theatres nation-wide. It was not until March 1940 that Wisten's Berlin ensemble could perform again. The final year and a half of the theatre's programmes consisted, for the most part, in escapist comedies, including such classics as Molière's *The Imaginary Invalid* (1940). They were mostly texts from abroad. Especially prevalent were fairy tales set in exotic places with such motifs as thwarted love, in Dimov's *Jusik* (spring 1940), or justice, in Ladisláv Fodor's *Fairy Tale of Justice*, about a French aristocrat and a cloakroom assistant whom he accuses of being a thief, after giving her an expensive gift. The man's father, a judge, acquits the girl. Even those plays with specifically Jewish themes, like Gordin's *Mirele Efros* (often called *The Jewish Queen Lear*, autumn 1940), focus on love and justice. This staple of the Yiddish theatre features an overbearing matriarch who presides over her son's courtship and marriage, is spurned by her children, and then is reaccepted by her family.[71]

The actual performances of these light dramas implicitly juxtaposed the threatening reality of the situation outside with the personal dramas behind the Kulturbund scenes. This is evident from a letter by a young actor, Kurt

Suessmann. He reveals an obsession with obtaining ship passage from Germany. Suessmann intersperses details about exit permits and papers with references to life at the theatre, where an opera singer suffered a stroke on stage and died later on the same night. At the same time, he refers to a foreign comedy in repertory as a 'small boost' from the 'desolation' he feels at the Kulturbund.[72] The play, Aldo de Benedetti's *Thirty Seconds of Love* (April 1941), depicts love, Italian style. In the play, a married woman, Grazia, injures Piero in a car accident. Piero sets his price: he will collect either 150,000 Lire or a thirty-second kiss from Grazia. It turns out that Piero was never really hurt. Grazia realizes how pleasant performing the penalty could be.

Just two months later, in June 1941, Suessmann acted in a modern Spanish comedy by Sancho López de la Puerta, *Señor Alan Out of Purgatory*, with music adapted from Offenbach.[73] Pink fliers affixed to the mimeographed programmes for the play warned theatre-goers what to do in case of air-raids during the performance, while on stage, a tale unfolded about a melancholy man who had died and gone to Hell. This satirical fantasy opposes a verse-speaking Devil with Señor Antonio Alan, who is ruining Hell with love songs and his refusal to behave badly. He is therefore permitted to return to Earth for two days to right the wrongs he had committed (adultery and an illegitimate child). Good proves victorious over the Devil's dark forces. The Devil decides that Heaven must take the love-struck man, who is too decent for Hell.

Repeat performance: *The Play's the Thing*

Given the real dark forces, like the Gestapo, posted outside Kulturbund premises, clever and entertaining comedies appealed more to the artists and their supporters than did didactic plays. 'We've enough tzaurus' was the motto of Max Ehrlich's Kulturbund-related cabaret.[74] And so, in retrospect, perhaps it is fitting that the Berlin Kulturbund's last play was a repeat performance of Molnár's *The Play's the Thing* in September 1941. Molnár's play within a play is a witty comedy of love saved and of creative energies replenished. The action takes place in an Italian castle, where a theatre director, his collaborator and a young composer overhear a love scene between the young man's fiancée (an actress) and her former lover. The director saves the relationship by writing a play (overnight) which includes a scene with the overheard dialogue and the overheard lovers. He then arranges to pass off the previous night's scene as a rehearsal. As a result, he has written a new hit comedy.

A play enacted and viewed constitutes, after all, theatre's reason for being. Eight years after an all-Jewish theatre was inaugurated in Nazi Germany, the Jewish actors replayed Molnár's comedy about actors and the creative process on the day that the Kulturbund was disbanded. In stubborn proof that the artistic spirit would endure, reality and theatrical illusion continued to blur in repeat performances of *The Play's the Thing* during the 1940s, outside Germany. The first was in Amsterdam at the Schouwburg and the second at Theresienstadt, directed for fellow inmates by Ben Spanier, who had directed the play at Berlin's Kulturbund two years earlier.[75]

The continuity of the human spirit

Can we understand the Jewish theatre within the historical context of Nazi Germany? Its eight years of repertory programmes did not exist in a cultural vacuum. As I have suggested throughout this chapter, the Jewish actors and musicians continued to perform plays and music which had been part of their dramatic heritage well before Hitler's Third Reich. In terms of basic repertory, the Kulturbund provided artists with a natural transition, since they continued to produce works by Shakespeare, Ibsen, Zweig and Schnitzler, albeit now for exclusively Jewish audiences. Such Western and Central European writers, Jewish or not, belonged to a theatrical tradition familiar to most of the Kulturbund artists, whose dramatic training and repertoires were rooted in the work of these playwrights. At the same time, their choice was limited. Lessing's *Nathan the Wise* was initially allowed, and Goethe and Hebbel were performed in 1934 and 1935. However, works by German non-Jews like Schiller and Kleist – considered Romantics of the true Germanic spirit – were denied them from the start. Moreover, the artists were eventually compelled to perform several works written by Jews, which presented Jewish themes or biblical characters. Plays like Zweig's *Jeremiah* and Beer-Hofmann's *Jacob's Dream* reintroduced many assimilated Kulturbund Jews to the Old Testament. Did the fact that the Nazis pressured the Jews into embodying Jewish heroes on stage amount to a renewal of Jewish culture?

Plays about the seventeenth-century heretic *Shabbatai Zevi* by Nathan Bistritzky (November 1936), or Portuguese history and the Jews in Karl Gutzkow's *Uriel Acosta* (January 1938), exposed artists and audience members to different interpretations of Jewish history. Dramaturgs translated and reworked plays originally written in Yiddish. The production of *The Trial* introduced audiences to Palestine's precarious political situation. Finally, accompanying lectures and programme notes aided those members who knew little about East European Jewish theatre or Zionism. These lectures were poorly attended, however.[76] Meanwhile, plans by Singer to provide actors with pedagogical training in Hebrew and Yiddish intonation do not appear to have been realized. It is true that Nazi censorship provoked discussion among Jews about the nature of Jewish identity and Jewish culture. But the Nazis under-mined the development of the separate Jewish culture that they pretended to encourage. They did so by censoring Jewish plays like *God's Hunt* as too Jewish and thus objectionable.

It is difficult to determine the extent to which Jews experienced a renewed sense of their culture. After all, Berlin Jews had a culture imposed on them that was not essentially theirs. Indeed, Kulturbund audiences preferred plays by authors familiar to them from the Weimar Republic rather than specifically 'Jewish' art imported from Eastern Europe and translated into German. Although many renowned – and Jewish – directors and actors (such as Max Reinhardt, Elisabeth Bergner and Fritz Kortner) had left Germany in 1933, well-known Weimar performers (who were also Jews) like Rosa Valetti, Camilla Spira and Max Ehrlich soon played to Kulturbund audiences. Other talented actors who had belonged to German repertory theatres before 1933 – Fritz Wisten, Lilly Kann and Jenny Bernstein-Schäffer among them – joined the Kulturbund, where they created art year after year.

Spira, Wisten, and most of their Kulturbund colleagues who survived the Holocaust to reflect on their role in Nazi Germany's 'Jewish' theatre have not emphasized the Jewish dimension of the theatre and its repertory. They stress the importance of artistic training and economic security. While a few actors have suggested being used by the Nazis in a 'showcase theatre', most of those interviewed remember the theatre as a haven, not a ghetto, where they could perform in their 'element' and be relatively content.[77]

A continuity of culture existed, despite Nazi attempts to stunt creation by Jews – and by association, 'Jewish' creation. Wisten told Freeden in 1946 that although the Nazis had misused them to show tolerance, the artists had exploited their playing as a form of protest against a cultural ghettoization. Freeden remembers the director's words: 'But even if they set a trap for us, things went differently from how they had planned. Night after night we proved that art does not stop affecting people, not even under the Gestapo's strict discipline. Today that sounds pathetic, but that is how it was.'[78] It appears that Kulturbund art, whether truly Jewish or not, did affect its audiences. Former audience members recall with pride the cultural outings provided them by the Kulturbund, whether in the Rhine Valley or in Berlin. At a gathering in honour of the singer Benya-Matz, several people reminisced about the theatre, agreeing on the high quality of 'first-rate' concerts and productions.[79]

Even in hindsight, the Kulturbund represents the continuity of the human spirit. One former Kulturbund musician has acknowledged: 'Music has a strong power over you. It helps you in situations. Keeps you going even when things get rough for awhile.'[80] Perhaps these artists compromised themselves by undermining their sense of Jewish identity or by working under Nazi censorship, but they none the less dedicated themselves to their art and to the task at hand. In this way, they maintained a sense of self as artists dedicated to their art and not just ones appropriated by a crippling regime and its stultifying political premises.

Notes

I would like to thank the American Council of Learned Societies and the Memorial Foundation for Jewish Culture for fellowships which have enabled me to carry out my present research.

1 For more on the various Nazi decrees barring Jews from the arts and the Reichs-kulturkammer, see the introduction to the present volume (pp. 8–9, 12–14); Alan E. Steinweis, *Art, Ideology, and Economics in Nazi Germany: The Reich Chambers of Music, Theatre, and the Visual Arts* (Chapel Hill: University of North Carolina Press, 1993), pp. 42–6, 105–6.

2 Shabtai Petrushka, for example, worked for Ufa film studios long after the official ban by Nazis. See *Premiere und Pogrom: der Jüdische Kulturbund 1933–1941, Texte und Bilder*, ed. by Eike Geisel and Henryk M. Broder (Berlin: Siedler, 1992), p. 190. The various chambers did not institute mass expulsions at the same time. See Steinweis, pp. 110–11.

3 This evidence has been corroborated by former Kulturbund artists from the Berlin group. For example, Mascha Benya-Matz recounts attending operas on the same evenings as Hitler and Göring (Geisel and Broder, p. 292). The passage of the Nuremberg Racial Laws, in September 1935, most certainly made it more difficult for Jews to mingle with German theatre-goers. Until the ordinance introducing the so-called Jewish identification card, the *Kennkarte*, for all Jews, however, effective in October 1938, and the Kristallnacht pogroms a month later, self-consciousness and discomfort were the primary deterrents to Jews from attending German theatre performances. Measures against the attendance of Jews at theatrical productions were only really enforceable after German Jews were ordered to display yellow stars in September 1941 (Steinweis, p. 115).

4 See Gerhard Hirschfeld, *Nazi Rule and Dutch Collaboration: The Netherlands under German Occupation 1940–1945*, trans. by Louise Willmot (Oxford: Berg, 1988). For Eike Geisel's views on the Dutch version of the Kulturbund, see his essays: 'Da Capo in Holland', in *Geschlossene Vorstellung: der Jüdische Kultur-bund in Deutschland, 1933–1941*, ed. by Akademie der Künste (Berlin: Hentrich, 1992), pp. 189–214; 'Reprise', in Geisel and Broder, pp. 294–313. See also Christine Fischer-Defoy's edited *'Mein C'est La Vie-Leben'*, in *einer bewegten Zeit: der Lebensweg der Jüdischen Künstlerin Paula Salomon-Lindberg* (Berlin: Im Verlag das Arsenal, 1992); Etty Hillesum, *Letters from Westerbork*, trans. by Arnold J. Pomerans (New York: Pantheon Books, 1986). It should be noted that Singer, despite his emigration to Amsterdam, was not involved in the Dutch Jewish theatre. He did belong to the Jewish advisory board committee for Jews in Holland.

5 For theatre and music in Westerbork, see *Lachen in het donker: Amusement in Kamp Westerbork*, ed. by Dirk Mulder and Ben Prinsen, Westerbork Cahiers, 4 (Hooghalen: Herinneringscentrum Kamp Westerbork; Assen: Van Gorcum, 1996).

6 Alfred Balthoff (Alfred Berliner), for example, began his Kulturbund career in Hamburg and then shuttled between there and Berlin. Max Ehrlich worked the cabaret circuit at various Kulturbund centres across Germany.

7 See Saul Friedländer, *Nazi Germany and the Jews*, 2 vols (New York: Harper-Collins, 1997–), I: *Years of Persecution, 1933–1939*, p. 66. Friedländer's study focuses on anti-semitism and the increasing persecution of Jews in Nazi Germany. He is not interested in examining the Kulturbund in detail, or evaluating its repertory, nor does he discuss the Jewish artists' motivations or life within the Kulturbund, except for attributing to 'some of the founders' the ambition of 'creating a cultural life to teach the Germans a lesson' (p. 66). More objectively presented references to the Kulturbund appear in Steinweis's book and in Michael Brenner's epilogue to *The Renaissance of Jewish Culture in Weimar Germany* (New Haven, CT: Yale University Press, 1995), pp. 213–20.

8 Herbert Freeden was Dramaturg in Berlin from autumn 1936 to early 1939. See his book, *Jüdisches Theater in Nazideutschland*, Schriftenreihe wissenschaftlicher Abhandlungen des Leo-Baecks-Instituts, 12 (Tübingen: J. C. B. Mohr, 1964); repr. Ullstein-Buch, 35233 (Frankfurt am Main: Ullstein, 1985). For preliminary English-language studies, see Freeden's only article in English on the subject, 'A Jewish Theatre under the Swastika', *Leo Baeck Institute Yearbook*, 1 (1956), 142–62; Bruce H. Zortman, 'Theatre in Isolation: The *Jüdischer Kulturbund* of Nazi Germany', *Educational Theatre Journal*, 24 (1972), 159–68; Glen W. Gadberry, 'Nazi Germany's Jewish Theatre', *Theatre Survey*, 21, no. 1 (May 1980), 15–32.

9 The 1992 exhibition resulted in two publications: the exhibition catalogue, *Geschlossene Vorstellung*, ed. by Akademie der Künste; and *Premiere und Pogrom*, ed. by Geisel and Broder. The latter includes several essays by the authors introducing transcribed interviews with Kulturbund artists who survived the Holocaust years. The majority of these interviews were filmed by the authors in 1988 for *Es waren wirklich Sternstunden* (SFB Rundfunk). The reference to a 'failed institution that was forced to exist' is in Jörg W. Gronius, 'Klarheit, Leichtigkeit, und Melodie', in *Geschlossene Vorstellung*, pp. 67–94 (p. 94).

10 For approaches to these problems, see Heidelore Riss, 'Das Theater des Jüdischen Kulturbundes, Berlin: zum gegenwärtigen Forschungsstand', in *Theatralia Judaica: Emanzipation und Antisemitismus als Momente der Theatergeschichte: von der Lessing-Zeit bis zur Shoa*, ed. by Hans-Peter Bayerdörfer, Theatron, 7 (Tübingen: Niemeyer, 1992), pp. 312–38; Barbara Müller-Wesemann, *Theater als geistiger Widerstand: der Jüdische Kulturbund in Hamburg, 1934–1941* (Stuttgart: M & P Verlag, 1996). I have begun to address some of these questions: see Rebecca Rovit, 'An Artistic Mission in Nazi Berlin: The Jewish Kulturbund Theatre as Sanctuary', *Theatre Survey*, 35, no. 2 (November 1994), 5–17; Rebecca Rovit, 'Collaboration or Survival, 1933–1938: Reassessing the Role of the *Jüdischer Kulturbund*', in *Theatre in the Third Reich, the Prewar Years: Essays on Theatre in Nazi Germany*, ed. by Glen W. Gadberry, Contributions to the Study of World History, 49 (Westport, CT: Greenwood Press, 1995), pp. 141–56.

11 Freeden, 'Vom geistigen Widerstand der deutschen Juden: ein Kapitel jüdischer Selbstbehauptung in den Jahren 1933 bis 1938', in *Widerstand und Exil 1933–1945*, ed. by Otto R. Romberg and others (Bonn: Bundeszentrale für Politische Bildung, 1986), pp. 47–59; Kurt Düwell, 'Jewish Cultural Centers in Nazi Germany: Expectations and Accomplishments', in *The Jewish Response to German Culture*, ed. by

Jehuda Reinharz and Walter Schatzberg (Hanover, NH: University Press of New England, 1985), pp. 294–316; Yehoyakim Cochavi, 'Kultur und Bildungsarbeit der deutschen Juden 1933–1941: Antwort auf die Verfolgung durch das NS Regime', *Neue Sammlung*, 26 (1986), 396–407. It should be emphasized that the Jewish Kulturbund ended up being virtually the only theatre open to Jewish performers and their Jewish audiences.

12 For a sensitive account of German Jewry during Weimar Germany, see Brenner. See also H. I. Bach, *The German Jew* (London: Oxford University Press, 1984).

13 Georg L. Mosse, 'Jewish Emancipation: Between *Bildung* and Respectability', in *The Jewish Response*, ed. by Reinharz and Schatzberg, pp. 2–5.

14 Avraham Barkai, *From Boycott to Annihilation: The Economic Struggle of German Jews, 1933–1943*, trans. by William Templer (Hanover, NH: University Press of New England, 1989), p. 1. Barkai cites a census study by U.O. Schmelz, 'Die demographische Entwicklung der Juden in Deutschland von der Mitte des 19. Jahrhunderts bis 1933', in *Zeitschrift für Bevölkerungswissenschaft*, 8 (1982), 31–72.

15 See Peter Sprengel's enlightening study, *Scheunenviertel-Theater: jüdische Schauspieltruppen und jiddische Dramatik in Berlin (1900–1918)* (Berlin: Fanei & Walz, 1995).

16 See Brenner, p. 53.

17 Heinz Condell, 'Stilprobleme des jüdischen Theaters', in *Jüdischer Kulturbund Berlin: Monatsblätter*, October 1936, pp. 27–9. This document is also in Berlin, Akademie der Künste, Sammlung Jüdischer Kulturbund, 1.53.104,8.

18 Letter to author from former Kulturbund musician, Kurt Michaelis, 29 January 1996.

19 Brenner, p. 142.

20 For a discussion of the controversial inaugural production of Lessing's *Nathan the Wise*, see Rovit, 'An Artistic Mission', pp. 8–9.

21 See play review by Dr Lutz Weltmann, '*Das Gericht*: Lebendiges Palästina', in *Israelitisches Familienblatt*, 12 May 1938. Weltmann was a director for the theatre.

22 Emil Bernhard (Cohn), *Die Jagd Gottes* (Berlin: Volksbühnen Verlags- und Vertriebe-GmbH, 1925), pp. 7–8. Unless stated otherwise, all translations from German are by Rebecca Rovit. The transliteration of the Hebrew that ends the cited passage was by the author of the play and has here been adapted slightly for accuracy according to English pronunciation.

23 Letter signed by Hinkel's secretary, Ursula Framm, 16 September 1933, Berlin, Akademie der Künste, Wiener Library binder, 2.53.20.

24 Schlösser to Hinkel, 26 October 1933, Berlin-Zehlendorf, Bundesarchiv Abtg. III, Reichskulturkammer, Box 041, File 01. This document is also in Berlin, Akademie der Künste, Wiener Library binder, 2.53.20. The document was reproduced in Joseph Wulf, *Theater und Film im Dritten Reich: eine Dokumentation* (Gütersloh: Sigbert Mohn, 1964), pp. 102–3, without explanatory notes. Saul Friedländer refers briefly to Wulf's reproduction of this letter (p. 67).

25 Letter from Hinkel to Singer, 20 October 1933, Berlin, Akademie der Künste, Wiener Library binder, 2.53.20. This letter is ostensibly in answer to Dr Werner Levie's letter of 9 October 1933, in which he requested information.

26 See the introduction to the present volume (pp. 11–12); Bogusław Drewniak, *Das Theater im NS-Staat: Szenarium deutscher Zeitgeschichte 1933–1945* (Düsseldorf: Droste, 1983), p. 34.

27 Eike Geisel suggests that Hinkel and Singer together made decisions on art (Geisel and Broder, pp. 318–19). A former actress, Ruth Anselm-Herzog, also told me that Hinkel and Singer would sit for hours drinking together in a bar near the theatre (personal interview, New York, 23 May 1995).

28 Letter to Schlösser, 5 March 1934; response, 9 March 1934; Berlin-Zehlendorf, Bundesarchiv, Abtg. III, Schlösser correspondence, Reichskulturkammer, Box 041, File 01.

29 Letter to Hinkel, 16 September 1935; answer from Hinkel on 20 September 1935 acknowledging request to give the list of forbidden composers immediately to theatre directorships; Berlin-Zehlendorf, Bundesarchiv, Abtg. III, Schlösser correspondence, Reichskulturkammer, Box 041, File 01.

30 Letter to the censor called 'Hermann', 23 February 1934, in answer to request by Hermann, 16 February 1934; Berlin-Zehlendorf, Bundesarchiv, Abtg. III, Schlösser correspondence, Reichskulturkammer, Box 041, File 01.

31 Letter to Hinkel, 5 April 1937, Berlin-Zehlendorf, Bundesarchiv, Abtg. III, Schlösser correspondence, Reichskulturkammer, Box 041, File 01. Schlösser ends his letter as if he might be swayed to make an exception under certain circumstances: 'In der Provinz, die freilich nicht viel Tantiemen bringen würde, ließe ich dagegen ohne Weiteres mit mir reden. Ich bitte um Rückäußerung.'

32 Examples in correspondence, Berlin, Akademie der Künste, Wiener Library binder, 2.53.22. Prior to the 1936 Olympics, there was a general loosening up of strictures for Jews, allowing international critics to visit the Kulturbund. According to Saul Friedländer, the Nazis permitted Louis Lochner to review Priestley's *People at Sea* in 1939 (p. 333).

33 Personal interview with Mira Rostovsky, New York, 24 May 1995.

34 The reference to the ban is in a letter to Gerhard Lehmann from a Kulturbund member and worker, Kurt Jutrosinki, 21 October 1935, Berlin, Akademie der Künste, Sammlung Jüdischer Kulturbund, 1.53.133. The reason for the ban is not mentioned in the letter.

35 Freeden, *Jüdisches Theater in Nazideutschland*, p. 48.

36 Protocol by Fritz Wisten with ministry official Erich Kochonowski, Berlin, Akademie der Künste, Fritz-Wisten-Archiv, FWA 74/86/5001/23, 1c, 5 January 1940. Interestingly enough, as detailed below (pp. 202–3), cuts were made to *The Winter's Tale* (February 1939).

37 These reports by the censor named 'Stehr' are from Berlin, Akademie der Künste, Wiener Library binder, 2.53.20.

38 The exchange between Hinkel and Singer may be followed in their correspondence: Hinkel wrote to Singer on 22 November 1933, to which Singer replied on 28 November 1933; Berlin, Akademie der Künste, Wiener Library binder, 2.53.20. Also in London, Wiener Library, microfilm, 500 series.

39 'Sabbatfeierfrohen, Lösungsjauchzendefreien Juden streiten über den Trümmer'; director Lutz Weltmann's script of Peretz's play, Berlin, Akademie der Künste, 8°-27.261, p. 20.

40 Letter from Singer to Hinkel, 28 November 1933, Berlin, Akademie der Künste, Wiener Library binder, 2.53.20.

41 Review in *Jüdische Rundschau*, 4 September 1936; Berlin, Akademie der Künste, press archives, 11/138.

42 Dr Oscar Liskowski, 'Jüdisches Theater von heute', *Nordische Rundschau Kiel*,

14 October 1936; Berlin, Akademie der Künste, press archives, 22/116. This review suggests an exception made by Hinkel to allow German critics to attend and review certain Jewish productions.

43 Stefan Zweig, *Jeremiah* (Leipzig: Insel, 1928), pp. 184–9 (director's original script); Berlin, Akademie der Künste, Fitz-Wisten-Archiv, 8°–27.265.

44 Hinkel's letter sent to Singer, 20 October 1933, along with galley proofs for the next issue of *Monatsblätter*, Berlin, Akademie der Künste, Wiener Library binder, 2.53.20.

45 Berlin, Akademie der Künste, Wiener Library binder, 2.53.25, p. 651. The original script no longer exists, but included among Kulturbund 'banned text' excerpts from Hinkel's office are typed out portions from the scene cited. These excerpts are under 'proposal # 2278; SJ 2059', undated.

46 *Jettchen Gebert* (Berlin: Oesterheld, 1928), p. 47; actor rolebook, Berlin, Akademie der Künste, Fritz-Wisten-Archiv, 74/86/1571.

47 Personal interview with musician Henry Bloch, New York, 10 November 1995. For the production script used for *The Winter's Tale* see Berlin, Akademie der Künste, Fritz-Wisten-Archiv, 8°–27.285, pp. 59–60.

48 Minutes, 14 December 1939, Berlin, Akademie der Künste, Fritz-Wisten-Archiv, 74/5001/21.

49 Berlin, Akademie der Künste, Fritz-Wisten-Archiv, 74/86/5080, 1, 2. Alfred Berliner and Jenny Bernstein-Schäffer were cast as Edmund and Ilona Kiss, the baker and his wife.

50 Minutes, Berlin, Akademie der Künste, Fritz-Wisten-Archiv, 86/75/5001.

51 Apparently it was seen by over 20,000 people. See Erik Levi, *Music in the Third Reich* (Basingstoke: Macmillan, 1994), p. 57. It is worth noting that an allowance for performance in Aryan theatres was made for this Jewish operetta early on in the regime. See Konrad Dussel, *Ein neues, ein heroisches Theater?: National-sozialistische Theaterpolitik und ihre Auswirkungen in der Provinz*, Literatur und Wirklichkeit, 26 (Bonn: Bouvier, 1988), p. 155.

52 Original libretto, Berlin, Akademie der Künste, Fritz-Wisten-Archiv, 74/86/74, p. 12. The librettists are Julius Brommer and Alfred Grunwald. Tassilo's cut lines appear on pp. 46, 51.

53 Promptbook from Kulturbund performance in Herbert Freeden's adaptation; Berlin, Akademie der Künste, Fritz-Wisten-Archiv, 74/86/48.

54 Original playscript rolebook for Diana Lismore, adapted for the Kulturbund stage by Kulturbund Dramaturg Leo Hirsch; Berlin, Akademie der Künste, Fritz-Wisten-Archiv, 74/86/47b.

55 *People at Sea*, adapted by Leo Hirsch, pp. 13, 14.

56 *People at Sea*, adapted by Leo Hirsch, pp. 43–4.

57 J. B. Priestley, *People at Sea* (London: Samuel French, 1938), p. 36.

58 Saul Friedländer concludes his book with a reference to this play performance by the Kulturbund Jews. His words are apocalyptic: 'The characters depicted on the stage are saved at the end. Those Jews seated in the Charlottenburg theater that night were doomed' (p. 333). But not all of those Jews in the theatre were doomed. Nor were they seated in a Charlottenburg theatre; the Kulturbund artists had long since moved to the former Herrnfeld Theatre on Kommandantenstraße in 1935. Friedländer uses Louis P. Lochner's review of the play from New York, Leo Baeck Institute, Max Kreuzberger Research Papers, AR 7183, Box 8, File 9.

59 For an example of Freeden's argument, see his 'Vom geistigen Widerstand der deutschen Juden'. Camilla Spira used the words 'breath of freedom' in Daniela Pogade, 'Atempause oder künstlerisches Ghetto', *Berliner Zeitung*, 25–6 January 1992.

60 G. B. Shaw, *Man kann nie wissen,* trans. by Siegfried Trebitsch (Berlin: Fischer, 1924), pp. 291–2; original script, Berlin, Akademie der Künste, Fritz-Wisten-Archiv, 8°–27.299.

61 Shaw, pp. 339–40.

62 The Kulturbund script used for Sophocles's *Antigone* belonged to Fritz Wisten, who played Creon; trans. by Georg Thudichum, ed. by Otto Güthling, 5th edn (Leipzig: Philipp Reclam, n.d.), Berlin, Akademie der Künste, Fritz-Wisten-Archiv, 8°–27.264. For Greek and English versions, see Sophocles, *Antigone. The Women of Trachis. Philoctetes. Oedipus at Colonus*, ed. and trans. by Hugh Lloyd-Jones, Loeb Classical Library, 21 (Cambridge, MA: Harvard University Press, 1994). When referring to the Kulturbund script, I use the Loeb edition to determine verse lines.

63 In order of citation, the following reviews are referenced according to the press material archives of the Berlin, Akademie der Künste: Eugen Roth, *Jüdische Allgemeine Zeitung*, 18 March 1936, 9/74; Hermann Sinsheimer, *Gemeindeblatt*, 22 March 1936, 9/75; Eugen Roth, *Jüdische Allgemeine Zeitung*; Dr Hugo Lachmanski, *CV-Zeitung*, 19 March 1936, 9/74; Arthur Eloesser, *Jüdische Rundschau*, 17 March 1936, 9/74.

64 Berlin, Akademie der Künste, Fritz-Wisten-Archiv, 8°–27.284, pp. 65–7. The Kulturbund script belonged to Fritz Wisten, who played Consul Bernick. The translation into German is by Wilhelm Lange. I follow James Walter McFarlane's translation in *The Oxford Ibsen*, ed. by James Walter McFarlane, 8 vols (London: Oxford University Press, 1960–77), V (1961), 19–126.

65 *The Oxford Ibsen*, p. 54; Kulturbund script of *Pillars of Society*, p. 31.

66 See Drewniak, p. 269. Another play was *Enemy of the People*.

67 *The Oxford Ibsen*, p. 119; Kulturbund script, p. 86.

68 *The Oxford Ibsen*, p. 25; Kulturbund script, p. 7.

69 Personal interview with Kulturbund actress Ruth Anselm-Herzog, New York, 23 May 1995.

70 'Was man außer Permit und Passage braucht', *Jüdisches Nachrichtenblatt*, 11 August 1939.

71 Like Gordin's *The Jewish King Lear*, *Mirele Efros* combined a stress on the respect due to parents (for the maintenance of the family unit) with an optimistic reversal of Shakespearean tragedy. See Nahma Sandrow, *A World History of Yiddish Theater: Vagabond Stars* (New York: Limelight Editions, 1986), p. 158.

72 Letter from Suessmann to Martin Brandt, 27 April 1941, Berlin, Akademie der Künste, Brandt Archives, 1.56.66. The Kulturbund script is in Berlin, Akademie der Künste, Fritz-Wisten-Archiv, 74/86/52.

73 This script is in Berlin, Akademie der Künste, Fritz-Wisten-Archiv, 74/86/53.

74 See Volker Kühn, 'Zores haben wir genug', in *Geschlossene Vorstellung*, ed. by Akademie der Künste, pp. 95–112 (p. 107); trans. in *Theatrical Performance During the Holocaust: Texts, Documents, Memoirs*, ed. by Rebecca Rovit and Alvin Goldfarb (Baltimore, MD: Johns Hopkins University Press, PAJ Books, 1999), pp. 40–57. 'Zores' or 'tzaurus' is the Yiddish word for troubles.

75 H. G. Adler, *Theresienstadt 1941–1945: Antlitz einer Zwangsgemeinschaft* (Tübingen: J. C. B. Mohr, 1960), p. 590.

76 See Herbert Freeden, 'Jüdischer Kulturbund ohne "jüdische" Kultur', in *Geschlossene Vorstellung*, ed. by Akademie der Künste, pp. 55–66 (p. 63).

77 Rovit, 'Collaboration or Survival', pp. 142–3.

78 Herbert Freeden, *Leben zur falschen Zeit* (Berlin: Transit, 1991), pp. 130–1.

79 I refer to the international conference, 'Soul of Ashkenaz: Music and Culture of German and Central European Jewry', Jewish Theological Seminary, New York, 9 November 1997. I attended a banquet where I spoke to three former audience members about their memories of the Kulturbund.

80 Personal interview with Henry Bloch, New York, 10 November 1995.

5

Non-German drama in the Third Reich

JOHN LONDON

Nazism is usually condemned as the most terrifying kind of nationalism inflicted on the twentieth century. Yet far from proclaiming a blanket xenophobia, spokesmen for the Third Reich were keen to assert the receptive, European nature of German culture. Weeks after the Theatre Chamber had been founded in 1933, its president, Otto Laubinger, declared that 'Shakespeare, Calderón, and Molière, just like the great Nordic-Germanic writers Ibsen, Bjørnson, Hamsun, etc.' were 'part of the permanent property of German theatre'. Half-way through the Second World War, one of the associates of the Nazi ideologue Alfred Rosenberg would claim: 'German theatre has always been a European theatre. No other country in our part of the world has striven like ours to make native in its theatres the drama of neighbouring or distant peoples.' In the final theatre season of the Nazi regime it was boasted that Berlin, by the range of contemporary and classical European drama presented in its theatres, had proved itself to be 'the intellectual and cultural heart of Europe'.[1]

Such statements spelt out the apparent success of explicit aims. Reichsdramaturg Rainer Schlösser had argued that the German mind should 'remain open' to foreign dramatists of stature.[2] Schlösser cited Goethe's notion of 'World Literature' (*Weltliteratur*), the idea that an awareness of national traditions other than one's own could be mutually enriching, without implying the disappearance of national literatures. In his opening address to the second Nazi Festival of Theatre, in 1935, Joseph Goebbels, minister for propaganda, stressed that art became international only when it had fulfilled its national capacity and then broke the boundaries of its own country. International worth came from specifically national sources: 'Shakespeare thus became a world artist (*Weltkünstler*), because he was the best Englishman, Corneille thus became a world artist, because he was the best Frenchman, and Goethe thus became a world artist, because he was the best German.' These authors created

222

their strength from the 'traditional national character' (*Volkstum*) out of which they had arisen.[3]

This position of ostensibly generous relativism, of an acknowledgement of excellence emanating from foreign sources, had a noble philosophical heritage in Germany which extended beyond Goethe. It was Johann Gottfried Herder (1744–1803) who maintained that every society had its own standards and ideals, and that a people's happiness lay in the development of its own national needs. Nations were defined by difference rather than superiority or inferiority. Herder was indeed used – albeit somewhat selectively – to provide a cultural alibi for Nazi ideology. In 1934 Hans Dahmen published a book entitled *The National Idea from Herder to Hitler* (*Die nationale Idee von Herder bis Hitler*). Although many Nazis converted Herder into a committed anti-semite, a founder of racial science and a defender of German superiority, Herder's desire to judge non-German culture on its own terms, as a product of different peoples, resurfaced in partial, sometimes distorted, forms throughout the Third Reich. It was a concept open to abuse as much as genuine understanding.[4]

Once a degree of praise had been granted to foreign traditions and an attempt had been made to understand them according to their own milieu, it was easy to convey a sense of cultural exchange and mutual respect. Tours to Latin America of several productions in German, including Shakespeare's *The Taming of the Shrew*, were therefore cause for celebration, and favourable press reviews from Buenos Aires were cited as evidence of the success of German theatre abroad. When a positive impression of theatre in Frankfurt was published in a London newspaper, the Nazis were quick to report on it. Even an academic, lecturing in New Mexico in 1936 on the theatre developed under the Nazis, could be quoted to prove the international quality of German culture.[5]

Moreover, Nazi rhetoric about the international repertoires of German theatres is far from hollow. Shakespeare was the dramatist most performed in Nazi Germany after Schiller and the reception of his plays merits close study, even if the fate of other selected foreign dramatists is also worthy of attention.[6] In the early stages of the regime, critics had no qualms about revealing the amount of foreign drama in German theatres. In a survey of 163 theatres during the winter of 1934–35, 15 per cent of all plays performed and 24 per cent of those by dead authors were found to be non-German. More significantly, 52 per cent of all productions in Berlin were of works by foreign writers.[7]

Of course, it could be argued that these figures were discussed in order to stir up more patriotism. However, as the regime became more entrenched, it transpired that the debate was not so much about whether foreign drama should be performed, but about exactly which non-German plays should grace the stages of the Third Reich. This is already obvious from the evocation of and subsequent distancing from Herder's ideas. After all, Goebbels's statements are not simply an interpretation based on the definition of a *Volk* or national people. They also constitute aesthetic judgements about the best culture to emerge from each *Volk*. One could be seen to be a good Nazi and a patriotic German precisely through the correct choice of non-German culture. It was only in this way that German theatre could be superior, simultaneously rely so heavily on non-German material, and therefore affirm its 'European' greatness. By 1940, translation had been labelled an explicitly 'political act' and a way of protecting Germany against the errors of its previous 'openness to the world'. Bridges for cultural development were to be built between countries, although the drama of friendly nations was a logical starting point because:

> Translations of foreign books and plays are [...] only meaningful and constitute a valuable addition, if they mediate the foreign people's mental values and knowledge to the German people and at the same time reproduce through this mediation the values of the foreign national character (*Volkstum*) in an artistic interpretation of high quality.[8]

An obvious alliance: Italian drama

Whatever the quality of its theatrical tradition, Fascist Italy seemed to be the most evidently 'friendly' country in the early days of Nazi rule. While representatives of the new order were taking over state theatres throughout Germany, an article on the 'The Fascist Revolution and the Theatre' appeared in the Nazi daily, the *Völkischer Beobachter*. It was a German translation of plans for the development of Italian theatre under Mussolini, written by the dramatist Rosso di San Secondo. Later reports in the theatrical press gave insights into Italian performance, although honest assessments (which pointed out the conservative nature of Italian audiences and the absence of German drama in Italy) soon gave way to more laudatory descriptions, which sought to establish aesthetic and ideological links between the two countries. These uniting factors had to be underlined at the expense of ignoring the relatively unsophisticated level of Italian theatrical infrastructure. Both regimes were therefore seen as popularizing the theatre by radically increasing audience numbers. After all, Mussolini seemed to coincide with Goebbels's intentions by declaring 'the theatre must be there for the people'. Rainer Schlösser compared the audience capacity of 20,000 for an open-air performance of *Rigoletto* in Milan with the size of the equally capacious auditorium offered by the Dietrich-Eckart-Bühne (originally designed as a stage for Nazi *Thing* plays).[9]

When it came to the production of Italian drama in Nazi Germany, an equally unrepresentative picture evolved. Within the first season to begin during the Third Reich, eleven towns were host to *Hundert Tage*, the German version of the play entitled *Campo di maggio* and co-authored, at least in name, by Benito Mussolini and Giovacchino Forzano. (In what must have seemed like a miraculous prophecy, the German premiere of the play had taken place on 30 January 1932 at the German National Theatre in Weimar, a year to the day before Hitler came to power.) The German title refers to the 'hundred days' following Napoleon's return from Elba, and the ensuing events could be glossed by Nazi commentators as showing that 'in times of emergency, parliaments can only fail and a people (*Volk*) gives itself up for lost if it deserts its leader (*Führer*) in times of need'. Another spate of politically associated productions came on 9 May 1940 with the German premiere of *Villafranca* (*Cavour* in German), ordered by Hermann Göring, perhaps to flatter the Duce at a crucial point. (Foreign minister von Ribbentrop had been to Rome in March and Hitler had talked personally with Mussolini on the Brenner shortly after.) This Mussolini–Forzano collaboration had Gustaf Gründgens's direction lavished on it at the Berlin Staatstheater, and (as with *Hundert Tage*) the famous actor Werner Krauss played the leading role. Programmes for the production carried images displaying Italian art, architecture and film, together with texts of appreciation for Italy by nineteenth-century German writers. The play celebrated Cavour as a major personality in the unification of Italy, but circumstances in May 1940 overtook nineteenth-century history. On the morning following the premiere, Hitler's western offensive began. At the end of the month, the Italian ambassador announced that his country would declare war in alliance with Germany within the next few days.[10]

Just how partial a view Nazi Germany received of worthwhile Italian theatre is illustrated by the fate of Pirandello. Whereas the two plays by Mussolini and Forzano were performed in a total of twenty-six theatres between 1933 and 1944, Italy's best-known modern playwright had a mere six 'Aryan' productions of his drama under Nazism. A prohibition which took place in early 1934 may explain the paucity of directors attracted to Pirandello. His libretto for the opera by Gian Francesco Malipiero, *The Changeling* (*La favola del figlio cambiato*), initially enjoyed some success. After the Braunschweig premiere there was praise from several critics. Then the opera was banned because it was found to be 'subversive and contrary to the policy of the German state'.

Pirandello himself thought that his text might have fallen foul of the censor because of what he called 'the Nazis' hypersensitivity in questions of racism'. The 'fable' told of a fisherman's wife in an imaginary country of the south whose beautiful son is replaced by an ugly baby who becomes paralysed, deformed and idiotic. A witch in the village tells the mother that evil spirits have taken her child and replaced him with the ugly, mentally retarded son of a king in a northern country. One day, a real prince comes to the village from a cold northern country and becomes attached to the fisherman's wife, who tells him the story of her lost child. When the king is killed, the ministers come to take away the real prince, but he refuses since he has discovered sunshine, freedom and maternal love. The idiot boy is thus presented as the new king instead. Although Pirandello insisted the countries were imaginary, the triumph of an imbecile in a cold land of the north probably encouraged too many parallels. The Vatican newspaper supported the Nazi prohibition and the story was banned from Italian radio.[11]

Yet Pirandello had expressed his admiration for Mussolini as early as 1923, and the Italian Fascist Party was the only party of which he had ever been a member. In 1936, the final year of his life, Pirandello accepted the Nazi-proposed replacement of his German translator Hans Feist with the racially pure Fred Angermayer. Pirandello even attended an international writers' congress in Berlin, but *Henry IV* was his only play to reach a wide audience after 1934.[12] It was performed in three cities during 1942–43 and it is tempting to see the depiction of an apparently mad, self-deluding but ultimately man-ipulative individual as a powerful dramatic analogy during wartime. (It was, in addition, given a Hungarian production in Budapest in the 1941–42 season.) Perhaps *Six Characters in Search of an Author* had been condemned because of the association with its Berlin production in 1924, by the Jewish director Max Reinhardt. Maybe Pirandello had simply passed out of fashion. In any case, the modernist innovations of the play were not to be seen by German audiences during the Third Reich and, in spite of receiving the Nobel Prize for Literature at the end of 1934, Pirandello remained an acknowledged name rather than a performed playwright.[13]

While Pirandello was virtually ignored, official cultural cooperation between Italy and Germany was thriving. A German theatre delegation, including the director Heinz Hilpert, the dramatist Eberhard Wolfgang Möller and Reichs-dramaturg Rainer Schlösser, visited Italy to see productions and discuss policies with their Italian colleagues. A cultural agreement was signed between the two countries in November 1938 and announced as heralding 'a second extensive renaissance', in political and cultural terms. The visit of Italian representatives in 1939 forged the theatrical aspect of this renaissance and there were Italian theatre weeks in Bremen (1940) and the southern city of Freiburg (in 1941). Some contemporary German plays were performed in Italy. Cycles of 'great Italian comedies' took place in Hamburg in 1941 and 1942.[14]

Since much time was spent during these occasions justifying the spiritual and aesthetic proximity between the two 'peoples', it is worth analyzing the

sorts of conclusion which could foster Italian drama under Nazism. A conference in Rome in 1940 was dedicated to the relationship between Italian and
German theatre. As well as recitals and the performance of scenes, lectures
revealed the connections supposedly at the heart of artistic comradeship.
Obvious differences emanating from the dominant role of Catholicism in Italy
were not avoided, although it was easier to concentrate on music. There was
talk of the Italian influence on Handel and Mozart. Monteverdi could lead
the way to Wagner's Leitmotif. Verdi drew on Schiller (for *Don Carlos*).
Wagner and Verdi were drawn together by their notions of the 'nation'. A
contemporary Italian dramatist complimented the Nazis on the quality and
quantity of German performances of Italian plays. Werner von der Schulenburg, the German translator of *Villafranca*, cited Pirandello, alongside Dante
and Michelangelo, when discussing Italian culture.[15]

One senses a certain desperation in the search for connections which did
not seem too obscure. By March 1943, when the German–Italian Days of
Culture took place in Hamburg, a more extreme reinterpretation of history
was called for. The Nazi Gauleiter of the city thought the events demonstrated
that 'the European desire for culture has remained alive even at the time of
hardest fighting'. An extraordinary lecture on 'Goethe and Italy', by Rainer
Schlösser, was reprinted in the booklet published to commemorate the festival.
Though describing the poet's artistic experiences in Italy, Schlösser implied
that Goethe could have written work apparently influenced by his stay without
having travelled to the country. More importantly, however, Goethe had built
the blocks of mutual understanding between the two nations: 'He laid the
poetic foundations which, one hundred and fifty years later, in accordance
with the will of the Führer and the Duce, would provide the monumental,
political domed building of a brotherhood-in-arms.' There were poetry and
musical recitals, but the only theatrical contributions by 'soldiers of culture'
(Schlösser's expression for the current generation of Germans and Italians)
were the German premiere of *Icaro*, by Pirandello's son, Stefano Landi, and
two Goldoni productions.[16]

Contemporary Italian playwrights such as Gherardo Gherardi, Alessandro
De Stefani and Dario Niccodemi were occasionally peformed during the Third
Reich, but it was indeed Goldoni (1707–98) who proved most durable. Again,
Goethe could be used as confirmation of Italian talent, since he recorded his
enthusiasm for an Italian performance of *The Chioggian Squabbles*. A German
version would later be performed for troops of the Reich in occupied France.
The author of a study of Goldoni written during the war joined in the rhetoric
of alliances by claiming Goldoni's comedies currently had a rich significance
for Germans, because they were rooted in the 'national character' (*Volkstum*)
of a country with which Germans were allied in a 'common fight'. The

Propaganda Ministry supported the translation of Goldoni's plays. When some directors were moving away from staging Shakespeare during the war, one in Potsdam substituted Goldoni's *The Liar* for *Twelfth Night*. The last performance at the Deutsches Theater in Berlin, before all the theatres were shut on 1 September 1944, was a production of Goldoni's *The Servant of Two Masters*.[17]

The extent of Goldoni's popularity appears undeniable. One play alone – *The Servant of Two Masters* – was performed in six different versions or translations. But the irony of such enthusiasm in political terms is that Germans were seeing comedies far removed from the Italian originals. Three of the most produced plays suffered numerous distorsions at the hands of adaptors and directors, who often had no knowledge of Italian and worked from existing translations. *La Locandiera* (called in English and German *Mirandolina*), had a Viennese version entitled *The Landlady from Venice*, whereas Goldoni's play takes place in Florence. Another adaptor, F. Knöller, freely admitted to eliminating minor episodes and changing elements which were not part of a current sensibility. A version of *The Servant of Two Masters*, premiered in Bremen in 1940, added songs and duets inspired by the *commedia dell'arte*, and there was a tendency in many productions to exaggerate what could be perceived as a typical Italian style. *The Liar* had moralizing phrases struck out and the ending changed, with the additional presence of a monkey. Misunderstandings became merely frivolous.[18]

Much German comment followed such changes by highlighting the harmlessness of Goldoni's comedies and their theatricality, rather than any relation they might bear to life. Yet it was Goldoni's greatest innovation to have brought Italian comedy closer to a social milieu by subordinating the improvisation of the *commedia dell'arte* and reducing its theatrical stock types. No wonder an Italian visitor to Vienna in 1943 thought a production of *The Venetian Twins* '100 per cent theatre' even though Goldoni was 'unrecognizable' in the show.[19] However friendly it was considered to be, a foreign culture had to be transformed in order to be appreciated.

The attractions of Spanish Golden-Age drama

The theatre of Calderón (1600–81) and Lope de Vega (1562–1635) had a longer history of German reception than Goldoni. Political developments also seemed ripe for a renewed appreciation of Spanish culture. Hitler had supported Franco's uprising (both militarily and economically) from the beginning of the Spanish Civil War in 1936 and, even before the Caudillo's troops had entered Madrid, a cultural agreement was signed between Germany and Spain in January 1939, in parallel to the Italo-German arrangement of two months before. By the end of 1939 Franco had been complimented with a hagiographic biography in German. While the Spanish Blue Division helped German offensives on the Russian front, Germany was sending opera companies to perform in Spain until April 1944.[20]

At least one detailed article appeared to inform German readers of contemporary Spanish drama. (It even included a summary of Lorca's work, although the date of the poet's death was omitted, doubtless because he was executed in 1936 by supporters of Franco's actions.) The experience of audiences in Germany, on the other hand, was confined to the plays of the Spanish Golden Age. A period of history indelibly linked to Spanish national unity, imperial expansion and an anti-semitic Inquisition had obvious attractions for the Nazis. Far less palatable were Counter-Reformation Catholicism and the ubiquitous presence of the 'honour' motif in the drama of the time. This was admitted even by those most enthusiastic about the genre. One academic critic said the concept of honour in Calderón's period 'is no longer understandable for us today'.[21] And yet Spanish Golden-Age drama amounted to almost 1 per cent of all productions performed in the Third Reich (approximately double the percentage proportion of the years 1929–33). Multiple changes had to be inflicted on literary identity for such an increase to be possible.

There was at least no argument among Nazis about one production: Hugo von Hofmannsthal's adaptation of Calderón's *The Great Theatre of the World*, directed by Max Reinhardt and premiered on 1 March 1933 in Berlin's Deutsches Theater. Albeit Catholic in inspiration, a text penned by a writer of Jewish origin and directed by a famous Jewish personality constituted an invitation for condemnation. Whereas non-Nazi critics reported applause, and underlined the drama and even the relevance of the production, reviewers in the National Socialist *Der Angriff* and the *Völkischer Beobachter* thought the event lacked spirit and theatricality. Calderón disappeared almost entirely in the Nazi attacks on Reinhardt and Hofmannsthal.[22]

It is, at first sight, therefore strange that another production of the play was performed in the same year on an outdoor stage in Heidenheim as a sign of support for the new regime. The choice of Joseph von Eichendorff's nineteenth-century version solved one problem. A radical staging of Calderón's play did the rest. On the day of the premiere the houses in the town were draped with flags. As a prelude to the performance, military guards and members of the Hitler Youth movement surrounded speakers who described Heidenheim as 'a stronghold of the awakened Germany'. The genre to which *The Great Theatre of the World* originally belonged was the *auto sacramental*, a one-act allegorical play performed at the feast of Corpus Christi. Calderón's text has eleven characters – such as the World, the Rich Man, the Poor Man – and an 'accompaniment'. The version in Heidenheim had at least 100 participants involved in a declamatory chorus (Figure 21). Added to a Catholic view of everything in its just place, the whole event resembled a Nazi *Thing* play. If this reclassification of seventeenth-century Christian theatre appears extreme, one has only to read the comparisons of the Hispanist Rudolf Großmann, expressed two years later. Großmann affirmed that while the *auto sacramental* depicted the miracle of transubstantiation during communion, the *Thing* play tried to represent 'the German miracle of the present'. He admitted that the genres differed technically and philosophically, but said that they both depended on audience receptivity and 'community experience'; what was 'once religious is now political'.[23]

Nazi acceptance of foreign drama so ritualistically Catholic could not last. Just as the official demise of the *Thing* play started towards the end of 1935, no predominantly religious Spanish play was performed after that year. There was one exception: Wilhelm von Scholz's version of *The Great Theatre of the World*, produced in Karlsruhe and Vienna during the war. Although much remains from Calderón's concept, the new title demonstrates how the genre could be allowed. Von Scholz called his version *The German Great Theatre of the World* (*Das deutsche große Welttheater*).

Together with adaptations of the comedy *The Phantom Lady* (*Dame Kobold*, in German) by other hands, it was von Scholz's version of *The Mayor*

21 Numerous actors and singers increase the cast size of *The Great Theatre of the World* by Calderón/Eichendorff in the town of Heidenheim, 1933.

of Zalamea which formed the most popular incarnation of Calderón's theatre during the Third Reich. Despite a well-established history on the German stage, it seems unusual that such publicity could be granted a play which culminates in the garrotting of a soldier for the rape of a daughter in a country setting. But once the actor Heinrich George had made the eponymous role his own in 1937 in Berlin's Schiller-Theater, *The Mayor of Zalamea* began a life which included a production tour round Europe. Other theatres staged further productions. George starred in a 1942 film – *The Long Shadow (Der große Schatten)* – as an actor-director whose life was intimately bound up with *The Mayor of Zalamea* and a modern version of the plot. The culpable soldier of the play may have been one of a troop stationed in the village, but this was no impediment to peformances in occupied Holland. The potential for current parallels (the German army in the Netherlands) was overlooked by the Nazis, because the text – with its violent justice exacted by the wily farmer/mayor/judge of the title – conveyed something much more important for the Third Reich: the triumph of a representative of country folk and the farming 'community'. Even though the translator had eliminated two comic characters, the harsh rules of Spanish 'honour' became acceptable because the regenerative roots of a whole people were being defended at source. An 'ancient right of a peasant farmer' was being claimed and an implicit lesson about *Blut und Boden* (blood and soil) ideology was inevitable.[24]

In any case, Wilhelm von Scholz's political credentials were never in doubt. He had signed a pledge of loyalty to Hitler in October 1933 and his memoirs, published in 1939, ended with a proleptic allusion to the Führer as an unknown soldier of the First World War who would lead 'people and fatherland' to 'new glory'. The production styles of von Scholz's translations were, moreover, largely traditional and transmitted a sense of what was typically Spanish in costume and manner. Rudolf Schröder's production of his version of Calderón's *Life is a Dream* was pompously regal and plentiful in attempts at period dress. The translation may have modernized the language, but it included phrases such as 'Heil, Sigismund!', which greeted Segismundo when he rightfully occupied the throne that had been denied him. The inevitability of heaven's will took on a new meaning in the era of National Socialism.[25]

Another version of *Life is a Dream* was premiered in Berlin in February 1943 and revived in the final season of the Reich. Gustaf Gründgens intervened to make sure the play would no longer be set in Poland (given military events at the time), but a different perception may have accounted for the eagerness to witness Segismundo's journey from imprisoned barbarian to sadistic ruler, and then wise king. Max Kommerell's translation had none of von Scholz's Hitlerite rhetoric and the illusion of earthly positions may have had attractions when it was obvious to some which way the war was going. Bernhard Minetti, who played Segismundo, later commented that it was as if the play 'described the political situation, in other words the right of the powerful to chain up the ill-bred, the non-conformist'.[26]

A much broader range of Lope de Vega's work was produced, largely due to the efforts of the contemporary translator Hans Schlegel. Although the repertories of German theatres were packed with Lope's comedies as well as some of his more serious plays, he had an advantage over Calderón because religion was not seen as being so significant in his theatre. What is more, with deliberate echoes of a nationalism closer to home, Nazi critics joined their Spanish colleagues in considering Lope the founder of Spanish theatre. Dramatists before Lope had created nothing durable and had not worked 'for the whole nation'. Lope, in contrast, had freed Spanish art from excessive foreign influences and created a national theatre which 'reached the hearts of everybody, the man of the people (*Volk*) just as the highest aristocrat'. Lope's position as undisputed 'leader (*Führer*) of his time in the area of theatre' allowed him to 'educate his people'. A lesson to all, indeed.[27]

The production of *Fuenteovejuna* (*Loderndes Dorf* or *Das brennende Dorf*) at the Staatliches Schauspielhaus in Hamburg provides an insight into exactly how relevant lessons could be learnt. The date of the premiere – 26 October 1935 – meant that the production could be part of the tercentenary commemorations of Lope's death, but this was no innocent celebration of foreign culture. Two weeks before the opening, a 'racial day' or 'day of race' had taken place at the Hamburg Ibero-American Institute. Diplomats and like-minded officials emphasized the common destiny shared by Spain and Germany.

Lope's play precedes many of the themes in *The Mayor of Zalamea*. A military leader, the Comendador, terrorizes the inhabitants of a village, called Fuenteovejuna, and is eventually killed in a popular revolt. The villagers claim collective responsibility for his death and are pardoned by the Catholic Monarchs, Ferdinand and Isabella, who reassert their sovereignty. The author of the Hamburg version, Günter Haenel, worked from an already inaccurate nineteenth-century adaptation to devise a mangled and abbreviated text for performance. The Comendador became more honourable in German and the rebellion more open to condemnation. Many sexual references were removed, but there was an aggressive military presence and more violence. Some cuts resulted in a superficial psychology or illogicality. The aristocratic personalities in the play were undervalued (perhaps in tone with the new Nazi order). When it came to staging, the Spanish local colour of realist houses was the backdrop for groups of singers and dancers. If any were unsure about the control exercised by the king at the end of the play, an official reception in a hotel after the premiere included speeches by Spanish critics sympathetic to the Nazi cause. One of them stated that Lope supported the *Führerprinzip* and that *Fuenteovejuna* was 'the first drama of National Socialism'.[28]

This reading of *Funteovejuna* was situated at the other end of the political spectrum from the left-wing interpretations of the play by Lorca and Communist directors. Popular rebellion had an allure when it was felt that extraneous forces were repressing innocent people. Maybe it is no coincidence that *Fuenteovejuna* was the only Spanish Golden-Age play to be published in Dutch during the occupation. With Queen Wilhelmina in exile clearly hostile to the Nazis and the German replacement of postage stamps bearing her picture, the re-establishment of monarchical power in the Netherlands would have implied the return of a free country. In a passage at the close of the play which departs slightly from Lope's original, a character describes what has happened in the village as 'tyranny'.[29] Only those who had suffered could really know.

Obligatory titles for the repertory

When there was no recourse to contemporary political allegiances, Nazi ideologues had to rely more heavily on particular critical interpretations to justify the continued presence of non-German drama. Ancient Greek drama was viewed academically as the background to German classical theatre. Aeschylus' *Oresteia* could be regarded as a criticism of democratic institutions, although Sophocles' plays proved more popular. (A concentration of productions of Ancient Greek drama accompanied the Italo-German occupation of Greece in the 1940–41 season.) Constant Nazi anti-Communist rhetoric could not dismiss Russian drama of the preceding century. Rainer Schlösser praised Gogol's *The Government Inspector* as an 'up-to-date play for combating corruption', with no mention of Meyerhold's legendary production. During the functioning of the Molotov–Ribbentrop Pact in 1939–41 there were several productions of Russian texts by authors such as Chekhov and Ostrovsky.[30]

No such alliance had to exist for the interest in Scandinavian drama. Even if Strindberg was not widely performed, he largely escaped attacks of the sort that plagued the so-called 'degenerate' modernism which his most innovative style had anticipated. Ibsen enjoyed the privilege not simply of being a great Nordic playwright ripe for recognition under a pan-German mantle, but also of Nazi attention dating from the 1920s. Dietrich Eckart had been editor of the *Völkischer Beobachter* and one of Hitler's intimate friends. He died of over-drinking in 1923 and the second part of *Mein Kampf* ended with Hitler's eulogy of Eckart, 'who devoted his life to the awakening of his, our people, in his writings and his thoughts and finally in his deeds'. It was this sort of reference which warranted the naming of a *Thingplatz* after him outside Berlin and the elevation of his racist version of *Peer Gynt* to untouchable Nazi status.[31]

One of the most spectacular productions of *Peer Gynt* to be mounted in the Third Reich occurred in 1936 in the Berlin Theater des Volkes, the Nazi name for what was Max Reinhardt's Grosses Schauspielhaus. Dances and Grieg's music bridged the many scene changes. The oriental exoticism of the Moroccan/Egyptian set and costumes (Act Four, in the original) formed a contrast to what one critic called 'the beautifully coloured traditional folk costumes in the Norwegian scenes'. In the storm of Act Five a ship actually moved across the stage. At one point, a voice was broadcast throughout the audience by loudspeakers. A huge cast was involved: farmgirls dancing around the bride encircled the whole stage. As with the *Thing* plays, a 'theatre of the people' meant that the maximum number of people felt a part of the experience. In spite of protests by Ibsen's daughter-in-law not to allow performances of Eckart's version, the Nazi *Peer Gynt* was given further productions.[32]

There were attempts to use Ibsen's *The Vikings at Helgeland*, *Pillars of Society* and *An Enemy of the People* as propaganda plays, without much success. Most idiosyncratic of all in the Nazi perception of Ibsen are the ruminations of Otto zur Nedden, Dramaturg at the German National Theatre in Weimar, on the colossal *Emperor and Galilean*. In the closing moments, Maximus declares: 'The third empire (*Reich* in German) shall come! The spirit of man shall reclaim its heritage.' Nedden spotted these words and cited more from an after-dinner speech in which Ibsen repeated the term 'third empire'. In the speech Ibsen looked forward almost mystically: 'I believe that an age is impending where the political and social concepts will cease to exist in their present forms, and that from these two things a unity will emerge containing within itself conditions for the potential happiness of mankind.' Nedden considered these words 'prophetic' and as 'forward-looking and significant' as similar and related thoughts by Nietzsche: 'They show us how strongly Ibsen was imbued with the ideology of a "third empire (*Reich*)".' In this perspective, his 'world-historic play', as Ibsen himself subtitled *Emperor and Galilean*, had a new meaning. But even so prophetic a dramatist as Ibsen had to be adjusted to fit into a larger historical project. During the war, the Propaganda Ministry banned plays such as *A Doll's House* and *Ghosts*, because they were deemed 'too depressing'.[33]

Nedden thought that French classical theatre, including Racine, Corneille and Molière, had produced 'no real political drama' or 'criticism of the times'. Yet when France became an enemy in war such classifications had little value: all French plays were forbidden, although exceptions were, on occasion, made for Molière and a minor, Nazi-supporting Frenchman called Eugène Gerber.

The former was even played for German troops in France. Rainer Schlösser had singled out Molière as worthy of consideration in 1934; he did, after all, belong to a France which had not yet had its best characteristics decimated by the Revolution and the Napoleonic Wars. After discussing *The Miser*, Schlösser concluded that 'even if it is not our blood', such creativity should be welcomed for the sake of its timing and linguistic skill. French classical drama nevertheless constituted half the proportion of the total national repertory compared to the percentage it had in the four years before the Third Reich (0.35 per cent, as compared to 0.69 per cent before). Among the better-known productions was Heinz Hilpert's direction of *Georges Dandin* at Berlin's Deutsches Theater in 1935.[34]

When Vichy replaced military conflict there were gestures towards relaxing previous restraints and transmitting an impression of theatre in occupied Paris. Positive remarks were made about the Comédie Française and acting in some other theatres. However, there was a tendency to condemn. The French had little talent for dance, because they lacked rhythm. For the French, Sacha Guitry was 'modern' although, a German critic ironically commented, Guitry was over sixty. (In fact, the playwright was born in 1885 and could not have been over sixty during the Vichy regime.) According to the German source, George Bernard Shaw was almost unknown in Paris, and Pirandello, together with all modern Italian drama, was despised.[35]

This kind of double-talk, of acknowledgement and simultaneous dismissal, was not unknown before the war. The house magazine of Berlin's Deutsches Theater included an article criticizing a certain vacuity in English comedy of manners, even though Somerset Maugham's *The Circle* would be performed in the same theatre after the criticisms had been published. Maybe a lighter genre was preferred officially. Oscar Wilde's comedies may have provoked nationalist criticism, but they filled theatres. Films of three plays by Wilde were made until the author was banned during the war. Even after a film version of 1934, *Charley's Aunt*, the 'irrepressibly funny farce' by Brandon Thomas, was part of the 'stock of every repertory'.[36]

The exceptional case of George Bernard Shaw

Shaw was another familiar English-speaking contemporary playwright throughout the period of the Third Reich. Given his approval of Stalin's achievements, his reputation in Socialist circles and his aversion to anti-semitism, Shaw may seem an unlikely choice for the Nazis. Alfred Rosenberg and other Nazis had indeed condemned him early on. In February 1933, a performance in Mannheim of *Too True to be Good* was disrupted by local Nazis, who hurled abuse at a Jewish actor and 'the Jew Shaw'. Yet Shaw ended up being the most successful non-German dramatist alive under Nazism and productions of his plays actually increased as the war broke out. In academic circles he was given an Irish, anti-English gloss and associated with healthy 'non-Jewish' drama. Schlösser thought Shaw had reached the status of a 'semi-classic of the Third Reich'. He was considered a pupil of Schopenhauer, Wagner, Ibsen and Nietzsche, while Goebbels and Hitler were in agreement in wanting to protect Shaw from censorship.[37]

Part of this acceptance must be attributable to the erratic nature of Shaw's own politics. His anti-parliamentarism led him to voice initial support for Mussolini and even Hitler. A play like *The Apple Cart*, with its arguments against the democratic foundations of modern parliament, became the dramatic representation of his ideas. Shaw's stance against British imperialism meant he could be seen as an Irish writer allied to much within the Nazi cause. And yet Shaw's German translator, Siegfried Trebitsch, was Jewish and Trebitsch's own works were banned. To circumvent this anomaly royalty payments were, from 1937, issued direct to the author and no questions were asked as to whether the 50 per cent due to the translator was in fact paid.[38]

Meanwhile, with Goebbels's support, *Pygmalion* was made into a film directed by Erich Engel. At Berlin theatres there were productions of *Man and Superman*, *Caesar and Cleopatra*, *Mrs Warren's Profession* and *The Doctor's Dilemma*. Before real theatre criticism was officially banned in 1936, some plays provoked greatly differing opinions in the press. In *On the Rocks* Shaw demonstrated how the 'Liberal Prime Minister' Sir Arthur Chavender solved his nation's problems, above all unemployment, through the creation of a totalitarian state, influenced by his analysis of Lenin and Marx. Despite this Communist influence, the text had attractions for the Nazis, because the mobilized unemployed at the end sang 'England arise!', a German translation of which became the title of the play for at least one production. The whole ideological gist could imply the necessity of National Socialism in Britain. Sympathetic voices hinted as much after a production in Berlin in 1934. According to the *Berliner Morgenpost* Shaw was still young enough to learn: 'Without the model of developments in Germany (and in Italy) the play would hardly have been written.' *Der Angriff* added that a prime reason for the laughter caused was the memory of 'the shadows and ghosts of our own parliamentary past'. In *Der Montag*, on the other hand, Shaw remained the same, but 'subject to alteration': 'The National Socialist Shaw is exactly the same old Shaw as the previous Communist or Socialist one.'[39]

When the runs of plays by Noel Coward and Somerset Maugham were cut short at the outbreak of hostilities with Britain in September 1939, exceptions were made for only two 'English' dramatists: Shakespeare and Shaw – the latter conveniently classified as Irish. Every so often, official concerns arose about Shaw's politics. Schlösser was worried by reports of a British actor impersonating Hitler in Shaw's *Geneva*, but when Goebbels insisted that Shaw should continue to be performed in Nazi Germany, Schlösser fended off attempts by the Gestapo to ban the play. In a rare instance of censorial lucidity in November 1939, Schlösser argued that Shaw could not be used so effectively for anti-English propaganda if it became known that one of his plays had been prohibited. But the game was played nevertheless: at the beginning of the occupation of Poland, the Polish actor who had played Hitler in *Geneva* was kept in prison for six months. A directive was issued to ignore one of Shaw's pro-British statements (which were more forthcoming from the end of 1940). By March 1941, Propaganda Ministry permission was needed for new productions of Shaw and Shakespeare.[40]

One of the plays performed until the theatres closed in 1944 was *Saint Joan*. In the last few months of the final season, audiences in Berlin, Vienna, Stuttgart, Braunschweig and Prague could experience what the Nazis regarded as the glorification of a people's martyr. The play was in the repertory of the Deutsches Theater from 1934 to 1936, under Heinz Hilpert's direction (Figure 22). Goebbels noted in his diary how Hitler thought this version of history stood 'high above' Schiller's *Die Jungfrau von Orleans*. In Goebbels's words (perhaps paraphrasing the Führer), Shaw was a 'great talent'. He could see history and 'expose' it. He was a 'really modern analyst'. It is therefore not surprising that the director of the Chemnitz Theatre chose the play in 1941 to commemorate the eighth anniversary of Hitler's coming to power.[41]

After the war had begun it was easy to perceive Shaw's version as a piece of anti-English propaganda. Joan of Arc had united the French against the English, and there were elements in the arguments about the nation in the fourth scene which could strike a chord in sympathetic German hearts. Cauchon claims: 'When she [Joan] threatens to drive the English from the soil of France she is undoubtedly thinking of the whole extent of country in which French is spoken.' This was exactly the kind of argument used for the initial expansion of Nazi Germany. Moreover, Cauchon calls her heresy 'anti-Christian'. In the epilogue, as if the military aspect of her actions needed emphasizing, Joan reminds the audience she was 'a regular soldier'.[42]

Joan of Arc was manipulated under Vichy as a suitably historic icon of anti-British sentiment. Every May the commemorative day named after her would be celebrated as a lesson of unity about 'the legitimate leader of the *patrie*'. The leader himself, Marshal Pétain, declared that, as 'a martyr of national unity', Joan was 'the symbol of France'. With such approbation, it was logical that the Nazis should support a Parisian performance of *Saint Joan* in late 1940. But there was another view of the saint and a different way of interpreting Shaw's play. Some were keen to transfer the message of the

22   George Bernard Shaw's *Saint Joan*, Deutsches Theater, Berlin, 1934. Director: Heinz Hilpert. Set designer: Ernst Schütte.

play and spotted in Jürgen Fehling's 1943 German production a setting located in Lübeck rather than Rouen and the River Meuse. (Later commentaries claimed that it was part of Fehling's strategy in attacking the totalitarian state.) Joan of Arc could equally well represent resistance to an occupying force. (This was the gloss given in a French radio broadcast of the time from London.) It is difficult to assign retrospective views which were initially unspoken, but there could well have been such subversive perceptions of *Saint Joan*, the subsequent performance in Paris of Charles Péguy's drama on the same legend, almost one year later, and Claude Vermorel's *Joan with us* (*Jeanne avec nous*) in 1942. Could not an audience hostile to Pétain and the Nazis mentally substitute the Germans for the English, whatever the intentions of those involved in the productions? Years after the war, when another unifying idea was needed – that of French national resistance to the occupation – it was indeed argued that audiences heard 'Germans' every time Joan said 'English'. If even a fraction of the public at these peformances did so, it proves that an officially sanctioned theatre of propaganda had backfired.[43]

Nazi variations on the German Shakespeare

Whereas George Bernard Shaw constituted an exception amongst foreign dramatists, Shakespeare enjoyed a status which rivalled that of German playwrights. Approximately 3 per cent of all productions in the Third Reich were of plays by Shakespeare. He was second only to Schiller in his share of the repertory, and there were seasons (such as 1935–36 and 1937–38) when Schiller had to take second place. The Badisches Landestheater of Karlsruhe was host to more plays by Shakespeare than Schiller up until 1939. When a week-long festival of the Reich's theatre was celebrated in Vienna in June 1938, three months after the annexation of Austria, *Hamlet* and *The Tempest* were in the programme alongside operas by Mozart and Wagner. Even in the first season of the Second World War, 1939–40, eighty-five Shakespeare productions across the Reich surpassed Schiller's eighty-two. *The Winter's Tale* remained in the last season of Berlin's Deutsches Theater under Nazi rule.[44]

By remaining a constant presence in German theatres, Shakespeare became emblematic of all non-German culture under Nazism. Shakespeare reception encapsulates a national psychosis only glimpsed in the fate of other authors. Nowhere were Herder's (and Goebbels's) gestures towards understanding different cultures more open to abuse. Harsh criticism could be counter-balanced by arguments for the legitimation of the regime. The definition of an author's racial identity evolved into a desperate form of self-assertion. Close reading revealed the need to tamper with the texts on which an apparently inviolate reputation was based. Diverse interpretations of classic plots allowed the possibility of a focus for opposition to the Third Reich.

Several Nazi critics and dramatists had no desire for Shakespeare to keep the status which would give rise to these phenomena. Hermann Wanderscheck cited the opinion of the contemporary dramatist Eberhard Wolfgang Möller, who thought that Shakespeare was one of the many foreign influences who had led German drama astray. At his best Shakespeare was 'typically unGerman' and thus had 'only made life a misery for German dramatists' when he had been taken as a model. Another young playwright, the Dramaturg at the Bavarian State Theatre in Munich, Curt Langenbeck, wanted to displace Shakespeare in favour of classical Greek drama.[45]

The few voices against Shakespeare could not suppress the long history of the reception of his drama in Germany or the Nazi adoption of the playwright's Germanic or Nordic identity. Drawing on, among other sources, Friedrich Gundolf's book of 1911, *Shakespeare und der deutsche Geist* (which included chapters on Herder, Goethe and Schiller), Nazi critics underlined the spiritual affinity between Shakespeare and German culture. It did not matter that Gundolf was Jewish. Shakespeare, after all, enjoyed the advantage of having written in an England free of Jews. Thilo von Trotha, an author who was Alfred Rosenberg's secretary, called Shakespeare 'the great creator of Nordic character drama' and 'one of the greatest liberators of the Germanic spirit'.[46]

A critic and Nazi bureaucrat went as far as to argue that performing Shakespeare was 'a duty to our own original national spirit (*völkischer Urgeist*)'. In the opening section (entitled 'Tragedy and Germanness') of his strange book of political aesthetics, *The German Path to Tragedy* (*Der deutsche Weg zur Tragödie*), Werner Deubel demonstrated how nationalism and foreign culture could be conflated: 'It is no coincidence that Germans – and Germans alone! – were the first to discover, translate, perform, and so keenly appropriate Shakespeare that the great tragedian, who "teaches, nurtures and educates Nordic people" (Herder), since then seems, in a deeper sense, to belong more to the Germans than the English.' Deubel stressed the heroic aspects of the death of characters such as Richard III and Macbeth. Shakespeare's 'tragic rank' is that, in a 'century intoxicated on the future, he is the only seer/prophet (*Seher*) from among the blind millions'. Likewise, Goebbels – doubtless with an eye on the present – thought it important that Shakespeare lived 'in London at the beginning of a world empire (*Weltreich*)'. He was 'right at the formation of history'.[47]

The German Shakespeare Society became a mouthpiece for declaring the contemporary importance of the dramatist. At its annual conference of 1936, the theatre historian Heinz Kindermann explained that Shakespeare had dramatic power 'today in the period of German rebirth'. Repeatedly evoking Herder's admiration for Shakespeare, he attempted to show how the playwright was virtually German because he used many so-called German sources and had a well-established German performance history. There was a close relationship between race and humour, so German comedies later reflected the Nordic features in Shakespeare's humour. In his closing comments, Kindermann brought his comparisons up to the present: 'We know that the writer who will give us the new people's national drama of the Third Reich will be, just as Shakespeare was for his nation, a dramatist of the political, national (*völkisch*) totality.'[48]

In an article entitled 'The German Shakespeare', Rainer Schlösser expanded this idea. Shakespeare was relevant today because he had created a living 'people's theatre (*Volkstheater*)': 'The political substance in Shakespeare exactly fulfilled the wish of his – and every! – people to see itself reflected in its essence on the stage.' But there was a contradiction here with other views. How could Shakespeare be so connected to his origins and yet at the same time be German? Besides stressing the central role of Shakespeare in German culture, Schlösser merely reproduced Nazi beliefs about *Weltkultur*. Richard Wagner had become 'world property' because he touched on German artistic feeling. So Shakespeare was rooted in his nation and thus extended beyond it. (If such opinions appear as muddled justifications to appropriate a great foreign culture, it is as well to remember that Fascist Italy was not oblivious to comparable reasoning; there Shakespeare was labelled Catholic.)[49]

Pseudo-historical and bogus anthropological arguments were not the only ways to reinforce Shakespeare's German identity. For the second German Shakespeare Week in Bochum in 1937, Professor Carl Niessen organized an exhibition entitled 'Shakespeare on the German Stage' with material from the theatre museum in Cologne. (Bochum had become a champion of Shakespeare through the efforts of the director Saladin Schmitt.) One part of the propaganda operation envisaged presenting this kind of event to the English as evidence of German appreciation of a fraternal spirit. The Nazi patron of the week in Bochum, Josef Wagner, prefaced the festival by proclaiming that it was 'living proof of the *weltoffen* (open-to-the-world) cultural mission of the new Germany'. He continued: 'It will contribute to a deeper understanding of both nations [Germany and Britain] on a spiritual level of mutual admiration for their great achievements.' The German theatrical press reported on British interest in the Bochum festival. The facts revealed far less 'mutual admiration': as Nazi officials confessed in private, an invitation to the event addressed to English students had met with very little response.[50]

It was not enough for Shakespeare to be German in spirit. From 1933 until 1936 a fierce debate raged about the language in which his plays could be performed. Hans Rothe's modern versions had started to rival the canonical nineteenth-century translations of August Wilhelm von Schlegel and Dorothea Tieck in the first two seasons of the Nazi period. His *As You Like It* and *Comedy of Errors* had been particularly successful in 1934–35. But Nazi critics, especially those in the Rosenberg camp, began to attack Rothe in virulent terms. A Berlin production of *Measure for Measure*, for example, was described as falling 'victim to the Rothean translation epidemic'. The epidemic appeared to be subsiding by the end of 1935 because, as one critic phrased it, 'word has got around that there are no cultural laurels to be gained [in using Rothe]'.[51]

Although the battle thus seemed to have been won, the beginning of 1936 witnessed an unprecedented campaign against Rothe's versions. It has to be admitted that, even when removed from the context of these controversies, Rothe's style and his often amputational view of Shakespeare are difficult to defend. His German is too modern and simplified to be dignified. He invents dialogues for Diana in *All's Well that Ends Well* and adds to a speech by Decius Brutus in *Julius Caesar*. He eliminates the power of black magic in *The Tempest*, and removes Prospero's 'epilogue', and with it much of the character's inner complexity.[52] However, what is interesting about Nazi objections to Rothe is that only a part of their energy was devoted to the analysis of such matters. For the Nazis, Rothe came to symbolize a whole series of aesthetic evils against which healthy German theatre could be defined.

According to Nazi critics, Rothe's 'boring naturalism makes Shakespeare unheroical'. Instead of keeping Shakespeare in the 'spiritual home of Germans', where Schlegel and Tieck had established him, Rothe had drawn him to 'international circles' of shallow, fashionable trends. The Schlegel–Tieck Shakespeare was compared to Luther's Bible (as indeed it still is) for its central importance to the German language. Rothe had argued that the new political epoch warranted a new set of translations. The problem for his opponents was that, far from ushering in a new regime, Rothe's style was contaminated with an immediate past the Nazis had already rejected. Hence 'Georg Kaiser's telegram style replaced Shakespeare's powerful linguistic orchestra', and this stemmed from a period of contemptible atonal music and Piscator's Bolshevist propaganda. It was also the time of despicable literary figures such as Alfred Döblin, Lion Feuchtwanger, Heinrich Mann, Bertolt Brecht, Ferdinand Bruckner and others. Whereas Rothe had argued that other German versions of Shakespeare written in the recent past were symptomatic of the need for a change from Schlegel–Tieck, Wolf Braumüller used the existence of these versions to point out just how wrong the theatre of the recent past was. (Besides being one of Rothe's most vituperative critics, Braumüller initially promoted the *Thing* play movement.) Just to make the coffin-lid secure, the principal organ for these attacks, *Bausteine zum Deutschen Nationaltheater*, reprinted a selection of aggressive reviews. Rothe's German was 'today's colourless city language' (*Münchener Neueste Nachrichten*). 'What there is left of Shakespeare here is almost just the characters' (*Das Schwarze Korps*).[53]

As the political ramifications of references to the Weimar Republic make clear, there was more at stake here than aesthetic tastes. Schlösser referred to Schlegel's comment that, as 'the genius of his people', Shakespeare was 'expert in the history of his fatherland'. Such notions of a national dramatist could be inextricably linked to the period in which the favoured Schlegel–Tieck translations were written. To perform the translations would enact the ideology of Romantic nationalist interpretation. Rothe could not approach this hallowed ground. Worse still, he was the subject of government moves to define him as once having been firmly on the political left. Some of his own plays had been anti-national and thus showed similarities with the lack of patriotism displayed by Ernst Toller and Walter Mehring.[54]

In May 1936 Goebbels used a speech he was due to make at a theatre festival as an opportunity to give his verdict on Rothe. Goebbels announced that he had consulted specialists and they all agreed that the Schlegel–Tieck translations were superior. (A report of the speech claims this statement was greeted with 'tumultuous applause'.) Goebbels said that classic authors had to be saved from 'literary experiments' which endangered the 'eternal value of their works'. There was virtually no performance of Rothe's versions afterwards. This effectively dictatorial arbitration of taste lies in stark contrast to the modernization apparently needed – and applauded – for great playwrights like Goldoni and Calderón. (Von Scholz's cutting of characters drawn by Calderón is comparable to Rothe's excisions.) His country of origin may not have been a political ally (unlike Italy and Spain), but Shakespeare was so much part of German culture that the form in which he had become most familiar had to be defended against prominent rivals. And yet, to illustrate the contradictions in Nazi thinking, evidence remains of performances (or at least authorization for productions) after 1936, not just of Rothe's own plays, but of Shakespearean versions by translators other than Schlegel–Tieck.[55]

When it came to judging productions, it was not as easy to dictate a uniform style. Objections to perceived lapses were, however, forthcoming. Mendelssohn's musical setting for A Midsummer Night's Dream was banned because of the composer's Jewish origin. A play could be made more 'German' by different choices. Heinz Hilpert's production of As You Like It at the Berlin Deutsches Theater in 1934 included music by Mozart, but in a probable allusion to the production, one Nazi critic thought what he called the 'Rococo style' interesting, but 'unnecessary'. When directors utilized elements nearer to the present, the reaction was one of outright condemnation. A Berlin production in the same season of A Midsummer Night's Dream was attacked as a 'blasphemy to Shakespeare' for its use of revue and cabaret interludes, considered 'Marxist'. Walther Brügmann's production of The Taming of the Shrew in Berlin's Theater des Volkes was similarly criticized for its revue content and 'clowning'. Such 'dramatic popularization' was said to distance the people (Volk) from Shakespeare and was reminiscent of Reinhardt's productions. If a further shorthand for the fate of Shakespeare under Weimar was needed, Leopold Jessner was continually cited for what he had 'perpetrated' on the 'genius of Shakespeare' with his 'Hamlet-in-tails production' of 1926. (What was not mentioned by Nazi critics was that Jessner's updating allowed him to parody the monarchy and contemporary militarism.)[56]

23 Adolf Mahnke's symmetrical, traditionally lavish design for *Hamlet* (Staatstheater, Dresden, 1937). Director: Georg Kiesau.

Given a certain reluctance to accept undue frivolity (at least in the Rosenberg camp), it is interesting to note that the Shakespeare play which received the most legal productions in the Third Reich (135 in total) was *Twelfth Night*. Second most popular was *The Taming of the Shrew* (101 productions), followed by *Hamlet* (94), *A Midsummer Night's Dream* (76), *Much Ado About Nothing* (57), *The Comedy of Errors* (48) and *As You Like It* (47). After that, the production figures drop below forty for each play during the entire period, so perhaps it is difficult to assume a widespread audience reception across the country, even though some productions made a considerable impact. But variations of performance figures from season to season are often noteworthy. *King Lear*, for instance, had a mere four performances in the season during which the Nazis came to power (1932–33). In the next season (1933–34) the number increased to thirty-four and by 1934–35 had reached ninety-eight. It is unclear if official ideology viewed the play as reinforcing the family rather than resigning it to tragedy.[57]

Despite Nazi adulation of Shakespeare, individual plays provided specific challenges to the National Socialist belief system. *Othello* was thus interpreted as a light-coloured 'Moor' rather than a 'negro' to avoid a racist conundrum, above all during the war. It is astounding that *Macbeth* – a play involving the murder of a king – should have been played continuously throughout the existence of the Reich. (There were a total of twenty-nine productions.) But stage presentations could transform meaning. A 1935 production in Mainz apparently showed Macbeth to be the real hero through a change in the sequence of scenes. In the same year, a staging outside the town hall in Lübeck, in Thilo von Trotha's version, made it into what one critic called 'a Nordic ballad of fate'. In 1940, the president of the Theatre Chamber, Ludwig Körner, suggested the play could be used as propaganda about the 'perfidy' of the British. The existence of two almost avant-garde productions, in Hamburg (in 1944) with abstract settings and at the Comédie Française in Paris, imply that some directors did not follow Körner's suggestion.[58]

In theory at least, *Hamlet* had also been given an 'heroic upgrading'. After the war had begun, it too was perceived as suitable anti-English fodder. Any deviation from such interpretations on stage thus had the potential to cause difficulties for those involved. Lothar Müthel's production at Berlin's Staatstheater in 1936 included Gustaf Gründgens wearing a blond wig in an energetic, active interpretation of the leading role. When Goebbels saw the actor in a revival of the same production he noted in his diary that it had been 'a great evening' and 'wonderfully coordinated acting'. Gründgens may have been 'somewhat decadent', but this was a 'pinnacle of German theatrical art': 'The audience is enthusiastic. A really great success. What a genius Shakespeare is! Everything is so small in comparison.' Not everybody was so 'enthusiastic' just after the production opened. Gründgens was condemned by Rosenberg's sector in the press for being 'degenerate, unGerman and decadent'. Gründgens took later references in the *Völkischer Beobachter* as personal attacks and threatened to leave Germany for good. Only through the intervention of Hermann Göring (under whose control the Staatstheater lay) were journalists sacked and the attacks brought to an end. With a record 130 performances, this *Hamlet* ended up being the most successful production of a classic to be mounted in the Staatstheater.[59]

Like Marlowe's *The Jew of Malta*, *The Merchant of Venice* could well be expected to have a great anti-semitic appeal. In 1933 alone there are records of eighty-six performances. A review of a provincial production pointed out how Shakespeare had a definite feeling for 'racial purity'. After Kristallnacht in 1938, a radio version was broadcast. For his production in September 1942, Paul Rose planted extras in the audience who started shouting abuse as soon as Shylock appeared. In Vienna's Burgtheater, in 1943, Werner Krauss played the 'Jewish' lead notoriously, under Lothar Müthel's direction. He had been Shylock before in 1921 (in Max Reinhardt's production) and later claimed to have changed the characterization of his subject from 'cheeky' to 'stupid'. But his theatrical mimicry was an open invitation to the prejudices of contemporary reviewers: 'The affected way of shuffling along, the hopping and stamping about in a rage, the clawing hand gestures, the raucous or mumbling voice – all this makes up the pathological picture of the East European racial type in all his external and internal human dirtiness, emphasizing danger through humour.' With an apparently 'garishly yellow' prayer shawl on his black gown, Krauss incarnated all that was evil in the Jew. The production stayed in the repertory for thirty-two performances and there were plans to make a film for propaganda purposes, based on the play, to be directed by Veit Harlan. (Krauss and Harlan had combined in 1940 for the anti-semitic film *Jew Süß* (*Jud Süß*).) The project was never completed, but the play continued its course. In December 1943 there was a staging by the Deutsches Theater of Minsk.[60]

There was, of course, plenty in Shakespeare's text which suited the Nazis. Critics depicted Shylock's desire for revenge as an abject, cowardly sentiment. Antonio was, in contrast, a noble human being willing to respect an unfair deal with the moneylender. The 'secret of these two worlds', commented one critic, is 'clear to us'; they are the 'expression of two racial opposites'. Shakespeare may not have had full knowledge of the contexts he was outlining, but he had treated a problem which 'has a current significance for us'.[61] Jessica's theft from her father in Act Two represented a way of ridding Jews of their fortunes which had actually occurred in Nazi Germany.

Reading it as an anti-semitic tract was not the only approach to *The Merchant of Venice*. In 1927 the Jewish actor Fritz Kortner had struggled amicably against his director Jürgen Fehling to portray a Shylock who, in Kortner's words, is 'treated inhumanely by the Christian environment, [and] degenerates into inhumanity'. There was another German Jewish interpretation which painted Shylock as a victim, this time of his daughter Jessica. In an exceptional essay, the poet Heinrich Heine argued that the real evil was to be found in her for her filial betrayal. She was a Jew only in name. (In a characteristic piece of nineteenth-century assimilatory optimism, Heine went on to underline the 'deep affinity' between the German and Jewish peoples.)[62]

The possibility of 'misinterpretations' or malign influences based on Jessica did not escape the Nazis. When productions of the play were encouraged in 1938, adjustments had to be made to the text. The Nazi writer Hermann Kroepelin had realized that the 'mixing of Aryan and Jewish blood' through the marriage of Jessica and Lorenzo went against the basic tenets of the Third Reich. Kroepelin, all the time claiming he had in no way distorted the play, suggested Jessica go to her father's help and thus leave Lorenzo. Solutions by others included insertions which would make it clear Jessica was adopted. In fact, the censors had to transform or omit all passages which conveyed Jewish family love or could be seen to show Shylock or the Jews in a positive light. Lines such as Launcelot's 'most beautiful pagan, most sweet Jew!' (II. 3.10–11) and Shylock's 'My own flesh and blood to rebel!' (III. 1.31) were thus removed.

To have the effect they desired, the Nazis had to reappropriate the text entirely.[63]

Cases have already been cited where the outbreak of war entailed a change in policy. Doubts were voiced in some circles as to whether Shakespeare productions should be performed at all, given the playwright's origins. Authorizations were probably refused in several instances. An analysis of the correspondence from official sources shows a lack of clarity in policy, although there was a definite urging towards stricter control during 1940–42. Certain unspoken rules seem to have worked. The history plays, for example, were too 'English' to survive after 1941.[64] Several comedies and tragedies nevertheless received new productions during the war. Among provincial theatres, Bielefeld was particularly active. New glosses evolved. When Heinz Hilpert directed *Antony and Cleopatra* in Berlin, Rosenberg's office judged the whole enterprise negatively; giving up the field of battle to join 'a loved one could hardly be reckoned positive in 1943. Others countered with a more symbolic view. The play was no longer a tragedy of love, because Antony had become the central figure. He may not have known about 'death as the highest sacrifice so that others can live', but he was 'imbued down to the last detail with his historical mission'.[65]

A German Shakespearian presence became important abroad. The Deutsches Theater in The Hague produced *Twelfth Night* in 1943, although it is worth noting how its reception in the legal Dutch press could not conform to German enthusiasm. One Dutch critic called the production 'pretty flat' and another pointed out how the theatre was 'not full'.[66] Yet for the Nazis, it was this sort of production which illustrated the German protection of Shakespeare. Ludwig Körner claimed that the British were inimical to the Germans, owing to the amount of German attention and the number of productions granted – even during wartime – to the greatest English dramatist: 'They therefore hate us because we defend Shakespeare against them.' As always, part of this defence involved defining how Shakespeare should not be treated. In March 1941, a Munich newspaper attacked an American Negro swing version of *A Midsummer Night's Dream* as an insult to Shakespeare.[67]

The possibility of an anti-Nazi Shakespeare

Like all public opposition within dictatorial regimes, cultural opposition is, by its very nature, more keenly defined and claimed when the dangers incurred through such opposition have disappeared and those who can prove they were righteous combatants can expect to gain from their past actions. Even before the abolition of cultural criticism in 1936 it would be difficult to imagine a mass of written evidence which acknowledged the anti-Nazi criticism supposedly implicit in theatrical productions. If references on stage had to be hidden, so did references in the press. When critics and directors retrospectively claim productions were oppositional, they may have personal reasons for doing so, salvaging their own integrity or the reputation of an artist whose personality would be tainted if he or she were simply an obedient collaborator. This was all the more necessary with somebody such as Erich Engel, who went on to work in Communist East Germany. Herbert Ihering wrote a list of anti-Nazi productions, but if he thought Jürgen Fehling's *Richard III* 'unmasked the whole falsifying and idealizing Hitlerite conception of history', he did not say so publicly until 1948.[68]

At the time of the premiere of Fehling's production in the Berlin Staatstheater on 2 March 1937, the evil of Richard III had already been related to his 'tragically inverted Nordic potential' by Rosenberg and other Nazi critics.[69] Fehling and his designer Traugott Müller had something more contemporary in mind. The enormous, sometimes almost empty, stage included objects from different periods, including chairs which looked as though they were from the 1930s. One of the backdrops with clouds is slightly reminiscent of the painting of Edvard Munch. The effect of the enormous space was to reduce the physical stature of the characters. If Werner Krauss can be redeemed by any production it is this one. His Richard became a grown-up child, although he was no perverse monster, but rather a cold, calculating figure. Given his blatant deformity and his advances to Anne in the second scene of the play, people have spoken about allusions to the limping, womanizing Goebbels. There were more overt references in the costumes of Clarence's murderers: they wore highboots (some describe them as jackboots) and a uniform like that of the Nazi Storm Troopers, with shoulder straps and belts. Richard had bodyguards wearing what looked like army helmets. (Photographs remain as evidence for this, but it is difficult to see how they could be allowed; from 1935 onwards prohibition orders were apparently administered strictly against the use of German military or Storm Trooper uniforms in the theatre.)[70] Once this sort of reference had been made, the field was open for further associations. Later commentators compared the ghosts which appeared before Richard (V.3) with the dead of the Night of the Long Knives, in 1934, when Ernst Röhm and others were killed on Hitler's orders.

In the five hours' duration of the evening, Fehling had the longest interval begin at the end of the fifth scene of the third act. During the interval there was apparently talk of 'cultural Bolshevism'. (In a letter to Goebbels in 1940, Schlösser, who had been present at the premiere, wrote that the production had been 'almost a cultural-Bolshevist experiment'.)[71] The Scrivener's monologue thus began the next part of the performance, laying emphasis on 'the indictment of the good Lord Hastings' (III. 6.1) and the Scrivener's comment

'Bad is the world' (III. 6.13). The Jewish musician Hans Neumark played a tune to accompany the march of the armies in the fifth act (but this affront to Aryanism was suppressed after a few performances). The biggest directorial adjustment came at the close. Fehling ended the spoken text with Richmond's words: 'The day is ours, the bloody dog is dead' (V. 4.15). There then followed a sung Bach *Te Deum*. Whereas Shakespeare, through the remaining words, reinforced the establishment of a new order, Fehling was still burying 'the bloody dog'.

Fehling's *Richard III* had twenty-one performances and was revived for a further seven. Werner Krauss chose it in 1938 as one of his performances to celebrate his twenty-fifth year on the Berlin stage. Could such a production really have meant what its later commentators claimed? The photographs are persuasive and an alert audience would doubtless be ready to make connections or interpret images and words creatively. But there is more than this. Karl Ruppel's newspaper review is remarkable because of its truth, which extends beyond the production. More remarkable still, it was actually reprinted in 1943. Ruppel was impressed by the whole production, but the musical end he found especially moving. A conclusion from which the word had been elimi- nated he thought 'possible, even necessary in a play which shows the word in its really fatal magic power, the word as a means for lying, distortion, trickery, sycophantic malice, nastiness with a smile, smirking deception – in short, the word as the true, effective means of the intellectually outstanding political criminal'. Ruppel may have gone on to mention a Renaissance context, but his own words could have only one meaning for those with a mind willing to understand them. Perhaps it is no wonder that Fehling only maintained his job because Gründgens told Göring he would resign if Fehling went.[72]

The opposition of Engel's *Coriolanus*, premiered in Berlin's Deutsches Theater on 26 March 1937, lay in a more aesthetic realm.[73] Engel had directed the play before, in 1925, in a sort of epic form. A French right-wing production, portraying Coriolanus as a strong leader in contrast to the Communist rable of Rome, had caused riots in Paris in the 1933–34 season. Nazi interpretations similarly underlined the history-shaping power of the eponymous hero. Productions, such as the one in Bochum in 1937, favoured pompous pro- cessions, sword-rattling, and magnificent sets with exotic costumes. Engel chose to shorten the fight scenes and create a more realistic, anti-heroic Coriolanus. It is difficult to judge how successful he was (Figure 24). Contrary to what one might expect, Nazi critics were confirmed in their view of the play. Volumnia was thus a 'mother of heroes' and Goebbels thought 'this Shakespeare is more up-to-date and more modern than all modern authors. [...] How he towers above Schiller!' If all agreed on the aesthetic worth, maybe in this case the opposition was in the eye of the beholder. Rudolf Heß admitted

24 *Coriolanus*, Deutsches Theater, Berlin, 1937. Director: Erich Engel. Set designer: Caspar Neher.

as much when he applauded a performance of *Julius Caesar*, but commented in private that it might prove a dangerous play if it fell into the wrong hands. Perhaps he was right. After the failed assassination attempt on Hitler on 20 July 1944, a copy of *Julius Caesar* was apparently discovered open on the desk of Graf von Stauffenberg, the colonel who was primarily responsible for the plot; Brutus's role was marked out.[74]

For every pro-Nazi or potentially critical production there were twenty stagings of comedies which had no ulterior motive other than amusement. His identity may have been German according to official dogma, but perhaps Shakespeare's overwhelming persona in the Third Reich was that of an entertainer. Early in the war, when a Berlin anti-aircraft unit took time off from guarding the skies, they put on *A Midsummer Night's Dream*. The same play was performed three times in Ludwig Berger's clandestine English-language production in Amsterdam in April 1944.[75]

A drama of victims and victors

There was inevitable hypocrisy in the promotion of foreign drama to represent a truly open-minded nation. Premieres of foreign plays had more than halved in the period 1933–38 as compared with the preceding five years, and the percentage dropped further during the war.[76] However, when a country involved in the war was occupied by German troops or at least not ostensibly hostile, then the Nazis could give the impression that a fresh cultural exchange was evolving. This picture could be painted even if the country in question, unlike Italy, could hardly be considered an inevitable ally.

A German theatre had been founded in 1933 in the town of Sibiu to cater for the estimated 800,000 ethnic Germans in Romania. It toured the country with plays by Schiller and Eberhard Wolfgang Möller, as well as Shakespeare and the Romanian dramatist Lucian Blaga in German. Nazi reports before the war, in the magazine *Die Bühne*, claimed that this German theatre was continually under threat from Romanian culture and the Jewish press, while audiences were increasingly enthusiastic: 156,000 had seen the productions on offer in the 1937–38 season. Once Romania began to support the German war effort under the command of General Antonescu, the tone changed. Romanian theatre itself became an object of interest and Caragiale's nineteenth-century comedy *A Lost Letter* was given a production in the Berlin Staatstheater in 1943.[77]

Whereas alliances and invasions defined military territory, dramatic territory often provided no clear indication of political allegiance. One of the most touching paradoxes within the culture of the Third Reich consisted in this dispute over appropriation. The Nazis' most abject victims were drawn to plays which made up the official face of the regime. In Sachsenhausen, two prisoners wrote a play on the model of *Charley's Aunt*, which was then performed in the camp. In Theresienstadt, Czech Jews put on Molière's *Georges Dandin* and Mirko Tuma translated *Measure for Measure* and *The Mayor of Zalamea* into Czech. Perhaps unaware of the success of Calderón's drama in Nazi Germany, Tuma called it a 'great anti-militaristic play'.[78]

After Belsen was liberated, the Old Vic Company from London, including Sybil Thorndike and Ralph Richardson, performed Shaw's *Arms and the Man* for Allied military staff who were desperately trying to save what lives they could. It was the one play by Shaw which had been banned from German theatres after the outbreak of the war, because of its pacifist tendencies. An author favoured by the Nazis could at least be shown in a sympathetic light. As usual, Shakespeare proved more problematic. German prisoners of war put on *Hamlet* in Mississippi and *Julius Caesar* in southern France. In 1945 the 'Theatre Officer' of the occupying US military authorities in Bavaria mentioned *Hamlet* in his recommendations for a future repertory (under the classification 'Corruption and Justice') and *Julius Caesar* in his blacklist ('considering the present mental and psychological status of Germans'). Among other recommendations were Ibsen's *Peer Gynt*, *Pillars of Society* and *An Enemy of the People* (all plays promoted by the Nazis in one form or another).[79]

In what was perhaps an oversight, the officer did not mention *The Merchant of Venice*, either positively or negatively. At the end of 1946 a proposal to stage the play in Frankfurt provoked widespread controversy, and the idea was postponed indefinitely, because it was thought that not enough time had elapsed since the end of ruling Nazism. Of course, it all depended on your point of view. In the same year a famous Yiddish *Merchant of Venice* was performed in London. When Hitler wielded supreme power in Germany – ten years earlier – the then exiled Leopold Jessner had portrayed Shylock as a victim of humiliation, with his Hebrew production in Palestine.[80]

The American officer's lists contained a category entitled 'The Pursuit of Happiness', consisting of comedies 'to show the free and easy ways of life in democratic countries, graciousness, charm, sense of humour, and the ability to rib and take a ribbing without becoming belligerent'. Among the texts listed was *Twelfth Night*, the play by Shakespeare which received most productions during the Third Reich. Even today it is debatable whether Shakespeare survived the Nazis unscathed or whether a certain approach to Shakespearian drama (and other non-German plays) extended beyond 1945.

Notes

1 Otto Laubinger, 'Aufgaben des Theaters im Dritten Reich: wie sieht das Volks-theater aus?', *Die Deutsche Bühne*, 25, no. 13 (16 October 1933), 214–15; Carl Stueber, 'Spanische Bühnenklassiker: zu den Erneuerungsversuchen Hans Schlegels', *Deutsche Dramaturgie*, 1, no. 8 (August 1942), 182–4 (p. 182); Dietmar Schmidt, 'Europäische Theater in Berlin', *Die Bühne*, 20 February 1944, pp. 17–18 (p. 17).

2 Rainer Schlösser, 'Nationalsozialismus und Weltliteratur', *Der neue Weg*, 63, no. 19 (31 December 1934), 472–5 (p. 472).

3 Joseph Goebbels, *Goebbels Reden: 1932–1945*, ed. by Helmut Heiber, 2 vols (Düsseldorf: Droste, 1971–72), I, 220–1.

4 The person who has done most in English to popularize a view of Herder as someone who rejected universal values in favour of understanding national tradi-tions is Isaiah Berlin. See, for example, his *Vico and Herder: Two Studies in the History of Ideas* (London: Hogarth, 1976), pp. 143–216; *The Crooked Timber of Humanity: Chapters in the History of Ideas*, ed. by Henry Hardy (London: John Murray, 1990), pp. 20–48. For Herder's reception in the Third Reich and his place in the history of anti-semitism, see respectively *Herder im 'Dritten Reich'*, ed. by Jost Schneider (Bielefeld: Aisthesis, 1994); Ritchie Robertson, '"Urheimat Asien": The Re-Orientation of German and Austrian Jews, 1900–1925', *German Life and Letters*, 49 (1996), 182–92. For Nazi abuse of the term *Volk* with regard to German theatre and drama, see the introduction to the present volume, especially pp. 15–18.

5 Ingolf Kuntze, 'Das Deutsche Süd-Amerika Gastspiel 1934', *Die Deutsche Bühne*, 26, no. 14 (10 November 1934), 287–9; 'Ausland: Buenos Aires', *Die Deutsche Bühne*, 27, no. 5 (25 April 1935), 94; *Die Bühne*, 1 September 1936, pp. 530–1

(theatre in Frankfurt); Dr Lester Raines, 'Ein Amerikaner über das deutsche Theater', trans. by Rudolf Ramlow, *Bausteine zum Deutschen Nationaltheater*, 4 (1936), 335–7 (lecture in New Mexico).

6 Unless otherwise indicated, all information relating to numbers of productions is derived from my own research, the database in the Institut für Theaterwissenschaft, Free University of Berlin, and Thomas Eicher, 'Theater im "Dritten Reich": eine Spielplananalyse der deutschen Schauspieltheater 1929–1944' (unpublished doctoral thesis, Free University of Berlin, 1992).

7 Hans Knudsen, 'Der Winter-Spielplan – statistisch gesehen', *Die Deutsche Bühne*, 27, nos. 7–8 (15 June 1935), 122–5.

8 Dr Hans Schirmer, 'Was soll man übersetzen?', *Die Bühne*, 11 October 1940, pp. 298–300 (p. 299).

9 Rosso di San Secondo, 'Die faschistische Revolution und das Theater', *Völkischer Beobachter* (North German edition – A), 3 March 1933; Karl Schück, 'Italienischer Theaterbrief', *Der neue Weg*, 63, no. 5 (15 March 1934), 104 (honest assessment); Nicola de Pirro, 'Zwei Nationen – zwei Theater des Volkes', *Die Bühne*, 5 December 1938, pp. 446–8 (p. 446: Mussolini quoted); Dr Rainer Schlösser, 'Italienische Freilichttheater', *Die Bühne*, 1 September 1937, pp. 417–18.

10 Bruno Fischli, *Die Deutschen-Dämmerung: zur Genealogie des völkisch-faschistischen Dramas und Theaters (1897–1933)*, Literatur und Wirklichkeit, 16 (Bonn: Bouvier, 1976), pp. 228–30 (on German premiere); Dr W[olfgang] von G[ordon], Review of published text of *Hundert Tage*, *Bausteine zum Deutschen Nationaltheater*, 1 (1933), 25 (gloss by Nazi commentator); Franz Groborz, 'Das Staatstheater am Gendarmenmarkt und das Deutsche Theater zur Zeit des Nationalsozialismus', 2 vols (unpublished Magisterarbeit, Free University of Berlin, 1987), I, 39–40 (on *Cavour*); Programme for *Cavour*, Schauspielhaus am Gendarmenmarkt, 1940–41 season, n.p., in Institut für Theaterwissenschaft, Free University of Berlin.

11 Michele Cometa, *Il teatro di Pirandello in Germania* (Palermo: Novecento, 1986), pp. 321–6 (details of censorship in Germany); Gaspare Giudice, *Luigo Pirandello* (Turin: UTET, 1963), p. 528 (Vatican); Maurizio Cesari, *La censura nel periodo fascista*, Le Istituzioni Culturali, 3 (Naples: Liguori, 1978), p. 66 (banning on Italian radio). For the fate of the opera in Italy, see Nino Borsellino, *Ritratto e immagini di Pirandello*, Biblioteca Universale Laterza, 347 (Bari: Laterza, 1991), p. 107. The libretto of *The Changeling* had been translated by the prominent Jewish musicologist H. F. Redlich, another possible 'racial' reason for the Nazi banning. See Chapter 3 of the present volume (pp. 162–3) for further details on the reception of this and other operas by Malipiero.

12 Cometa, p. 321 (Berlin congress). There had been a break between Pirandello and Feist in the late 1920s, although only in 1936 did Pirandello announce the preparation of new, Aryan translations; see Oscar Büdel, 'Pirandello sulla scena tedesca', *Quaderni del Piccolo Teatro della Città di Milano*, 1 (1961), 99–122 (pp. 106–7). For Pirandello's relationship with Fascism see Alberto Cesare Alberti, *Il teatro nel fascismo: Pirandello e Bragaglia: documenti inediti negli archivi italiani*, Biblioteca Teatrale, 15 (Rome: Bulzoni, 1974); Giudice, pp. 412–64; Gianfranco Pedullà, *Il teatro italiano nel tempo del fascismo*, Saggi, 416 (Bologna: Il Mulino, 1994), especially pp. 31–3, 301–2; Gian Franco Vené, *Pirandello fascista: la coscienza borghese tra ribellione e rivoluzione* (Venice: Marsilio, 1981).

13 In his review of the polemical Berlin premiere of *Tonight we Improvise*, in 1930, Herbert Ihering had claimed that 'the fashion for Pirandello was never genuine in Germany' (repr. in *Luigi Pirandello in the Theatre: A Documentary Record*, ed. by Susan Bassnett and Jennifer Lorch, Contemporary Theatre Studies, 3 (Chur: Harwood Academic, 1993), pp. 165–6 (p. 165)). (As a demonstration of the actual popularity of Pirandello in Weimar, which had indeed faded by the late 1920s, Büdel provides a list of German productions of Pirandello (pp. 110–22); it is not complete for the Third Reich period.) *Six Characters in Search of an Author* was performed for Jewish audiences by Berlin's Jüdischer Kulturbund in 1935.

14 Dr Giovanni Lerda, 'Freundschaftstage mit der deutschen Delegation in Italien', *Die Bühne*, 1 September 1937, pp. 420–3 (German visit to Italy); *Die Bühne*, 5 December 1938, p. 447 (cultural agreement); 'Italienische Vertreter der Bühnenschaffenden studieren das Theaterwesen in Deutschland', *Die Bühne*, 5 March 1939, pp. 101–2 (Italian visit); Bogusław Drewniak, *Das Theater im NS-Staat: Szenarium deutscher Zeitgeschichte 1933–1945* (Düsseldorf: Droste, 1983), pp. 140, 208, 242, 263 (visits of Italian and German opera and theatre companies; German plays in Italy; Italian weeks).

15 Otto zur Nedden, 'Deutsche und italienische Opernmusik in Vergangenheit und Gegenwart'; Alessandro De Stefani, 'Teatro italiano e tedesco'; Werner von der Schulenburg, 'Römische Theatereindrücke'; all in *Wechselbeziehungen des deutschen und des italienischen Theaters: eine deutsch-italienische Theaterwoche in Rom im Palazzo Zuccari 5.–9. März 1940: Tagungsbericht (in deutscher und italienischer Sprache)*, ed. by Otto C. A. zur Nedden, 'Das Nationaltheater': Schriftenreihe des Theaterwissenschaftlichen Instituts der Friedrich-Schiller-Universität Jena, 5 (Würzburg: Konrad Triltsch, 1940), respectively pp. 5–21 (pp. 7, 14, 19: Leitmotif, *Don Carlos*, nation); pp. 72–4 (p. 73: quality and quantity); pp. 26–34 (p. 27: Pirandello).

16 Karl Kaufmann (Gauleiter of Hamburg), untitled introduction; Dr Rainer Schlösser, 'Goethe und Italien'; details of theatrical productions; all in *Deutsch-Italienische Kulturtage der Hansestadt Hamburg: 1943*, a special edition of *Die Rampe: Blätter des Staatlichen Schauspielhauses Hamburg*, ed. by Henry Flebbe (Hamburg: Conrad Kayser, [1943]), respectively, p. 1; pp. 16–25 (pp. 20–1); pp. 2–3, 9–12.

17 *Deutsch-Italienische Kulturtage*, pp. 29–30 (Goethe quoted); Mathilde Kühle, *Carlo Goldonis Komödien auf dem deutschen Theater des 20. Jahrhunderts*, Italienische Studien, 7 (Cologne: Petrarca-Haus; Stuttgart: Kommissionsverlag Deutsche Verlags-Anstalt, 1943), pp. 97 (performance for German troops), 104 ('common fight'); Drewniak, p. 263 (Propaganda Ministry support); Eicher, p. 42 (substitution in Potsdam); Michael Dillmann, *Heinz Hilpert: Leben und Werk* (Berlin: Akademie der Künste/Hentrich, 1990), p. 191 (last performance at the Deutsches Theater).

18 Kühle, pp. 23 (*The Landlady from Venice*), 37–8 (Knöller), 35–6 (Bremen production), 39–41 (*The Liar*). For an alternative view to Kühle's judgement of some translations, see W. Theodor Elwert, 'Goldoni in Germania', in *Studi goldoniani*, ed. by Vittore Branca and Nicola Mangini, Civiltà Veneziana: Studi, 6, 2 vols (Venice: Istituto per la Collaborazione Culturale, 1960), II, 259–76.

19 Kühle, p. 90 (German comment); F. De Crucciati, 'Itinerario teatrale attraverso l'Europa in guerra', *Scenario*, 12 (1943), 114–16 (p. 115: 'unrecognizable').

20 Johann Froembgen, *Franco: ein Leben für Spanien* (Leipzig: Goten-Verlag Herbert Eisentraut, 1939) (hagiography); Drewniak, pp. 141–2 (opera companies).

21 Edmund Schramm, 'Spanisches Theater der Gegenwart', *Die Bühne*, 5 May 1939, pp. 218–21 (on contemporary Spanish drama); Stueber, p. 183 (admission); Gertrud Wieser, 'Wilhelm von Scholz' Nachdichtungen des Calderón' (unpublished doctoral thesis, University of Vienna, 1939), p. 63 ('no longer understandable').

22 Compare F[echter], *Deutsche Allgemeine Zeitung*, 2 March 1933 (evening edition); K.M.-Fr., *Der Angriff*, 2 March 1933; Arenhövel, *Völkischer Beobachter* (North German edition), 3 March 1933.

23 Brigitte Schöpel, '*Naturtheater': Studien zum Theater unter freiem Himmel in Südwestdeutschland*, Volksleben, 9 (Tübingen: Tübinger Vereinigung für Volkskunde, 1965), pp. 79, 105 (Heidenheim production); R[udolf] Großmann, 'Lope, der Dichter des ewigen Spanien', *Ibero-Amerikanische Rundschau*, 1 (1935–36), 215–18 (p. 217).

24 See, for example, the reviews of *Der Richter von Zalamea* by Conrad Neckels, *Lübecker Zeitung*, 28 May 1943 ('community'); Günther Mann, *Kreuz Zeitung*, 10 January 1937 ('ancient right').

25 Wilhelm von Scholz, *Am Ilm und Isar: Lebenserinnerungen* (Leipzig: Paul List, 1939), p. 309 (proleptic allusion); *Künstlerbuch der Sächsischen Staatstheater*, ed. by Dr Alexander Schum (Dresden: [Staatstheater], [1934]), p. 106 (Adolf Mahnke's design of *Life is a Dream* in Schröder's production, Dresden); Wieser, pp. 64–5 (example of modernization of language); Calderón de la Barca and Wilhelm von Scholz, *Welttheater* (Leipzig: Paul List, 1942), p. 346 ('Heil, Sigismund!').

26 Bernhard Minetti, *Erinnerungen eines Schauspielers*, ed. by Günther Rühle (Stuttgart: Deutsche Verlags-Anstalt, 1985), p. 134. For further details of Calderón in the Third Reich, see John London, 'Algunos montajes de Calderón en el Tercer Reich', in *Texto e imagen en Calderón: undécimo coloquio anglogermano sobre Calderón: St Andrews, Escocia, 17–20 de julio de 1996*, ed. by Manfred Tietz, Archivum Calderonianum, 8 (Stuttgart: Franz Steiner, 1998), pp. 143–57 (with illustrations); Henry Sullivan, *Calderón in the German Lands and the Low Countries: His Reception and Influence, 1654–1980* (Cambridge: Cambridge University Press, 1983), pp. 355–8, 364–73.

27 Hans Schlegel, 'El problema de la traducción de los clásicos del teatro español', *Ensayos y Estudios*, 2 (1940), 24–45 (on Schlegel's style of translation); Adalbert Hämel, 'Lope de Vega', *Ibero-Amerikanisches Archiv*, 9 (1935–36), 94–100 (pp. 95–6: Lope as the founder of Spanish theatre).

28 My account of the Hamburg production and the events which accompanied it is derived from H. W. Seliger, '*Fuenteovejuna* en Alemania: de la traducción a la falsificación', *Revista Canadiense de Estudios Hispánicos*, 8 (1983–84), 381–403. Seliger is wrong to imply that *Fuenteovejuna* was not put on again in the Third Reich after the Hamburg production. Another production took place in Regensburg in 1939.

29 Derek Gagen, *Coming to Terms with the Civil War: Modern Productions of Lope de Vega's 'Fuenteovejuna'* (Swansea: University College of Swansea, 1993) (left-wing productions of the play); Werner Warmbrunn, *The Dutch under German Occupation: 1940–1945* (Stanford, CA: Stanford University Press; London: Oxford University Press, 1963), p. 44 (Nazi measures against the Dutch royal family); Lope de Vega, *Fuente Ovejuna*, trans. by Dr G. C. Van 'T Hoog (Amsterdam:

Wereldbibliotheek, 1941), p. 130 ('tyranny'). The Dutch translator's introduction (pp. 5–14) shows him to be well aware of the potential of the play and some of its reception outside Spain.

30 Dr Gottfried Müller, *Dramaturgie des Theaters und des Films*, 'Das National-theater': Schriftenreihe des Theaterwissenschaftlichen Instituts der Friedrich-Schiller-Universität Jena, 6, 2nd edn (Würzburg: Konrad Triltsch, 1942) (academic view of Ancient Greek drama); Schlösser, 'Nationalsozialismus und Weltliteratur', p. 474 ('up-to-date play'); Drewniak, pp. 275–6 (several productions of Russian texts). Chekhov's niece, whose name had the Germanized spelling Olga Tsche-chowa, became a famous actress in the Third Reich, and was especially well known for her film roles. Photographed with Hitler, she was also a spy for Stalin. Thanks to her the Nazis protected Chekhov's house in Yalta. See Donald Rayfield, *Anton Chekhov: A Life* (London: HarperCollins, 1997), p. 602.

31 W.Fr. Könitzer, 'Zu Henrik Ibsens 30. Todestag: der Dichter seiner Zeit', *Völki-scher Beobachter* (North German edition – A), 23 May 1936 (Nordic playwright); Adolf Hitler, *Mein Kampf*, trans. by Ralph Manheim (London: Pimlico, 1992), p. 627; Christoph P. Saxer, 'Dietrich Eckarts Interpretation des *Peer Gynt*' (unpub-lished doctoral thesis, University of Vienna, 1940) (on Eckart's translation). There were numerous eulogies of Eckart during the Nazi period. For example, see Richard Euringer, *Dietrich Eckart* (Hamburg: Hanseatische Verlagsanstalt, 1935).

32 Yvonne Shafer, 'Nazi Berlin and the *Grosses Schauspielhaus*', *Theatre Survey*, no. 34 (May 1993), 71–90 (pp. 84–7: 1936 production of *Peer Gynt*); Drewniak, p. 269 (protests against Eckart's version).

33 Drewniak, p. 269 (propaganda plays; banning of plays during the war); *The Oxford Ibsen*, ed. by James Walter McFarlane, 8 vols (London: Oxford University Press, 1960–77), IV (1963), 458 ('The third empire'), 608 ('I believe that an age'); Dr Otto C.A. zur Nedden, *Drama und Dramaturgie im 20. Jahrhundert: Abhand-lungen zum Theater und zur Theaterwissenschaft der Gegenwart*, 'Das Nationaltheater': Schriftenreihe des Theaterwissenschaftlichen Instituts der Friedrich-Schiller-Universität Jena, 4, 3rd edn (Würzburg: Konrad Triltsch, 1944), pp. 27–8 (Nedden's quotation and comments on Ibsen's words).

34 Nedden, *Drama*, p. 77; Drewniak, p. 262 (Gerber, here misspelt); Schlösser, 'Nationalsozialismus und Weltliteratur', p. 474; Eicher, p. 75 (percentages). The decrease in the production of plays by Molière was compensated for by the increased number of productions of comedies by Goldoni, Calderón, Lope de Vega, Moreto and Tirso de Molina.

35 German comments on Parisian theatre from Dr Julius Lothar Schücking, 'Theater in Frankreich', *Deutsche Dramaturgie*, 2, no. 2 (February 1943), 42–6.

36 Franz Woertz, 'Politisches Gesellschaftsstück?', *Blätter des Deutschen Theaters und der Kammerspiele*, 1937–38 season, pp. 37–40 (on English comedy of manners); Bettina Schültke, *Theater oder Propaganda?: die städtischen Bühnen Frankfurt am Main 1933–1945*, Studien zur Frankfurter Geschichte, 40 (Frankfurt am Main: Waldemar Kramer, 1997), pp. 242–3 (examples of reception and popularity of Wilde); Drewniak, p. 255 (details of Wilde films); Karl Künkler, 'Theater in Berlin', *Bausteine zum Deutschen Nationaltheater*, 5 (1937), 17–24 (p. 24: 'irrepressibly funny farce').

37 Glenn R. Cuomo, '"Saint Joan before the Cannibals": George Bernard Shaw in the Third Reich', *German Studies Review*, 16 (1993), 435–61 (pp. 441: Mannheim

production; 443: 'semi-classic'; 444: Goebbels and Hitler in agreement); Else Pilger, 'George Bernard Shaw in Deutschland' (unpublished doctoral thesis, University of Münster, 1940), pp. 12, 28, 70 (academic circles); Müller, p. 89 (Schopenhauer etc.).

38 Cuomo, p. 450 (on royalties). There was some anti-semitic criticism of Trebitsch's versions (Pilger, pp. 32–3, 38).

39 Cuomo, p. 442 (about *On the Rocks*); 'Diskussion um Shaw', *Blätter der Volksbühne Berlin*, May–June 1934, pp. 6–8 (repr. of comments in *Berliner Morgenpost*, *Der Angriff* and *Der Montag*).

40 Cuomo, pp. 445 (exceptions made), 447 (on *Geneva*), 449 (directive); *The Nazi 'Kultur' in Poland* (London: His Majesty's Stationery Office, 1945), p. 192 (actor imprisoned).

41 Cuomo, pp. 445 (people's martyr), 450 (Chemnitz Theatre); Joseph Goebbels, *Die Tagebücher von Joseph Goebbels: sämtliche Fragmente*, Teil I: *Aufzeichnungen 1924–1941*, 4 vols, ed. by Elke Fröhlich (Munich: K. G. Saur, 1987), III, 424–5 (Goebbels's diary entry, 1 February 1938).

42 *The Complete Plays of Bernard Shaw* (London: Constable, 1931), pp. 984, 1004.

43 Serge Added, *Le Théâtre dans les années-Vichy: 1940–1944* (Paris: Ramsay, 1992), p. 292, n. 18 (commemoration and Pétain's view), n. 19 (broadcast from London); Richard Biedrzynski, *Schauspieler: Regisseure: Intendanten* (Heidelberg: Verlagsanstalt Hüthig, 1944), pp. 10–11 (Fehling's production); Groborz, I, 76–7 (later commentaries); [Béatrix] Dussane, *Notes de théâtre: 1940–1950* (Paris: Lardanchet, 1951), pp. 121–2 (example of subsequent interpretation based on a view of resistance to the occupation). Added (pp. 262–73) is more cynical about claims for resistance through the Joan of Arc legend, and judges possibilities according to the exact chronological context and the intentions of those involved.

44 Eicher, pp. 35–6 (on percentages and Schiller versus Shakespeare); Konrad Dussel, *Ein neues, ein heroisches Theater?: Nationalsozialistische Theaterpolitik und ihre Auswirkungen in der Provinz*, Literatur und Wirklichkeit, 26 (Bonn: Bouvier, 1988), p. 283 (Karlsruhe); 'Reichs-Theaterfestwoche in Wien', *Die Bühne*, 5 June 1938, p. 161 (festival in Vienna).

45 Dr Hermann Wanderscheck, *Deutsche Dramatik der Gegenwart* (Berlin: Bong, 1938), p. 40 (reference to Möller's comments). Joseph Wulf implies the opinions are directly those of Wanderscheck; see Wulf's *Theater und Film im Dritten Reich: eine Dokumentation*, Ullstein Buch, 33031 (Frankfurt am Main: Ullstein, 1983), pp. 251–2. For an account of Langenbeck's views see Ernst Leopold Stahl, *Shakespeare und das deutsche Theater: Wanderung und Wandelung seines Werkes in dreiundeinhalb Jahrhunderten* (Stuttgart: W. Kohlhammer, 1947), pp. 645–8.

46 Stahl; and Simon Williams [and Wilhelm Hortmann], *Shakespeare on the German Stage*, 2 vols (Cambridge: Cambridge University Press, 1990–98); I: *1586–1914* (by Williams, 1990) (history of reception in Germany); Eicher, p. 34 (Nordic identity in Nazi period); Werner Habicht, 'Shakespeare and Theatre Politics in the Third Reich', in *The Play Out of Context: Transferring Plays from Culture to Culture*, ed. by Hanna Scolnicov and Peter Holland (Cambridge: Cambridge University Press, 1989), pp. 110–20 (pp. 111–13: Gundolf and Nazi theories); Thilo von Trotha, *NS-Monatshefte*, 1934, p. 1147 (quoted in Günther Rühle, 'Einleitung', in *Zeit und Theater*, ed. by Günther Rühle, 6 vols (Frankfurt am Main: Ullstein/ Propyläen, 1980), V: *Diktatur und Exil*, pp. 7–75 (p. 49)). Gundolf had taught Goebbels at Heidelberg.

47 Walter Thomas, 'Shakespeare und das deutsche Theater', *Prisma*, 12 (1935–36), 115 (quoted in Bernd Schmidt, 'Die Entwicklung des Bochumer Theaters bis 1944: unter besonderer Berücksichtigung der Festwochen in der Zeit von 1933 bis 1944' (unpublished Magisterarbeit, Free University of Berlin, 1982), p. 87: 'duty'); Werner Deubel, *Der deutsche Weg zur Tragödie* (Dresden: Wolfgang Jess, 1935), pp. 5, 32; Goebbels, *Die Tagebücher*, III, 424.

48 Heinz Kindermann, 'Shakespeare und das deutsche Volkstheater: Festvortrag bei der Jahrestagung 1936 der Deutschen Shakespeare-Gesellschaft', *Shakespeare-Jahrbuch*, 72 (1936), 9–41 (pp. 9: 'German rebirth'; 14: Herder; 15: German sources; 23: humour; 41: 'We know …').

49 Dr Rainer Schlösser, 'Der deutsche Shakespeare: ein Beitrag zur Bochumer Shakespeare-Woche', *Shakespeare-Jahrbuch*, 74 (1938), 20–30 (pp. 25: 'people's theatre'; 21–2: *Weltkultur*); Silvio D'Amico, 'Shakespeare cattolico?', *Scenario*, 4 (1935), 62–6.

50 Schmidt, 'Die Entwicklung', pp. 93–4 (exhibition), 86 (Josef Wagner, invitations to English students); 'Deutschland wirbt in England für Shakespeare', *Die Bühne*, 1 September 1937, p. 435 (theatrical press).

51 'Theater in Berlin', *Bausteine zum Deutschen Nationaltheater*, 3 (1935), 339–42 (p. 341: 'victim'); Wolf Braumüller, 'Die Spielzeit der Klassiker: Überblick über die ersten drei Monate der Theaterspielzeit 1935/36', *Bausteine zum Deutschen Nationaltheater*, 4 (1936), 5–10 (p. 6: 'word has got around'). The Schlegel–Tieck Shakespeare – as the translations are commonly known – was completed, under the supervision of Ludwig Tieck, by Tieck's daughter Dorothea and Graf W. H. Baudissin.

52 On Rothe's omissions and adaptations, see Angel-Luis Pujante and Dagmar Scheu, 'El Shakespeare de Hans Rothe o el mito de la traducción teatral', *Livius*, 2 (1992), 253–62; Simon Williams and Wilhelm Hortmann, *Shakespeare on the German Stage*, [II]: *The Twentieth Century* (by Hortmann, 1998), pp. 87–9.

53 'Ein Theater-Urteil zu Rothes Shakespeare-Übersetzung', *Die Bühne*, 1 January 1936, pp. 2–3 ('boring naturalism'); Dr Reinhold [Zickel] von Jan, '"Gründe, die gegen eine Neuübersetzung Shakespeares sprechen": ein Wort zur Shakespeare-Übersetzung von Hans Rothe', *Bausteine zum Deutschen Nationaltheater*, 3 (1935), 33–42 (p. 35: Luther); Dr Reinhold Zickel von Jan, 'Wir brauchen Shakespeare!', *Bausteine zum Deutschen Nationaltheater*, 4 (1936), 47–51 (p. 48: 'Georg Kaiser'); Wolf Braumüller, '"Der Kampf um Shakespeare": eine Entgegnung auf Hans Rothes Bericht', *Bausteine zum Deutschen Nationaltheater*, 4 (1936), 51–62 (pp. 51: Alfred Döblin etc.; 57: on other versions); *Bausteine zum Deutschen Nationaltheater*, 4 (1936), 65 ('city language'), 64 ('just the characters').

54 Schlösser, 'Der deutsche Shakespeare', p. 22; Eicher, p. 72 (government moves).

55 'Bericht über die Reichs-Theaterfestwoche in München: 10.–17. Mai 1936', *Die Bühne*, 1 June 1936, pp. 341–54 (p. 346: extracts from speech by Goebbels); Eicher, p. 73 (authorizations for Rothe's plays); Drewniak, p. 250 (other Shakespeare versions).

56 Karl Künkler, 'Theater in Berlin: Grundsätzliches zu einer Shakespeare-Inszenierung', *Bausteine zum Deutschen Nationaltheater*, 2 (1934), 323–4 (*As You Like It*, *A Midsummer Night's Dream*); 'Theater in Berlin', *Bausteine zum Deutschen Nationaltheater*, 3 (1935), 339–42 (pp. 339–40: *The Taming of the Shrew*); Karl Künkler, 'Hans Rothe und das Theater', *Bausteine zum Deutschen*

Nationaltheater, 4 (1936), 43–7 (p. 46: Jessner). For a summary of Hilpert's style for Shakespeare, see Hortmann, who analyzes Shakespeare productions of several Berlin directors (pp. 124–61).

57 For these figures and a table of all plays, see Eicher, pp. 45, 61.

58 Eicher, pp. 60 ('Moor'), 61–2 (*Macbeth* in Mainz); Stahl, pp. 704 (Lübeck), 723–4 (Hamburg), 727 (Paris); Ludwig Körner, '"Sprich eine Lüge und bleib dabei!": die *Times* wird interviewt', *Die Bühne*, 25 July 1940, pp. 194–202 (p. 200).

59 Habicht, 'Shakespeare and Theatre Politics', p. 115 ('heroic upgrading'); Goebbels, *Die Tagebücher*, III, 454; Drewniak, p. 248 (attacks on Gründgens); Groborz, I, 43 (success at Staatstheater).

60 Wulf, pp. 278–9 (*The Jew of Malta*), 280 (performance numbers), 281 (Paul Rose production); Ernst Heiß, *Lippische Staatszeitung*, 17 October 1933 (quoted by Ron Engle, 'Theatre in Detmold 1933–1939: A Case Study of Provincial Theatre During the Nazi Prewar Era', in *Theatre in the Third Reich, the Prewar Years: Essays on Theatre in Nazi Germany*, ed. by Glen W. Gadberry, Contributions to the Study of World History, 49 (Westport, CT: Greenwood Press, 1995), pp. 33–45 (p. 37: provincial production)); Drewniak, p. 251 (radio); Werner Krauss, *Das Schauspiel meines Lebens: einem Freund erzählt* (Stuttgart: Henry Govert, 1958), pp. 206–9 (Krauss's account of his performance); Karl Lahm, 'Shylock der Ostjude', *Deutsche Allgemeine Zeitung*, 19 May 1943 (repr. in Wulf, pp. 282–3: 'the affected way'); Biedrzynski, p. 35 ('garishly yellow'); Stahl, p. 726, and Hans Daiber, *Schaufenster der Diktatur: Theater im Machtbereich Hitlers* (Stuttgart: Günther Neske, 1995), p. 329 (Minsk). Hortmann (pp. 134–6) claims that *The Merchant of Venice* was relatively neglected as a propaganda weapon.

61 Dr Karl Pempelfort, 'Er besteht auf seinem Schein', *Königsberger Tageblatt*, 31 March 1935 (Wulf, pp. 280–1).

62 Fritz Kortner, *Alle Tage Abend*, dtv, 556, 2nd edn (Munich: Deutscher Taschenbuch Verlag, 1970), p. 242; Heinrich Heine, *Säkularausgabe* (Berlin: Akademie-Verlag; Paris: Editions du CNRS, 1970–), IX: *Prosa: 1836–1840*, ed. by Fritz Mende (1979), pp. 218–26.

63 For details of changes to the text see Eicher, pp. 49–57. For the history of anti-semitic views of Shylock, see John Gross, *Shylock: A Legend and its Legacy* (New York: Simon and Schuster, 1994).

64 For the changes of policy during the war, see Eicher (pp. 38–43), who corrects Drewniak's claim (p. 249) that Shakespeare was actually banned for a month.

65 Drewniak, p. 252 (negative view of *Antony and Cleopatra*); Franz Köppen, 'Politische Dramen: Berliner Theater im totalen Krieg', *Deutsche Zeitung in den Niederlanden*, 27 April 1943 (more symbolic view).

66 Compare the reviews of Kurt Herwarth Ball, *Deutsche Zeitung in den Niederlanden*, 27 April 1943 (German reception); B. V. Eysselsteijn, *Haagsche Courant*, 27 April 1943 ('pretty flat'); G. K. Krop, *Het Volk*, 29 April 1943 ('not full').

67 Körner, p. 199; *Münchner Illustrierte Presse*, 27 March 1941 (quoted in Terry Charman, '"Swingmusik ist verboten": Popular Music Policy and "Swing Youth" in Nazi Germany', *Imperial War Museum Review*, no. 3 (October 1988), 80–6 (p. 86: Munich newspaper)).

68 Herbert Ihering, *Berliner Dramaturgie* (Berlin: Aufbau Verlag, 1948), p. 110. Jutta Wardetzky wrote of the anti-fascist nature of that production and Engel's *Coriolanus* from a firmly East German perspective. See her *Theaterpolitik im*

faschistischen Deutschland: Studien und Dokumente ([East] Berlin: Henschel, 1983), pp. 202–3.

69 For Nazi views of Richard III, see Habicht, 'Shakespeare and Theatre Politics', p. 115. Details of Fehling's production are taken from the reconstructions in Groborz, I, 100–16; Hortmann, pp. 137–41; Hans-Thies Lehmann, 'Richard der Dritte, 1937 – eine Skizze' (with photographs), in *Das Theater des deutschen Regisseurs Jürgen Fehling*, 2nd edn, ed. by Gerhard Ahrens (Weinheim: Quadriga, 1987), pp. 172–83.

70 Barbara Panse, 'Censorship in Nazi Germany: The Influence of the Reich's Ministry of Propaganda on German Theatre and Drama, 1933–1945', trans. by Meg Mumford, in *Fascism and Theatre: Comparative Studies on the Aesthetics and Politics of Performance in Europe, 1925–1945*, ed. by Günter Berghaus (Providence, RI: Berghahn Books, 1996), pp. 140–56 (p. 147: on ruling against uniforms).

71 Eicher, p. 65.

72 Karl H. Ruppel, *Berliner Schauspiel: Dramaturgische Betrachtungen: 1936 bis 1942* (Berlin: Paul Neff, 1943), p. 15; Curt Riess, *Gustaf Gründgens: die klassische Biographie des grossen Künstlers* (Hamburg: Hoffmann & Kampe, 1965), p. 214 (Gründgens's stance).

73 For details of Engel's production, see Groborz, I, 134–48. Hortmann (p. 150) includes a photograph in which the Roman greeting looks like the Nazi salute.

74 Alan Chamberlain, 'Theatre and the French Right in the 1920s and 1930s: Nostalgia for "un chef fort et autoritaire"', in *The Attractions of Fascism: Social Psychology and the Aesthetics of the 'Triumph of the Right'*, ed. by John Milfull (New York: Berg, 1990), pp. 124–36 (pp. 134–5: *Coriolanus* in Paris); Schmidt, 'Die Entwicklung', pp. 88–91 (the Nazi *Coriolanus*); Willi F. Könitzer, *Völkischer Beobachter* (Berlin edition), 28–29 March 1937 (quoted in Groborz, I, 147: 'mother of heroes'); Goebbels, *Die Tagebücher*, III, 93; Werner Habicht, 'Shakespeare in the Third Reich', in *Anglistentag (1984, Passau)*, ed. by Manfred Pfister (Gießen: Hoffmann, 1985), pp. 194–204 (p. 199: Rudolf Heß); Minetti, p. 108 (Stauffenberg). *Julius Caesar* was one of the plays from which Stauffenberg, his brothers and their friends acted scenes when they were at school. See Peter Hoffmann, *Stauffenberg: A Family History, 1905–1944* (Cambridge: Cambridge University Press, 1995), p. 17.

75 Gerwin Strobl, 'Shakespeare and the Nazis', *History Today*, 47, no. 5 (May 1997), 16–21 (p. 16: anti-aircraft unit); E. F. Verkade-Cartier van Dissel, 'Ludwig Berger in Nederland (1937–1945)', in Hana Bobková and others, *Scenarium, 6: Toneel in crisis- en bezettingstijd* (Zutphen: De Waldburg Pers, 1982), pp. 108–27 (pp. 118 24: Amsterdam production). It is hard not to conclude that almost all the operas inspired by Shakespeare and performed in the Third Reich were also essentially non-ideological. See Chapter 3 of the present volume (pp. 145, 160, 164–5, 182 n. 22).

76 The figures for German-language premieres of foreign plays are 444 for 1927–33 and 208 for 1933–38. See the figures compiled from the journal *Die neue Literatur* by Glen Gadberry, in Chapter 2 of the present volume (p. 99). Eicher (pp. 393–4) calculates that foreign plays (not including Shakespeare) constituted 25 per cent of the total repertory in 1929–33 and that this figure had diminished to 8 per cent in the 1933–34 season.

77 P. D., 'Vier Jahre Deutsches Landestheater in Rumänien', *Die Bühne*, 15 August

1937, p. 393 (Blaga, threat of Romanian culture, Jewish press); 'Deutsches Theater in Rumänien – stop!', *Die Bühne*, 20 January 1939, pp. 30–1 (p. 31: 156,000); K. Gebauer, 'Der Stil des rumänischen Theaters', *Die Bühne*, 20 March 1944, p. 41 (on Romanian theatre). See also 'Landestheater der deutschen Volksgruppe in Rumänien', *Die Bühne*, 20 September 1944, p. 138.

78 Harry Naujoks, *Mein Leben im KZ Sachsenhausen: 1936–1942: Erinnerungen des ehemaligen Lagerältesten* ([East] Berlin: Dietz Verlag, 1989), p. 298 (*Charley's Aunt*); personal interview with Zdenka Ehrlich (actress in Theresienstadt), London, 29 November 1996 (*Georges Dandin*); Mirko Tuma, 'Memories of Theresienstadt', *Performing Arts Journal*, 1, no. 2 (Fall 1976), 12–18 (p. 17: 'anti-militaristic').

79 John Miller, *Ralph Richardson: The Authorized Biography* (London: Sidgwick and Jackson, 1995), pp. 92–3 (*Arms and the Man*); Stahl, p. 739 (productions by German prisoners of war); Christiane Wilke, *Das Theater der großen Erwartungen: Wiederaufbau des Theaters 1945–1948 am Beispiel des Bayerischen Staatstheaters*, Europäische Hochschulschriften, Reihe III: Geschichte und ihre Hilfswissenschaften, 507 (Frankfurt am Main: Lang, 1992), pp. 313–18 (Theatre Officer's recommendations and blacklists). Other non-German plays recommended include work by Calderón, Shaw, Gogol and Molière.

80 Stahl, p. 738 (Frankfurt proposal); Anna Tzelniker, *Three for the Price of One* (London: Spiro Institute, 1991), pp. 164–8 (Yiddish version); Freddie Rokem, 'Hebrew Theater from 1889 to 1948', in *Theater in Israel*, ed. by Linda Ben-Zvi (Ann Arbor: University of Michigan Press, 1996), pp. 51–84 (pp. 78–80: Jessner's production).

6

Nazi performances in the occupied territories: the German Theatre in Lille

WILLIAM ABBEY AND KATHARINA HAVEKAMP

In the wake of the German armies which moved across much of Europe from 1938 onwards, the Nazis conducted a cultural campaign in which theatre, in all its forms, was a major component.[1] The varied nature of the institutions they set up reflected their short- and longer-term geopolitical aims, but with regard to the theatre, the principal purpose of the campaign, and one that was constant across all the assimilated and occupied territories, was to provide German theatre for German audiences.

The policy was seen at its simplest in areas which had substantial German-speaking communities and which were incorporated (or in Nazi eyes, reincorporated) into the Reich. The theatres of Alsace-Lorraine were cleared of all French employees and reopened as German establishments, staffed by Germans. Luxembourg, with no permanent ensemble, now received visiting productions from neighbouring German theatres rather than French companies. Existing German-language theatres in Danzig (Gdansk, in Polish) and Zoppot (Sopot) were given extra support. In assimilated areas of Poland, where a German theatre tradition had been kept alive by amateur companies and visits of German theatrical troupes arranged by local theatre societies, the tradition was to be strengthened through the establishment of permanent professional companies in towns such as Bromberg (Bydgoszcz), Thorn (Toruń) and Graudenz (Grudziądz).

In Czechoslovakia, German theatres in the Sudetenland, already sympathetic to the Nazis, became part of the municipal system that prevailed throughout the Reich. Elsewhere, in what was renamed the Reich Protectorate of Bohemia and Moravia, selected Czech theatres were taken over for use by the Germans. Many of them had been German-speaking until the Czech Republic was set up after the First World War, and this German 'tradition' was justification

262

enough for the occupying forces. In Prague, there was a genuine, well-established tradition of German theatre, which the Nazis now enhanced and expanded, but the tradition to which they often appealed elsewhere was frequently little more than the assertion that German-language drama had been performed, however fleetingly, however long ago, in a particular place.

Directly assimilated areas were regarded as part of the Greater German Reich. Any soldiers stationed there were not classified as occupation forces and the theatres were catering for the German civilian population. Theatrical activity in other languages was forbidden, and no acknowledgement was made of any parallel culture. The establishment of new theatres, with their own companies, the extra support given to existing houses, the expansion of the touring network (in annexed parts of Poland for example) and the integration of all these measures into the overall theatre administration of the Reich were undoubtedly intended to demonstrate Berlin's commitment to its newly acquired communities and to cement their place within the greater German empire. A theatre was both a sign of confidence and a signal of permanence.

Beyond the assimilated territories, the picture was less straightforward. Broader political and cultural considerations always coloured theatre policy. Newly created German theatres in Oslo, Lille and The Hague were designed to cater in the first instance for the German occupying forces, but they were also part of a wider initiative to win over the local (Germanic) populations. In Poland and the Soviet Union, there was no such secondary motive: German theatres were there for the Germans. Throughout the east and the Balkans, theatre buildings were taken over for use as 'front(-line) theatres' or soldiers' theatres.[2] In some cases, plans for more permanent establishments never reached beyond the planning stage; in others, the theatres did not survive more than a season before the course of the war swept them aside. Wherever they were set up, east or west, German theatres were to send that same message of permanence: the Germans were there to stay. They were to underline that Germany's hegemony was cultural as well as military and to demonstrate that cultural activities were an essential part of the Nazi way of life. The discrepancy between the people of culture and the brutality of its occupation cannot have been lost on local populations.

The extent to which theatre in any language other than German was permitted, tolerated or fostered also varied considerably. In France, the Nazis encouraged the reopening of theatres and cinemas as a sign that life was returning to normal. In Belgium and northern France, Flemish theatre was actively supported. In the east, where Polish activity was allowed at all, it was restricted to the trivial or the frivolous. The productions of the City Theatre of Warsaw were an isolated exception. In the longer term, if Nazi plans to incorporate the *Generalgouvernement* (the occupied but unassimilated area of Poland) into the Reich had come to fruition, Polish theatre would have disappeared altogether. Czechs and Slovaks were allowed their own theatres, but after 1942, little serious work could be staged.[3] Very strict control was maintained over all non-German theatres. Their personnel and their repertoires were subjected to close scrutiny. In an effort to see more German drama staged in other languages, the Germans even commissioned new translations of plays.

Cooperation between German and local theatre companies, and the participation of other nationals in German productions, also differed from place to place. It was encouraged, for example, in Flemish-speaking areas, and in the 'liberated' countries of the east, the Ukraine and the Baltic States. In Poland, it did not happen unless Germany's labour shortage made it absolutely unavoidable. In the further reaches of the conquered territories, though, on the Russian fronts, locals might be admitted to, or even allowed to take part in, performances in front-line theatres.

Lille

The French city of Lille fell to the Germans in the campaign that led to Dunkirk. Troops were still disembarking from the beaches a few miles away as French soldiers under General Molinié in Lille and to its southeast surrendered after stiff resistance.[4] When France fell a few weeks later, two *départements* or regions, Nord (including Lille) and Pas de Calais, were administratively separated from the rest of northern, occupied France and placed under the jurisdiction of General Alexander von Falkenhausen, the German military governor in Belgium. The Germans had plans, never realized but never totally abandoned either, for some sort of Flemish state, but the measure also proved a useful lever in their negotiations with the French, who were always concerned that the division would be made permanent. In October 1941, for example, Oberregierungsrat Gerhart Scherler, a senior official from Abteilung T in the Propaganda Ministry in Berlin, visiting Lille to assess the theatre's progress, passed on a report that the French foreign minister had asked for a promise that the two regions would be returned.[5] Lille and the surrounding area were of high industrial and strategic importance for the duration of the occupation: as long as the invasion of Britain remained a possibility, troops gathered here in preparation. When later an Allied invasion became imminent, the Pas de Calais was, until the last moment, one of the obvious possible landing sites. For most of the war, the area was part of a huge section of northern and eastern France that was virtually a forbidden zone. For the local population especially, communication with the rest of France was difficult: it was largely cut off from much of its rural hinterland, which meant that basic foodstuffs were often lacking.

The high concentration of armed forces, the likelihood that they would be there for some time, and the need to keep them entertained led General Ernst Busch, commander-in-chief of the 16th Army, to suggest in September 1940 the establishment of a permanent German theatre. From the outset, it was envisaged that the theatre would not only serve troops stationed in the immediate area, but from its fixed base could also undertake extensive touring of military installations throughout Belgium and across the whole of northern France. It would replace the usual tours and visits arranged by the Kraft durch Freude (Strength through Joy) organization (under the direction of Robert Ley) and at the same time relieve the army of a considerable administrative burden. Such a project would underline the long-term nature of Germany's commitment to the area and would ensure a German cultural presence in areas where there was otherwise only a military one.

Setting up the theatre

Busch's proposal was taken up in Berlin and discussions began at the Propaganda Ministry as to how the theatre should be organized.[6] At a very early stage (the exact date is not clear), Ernst Andreas Ziegler was appointed as director of the theatre or *Intendant*. Ziegler had trained as an actor and dancer; he had been literary manager (Dramaturg) and director at the National Theatre in Weimar and was a leading light in the Hitler Youth in Thuringia.[7] Initial hopes that the theatre would be up and running in time for Christmas 1940 proved overly optimistic, and only in January 1941 was Ziegler given formal permission to go ahead and form a company. He knew he would eventually be able to get French stagehands and non-German musicians to make up the numbers backstage and in the planned orchestra, but it was his responsibility to find German performers for the drama, opera, operetta and dance companies, and German nationals for the administrative posts and senior backstage positions.

Since 1937, the Kraft durch Freude organization, part of the Deutsche Arbeitsfront (German Labour Front), had been jointly responsible with the army for the entertainment of the troops. With the outbreak of war in 1939, the Propaganda Ministry, which had previously exercised a supervisory role as it did over all things theatrical, became more closely involved, via its Special Bureau for the Troops' Welfare (Truppenbetreuung), set up in July 1940 under Hans Hinkel. The initial plan was that Hinkel would be responsible for setting up the new theatre as an army institution. Inevitably, though, the question of finance moved to the centre of the discussions. Since entrance to performances would be free to members of the armed forces, and they would form the bulk of the audiences, the theatre could never expect to generate any substantial income from the sale of tickets. In the ensuing negotiations, tensions between the Propaganda Ministry, the Ministry of Finance and the army were never far from the surface, but an agreement was eventually reached. Lille, now more the equivalent of a civic theatre than an army institution, was to be directly responsible to the Propaganda Ministry, with the local army command playing a role similar to a municipal authority. The level of support, to which the Ministry of Finance now agreed and which was to be payable via the Propaganda Ministry, would correspond to that awarded to municipal theatres of a certain size within the Reich: approximately one million Reichsmarks per year, the equivalent, in round terms, of the amount given to provincial theatres in Aussig, Gera or Gladbach-Rheydt.[8] Army involvement remained strong but, with civic status, the theatre now fell outside the remit of Hinkel's Special Bureau and his name disappeared from the documents. From early 1941 onwards, all Lille's dealings were with the officials of Abteilung T, with the Reichsdramaturg Rainer Schlösser, or with Goebbels himself. Ziegler clearly became very friendly with Schlösser. The formal correspondence between the two runs parallel to a second layer of contacts, the whole tone of which is much less official and far more intimate. In late 1943, Schlösser's daughter Renate ('Reni') came to work as a volunteer in the theatre administration in Lille, staying at the Ziegler family house while she did so.

The selection of Lille as the site of the theatre rather than Brussels or even Paris, both of which seem more obvious choices, reflected the Germans' proprietary interest in the theatre itself: when they occupied Lille during the First World War, they had found the Lille architect Louis Cordonnier's new building finished but for its lighting and seating, delivery of which had been prevented by the fighting; they cleared the building of construction rubble and completed the refitting before going on to use it as a front-line theatre, opening with Goethe's *Iphigenie* on Christmas Day in 1915. Now, with this second occupation, they had the opportunity to renew a tradition[9] and to make up for what they condemned as an interlude of British vandalism followed by years of French neglect of 'their' (German) theatre, by bringing its facilities up to date once again. Ernst Lemperle, the theatre's set designer, wrote disparagingly about the technical facilities in Lille, and in a report in October 1941, a Propaganda Ministry official suggested many of the theatre's fittings had been so neglected they were now unsafe. Similar complaints had been made about the theatre in Metz.[10]

By the time of the official opening, a theatre with an unusually large company had been set up, a company extensive and varied enough to undertake a full programme of opera, operetta, drama, orchestral concerts and dance performances, as well as smaller events. The personnel totalled 430 and included 200 non-German stagehands and other backstage workers. The core

25   The German Theatre in Lille, 1941.

of the company, some fifty individuals, was made up of soldiers with a theatrical background or some theatre experience; they were transferred to the theatre from units in the Lille area (including air force and navy units), but there were clearly never going to be enough of them to staff an organization of the size that was being planned; hence Ziegler's efforts early in 1941. Germany's labour shortage, though, was already in evidence and many places in the orchestra (as many as two-thirds) had to be filled by French and Flemish musicians; much of the backstage staff was of necessity made up of French stagehands and technicians, some of whom were prisoners of war released specifically for this purpose. Some administrative posts could not be filled adequately, if at all, and one recurring problem for the theatre was therefore present from the outset.

Although Ziegler was recognized by his superiors as a committed Nazi Party member, his theatre nevertheless embodied many of the contradictions between stated policy and actual practice that typify theatrical life under the Nazis. Recollections of members of the company, for example (there is nothing in the official records), make it clear that Ziegler employed many actors who were not only well known as homosexuals, but who made little effort to conceal their sexuality. However, the flamboyant dress and extravagant behaviour that aroused such concern in their friends and colleagues do not seem to have been reflected in any way on stage. It is also evident that a number of the male civilian actors joined what they regarded as an army theatre in the hope of avoiding being called up to the army itself. As things turned out, they were to be disappointed, but for a short time at least, Lille, a flagship of the Nazi cultural campaign in France, was seen, paradoxically, as a haven from some of the unpleasant realities of the Third Reich. The theatre did have its hard core of dedicated Nazis, but they were a small group led by Ziegler and his wife Annelies, who, despite her training as a medical technician and apparent lack of any relevant theatrical experience, was the theatre's literary manager.

Administratively, the theatre was ultimately answerable to the Propaganda Ministry, from which it received its substantial annual subsidy and to which estimates, reports, accounts and requests for extra funds had to be submitted. The army exercised considerable local control: members of the company, even the civilians, were subject to army discipline and regulations where applicable (though some of them did not know or do not remember this). The army also made available commandeered hotels as well as other private accommodation around the town. It provided, to begin with at least, free rail transport and a catering service, and would make available transport for sets and luggage when the company went on tour. For its part, the city of Lille was forced to agree to maintain both the hotels and the three principal buildings the theatre would use. Many other expenses, among them the printing of programmes and posters, the costs of newspaper advertising, and the theatre's postal and phone costs, fell to the city, as did the wages of non-German stagehands, cloakroom attendants, technicians and other backstage employees in the various workshops.

These three strands – Lille, the army and the Propaganda Ministry – were the channels by which the theatre was financed. At this early stage, there was still optimism that some income might come from the sale of tickets to the locals, and it was confidently expected that by the end of 1941, Kraft durch Freude would agree to sponsor a certain number of performances each month. This confidence proved to be justified and, in November 1941, Kraft durch Freude agreed to 'buy' performances to the value of 45,000 Reichsmarks per month from 1 January 1942 onwards, to pay supplementary tour costs and to prepare the theatres that would be used on tours.[11] For this, the organization brought a few guest productions or events to the theatre in Lille, but in general the performances it sponsored were part of the theatre's normal repertoire. They could be designated as Kraft durch Freude events and the organization's name could be added prominently to playbills and programmes. When the contract was renewed for a second year, the basic monthly figure was increased to 55,000 Reichsmarks.[12]

Whatever other purposes the theatre may have been designed to serve, its prime aim was to entertain the troops. This was asserted by Oberregierungsrat Keppler to Goebbels in January 1941 and often repeated thereafter.[13] The actress Wilfried Krafft remembers that the overriding consideration was that the repertoire should be neither too intellectually demanding nor too boring.[14] General von Falkenhausen, writing to Goebbels in February of the same year, felt the theatre should not only contribute to the troops' cultural welfare but also help to keep them mentally alert.[15] In a speech of May 1942, Ziegler felt the theatre should offer soldiers not only entertainment and distraction, but also German classics and plays dealing with contemporary problems.[16] In another ministry report of January 1943, Oberregierungsrat Scherzer felt the theatre was offering its audiences more demanding fare than they would have had from a simple front-line theatre and also providing a bridge to home within an overwhelmingly hostile environment.[17] And in a later memo of November 1943 to Goebbels, Scherzer recommends making special arrangements to supply theatre tickets to troops passing through Lille in order to keep them out of French or Belgian places of entertainment during their brief stays.[18] Brothels seem to have been uppermost in his mind.

The theatrical and operatic repertoire

The honour of putting on the first production in the theatre fell to the Städtische Bühne of Bochum, with a guest performance directed by Saladin Schmitt of Kleist's *Prinz Friedrich von Homburg* in February 1941, but the formal inauguration and the first performance by the theatre's own company followed some weeks later, when Goethe's *Egmont* was staged in the Grosses Haus on 10 May 1941. According to the director Otto Roland, the play was chosen because it was set in the Netherlands.[19] Whether the oppressive and unpopular occupation in the play was considered, he does not say. Ernst Lemperle's set was dominated by a flight of steps, but surviving sketches and unclear photographs suggest nineteenth-century historical realism rather than Leopold Jessner's austere Expressionism.[20]

A few days later, after scaffolding in the auditorium had been dismantled earlier the same day, the companion Kleines Theater opened with A. A. Zinn's *Lucky Seven (Die gute Sieben)*. The play is typical of the romantic comedies that would make up a large proportion of the theatre's output. A film actor invites his six ex-wives to a house-warming. His son's girlfriend seems in danger of becoming number seven, only for him to realize the first is the one he has always loved. The six ex-wives were all dressed in different colours and in varying styles which were supposed to reflect their characters.

Both buildings required further substantial fitting and conversion over the summer months, and the company had to make heavy use of a third venue, the Théâtre Sébastopol, in August and September. Once again, the army, the Propaganda Ministry and the city of Lille paid the bills. Much of the work was supervised by Otto Junker, who had also worked for the theatre during the First World War. Both theatres were equipped with air-raid shelters, a precaution all theatres in the Reich had had to take since the outbreak of war.

On 1 November 1941, the theatre reopened for its second season with Wagner's *Tannhäuser* at the Grosses Haus, the only Wagner opera the company staged. Eight further performances were given in Lille, and two in Brussels. Ralph Benatzky's operetta *My Sister and I* (*Meine Schwester und ich*) opened the Kleines Theater four days later. And from then on, the theatre put on performances in Lille, throughout Belgium and across the whole of northern, occupied France, a territory later extended to the southern region (formerly Vichy France) after the end of 1942, when the Germans took over the entire country. Showpiece and more ambitious productions were put on in the Grosses Haus and, if they went on tour at all, it was to major centres such as Brussels, Antwerp or Paris. The productions at the Kleines Theater were less elaborate and so more easily transferred, often having only a single simple set; it was these that went on tours of the occupied areas, visiting military installations of all kinds and sizes (Figures 26 and 29). Wherever possible, local French theatres were used, but they were often in a state of serious neglect, sometimes even dangerous to work in. On occasion, there was insufficient space to erect the whole set and only a table and a couple of chairs could be used. The actors had to adjust the volume of their performances to suit the varying acoustics of the rooms they found themselves in. And, last but by no means least, they rarely found anywhere for those post-performance dinners that are part of the acting tradition.

In the three short years of its life, the theatre put on drama, opera and operetta, musical comedy, dance and music; its repertoire was set locally by Ziegler and his wife, working in close collaboration with the Reichsdramaturg in Berlin (to whom all programmes had to be submitted), the Brussels division of the Propaganda Ministry and, at the insistence of the army, an army liaison officer. The latter's principal role was to watch out for productions that could turn out to be too expensive rather than to have any literary or ideological input into the choice of pieces. Once Kraft durch Freude was contractually bound in with the theatre, it had the right to approve a whole season's programme in advance. On the face of it, this right contradicted that of the Propaganda Ministry to vet all programmes, but there is no indication as to how any conflict would have been resolved or that any occurred.

Even while negotiations about the final form of the theatre were still going on, Ziegler sent a long list of over fifty possible titles (no authors are given) to Abteilung T.[21] Several of the titles have question marks pencilled alongside

26   The tour bus moves on. The caption in the bottom left-hand corner reads 'A fond farewell'.

them, and an internal Propaganda Ministry memorandum called the list a hotch-potch that needed urgent revision, picking out *The Sixth Wife* (*Die sechste Frau*), a play by Max Christian Feiler about Henry VIII of England, and Wagner's *Die Meistersinger* as totally unsuitable.[22] A play by Otto Erler was also condemned, but it is impossible to say whether the criticism applied to *Tsar Peter* (*Zar Peter*), or to *St Bartolus's Trousers* (*Die Hosen des heiligen Bartolus*), perhaps for the suggestiveness of its title, though it was, surely, no worse than some of the plays that were eventually put on. The French subject matter of *Napoleon* by Grabbe and *The Duke of Enghien* (*Der Herzog von Enghien*), another play about Napoleon by Fritz Helke, would have made them unsuitable for performance in Lille. Yet Hans Müller-Schlösser's *Wibbel the Tailor* (*Schneider Wibbel*), which centred on the French occupation of the Rhineland in 1812, was eventually staged. Gogol's *The Inspector General* could not have survived beyond June 1941, when all works by Russian dramatists were banned with the invasion of the Soviet Union. And we may assume that two suggested plays with Russian themes – *Tsar Peter* and Friedrich Wilhelm Hymmen's *Coronation in St Petersburg* (*Petersburger Krönung*) – were also felt to be too sensitive, although such plays were not officially banned until February 1942. Also questioned was Werner von der Schulenburg's *Black Bread and Croissants* (*Schwarzbrot und Kipfel*): perhaps someone in the ministry recalled the temporary banning of all his plays in 1936.[23] Schulenburg had gone on to translate *Villafranca* (as *Cavour*) by Benito Mussolini and Giovacchino Forzano. In the event, though, neither his play nor any of those Schlösser had marked were ever produced in Lille, though *Cavour* was. About a third of the titles did eventually reach the stage.

From the end of 1941 onwards, Ziegler's monthly reports to Berlin usually included a note of new productions to be put on in the following month, but there is no record of how decisions were reached. Nor is it clear why a work might have been announced, but then never performed. Among these were Goethe's *Faust* and Ibsen's *Peer Gynt*. Perhaps in those cases that would have called for more elaborate productions, the army liaison officer had made his presence felt.

At the time of the theatre's opening, Ziegler looked forward to a repertoire comprising great works of the German past (Goethe, Schiller, Lessing, Kleist, Hebbel and Grabbe were the specific authors he named), contemporary plays by young Germans and classics by foreign authors. Classic and modern comedy were to be the mainstay of the Kleines Haus.[24] In the event, that prime objective, the entertainment of the troops, clearly formed the guiding principle, and the resulting repertoire was safe, shallow and unadventurous. With one exception, everything chosen was firmly established on the stages of the Third Reich and had been widely performed elsewhere. (Indeed, many of the works selected had already been filmed, though interestingly, members of the company did not necessarily know this and had not seen the films concerned.) The single exception, where Lille is listed as holding the world premiere, was *The Flax Field* (*Der Flachsacker*), a play by Nora Reinhard based on themes from a novel by the Flemish author Stijn Steuvels (1871–1969), first staged in 1942. The play is a rural melodrama centring on a father–son conflict, which the actress Almut Sandstede, who had a minor role as a farm girl, remembers as 'a really stupid story'.[25] It is the only work put on in Lille which had any obvious Flemish connection. There is no indication that other possibilities, such as works by Cyriel Verschaeve, a Flemish nationalist writer supported by the Nazis, or the slightly better-known Felix Timmermanns, were ever considered.

Where there had been some dispute about certain works, the battles had been fought to a conclusion before the theatre in Lille had even opened. Franz Lehár, Eduard Künneke and Richard Strauss, for example, had all worked with Jewish librettists. In addition, both Lehár and Künneke had Jewish family connections through their wives. Strauss's standing in the world of music carried him through, though not without difficulties, and little could be done against Lehár in the face of Hitler's well-known enthusiasm for *The Merry Widow*.[26] But it took a directive from Goebbels, acting on a personal decision by Hitler, to clear the way for Künneke. Ralph Benatzky was not Jewish, but had already left Germany when his works, accused of being un-German, were banned in 1935. Their enormous popularity led to their reinstatement three years later, but Benatzky did not return. And it was the enduring popularity

27   The cast of Lessing's *Minna von Barnhelm*, 1942. The director, Jost Dahmen, is fourth from the left.

of the works of Johann Strauss that led to the suppression of the fact that he was Jewish and had worked with Jewish librettists, so that his works could still be performed.[27] At one time or another, Lille put on productions of works by all these composers.

Of the German classics Ziegler had mentioned, Grabbe and Hebbel were not performed. Nor was Grillparzer. Goethe's *Iphigenie* and *Egmont* were put on, as were Schiller's *Maria Stuart* and *Wallenstein*, though invariably for comparatively few performances. A shortened version of the *Wallenstein* trilogy, for example, received only four performances in Lille, four in Paris and one in Brussels, before disappearing from the repertoire. *Maria Stuart* was dropped from the programme after only six performances in Lille. Although again only two plays by each author were staged, Lessing and Kleist fared rather better, *Minna von Barnhelm*, *Emilia Galotti*, *Amphitryon* and *The Broken Jug* (*Der zerbrochene Krug*) with their smaller casts and simpler sets touring widely (Figure 27). *Amphitryon* was unusual in being rehearsed and first performed in Paris, before returning to Lille and then touring.

It comes as no surprise that Shakespeare was the only English author, represented by *Hamlet* and *The Taming of the Shrew*. Neither play enjoyed many performances. *Hamlet*, in addition to eight nights in Lille, was given three times in Brussels and twice in Paris, and *The Taming of the Shrew* was performed six times in Paris and five in Lille. The only other genuine foreign classic put on was Goldoni, whose *Coffee House* was staged. Translations of two Calderón plays – *Beware of Still Waters* and *Tomorrow is Another Day* – were prepared by Carl Balhaus, an actor and director with the company, together with Carlo Schmid, an army legal expert with a keen interest in literature and the theatre (and a prominent post-war Social Democrat), but neither was performed. More modern Italian drama included Dario Niccodemi's *Scampolo* and Alessandro de Stefani's *The Ugly Duckling* (*Dopo divorzieremo* in Italian). The latter was first translated by Werner von der Schulenburg as *Love in the USA* (*Liebe in USA*). The alternative title was adopted, presumably to avoid mentioning an enemy country, but a review by August Haussleiter makes it clear that nothing else was changed: the setting was unmistakably New York and he was disappointed that the play, set in a girls' hostel, did not develop into a satire on American moral hypocrisy (Figure 28).[28] The only other English-speaking dramatist represented was George Bernard Shaw, regarded as Irish, appreciated by the Nazis for his anti-English sentiments and widely performed throughout the Third Reich. His *Candida* and *Widowers' Houses* (as *Die Häuser des Herrn Sartorius*) were both staged, though by the time they were put on, all proposed productions of Shaw, and Shakespeare, required special permission.[29]

Notable for their absence are many of those regarded as the more important Nazi dramatists. Nothing by Euringer, Billinger, Möller, Langenbeck, Kolbenheyer, Rehberg or Bethge, for example, was staged at all. Felix Dhünen's *Uta von Naumburg* was put on, as was Otto Erler's *Struensee* (both historical plays), but, in general, if contemporary plays were staged, they were now-forgotten comedies and farces such as *A Touch of Grey* (*Der Mann mit den grauen Schläfen*) by Leo Lenz, and Heinrich Zerkaulen's *A Break from Routine* (*Der Sprung aus dem Alltag*). They, and many similar plays, were among the most popular and widely performed of the Third Reich, and the Lille management took no risks by staging them. Despite the Nazis' attempts to encourage the creation of National Socialist comedy (whatever that might have looked like), and the dramatists' efforts to oblige, these works had little explicit ideological content. *A Touch of Grey*, for example, was a romantic comedy in which the young son of a Romanian millionaire, in order to win the love of a Berlin girl (who thinks she prefers older men), pretends to be his own father, thereby arousing the interest of her mother too. *A Break from Routine* was described by one reviewer as 'two and a half hours of Rhineland humour'.[30] Carl Balhaus's production emphasized the comic over the farcical, and made use of music and songs throughout. It opened with six nights in Paris and toured to Bordeaux, Dax, Biarritz and Bayonne before returning to Lille.

28   A scene from Alessandro de Stefani's, *The Ugly Duckling*, November 1943.

These contemporary comedies were supplemented by a handful of older works which had been established in the repertoire of the German stage since before the advent of the Nazis and which now enjoyed something of a revival, since so many other plays were banned: *The Rape of the Sabine Women* (*Der Raub der Sabinerinnen*) by Franz and Paul von Schönthan, and August Hinrichs's *Much Ado about Iolanthe* (*Krach um Iolanthe*) – where Iolanthe is a pig – are two of the best-known examples. It is clear that some plays were chosen for their small casts: Manfred Rössner's *Charles III and Anne of Austria* (*Karl III und Anna von Österreich*), a domestic comedy rather than the history play its title suggests, had only two characters, and there is some evidence that when Curt Goetz's one-act plays were put on, only those with casts of four or five were done and others were ignored.

In other instances, it was apparently the composition of the cast rather than its size that was decisive: Wilfried Krafft remembers the importance attached to having plenty of female characters in the plays chosen for performance, and there are several titles which confirm this. The principal parts in A. A. Zinn's *Lucky Seven* consist of a man and his six ex-wives, and *Revolt at the Rest Home* (*Aufruhr im Damenstift*) by the Dane Axel Breidahl has a cast of twelve, all female. The title of another play by Leo Lenz, *Adrian's Five Women* (*Fünf Frauen um Adrian*), suggests something similar. Lille, though, did not resort to *360 Women* (*360 Frauen*) by Hans and Johanna von Wentzel.[31] Significantly, these plays were being staged long before the theatre really started to suffer from the recall and call-up of male members of the company, the problem that led to an impassioned plea to Berlin for plays with fewer male and more female parts.[32] Other titles give some clue to the nature of the plays: *Honeymoon without a Husband* (*Hochzeitsreise ohne Mann*), by Leo Lenz again, and *Marrying my Aunt* (*Ich heirate meine Tante*) by Jupp Hussels. In fact, the cast was so unhappy with the latter, a farce set in a bankrupt family hotel, that they complained to Frau Ziegler, who had selected it. Their protest that the play was insulting to both audience and players, and little better than pornography, led shortly afterwards to a full assembly in the theatre, where Ziegler harangued the company with a long speech about mutiny and sabotage. Performances went ahead as planned.[33]

Musical theatre in Lille showed a similar pattern. There were productions of a comparatively small number of German and Austrian operatic classics – among them Richard Strauss's *Rosenkavalier*, *Hänsel und Gretel* by Humperdinck, and Mozart's *The Magic Flute* and *The Marriage of Figaro* – and a handful of Italian works: Puccini's *La Bohème* and *Madame Butterfly*, and Mascagni's *Cavalleria rusticana*. Somewhat lighter were Friedrich von Flotow's *Martha*, Albert Lortzing's *The Armourer* (*Der Waffenschmied*) and C. M. Weber's *Abu Hassan*. Musical comedy, a genre that figured prominently in Lille's repertoire, included *Eve in Evening Dress* (*Eva im Abendkleid*) by Franz Gribitz and Nico Dostal, and works by Benatzky. Despite its promising title, Lortzing's *Flemish Adventure* (*Das flandrische Abenteuer*) was not put on.

Bizet's *Carmen* was something of a special case in that it was the only French work included in either the drama or the musical theatre programme. It was aimed, albeit in a German-language production, at the French population, but even after this objective had clearly failed, its enormous popularity ensured that it was retained in the repertoire. The records are incomplete, but after the first performance in April 1942, it was repeated at least twenty times in Lille. In November 1942, there were six performances in Paris, followed by two in Antwerp the following February. Within the company, it was, somewhat unkindly, remembered for the occasion when Flemish singers appeared as guests in leading roles, their quaint pronunciation of the German text remaining a source of great amusement for some time afterwards: 'Du levst mi ni mey! – Ney! (Ya don luv ma any mo! – Na!)'[34]

The same pattern can be detected in the theatre's dance programme: a handful of ballet classics such as *The Legend of Joseph* (*Josephslegende*), with music by Richard Strauss, *Coppélia* (Delibes), and many more popular, shorter pieces, inserted into the variety shows.

The programme of dramatic and musical works was supplemented by countless smaller productions of revues and selections of favourite songs and dances. These were given a variety of titles, and all had small casts, and modest sets that could be erected almost anywhere. *New Year Punch (Silvesterpunsch)*, put together by Heinz Lehmann and Harald Fürstenau, may be taken as representative. It opened with Norbert Schultze's song 'At the Barracks Gate' ('Vor dem Kasernentor') and ended with the same composer's 'Lili Marlene', to which the whole audience sang along. In between were jokes and sketches, one of which was entitled 'Paradise sent up' ('Paradies total veräppelt'). There was an aria from *The Barber of Seville*, and the dances included a cancan, a sailors' hornpipe, and a ballet piece 'In the Green Meadow' ('Auf der grünen Wiese'). A display of national dances featured Hungary, Spain, Italy, Japan, Holland and Germany, the choice of countries sending a message of its own and implying a canon of folkloric culture based on political alliances. It contrasted sharply, and no doubt deliberately, with the number that followed it in the show, a frenetic parody of American 'swing' dancing.

The quality of the productions

What did the theatre achieve with this programme? In statistical terms, it put on 3889 performances between 10 May 1941 and 31 July 1944, of which 1090 were staged in Lille and the remaining 2799 elsewhere in France and Belgium. Audiences for the same period totalled well over two million. Performances of plays and musical comedies outnumbered all other categories. While the reviews usually speak of overflowing auditoria, the surviving figures, which cover the period from November 1941 until October 1943, indicate that the monthly numbers varied between 70 per cent and 98 per cent of capacity, averaging around 84 per cent. The emphasis on entertainment and the generally apolitical content of the repertoire are features of German provincial theatre during the war years, as is the low number of foreign plays or plays with serious themes.[35] While it can be argued that a non-political repertoire, which distracts its audience from the reality around it, is by its very nature part of a political programme, the overwhelmingly light, not to say trivial, nature of Lille's offerings from the very beginning suggests an awareness that the soldiers would have stayed away from anything too intellectual or overtly propagandistic. The local population, which did stay away, was impressed, if at all, only by the fact that the Germans set up a theatre, and seemed prepared to pour so much time, money and effort into it.

It is difficult to go beyond the bare figures to assess the quality of the performances. The actors who took part in the plays found many of them poor, and the productions, even of the classics, lacklustre, offering little beyond the routine, either to the performers or to the audience. Ulrike Thimme, who

29 Soldiers queue for a tour performance.

worked in the theatre administration, remembers the standard of the performances as not bad, despite the frequently dismal quality of the material being
presented.[36] The actress Edith Lechtape, who was with the company from
beginning to end, remembers only two of the many productions in which she
appeared as offering any intellectual challenge or professional satisfaction:
Kleist's *Amphitryon*, directed by Jost Dahmen, and Shaw's *Candida*, into
which the director Carl Balhaus successfully introduced the intimate tone of
a chamber play.[37] Frau Ziegler's dramaturgical skills are remembered chiefly
for their absence; she herself was not popular and interfered in everything.
Even Berlin became uneasy at her *de facto* assumption of the role of deputy-
Intendant.

Surviving reviews are not helpful. They usually appear in army newspapers
and their authors are presumably army journalists. Even without the Goebbels
edict of late 1936 prohibiting criticism of the arts, they would not be the place
to look for the slightest suggestion that the plays in question were of poor
literary quality, let alone ideologically suspect. And no such suggestion is
evident. This is not to say that there is no criticism at all, but occasional notes
of disquiet about a particular set, or the performance by an individual actor,
are invariably overwhelmed by the weight of purely descriptive text, plot
outline and praise, often lavish, of other aspects of the production. If mentioned, audience reaction is, without exception, prolonged and enthusiastic.

Observations on the theatre's work can also be gleaned from the reports of the various Berlin officials of the Propaganda Ministry, who went to Lille, sometimes to Paris, and saw performances, usually in the context of some wider investigation. The earliest and briefest of these was by the Reichsdramaturg, Rainer Schlösser. He attended the opening in place of Goebbels and six days later wrote a short memo to his superior, describing the *Egmont* performance as the equivalent of a solid provincial production that one could see, say, in Braunschweig.[38] In his report dated 23 January 1943, Scherzer commented on a number of productions.[39] He enjoyed some of the leading performances in Kleist's *Amphitryon*, but not the set. Considering there had been time for only ten rehearsals, he thought the production attained a good provincial level. He felt the production of the operetta *Fresh Wind from Sumatra* (*Frischer Wind aus Sumatra*) in the Kleines Theater could hold its own in any German city.[40] In Strauss's *Der Rosenkavalier* at the Grosses Haus, he found the three female leads were only up to good provincial standard, Lore Eckhardt in particular lacking the musical depth needed for the role of Octavian: he judged her casting as a failed experiment.[41] Scherzer recognized Herbert Charlier as an extremely competent musical director, who could, however, lose interest in a performance and did not rise above the standard of Essen, Halle or Stettin. The drama director Jost Dahmen made a good impression: he was reliable even though not a member of the Nazi Party. The other directors Scherzer found colourless in comparison. Surviving members of the acting company recall things differently, tending to regard Carl Balhaus as the most able play director, recalling Charlier as particularly gifted and Werner Jacob as an excellent director of opera.[42]

Political considerations clearly coloured Scherzer's and Schlösser's assessments of individuals, and they must be viewed with caution. And the references to the provincial standard of the theatre's work are so persistent it is hard to avoid the conclusion that Goebbels was being told what he expected to hear: the intention had been to set up a provincial theatre, so that is precisely what has been achieved. The actress Wilfried Krafft confirms that this was the general level of the theatre's work: 'What was put on was equivalent to the programmes of German provincial theatres.'[43]

The reports that went back to Berlin were generally favourable, though recognizing the problems, and sympathetic in tone towards Ziegler, even if his problems (and his limitations) did not go unnoticed.[44] Perhaps the only genuinely honest response to the theatre's work is an enthusiastic letter from the officer commanding Field Unit 31 287 E to Ziegler.[45] He acknowledged that the performers had had to work in primitive conditions with poor stage facilities, but his men had appreciated their commitment and had thoroughly

30 A scene from *The Four Companions* (*Die vier Gesellen*), by Jochen Huth, late 1941.

enjoyed the poems by Joachim Ringelnatz, the witty one-act plays by Goetz and the singsongs.

Behind the scenes

Away from the field-grey uniforms that dominated the audiences, life for the ensemble was much the same as in any larger provincial theatre. Surviving company members look back and in the main remember their time in Lille as a stepping stone in a professional career. They could act, in German, before German-speaking audiences; if they did not want to, they needed never to leave a German-language environment, so heavy and all-pervading was the military presence in Lille. Lille was not Paris, but retained enough of the perceived charm and elegance of the French way of life to make it an attractive posting and a welcome change from the austerity at home in Germany. For many of the younger actresses in particular, Lille represented not only their first professional engagement, but also their first visit abroad. If they ever thought of themselves as part of the occupying power, it was probably on Bastille Day each year, when the entire company (with the soldiers among them in uniform) was required to remain within the confines of the theatre for the whole day.

For Ziegler, though, 1942 and 1943 brought a series of personnel and financial problems. The theatre had always been short of administrative staff, but now seconded soldiers were recalled to their units, and civilians began to be called up. It became ever harder to fill vacant posts, especially since Ziegler remained unwilling to employ French and Flemish citizens in positions of responsibility. One consequence was that Ziegler, burdened by administrative matters he could not or would not delegate, was never able to make the artistic contribution to the work of the theatre that he had hoped. Financial pressures resulted from the Armistice Commission's decision to reduce Lille's contribution to the theatre's upkeep and from the army's reduction of transport allowances and catering support. As Allied air-raids increasingly disrupted the theatre's tours, causing it to fail in its contractual obligations to Kraft durch Freude, it lost the corresponding income.

Ziegler constantly blamed the war for the shortage of materials that he needed. There is no indication, though, that productions suffered in any way, and surviving actresses still remember the quality of their costumes. Basic requirements such as typewriters were hard to find, and Ziegler never managed to obtain a safe. Members of the company recall their *Intendant* carrying cash in his pockets and paying them as he passed. Small wonder that he sometimes lost track of payments he had made, or that officials in Berlin occasionally questioned his record-keeping or the way his estimates were presented.[46] Ziegler's normal response to problems was a request to Berlin for more funding, coupled with frequent reminders to Goebbels of the theatre's status as his (i.e. Goebbels's) gift to the soldiers.

By January 1944, the theatre's activities began to be scaled down in view of the impending invasion. Such tours as could be undertaken in the early months of 1944 were frequently disrupted by air-raid warnings, even in southern France, where landings from Italy were expected. Nevertheless, even as plans were being made to transfer personnel and equipment out of Lille, Rudolf Zloch, the theatre's director of administration, was still trying to build up its stock of costumes by suggesting the purchase of a collection from Charleroi.[47] Over the next few months, family members were sent to Vittel and Contrexéville if possible, or otherwise back to Germany. Negotiations began with the Bavarian Ministry of the Interior to find accommodation for wives and children who had nowhere else to go. Like clockwork, Ziegler pointed out to Berlin that the withdrawal from Lille would incur costs that had not been included in his estimates for the year. While these might be partly offset by the reduction in the number of new productions they were able to put on, the ministry might well have to step in, if, as Goebbels wished, the company was to be kept together and if accumulated collections of sets and costumes of considerable value were to be saved.

By May 1944, much of the theatre and operetta personnel had moved to Spa, where rehearsals for the 1944–45 season were under way. The opera company was on leave, with orders to reassemble in July in Strasbourg. In view of the military situation both immediately before and after the Allied landings, tours were impossible, though Ziegler continued to plan for their resumption, staying in close touch with both the army and Kraft durch Freude. Even after the invasion had taken place, with the Allies advancing and all forms of communication deteriorating, Berlin too tried to carry on as normal, asking for regular weekly activity reports to be delivered by Saturday. If they were sent, they did not survive the war. By early July, Ziegler's company was scattered: some were still in Lille and Spa, giving sporadic local performances of the musical comedy by Franz Gribitz and Nico Dostal, *Eve in Evening Dress*, in Spa, Verviers and Liège. Ziegler was making plans to take the production to Brussels, Antwerp and even Paris, though the 9.00 p.m. curfew in Belgium was making things difficult.[48] Communications, he reported, were appalling: train journeys from Lille to Brussels could take up to thirty-six hours and it was impossible to obtain passes for couriers; bulletins from the Reich Theatre Chamber were taking four to six weeks to arrive and ought now to be dispatched via the more reliable Propaganda Ministry courier. Even so, he could still write of taking a small revue *Singing, Ringing Love* (*Liebe, wie sie singt und klingt*) to the battlefront.

But the theatre's days were numbered and its closure at the end of August 1944, when all theatres of the Third Reich were shut down, confirmed that there would be no more tours. By that time, German occupation forces in Lille were in full retreat; all remaining members of the company had received orders to report for war service, the males to the armed forces (mainly reserve battalions), the actresses chiefly to armaments and munitions factories. Some of the actresses found themselves called to the National Theatre in Weimar, which had been taken over by Siemens. Ziegler was also transferred to Weimar, where he wound up the Lille theatre's affairs before reporting to the Propaganda Section in Potsdam. The army liaison officer, Professor Rang, was among the very last to leave Lille, in a hired car, on 2 September 1944. By the end of the next day, the Allied liberation of the city was complete.

The impact on the local population

If the quality of the theatre's output is difficult to judge at this distance, its cultural-political role and any effect it might have had are even harder to assess. It is clear that both Ziegler and the Propaganda Ministry saw it as having such a role for the local population, a role which was frequently mentioned. Its exact nature and purpose, however, are never explicitly spelled out, and the ambiguous and sometimes contradictory nature of the evidence that can be sifted from surviving documents compounds the problem.[49]

While the theatre was being set up, it was envisaged that the local population would be admitted to certain performances, an intention confirmed in the first financial estimates submitted in February 1941, where some income, though not a great deal, was expected from ticket sales.[50] Shortly after the opening, however, Schlösser could assure the local army commander in Lille, General Heinrich Niehoff, that no involvement of the local population was being considered.[51] By March 1942, Ziegler's chief administrator Ludwig Apel had virtually written off the prospect of generating any income from the sale of tickets to the locals, recognizing that the theatre was suffering the effects of a near-total political boycott.[52] The monthly statistics bear him out: ticket sales were consistently low. In December 1941, the first month for which figures survive, 127 tickets were sold and raised 317 Reichsmarks (RM); sales in the following months, however, never again reached these giddy heights: less than 30 RM per month came in during January, March and April 1942, 153.50 RM in May, 56.75 RM in June and a lamentable 7.50 RM in July. Thereafter, Ziegler's monthly reports to Berlin exclude financial details altogether.

In his speech in May 1942, Ziegler could still mention the visits of the French and Flemish population to those performances open to them.[53] He also talked of working with local cultural forces – a statement that even on the most charitable of interpretations can only be half true: there is no evidence of any cooperation with the French during that first season, though plans for working with the Flemish theatres in Antwerp, Brussels and Ghent in the 1942–43 season were well advanced. Members of the Lille company were to direct operas and operettas at Flemish theatres, musical directors were to be exchanged and one of Lille's drama directors was to work in Ghent and Brussels. Lille's set and costume designers were at the disposal of Flemish theatres, as was some technical support (with a view to enforcing standardization, by which was understood German standards, across the region). And Lille's workshops were also made available to Flemish theatres, generating some income by the work they did. A branch of the costume and tailoring workshop was even opened in Antwerp. There was a suggestion that the Lille workshops might do some work for theatres within the Reich whose own facilities had been damaged by Allied bombing, and there were plans to educate Flemish technicians up to a satisfactory German level, another route by which standardization might be imposed. A German-Flemish modern dance company was proposed and Flemish singers learned opera parts in German so as to appear in Lille; members of Lille's company returned the compliment and learned parts in Flemish. The Flemish theatres in Brussels, Antwerp and Ghent were run by people generally sympathetic to the Nazis, and many of these plans were put into effect. Even so, this programme of cooperation could be interrupted by, for example, the temporary closure of the theatres in Brussels in early 1943 as a German response to local unrest.

The French were boycotting the theatre, which was doing little for them, but the Nazis clearly felt that the mere presence of a permanent, active theatre could be an effective part of a wider propaganda campaign. When the Ministry of Finance suggested that opera and other expensive productions should be dropped from Lille's programme, Scherzer responded that any such cuts would send the wrong message to the French about German interest in the area.[54] There is no doubt that Ziegler also felt that a strong theatrical presence could contribute to the establishment of German dominance. Looking to the future, he foresaw the need to increase German influence in Flanders once final victory had been achieved, whatever the eventual political shape of the region. French linguistic and cultural dominance would have to give way to German, and the pervasive Parisian influence on the region would have to be overcome. Ziegler does not say so, but no theatre, however imposing its physical presence or extensive the range of its activities, could achieve this alone. There would have to be a wider language policy, perhaps along the lines that had been introduced in the Protectorate of Bohemia and Moravia.[55] In fact, Ziegler conceded that Lille was likely to remain a French city and that his theatre might be more effective if situated elsewhere. The German theatres in The Hague and the border areas of the Reich were not sufficient to exercise the necessary influence, and efforts should start now to set up a permanent theatre in Brussels: a suitable building should be found and purchased as soon as possible. Later on, the Germans could build a new theatre of their own. Schlösser forwarded Ziegler's suggestions to Goebbels, but no action was taken.[56]

In November 1942, Ziegler wrote to Schlösser that he was coming under increasing pressure from the German embassy in Paris and from the military to do more for the French, especially for groups such as university students and school children, but also to a limited extent for the general population. If he did take any steps, it is not reflected in the repertoire, but the actress Almut Sandstede does remember classes of French students coming to certain performances of the classics, so it is possible some such visits were encouraged.[57] Scherzer's report of January 1943 recommended more tours in France: these would be effective propaganda because they were *not* aimed at the French, but would nevertheless impress the French by the mere fact of the Germans' efforts.[58] By January 1944, however, Ziegler was writing to the Propaganda Ministry that no public performances for the general French population were envisaged, and that they could only cater for a small circle of interested visitors: the income from ticket sales would be minimal. It must have been clear that the local people were overwhelmingly and increasingly hostile to the occupation in all its manifestations. The winter of 1943–44 was to be the most severe of the war for them, and the imminence of an Allied invasion was apparent to French and Germans alike. There was a wave of ambushes and sabotage attacks by the local resistance, and strikes and other forms of industrial unrest were widespread.[59]

Even as late as August 1944, after D-Day and when most of his company had already left Lille, Ziegler could write to Schlösser about the future German theatre in Brussels with the Lille company as its nucleus, still imagining it could go ahead when circumstances allowed. Yet he felt that Nazi Party comrades in Brussels were being overoptimistic in thinking this would be possible by the end of the year.[60] Events rendered all these plans redundant. Once the Germans were driven out of Lille at the very beginning of September (Brussels itself falling to the Allies shortly afterwards), they did not return. Brussels never witnessed a German theatre under National Socialist control.

A unique failure

Looking back, it is clear that the diverse nature of the actual and potential audiences of the Deutsches Theater in Lille and its aims, however ill-defined, towards those audiences, combined to make it distinct from any other theatre in Nazi-occupied Europe. In every region, the theatre was part of that second, cultural, onslaught that followed on the heels of a successful German military offensive. Lille was not in one of those areas, in the east or the west, that were entirely German-speaking. Nor did it have a substantial German-speaking community. True, Lille's status as a civic theatre did link it in administrative terms to the theatres of the annexed regions, but the actual audiences for whom it catered on a daily basis and the extensive involvement of the army in its local administration put it into a different category: these are factors that clearly invite comparison with the many front-line theatres, set up to bring entertainment exclusively to the armed forces and others in the occupation administration. However, Lille's combination of a fixed base, a permanent ensemble, touring responsibilities and the sheer size of its organization distinguish it from the more modest travelling front-line theatres that circulated in regions not annexed to the Reich.

Certainly Ziegler's hackles rose at any suggestion that his theatre was simply a front-line theatre, and the army too regarded Lille as something more than that. Its objectives for the local population (especially the Flemish speakers), however unevenly realized in practice, raised it to a different level, and the closest parallels were then with the German theatres set up in The Hague and

Oslo, which hoped to draw the local Germanic populations into the Nazi fold. Both of these theatres had, like Lille, a dual role: the entertainment of the troops and other locally stationed Germans, and a cultural-political role for the local population; both had a fixed base and toured their respective countries. Oslo's company was made up of Germans and Norwegians, and tended to concentrate on opera; accounts differ, but it seems to have been marginally less unsuccessful than Lille in appealing to the locals, though it filled empty seats with local military personnel when necessary.[61] Administered to a large extent by the Theater des Volkes in Berlin, it was responsible to Josef Terboven, the local Reich Commissar.

The German Theatre in The Hague also came under the control of the local Reich Commissar, here Arthur Seyss-Inquart, rather than the Propaganda Ministry, and seems to have been largely boycotted by the people whom it was trying to reach. There was some territorial friction with Lille and, despite its ambitions, the theatre in The Hague never managed to reach Paris.

One other element further distinguished Lille from other theatres in occupied areas, namely the presence of a third group – the French-speaking community – for whom it had to cater. However, as we have seen, its attempts in this area were largely fruitless and the French had remained hostile. One reason for this was that, since the Germans had encouraged the reopening of theatres and cinemas, the French had somewhere else to go. Films and plays were strictly controlled by the Vichy government or the German censor in Paris, but the years of occupation were a period when both French film and theatre flourished.[62] Both Wilfried Krafft and Edith Lechtape, for example, used their free time in Paris to see most of the major French actors on stage.[63] What for the Germans in the audience of these French plays was a treat was for the French a way of asserting their cultural identity and independence. It was also, during the winter months, a popular way of keeping warm for an hour or two.

The Deutsches Theater in Lille lived and died with the German occupation. Whatever longer-term ambitions the Germans may have had, they would always have depended on the presence of a substantial German community to provide an audience. In its short life, the theatre did nothing to put down roots in the area or to reach out in any genuine way to the local community. Artistically, it was hampered by the lack of any truly creative leadership which might have allowed it to produce quality work even under the restrictions of the National Socialist regime. It has left no legacy of any sort, but as an example of a dictatorial regime's belief in the importance of theatre within its cultural policy, it remains a revealing episode in German theatre history.

Notes

1 This brief survey is based on the more detailed accounts in Hans Daiber, *Schaufenster der Diktatur: Theater im Machtbereich Hitlers* (Stuttgart: Günther Neske, 1995); Bogusław Drewniak, *Das Theater im NS-Staat: Szenarium deutscher Zeitgeschichte 1933–1945* (Düsseldorf: Droste, 1983); Geerte Murmann, *Komödianten für den Krieg: deutsches und alliiertes Fronttheater* (Düsseldorf: Droste, 1992).

2 Though the distinction was often ignored in practice (and further confused by the use of *Truppentheater* and *Armeetheater*), the terms *Fronttheater* and *Soldatentheater* did have exact meanings. See Drewniak, p. 87; Murmann, p. 91.

3 Callum MacDonald and Jan Kaplan, *Prague in the Shadow of the Swastika* (London: Quartet, 1995), p. 148.

4 For details of the campaign, see, for example, Nicholas Harman, *Dunkirk: The Necessary Myth* (London: Hodder and Stoughton, 1980); Janusz Piekalkiewicz, *Ziel Paris: der Westfeldzug 1940* (Augsburg: Bechtermünz, 1998). These are two titles among many.

5 Potsdam, Bundesarchiv (formerly Zentrales Staatsarchiv der DDR), 50.01 (Reichsministerium für Volksaufklärung und Propaganda), Files 513–15 (Deutsches Theater Lille), here 515, Document 592. Cited hereafter as Potsdam, Bundesarchiv, file plus document number (with the particular reference/quotation in parentheses).

6 This account of the German Theatre in Lille is based on the records at the Bundesarchiv, Potsdam, which are unfortunately incomplete, and on surviving documents of the theatre itself, such as programmes and playbills. We are grateful to the staff in Potsdam and elsewhere for their help.

7 Keppler (Abteilung T) to Goebbels, 30 January 1941, Potsdam, Bundesarchiv, 513/23–8 (27). Ernst Andreas Ziegler should not be confused with his namesake Hans Severus Ziegler, also a director but apparently not a relative, who came to Lille as a guest director on one occasion.

8 Keppler (Abteilung T) to Goebbels, 30 January 1941, Potsdam, Bundesarchiv, 513/23–8 (25).

9 Propaganda Ministry memorandum, undated but internal evidence suggests late 1940, Potsdam, Bundesarchiv, 513/5–6 (5).

10 Ernst Lemperle, 'Wir werden gutes Theater spielen', *Feldzeitung der Armee an Scheide, Somme, Seine: Beilage*, 11 May 1941; Report on a visit to Brussels, Lille and Paris by Oberregierungsrat Scherler, dated 18 October 1941, Potsdam, Bundesarchiv, 515/588–95 (590); Drewniak, p. 109 (Metz).

11 Report by Regierungsrat Schwebel, 'Bericht über meine Feststellungen bei dem Deutschen Theater in Lille', dated 11 December 1941, Potsdam, Bundesarchiv, 515/736–41 (736).

12 Contract between Lille and the Deutsche Arbeitsfront, Potsdam, Bundesarchiv, 514/48–51.

13 Keppler to Goebbels, 30 January 1941, Potsdam, Bundesarchiv, 513/23–8 (24).

14 Wilfried Krafft, letter of 16 November 1992 to Katharina Havekamp. We are grateful to Wilfried Krafft and to other surviving members of the company for sharing their memories and mementoes with us, contributing to the overall picture even where they are not directly quoted. In this respect, our thanks go to Almut

Dorowa, Toni Koch-Schauer, Edith Lechtape, Almut Sandstede and Ulrike Thimme. All translations are the authors' own.

15 Falkenhausen to Goebbels, 27 February 1941, Potsdam, Bundesarchiv, 513/112.

16 Speech by Ziegler to representatives of the cultural press, 1 May 1942, Potsdam, Bundesarchiv, 513/605–18.

17 Report 'Deutsches Theater Lille: Reisebericht 11.–16. Januar 1943', dated 23 January 1943, by Oberregierungsrat Scherzer, Potsdam, Bundesarchiv, 513/734-45 (734).

18 Memo to Goebbels, dated 18 November 1943, Potsdam, Bundesarchiv, 514/151–2.

19 Otto Roland, 'Oberspielleiter des Schauspiels Otto Roland inszenierte den Egmont', *Die Brücke: Blätter des Deutschen Theaters Lille*, 1, no. 1 (May 1941), 10.

20 Leopold Jessner (1878–1945), leading Expressionist director. The centrepiece of many of his sets in Berlin in the 1920s was a symbolic staircase.

21 Repertoire suggestions ('Spielplan-Vorschläge'), Potsdam, Bundesarchiv, 513/47–9.

22 Otherwise unidentified discussion agenda, Potsdam, Bundesarchiv, 513/120.

23 Daiber, p. 141, though with no supporting documentation.

24 Ernst Andreas Ziegler, 'Deutsches Theater im fremden Land', *Feldzeitung der Armee an Schelde, Somme, Seine: Beilage*, 11 May 1941.

25 Almut Sandstede, in interview with Katharina Havekamp, Hamburg, 3 October 1992.

26 See, for example, Brigitte Hamann, *Hitlers Wien: Lehrjahre eines Diktators*, Serie Piper, 2653 (Munich: Piper, 1998), p. 46; Ian Kershaw, *Hitler*, 2 vols (London: Penguin, 1998–), I: *1889–1936: Hubris*, p. 42. Kershaw also mentions Hitler's fondness for the works of Johann Strauss.

27 For more detailed accounts, see Drewniak, pp. 282–343; Ingo Fulfs, *Musiktheater im Nationalsozialismus* (Marburg: Tectum, 1995), pp. 72–5; Klaus Kieser, *Das Gärtnerplatztheater in München 1932–1944: zur Operette im Nationalsozialismus*, Europäische Hochschulschriften, Reihe 30: Theater- , Film- und Fernsehwissens-chaften, 43 (Frankfurt am Main: Lang, 1991), pp. 28–32; Erik Levi, 'Music and National Socialism: the Politicisation of Criticism, Composition and Performance', in *The Nazification of Art, Design, Music, Architecture and Film in the Third Reich*, ed. by Brandon Taylor and Wilfried van der Will (Winchester: Winchester Press, 1990), pp. 158–82. On individual composers, see Tim Ashley, *Richard Strauss* (London: Phaidon, 1999); Fritz Hennenberg, *Es muß was Wunderbares sein …: Ralph Benatzky zwischen 'Weißem Rößl' und Hollywood* (Vienna: Zsol-nay, 1998); Leif Ludwig Albertsen, 'Eduard Künneke im Dritten Reich', in *Idee, Gestalt, Geschichte: Festschrift Klaus von See: Studien zur europäischen Kultur-tradition*, ed. by Gerd Wolfgang Weber (Odense: Odense University Press, 1988), pp. 563–603. For further examples of these contradictions, see Chapter 3 of the present volume (pp. 139–41, 144, 146–7, 168).

28 August Haussleiter, '*Das häßliche Entlein*: eine italienische Komödie im Deutschen Theater Lille', *Wacht am Kanal*, 22 November 1943. The alternative titles are both listed in Friedrich Ernst Schulz, *Dramen-Lexikon* (Berlin: Drei Masken, 1941), pp. 82, 125.

29 See Glenn R. Cuomo, ' "Saint Joan before the Cannibals": George Bernard Shaw in the Third Reich', *German Studies Review*, 16 (1993), 435–61. For a detailed account of non-German authors in the Third Reich, see Chapter 5 of the present volume.

30 Albert Buesche, 'Neujahr im Empire: Erstaufführung *Sprung aus dem Alltag*', unidentified newspaper cutting, Potsdam, Filmmuseum, Carl-Balhaus-Archiv. The documents are not sorted or numbered.

31 Murmann, p. 225.

32 Internal ministry memorandum dated 31 August 1943, passing on Lille's urgent request for titles of plays with few male characters, Potsdam, Bundesarchiv, 514/127.

33 Edith Lechtape, in interview with Katharina Havekamp, Strasbourg, 26 December 1992.

34 Toni Koch-Schauer, 'Erinnerungen an den Winter 1942/43 in Lille am Deutschen Theater', unpublished typescript in the possession of Katharina Havekamp.

35 See the analyses in Konrad Dussel, *Ein neues, ein heroisches Theater?: National-sozialistische Theaterpolitik und ihre Auswirkungen in der Provinz*, Literatur und Wirklichkeit, 26 (Bonn: Bouvier, 1988); Thomas Salb, *Trutzburg deutschen Geistes: das Stadttheater Freiburg in der Zeit des Nationalsozialismus* (Freiburg: Rombach, 1993); Bettina Schültke, *Theater oder Propaganda?: die städtischen Bühnen Frankfurt am Main 1933–1945*, Studien zur Frankfurter Geschichte, 40 (Frankfurt am Main: Waldemar Kramer, 1997).

36 Ulrike Thimme, letter of 6 August 1992 to Katharina Havekamp.

37 Edith Lechtape, in interview with Katharina Havekamp, Strasbourg, 26 December 1992.

38 Schlösser to Goebbels, 16 May 1941, Potsdam, Bundesarchiv, 513/205–6 (205).

39 Report dated 23 January 1943 by Oberregierungsrat Scherzer, Potsdam, Bundes-archiv, 513/734–45 (736–7).

40 *Fresh Wind from Sumatra*, by Hans Müller with song lyrics by Hans Fritz Beckmann, was originally called *Fresh Wind from Canada* (*Frischer Wind aus Kanada*). It was performed under that title before the war, in Frankfurt for example, and even filmed in 1935. As with *Love in the USA*, the title was presumably changed to avoid mentioning an enemy country, but nothing else was altered, and the original title was still listed in Schulz, *Dramen-Lexikon*, p. 41. In Wilhelm Allgayer, *Dramenlexikon* (Cologne: Kiepenheuer und Witsch, 1958), the title has become *Frischer Wind* and the author Hans Müller-Nürnberg (p. 119).

41 The role of Octavian is taken by a soprano or mezzo-soprano and it is not clear what was experimental about the casting. However, this is the only occasion in the Lille documents where the word 'experiment' occurs and so should not pass unmarked.

42 Almut Sandstede, in interview with Katharina Havekamp, Hamburg, 3 October 1992.

43 Wilfried Krafft, letter of 16 January 1992 to Katharina Havekamp.

44 See, for example, Scherzer's confidential addendum to his report of January 1943, Potsdam, Bundesarchiv, 513/761.

45 Letter to Ziegler dated 20 March 1943, Potsdam, Bundesarchiv, 513/808. The letter mentions 'our island'.

46 See, for example, an internal Propaganda Ministry memorandum of November 1942 criticizing Ziegler's application for extra funding (Potsdam, Bundesarchiv, 513/367), or the report of the Reich Audit Office dated 29 October 1942 (Potsdam, Bundesarchiv, 515/420–6).

47 Letter from Zloch to the Propaganda Ministry, dated 11 March 1944, Potsdam, Bundesarchiv, 515/144.

48 Ziegler to the Propaganda Ministry, 9 July 1944, Potsdam, Bundesarchiv, 514/490–3.

49 There are references to the 'French population', for example, when it is impossible to say whether the French-*speaking* community is meant (as distinct from the Flemish speakers), or the local inhabitants in their entirety.

50 Theatre estimates ('Haushalts-Voranschlag'), Potsdam, Bundesarchiv, 513/105–8 (105).

51 Schlösser to Goebbels, 16 May 1941, Potsdam, Bundesarchiv, 513/205–6 (206).

52 Apel to the Propaganda Ministry, 31 March 1942, Potsdam, Bundesarchiv, 515/306–7 (306).

53 Speech by Ziegler to representatives of the cultural press, 1 May 1942, Potsdam, Bundesarchiv, 513/605–18.

54 Ministry of Finance to the Propaganda Ministry, 15 December 1942, Potsdam, Bundesarchiv, 513/374; Report dated 23 January 1943 by Oberregierungsrat Scherzer, Potsdam, Bundesarchiv, 513/734–45 (734).

55 MacDonald and Kaplan, p. 42.

56 Schlösser to Goebbels, 15 May 1942, passing on Ziegler's views, Potsdam, Bundesarchiv, 513/559–60 (560).

57 Almut Sandstede, in interview with Katharina Havekamp, Hamburg, 3 October 1992.

58 Report dated 23 January 1943 by Oberregierungsrat Scherzer, Potsdam, Bundesarchiv, 513/734–45 (735).

59 Petra Weber, *Carlo Schmid 1896–1979: eine Biographie* (Munich: Beck, 1996), pp. 178–83.

60 Ziegler to Schlösser, 16 August 1944, Potsdam, Bundesarchiv, 514/510.

61 Drewniak, p. 127.

62 See Evelyn Ehrlich, *Cinema of Paradox: French Filmmaking under the German Occupation* (New York: Columbia University Press, 1985), pp. x–xi; Patrick Marsh, 'The Theatre: Compromise or Collaboration?', in *Collaboration in France: Politics and Culture during the Nazi Occupation, 1940–1944*, ed. by Gerhard Hirschfeld and Patrick Marsh (Oxford: Berg, 1989), pp. 142–61 (p. 142). For an introduction to theatre under the Vichy regime, see Serge Added, *Le Théâtre dans les années-Vichy 1940–1944* (Paris: Ramsay, 1992).

63 Wilfried Krafft, letter of 16 January 1992 to Katharina Havekamp; Edith Lechtape, in interview with Katharina Havekamp, Strasbourg, 26 December 1992.

Select bibliography

Archives

Agnes Straub Archive, Gries, Austria.
Akademie der Künste, Berlin.
Bundesarchiv, Berlin-Zehlendorf (formerly Berlin Document Centre).
Bundesarchiv, Koblenz.
Bundesarchiv, Potsdam (formerly Zentrales Staatsarchiv der DDR).
Carl Balhaus Archiv, Filmmuseum, Potsdam.
Deutsches Rundfunkarchiv, Frankfurt am Main.
Geheimes Staatsarchiv, Berlin.
Hauptstaatsarchiv, Wiesbaden.
Historisches Museum, Vienna.
Institut für Theaterwissenschaft (Library and Walter Unruh Collection), Free University of Berlin.
Institute of Germanic Studies, University of London.
Leo Baeck Institute, New York.
Musikarchiv 'Komponisten als Opfer der Gewalt', Staatliche Hochschule für Musik und darstellende Kunst, Stuttgart.
Österreichisches Theatermuseum, Vienna.
Political Archive of the Auswärtiges Amt, Bonn.
Staatsarchiv, Bremen.
Staatsarchiv, Hamburg.
Stadtarchiv, Heidelberg.
Terezín Music Memorial Project, University of Tel Aviv, Israel.
Theatersammlung of the Austrian National Library, Vienna.
Theatersammlung, University of Hamburg.
Theaterwissenschaftliche Sammlung, University of Cologne.
Wiener Library, London.
Wiener Library, Tel Aviv.
Wilhelm Fürtwängler Archives, Zurich.

Newspapers and magazines

Allgemeine Thüringische Landeszeitung Deutschland
Der Angriff
Badische Presse
Badischer Beobachter
Bayerische Volkszeitung

Bayerischer Anzeiger
Berliner Börsen-Zeitung
Berliner Illustrirte/Illustrierte Zeitung
Berliner Lokalanzeiger
Berliner Morgenpost
Berliner Tageblatt und Handels-Zeitung
Bielefelder Generalanzeiger
Braunschweiger Neueste Nachrichten
Breslauer Neueste-Nachrichten
Brünner Tagblatt
Brüsseler Zeitung
B. Z. am Mittag
CV-Zeitung
Der Deutsche
Deutsche Allgemeine Zeitung
Deutsche Arbeiter-Korrespondenz
Deutsche Nachrichten in Griechenland
Deutsche Ostfront
Deutsche Tageszeitung
Deutsche Ukraine Zeitung
Deutsche Wochenschau
Deutsche Zeitung
Deutsche Zeitung im Ostland
Deutsche Zeitung in den Niederlanden
Deutsche Zeitung in Kroatien
Deutsche Zeitung in Norwegen
Deutsche Zukunft
Deutsches Volksblatt
Donaubote
Donauzeitung
Dortmunder Zeitung
Dresdner Anzeiger
Dresdner Nachrichten
Dresdner Neueste Nachrichten
FAZ (R)
Frankfurter Volksblatt
Frankfurter Zeitung
Fränkische Tageszeitung
Fränkischer Kurier
Der Führer
Gemeindeblatt
General-Anzeiger
Der Grenzbote
Haagsche Courant
Hakenkreuzbanner
Hamburger Fremdenblatt
Hamburger Tageblatt
Heidelberger Neueste Nachrichten
Het Volk

Ingolstädter Zeitung
Innsbrucker Nachrichten
Israelitisches Familienblatt
Jüdische Allgemeine Zeitung
Jüdische Rundschau
Jüdisches Nachrichtenblatt
Katholisches Wochenblatt
Kölnische Zeitung
Krakauer Zeitung
Kreuz Zeitung
Leipziger Neueste Nachrichten
Lübecker Zeitung
Märkisches Tageblatt
Minsker Zeitung
Der Mittag
Der Mitteldeutsche
Der Montag
Münchener Neueste Nachrichten
National-Zeitung
Neue Badener Zeitung
Der neue Tag
Neues Wiener Tagblatt
Neueste Zeitung
Niederdeutscher Beobachter
NS-Grenzwacht
NS-Kurier
NS-Monatshefte
NS-Tageszeitung
Pariser Zeitung
Pfälzer Bote
Das Reich
Revaler Zeitung
Rheinische Landeszeitung
Rheinisch-Westfälische Zeitung
Rote Erde
Das Schwarze Korps
Der Stern
Der Stürmer
Sudetendeutsche Tageszeitung
Tagespost
Völkische Kultur
Völkischer Beobachter (Berlin edition; North German edition; Vienna edition)
Volksgemeinschaft
Vossische Zeitung
Warschauer Zeitung
Westdeutscher Beobachter
Westfälische Landeszeitung
Westfälische Neueste Nachrichten
Westfälische Zeitung-Bielefelder Tageblatt

Wiener Neueste Nachrichten
Wilnaer Zeitung
12-Uhr-Blatt

Theatre periodicals, internal government newsletters, annual publications and other relevant periodicals of the Third Reich

Allgemeine Musik-Zeitung
Amtliche Mitteilungen der Reichsmusikkammer
Amtliches Nachrichtenblatt der DAF
Auto
Bausteine zum Deutschen Nationaltheater
Bayerische Staatstheater
Bayreuther Blätter
Blätter der Schauspiele Baden-Baden
Blätter der Staatsoper [Berlin]
Blätter der Städtischen Bühnen Frankfurt am Main/Der 30. Januar: Braune Blätter der
*   Städtischen Bühnen*
Blätter der Volksbühne Berlin
Blätter des Deutschen Theaters und der Kammerspiele
Die Blätter des Reichsgautheater in Posen
Blätter des Staatstheaters des Generalgouvernements
Börsenblatt für den deutschen Buchhandel
Braunschweiger Bühnenblätter
Die Brücke: Blätter des Deutschen Theaters Lille
Die Brücke: Blätter des Deutschen Grenzlandtheaters Görlitz
Die Bücherei
Bücherkunde
Die Bühne
Bühnenblätter der Deutschen Volksgruppe in Rumänien
Bühnentechnische Rundschau
Die Deutsche Artistik
Deutsche Bühne
Die Deutsche Bühne
Deutsche Bühnenkorrespondenz
Die Deutsche Dichtung
Das Deutsche Drama in Geschichte und Gegenwart
Deutsche Dramaturgie
Deutsche Kultur-Wacht
Deutsche Musikkultur
Deutsche Musik-Zeitung Köln
Deutsche Presse
Der deutsche Schriftsteller
Der deutsche Student
Deutsche Tanz-Zeitschrift
Deutsche Theater-Zeitung
Das Deutsche Volksspiel
Das Deutsche Wort

Deutscher Bühnenspielplan
Deutscher Kulturdienst: Informationsdienst für die deutschen Bühnen
Deutscher Kulturdienst: Kulturnachrichten des Deutschen Nachrichtenbüros
Deutscher Theaterdienst
Deutsches Bühnen-Jahrbuch
Deutsches Volkstum
Dichtung und Volkstum
Film-Kurier
Frankfurter Theater Almanach
Geist der Zeit
Hamburgisches Jahrbuch für Theater und Musik
Hammer
Der Hochwart
Informationen des Kulturpolitischen Archivs
Das innere Reich
Jahrbuch der Grabbe-Gesellschaft
Jahrbuch deutscher Städte
Jahrbuch (Gesellschaft für Wiener Theaterforschung)
Jahrbuch—Staatstheater des Generalgouvernements
Jahresliste des schädlichen und unerwünschten Schrifttums
Jüdischer Kulturbund Berlin: Monatsblätter
Kritische Gänge
Kulturdienst der Nationalsozialistischen Kulturgemeinde
Kulturinformationen für das Ostland
Kulturpolitisches Mitteilungsblatt der Reichspropagandaleitung der NSDAP
Künstler-Almanach für Bühne und Film
Kunst und Kultur (Hamburger Theater-Woche)
Die Literatur
Maandblad der Nederlandsch-Duitsche Kultuurgemeenschap/Monatsschrift der
    Niederländisch-Deutschen Kulturgemeinschaft
Melos/Neues Musikblatt
Die Musik
Musik im Kriege
Musik in Jugend und Volk
Musik und Theater: Blätter der Städtischen Bühnen Nürnberg
Die Musik-Woche
Nachrichten aus dem deutschen Kulturleben
Nachrichtenblatt der Deutschen Bühne
Nachrichtenblatt des Reichsministers für Volksaufklärung und Propaganda
Das Nationaltheater
Die neue Literatur
Der Neue Rundfunk
Die neue Rundschau
Der neue Weg
Odal: Organ für Blut und Boden
Ostdeutsche Monatshefte
Die Rampe: Blätter des Staatlichen Schauspielhauses Hamburg
Reichsgesetzblatt
Reichsliste für kleinere städtische Büchereien

Die RKK, Amtliches Mitteilungsblatt
Shakespeare-Jahrbuch
Schriften der Deutschen Shakespeare-Gesellschaft
Der Schriftsteller
Signale für die musikalische Welt
Sonderdienst der Reichspropagandaleitung
Die Spielgemeinde
Städtische Bühnen Hannover: Blätter des Schauspielhauses
Der Tanz
Theater-Tageblatt
Theater der Welt
Theater zu Litzmannstadt
Theaterwelt (Düsseldorf)
Theaterzeitung des Staatstheaters Danzig
Unser Wille und Weg
Volk an der Arbeit
Völkische Kultur
Volkstum und Heimat
Die Weltliteratur
Die Westmark
Wille und Macht
Zeitschrift für deutsche Bildung
Zeitschrift für Deutschkunde
Zeitschrift für Musik

Published *Thing* plays (*Thingspiele*) and selected *Thing* play theory

Barthel, Max, *Feierliche Übergabe der Thingstätte durch den Arbeitsdienst* (Berlin: Volkschaft-Verlag, 1934).

Bauer, Josef Martinus, *Ein Volksspiel von Winternot und Menschengüte* (Berlin: Langen/Müller, 1933).

Becker, Julius Maria, *Deutsche Notwende: epischer Sprechchor in zwei Teilen* (Munich: Val. Höfling, 1933).

Bertling, Klaus, and Johannes Menge, *Prometheus: ein chorisches Spiel vom Licht* (Leipzig: Arwed Strauch, 1933).

Beyer, Paul, *Düsseldorfer Passion: ein deutsches National-Festspiel* (Munich: Franz Eher, 1933).

Braumüller, Wolf, *Freilicht- und Thingspiele: Rückschau und Forderungen*, Schriften zum deutschen Volksspiel, 1 (Berlin: Volkschaft-Verlag, 1935).

Brockmeier, Wolfram, *Ewiges Volk* (Leipzig: Goten-Verlag Herb. Eisentraut, 1934).

Eckart, Walther, *Deutschland erwache!: ein Weihespiel* (Munich: Val. Höfling, 1934).

Eggers, Kurt, *Annaberg* (Berlin: Volkschaft-Verlag, 1933).

—— *Das Spiel von Job dem Deutschen: ein Mysterium* (Berlin: Volkschaft-Verlag, 1933).

—— *Das große Wandern: ein Spiel vom ewigen deutschen Schicksal* (Berlin: Volkschaft-Verlag, 1934).

Euringer, Richard, *Deutsche Passion 1933: Hörwerk in sechs Sätzen* (Oldenburg: Gerhard Stalling, 1933).

—— 'Thingspiel-Thesen I', *Der Führer*, no. 182 (5 July 1934).

—— *Totentanz: ein Tanz der lebendig Toten und der erweckten Muskoten* (Hamburg: Hanseatische Verlagsanstalt, 1935).

Goes, Gustav, *Aufbricht Deutschland: ein Stadionspiel der nationalen Revolution* (Berlin: Traditions-Verlag Kolk, 1933).

—— *Opferflamme der Arbeit: ein Freilichtspiel* (Berlin: Traditions-Verlag Kolk, 1934).

Heynicke, Kurt, *Neurode: ein Spiel von deutscher Arbeit* (Berlin: Volkschaft-Verlag, 1934).

—— *Neurode* and *Der Weg ins Reich* (Berlin: Volkschaft-Verlag, 1935).

Krug, Konrad, 'Erziehung zur Gemeinschaft im deutschen Thingspiel', *Volk im Werden*, 3 (1935), 453–64.

Kühn, Walter, 'Thingspiel, das Spiel der völkischen Gemeinschaft', *Schlesische Monatshefte*, 11 (1934), 456–63.

Michels, Wilhelm, and Heinrich Lersch, *Thingweihe: Werdendes Volk* (Koblenz: Manuskript der Spielgemeinschaft für Nationalsozialistische Festgestaltung, 1935).

Möller, Eberhard Wolfgang, *Das Frankenburger Würfelspiel*, in *Zeit und Theater*, ed. by Günther Rühle, 6 vols (Frankfurt am Main: Ullstein/Propyläen, 1980), V: *Diktatur und Exil*, 335–78.

Moshamer, Ludwig, 'Freilichttheater und Thingplätze: ein Beitrag zu ihrer architektonischen Durchbildung', *Bauamt und Gemeindebau*, 16, no. 1 (1934), 3–8.

—— 'Die Thingplätze und ihre Bedeutung für das kommende deutsche Theater', *Bauwelt*, 26, no. 45 (1935), 1–8.

Müller-Schnick, Erich, *Soldaten der Scholle: ein chorisches Spiel aus deutscher Geschichte* (Berlin: Langen/Müller, 1934).

Nelissen-Haken, Bruno, 'Das Volks- und Thingspiel', *Hochschule und Ausland*, 13, no. 8 (1935), 55–65.

Neuschaefer, Wolfgang, *Thing am heiligen Berg: Schau eines völkischen Kultes* (Mühlhausen: Friedrich Lamade, 1935).

Nierentz, Hans Jürgen, *Segen der Bauernschaft: ein chorisches Erntespiel* (Berlin: Langen/Müller, 1933).

—— *Symphonie der Arbeit* (Berlin: Langen/Müller, 1933).

Nowak, Bruno, *Der Bauer: ein Spiel der Mahnung* (Berlin: Langen/Müller, 1935).

—— *Das Opfer der Notburga: ein Spiel der Mahnung* (Berlin: Langen/Müller, 1935).

Oppenberg, Ferdinand, *Wir bauen einen Dom: Chöre von Gott und Werk* (Berlin: Langen/Müller, 1935).

Schlosser, Johannes G., *Deutsche Feier* (Berlin: Langen/Müller, 1935).

—— *Ich rief das Volk* (Berlin: Langen/Müller, 1934/5).

Schlösser, Rainer, *Das Volk und seine Bühne: Bemerkungen zum Aufbau des deutschen Theaters* (Berlin: Langen/Müller, 1935).

Schramm, Wilhelm von, *Neubau des deutschen Theaters: Ergebnisse und Forderungen* (Berlin: Schlieffen, 1934).

Zerkaulen, Heinrich, *Der Arbeit die Ehr'* (Berlin: Volkschaft-Verlag, 1935).

Secondary sources and documents from the period 1933–45

Abbetmeyer, Theo, *Über moderne Theater-Unkultur: zur Enteignung des deutschen Theaters durch Marxismus und Bolschewismus: mit besonderer Berücksichtigung der stadthannoverschen Verhältnisse und mit Richtlinien für den Aufbau wahrer deutscher Theater-Kultur* (Süd-Hannover-Braunschweig: NSDAP des Gaues, 1933).

Aders, Egon F., *Theater, wohin?* (Stuttgart: Muth, 1935).

Anheisser, Siegfried, *Für den deutschen Mozart: das Ringen um gültige deutsche Sprach-form der italienischen Opern Mozarts: ein Vermächtnis an das deutsche Volk*, Die Schaubühne: Quellen und Forschungen zur Theatergeschichte, 26 (Emsdetten: H. & J. Lechte, 1938).

Atkins, Henry G., *German Literature through Nazi Eyes* (London: Methuen, 1941).

Bach, Rudolf, *Die Frau als Schauspielerin* (Tübingen: Rainer Wunderlich, 1937).

Bäcker, Hans, 'Die Gestalt Brünhilds im deutschen Drama' (unpublished doctoral thesis, Friedrich-Wilhelm University, Bonn, 1938).

Bacmeister, Ernst, *Die Tragödie ohne Schuld und Sühne* (Wolfshagen-Scharbeutz: West-phal, 1940).

—— *Der deutsche Typus der Tragödie: dramaturgisches Fundament* (Berlin: Langen/Müller, 1943).

Baden, Hans J., *Das Tragische: die Erkentnisse der griechischen Tragödie* (Berlin: de Gruyter, 1941).

Bartels, Adolf, *Geschichte der deutschen Literatur: mit Nachträgen über allerneueste Zeit*, 11th–12th edn (Braunschweig: Westermann, 1933); 19th edn (Braunschweig: Westermann, 1943).

Bayerische Versicherungskammer München, *Satzung der Versorgungsanstalt der Deut-schen Bühnen vom 25. Februar 1938: Anhang: 1. Tarifordnung für die deutschen Theater* ... (Munich: [Versorgungsanstalt der Deutschen Bühnen], 1938).

Becker-Glauch, Woldemar, *Heinrich Bulthaupt als Dramaturg: ein Beitrag zum Problem des Epigonentums*, Die Schaubühne: Quellen und Forschungen zur Theatergeschichte, 27 (Emsdetten: H. & J. Lechte, 1938).

Bergmann, Alfred, *Meine Grabbe-Sammlung: Erinnerungen und Bekentnisse* (Detmold: Ernst Schnelle, 1942).

Berten, Walther, *Musik und Musikleben der Deutschen* (Hamburg: Hanseatische Ver-lagsanstalt, 1933).

Bertram, Johannes, *Der Seher von Bayreuth: Deutung des Lebens und Werkes Richard Wagners* (Berlin: Büchergilde Gutenberg, 1943).

Best, Walter, *Völkische Dramaturgie* (Würzburg: Konrad Triltsch, 1940).

Beyer, Paul, *Nationaldramaturgie: ein erster Versuch: praktische Untersuchungen über die nahe Zukunft der Dramatik in Deutschland*, Schriftenreihe des Theater-Tageblattes, 1 (Berlin: Theater-Tageblatt, 1933).

Bie, Richard, and Alfred Mühr, *Die Kulturwaffen des neuen Reiches: Briefe an Führer, Volk und Jugend* (Jena: Diederichs, 1933).

Biedrzynski, Richard, *Schauspieler: Regisseure: Intendanten* (Heidelberg: Hüthig, 1944).

Bielfeldt, Franz, *Hebbels Menschengestaltung als dichterischer Ausdruck nordisch-deutschen Wesens: ein Beitrag zur literarhistorischen Anthropologie des 19. Jahrhunderts*, Germanische Studien, 209 (Berlin: Ebering, 1939).

Blanck, Karl, and Heinz Haufe, *Unbekanntes Theater: ein Buch von der Regie* (Stuttgart: J. G. Cotta'sche Buchhandlung Nachfolger, 1941).

Blunck, Hans Friedrich, *Deutsche Kulturpolitik* (Munich: Langen/Müller, 1934).

Bonn, Friedrich, *Jugend und Theater*, Die Schaubühne: Quellen und Forschungen zur Theatergeschichte, 30 (Emsdetten: H. & J. Lechte, 1939).

Braun, Hanns, *Vor den Kulissen* (Munich: Heimeran, 1938).

Brendler, Erich, 'Die Tragik im deutschen Drama vom Naturalismus bis zur Gegenwart' (unpublished doctoral thesis, University of Tübingen, 1940).

Brinker, Käthe, *Hannelore Schroth, Käte Haack: Mutter und Tochter* (Berlin: Gründler, 1940).

Bücken, Ernst, *Musik der Deutschen* (Cologne: Staufen Verlag, 1941).

Bunte Bilder, Deutsche Bühne (Dresden: Sächsische Staatstheater, [1938]).

Casper, Siegfried, *Der Dramatiker Hanns Johst* (Munich: Langen/Müller, 1935).

—— *Hanns Johst* (Munich: Langen/Müller, 1940).

—— ed., *Hanns Johst spricht zu Dir: eine Lebenslehre aus seinen Werken und Reden* (Berlin: Nordland Verlag, 1941).

Conrad, Leopold, *Mozarts Dramaturgie der Oper*, 'Das Nationaltheater': Schriftenreihe des Theaterwissenschaftlichen Instituts der Friedrich-Schiller-Universität Jena, 8 (Würzburg: Konrad Triltsch, 1943).

Cysarz, Herbert, *Schiller* (Halle: Niemeyer, 1934).

Czech, Stan, *Das Operettenbuch: ein Wegweiser durch die Operetten und Singspiele des Bühnenspielplans der Gegenwart und Vergangenheit* (Dresden: E. Wulffen, [1936]); 2nd edn (Dresden: E. Wulffen, 1939).

Das deutsche Puppenspiel: Einsatz, Erfolge und Zielsetzung (Berlin: Verlag der Deutschen Arbeitsfront, 1939).

Das Deutsche Volkstheater Erfurt als Theater der Hitler-Jugend (Erfurt: Volkstheater, 1941).

Das Theater des Führers: Festschrift anläßlich der Weihe des Gautheater ... zu Saarbrücken (Saarbrücken: no publ., 1935).

Das Volksspiel im nationalsozialistischen Gemeinschaftsleben (Munich: Franz Eher, 1943).

Daube, Otto, *Siegfried Wagner und die Märchenoper* (Leipzig: Deutscher Theater Verlag, M. Schleppengerl, 1936).

—— ed., *Amtlicher Führer durch die Richard-Wagner-Festwoche, Detmold 1937* (Detmold: Ernst Schnelle, 1937).

Deubel, Werner, *Der deutsche Weg zur Tragödie* (Dresden: Wolfgang Jess, 1935).

Dippel, Paul Gerhard, ed., *Künder und Kämpfer: die Dichter des neuen Deutschlands* (Munich: Deutscher Volksverlag, n.d.).

Dresler, Adolf, *Dietrich Eckart* (Munich: Deutscher Volksverlag, 1938).

Dreyer, Ernst Adolf, ed., *Deutsche Kultur im neuen Reich: Wesen, Aufgabe und Ziel der Reichskulturkammer*, Schlieffen-Bücherei Geist von Potsdam, 7 (Berlin: Schlieffen-Verlag, 1934).

Eckert, Gerhard, *Gestaltung eines literarischen Stoffes in Tonfilm und Hörspiel*, Neue Deutsche Forschung, 67 (Berlin: Junker und Dünnhaupt, 1936).

Eichenauer, Richard, *Musik und Rasse*, 2nd edn (Munich: Lehmann, 1937).

Eichert, Ellynor, *Das geistliche Spiel der Gegenwart in Deutschland und Frankreich* (Berlin: Junker und Dünnhaupt, 1941).

Eichler, Fritz, *Das Wesen des Handpuppen- und Marionettenspiels*, Die Schaubühne: Quellen und Forschungen zur Theatergeschichte, 17 (Emsdetten: H. & J. Lechte, 1937).

Elsner, Richard, *Die deutsche Nationalbühne*, Deutsche Zukunft, 1 (Berlin: Wolf Heyer, 1934).

Emmel, Felix, *Theater aus deutschem Wesen* (Berlin: Stilke, 1937).

Engel, Hans, *Deutschland und Italien in ihren musikgeschichtlichen Beziehungen* (Regensburg: Gustav Bosse, 1944).

Engelbrecht, Kurt, *Deutsche Kunst im totalen Staat* (Lahr in Baden: no publ., 1933).

—— *Faust im Braunhemd* (Jena: Adolf Klein, 1933).

Erdmann, Walter, *Ferdinand Raimund: dichterische Entwicklung, Persönlichkeit und Lebensschicksal*, 'Das Nationaltheater': Schriftenreihe des Theaterwissenschaftlichen Instituts der Friedrich-Schiller-Universität Jena, 9 (Würzburg: Konrad Triltsch, 1943).

Euringer, Richard, *Dietrich Eckart* (Hamburg: Hanseatische Verlagsanstalt, 1935).

Fabricius, Hans, *Schiller als Kampfgenosse Hitlers: Nationalsozialismus in Schillers Dramen* (Bayreuth: N. S. Kultur-Verlag, 1932); 2nd edn (Berlin: Deutsche Kultur-Wacht, 1934).

Faßbinder, Joseph, *Heinrich von Kleist: 'Die Hermannsschlacht'* (Paderborn: Schöningh; Vienna: Beck, 1941).

Fischer, Hans, *Das Land ohne Musik: Kreuz und quer durch 'englische Musikkultur'* (Berlin: Vieweg, 1940).

—— ed., *Wege zur deutschen Musik: die Musik im Schaffen der großen Meister und im Leben des Volkes*, 2nd edn (Berlin: Vieweg, 1941).

Frauenfeld, Albert Eduard, *Der Weg zur Bühne*, 2nd edn (Berlin: Wilhelm Limpert, 1941).

Freisburger, Walther, *Theater im Film: eine Untersuchung über die Grundzüge und Wandlungen in den Beziehungen zwischen Theater und Film*, Die Schaubühne: Quellen und Forschungen zur Theatergeschichte, 13 (Emsdetten: H. & J. Lechte, 1936).

Frenzel, Elisabeth, *Judengestalten auf der deutschen Bühne: ein notwendiger Querschnitt durch 700 Jahre Rollengeschichte* (Munich: Deutscher Volksverlag, 1942).

Frenzel, Herbert A., *Eberhard Wolfgang Möller* (Munich: Deutscher Volksverlag, 1938).

Freund, Hans, and Wilhelm Reinking, *Musikalisches Theater in Hamburg* (Hamburg: Christians, 1938).

Friedrichs, Axel, ed., *Die Nationalsozialistische Revolution 1933*, Dokumente der deutschen Politik, 1 (Berlin: Junker und Dünnhaupt, 1935); 3rd edn (Berlin: Junker und Dünnhaupt, 1938).

Friesicke, Joachim K., 'Der Gegensatz zwischen Vater und Sohn in der deutschen Dramatik von Hasenclevers *Sohn* bis Rehbergs *Friedrich Wilhelm I*' (unpublished doctoral thesis, University of Munich, 1942).

Fritsch, Theodor, ed., *Handbuch der Judenfrage: eine Zusammenstellung des wichtigsten Materials zur Beurteilung des jüdischen Volkes* (Leipzig: Hammer, 1944).

Fünf Jahre Theaterverlag Albert Langen Georg Müller: eine Übersicht über die Entwicklung des Verlagswerks von 1933 bis 1938 (Berlin: Langen/Müller, 1938).

Gabler, Karl, *Faust und Mephisto, der deutsche Mensch* (Berlin: Theodor Fritsch, 1938).

Gaillard, Otto Friedrich, *Hans Rehberg, der Dichter der Preußendramen*, Rostocker Studien, 9 (Rostock: Hinstorff, 1941).

Geisow, Hans, *Bühne und Volk* (Leipzig: Armanen-Verlag, 1933).

Gentsch, Adolf, *Die politische Struktur der Theaterführung*, Leipziger Beiträge zur Erforschung der Publizistik, 8 (Dresden: Dittert, 1942).

Gerhart Hauptmann zum 80. Geburtstage am 15. November 1942 (Breslau: Schlesien-Verlag, 1942).

Gerlach-Bernau, Kurt, *Drama und Nation: ein Beitrag zur Wegbereitung des nationalsozialistischen Dramas* (Breslau: Ferd. Hirt, 1934).

Gerth, Werner, 'Die Theaterkritik der liberalistischen Epoche im Vergleich zur nationalsozialistischen Kritik' (unpublished doctoral thesis, University of Leipzig, 1936).

Glanz, Lucia, *Das Puppenspiel und sein Publikum* (Berlin: Junker und Dünnhaupt, 1941).

Golz, Bruno, *Die nationale Selbstbesinnung und das Theater* (Leipzig: Reichsverband 'Deutsche Bühne', 1933).

Gregor, Joseph, *Meister deutscher Schauspielkunst: Krauß, Klöpfer, Jannings, George* (Bremen: Carl Schünemann, 1939).

—— *Richard Strauss der Meister der Oper* (Munich: Piper, 1939).

—— *Kulturgeschichte der Oper: ihre Verbindung mit dem Leben, den Werken des Geistes und der Politik* (Vienna: Gallus, 1941).

—— *Das Theater des Volkes in der Ostmark* (Vienna: Deutscher Verlag für Jugend und Volk, 1943).

Großmann, R[udolf], 'Lope, der Dichter des ewigen Spanien', *Ibero-Amerikanische Rundschau*, 1 (1935–36), 215–18.

Günther, Johannes, *Der Schauspieler Lothar Müthel* (Berlin: Hendriock, 1934).

Hain, Mathilde, *Studien über das Wesen des frühexpressionistischen Dramas*, Frankfurter Quellen und Forschungen zur germanischen und romanischen Philologie, 5 (Frankfurt am Main: Moritz Diesterweg, 1933).

Hamburger Bühnen-Almanach 1938–1939 (Hamburg: Bruno Sachse, 1938).

Hartz, Erich von, *Wesen und Mächte des heldischen Theaters*, Bücherei für Spiel und Theater, 3 (Berlin: Langen/Müller, 1934).

Hase, Hellmuth von, and Albert Dreetz, eds, *Jahrbuch der deutschen Musik: im Auftrag der Abteilung Musik des Reichsministeriums für Volksaufklärung und Propaganda*, 2 vols (Leipzig: Breitkopf und Härtel, 1943–44).

Haußwald, Günter, *Die deutsche Oper*, 2nd edn (Cologne: Schaffstein, 1941).

Heering, Hans, *Idee und Wirklichkeit bei Hanns Johst* (Berlin: Junker und Dünnhaupt, 1938).

Heidrich, Walter, ed., *Die Sudetenbühne* (Reichenberg [Liberec]: Sudetendt. Verlag, 1934).

Hellwig, Gerhard, *Nationalsozialistische Feiern im Rahmen eines Hitlerjahres für Schule und Gemeinde des 3. Reiches* (Berlin: N. B. Buchvertrieb, 1934).

Hellwig, L. W., *Olga Tschechowa: die Karriere einer Schauspielerin* (Berlin: AGV-Verlag, 1939).

Henry XLV, Prince of Reuss, *Das deutsche Theater im Kulturaufbau des dritten Reiches* (Szeged: Városi Nyomda és Könyvikiadó, 1940).

Herterich, Fritz, *Theater und Volkswirtschaft* (Munich: Duncker und Humblot, 1937).

Heyde, Ludwig, *Presse, Rundfunk und Film im Dienste der Volksführung* (Dresden: Dittert, 1943).

Hieronimi, Martin, 'Französische Literatur- und Theaterkrise', *Bücherkunde*, 5 (1938), 295–8.

Hildebrant, Gustav, *Das Theater des deutschen Volkes: vom Allerweltstheater zum Nationaltheater* (Berlin: Volksbuchgesellschaft, 1934).

Hilpert, Heinz, *Formen des Theaters: Reden und Aufsätze* (Vienna: Ibach, 1944).

Hinkel, Hans, ed., *Handbuch der Reichskulturkammer* (Berlin: Deutscher Verlag für Politik und Wirtschaft, 1937).

Hitler, Adolf, *Mein Kampf*, 36th edn (Munich: Franz Eher, 1933).

Hoffmann, H., ed., *Theaterrecht – Bühne und Artistik: Zusammenfassende Darstellung des gesamten Theaterrechts unter Berücksichtigung der Anordnungen der Reichskulturkammer und Reichstheaterkammer sowie der Bestimmungen der Reichsgewerbeordnung nebst Text mit Anmerkungen* (Berlin: Vahlen, 1936).

Holl, Werner, *Gustav Fröhlich, Künstler und Mensch* (Berlin: Wendt, 1936).

Horn, Walter, *Hanns Johst* (Munich: Deutscher Volksverlag, 1938).

Hotzel, Curt, *Hanns Johst: der Weg des Dichters zum Volk* (Berlin: Frundsberg, 1933).

Huch, Rudolf, *William Shakespeare: eine Studie* (Hamburg: Hanseatische Verlagsanstalt, 1941).

Ibach, Alfred, *Die Wessely: Skizze ihres Werdens* (Vienna: Frick, 1943).

Ihering, Herbert, *Emil Jannings: Baumeister seines Lebens und seiner Filme* (Heidelberg: Hüthig, 1941).

—— *Von Josef Kainz bis Paula Wessely: Schauspieler von gestern und heute* (Heidelberg: Hüthig, 1942).

—— *Regie* (Berlin: Hans von Hugo, 1943).

—— *Käthe Dorsch* (Munich: Zinnen-Verlag, 1944).

Ihlert, Heinz, *Die Reichsmusikkammer: Ziele, Leistungen und Organisation* (Berlin: Junker und Dünnhaupt, 1935).

Intendanz der Staatlichen Schauspiele Berlin, *150 Jahre: Schauspielhaus am Gendarmenmarkt: 5. Dezember 1786–5. Dezember 1936* (Berlin: [Schauspielhaus am Gendarmenmarkt], [1936]).

Iwanow, Wiatscheslaw, 'Der Sinn der antiken Tragödie', *Hochland*, 34 (1936–37), 232–43.

Jedzek, Klaus, *Theater als politische Kraft* (Eisenach: Erich Röth, 1935).

Jerger, Wilhelm, *Die Wiener Philharmoniker: Erbe und Sendung* (Vienna: Wiener Verlagsgesellschaft, 1942).

Johst, Hanns, *Standpunkt und Fortschritt*, Schriften an die Nation, 58 (Oldenburg: Gerh. Stalling, 1933).

—— 'Vom neuen Drama', *Hochschule und Ausland*, 11, no. 11 (1933), 5–11.

—— *Maske und Gesicht: Reise eines Nationalsozialisten von Deutschland nach Deutschland* (Munich: Langen/Müller, 1936).

Junghans, Ferdinand, *Das dramatische Theater deutscher Nation* (Berlin: Die Runde, 1934).

Kadner, Siegfried, *Rasse und Humor* (Munich: Lehmann, 1936).

Kapp, Julius, *Geschichte der Staatsoper Berlin* (Berlin: Hesse, 1942).

Kaun, Axel, ed., *Berliner Theater-Almanach: 1942* (Berlin: Paul Neff, [1942]).

Kindermann, Heinz, ed., *Kampf um das soziale Ordnungsgefüge* (Leipzig: Reclam, 1939).

—— *Ferdinand Raimund* (Vienna: Luser, 1940).

—— *Kampf um die deutsche Lebensform: Reden und Aufsätze über die Dichtung im Aufbau der Nation* (Vienna: Wiener Verlagsgesellschaft, 1941).

—— *Max Halbe und der deutsche Osten*, Danzig in Geschichte und Gegenwart, 4 (Danzig [Gdansk]: Rosenberg, 1941).

—— *Hölderlin und das deutsche Theater* (Vienna: Frick, 1943).

—— *Theater und Nation*, Reclams Universal-Bibliothek, 7563 (Leipzig: Reclam, 1943).

—— *Die europäische Sendung des deutschen Theaters*, Wiener Wissenschaftliche Vorträge und Reden, 10 (Vienna: Verlag der Ringbuchhandlung, 1944).

Knoth, Werner, and Wolfgang Golther, *Bayreuth im Dritten Reich: ein Buch des Dankes und der Erinnerung* (Hamburg: Alster-Verlag, 1933).

Knudsen, Hans, *Wesen und Grundlagen der Theaterkritik* (Berlin: Langen/Müller, 1935).

—— 'Vom Standort des neuen Dramas', *Zeitschrift für deutsche Geisteswissenschaft*, 2 (1939–40), 193–204.

Koener, Raymund, 'Das Theater als öffentliche Aufgabe' (unpublished doctoral thesis, University of Würzburg, 1938).

Kölli, Josef G., 'Die notwendige Wiedergeburt der Tragödie', *Monatsschrift für das deutsche Geistesleben*, 42 (1941), 280–2.

—— 'Die Sendung der Dichtung und die Möglichkeit der Tragödie', *Volk im Werden*, 10 (1942), 178–83.

Krauß, Rudolf, *Modernes Schauspielbuch: ein Führer durch den deutschen Theaterspielplan der neueren Zeit*, 9th edn (Stuttgart: Muth, 1934).

Kröjer, Maxim, *Het Nationaal-Socialistisch tooneel* (Antwerp: Standaard, 1940).

Kruse, G. R., *Reclams Opernführer* (Leipzig: Reclam, 1938).

Kühle, Mathilde, *Carlo Goldonis Komödien auf dem deutschen Theater des 20. Jahrhunderts*, Italienische Studien, 7 (Cologne: Petrarca-Haus; Stuttgart: Kommissionsverlag Deutsche Verlags-Anstalt, 1943).

Kummer, Friedrich, *Dresden und seine Theaterwelt* (Dresden: Verlag Heimatwerk Sachsen, 1938).

Kurtz, Rudolf, *Emil Jannings: das Filmbuch* (Berlin: UFA, 1942).

Kutscher, Artur, *Vom Salzburger Barocktheater zu den Salzburger Festspielen* (Düsseldorf: Pflugschar-Verlag, 1939).

Langenbeck, Curt, 'Über Sinn und Aufgabe der Tragödie in unserer Epoche', *Völkische Kultur*, 3 (1935), 241–52.

—— 'Wiedergeburt des Dramas aus dem Geist der Zeit', *Das innere Reich*, 6 (1939–40), 923–57.

—— *Tragödie und Gegenwart: die Rede des Preisträgers des rheinischen Literaturpreises* (Munich: Langen/Müller, 1940).

Langenbucher, Hellmuth, *Volkhafte Dichtung der Zeit*, 6th edn (Berlin: Junker und Dünnhaupt, 1933); 9th–10th edn (Berlin: Junker und Dünnhaupt, 1944).

Lehnerdt, Irmgard, 'Das Theaterrecht des nationalsozialistischen Staates' (unpublished doctoral thesis, University of Kiel, 1939).

Leip, Hans, *Max und Anny, romantischer Bericht vom Aufstieg zweier Sterne* (Hamburg: Broschek, 1935).

Lembert, R., *Dietrich Eckart* (Munich: Franz Eher, 1934).

Lenk, Wolfgang, 'Das kommunale Theater' (unpublished doctoral thesis, University of Berlin, 1933).

Lennartz, Franz, *Die Dichter unserer Zeit: Einzeldarstellungen zur deutschen Dichtung der Gegenwart*, 3rd edn (Stuttgart: Alfred Kröner, 1940).

Lepel, Felix von, *Die Dresdner Oper als Weltkulturstätte: eine Studie* (Dresden: Spohr, 1942).

Ley, Robert, *Wir alle helfen dem Führer* (Munich: Franz Eher, 1937).

Liess, Andreas, *L. van Beethoven und Richard Wagner im Pariser Musikleben* (Hamburg: Hoffmann & Campe, 1939).

Linden, Walther, *Geschichte der deutschen Literatur von den Anfängen bis zur Gegenwart* (Leipzig: Reclam, 1937); 5th edn (Leipzig: Reclam, 1944).

Lindner, Josef, 'Das deutsche Theater der Gegenwart' (unpublished doctoral thesis, University of Vienna, 1940).

Linkenbach, Baldur, *Das Prinzip des Tragischen* (Munich: Einhorn, 1934).

Margendorff, Wolfgang, *Imre Madách: 'Die Tragödie des Menschen'*, 'Das Nationaltheater': Schriftenreihe des Theaterwissenschaftlichen Instituts der Friedrich-Schiller-Universität Jena, 7, 2nd edn (Würzburg: Konrad Triltsch, 1943).

Marrenbach, Otto, ed., *Fundamente des Sieges: die Gesamtarbeit der Deutschen Arbeitsfront von 1933–1940* (Berlin: Verlag der Deutschen Arbeitsfront, 1940).

Meerstein, Günter, 'Das Kabarett im Dienste der Politik' (unpublished [doctoral] thesis, University of Leipzig, 1938).

Meffert, Erich, *Das Haus der Staatsoper und seine Baumeister: dargebracht zum Jahrestage des 200jährigen Bestehens der Berliner Staatsoper vom preussischen Finanzministerium* (Leipzig: Max Beck, 1942).

—— *Das Haus der Staatsoper und seine neue Gestaltung: eine baugeschichtliche Studie* (Leipzig: Max Beck, 1944).

Mettin, Hermann-Christian, *Der politische Schiller*, Bücherei für Spiel und Theater, 5 (Berlin: Langen/Müller, 1937).

—— *Die Situation des Theaters* (Vienna: Sexl, 1942).

Meyer, Rudolf, *Hecken- und Gartentheater in Deutschland im 17. und 18. Jahrhundert*, Die Schaubühne: Quellen und Forschungen zur Theatergeschichte, 6 (Emsdetten: H. & J. Lechte, 1934).

Meyer, Walther, *Die Entwicklung des Theaterabonnements in Deutschland*, Die Schaubühne: Quellen und Forschungen zur Theatergeschichte, 32 (Emsdetten: H. & J. Lechte, 1939).

Möller, Eberhard Wolfgang, *Rede in Lauchstädt* (Merseburg: Landeshauptmann der Provinz Sachsen, 1938).

Mühr, Alfred, *Werner Krauß, das Schicksal auf der Bühne* (Berlin: Frundsberg, 1933).

—— *Gustaf Gründgens, aus dem Tagewerk des Schauspielers* (Hamburg: Toth, 1943).

Müller, Gottfried, *Dramaturgie des Theaters und des Films*, 'Das Nationaltheater': Schriftenreihe des Theaterwissenschaftlichen Instituts der Friedrich-Schiller-Universität Jena, 6, 2nd edn (Würzburg: Konrad Triltsch, 1942).

Müller, Irmgard, *Gerhart Hauptmann und Frankreich* (Breslau: Priebatsch, 1939).

Mulot, Arno, *Die deutsche Dichtung unserer Zeit*, 6 vols (Stuttgart: Metzler, 1937–42); 2nd edn (Stuttgart: Metzler, 1944).

Nedden, Otto C. A. zur, *Drama und Dramaturgie im 20. Jahrhundert: Abhandlungen zum Theater und zur Theaterwissenschaft der Gegenwart*, 'Das Nationaltheater': Schriftenreihe des Theaterwissenschaftlichen Instituts der Friedrich-Schiller-Universität Jena, 4 (Würzburg: Konrad Triltsch, 1940); 3rd edn (1944).

—— ed., *Wechselbeziehungen des deutschen und des italienischen Theaters: eine deutsch-italienische Theaterwoche in Rom im Palazzo Zuccari 5.–9. März 1940: Tagungsbericht (in deutscher und italienischer Sprache)*, 'Das Nationaltheater': Schriftenreihe des Theaterwissenschaftlichen Instituts der Friedrich-Schiller- Universität Jena, 5 (Würzburg: Konrad Triltsch, 1940).

Netzle, Hans, *Das süddeutsche Wander-Marionettentheater* (Munich: Filser, 1938).

Niessen, Carl, *Shakespeare auf der deutschen Bühne: eine Ausstellung zur 2. deutschen Shakespeare-Woche* (Bochum: no publ., 1937).

—— *Deutsches Theater und Immermanns Vermächtnis*, Die Schaubühne: Quellen und Forschungen zur Theatergeschichte, 35 (Emsdetten: H. & J. Lechte, 1940).

—— *Die deutsche Oper der Gegenwart* (Regensburg: Gustav Bosse, 1944).

Ongyerth, Gust, ed., *10 Jahre Landestheater der Deutschen Volksgruppe in Rumänien* (Sibiu: Landestheater, 1942).

Ortloff, Alfred, 'Heinrich von Kleist und das deutsche Nationaldrama' (unpublished doctoral thesis, University of Würzburg, 1935).

Paul Ernst und das Drama (Langensalza: Beltz/Jahrbuch der Paul-Ernst-Gesellschaft, 1939).

Perger, Arnulf, *Die Wandlung der dramatischen Auffassung* (Berlin: Elsner, 1936).

—— *Probleme des Theaters*, Wissenschaft und Volk, 3 (Prague: Noebe, 1944).

Petersen, Julius, *Geschichtsdrama und nationaler Mythos: Grenzfragen zur Gegenwartsform des Dramas* (Stuttgart: Metzler, 1940).

Petsch, Robert, 'Drei Haupttypen des Dramas', *Deutsche Vierteljahrsschrift*, 12 (1934), 210–44.

—— 'Die Darbietungsformen der dramatischen Dichtung', *Germanisch-Romanische Monatsschrift*, 23 (1935), 321–48.

Petzet, Wolfgang, *Otto Falckenberg: mein Leben – mein Theater: nach Gesprächen und Dokumenten aufgezeichnet* (Munich: Zinnen-Verlag, 1944).

Pfeiffer, Arthur, *Ursprung und Gestalt des Dramas: Studien zu einer Phänomenologie der Dichtkunst und Morphologie des Dramas* (Berlin: Junker und Dünnhaupt, 1943).

Pfitzenreiter, Werner, ed., *Das Theater des Führers: Festschrift anläßlich der Weihe des Gautheaters Saarpfalz am 9 Otk. 1938 zu Saarbrücken* (Saarbrücken: NSZ-Rheinfront, 1938).

Pilger, Else, 'George Bernard Shaw in Deutschland' (unpublished doctoral thesis, University of Münster, 1940).

Pirklbauer, Franz, 'Richard Billinger: Dramen und Brauchtum' (unpublished doctoral thesis, University of Vienna, 1940).

Poensgen, Wolfgang, *Der deutsche Bühnen-Spielplan im Weltkriege* (Berlin: Gesellschaft für Theatergeschichte, 1934).

Raabe, August, *Goethes Sendung im Dritten Reich* (Bonn: Röhrscheid, 1934).

Raabe, Peter, *Die Musik im dritten Reich: Kulturpolitische Reden und Aufsätze* (Regensburg: Gustav Bosse, 1935).

—— *Kulturwille im deutschen Musikleben: Kulturpolitische Reden und Aufsätze* (Regensburg: Gustav Bosse, 1936).

Raeck, Kurt, ed., *Heinrich George: 25 Jahre Schauspieler* (Berlin: Berek, 1937).

Raupp, Wilhelm, *Max von Schillings: der Kampf eines deutschen Künstlers* (Hamburg: Hanseatische Verlagsanstalt, 1935).

Redder, Joachim, 'Die Führung und Verwaltung des Theaters nach dem neuen deutschen Theaterrecht' (unpublished doctoral thesis, University of Leipzig, 1938).

Reichsministerium für Volksaufklärung und Propaganda, Abteilung Schrifttum, *Verzeichnis englischer und nordamerikanischer Schriftsteller* (Leipzig: Verlag des Börsenvereins, 1942).

Reinemer, Edith, 'Form und Stil in den Werken Richard Billingers' (unpublished doctoral thesis, University of Vienna, 1940).

Renner, Hans, *Die Wunderwelt der Oper: der große Führer durch die Oper und die klassische Operette* (Berlin: Vier Falken-Verlag, 1938).

Resch, H., 'Zum Kampf um die Tragödie', *Zeitschrift für deutsche Kulturphilosophie*, 7 (1941), 63–73.

Riecke, Heinz, *Gruppenspiele als volkskulturelle Aufgabe* (Hamburg: Hamburger Verlagsanstalt, 1934).

Riedel, Richard, *Neues Weltbild und Lebendiges Theater*, Deutsche Entscheidungen, 3 (Potsdam: Protte, 1933).

Riesen, Gerhard, *Die Erziehungsfunktion der Theaterkritik*, Neue Deutsche Forschungen: Abteilung Neuere Deutsche Literaturgeschichte, 5 (Berlin: Junker und Dünnhaupt, 1935).

Rock, Christa Maria, and Hans Brückner, eds, *Judentum und Musik: mit dem ABC jüdischer und nichtarischer Musikbeflissener* (Munich: Hans Brückner, 1936).

Rosenberg, Alfred, *Gestaltung der Idee: Reden und Aufsätze von 1933–1935* (Munich: Franz Eher, 1936); 15th edn (Munich: Franz Eher, 1943).

—— ed., *Dietrich Eckart: ein Vermächtnis* (Munich: Zentralverlag der NSDAP, 1938).

—— *Der Mythus des 20. Jahrhunderts: eine Wertung der seelisch-geistigen Gestaltenkämpfe unserer Zeit*, 147th–148th edn (Munich: Hoheneichen, 1939).

Rothe, Hans, *Der Kampf um Shakespeare* (Leipzig: List, 1936).

Ruppel, Karl H., *Berliner Schauspiel: dramaturgische Betrachtungen: 1936 bis 1942* (Berlin: Paul Neff, 1943).

Saxer, Christoph P., 'Dietrich Eckarts Interpretation des *Peer Gynt*' (unpublished doctoral thesis, University of Vienna, 1940).

Schiedermair, Ludwig, *Die deutsche Oper: Grundzüge ihres Werdens und Wesens*, 2nd edn (Bonn: Dümmler, 1940).

Schiller, Friedrich, *Der Weg zur Vollendung: Erkenntnisse, Betrachtungen, Anweisungen*, ed. by Hartfrid Voss (Ebenhausen bei München: Langewiesche-Brandt, 1938).

Schlamp, Hans Joachim, *Hans Albers* (Berlin: Robert Mölich, 1939).

—— *Karl Ludwig Diehl* (Berlin: Robert Mölich, 1939).

—— *Willy Birgel* (Berlin: Robert Mölich, 1939).

Schlösser, Rainer, *Das Volk und seine Bühne: Bemerkungen zum Aufbau des deutschen Theaters* (Berlin: Langen/Müller, 1935).

—— *Politik und Drama* (Berlin: Verlag Zeitgeschichte, 1935).

—— *Grabbes Vermächtnis*, Westfalen-Bücher, 10 (Münster: Coppenrath, 1937).

Schlötermann, Heinz, *Das deutsche Weltkriegsdrama 1919 bis 1937, eine wertkritische Analyse*, 'Das Nationaltheater': Schriftenreihe des Theaterwissenschaftlichen Instituts der Friedrich-Schiller-Universität Jena, 2 (Würzburg: Konrad Triltsch, 1939).

Schlötermann-Kuffner, Liselotte, *Erwin Guido Kolbenheyers 'Dritte Bühne'*, 'Das Nationaltheater': Schriftenreihe des Theaterwissenschaftlichen Instituts der Friedrich-Schiller-Universität Jena, 1 (Würzburg: Konrad Triltsch, 1939); 2nd edn (Würzburg: Konrad Triltsch, 1944).

Schmidt-Leonhardt, Hans, *Die Reichskulturkammer* (Berlin: Spaeth & Linde, 1936).

Schneider, Hans, 'Der Tragiker Paul Ernst in der Reihe seiner Dramen *Demetrios* bis *Brunhild*: Versuch einer Würdigung vom Standpunkt nationalsozialistischer Weltanschauung' (unpublished doctoral thesis, University of Münster, 1935).

Scholtze, Johannes, *Opernführer: Oper, Operette, Ballet, Schauspielmusik* (Leipzig: J. Dörner, 1935).

Schrade, Hubert, *Bauten des Dritten Reiches* (Leipzig: Bibliographisches Institut, 1937).

Schramm, Wilhelm von, *Die Theaterkritik im neuen Deutschland*, Schriftenreihe des Theater-Tageblatts, 2 (Berlin: Theater-Tageblatt, 1933).

Schrieber, Karl-Friedrich, *Die Reichskulturkammer: Organisation und Ziele der deutschen Kulturpolitik* (Berlin: Junker und Dünnhaupt, 1934).

—— ed., Das Recht der Reichskulturkammer, 5 vols (Berlin: Junker und Dünnhaupt, 1935).

Schrott, Ludwig, *Hans Pfitzner, Leben und Werk* (Berlin-Halensee: M. Hesse, n.d.).

Schuberth, Ottmar, *Rahmen- oder Raum-Bühne, höfisches oder Volks-Theater?* (Munich: Callwey, 1940).

Schultz, Wolfgang, *Grundgedanken nationalsozialistischer Kulturpolitik* (Munich: Franz Eher, 1939).

Schultze, Hermann, *Das deutsche Jugendtheater* (Leipzig: A. Strauch, 1941).

Schulz, Friedrich Ernst, *Dramen-Lexikon* (Berlin: Drei Masken, 1941).

—— *Nachtrag I zum Dramen-Lexikon, Herbst 1942* (Berlin: Drei Masken, 1942).

—— *Nachtrag II zum Dramen-Lexikon, Frühjahr 1944* (Berlin: Drei Masken, 1944).

Schulz-Heising, Otto, *Handpuppenspiel in der Kriegsmarine* (Potsdam: Voggenreiter, 1944).

Schum, Alexander, ed., *Künstlerbuch der Sächsischen Staatstheater* (Dresden: [Staatstheater], [1934]).

Schumann, Otto, *Meyers Opernbuch*, 2nd edn (Leipzig: Bibliographisches Institut, 1936).

—— *Geschichte der deutschen Musik* (Leipzig: Bibliographisches Institut, 1940).

Seelig, Ludwig, *Geschäftstheater oder Kulturtheater?* (Berlin: Reichsverband Deutscher Bühnenangehörigen, [1935]).

Seitz, Franz, 'Drama und Spiel', *Volk im Werden*, 4 (1936), 587–96.

—— 'Zur Kritik des Dramas', *Die Tat*, 30 (1939), 832–41.

Sellmair, Joseph, 'Katharsis oder der Sinn der Tragödie', *Zeitschrift für deutsche Geisteswissenschaft*, 1 (1938–39), 269–79.

Sengle, Friedrich, 'Vom Absoluten in der Tragödie', *Deutsche Vierteljahrsschrift*, 20 (1942), 265–72.

Sievers, Heinrich, Albert Trapp and Alexander Schum, *250 Jahre Braunschweigisches Staatstheater 1690–1940* (Braunschweig: E. Appelhans, 1941).

Sievert, Ludwig, *Lebendiges Theater: drei Jahrzehnte deutscher Theaterkunst* (Munich: Bruckmann, 1944).

Skraup, Siegmund, *Die Oper als lebendiges Theater*, 'Das Nationaltheater': Schriftenreihe des Theaterwissenschaftlichen Instituts der Friedrich-Schiller-Universität Jena, 10 (Würzburg: Konrad Triltsch, 1942).

Stang, Walter, *Grundlagen nationalsozialistischer Kulturpflege* (Berlin: Junker und Dünnhaupt, 1935).

—— *Weltanschauung und Kunst (Grundlagen nationalsozialistischer Kulturpflege 2)* (Berlin: Junker und Dünnhaupt, 1937).

Staudinger, Friedrich, 'Die berufsständische Idee des Bühnenkünstlers in ihrer Entwicklung' (unpublished doctoral thesis, University of Heidelberg, 1935).

Stein, Irmgard von, *Wir vom Fronttheater* (Berlin: Scherl, 1937).

Stemmle, Robert A., *Die Zuflöte: Theater- und Filmanekdoten* (Berlin: Herbig, 1940).

Stemplinger, Eduard, *Von berühmten Schauspielern: Anekdoten aus authentischen Quellen gesammelt* (Munich: Piper, 1939).

Stengel, Theo, and Herbert Gerigk, eds, *Lexikon der Juden in der Musik* (Berlin: Bernhard Hahnemann, 1940).

Stigler-Fuchs, Margarete, *Wiener Theater vor und hinter den Kulissen* (Vienna: Andermann, 1943).

Strantz, Ferdinand von, *Opernführer*, rev. by Walter Abdendroth (Berlin: Weichert, 1935).

Straub, Agnes, *Im Wirbel des neuen Jahrhunderts* (Heidelberg: Hüthig, 1942).

Stroedel, Wolfgang, *Shakespeare auf der deutschen Bühne: vom Ende des Weltkrieges bis zur Gegenwart*, Schriften der Deutschen Shakespeare Gesellschaft, NF, 2 (Weimar: Böhlau, 1938).

Stumpfl, Robert, *Unser Kampf um ein deutsches Nationaltheater* (Berlin: Junker und Dünnhaupt, 1935).

—— *Kultspiele der Germanen als Ursprung des mittelalterlichen Dramas* (Berlin: Junker und Dünnhaupt, 1936).

Thomas, Walter, ed., *Festschrift zur zweiten deutschen Shakespeare-Woche: Bochum 1937* (Bochum: Schürmann & Klagges, 1937).

—— *Vom Drama unserer Zeit* (Leipzig: Max Beck, 1938).

Tieche, Edouard, *Thespis* (Leipzig: Teubner, 1933).

Türk, Franz, ed., *Sprechchöre für die nationalsozialistische Deutsche Schule* (Frankfurt am Main: Moritz Diesterweg, 1935).

Vonden, Hubert, 'Die weltanschaulichen Grundlagen des ernsten Dramas unserer Zeit: Untersucht am Beispiel verschiedener Dramen von Paul Ernst, Ernst Bacmeister, Erwin Guido Kolbenheyer und Curt Langenbeck' (unpublished doctoral thesis, University of Hamburg, 1945).

Vowinckel, Hans August, *Schiller, der Dichter der Geschichte: eine Auslegung des 'Wallenstein'*, Neue Deutsche Forschung: Abteilung: Neuere deutsche Literaturgeschichte, 16 (Berlin: Junker und Dünnhaupt, 1938).

Waldmann, Guido, ed., *Rasse und Musik* (Berlin: Vieweg, 1939).

Walz, Josef, 'Reichsverfassung und Zensur' (unpublished doctoral thesis, University of Heidelberg, 1933).

Walzel, Oskar, 'Vom Wesen des Tragischen', *Euphorion*, 34 (1933), 1–37.

Wanderscheck, Hermann, *Deutsche Dramatik der Gegenwart* (Berlin: Bong, 1938).

—— *Heinrich Zerkaulen* (Munich: Deutscher Volksverlag, 1939).

—— *Dramaturgische Appassionata* (Leipzig: Max Beck, [1943]).

Watzinger, Carl H., 'Die theatralische Sendung der jungen Generation', *Klingsor*, 10 (1933), 268–9.

Wehner, Josef Magnus, *Vom Glanz und Leben deutscher Bühne: eine Münchner Dramaturgie: Aufsätze und Kritiken, 1933–1941* (Hamburg: Hanseatische Verlagsanstalt, 1944).

Weinschenk, Harry E., *Wir von Bühne und Film* (Berlin: Wilhelm Limpert, 1939).

—— *Schauspieler erzählen* (Berlin: Wilhelm Limpert, 1941).

—— *Unser Weg zum Theater* (Berlin: Wilhelm Limpert, 1942).

Weller, Maximilian, *Die fünf grossen Dramenvorleser: zur Stilkunde und Kulturgeschichte des deutschen Dichtungsvortrags von 1800–1880*, 'Das Nationaltheater': Schriftenreihe des Theaterwissenschaftlichen Instituts der Friedrich-Schiller-Universität Jena, 3 (Würzburg: Konrad Triltsch, 1939).

Welter, Friedrich, *Führer durch die Opern* (Leipzig: Hachmeister und Thal, 1937).

Werkhäuser, Fritz Richard, ed., *150 Jahre Theater der Stadt Koblenz* (Koblenz: Stadt Koblenz, 1937).

Westerhagen, Curt von, *Richard Wagners Kampf gegen seelische Fremdherrschaft* (Munich: Lehmann, 1935).

Wichmann, Heinz, *Der neue Opernführer* (Berlin: P. Franke, 1936); 8th edn (Berlin: P. Franke, 1943).

Wiedeburg, Paul H., 'Dietrich Eckart' (unpublished doctoral thesis, University of Hamburg, 1939).

Wiese, Benno von, *Die Dramen Schillers: Politik und Tragödie*, Meyers kleine Handbücher, 12 (Leipzig: Bibliographisches Institut, 1938).

—— 'Geschichte und Drama', *Deutsche Vierteljahrsschrift*, 20 (1942), 412–34.

Wieser, Gertrud, 'Wilhelm von Scholz' Nachdichtungen des Calderón' (unpublished doctoral thesis, University of Vienna, 1939).

Wigman, Mary, *Deutsche Tanzkunst* (Dresden: Carl Reissner, 1935).

Winterstein, Eduard von, *Mein Leben und meine Zeit: ein halbes Jahrhundert deutscher Theatergeschichte* (Berlin: Arnold, 1942).

Zander, Otto, and Walter Thomas, eds, *Dramatiker der Hitler-Jugend: Sonderheft zur Theaterwoche der Hitler-Jugend verbunden mit einer Reichstheatertagung der Theater-Jugend vom 11.–18. April* (Bochum: Schürmann & Klagges, 1937).

Ziegenspeck, Erich, 'Das Drama: eine Hochform politischer Dichtung', *Politische Erziehung*, 1 (1933–34), 354–7.

Ziegler, Hans S., *Das Theater des deutschen Volkes: ein Beitrag zur Volkserziehung und Propaganda* (Leipzig: Voigtländer, 1933).

—— *Wende und Weg: kulturpolitische Reden und Aufsätze* (Weimar: Fink, 1937).

—— *Entartete Musik: eine Abrechnung* (Düsseldorf: Völkischer Verlag, 1939).

Post-1945 secondary sources covering theatre, opera and dance in the Third Reich and related fields

A guide to further studies on individual dramatists can be found in Michael Patterson, *German Theatre: A Bibliography from the Beginning to 1995* (Leicester: Motley Press; New York: G. K. Hall, 1996).

Albert, Claudia, ed., *Deutsche Klassiker im Nationalsozialismus: Schiller: Kleist: Hölderlin* (Stuttgart: Metzler, 1994).

Albertsen, Leif Ludwig, 'Eduard Künneke im Dritten Reich', in *Idee, Gestalt, Geschichte: Festschrift Klaus von See: Studien zur europäischen Kulturtradition*, ed. by Gerd Wolfgang Weber (Odense: Odense University Press, 1988), pp. 563–603.

Alth, Minna von, ed., *Burgtheater, 1776–1976: Aufführungen und Besetzungen von zweihundert Jahren*, 2 vols (Vienna: Überreuter, 1979).

Altmeyer, Katrin, 'Das Theater in Saarbrücken in der Zeit des Nationalsozialismus' (unpublished Magisterarbeit, Free University of Berlin, 1991).

Appignanesi, Lisa, *The Cabaret* (London: Studio Vista, 1975), pp. 153–9.

Ashley, Tim, *Richard Strauss* (London: Phaidon, 1999).

Axt, Eva Maria, *Musikalische Form als Dramaturgie: Prinzipien eines Spätstils in der Oper 'Friedenstag' von Richard Strauss und Joseph Gregor* (Munich: Katzbuchler, 1989).

Bair, Henry, 'National Socialism and Opera: The Berlin Opera Houses, 1933–1939', *Opera*, 35 (1984), 17–23, 129–37.

Barbian, Jan-Pieter, *Literaturpolitik im 'Dritten Reich': Institutionen, Kompetenzen, Betätigungsfelder* (Frankfurt am Main: Buchhandler-Vereinigung, 1993).

Bartetzko, Dieter, *Illusionen in Stein: Stimmungsarchitektur im deutschen Faschismus: ihre Vorgeschichte in Theater- und Film-Bauten*, rororo, 7889 (Reinbek bei Hamburg: Rowohlt, 1985).

—— *Zwischen Zucht und Ekstase: zur Theatralik von NS-Architektur* (Berlin: Mann, 1985).

Baumgarten, Michael, 'Gerhart Hauptmann-Inszenierungen am Berliner Rose-Theater 1933–1944' (unpublished doctoral thesis, Free University of Berlin, 1991).

—— and Ruth Freydank, *Das Rose-Theater: ein Volkstheater im Berliner Osten 1906–1944*, Reihe deutsche Vergangenheit: Stätten der Geschichte Berlins, 64 (Berlin: Hentrich, 1991).

Baxmann, Inge, 'Tanz als Kulturkritik und Projekt der Gemeinschaftsbildung', in *Entre Locarno et Vichy: les relations culturelles franco-allemandes dans les années 1930*, ed. by Hans Manfred Bock, Reinhart Meyer-Kalkus and Michel Trebitsch, 2 vols (Paris: CNRS, 1993), I, 527–48.

Becker, Max, ed., *Rudolf Wagner-Régeny: an den Ufern der Zeit: Schriften, Briefe, Tagebücher* (Leipzig: Reclam, 1989).

Becker, Paul W., 'Der Dramatiker Dietrich Eckart: ein Beitrag zur Dramatik des Dritten Reiches' (unpublished doctoral thesis, University of Cologne, 1970).

Bellmann, Günther, *Schauspielhausgeschichten: 250 Jahre Theater und Musik auf dem Berliner Gendarmenmarkt* (Berlin: Christoph Links, 1993).

Berglund, Gisela, *Der Kampf um den Leser im Dritten Reich: die Literaturpolitik der 'Neuen Literatur' (Will Vesper) und der 'Nationalsozialistischen Monatshefte'*, Deutsches Exil 1933–45, 11 (Worms: Heintz, 1980).

Birkin, Kenneth, 'Friedenstag' and 'Daphne': An Interpretative Study of the Literature and Dramatic Sources of Two Operas by Richard Strauss (New York: Garland, 1989).

Birmans, Manfred, Oecher Schängche: Geschichte des Aachener Puppenspiels von der Gründung bis zum Ende des Dritten Reiches (Aachen: Alano, 1990).

Blunden, Allan, Thomas Mann: Pro and Contra Wagner (Chicago: University of Chicago Press, 1985).

Bochow, Jörg, 'Berliner Theater im Dritten Reich: repräsentative Ästhetik oder/und "Bewahrer kultureller Werte"?: Linien und Brüche der Moderne im Berliner Theater der dreißiger Jahre', in Berliner Theater im 20. Jahrhundert, ed. by Erika Fischer-Lichte, Doris Kolesch and Christel Weiler (Berlin: Fannei & Walz, 1998), pp. 147–69.

Boeswald, Alfred, Werner Egk (Tutzing: Schneider, 1997).

Bohlmeier, Gerd, 'Kasper, Jude, Kdf-Kulturpolitik und Puppentheater', in Deutsche Kunst: 1933–1945 in Braunschweig: Kunst im Nationalsozialismus, ed. by Städtisches Museum Braunschweig and Hochschule für Bildende Künste Braunschweig, exhibition catalogue (Hildesheim: Georg Olms), pp. 83–5.

Bollmus, Reinhard, Das Amt Rosenberg und seine Gegner: Studien zum Machtkampf im nationalsozialistischen Herrschaftssystem (Stuttgart: Deutsche Verlags-Anstalt, 1970).

Bortenschläger, Wilhelm, Der unbekannte Billinger (Innsbruck: Wagner, 1985).

Boyden, Matthew, Richard Strauss: The Conquest of Conscience (London: Weidenfeld and Nicolson, 1999).

Brenner, Hildegard, Die Kunstpolitik des Nationalsozialismus (Reinbek bei Hamburg: Rowohlt Taschenbuch, 1963).

Breßlein, Erwin, Völkisch-faschistoides und nationalsozialistisches Drama: Kontinuitäten und Differenzen (Frankfurt am Main: Haag & Herchen, 1980).

Broer, Werner, and Detlev Kopp, eds, Grabbe im Dritten Reich: zum nationalsozialistischen Grabbe-Kult (Bielefeld: Aisthesis, 1986).

Brosche, Günter, ed., Briefwechsel Richard Strauss-Clemens Krauss (Tutzing: Schneider, 1997).

Buchholtz, Wolfhard, 'Die nationalsozialistische Gemeinschaft Kraft durch Freude' (unpublished doctoral thesis, University of Munich, 1976).

Büdel, Oscar, 'Pirandello sulla scena tedesca', Quaderni del Piccolo Teatro della Città di Milano, 1 (1961), 99–122.

Bumm, Peter H., Drama und Theater der konservativen Revolution (Munich: UNI-Druck, 1971).

Busch, Rolf, Imperialistische und faschistische Kleist-Rezeption 1890–1945 (Frankfurt am Main: Akademische Verlagsgesellschaft, 1974).

Busch, Stefan, 'Und gestern, da hörte uns Deutschland': NS-Autoren in der Bundesrepublik: Kontinuität und Diskontinuität bei Friedrich Griese, Werner Beumelburg, Eberhard Wolfgang Möller und Kurt Ziesel, Studien zur Literatur- und Kulturgeschichte, 13 (Würzburg: Königshausen & Neumann, 1998).

Butzlaff, Wolfgang, 'Nazismo e seconda guerra mondiale nel teatro tedesco', Ponte, 22 (1966), 370–87.

Cadigan, Rufus J., 'Richard Billinger, Hanns Johst, and Eberhard W. Möller: Three Representative National Socialist Playwrights' (unpublished doctoral thesis, University of Kansas, 1979).

Cahn, Peter, and Wolfgang Osthoff, eds, Hans Pfitzner: das Herz und der Übergang zum Spätwerk (Tutzing: Schneider, 1997).

Cepl-Kaufmann, Gertrude, Winfried Hartkopf and Winrich Meiszies, eds, *Bilanz Düsseldorf '45: Kultur und Gesellschaft von 1933 bis in die Nachkriegszeit* (Düsseldorf: Grupello, 1992).

Černý, František, '*Weh' dem, der lügt!* und *Der Traum ein Leben* in den Inszenierungen des Prager Nationaltheaters zur Zeit der nazistischen Okkupation', in '*Stichwort Grillparzer*', ed. by Hilde Haider-Pregler and Evelyn Deutsch-Schreiner, Grillparzer Forum, 1 (Vienna: Böhlau, 1994), pp. 159–70.

Claussen, Horst, and Norbert Oellers, eds, *Beschädigtes Erbe: Beiträge zur Klassikerrezeption in finsterer Zeit*, Schriften des Arbeitskreises selbständiger Kultur-Institute, 1 (Bonn: Bouvier, 1984).

Clemons, Leigh, 'Gewalt, Gott, Natur, Volk: The Performance of Nazi Ideology in Kolbenheyer's *Gregor und Heinrich*', in *Essays on Twentieth-Century German Drama and Theater: An American Reception (1977–1999)*, ed. by Hal H. Rennert (Berne: Lang, forthcoming).

Cometa, Michele, *Il teatro di Pirandello in Germania* (Palermo: Novecento, 1986).

Creyghton, Job, 'Toneel en ideologie in nationaalsocialistisch Duitsland', in Hana Bobková and others, *Scenarium, 6: Toneel in crisis- en bezettingstijd* (Zutphen: De Waldburg Pers, 1982), pp. 9–22.

Cuomo, Glenn R., ' "Saint Joan before the Cannibals": George Bernard Shaw in the Third Reich', *German Studies Review*, 16 (1993), 435–61.

—— ed., *National Socialist Cultural Policy* (New York: St Martin's Press, 1995).

Daiber, Hans, *Gerhart Hauptmann oder der letzte Klassiker* (Vienna: Molden, 1971).

—— *Deutsches Theater seit 1945: Bundesrepublik Deutschland, Deutsche Demokratische Republik, Österreich, Schweiz* (Stuttgart: Reclam, 1976).

—— *Schaufenster der Diktatur: Theater im Machtbereich Hitlers* (Stuttgart: Günther Neske, 1995).

Demange, Camille, 'Le Théâtre allemand et la deuxième guerre mondiale', in *Le Théâtre moderne, II: Depuis la deuxième guerre mondiale* (Paris: Centre National de la Recherche Scientifique, 1967), pp. 201–8.

Denkler, Horst, and Eberhard Lämmert, eds, '*Das war ein Vorspiel nur ...*': Berliner Colloquium zur Literaturpolitik im '*Dritten Reich*', Schriftenreihe der Akademie der Künste, [16] (Berlin: Akademie der Künste, 1985).

Denkler, Horst, and Karl Prümm, eds, *Die deutsche Literatur im Dritten Reich: Themen, Traditionen, Wirkungen* (Stuttgart: Reclam, 1976).

Detig, Christian, *Deutsche Kunst, deutsche Nation: der Komponist Max von Schillings* (Kassel: Gustav Bosse, 1998).

Deutsch-Schreiner, Evelyn, 'Die verlorene Heldin: Frauenbilder und Schauspielerinnen in der Aufführungspraxis des Deutschen Volkstheaters Wien 1938–1944', *Maske und Kothurn*, 37: *Festschrift für Margret Dietrich* (1991), 327–53.

—— 'Der "vierfach männliche Blick" auf die Frau: das Frauenbild auf der Bühne im nationalsozialistischen Deutschland', *Zeitschrift für Literaturwissenschaft und Linguistik*, 24, no. 95 (1994), 91–105.

—— ' "Blonde Mütter für das Reich?": zum Bild der Mutter auf dem NS-Theater', in *Verklärt, verkitscht, vergessen: die Mutter als ästhetische Figur*, ed. by Renate Möhrmann (Stuttgart: Metzler, 1996), pp. 242–60.

—— 'Das Theater im "Reichskanzleistil": Aspekte zur NS-Bühnenästhetik in Österreich', in *Macht—Literatur—Krieg: österreichische Literatur im Nationalsozialismus*, ed. by Uwe Baur and others, Fazit, 2 (Vienna: Böhlau, 1998), pp. 346–56.

—— 'Theater im Schatten der Gewaltherrschaft: innere Emigration an österreichischen

Theatern', in *Literatur der 'Inneren Emigration' aus Österreich*, ed. by Johann Holzner and Karl Müller, Zwischenwelt, 6 (Vienna: Döcker, 1998), pp. 295–312.

Diller, Ansgar, *Die Rundfunkpolitik im Dritten Reich*, dtv, 3184 (Munich: Deutscher Taschenbuch Verlag, 1980).

Dittmer, Frank, 'Freilufttheater: Dramatisches ohne Dach im 20. Jahrhundert: dargestellt an Berliner Beispielen' (unpublished doctoral thesis, Free University of Berlin, 1991).

Döhl, Reinhard, *Das Hörspiel zur NS-Zeit: Geschichte und Typologie des Hörspiels* (Darmstadt: Wissenschaftliche Buchgesellschaft, 1992).

Dreifuss, Alfred, *Deutsches Theater Berlin: Schumannstraße 13a: Fünf Kapitel aus der Geschichte einer Schauspielbühne* ([East] Berlin: Henschel, 1987).

Drewniak, Bogusław, *Das Theater im NS-Staat: Szenarium deutscher Zeitgeschichte 1933–1945* (Düsseldorf: Droste, 1983).

Dultz, Michael, 'Der Aufbau der nationalsozialistischen Thingspielorganisation 1933/34', in Henning Eichberg and others, *Massenspiele: NS-Thingspiele, Arbeiterweihespiel und olympisches Zeremoniell*, Problemata, 58 (Stuttgart: Frommann-Holzboog, 1977), pp. 203–34.

Dümling, Albrecht, and Peter Girth, eds, *Entartete Musik: eine kommentierte Rekonstruktion* (Düsseldorf: Kleinherne, 1988).

Dunzinger, Christian, 'Staatliche Eingriffe in das Theater von 1934–1938 als Teil austrofaschistischer Kulturpolitik' (unpublished Diplomarbeit, University of Vienna, 1995).

Dussel, Konrad, 'Theatergeschichte der NS-Zeit unter sozialgeschichtlichem Aspekt: Ergebnisse und Perspektiven der Forschung', *Neue politische Literatur*, 32 (1987), 233–45.

—— *Ein neues, ein heroisches Theater?: Nationalsozialistische Theaterpolitik und ihre Auswirkungen in der Provinz*, Literatur und Wirklichkeit, 26 (Bonn: Bouvier, 1988).

—— 'Von Bert Brecht zu Hanns Johst?: deutsches Provinztheater 1918–1944 im Spiegel seiner Spielpläne', *Universitas*, 43 (1988), 976–89.

—— 'Provinztheater in der NS-Zeit', *Vierteljahrshefte für Zeitgeschichte*, 38 (1990), 75–111.

Eckardt, Jo-Jacqueline, *Lessing's 'Nathan the Wise' and the Critics: 1779–1991* (Columbia, SC: Camden House, 1993).

Egk, Werner, *Musik- Wort- Bild: Texte und Anmerkungen: Betrachtungen und Gedanken* (Munich: Langen Müller, 1960).

—— *Die Zeit wartet nicht* (Mainz: Wilhelm Goldmann, 1971).

Ehrlich, Lothar, 'Eine völkische Wiedergeburt: zur faschistischen Grabbe-Rezeption', in *Traditionen und Traditionssuche des deutschen Faschismus*, ed. by Günter Hartung and Hubert Orlowski (Halle/Saale: Wissenschaftspublizistik der Martin-Luther-Universität Halle-Wittenberg, 1983), pp. 146–65.

—— 'Zur Rezeption der Dramaturgie Schillers durch faschistische Dramatiker am Beispiel von Curt Langenbeck', in *Traditionen und Traditionssuche des deutschen Faschismus*, ed. by Günter Hartung and Hubert Orlowski, Seria Filologia Germanska, 29 (Poznań: Adam Mickiewicz University Press, 1988), pp. 29–40.

——, Jürgen John and Justus H. Ulbricht, eds, *Das Dritte Weimar: Klassik und Kultur im Nationalsozialismus* (Cologne: Böhlau, 1999).

Eichberg, Henning, 'Das nationalsozialistische Thingspiel: Massentheater im Faschismus und Arbeiterkultur', *Ästhetik und Kommunikation*, no. 26 (July 1976), 60–9.

—— 'The Nazi *Thingspiel*: Theater for the Masses in Fascism and Proletarian Culture', *New German Critique*, 11 (1977), 133–50.

—— and others, *Massenspiele: NS-Thingspiele, Arbeiterweihespiel und olympisches Zeremoniell*, Problemata, 58 (Stuttgart: Frommann-Holzboog, 1977).

Eicher, Thomas, 'Theater im "Dritten Reich": eine Spielplananalyse der deutschen Schauspieltheater 1929–1944' (unpublished doctoral thesis, Free University of Berlin, 1992).

Erdmann, Ulrich, *Vom Naturalismus zum Nationalsozialismus?: zeitgeschichtlich-biographische Studien zu Max Halbe, Gerhart Hauptmann, Johannes Schlaf und Hermann Stehr: mit unbekannten Selbstzeugnissen* (Frankfurt am Main: Lang, 1997).

Euler, Friederike, 'Theater zwischen Anpassung und Widerstand: die Münchner Kammerspiele im Dritten Reich', in *Bayern in der NS-Zeit*, ed. by Martin Broszat and others, 6 vols (Munich: Oldenbourg, 1977–83), II: *Herrschaft und Gesellschaft im Konflikt* (1979), pp. 91–173.

Faber, Christiane, and Walburga Steinki, 'Unterhaltung um 1933: Berliner Kabarett und Varieté', in *Projekt: Spurensicherung: Alltag und Widerstand im Berlin der 30er Jahre*, ed. by Karl-Heinz Breidt and others, exhibition catalogue (Berlin: Elefanten Press, 1983), pp. 227–52.

Feldens, Fritz, *75 Jahre Städtische Bühnen Essen: Geschichte des Essener Theaters 1892–1967* (Essen: Rheinisch-Westfälische Verlagsgesellschaft, 1967).

Fetting, Hugo, *Die Geschichte der Deutschen Staatsoper* (Berlin: Werbung Berolina, 1955).

Fiedler, Ralph, *Die späten Dramen Gerhart Hauptmanns: Versuch einer Deutung* (Munich: Bergstadtverlag, 1954).

Fischli, Bruno, *Die Deutschen-Dämmerung: zur Genealogie des völkisch-faschistischen Dramas und Theaters (1897–1933)*, Literatur und Wirklichkeit, 16 (Bonn: Bouvier, 1976).

—— 'Zur Herausbildung von Formen faschistischer Öffentlichkeit in der Weimarer Republik', in *Die Weimarer Republik*, ed. by Kunstamt Kreuzberg, Berlin, and Institut für Theaterwissenschaften, University of Cologne, exhibition catalogue (Berlin: Elefanten Press, 1977), pp. 891–922.

Fontana, Oskar M., *Das große Welttheater: Theaterkritiken 1909–1967*, selected by Paul Wimmer (Vienna: Amalthea, 1976).

Freydank, Ruth, *Theater in Berlin: von den Anfängen bis 1945* ([East] Berlin: Argon, 1988).

Friedländer, Saul, and Jörn Rüsen, eds, *Richard Wagner im Dritten Reich: ein Schloß Elmau-Symposion*, Beck'sche Reihe, 1356 (Munich: Beck, 2000).

Fritsch-Vivié, Gabriele, *Mary Wigman*, Rowohlts Monographien, 50597 (Reinbek bei Hamburg: Rowohlt, 1999).

Fröhlich, Elke, 'Die kulturpolitische Pressekonferenz des Reichspropagandaministeriums', *Vierteljahrshefte für Zeitgeschichte*, 22 (1974), 347–81.

Fulfs, Ingo, *Musiktheater im Nationalsozialismus* (Marburg: Tectum, 1995).

Fuller, Steven N., *The Nazis' Literary Grandfather: Adolf Bartels and Cultural Extremism, 1871–1945*, Studies in Modern German Literature, 62 (New York: Lang, 1996).

Funke, Christoph, and Dieter Kranz, *Theaterstadt Berlin* ([East] Berlin: Henschel, 1978).

—— and Wolfgang Jansen, *Theater am Schiffbauerdamm: die Geschichte einer Berliner Bühne* (Berlin: Christoph Links, 1992).

Gadberry, Glen W., 'E. W. Möller and the National Drama of Nazi Germany: A Study of the *Thingspiel* and of Möller's *Das Frankenburger Würfelspiel*' (unpublished master's thesis, University of Wisconsin–Madison, 1972). Includes English translation of Möller's play (pp. 85–120).

—— 'Eberhard Wolfgang Möller's *Thingspiel Das Frankenburger Würfelspiel*', in Henning Eichberg and others, *Massenspiele: NS-Thingspiele, Arbeiterweihespiel und olympisches Zeremoniell*, Problemata, 58 (Stuttgart: Frommann-Holzboog, 1977), pp. 235–51.

—— 'The *Thingspiel* and *Das Frankenburger Würfelspiel*', *Drama Review*, 24, no. 1 (1980), 103–14.

—— 'Dramatic Contraries: The Paine Histories of Hanns Johst and Howard Fast', *Text and Presentation*, 9 (1989), 61–72.

—— '*The Stedingers*: Nazi Festival Drama of the Destruction of a People', *Theatre History Studies*, 10 (1990), 105–26.

—— 'The Theatre of the Third Reich: Issues and Concerns', in *Nordic Theatre Studies: Special International Issue: New Directions in Theatre Research: Proceedings of the XIth FIRT/IFTR Congress, Stockholm, 1989*, ed. by Willmar Sueter (Copenhagen: Munksgaard, 1990), pp. 75–8.

—— 'The Black Medeas of Weimar and Nazi Berlin: Jahnn-Straub and Straub-Grillparzer', *Theatre Survey*, 33, no. 2 (November 1992), 154–66.

—— ed., *Theatre in the Third Reich, the Prewar Years: Essays on Theatre in Nazi Germany*, Contributions to the Study of World History, 49 (Westport, CT: Greenwood Press, 1995).

—— 'The Theater in and of the Third Reich: The German Stage *"in Extremis"*'; 'An "Ancient German Rediscovered" – The Third Reich History Play'; 'Stages of Reform: *Caroline Neuber/Die Neuberin* in the Third Reich'; 'Gerhart Hauptmann's *Ratten* (1911) at the Rose (1936)', in *Essays on Twentieth-Century German Drama and Theater: An American Reception (1977–1999)*, ed. by Hal H. Rennert (Berne: Lang, forthcoming).

Garten, H. F., *Modern German Drama* (London: Methuen, 1959).

Geisenheyner, Max, *Kulturgeschichte des Theaters: Volk und Drama* (Berlin: Safari, 1951).

George, David E. R., *Henrik Ibsen in Deutschland: Rezeption und Revision*, trans. by Heinz Arnold and Bernd Glasenapp (Göttingen: Vandenhoeck & Ruprecht, 1968).

Gerstinger, Heinz, 'Richard Billinger als Dramatiker' (unpublished doctoral thesis, University of Vienna, 1947).

Gilman, Sander, ed., *NS-Literaturtheorie: eine Dokumentation* (Frankfurt am Main: Athenäum, 1971).

Göbel, Helmut, 'Zum politischen Drama und Theater im Nationalsozialismus: Hanns Johsts *Schlageter* als politisches Märtyrerdrama und die nationalsozialistischen Massenveranstaltungen', in *Aspekte des politischen Theaters und Dramas von Calderón bis Georg Seidel: deutsch-französische Perspektiven*, ed. by Horst Turk and Jean-Marie Valentin, with Peter Langemeyer, Jahrbuch für internationale Germanistik, Reihe A: Kongreßberichte, 40 (Berne: Lang, 1996), pp. 269–88.

Goerden, Elmar, 'Shylock on the German Stage' (unpublished master's thesis, University of Rochester, New York, 1989).

Goertz, Heinrich, *Lachen und Heulen: Roman* (Munich: List, 1982).

Goltschnigg, Dietmar, 'Zur Ideologisierung der Literaturwissenschaft: am Beispiel Goethes', *Wirkendes Wort*, 28 (1978), 232–42.

—— ed., *Büchner im 'Dritten' Reich: Mystifikation–Gleichschaltung–Exil: eine Dokumentation* (Bielefeld: Aisthesis, 1990).

Gradl, Bergita, 'Rudolf Geck: Theaterkritiker der *FZ* 1898–1935' (unpublished doctoral thesis, Free University of Berlin, 1968).

Gräfe, Axel, 'Das Deutsche Schauspielhaus Hamburg 1929–1943/44' (unpublished Magisterarbeit, Free University of Berlin, 1992).

Graff, Sigmund, *Von S. M. zu N. S.: Erinnerungen eines Bühnenautors, 1900 bis 1945* (Munich: Welsermühl, 1963).

Gramberger, Tanja, 'Das Theater als Propagandainstrument des NS-Regimes am Beispiel der Städte Salzburg und Linz' (unpublished Diplomarbeit, University of Salzburg, 1996).

Grange, William, 'Ersatz Comedy in the Third Reich', in *Essays on Twentieth-Century German Drama and Theater: An American Reception (1977–1999)*, ed. by Hal H. Rennert (Berne: Lang, forthcoming).

Gregor-Dellin, Martin, *Richard Wagner: sein Leben, sein Werk, sein Jahrhundert* (Munich: Goldmann; Mainz: Schott, 1983).

Groborz, Franz, 'Das Staatstheater am Gendarmenmarkt und das Deutsche Theater zur Zeit des Nationalsozialismus', 2 vols (unpublished Magisterarbeit, Free University of Berlin, 1987).

Grossman-Vendrey, Susanna, with Felix Schneider, *Bayreuth in der deutschen Presse: Beiträge zur Rezeptionsgeschichte Richard Wagners und seiner Festspiele*, Arbeitsgemeinschaft 100 Jahre Bayreuther Festspiele, 10 (Regensburg: Gustav Bosse, 1977).

Grun, Bernard, *Kulturgeschichte der Operette* ([East] Berlin: Lied der Zeit Musikverlag, 1967).

Grunberger, Richard, *A Social History of the Third Reich* (Harmondsworth: Penguin, 1991), pp. 457–74. (Originally published in 1971)

Gschwendtner, Brigitte, 'Das Schauspiel des Hofer Theaters von 1933–1944' (unpublished Magisterarbeit, Free University of Berlin, 1991).

Guthke, Karl S., 'Der "König der Weimarer Republik": Gerhart Hauptmanns Rolle in der Öffentlichkeit zwischen Kaiserreich und Nazi-Regime', *Schweizer Monatshefte*, 61 (1981), 787–806.

Gutzeit, Jutta, 'Staatliches Schauspielhaus und Thalia-Theater in Hamburg 1939–1945' (unpublished Magisterarbeit, University of Hamburg, 1989).

Habicht, Werner, 'Shakespeare in the Third Reich', in *Anglistentag (1984, Passau)*, ed. by Manfred Pfister (Gießen: Hoffmann, 1985), pp. 194–204.

——— 'Shakespeare and Theatre Politics in the Third Reich', in *The Play Out of Context: Transferring Plays from Culture to Culture*, ed. by Hanna Scolnicov and Peter Holland (Cambridge: Cambridge University Press, 1989), pp. 110–20.

Hager, Alfred, 'Krieg und Theater nach den Spielplänen der Wiener Bühnen von 1938–1944' (unpublished doctoral thesis, University of Vienna, 1950).

Haider-Pregler, Hilde, 'Das Dritte Reich und das Theater', *Maske und Kothurn*, 17 (1971), 203–14.

——— and Beate Reiterer, eds, *Verspielte Zeit: österreichisches Theater der dreißiger Jahre* (Vienna: Picus, 1997).

Hammerschmidt, Ulrich, 'Theaterkritik im Dritten Reich' (unpublished Magisterarbeit, Friedrich-Alexander University of Erlangen-Nuremberg, 1989).

Happl, Doris, 'Theater zwischen Kult und Propaganda: Spielstil und Ideologie im Nationalsozialismus' (unpublished doctoral thesis, University of Vienna, 1989).

Hartung, Günter, 'Faschistische Tragiker im Verhältnis zu Schiller und Paul Ernst', in *Traditionen und Traditionssuche des deutschen Faschismus*, ed. by Günter Hartung and Hubert Orlowski, Seria Filologia Germanska, 29 (Poznań: Adam Mickiewicz University Press, 1988), pp. 117–28.

Härtwig, Dieter, *Rudolf Wagner-Régeny: der Opernkomponist* ([East] Berlin: Henschel, 1965).

Heiber, Helmut, *Die Katacombe wird geschlossen* (Munich: Scherz, 1966).

Hein, Annette, '*Es ist viel "Hitler" in Wagner': Rassismus und antisemitische Deutschtumsideologie in den 'Bayreuther Blättern' (1878 bis 1938)*, Conditio Judaica, 13 (Tübingen: Niemeyer, 1996).

Heister, Hans-Werner, and Hans-Günter Klein, eds, *Musik und Musikpolitik im faschistischen Deutschland* (Frankfurt am Main: Fischer, 1984).

Henderson, Archibald, 'Shaw-Aufführungen in Deutschland von 1931/32 bis 1952', unpublished typescript, Institut für Theaterwissenschaft, Free University of Berlin, 1955.

Hennenberg, Fritz, *Es muß was Wunderbares sein. . .: Ralph Benatzky zwischen 'Weißem Rößl' und Hollywood* (Vienna: Zsolnay, 1998).

Hepp, Fred, 'Der geistige Widerstand im Kulturteil der *Frankfurter Zeitung* gegen die Diktatur des totalen Staates 1933–1943' (unpublished doctoral thesis, University of Munich, 1950).

Hernø, Leif, 'Das Thingspiel: Fragen zu seiner literarischen Untersuchung', *Text und Kontext*, 8 (1980), 337–52.

Hildebrand, Alexander, Eva Christina Vollmer and Karl Heinz Roland, *Theater in Wiesbaden 1765–1978* (Wiesbaden: Hessisches Staatstheater, 1978).

Hillesheim, Elisabeth, *Die Erschaffung des Märtyrers: das Bild Albert Leo Schlageters in der deutschen Literatur von 1923 bis 1945*, Studien zur deutschen Literatur des 19. und 20. Jahrhunderts, 26 (Frankfurt am Main: Lang, 1994).

Hillesheim, Jürgen, '*Heil Dir Führer! Führ uns an! . . .': der Augsburger Dichter Richard Euringer* (Würzburg: Königshausen & Neumann, 1995).

—— and Elisabeth Michael, *Lexikon Nationalsozialistischer Dichter: Biographien–Analysen–Bibliographien* (Würzburg: Königshausen & Neumann, 1993).

Hinck, Walter, *Das moderne Drama in Deutschland: vom expressionistischen zum dokumentarischen Theater* (Göttingen: Vandenhoeck & Ruprecht, 1973).

—— ed., *Handbuch des deutschen Dramas* (Düsseldorf: Bagel, 1980).

Hinüber, Georg von, 'Theaterleben im Dritten Reich am Beispiel des Kempter Stadttheaters' (1997), Net site: http://www.allgaeu.org/ag/material/facharb/theater/theater.htm

Hoffmann, Erich, 'Die "Gleichschaltung" des Flensburger Grenzlandtheaters und der szenische Untergang des "Landesverräters" Carsten Holm', in '*Wir bauen das Reich': Aufstieg und erste Herrschaftsjahre des Nationalsozialismus in Schleswig-Holstein*, ed. by Erich Hoffmann and Peter Wulf (Neumünster: Wachholtz, 1983), pp. 253–70.

Hoffmann, Paul Theodor, *Theater und Drama im deutschen Geistesschicksal*, Hamburger Theaterbücherei, 5 (Hamburg: Toth, 1948).

Holst, Renate, 'Die Württembergischen Staatstheater von 1933–1945' (unpublished Magisterarbeit, Free University of Berlin, 1990).

Höntsch, Winfried, and Ursula Püschel, eds, *300 Jahre Dresdner Staatstheater* ([East] Berlin: Henschel, 1967).

Hopster, Norbert, Petra Josting and Joachim Neuhaus, *Literaturlenkung im 'Dritten Reich': eine Bibliographie*, 2 vols (Hildesheim: Georg Olms, 1993–94).

Hortmann, Wilhelm, and Simon Williams, *Shakespeare on the German Stage*, 2 vols (Cambridge: Cambridge University Press, 1990–98), [II]: *The Twentieth Century* (by Hortmann, 1998), pp. 112–73.

Howe, Diane S., *Individuality and Expression: the Aesthetics of the New German Dance, 1901–1936*, New Studies in Aesthetics, 24 (New York: Lang, 1996).

Ihering, Herbert, *Berliner Dramaturgie* (Berlin: Aufbau Verlag, 1948).

—— *70 Jahre Deutsches Theater, 1883–1953* ([East] Berlin: VEB Berliner Bruckhaus, n.d.).

Jacobsen, Astrid, 'Möglichkeiten und Grenzen der politischen Meinungsbildung während des Dritten Reiches, dargestellt am publizistischen Medium des deutschsprachigen politischen Kabaretts' (unpublished doctoral thesis, University of Vienna, 1967).

Jelavich, Peter, *Berlin Cabaret* (Cambridge, MA: Harvard University Press, 1993).

Jeziorkowski, Klaus, 'Der getretene Schiller: zum Katalog der Ausstellung Klassiker in finsteren Zeiten 1933–1945', in Klaus Jeziorkowski, *Eine Iphigenie rauchend: Aufsätze und Feuilletons zur deutschen Tradition* (Frankfurt am Main: Suhrkamp, 1987), pp. 10–21.

Kabel, Rainer, and Peter Kröger, eds, *Theater in Deutschland 1928–1948: Materialien zur neueren Geschichte des deutschen Theaters* (Berlin: Presse- und Informationsstelle des Senders Freies Berlin, 1981).

Kahmann, Wolfgang, 'Das Gießener Stadttheater im Nationalsozialismus' (unpublished Diplomarbeit, University of Gießen, 1981).

Karasek-Langer, Alfred, and Josef Lanz, *Das deutsche Volksschauspiel in der Bukowina*, Schriftenreihe der Kommission für Ostdeutsche Volkskunde in der Deutschen Gesellschaft für Volkskunde, 9 (Marburg: Elwert, 1971).

Karbaum, Michael, *Studien zur Geschichte der Bayreuther Festspiele (1876–1976)* (Regensburg: Gustav Bosse, 1976).

Karina, Lilian, and Marion Kant, *Tanz unterm Hakenkreuz: eine Dokumentation* (Berlin: Henschel, 1996).

Kater, Michael H., 'Carl Orff im Dritten Reich', *Vierteljahrshefte für Zeitgeschichte*, 43 (1995), 12–35.

—— *The Twisted Muse: Musicians and their Music in the Third Reich* (New York: Oxford University Press, 1997).

—— *Composers of the Nazi Era: Eight Portraits* (New York: Oxford University Press, 2000).

Kaubek, Marianne, 'Führermodelle im Drama des Dritten Reiches' (unpublished doctoral thesis, University of Vienna, 1975).

Kaufmann, Erika, 'Medienmanipulation im Dritten Reich: Ziele und Wirkungsabsichten mit dem Einsatz von Theater und Fronttheater' (unpublished doctoral thesis, University of Vienna, 1987).

Kaufmann, Wolfgang, 'Aspekte zur Wechselwirkung von Theater und Politik: dargestellt an kritischen Reminiszenzen und ausgewählten Beispielen aus einem halben Jahrhundert deutscher Theater- und Zeitgeschichte von 1910 bis 1960' (unpublished doctoral thesis, University of Vienna, 1984).

Keckeis, Hermann, *Das deutsche Hörspiel 1923–1973: ein systematischer Überblick mit kommentierter Bibliographie* (Frankfurt am Main: Athenäum, 1973).

Keiser-Hayne, Helga, *Beteiligt euch, es geht um eure Erde: Erika Mann und ihr politisches Kabarett die 'Pfeffermühle' 1933–1937* (Munich: Spangenberg, 1990).

Kemmler, Richard S., 'The National Socialist Ideology in Drama' (unpublished doctoral thesis, New York University, 1973).

Kemnitz, Helmut, *'Die Kluge' von Carl Orff* (Berlin: Lienau, 1994).

Kennedy, Michael, *Richard Strauss* (Cambridge: Cambridge University Press, 1999).

Ketelsen, Uwe-Karsten, *Heroisches Theater: Untersuchungen zur Dramentheorie des Dritten Reichs*, Literatur und Wirklichkeit, 2 (Bonn: Bouvier, 1968).

—— *Von heroischem Sein und völkischem Tod: zur Dramatik des Dritten Reiches*, Abhandlungen zur Kunst-, Musik- und Literaturwissenschaft, 96 (Bonn: Bouvier, 1970).

—— *Völkisch-nationale und nationalsozialistische Literatur in Deutschland 1890–1945*, Sammlung Metzler, 142 (Stuttgart: Metzler, 1976).

—— 'Kulturpolitik im III. Reich und Ansätze zu ihrer Interpretation', *Text und Kontext*, 8 (1980), 217–42.

—— Review of Bogusław Drewniak, *Das Theater im NS-Staat: Szenarium deutscher Zeitgeschichte 1933–1945* (Düsseldorf: Droste, 1983), *Forum Modernes Theater*, 1 (1986), 103–8.

—— 'Hanns Johsts *Thomas Paine*—ein imaginierter Held der Nationalsozialisten', in *Fascism and European Literature: Faschismus und europäische Literatur*, ed. by Stein Ugelvik Larsen and Beatrice Sandberg, with Ronald Speirs (Berne: Lang, 1991), pp. 38–57.

—— *Literatur und Drittes Reich* (Schernfeld: SH-Verlag, 1992).

—— Review of *Theatre in the Third Reich, the Prewar Years: Essays on Theatre in Nazi Germany*, ed. by Glen W. Gadberry, Contributions to the Study of World History, 49 (Westport, CT: Greenwood Press, 1995), *Comparative Drama*, 31 (1997), 329–32.

Kieser, Klaus, *Das Gärtnerplatztheater in München, 1932–1944: zur Operette im Nationalsozialismus*, Europäische Hochschulschriften: Reihe 30: Theater-, Film- und Fernsehwissenschaften, 43 (Frankfurt am Main: Lang, 1991).

Kirsch, Mechthild, 'Zur Geschichte des Instituts für Theaterwissenschaft an der FU-Berlin' (unpublished Magisterarbeit, Free University of Berlin, 1991).

Klausnitzer, Ralf, ' "Wir rücken die Burgen unseres Glaubens auf die Höhen des Kaukasus": "Reichsdramaturg" Rainer Schlösser zwischen Jena-Weimar und Führerbunker', *Zeitschrift für Germanistik*, Neue Folge 9 (1999), 294–317.

Klein, Hans-Günter, 'Atonalität in den Opern von Klenau und Zillig: zur Duldung einer im Nationalsozialismus verfemten Kompositionstechnik', in *Bericht über den internationalen musikwissenschaftlichen Kongreß Bayreuth 1981*, ed. by Christoph-Hellmut Mahling and Sigrid Weismann (Basel: Bärenreiter, 1984), pp. 490–4.

Kliesch, Hans-Joachim, 'Die Film- und Theaterkritik im NS-Staat' (unpublished doctoral thesis, University of Berlin, 1957).

Kloss, Wolfgang, 'Die nationalsozialistische Thingspiele: die Massenbasis des Faschismus 1933–1935 in seinem trivialen Theater: eine parataktische Darstellung' (unpublished doctoral thesis, University of Vienna, 1981).

Klusacek, Christine, 'Die Gleichschaltung der Wiener Bühnen', in *Wien 1938*, ed. by Felix Czeike, Forschungen und Beiträge zur Wiener Stadtgeschichte, 2 (Vienna: Verein für Geschichte der Stadt Wien, 1978), pp. 248–57.

Koegler, Horst, 'Tanz in die dreissiger Jahre', in *Ballett: Chronik und Bilanz des Ballettjahres* (Velber bei Hannover: Erhard Friedrich, 1972), pp. 39–51.

—— 'In the Shadow of the Swastika: Dance in Germany, 1927–1936', *Dance Perspectives*, 57 (Spring 1974), n.p.

—— 'Vom Ausdruckstanz zum "Bewegungschor" des deutschen Volkes: Rudolf von Laban', in *Intellektuelle im Bann des Nationalsozialismus*, ed. by Karl Corino (Hamburg: Hoffmann & Campe, 1980), pp. 165–79.

Köhler, F. H., *Die Struktur der Spielpläne deutschsprachiger Opernbühnen von 1896 bis 1966: eine statistische Analyse* (Koblenz: Statistische Amt, 1968).

Kolland, Hubert, 'Wagner-Rezeption im deutschen Faschismus', in *Bericht über den internationalen musikwissenschaftlichen Kongreß Bayreuth 1981*, ed. by Christoph-Hellmut Mahling and Sigrid Weismann (Basel: Bärenreiter, 1984), pp. 494–503.

Königstein, Horst, *Die Schiller Oper in Altona: eine Archäologie der Unterhaltung* (Frankfurt am Main: Suhrkamp, 1983).

Kopp, Detlev, ed., *Studien zur Literaturwissenschaft im Dritten Reich: zur Rezeption der Dramatiker Büchner, Grabbe, Grillparzer, Hebbel und Kleist 1933–45* (Bielefeld: Aisthesis, 1988).

Kothes, Franz-Peter, *Die theatralische Revue in Berlin und Wien 1900–1938: Typen, Inhalte, Funktionen* (Wilhelmshaven: Heinrichshofen, 1977).

Kraft, Zdenko von, *Der Sohn: Siegfried Wagners Leben und Umwelt* (Graz: Stocker, 1969).

Krause, Ernst, *Richard Strauss: Gestalt und Werk* (Leipzig: Breitkopf & Härtel, 1955).

—— *Werner Egk: Oper und Ballet* (Wilhelmshaven: Heinrichshofen, 1971).

Kressin, Heide, 'Die Entwicklung des Theaterprogrammheftes in Deutschland von 1894–1941' (unpublished doctoral thesis, Free University of Berlin, 1968).

Kretschmer, Vera, 'Die württembergische Landesbühne Esslingen von 1933 bis 1948', in *Von Weimar bis Bonn: Esslingen 1919–1949*, exhibition catalogue (Esslingen: Stadt Esslingen, 1991), pp. 309–25.

Krüger, Christian, *Geschichte der Oper am Landestheater Oldenburg 1921–1938* (Oldenburg: Holzberg, 1984).

Kühn, Volker, ed., *Deutschlands Erwachen: Kabarett unterm Hakenkreuz 1933–1945*, Kleinkunststücke, 3 (Weinheim: Quadriga, 1989).

Kulturamt der Stadt Düsseldorf, ed., *Musik, Theater, Literatur und Film zur Zeit des Dritten Reiches (1937: Europa vor dem 2. Weltkrieg: September 1987 bis Januar 1988: ein Gemeinschaftsprojekt Düsseldorfer Kulturinstitute)* (Düsseldorf: Goethe Buchhandlung Teubig, 1987).

Kuschnia, Michael, and others, eds, *100 Jahre Deutsches Theater Berlin: 1883–1983* ([East] Berlin: Henschel, 1983).

Kvam, Wayne, 'The Nazification of Max Reinhardt's Deutsches Theater Berlin', *Theatre Journal*, 40 (1988), 357–74.

Laux, Karl, *Musik und Musiker der Gegenwart* (Essen: Spael, 1949).

—— *Joseph Haas* ([East] Berlin: Henschel, 1954).

—— *Ottmar Gerster: Leben und Werk*, Reclams Universal-Bibliothek, 8928/29 (Leipzig: Reclam, 1961).

Lebedur, Ruth von, 'Der deutsche Geist und Shakespeare: Anmerkungen zur Shakespeare-Rezeption 1933–1945', in *Wissenschaft und Nationalsozialismus: eine Ringvorlesung an der Universität, Gesamthochschule, Siegen*, ed. by Rainer Geißler, Kultur, Literatur, Kunst, 8 (Essen: Die Blaue Eule, 1988), pp. 197–225.

Leppmann, Wolfgang, *Gerhart Hauptmann: Leben, Werk und Zeit* (Berne: Scherz, 1986).

Levi, Erik, *Music in the Third Reich* (Basingstoke: Macmillan, 1994).

—— 'Towards an Aesthetic of Fascist Opera', in *Fascism and Theatre: Comparative Studies on the Aesthetics and Politics of Performance in Europe, 1925–1945*, ed. by Günter Berghaus (Providence, RI: Berghahn Books, 1996), pp. 260–76.

Loewy, Ernst, *Literatur unterm Hakenkreuz: das Dritte Reich und seine Dichtung: eine Dokumentation*, 3rd edn (Cologne: Europäische Verlagsanstalt, 1977).

London, John, 'Algunos montajes de Calderón en el Tercer Reich', in *Texto e imagen en Calderón: undécimo coloquio anglogermano sobre Calderón: St Andrews, Escocia, 17–20 de julio de 1996*, ed. by Manfred Tietz, Archivum Calderonianum, 8 (Stuttgart: Franz Steiner, 1998), pp. 143–57.

Losada, Basilio, 'Paz y guerra en el teatro alemán (1933–1950)', *Estudios Escénicos: Cuadernos del Instituto del Teatro*, 12 (1966), 55–100.

Łucejko-Drewniak, Helena, 'Literatura piękna na listach piśmiennictwa niepożądanego w Trzeciej Rzeszy (1933–1944)' (unpublished doctoral thesis, University of Gdansk), 1978).

Lück, Monika, 'Die Programmhefte des Bayerischen Staatsschauspiels München und der Münchner Kammerspiele aus den Jahren 1933/34 bis 1940/41: zwei Möglichkeiten der Programmheftgestaltung im Dritten Reich' (unpublished Magisterarbeit, University of Munich, 1978).

Lukas, Hans-Willi, 'Das Theater in Wuppertal zur Zeit des Dritten Reiches', in *Wuppertal in der Zeit des Nationalsozialismus*, ed. by Klaus Goebel (Wuppertal: Hammer, 1984), pp. 133–46.

Lurz, Meinhold, *Die Heidelberger Thingstätte: die Thingbewegung im Dritten Reich: Kunst als Mittel politischer Propaganda: Dokumentation* (Heidelberg: Schutzgemeinschaft Heiligenberg, 1975).

Lüth, Erich, *Hamburger Theater 1933–1945: ein theatergeschichtlicher Versuch* (Hamburg: Verlag der Werkberichte Justus Bueckschmitt, 1962).

Mahl, Bernd, *Goethes 'Faust' auf der Bühne (1806–1996): Fragment: Ideologiestück: Spieltext* (Stuttgart: Metzler, 1998).

Malth, Rainer, *Ottmar Gerster: Leben und Werk* (Leipzig: Peters, 1988).

Mämpel, Arthur, 'Das Dortmunder Theater von seinen Anfängen bis zur Gegenwart: ein Überblick', *Beiträge des Historischen Vereins für Dortmund und die Grafschaft Mark*, 47 (1948), 99–138.

—— *Theater am Hiltropwall: 40 Jahre im Hause von Martin Dülfer (1904–1944)* (Dortmund: no publ., 1955).

Mandelkow, Karl Robert, ed., *Goethe im Urteil seiner Kritiker: Dokumente zur Wirkungsgeschichte Goethes in Deutschland*, 4 vols (Munich: Beck, 1975–84), IV: *1918–1982* (1984).

—— *Goethe in Deutschland: Rezeptionsgeschichte eines Klassikers*, 2 vols (Munich: Beck, 1980–9), II: *1919–1982* (1989), pp. 78–117.

Manning, Susan, *Ecstasy and the Demon: Feminism and Nationalism in the Dances of Mary Wigman* (Berkeley: University of California Press, 1993).

May, Ursula, 'Das Mannheimer Nationaltheater 1933–1945' (unpublished Magisterarbeit, Free University of Berlin, 1986).

Mayer, Hans, *Gerhart Hauptmann*, Friedrichs Dramatiker des Welttheaters, 23 (Velber bei Hannover: Erhard Friedrich, 1967).

Meier, Monika, Peter Roessler and Gerhard Scheit, *Theater: Wissenschaft und Faschismus* (Berlin: Peter Roessler, 1981).

Melchior, Andrea, 'Gerhart Hauptmanns *Florian Geyer*: Interpretation eines Dramas' (unpublished doctoral thesis, University of Zurich, 1979).

Mellen, Peter J., 'The Third Reich Examined as the Dramatic Illusion of Ritual Performance' (unpublished doctoral thesis, Bowling Green State University, 1988).

Mennemeier, Franz Norbert, *Modernes deutsches Drama: Kritiken und Charakteristiken*, 2 vols (Munich: Fink, 1973–75).

—— 'Nationalsozialistische Dramatik', in *Deutsche Literatur: eine Sozialgeschichte*, ed. by Horst Albert Glaser, 10 vols (Reinbek bei Hamburg: Rowohlt, 1980–), IX: - *Weimarer Republik–Drittes Reich: Avantgardismus, Parteilichkeit, Exil 1918–1945*, ed. by Alexander von Bormann and Horst Albert Glaser (1983), pp. 283–92.

Menz, Egon, 'Sprechchor und Aufmarsch: zur Entstehung des Thingspiels', in *Die deutsche Literatur im Dritten Reich: Themen, Traditionen, Wirkungen*, ed. by Horst Denkler and Karl Prümm (Stuttgart: Reclam, 1976), pp. 330–46.

Messmer, Franzpeter, ed., *Kritiken zu den Uraufführungen der Bühnenwerke von Strauss* (Pfaffenhofen: Ludwig, 1989).

Meyer, Michael, *The Politics of Music in the Third Reich*, American University Studies: Series 09, 49 (New York: Lang, 1991).

Milfull, John, ed., *The Attractions of Fascism: Social Psychology and the Aesthetics of the 'Triumph of the Right'* (New York: Berg, 1990).

Mohr, Albert Richard, *Hans Meissner und das Frankfurter Theater* (Frankfurt am Main: Waldemar Kramer, 1968).

—— *Die Frankfurter Oper, 1924–1944: ein Beitrag zur Theatergeschichte mit zeitgenössischen Berichten und Bildern* (Frankfurt am Main: Waldemar Kramer, 1971).

—— *Das Frankfurter Schauspiel 1929–1944: eine Dokumentation zur Theatergeschichte mit zeitgenössischen Berichten und Bildern* (Frankfurt am Main: Waldemar Kramer, 1974).

Mosse, George, *Nazi Culture: Intellectual, Cultural and Social Life in the Third Reich*, trans. by Salvator Attanasio and others (New York: Grosset & Dunlap, 1968).

—— 'Die NS-Kampfbühne', trans. by Reinhold Grimm, in *Geschichte im Gegenwartsdrama*, ed. by Reinhold Grimm and Jost Hermand, Sprache und Literatur, 99 (Stuttgart: Kohlhammer, 1976), pp. 24–38.

Mrukwa, Michael, 'Das Bremer Staatstheater und das Bremer Schauspielhaus von 1933–1945' (unpublished Magisterarbeit, Free University of Berlin, 1987).

Mühleder, Eva, 'Faschismus- und NS-Kritik im Wiener Kabarett der 30er Jahre' (unpublished Magisterarbeit, University of Vienna, 1986).

Müller, Hedwig, *Mary Wigman: Leben und Werk der großen Tänzerin* (Weinheim: Quadriga, 1986).

—— and Patricia Stöckermann, '… jeder Mensch ist ein Tänzer': Ausdruckstanz in Deutschland zwischen 1900 und 1945*, exhibition catalogue (Gießen: Anabas, 1993).

Murmann, Geerte, *Komödianten für den Krieg: deutsches und alliiertes Fronttheater* (Düsseldorf: Droste, 1992).

Muschelknautz, Johanna, '"Kautschukmann muß man sein": zur szenografischen Arbeit Traugott Müllers im Dritten Reich' (unpublished Magisterarbeit, Free University of Berlin, 1989).

Namowicz, Tadeusz, 'Zur Instrumentalisierung des Goethebildes im Dritten Reich', in *Traditionen und Traditionssuche des deutschen Faschismus*, ed. by Günter Hartung and Hubert Orlowski (Halle/Saale: Wissenschaftspublizistik der Martin-Luther-Universität Halle-Wittenberg, 1983), pp. 61–78.

—— 'Friedrich Schiller in der Literaturforschung des Dritten Reiches', in *Traditionen und Traditionssuche des deutschen Faschismus*, ed. by Günter Hartung and Hubert Orlowski, Seria Filologia Germanska, 29 (Poznań: Adam Mickiewicz University Press, 1988), pp. 7–27.

Naso, Eckart von, *Ich liebe das Leben: Erinnerungen aus fünf Jahrzehnten* (Hamburg: Wolfgang Krüger, 1953).

Nijssen, Hub, 'Peter Huchel als Propagandist?: über die Autorschaft des Hörspiels *Die Greuel von Denshawai*', *Neophilologus*, 77 (1993), 625–57.

Niven, William J., *The Reception of Friedrich Hebbel in Germany in the Era of National Socialism*, Stuttgarter Arbeiten zur Germanistik, 142 (Stuttgart: Hans-Dieter Heinz, 1984).

—— 'Apocalyptic Elements in National Socialist *Thingspiele* and in Drama of the Weimar Republic', *German Life and Letters*, 48 (1995), 170–83.

—— 'The Procreative Male: Male Images of Masculinity and Femininity in Right-Wing German Literature of the 1918–1945 Period', *Forum for Modern Language Studies*, 34 (1998), 226–36.

Oellers, Norbert, ed., *Schiller—Zeitgenosse aller Epochen: Dokumente zur Wirkungsgeschichte Schillers in Deutschland*, 2 vols (Frankfurt am Main: Athenäum; Munich: Beck, 1970–76), II: *1860–1966* (1976).

Orff, Godela, *Mein Vater und ich: Erinnerungen an Carl Orff* (Munich: Piper, 1992).

Otto, Rainer, and Walter Rösler, *Kabarettgeschichte: Abriß des deutschsprachigen Kabaretts*, 2nd edn ([East] Berlin: Henschel, 1981).

Otto, Werner, *Geschichte der Deutschen Staatsoper Berlin: von der Gründung der Kapelle bis zur Gegenwart*, 6th edn ([East] Berlin: Deutsche Staatsoper, 1982).

Pachl, Peter, *Siegfried Wagners musikdramatisches Schaffen* (Tutzing: Schneider, 1979).

—— *Siegfried Wagner: Genie im Schatten* (Munich: Nymphenburger, 1988).

Panse, Barbara, ' "Diese Künstler sind wie Kinder": die Theatermacher und die Macht', *Theater Heute*, 30, no. 9 (September 1989), 4–5.

—— 'Autoren, Themen und Zensurpraxis: zeitgenössische deutschsprachige Dramatik im Theater des Dritten Reiches' (unpublished Habilitation Thesis, Free University of Berlin, 1993).

—— 'Censorship in Nazi Germany: The Influence of the Reich's Ministry of Propaganda on German Theatre and Drama, 1933–1945', trans. by Meg Mumford, in *Fascism and Theatre: Comparative Studies on the Aesthetics and Politics of Performance in Europe, 1925–1945*, ed. by Günter Berghaus (Providence, RI: Berghahn Books, 1996), pp. 140–56.

—— 'Theater im "Dritten Reich": die Zensur von Stücken über den Ersten Weltkrieg', in *Theater als Ort der Geschichte: Festschrift für Henning Rischbieter*, ed. by Theo Girshausen and Henry Thorau ([Seelze]: Friedrich Verlag Velber, 1998), pp. 167–84.

Papke, Gabriele, *Wenns löfft, donn löfft's: die Geschichte des Theaters in Bamberg von 1860 bis 1978: Alltag einer Provinzbühne* (Bamberg: Bayerische Verlagsanstalt, 1985).

Parker, Stephen, 'Peter Huchel als Propagandist: Huchels 1940 entstandene Adaption von George Bernard Shaws *Die Greuel von Denshawai*', *Rundfunk und Fernsehen*, 39 (1991), 343–52.

Parkes-Perret, Ford B., *Hanns Johst's Nazi Drama 'Schlageter': Translated with an Introduction*, Stuttgarter Textbeiträge, 5 (Stuttgart: Hans-Dieter Heinz, 1984).

Pelzer, Jürgen, 'Satire oder Unterhaltung? Wirkungskonzepte im deutschen Kabarett zwischen Bohémerevolte und antifaschistischer Opposition', *German Studies Review*, 9 (1986), 45–65.

Pesch, Jessica, *Festspiele für ein neues Deutschland?: Saladin Schmitts 'Klassikerwochen' am Schauspielhaus Bochum im Dritten Reich* (Herne: Verlag für Wissenschaft und Kunst, 1999).

Peter, Erich, *Geschichte des Oberschlesischen Landestheaters und Landesorchesters in Beuthen OS: ein Dokumentationsbericht*, Veröffentlichungen der Ostdeutschen Forschungsstelle im Lande Nordrhein-Westfalen: Reihe A, 24 (Dortmund: [Ostdeutsche Forschungsstelle im Lande Nordrhein-Westfalen], 1972).

Peter, Frank-Manuel, ed., *Der Tänzer Harald Kreutzberg* (Berlin: Hentrich, 1997).

Peters, Hans Georg, *Vom Hoftheater zum Landestheater: die Detmolder Bühne von 1825–1969*, Lippische Studien: Forschungsreihe des Landesverbandes Lippe, 1 (Detmold: Landesverband Lippe, 1972).

Petzet, Wolfgang, *Theater: die Münchner Kammerspiele 1911–1972* (Munich: Desch, 1973).

Pfanner, Helmut F., *Hanns Johst: vom Expressionismus zum Nationalsozialismus* (The Hague: Mouton, 1970).

Pfennings, Daniele, 'Das Schillertheater Berlin 1933–1944' (unpublished Magisterarbeit, Free University of Berlin, 1991).

Pitsch, Ilse, 'Das Theater als politisch-publizistisches Führungsmittel im Dritten Reich' (unpublished doctoral thesis, University of Münster, 1952).

Plewnia, Margarete, *Auf dem Weg zu Hitler: der 'völkische' Publizist Dietrich Eckart* (Bremen: Schünemann, 1970).

Plötzeneder, Irene, 'Die Kulturpolitik des Nationalsozialismus im Bereich von Literatur, Theater und Bildender Kunst und die Auswirkungen auf den Ständestaat' (unpublished Diplomarbeit, Universität für Bildungswissenschaft, Klagenfurt, 1991).

Potter, Pamela M., 'Richard Strauss's *Friedenstag*: A Pacifistic Attempt at Political Resistance', *Musical Quarterly*, 69 (1983), 408–20.

—— 'Strauss and the National Socialists: The Debate and its Relevance', in *Richard Strauss: New Perspectives on the Composer and his Work*, ed. by Bryan Gilliam (Durham, NC: Duke University Press, 1992), pp. 93–113.

—— *Most German of the Arts: Musicology and Society from the Weimar Republic to Hitler's Reich* (New Haven, CT: Yale University Press, 1998).

Prawy, Marcel, *Die Wiener Oper: Geschichte und Geschichten* (Vienna: Molder, 1978).

Preston-Dunlop, Valerie, 'Laban and the Nazis', *Dance Theatre Journal*, 6, no. 2 (July 1988), 4–7.

Prieberg, Fred K., *Musik im NS-Staat*, Fischer Taschenbücher, 6901 (Frankfurt am Main: Fischer Taschenbuch, 1982).

Probst, Gerhard F., 'Zur Klassik-Rezeption im Dritten Reich: prinzipielle Überlegungen und Analyse eines "Hausbuches"', *Jahrbuch für Internationale Germanistik*, Reihe A5 (1979), 148–57.

Puffett, Derrick, *The Song-Cycles of Othmar Schoeck* (Berne: Paul Haupt, 1982).

Pujante, Angel-Luis, and Dagmar Scheu, 'El Shakespeare de Hans Rothe o el mito de la traducción teatral', *Livius*, 2 (1992), 253–62.

Rabenstein, Edith, *Dichtung zwischen Tradition und Moderne: Richard Billinger: Untersuchungen zur Rezeptionsgeschichte und zum Werk*, Europäische Hochschulschriften: Reihe 1: Deutsche Sprache und Literatur, 1052 (Frankfurt am Main: Lang, 1988).

Radvan, Florian, 'Überlegungen zur Wiederaufführung nationalsozialistischer Dramatik auf deutschen Bühnen: Hanns Johsts Schauspiel *Schlageter* (UA 1933) als Beispiel', *Forum Modernes Theater*, 13 (1998), 165–83.

Rathkolb, Oliver, *Führertreu und gottbegnadet: Künstlereliten im Dritten Reich* (Vienna: Österreichischer Bundesverlag, 1991).

Reeve, William C., *Kleist on Stage, 1804–1987* (Montreal: McGill-Queen's University Press, 1993).

Reichel, Peter, *Der schöne Schein des Dritten Reiches: Faszination und Gewalt des Faschismus*, 2nd edn (Frankfurt am Main: Fischer Taschenbuch, 1993), pp. 336–45.

Reichert, Franz, *Durch meine Brille: Theater in bewegter Zeit (1925–1950)* (Vienna: Österreichischer Bundesverlag, 1986).

Reichl, Johannes, *Das Thingspiel: über den Versuch eines nationalsozialistischen Lehrstück-Theaters* (Frankfurt am Main: Mißlbeck, 1988).

Requardt, Walter, 'Gerhart Hauptmann und der Nationalsozialismus – die Nationalsozialisten und Gerhart Hauptmann', in *Nationalsozialismus und Widerstand in Schlesien*, ed. by Lothar Bossle and others, Schlesische Forschungen, 3 (Sigmaringen: J. Thorbecke, 1989), pp. 41–71.

Reynolds, Dee, 'Dancing as a Woman: Mary Wigman and "Absolute Dance"', *Forum for Modern Language Studies*, 35 (1999), 297–310.

Richard-Billinger-Gedächtnisausstellung (Linz: Oberösterreichischer Landesverlag, 1975); 2nd edn (Linz: Adalbert-Stifter-Institut, 1985).

Riethmüller, Albrecht, 'Komposition im deutschen Reich um 1936', *Archiv für Musikwissenschaft* 38 (1981), 241–78.

Ritchie, James MacPherson, 'Johst's *Schlageter* and the End of the Weimar Republic', in *Weimar Germany: Writers and Politics*, ed. by A. F. Bance (Edinburgh: Scottish Academic Press, 1982), pp. 153–67.

—— *German Literature under National Socialism* (London: Croom Helm; Totowa, NJ: Barnes & Noble, 1983).

Roder-Breymann, Susanne, *Die Wiener Staatsoper in den Zwischenkriegsjahren* (Tutzing: Schneider, 1994).

Roessler, Peter, and Gerhard Scheit, eds, *Wespennest*, no. 56: *Theater und Faschismus* (Vienna: Verein Gruppe Wespennest, 1984).

Ronsdorf, Renate, 'Das Wuppertaler Theater von 1933 bis 1945' (unpublished Magisterarbeit, Free University of Berlin, 1989).

Rösler, Walter, ed., *Gehn ma halt a bisserl unter: Kabarett in Wien von den Anfängen bis heute* (Berlin: Henschel, 1991), pp. 269–306.

Rost, Nico, *Goethe in Dachau* (Hamburg: Konkret Literatur-Verlag, 1981).

Rühle, Günther, 'Die Thingspielbewegung', in Henning Eichberg and others, *Massenspiele: NS-Thingspiele, Arbeiterweihespiel und olympisches Zeremoniell*, Problemata, 58 (Stuttgart: Frommann-Holzboog, 1977), pp. 181–202.

—— ed., *Zeit und Theater*, 6 vols (Frankfurt am Main: Ullstein/Propyläen, 1980).

Ruhrberg, Karl, 'Zwischen Anpassung und Widerstand: das Theater unter dem Hakenkreuz', and 'NS-Gesinnungsstücke in Düsseldorf von 1933–1940', in *Musik, Theater, Literatur und Film zur Zeit des Dritten Reiches (1937: Europa vor dem 2. Weltkrieg: September 1987 bis Januar 1988: ein Gemeinschaftsprojekt Düsseldorfer Kulturinstitute)*, ed. by Kulturamt der Stadt Düsseldorf (Düsseldorf: Goethe Buchhandlung Teubig, 1987), pp. 39–46, 49–61.

Ruppel, Karl H., *Großes Berliner Theater: Gründgens, Fehling, Müthel, Hilpert, Engel* (Velber bei Hannover: Erhard Friedrich, 1962).

Ruppelt, Georg, *Schiller im nationalsozialistischen Deutschland: der Versuch einer Gleichschaltung* (Stuttgart: Metzler, 1979).

Salb, Thomas, *'Trutzburg deutschen Geistes?': das Stadttheater Freiburg in der Zeit des Nationalsozialismus* (Freiburg im Breisgau: Rombach, 1993).

Sauer, Klaus, and German Werth, *Lorbeer und Palme: Patriotismus in deutschen Festspielen*, dtv, 795 (Munich: Deutscher Taschenbuch Verlag, 1971).

Scanzoni, Signe, *Wiener Oper: Wege und Irrwege* (Stuttgart: Frick, 1956).

Schauwecker, Detlev, 'Japanisches auf Bühnen der nationalsozialistischen Zeit', in *Deutschland–Japan in der Zwischenkriegszeit*, ed. by Josef Kreiner and Regine Mathias, Studium Universale, 12 (Bonn: Bouvier, 1990), pp. 403–40.

Schebera, Jürgen, *Kurt Weill: An Illustrated Life* (New Haven, CT: Yale University Press, 1995).

Schellack, Fritz, *Nationalfeiertage in Deutschland von 1871 bis 1945*, Europäische Hochschulschriften: Reihe 3, 415 (Frankfurt am Main: Lang, 1990).

Schiedermair, Ludwig F., *Deutsche Oper in München* (Munich: Langen Müller, 1992).

Schlesinger, Robert, *'Gott sei mit unserem Führer': der Opernbetrieb im deutschen Faschismus* (Vienna: Löcker, 1997).

Schliebs, Siegfried, 'Mythos als Geschichtsersatz im nationalsozialistischen Heimkehrerdrama bis 1933' (unpublished Magisterarbeit, Free University of Berlin, 1985).

Schlötterer, Roswitha, *Richard Strauss–Rudolf Hartmann: ein Briefwechsel* (Tutzing: Schneider, 1984).

Schmidl, Michael, 'Das Nürnberger Stadttheater von 1922 bis 1939: die Ära des Intendanten Dr Johannes Maurach' (unpublished Magisterarbeit, Free University of Berlin, 1987).

Schmidt, Bernd, 'Die Entwicklung des Bochumer Theaters bis 1944: unter besonderer Berücksichtigung der Festwochen in der Zeit von 1933 bis 1944' (unpublished Magisterarbeit, Free University of Berlin, 1982).

Schmidt, Hugo Wolfram, *Carl Orff: sein Leben und sein Werk in Wort, Bild und Noten* (Cologne: Wienand, 1971).

Schoeps, Karl-Heinz Joachim, *Literatur im Dritten Reich*, Deutsche Literatur zwischen den Weltkriegen, 3, Germanistische Lehrbuchsammlung, 43 (Berne: Lang, 1992).

Schonauer, Franz, *Deutsche Literatur im Dritten Reich: Versuch einer Darstellung in polemisch-didaktischer Absicht* (Olten: Walter, 1961).

Schöndienst, Eugen, *Geschichte des deutschen Bühnenvereins: ein Beitrag zur Geschichte des Theaters 1846–1935* (Frankfurt am Main: Propyläen, 1979).

—— 'Kulturelle Angelegenheiten: Theater und Orchester (1933–1945)', in *Deutsche Verwaltungsgeschichte*, ed. by Kurt G. A. Jeserich and others, 6 vols (Stuttgart: Deutsche Verlags-Anstalt, 1983–88), IV: *Das Reich als Republik und in der Zeit des Nationalsozialismus* (1985), pp. 988–98.

Schöpel, Brigitte, *'Naturtheater': Studien zum Theater unter freiem Himmel in Südwestdeutschland*, Volksleben, 9 (Tübingen: Tübinger Vereinigung für Volkskunde, 1965).

Schreiner, Evelyn, 'Nationalsozialistische Kulturpolitik in Wien 1938–1945 unter spezieller Berücksichtigung der Wiener Theaterszene' (unpublished doctoral thesis, University of Vienna, 1980).

—— ed., *100 Jahre Volkstheater: Theater, Zeit, Geschichte* (Vienna: Jugend und Volk, 1989).

Schreyvogl, Friedrich, *Das Burgtheater: Wirklichkeit und Illusion* (Vienna: Speidel, 1965).

Schrott, Ludwig, *Die Persönlichkeit Hans Pfitzners* (Zurich: Atlantis, 1959).

Schuh, Willi, ed., *A Confidential Matter: The Letters of Richard Strauss and Stefan Zweig, 1931–1935* (Berkeley: University of California Press, 1977).

Schültke, Bettina, 'Das Frankfurter Schauspielhaus 1933 bis 1944' (unpublished Magisterarbeit, Free University of Berlin, 1987).

—— '"Was war mir die Politik! Gar nichts — und die Kunst alles": die Entnazifizierung des ehemaligen Frankfurter Generalintendanten Hans Meissner', *Theaterzeitschrift*, 28 (1989), 22–33.

—— 'The Municipal Theatre in Frankfurt-on-the-Main: A Provincial Theatre under National Socialism', trans. by Laura Tate and Günter Berghaus, in *Fascism and Theatre: Comparative Studies on the Aesthetics and Politics of Performance in Europe, 1925–1945*, ed. by Günter Berghaus (Providence, RI: Berghahn Books, 1996), pp. 157–71.

—— *Theater oder Propaganda?: die städtischen Bühnen Frankfurt am Main 1933–1945*, Studien zur Frankfurter Geschichte, 40 (Frankfurt am Main: Waldemar Kramer, 1997).

Seebohm, Andrea, *Die Wiener Oper: 350 Jahre Glanz und Tradition* (Vienna: Ueberreuter, 1986).

Segel, Harold B., *The Body Ascendant: Modernism and the Physical Imperative* (Baltimore, MD: Johns Hopkins University Press, 1998).

Seidel, Klaus Jürgen, *Das Prinzregenten-Theater in München* (Nuremberg: Drei W Druck, 1984).

Seliger, H. W., '*Fuenteovejuna* en Alemania: de la traducción a la falsificación', *Revista Canadiense de Estudios Hispánicos*, 8 (1983–84), 381–403.

Shafer, Yvonne, 'Nazi Berlin and the *Grosses Schauspielhaus*', *Theatre Survey*, 34, no. 1 (May 1993), 71–90.

Sharpe, Lesley, 'National Socialism and Schiller', *German Life and Letters*, 36 (1982–83), 156–65.

Smelser, Ronald, *Robert Ley: Hitler's Labor Front Leader* (New York: Berg, 1988).

Sonnega, William, 'Anti-war Discourse in War Drama: Sigmund Graff and *Die endlose Straße*', in *Essays on Twentieth-Century German Drama and Theater: An American Reception (1977–1999)*, ed. by Hal H. Rennert (Berne: Lang, forthcoming).

Sonntag, Brunhilde, ' "Lied eines Gefangenen" oder "Ein deutsches Gloria": Musik in der Zeit des Nationalsozialismus', *Forschung: Mitteilungen der DFG*, 1 (1996), 18–21.

Sorell, Walter, ed., *The Mary Wigman Book: Her Writings Edited and Translated* (Middletown, CT: Wesleyan University Press, 1975).

Spenlen, Heinz-Rüdiger, 'Theater in Aachen, Köln, Bonn und Koblenz 1931–1944' (unpublished doctoral thesis, University of Bonn, 1984).

Splitt, Gerhard, *Richard Strauss 1933–1935* (Pfaffenweiler: Centaurus, 1987).

Spotts, Frederic, *Bayreuth: A History of the Wagner Festival* (New Haven, CT: Yale University Press, 1994).

Stahl, Ernst Leopold, *Shakespeare und das deutsche Theater: Wanderung und Wandelung seines Werkes in dreiundeinhalb Jahrhunderten* (Stuttgart: Kohlhammer, 1947).

Steiger, Martina, '*Die Liebe der Danae' von Richard Strauss* (Mainz: Schott, 1999).

Steinweis, Alan E., 'The Professional, Social, and Economic Dimensions of Nazi Cultural Policy: The Case of the Reich Theater Chamber', *German Studies Review*, 13 (1990), 442–59.

—— *Art, Ideology, & Economics in Nazi Germany: The Reich Chambers of Music, Theater, and the Visual Arts* (Chapel Hill: University of North Carolina Press, 1993).

Stollmann, Rainer, 'Theater im Dritten Reich', in *Leid der Worte: Panorama des literarischen Nationalsozialismus*, ed. by Jörg Thunecke, Abhandlungen zur Kunst-, Musik- und Literaturwissenschaft, 367 (Bonn: Bouvier, 1987), pp. 72–89.

Stommer, Rainer, 'Thingplatz und Sprechchor im Dienst der "Volksgemeinschaft": Ansätze zu einer nationalsozialistischen "Volkskultur" in der Thing-Bewegung 1933–1936', *Text und Kontext*, 8 (1980), 309–36.

—— ' "Da oben versinkt einem der Alltag ...": Thingstätten im Dritten Reich als Demonstration der Volksgemeinschaftsideologie', in *Die Reihen fast geschlossen: Beiträge zur Geschichte des Alltags unterm Nationalsozialismus*, ed. by Detlev Peukert and Jürgen Reulecke (Wuppertal: Hammer, 1981), pp. 149–73.

—— *Die inszenierte Volksgemeinschaft: die 'Thing-Bewegung' im Dritten Reich* (Marburg: Jonas, 1985).

—— and Marina Dalügge, 'Masse—Kollektiv—Volksgemeinschaft', in *Berlin Moscow: 1900–1950*, ed. by Irina Antonowa [sic] and Jörn Merkert, exhibition catalogue (Munich: Prestel, 1995), pp. 349–55.

Stompor, Stephen, 'Oper in Berlin von 1933 bis 1945', *Beiträge zur Musikwissenschaft*, 28 (1986), 23–38.

Storck, Gerhard, 'Probleme des modernen Bauens und die Theaterarchitektur des 20. Jahrhunderts in Deutschland' (unpublished doctoral thesis, Friedrich-Wilhelm University, Bonn, 1971).

Strauss, Richard, *Dokumente, Aufsätze, Aufzeichnungen, Vorworte, Reden, Briefe*, Universal-Bibliothek, 830 (Leipzig: Reclam, 1980).

Strobl, Gerwin, 'Shakespeare and the Nazis', *History Today*, 47, no. 5 (May 1997), 16–21.

Strothmann, Dietrich, *Nationalsozialistische Literaturpolitik; ein Beitrag zur Publizistik im Dritten Reich*, Abhandlungen zur Kunst-, Musik- und Literaturwissenschaft, 13, 4th edn (Bonn: Bouvier, 1985).

Stuchlik, Gerda, *Goethe im Braunhemd: Universität Frankfurt 1933–1945* (Frankfurt am Main: Röderberg, 1984).

Sullivan, Henry, *Calderón in the German Lands and the Low Countries: His Reception and Influence, 1654–1980* (Cambridge: Cambridge University Press, 1983).

Székely, György, 'A *Csongor és Tünde* német előadásai', *Színház*, 27, no. 12 (December 1994), 29–32.

Tambling, Jeremy, *Opera and the Culture of Fascism* (Oxford: Clarendon Press, 1996).

Taylor, Jennifer Ann, 'The Third Reich in German Drama, 1933–56' (unpublished doctoral thesis, University of London, 1977).

Taylor, Ronald, *Literature and Society in Germany: 1918–1945*, Harvester Studies in Contemporary Literature and Culture, 3 (Brighton: Harvester Press; Totowa, NJ: Barnes & Noble, 1980).

Thomas, Walter, *Bis der Vorhang fiel: berichtet nach Aufzeichnungen aus den Jahren 1940 bis 1945* (Dortmund: Schwalvenberg, 1947).

—— and Karl Brinkmann, *Shakespeare in Deutschland 1864–1964* (Bochum: Deutsche Shakespeare-Gesellschaft, 1964).

Töteberg, Michael, '"Ich möchte hier den Vorhang des Schweigens herunterlassen": über die Darstellung des Dritten Reiches in Schauspieler-Memoiren; mit einem Exkurs über den Theaterkritiker Herbert Ihering', in *Im Rampenlicht der 'dunklen Jahre': Aufsätze zum Theater im 'Dritten Reich', Exil und Nachkrieg*, ed. by Helmut G. Asper (Berlin: Sigma, 1989), pp. 123–48.

Trommler, Frank, 'Komödie und Öffentlichkeit nach dem Zweiten Weltkrieg', in *Die deutsche Komödie im zwanzigsten Jahrhundert: sechstes Amherster Kolloquium zur modernen deutschen Literatur, 1972*, ed. by Wolfgang Paulsen (Heidelberg: Stiehm, 1976), pp. 154–86.

Tschulik, Norbert, *Musiktheater in Österreich: die Oper im 20. Jahrhundert* (Vienna: Österreichischer Bundesverlag, 1984).

Ulischberger, Emil, *Schauspiel in Dresden: ein Stück Theatergeschichte von den Anfängen bis in die Gegenwart in Wort und Bild* ([East] Berlin: Henschel, 1989).

Ulrich, Paul S., *Biographisches Verzeichnis für Theater, Tanz und Musik: Biographical Index for Theatre, Dance and Music: Fundstellennachweis aus deutschsprachigen Nachschlagewerken und Jahrbüchern*, 2 vols, 2nd edn (Berlin: Arno Spitz, 1997).

Unseld, Claudia, 'Zwischen "Thingspielen" und "politischem" Forum: eine kurze Geschichte der Studiobühne', in *Nachhilfe der Erinnerung: 600 Jahre Universität zu Köln*, ed. by Wolfgang Blaschke (Cologne: Pahl-Rugenstein, 1988), pp. 132–8.

Valentin, Petra Maria, 'Die Bayerische Staatsoper im Dritten Reich' (unpublished Magisterarbeit, University of Munich, 1985).

Van Zandt Moyer, Laurence, 'The *Kraft durch Freude* Movement in Nazi Germany: 1933–1939' (unpublished doctoral thesis, Northwestern University, 1967).

Vasold, Manfred, 'Theater im Dritten Reich: das Beispiel Hagen', *Geschichte im Westen*, 7 (1992), 69–86.

Vondung, Klaus, *Magie und Manipulation: ideologischer Kult und politische Religion des Nationalsozialismus* (Göttingen: Vandenhoeck & Ruprecht, 1971).

—— *Völkisch-nationale und nationalsozialistische Literaturtheorie*, Taschenbücher der Wissenschaft, 1465 (Munich: List, 1973).

—— 'Das Bild der "faschistischen Persönlichkeit" in der nationalsozialistischen Literatur nach 1933: am Beispiel chorischer Dichtungen Gerhard Schumanns', in *Fascism and European Literature: Faschismus und europäische Literatur*, ed. by Stein Ugelvik Larsen and Beatrice Sandberg, with Ronald Speirs (Berne: Lang, 1991), pp. 58–64.

Wackwitz, Günter, 'Mit Schiller heim ins Reich: Bemerkungen zu einigen Aspekten der Schillerrezeption in Sudetendeutschtum', in *Traditionen und Traditionssuche des deutschen Faschismus*, ed. by Günter Hartung and Hubert Orlowski, Seria Filologia Germanska, 29 (Poznań: Adam Mickiewicz University Press, 1988), pp. 55–67.

Wagner, Hans, *200 Jahre Münchner Theaterchronik 1750–1950: Theatergründungen, Ur- und Erstaufführungen, berühmte Gastspiele und andere Ereignisse und Kuriosa aus dem Bühnenleben* (Munich: Lerche, 1958).

Wagner-Régeny, Rudolf, *Begegnungen: Biographische Aufzeichnungen, Tagebücher, und sein Briefwechsel mit Caspar Neher* ([East] Berlin: Henschel, 1968).

Wallner, Regina, 'Erfolgreiche Komödien im Nationalsozialismus' (unpublished Magisterarbeit, Free University of Berlin, 1991).

Walter, Michael, *Hitler in der Oper: deutsches Musikleben 1919–1945* (Stuttgart: Metzler, 1995).

Walton, Chris, *Othmar Schoeck* (Zurich: Atlantis, 1994).

Wamlek-Junk, Elisabeth, ed., *Hans Pfitzner und Wien: sein Briefwechsel mit Viktor Junk und andere Dokumente* (Tutzing: Schneider, 1986).

Wardetzky, Jutta, *Theaterpolitik im faschistischen Deutschland: Studien und Dokumente* ([East] Berlin: Henschel, 1983).

Weber, Karl, *Geschichte des Theaterwesens in Schlesien: Daten und Fakten von den Anfängen bis zum Jahre 1944*, Veröffentlichungen der Forschungsstelle Ostmitteleuropa: Reihe A, 29 (Dortmund: Forschungsstelle Ostmitteleuropa, 1980).

Wegner, P. Ch., 'Gerhart Hauptmanns Griechendrama: ein Beitrag zu dem Verhältnis von Psyche und Mythos' (unpublished doctoral thesis, University of Kiel, 1968).

Weinzierl, Berta Brigitte, 'Spielplanpolitik im Dritten Reich und das Spielplanprofil 1932/33 bis 1943/44 des Bayerischen Staatsschauspiels München' (unpublished doctoral thesis, University of Munich, 1981).

Wenger, Sabine, 'Das Badische Staatstheater Karlsruhe von 1933–1945' (unpublished Magisterarbeit, Free University of Berlin, 1989).

Wenzel, Joachim E., *Geschichte der Hamburger Oper 1678–1978* (Hamburg: Hamburgische Staatsoper, 1978).

Wessels, Wolfram, *Hörspiele im Dritten Reich: zur Institutionen-, Theorie- und Literaturgeschichte*, Abhandlungen zur Kunst-, Musik- und Literaturwissenschaft, 366 (Bonn: Bouvier, 1985).

Wessling, Berndt Wilhelm, ed., *Bayreuth im Dritten Reich: Richard Wagners politische Erben: eine Dokumentation* (Weinheim: Beltz, 1983).

Wicclair, Walter, 'Das fatale Loch in der Berliner Theatergeschichte: Vortrag über Persönlichkeiten des Berliner Theaterlebens und ihre NS-Vergangenheit', in *Im Rampenlicht der 'dunklen Jahre': Aufsätze zum Theater im 'Dritten Reich', Exil und*

Nachkrieg, ed. by Helmut G. Asper, Sigma-Medienwissenschaft, 3 (Berlin: Sigma, 1989), pp. 17–42.

Wilhelm, Kurt, *Fürs Wort brauch ich Hilfe: die Geburt der Oper 'Capriccio' von Richard Strauss und Clemens Krauss* (Munich: Nymphenburger, 1988).

Willeke, Audrone B., *Georg Kaiser and the Critics: A Profile of Expressionism's Leading Playwright* (Columbia, SC: Camden House, 1995).

Willett, John, *The Theatre of the Weimar Republic* (New York: Holmes & Meier, 1988), pp. 179–204.

Williamson, John, *The Music of Hans Pfitzner* (Oxford: Clarendon Press, 1992).

Willnauer, Franz, ed., *'Carmina Burana' von Carl Orff: Entstehung – Wirkung – Text* (Munich: Piper, 1995).

Wolf, Friedrich, 'Die Dramatik des deutschen Faschismus', in *Gesammelte Werke*, ed. by Else Wolf and Walther Pollatschek, 16 vols (Berlin: Aufbau-Verlag, 1960–68), XV: *Aufsätze* (1967), pp. 480–91.

Wolf-Sykes, Barbara, 'Sprechtheater im nationalsozialistischen Köln unter besonderer Berücksichtigung der Jahre 1939–1944' (unpublished Magisterarbeit, University of Cologne, 1986).

Wulf, Joseph, *Literatur und Dichtung im Dritten Reich: eine Dokumentation* (Gütersloh: Sigbert Mohn, 1963); repr. Ullstein Buch, 33029 (Frankfurt am Main: Ullstein, 1983).

—— *Musik im Dritten Reich: eine Dokumentation* (Gütersloh: Sigbert Mohn, 1963); repr. Ullstein Buch, 33032 (Frankfurt am Main: Ullstein, 1983).

—— *Theater und Film im Dritten Reich: eine Dokumentation* (Gütersloh: Sigbert Mohn, 1964); repr. Ullstein Buch, 33031 (Frankfurt am Main: Ullstein, 1983).

Würffel, Stefan Bodo, '"... denn heute hört uns Deutschland": Anmerkungen zum Hörspiel im Dritten Reich', in *Kunst und Kultur im deutschen Faschismus*, ed. by Ralf Schnell (Stuttgart: Metzler, 1978), pp. 203–20.

Yates, W. E., *Theatre in Vienna: A Critical History, 1776–1995* (Cambridge: Cambridge University Press, 1996).

Young, Harry F., *Maximilian Harden, censor Germaniae: The Critic in Opposition from Bismarck to the Rise of Nazism* (The Hague: Nijhoff, 1959); in German as *Maximilian Harden: ein Publizist im Widerstreit von 1892–1927* (Münster: Regensburg, 1971).

Zeidler, Ulrike, 'Das Essener Theater von 1927 bis 1944' (unpublished Magisterarbeit, Free University of Berlin, 1990).

Zelinsky, Hartmut, *Richard Wagner – ein deutsches Thema: eine Dokumentation zur Wirkungsgeschichte Richard Wagners 1876–1976* (Frankfurt am Main: Zweitausendeins, 1976).

Zeller, Bernhard, ed., *Klassiker in finsteren Zeiten, 1933–1945: eine Ausstellung des Deutschen Literaturarchivs im Schiller-Nationalmuseum Marbach am Neckar*, 2 vols (Marbach am Neckar: Deutsche Schillergesellschaft, 1983).

Zimmer, Dieter E., 'Max Reinhardts Nachlaß: ein Drama um Kunst und Kommerz', *Die Zeit*, 15 July 1994, pp. 9–12.

Zortman, Bruce Harold, 'The Theater of Ideology in Nazi Germany' (unpublished doctoral thesis, University of California, Los Angeles, 1969; Uni. Microfilms, Ann Arbor, MI).

—— 'The Theater of Ideology in Nazi Germany', *Quarterly Journal of Speech*, 57 (1971), 153–62.

—— *Hitler's Theater: Ideological Drama in Nazi Germany* (El Paso, TX: Firestein Books, 1984).

Zum Jubiläum des Landestheaters: 150 Jahre Theater in Detmold (Detmold: Landes-theater Detmold, 1975).

Zygulski, Zdzislaw, *Gerhart Hauptmann: Czlowiek i twórca* (Łodz: [Łodzkie Towarzy-stwo Naukowe], 1968).

Jewish theatre, and theatre and music in ghettos and concentration camps

Adler, H. G., *Theresienstadt 1941–1945: das Antlitz einer Zwangsgemeinschaft* (Tüb-ingen: J. C. B. Mohr, 1960).

Akademie der Künste, ed., *Fritz Wisten: Drei Leben für das Theater* (Berlin: Hentrich, 1990).

—— ed., *Geschlossene Vorstellung: der Jüdischer Kulturbund in Deutschland 1933–1941*, exhibition catalogue (Berlin: Hentrich, 1992).

Bayerdörfer, Hans-Peter, ed., *Theatralia Judaica: Emanzipation und Antisemitismus als Momente der Theatergeschichte: von der Lessing-Zeit bis zur Shoa*, Theatron, 7 (Tübingen: Niemeyer, 1992).

Bloch, Max, 'Viktor Ullmann: A Brief Biography and Appreciation', *Journal of the Arnold Schoenberg Institute*, 2 (1979), 150–77.

Bor, Josef, *The Terezín Requiem*, trans. by Edith Pargeter (New York: Alfred. A. Knopf, 1963).

Brenner, Michael, *The Renaissance of Jewish Culture in Weimar Germany* (New Haven, CT: Yale University Press, 1995).

Broder, Henryk M. (with Eike Geisel), *Es Waren Wirklich Sternstunden*, film including interviews, Bayrischer Rundfunk, Sender Freies Berlin, Akademie der Künste, 1988.

Cochavi, Yehoyakim, 'Kultur und Bildungsarbeit der deutschen Juden 1933–1941: Ant-wort auf die Verfolgung durch das NS Regime', *Neue Sammlung*, 26 (1986), 396–407.

Crome, Len, *Unbroken: Resistance and Survival in the Concentration Camps* (London: Lawrence & Wishart, 1988).

Dahm, Volker, 'Kulturelles und geistiges Leben', in *Die Juden in Deutschland 1933–1945*, ed. by Wolfgang Benz (Munich: Beck, 1989), pp. 75–267.

Dalinger, Brigitte, *'Verloschene Sterne': Geschichte des jüdischen Theaters in Wien* (Vienna: Picus, 1998).

Daniel, Curt, ' "The Freest Theatre in the Reich": In the German Concentration Camps', *Theatre Arts*, 25 (1941), 801–7.

Düwell, Kurt, 'Jewish Cultural Centers in Nazi Germany: Expectations and Accom-plishments', in *The Jewish Response to German Culture*, ed. by Jehuda Reinharz and Walter Schatzberg (Hanover, NH: University Press of New England, 1985), pp. 294–316.

Edelman, Samuel M., 'Singing in the Face of Death – A Study of Jewish Cabaret and Opera During the Holocaust', in *The Publications of the World Union of Jewish Studies* (Jerusalem: Publications of the World Union of Jewish Studies, 1986), pp. 205–11.

Ehrlich-Fantlová, Zdenka, *Klíd je síla, řek' tatínek* (Prague: Primus, 1996).

Fass, Moshe, 'Theatrical Activities in the Polish Ghettos During the Years 1939–1942', *Journal of Jewish Social Studies*, no. 38 (Winter 1976), 54–72.

Feder, Sammy, 'The Yiddish Theatre of Belsen', in *Belsen* (Tel Aviv: Irgun Sheerit Hapleita Me'Haezor Habriti, 1957), pp. 135–9.

Felsmann, Barbara, and Karl Prümm, *Kurt Gerron – gefeiert und gejagt* (Berlin: Hentrich, 1992).

František Zelenka: Scenographer: 1904–1944, exhibition catalogue (London: London Institute, 1994).

Freeden, Herbert, 'A Jewish Theatre under the Swastika', *Leo Baeck Institute Yearbook*, 1 (1956), 142–62.

—— *Jüdisches Theater im Nazideutschland*, Schriftenreihe wissenschaftlicher Abhandlungen des Leo-Baecks-Instituts, 12 (Tübingen: J. C. B. Mohr, 1964); repr. Ullstein-Buch, 35233 (Frankfurt am Main: Ullstein, 1985).

—— 'Vom geistigen Widerstand der deutschen Juden: ein Kapitel jüdischer Selbstbehauptung in den Jahren 1933 bis 1938', in *Widerstand und Exil 1933–1945*, ed. by Otto R. Romberg and others (Bonn: Bundeszentrale für Politische Bildung, 1986), pp. 47–59.

—— *Leben zur falschen Zeit* (Berlin: Transit, 1991).

—— *The Jewish Press in the Third Reich*, trans. by William Templer (Providence, RI: Berg, 1993).

Gadberry, Glen W., 'Nazi Germany's Jewish Theatre', *Theatre Survey*, 21, no. 1 (May 1980), 15–32.

Geisel, Eike, and Henryk M. Broder, eds, *Premiere und Pogrom: der Jüdische Kulturbund 1933–1941, Texte und Bilder* (Berlin: Siedler, 1992).

Geisel, Eike, 'Premiere und Pogrom: der Jüdische Kulturbund 1933–1941', *Jüdischer Almanach* (1993), 35–44.

Goldfarb, Alvin, 'Theatrical Activities in Nazi Concentration Camps', *Performing Arts Journal*, 1, no. 2 (Fall 1976), 3–11.

—— 'Theatre and Drama and the Nazi Concentration Camps' (unpublished doctoral thesis, University of New York City, 1978).

Goldsmith, Martin, *The Inextinguishable Symphony: A True Story of Music and Love in Nazi Germany* (New York: John Wiley, 2000).

Hiller, Carl, 'Survival Tactics: Jewish Opera under the Nazis', *Opera*, 51 (2000), 777–90.

Hoffmann, Heidi Tamar, and Hans-Günter Klein, *Musik in Theresienstadt: die Komponisten Pavel Haas, Gideon Klein, Hans Krása, Viktor Ullmann, Erwin Schulhoff (gestorben in KZ Wülzburg) und ihre Werke* (Berlin: Musica Reanimata, 1991).

Jelavich, Peter, *Berlin Cabaret* (Cambridge, MA: Harvard University Press, 1993).

John, Eckhard, 'Musik und Konzentrationslager: eine Annäherung', *Archiv für Musikwissenschaft*, 48 (1991), 1–36.

Karas, Joža, *Music in Terezín 1941–1945* (New York: Beaufort Books, 1985).

Kift, Roy, 'Comedy in the Holocaust: the Theresienstadt Cabaret', *New Theatre Quarterly*, 12 (1996), 299–308; repr. as: 'Reality and Illusion in the Theresienstadt Cabaret', in *Staging the Holocaust: The Shoah in Drama and Performance*, ed. by Claude Schumacher (Cambridge: Cambridge University Press, 1998), pp. 147–68.

Klein, Hans-Günter, ed., *Viktor Ullmann: Materialien* (Hamburg: von Bockel, 1992).

—— *... es wird der Tod zum Dichter: die Referate des Kolloquiums zur Oper 'Der Kaiser von Atlantis' von Viktor Ullmann in Berlin 4–5 November 1995* (Hamburg: von Bockel, 1997).

Kramer, Aaron, 'Creative Defiance in a Death-Camp', *Journal of Humanistic Psychology*, 38 (1998), 12–24.

Kuna, Milan, *Musik an der Grenze des Lebens: Musikerinnen und Musiker aus böhmischen Ländern in nationalsozialistischen Konzentrationslagern und Gefängnissen* (Frankfurt am Main: Zweitausendeins, 1993).

Laks, Szymon, *Music of Another World*, trans. by Chester A. Kisiel (Evanston, IL: Northwestern University Press, 1989).

Langhoff, Wolfgang, *Die Moorsoldaten: 13 Monate Konzentrationslager* (Munich: Zinnen-Verlag, 1946).

Malík, Jan, *Puppetry in Czechoslovakia*, trans. by B. Goldreich (Prague: Orbis, 1948).

Margry, Karel, ' "Theresienstadt" (1944–45): The Nazi Propaganda Film Depicting the Concentration Camp as Paradise', *Historical Journal of Film, Radio and Television*, 12 (1992), 145–62.

Mechanicus, Philip, *Year of Fear: A Jewish Prisoner Waits for Auschwitz*, trans. by Irene Gibbons (New York: Calder & Boyars, 1968).

Metzger, Angela Esther, *Wahrheit aus Tränen und Blut: Theater in nationalsozialistischen Konzentrationslagern von 1933–1945; eine Dokumentation* (Hagen: Erich Walter, 1996).

Migdal, Ulrike, ed., *Und die Musik spielt dazu: Chansons und Satiren aus dem KZ Theresienstadt* (Munich: Piper, 1986).

Mulder, Dirk, and Ben Prinsen, eds, *Lachen in het donker: Amusement in Kamp Westerbork*, Westerbork Cahiers, 4 (Hooghalen: Herinneringscentrum Kamp Westerbork; Assen: Van Gorcum, 1996).

Müller-Wesemann, Barbara, *Theater als geistiger Widerstand: der Jüdische Kulturbund in Hamburg 1934–1941* (Stuttgart: M & P Verlag, 1996).

Münchner Stadtmuseum, ed., *Die gefesselte Muse: das Marionettentheater im Jüdischen Kulturbund 1935–1937* (Munich: Buchendorfer Verlag, 1994).

Patterson, Michael, with Louise Stafford-Charles, 'The Final Chapter: Theatre in the Concentration Camps of Nazi Germany', in *Theatre in the Third Reich, the Prewar Years: Essays on Theatre in Nazi Germany*, ed. by Glen W. Gadberry, Contributions to the Study of World History, 49 (Westport, CT: Greenwood Press, 1995), pp. 157–65.

Pulaver, Moishe, *Geven is a geto* (Tel Aviv: I. L. Peretz, 1963).

Riss, Heidelore, *Jüdisches Theater in Berlin: Ansätze zu einer Geschichte des jüdischen und deutsch-jüdischen Theaters (1890–1936)* (Tübingen: Niemeyer, 2000).

Rogge-Gau, Sylvia, *Die doppelte Wurzel des Daseins: Julius Bab und der Jüdische Kulturbund Berlin*, Dokumente-Texte-Materialien, 30 (Berlin: Metropol, 1999).

Rovit, Rebecca, 'An Artistic Mission in Nazi Berlin: The Jewish Kulturbund Theatre as Sanctuary', *Theatre Survey*, 35, no. 2 (November 1994), 5–17.

—— 'Collaboration or Survival, 1933–1938: Reassessing the Role of the *Jüdischer Kulturbund*', in *Theatre in the Third Reich, the Prewar Years: Essays on Theatre in Nazi Germany*, ed. by Glen W. Gadberry, Contributions to the Study of World History, 49 (Westport, CT: Greenwood Press, 1995), pp. 141–56.

—— and Alvin Goldfarb, eds, *Theatrical Performance During the Holocaust: Texts, Documents, Memoirs* (Baltimore, MD: Johns Hopkins University Press, PAJ Books, 1999).

Schultz, Ingo, ed., *Viktor Ullmann: 26 Kritiken über musikalische Veranstaltungen in Theresienstadt* (Hamburg: von Bockel, 1993).

Seidel, Sonja, *Kultur und Kunst im antifaschistischen Widerstandskampf im Konzentrationslager Buchenwald*, Buchenwaldheft, 18 (Weimar: Nationale Mahn- und Gedenkstätte Buchenwald, 1983).

Somorová, Eva, *Divadlo v Terezíne (1941/1945)* (Ústí nad Labem: Památník Terezín, 1973).

—— 'Kabarett im Konzentrationslager Terezín (Theresienstadt), 1941–1945', *Kassette*, 5 (1981), 161–9.

Staar, Sonja, *Kunst, Widerstand und Lagerkultur: eine Dokumentation*, Buchenwaldheft, 27 (Weimar: Nationale Mahn- und Gedenkstätte Buchenwald, 1987).

Steinweis, Alan E., 'Hans Hinkel and German Jewry, 1933–1941', *Leo Baeck Institute Yearbook*, 38 (1993), 209–19.

Tillion, Germaine, *Ravensbrück* (Paris: Seuil, 1973).

Tory, Avraham, *Surviving the Holocaust* (Cambridge, MA: Harvard University Press, 1990).

Tuma, Mirko, 'Memories of Theresienstadt', *Performing Arts Journal*, 1, no. 2 (Fall 1976), 12–18.

Turkov, Yonas, 'Teater un Kontsertn in di Getos un Kontsentratsye Lagern', in *Yidisher Teater in Yirope . . . Poylen* (New York: Knight, 1968), pp. 415–573.

Wolff, David, 'Drama Behind Barbed Wire', *Theatre Arts Committee Magazine*, no. 1 (March 1939), 15–16.

Zaich, Katja B., 'Operette am Rande des Grabes: jüdische Kabarettisten und Unter-haltungskünstler in den besetzten Niederlanden 1940–1944', *Theater Heute*, 39, nos 8–9 (August–September 1998), 38–43.

Zortman, Bruce H., 'Theatre in Isolation: The *Jüdischer Kulturbund* of Nazi Germany', *Educational Theatre Journal*, 24 (1972), 159–68.

Theatre in the assimilated and occupied territories

Austria is included above in post-1945 secondary sources, pp. 309–30.

Abirached, Robert, ed., *La Décentralisation théâtrale – le premier âge 1945–1958*, Cahiers Théâtre Éducation, 5 (Arles: Actes Sud-Papiers, 1992).

Added, Serge, *Le Théâtre dans les années-Vichy 1940–1944* (Paris: Ramsay, 1992).

—— 'Jacques Copeau and "Popular Theatre" in Vichy France', trans. by Robin Slaughter, in *Fascism and Theatre: Comparative Studies on the Aesthetics and Politics of Performance in Europe, 1925–1945*, ed. by Günter Berghaus (Providence, RI: Berghahn Books, 1996), pp. 247–59.

Barrault, Jean-Louis, *Souvenirs pour demain* (Paris: Seuil, 1972).

Bobková, Hana, and others, *Scenarium, 6: Toneel in crisis- en bezettingstijd* (Zutphen: De Waldburg Pers, 1982).

Burrin, Philippe, *Living with Defeat: France under the German Occupation, 1940–1944*, trans. by Janet Lloyd (London: Arnold, 1996).

Cardinne-Petit, Robert, *Les Secrets de la Comédie Française 1936–1945* (Paris: Nouvelles Éditions Latines, 1958).

Černý, František, '*Weh' dem, der lügt!* und *Der Traum ein Leben* in den Inszenierungen des Prager Nationaltheaters zur Zeit der nazistischen Okkupation', in '*Stichwort Grillparzer*', ed. by Hilde Haider-Pregler and Evelyn Deutsch-Schreiner, Grillparzer Forum, 1 (Vienna: Böhlau, 1994), pp. 159–70.

Cogniat, Raymond, and Michel Florisoone, *Un an de théâtre*, 3 vols (Lyons: Éditions Françaises Nouvelles, 1940–41 [with Yves Bonnat], 1941–42, 1942–43).

Dussane, [Béatrix], *Notes de théâtre: 1940–1950* (Paris: Lardanchet, 1951).

Flügge, Manfred, *Jean Anouilhs 'Antigone': Symbolgestalt des französischen Dilemmas 1940–1944*, 2nd edn (Rheinfelden: Schäuble, 1994).

Forkey, Leo O., 'The Theater of Paris During the Occupation', *French Review*, 22 (1949), 229–305.

—— 'The Comédie Française and the German Occupation', *French Review*, 24 (1951), 480–9.

Fröhlich, Elke, 'Die Anweisungen des Reichsministeriums für Volksaufklärung und Propaganda bezüglich des Kulturproblems in okkupierten Gebieten', in *Inter arma non silent Musae: The War and the Culture 1939–1945*, ed. by Czeslaw Madajczyk (Warsaw: Państwowy Instytut Wydawniczy, 1977), pp. 217–44.

Fuchs-Betteridge, Annette, 'Le Théâtre dramatique en France pendant l'occupation allemande 1940–1944' (unpublished [doctoral] thesis, University of Paris, 1969).

Galster, Ingrid, *Le Théâtre de Jean-Paul Sartre devant ses premiers critiques: les pièces créées sous l'occupation allemande: 'Les Mouches' et 'Huis clos'* (Tübingen: Gunter Narr; Paris: Jean-Michel Place, 1986).

Gautier, Jean-Jacques, *Paris sur scène: dix ans de théâtre 1941–1951* (Paris: Jacques Vautrin, 1951).

Golsan, Richard J., 'Henry de Montherlant: Itinerary of an Ambivalent Fascist', in *Fascism, Aesthetics, and Culture*, ed. by Richard J. Golsan (Hanover, NH: University Press of New England, 1992), pp. 143–63.

Gontard, Denis, *La Décentralisation théâtrale en France 1895–1952* (Paris: Sédès, 1973).

Guitry, Sacha, *Quatre ans d'occupation* (Paris: L'Élan, 1947).

Halimi, André, *Chantons sous l'Occupation*, documentary film, Paris, 1976; book (Verviers: Marabout, 1976).

Hirschfeld, Gerhard, and Patrick Marsh, eds, *Collaboration in France: Politics and Culture during the Nazi Occupation, 1940–1944* (Oxford: Berg, 1989).

Hoffmann, Gabriele, *NS-Propaganda in den Niederlanden: Organisation und Lenkung der Publizistik unter deutscher Besatzung, 1940–1945*, Kommunikation und Politik, 5 (Munich: Dokumentation, 1972).

Joubert, Marie-Agnès, *La Comédie-Française sous l'occupation* (Paris: Tallandier, 1998).

Jouvet, Louis, *Prestiges et Perspectives du théâtre français* (Paris: Gallimard, 1945).

Kantor, Tadeusz, *A Journey Through Other Spaces: Essays and Manifestos, 1944–1990*, ed. and trans. by Michal Kobialka (Berkeley: University of California Press, 1993).

Kleßmann, Christoph, *Die Selbstbehauptung einer Nation: nationalsozialistische Kulturpolitik und polnische Widerstandsbewegung im Generalgouvernement 1939–1945*, Studien zur modernen Geschichte, 5 (Düsseldorf: Bertelsmann, 1971).

Launay, Jacques de, and Jacques Offergeld, *Belgen en bezetters: het dagelijkse leven tijdens de bezetting 1940–1945*, trans. by Jan Van den Dries, revised by Jan Van den Dries and Walter Soethoudt (Antwerp: Soethoudt, 1983).

Le Boterf, Hervé, *La Vie parisienne sous l'occupation, 1940–1944* (Paris: France-Empire, 1997).

Lenormand, Henri-René, *Les Confessions d'un auteur dramatique* (Paris: Albin Michel, 1953).

Malachy, Thérèse, 'Le Mythe grec en France avant et pendant l'Occupation (Giraudoux, Sartre, Anouilh)', *Revue d'Histoire du Théâtre*, 51 (1999), 53–60.

Marczak-Oborski, Stanislaw, *Teatr czasu wojny: Polskie życie teatralne w latach II wojny światowej 1939–1945* (Warsaw: Państwowy Instytut Wydawniczy, 1967).

Marsh, Patrick, 'Le Théâtre à Paris sous l'occupation allemande', *Revue d'Histoire du Théâtre*, 33 (1981), 197–369.

—— 'The Theatre: Compromise or Collaboration?', in *Collaboration in France: Politics and Culture during the Nazi Occupation, 1940–1944*, ed. by Gerhard Hirschfeld and Patrick Marsh (Oxford: Berg, 1989), pp. 142–61; German version in *Kollaboration in Frankreich: Politik, Wirtschaft und Kultur während der national-sozialistischen*

Besetzung 1940–1944, ed. by Patrick Marsh and Gerhard Hirschfeld (Frankfurt am Main: Fischer, 1991), pp. 178–97.

Mulder, Hans, *Kunst in crisis en bezetting: een onderzoek naar de houding van Nederlandse kunstenaars in de periode 1930–1945* (Utrecht: Het Spectrum, 1978).

Murmann, Geerte, *Komödianten für den Krieg: deutsches und alliiertes Fronttheater* (Düsseldorf: Droste, 1992).

Ousby, Ian, *Occupation: The Ordeal of France, 1940–1944* (London: John Murray, 1997).

Perrault, G., and J.-P. Azéma, *Paris sous l'Occupation* (Paris: Belfond, 1987).

Prod'homme, J.-G., 'Les Théâtres parisiens sous l'Occupation', *Revue d'Histoire du Théâtre*, 1 (1948), 52–3.

Rebatet, Lucien, *Les Tribus du cinéma et du théâtre* (Paris: Nouvelles Éditions Françaises, 1941).

Rioux, J.-P., ed., *La Vie culturelle sous Vichy* (Brussels: Complexe, 1990).

Rosenberg, Merrill A., 'Montherlant and the Critics of the French Resistance', *French Review*, 44 (1970–71), pp. 839–51.

Schmid, Carlo, *Erinnerungen* (Berne: Scherz, 1979).

The Nazi 'Kultur' in Poland (London: His Majesty's Stationery Office, 1945).

Verhoeyen, Etienne, *Belgie bezet: 1940–1944: een synthese* (Brussels: BRTN-Instructieve Omroep, 1993).

Weber, Petra, *Carlo Schmid, 1896–1979: eine Biographie* (Munich: Beck, 1996).

Personalities: directors, set designers, conductors, singers and actors

Ahrens, Gerhard, ed., *Das Theater des deutschen Regisseurs Jürgen Fehling*, 2nd edn (Weinheim: Quadriga, 1987).

Ambesser, Axel von, *Nimm einen Namen mit A* (Berlin: Ullstein, 1985).

August, Wolf-Eberhard, 'Die Stellung der Schauspieler im Dritten Reich: Versuch einer Darstellung der Kunst- und Gesellschaftspolitik in einem totalitären Staat am Beispiel des "Berufsschauspielers"' (doctoral thesis, University of Cologne, 1973).

Bachmann, Robert C., *Karajan: Notes on a Career* (London: Quartet, 1990).

Barkhoff, Hermann, *Ernst Legal*, Theater und Film, 7 ([East] Berlin: Henschel, 1965).

Berger, Erna, *Auf Flügeln des Gesänges: Erinnerungen einer Sängerin* (Berlin: Henschel, 1990).

Berger, Ludwig, *Käthe Dorsch*, Rembrandt-Reihe: Bühne und Film, 2 (Berlin: Rembrandt, 1957).

Bernauer, Rudolf, *Das Theater meines Lebens: Erinnerungen* (Berlin: Blanvalet, 1955).

Biedrzynski, Richard, *Schauspieler: Regisseure: Intendanten* (Heidelberg: Hüthig, 1944).

Blanck, Karl, and Heinz Haufe, *Unbekanntes Theater: ein Buch von der Regie* (Stuttgart: J. G. Cotta'sche Buchhandlung Nachfolger, 1941).

Böhm, Karl, *Ich erinnere mich ganz genau: Autobiographie* (Frankfurt am Main: Gutenberg, 1968); English trans. by John Kehoe, *A Life Remembered: Memoirs* (London: Boyars, 1992).

Borgelt, Hans, *Grete Weiser: Herz mit Schnauze*, rororo, 1741 (Reinbek bei Hamburg: Rowohlt, 1974).

Brinkmann, Joachim, ed., *Festschrift für Heinz Hilpert* (Göttingen: Druckerei- und Verlagsgesellschaft, 1960).

Busch, Fritz, *Aus dem Leben eines Musikers* (Frankfurt am Main: Fischer, 1982); English trans. by Marjorie Strachey, *Pages from a Musician's Life* (Westport, CT: Greenwood Press, 1971).

Busch, Grete, *Fritz Busch, Dirigent* (Frankfurt am Main: Fischer, 1970).

Dagover, Lil, *Ich war die Dame* (Munich: Schneekluth, 1979).

Dillmann, Michael, 'Die Theaterarbeit Heinz Hilperts im Spannungsfeld der Kultur-politik des Dritten Reiches' (unpublished Magisterarbeit, Friedrich-Alexander University of Erlangen-Nuremberg, 1988).

—— *Heinz Hilpert: Leben und Werk* (Berlin: Akademie der Künste/Hentrich, 1990).

Doublier, Gerda, and Fritz Fuhrich, eds, *Hermann Thimig: ein Leben in Dokumenten*, Museion: Veröffentlichungen der Österreichischen Nationalbibliothek, Neue Folge, 1. Reihe, 6 (Vienna: Brüder Hollinek, 1972).

Drews, Berta, *Wohin des Wegs: Erinnerungen*, 4th edn (Munich: Langen Müller, 1987).

Drews, Wolfgang, *Die grossen Zauberer: Bildnisse deutscher Schauspieler aus zwei Jahrhunderten* (Vienna: Donau-Verlag, 1953).

—— *Festgabe für Heinz Hilpert* (Göttingen: Drückerei- und Verlagsgesellschaft, 1965).

Einem, Gottfried von, and Siegfried Melchinger, eds, *Caspar Neher* (Velber bei Hannover: Erhard Friedrich, 1966).

Elwood, William R., 'Werner Krauß and the Third Reich', in *Theatre in the Third Reich, the Prewar Years: Essays on Theatre in Nazi Germany*, ed. by Glen W. Gadberry, Contributions to the Study of World History, 49 (Westport, CT: Greenwood Press, 1995), pp. 91–101.

Endler, Franz, *Karl Böhm: ein Dirigentenleben* (Hamburg: Hoffmann & Campe, 1981).

Endres, Ria, 'Gesichter ohne Entscheidung: Notizen zu Gründgens', *Autonomie*, 14 (1979), 16–25.

Engel, Erich, *Schriften: über Theater und Film* ([East] Berlin: Henschel, 1971).

Evans, Joan, *Hans Rosbaud: A Bio-bibliography* (New York: Greenwood, 1992).

Falkenberg, Hans-Geert, *Heinz Hilpert: das Ende einer Epoche* (Göttingen: Vandenhoeck & Ruprecht, 1968).

Fechter, Paul, *Große Zeit des deutschen Theaters: Gestalten und Darsteller*, Das Kleine Buch, 4 (Gütersloh: Bertelsmann, 1950).

Fehling, Jürgen, *Die Magie des Theaters* (Velber bei Hannover: Erhard Friedrich, 1965).

Fernau, Rudolf, *Als Lied begann's: Lebenstagebuch eines Schauspielers* (Frankfurt am Main: Ullstein, 1972).

Finck, Werner, *Alter Narr, was nun?: die Geschichte meiner Zeit* (Munich: Herbig, 1972).

Fischer, Helmar Harald, 'Was gestrichen ist, kann nicht durchfallen', *Theater Heute*, 30, no. 9 (September 1989), 1–3, 6–19.

—— 'Theatergeschichte: Schauspieler und Diktatur', *Theater Heute*, 33, no. 2 (February 1992), 19–28.

Flickenschildt, Elisabeth, *Kind mit roten Haaren: ein Leben wie ein Traum* (Hamburg: Hoffmann & Campe, 1971).

Flimm, Jürgen, ed., *Will Quadflieg: ein Leben für das Wort in Texten und Bildern* (Hamburg: Arche, 1994).

Fontana, Oskar Maurus, *Wiener Schauspieler: von Mitterwurzer bis Maria Eis* (Vienna: Amandus, 1948).

—— *Paula Wessely*, Rembrandt-Reihe: Bühne und Film, 14 (Berlin: Rembrandt, 1959).

—— *Hans Moser: Volkskomiker und Menschendarsteller* (Vienna: Buchgemeinschaft Donauland, 1965).

Ford, Charles, *Emil Jannings*, Anthologie du Cinéma, 46 (Paris: L'Avant-Scène du Cinéma, 1969).

Fricke, Kurt, *Spiel am Abgrund: Heinrich George – eine politische Biographie* (Halle: Mitteldeutscher Verlag, 2000).

Fritsch, Willy, ... *das kommt nicht wieder: Erinnerungen eines Schauspielers* (Zurich: Classen, 1963).

Fröbe, Gert, *Auf ein Neues, sagte er ... und dabei fiel ihm das Alte ein: Geschichte aus meinem Leben* (Munich: Albrecht Knaus, 1988).

Fröhlich, Gustav, *Waren das Zeiten: mein Film-Heldenleben* (Munich: Herbig, 1982).

Funke, Christoph, 'Heinrich George – ein Komödiant im Dritten Reich: Versuch einer Deutung', in *Sachsenhausen bei Berlin: Speziallager Nr. 7 1945–1950*, ed. by Günter Adge (Berlin: Aufbau Verlag, 1994), pp. 216–28.

Goertz, Heinrich, *Gustaf Gründgens* (Reinbek bei Hamburg: Rowohlt, 1965).

Goetz, Wolfgang, *Werner Krauß* (Hamburg: Hoffmann & Campe, 1954).

Grange, William, *Partnership in the German Theatre: Zuckmayer and Hilpert, 1925–1961*, Studies in Modern German Literature, 43 (New York: Lang, 1991).

—— 'Ordained Hands on the Altar of Art: Gründgens, Hilpert, and Fehling in Berlin', in *Theatre in the Third Reich, the Prewar Years: Essays on Theatre in Nazi Germany*, ed. by Glen W. Gadberry, Contributions to the Study of World History, 49 (Westport, CT: Greenwood Press, 1995), pp. 75–89.

Grawert-May, Erik, *Theatrum eroticum: ein Plädoyer für den Verrat an der Liebe* (Tübingen: Konkursbuchverlag, 1981).

Gregor, Joseph, *Meister deutscher Schauspielkunst: Krauß, Klöpfer, Jannings, George* (Bremen: Carl Schünemann, 1939).

—— *Clemens Krauss: seine musikalische Sendung* (Bad Bocklet: W. Krieg, 1953).

Greisenegger-Georgila, Vana, and Hans Jörg Jans, eds, *Was ist die Antike wert?: Griechen und Römer auf der Bühne von Caspar Neher*, Cortina: Materialien aus dem Österreichischen Theatermuseum, 18 (Vienna: Böhlau, 1995).

Gründgens, Gustaf, *Briefe, Aufsätze, Reden*, ed. by Rolf Badenhausen and Peter Gründgens-Gorski, dtv, 694 (Munich: Deutscher Taschenbuch Verlag, 1970).

Gustaf Gründgens: eine Dokumentation des Dumont-Lindemann-Archivs, 2nd edn (Munich: Langen Müller, 1981).

Haack, Käthe, *In Berlin und anderswo* (Munich: Herbig, 1971).

Haan, Christa, 'Werner Krauß und das Burgtheater' (unpublished doctoral thesis, University of Vienna, 1970).

Hadamowsky, Franz, *Caspar Nehers szenisches Werk: ein Verzeichnis des Bestandes der Theatersammlung der Österreichischen Nationalbibliothek* (Vienna: Hollinek, 1972).

Haider-Pregler, Hilde, with Isabella Suppanz, *Überlebens-Theater: der Schauspieler Reuss* (Vienna: Holzhausen, 1998).

Harlan, Veit, *Im Schatten meiner Filme: Selbstbiographie* (Gütersloh: Sigbert Mohn, 1966).

Hartmann, Rudolf, *Das geliebte Haus: mein Leben mit der Oper* (Munich: Piper, 1975).

—— *Richard Strauss, die Bühnenwerke von der Uraufführung bis heute* (Munich: Piper, 1980); trans. by Graham Davies, *Richard Strauss: The Staging of his Operas and Ballets* (Oxford: Oxford University Press, 1981).

Hasse, Otto Eduard, *O. E.: unvollendete Memoiren* (Munich: Bertelsmann, 1979).

Heesters, Johannes, *Es kommt auf die Sekunde an: Erinnerungen an ein Leben im Frack* (Munich: Blanvalet, 1978).

Heyder, Gerhild, and Annette Niewöhner, 'Gustaf Gründgens als Theaterpraktiker im

Dritten Reich, dargestellt an seinen deutschen Klassiker-Inszenierungen' (unpublished Magisterarbeit, Free University of Berlin, 1982).

Heyworth, Peter, *Otto Klemperer: His Life and Times*, 2 vols (Cambridge: Cambridge University Press, 1983–96).

Ihering, Herbert, *Von Josef Kainz bis Paula Wessely: Schauspieler von gestern und heute* (Heidelberg: Hüthig, 1942).

—— *Regie* (Berlin: Hans von Hugo, 1943).

—— *Junge Schauspieler* (Munich: Desch, 1948); 2nd edn (Berlin: Henschel, 1948).

—— and Eva Wisten, *Eduard von Winterstein*, Theater und Film, 1 ([East] Berlin: Henschel, 1968).

Jannings, Emil, *Theater, Film – das Leben und ich: Autobiographie* (Berchtesgaden: Zimmer & Herzog, 1951).

Jefferson, Allan, *Elisabeth Schwarzkopf* (London: Gollancz, 1996).

Jürgen Fehling der Regisseur (Berlin: Akademie der Künste, 1978).

Jürgens, Curd, *... und kein bißchen weise* (Munich: Droemer Knaur, 1976).

Kende, Götz Klaus, *Höchste Leistung aus begeistertem Herzen: Clemens Krauss als Direktor der Wiener Staatsoper* (Salzburg: Residenzverlag, 1971).

Kern, Rosemarie, 'Hans Thimig und das Theater' (unpublished doctoral thesis, University of Vienna, 1967).

Knuth, Gustav, *Mit einem Lächeln im Knopfloch* (Hamburg: R. Glöss, 1974).

Koesters, Ferdinand, *Peter Anders: Biographie eines Tenors* (Stuttgart: Metzler, 1995).

Kowa, Viktor de, *Als ich noch Prinz war von Arkadien* (Nuremberg: Glock und Lutz, 1955).

—— *Achduliebezeit: aus dem Libretto meines Lebens: aufgeschnappt, aufgeschrieben, verdichtet und gedichtet* (Stuttgart: Deutsche Verlags-Anstalt, 1971).

Krauss, Werner, *Das Schauspiel meines Lebens: einem Freund erzählt*, ed. by Hans Weigel (Stuttgart: Henry Govert, 1958).

Kresse, Dodo, and Michael Horvath, *Nur ein Komödiant?: Hans Moser in den Jahren 1938 bis 1945* (Vienna: Österreichische Staatsdruckerei, 1994).

Kuckhoff, Armin-G., ed., *Hans Otto: Gedenkbuch für einen Schauspieler und Kämpfer* (Berlin: Henschel, 1948).

Kühlken, Edda, *Die Klassiker-Inszenierungen von Gustaf Gründgens* (Meisenheim: Hain, 1972).

Leander, Zarah, *Es war so wunderbar: mein Leben* (Hamburg: Hoffmann & Campe, 1973).

Leider, Frieda, *Das war mein Teil: Erinnerungen einer Opernsängerin* ([East] Berlin: Henschel, 1981).

Liebe, Ulrich, *'Verehrt, verfolgt, vergessen': Schauspieler als Naziopfer* (Weinheim: Quadriga, 1992).

Lindt, Lotte Walter, ed., *Bruno Walter: Briefe 1894–1962* (Frankfurt am Main: Fischer, 1969).

Lingen, Theo, *Ich über mich: Interview eines Schauspielers mit sich selbst*, Reihe Theater Heute, 9 (Velber bei Hannover: Erhard Friedrich, 1963).

—— *Ich bewundere ... Liebeserklärungen an das Theater* (Munich: Piper, 1969).

London, John, 'Being a Good German in the Third Reich', *Jewish Quarterly*, no. 160 (Winter 1995), 52–5.

Luft, Friedrich, *Gustaf Gründgens*, Rembrandt-Reihe: Bühne und Film, 3 (Berlin: Rembrandt, 1958).

Maisch, Herbert, *Helm ab, Vorhang auf: 70 Jahre eines ungewöhnlichen Lebens* (Emsdetten: H. & J. Lechte, 1968).

Mann, Klaus, *Mephisto: Roman einer Karriere*, rororo, 1490 (Reinbek bei Hamburg: Rowohlt, 1981); trans. by Robin Smyth (Harmondsworth: Penguin, 1983).

Mantler, Anton, *Paul Hörbiger, Hans Moser: zwei Wiener Schauspiel-Legenden*, ed. by Herwig Würtz (Vienna: Wiener Stadt- und Landesbibliothek, 1994).

Markus, Georg, *Hans Moser: das Leben des genialen Volksschauspielers in Bildern*, Heyne-Bücher: 01, Heyne Allgemeine Reihe, 8837 (Munich: Heyne, 1993).

Maser, Werner, *Heinrich George: Mensch aus Erde gemacht: die politische Biographie* (Berlin: Edition Q, 1998).

Matzigkeit, Michael, and Winrich Meiszies, eds, *Gustaf Gründgens – Ansichten eines Schauspielers: Bilder einer Legende*, Dokumente zur Theatergeschichte (Düsseldorf: Theatermuseum Düsseldorf, 1999).

Mesalla, Horst, 'Heinrich George: Versuch der Rekonstruktion der schauspielerischen Leistung unter besonderer Berücksichtigung der zeitgenössischen Publizistik' (unpublished doctoral thesis, Free University of Berlin, 1969).

Meyhöfer, Annette, 'Schauspielerinnen im Dritten Reich', in *Die Schauspielerin: zur Kulturgeschichte der weiblichen Bühnenkunst*, ed. by Renate Möhrmann (Frankfurt am Main: Insel, 1989), pp. 300–20.

Michalzik, Peter, *Gustaf Gründgens: der Schauspieler und die Macht* (Berlin: Quadriga, 1999).

Minetti, Bernhard, *Erinnerungen eines Schauspielers*, ed. by Günther Rühle (Stuttgart: Deutsche Verlags-Anstalt, 1985).

Mira, Brigitte, *Kleine Frau – was nun?: Erinnerungen an ein buntes Leben* (Munich: Herbig, 1988).

Mühr, Alfred, *Großes Theater: Begegnungen mit Gustaf Gründgens* (Berlin: Arnold, 1950).

—— *Mephisto ohne Maske: Gustaf Gründgens, Legende und Wahrheit* (Munich: Langen Müller, 1981).

Osborne, Richard, *Herbert von Karajan: A Life in Music* (London: Chatto & Windus, 1998).

Pichel, Gertrud, 'Paul und Attila Hörbiger' (unpublished [doctoral] thesis, University of Vienna, 1949).

Pospischill, E., 'Hermann Thimig: eine Schauspielerbiographie' (unpublished doctoral thesis, University of Vienna, 1950).

Prieberg, Fred K., *Trial of Strength: Wilhelm Furtwängler and the Third Reich*, trans. by Christopher Dolan (London: Quartet, 1991).

Quadflieg, Will, *Wir spielen immer: Erinnerungen* (Frankfurt am Main: Fischer, 1976).

Reinhardt, Gottfried, *Der Liebhaber: Erinnerungen seines Sohnes Gottfried Reinhardt an Max Reinhardt* (Munich: Droemer Knaur, 1973).

Riess, Curt, *Gustaf Gründgens: die klassische Biographie des grossen Künstlers* (Hamburg: Hoffmann & Campe, 1965).

Rischbieter, Henning, ed., *Gründgens: Schauspieler, Regisseur, Theaterleiter* (Velber bei Hannover: Erhard Friedrich, 1963).

—— ed., 'Gründgens unter den Nazis', *Theater Heute*, 22, no. 4 (April 1981), 47–57.

Rökk, Marika, *Herz mit Paprika* (Berlin: Universitas Verlag, 1974).

Rosvaenge, Helge, *Mach es besser, mein Sohn: ein Tenor erzählt aus seinem Leben* (Leipzig: Koehler & Amelang, 1963).

Rühmann, Heinz, *Das war's: Erinnerungen*, 2nd edn (Berlin: Ullstein, 1982).

Russell, John, *Erich Kleiber: A Memoir* (London: Deutsch, 1957).

Scanzoni, Signe, and Götz Klaus Kende, *Der Prinzipal: Clemens Krauss: Fakten, Vergleiche, Rückschlüsse* (Tutzing: Schneider, 1988).

Schönböck, Karl, *Wie es war durch achtzig Jahr: Erinnerungen* (Munich: Langen Müller, 1988).

Schröder, Ernst, *Das Leben – verspielt* (Frankfurt am Main: Fischer, 1978).

Schroth, Carl-Heinz, *Keine Angst vor schlechten Zeiten* ... (Munich: Herbig, 1984).

Schulz, Hedi, *Hans Moser: der grosse Volksschauspieler, wie er lebte und spielte* (Vienna: Molden, 1980).

Schulz, Wilfried, ed., *'Gründgens' von Johann Kresnik nach einer Vorlage von Werner Fritsch* (Hamburg: Deutsches Schauspielhaus in Hamburg, 1995).

Shirakawa, Sam H., *The Devil's Music Master: The Controversial Life and Career of Wilhelm Furtwängler* (New York: Oxford University Press, 1992).

Smith, Amy, *Hermine Körner* (Berlin: Kranich-Verlag, 1970).

Söderbaum, Kristina, *Nichts bleibt immer so: Rückblenden auf ein Leben vor und hinter der Kamera* (Bayreuth: Hestia, 1983).

Söhnker, Hans, *... und kein Tag zuviel* (Hamburg: R. Glöss, 1974).

Spangenberg, Eberhard, *Karriere eines Romans: Mephisto, Klaus Mann und Gustaf Gründgens: ein dokumentarischer Bericht aus Deutschland und dem Exil 1925–1981* (Munich: Ellermann, 1982).

Steiner, Maria, *Paula Wessely: die verdrängten Jahre* (Vienna: Verlag für Gesellschaftskritik, 1996).

Steinhoff, Johannes, ed., *Deutsche im Zweiten Weltkrieg: Zeitzeugen sprechen* (Munich: Schneekluth, 1989).

Stemmle, Robert A., *Theater- und Film-Anekdoten* (Berlin–Grunewald: Non Stop-Bücherei, 1957).

Tassié, Franz, *Helge Rosvaenge* (Augsburg: Schrott, 1975).

Thomalla, Georg, *In aller Herzlichkeit: Erinnerungen* (Munich: Langen Müller, 1988).

Töteberg, Michael, '"Ich möchte hier den Vorhang des Schweigens herunterlassen": über die Darstellung des Dritten Reiches in Schauspieler-Memoiren; mit einem Exkurs über den Theaterkritiker Herbert Ihering', in *Im Rampenlicht der 'dunklen Jahre': Aufsätze zum Theater im 'Dritten Reich', Exil und Nachkrieg*, ed. by Helmut G. Asper, Sigma-Medienwissenschaft, 3 (Berlin: Sigma, 1989), pp. 123–48.

Trepte, Curt, and Jutta Wardetzky, *Hans Otto: Schauspieler und Revolutionär* ([East] Berlin: Henschel, 1970).

Tretow, Christine, and Helmut Gier, eds, *Caspar Neher – der größte Bühnenbauer unserer Zeit* (Opladen: Westdeutscher Verlag, 1997).

Tschechowa, Olga, *Ich verschweige nichts!: Autobiographie*, ed. by C. C. Bergius (Berchtesgaden: Zimmer & Herzog, 1952).

—— *Meine Uhren gehen anders* (Munich: Herbig, 1973).

Turing, Penelope, *Hans Hotter: Man and Artist* (London: Calder, 1983).

Uhlen, Gisela, *Mein Glashaus: Roman eines Lebens* (Bayreuth: Hestia, 1978).

Ullrich, Luise, *Komm auf die Schaukel, Luise: Balance eines Lebens* (Percha am Starnberger See/Kempfenhausen am Starnberger See: R. S. Schulz, 1973).

Ursuleac, Viorica, *Singen für Richard Strauss: Erinnerungen und Dokumente* (Vienna: Doblinger, 1986).

Wagner, Wolfgang, *Lebens-Akte: Autobiographie* (Munich: Goldmann, 1994).

Walach, Dagmar, *Aber ich habe nicht mein Gesicht: Gustaf Gründgens – eine deutsche Karriere* (Berlin: Henschel, 1999).

Walter, Bruno, *Theme and Variations: An Autobiography*, trans. by James A. Galston (London: Hamish Hamilton, 1947).

Wangenheim, Inge von, *Die tickende Bratpfanne: Kunst und Künstler aus meinem Stundenbuch* (Rudolstadt: Greifenverlag, 1974).

Weinschenk, H. E., *Schauspieler erzählen* (Berlin: Wilhelm Limpert, 1941).

Wessling, Berndt Wilhelm, *Hans Hotter* (Bremen: Schünemann, 1966).

—— *Wieland Wagner: der Enkel* (Cologne: Tonger, 1997).

Willett, John, *Caspar Neher: Brecht's Designer* (London: Methuen, 1986).

Index

The alphabetical order is English, regardless of diacritical marks. The titles of plays and operas are listed under authors' and composers' names. Page numbers in *italic* refer to illustrations; 'n.' after a page reference indicates the number of a note on that page.